The Marquess of Londonderry

CW01646476

The Marquess of Londonderry

Aristocracy, Power and Politics in Britain and Ireland

Revised Edition

N. C. Fleming

BLOOMSBURY ACADEMIC
LONDON • NEW YORK • OXFORD • NEW DELHI • SYDNEY

BLOOMSBURY ACADEMIC
Bloomsbury Publishing Plc
50 Bedford Square, London, WC1B 3DP, UK
1385 Broadway, New York, NY 10018, USA
29 Earlsfort Terrace, Dublin 2, Ireland

BLOOMSBURY, BLOOMSBURY ACADEMIC and the Diana logo are trademarks of Bloomsbury Publishing Plc

First published in 2005 by Tauris Academic Studies, an imprint of I.B. Tauris & Co Ltd.
This paperback edition first published by Bloomsbury Academic in 2024

Copyright © N. C. Fleming, 2005, 2024

N. C. Fleming has asserted his right under the Copyright, Designs and Patents Act, 1988, to be identified as Author of this work.

For legal purposes the Acknowledgements on p. ix constitute an extension of this copyright page.

Cover image © Lord Londonderry leaves his home with his wife to attend the Knights of the Garter service at Windsor, 1937. Photo by Hulton-Deutsch/Hulton-Deutsch Collection/Corbis via Getty Images

All rights reserved. No part of this publication may be reproduced or transmitted in any form or by any means, electronic or mechanical, including photocopying, recording, or any information storage or retrieval system, without prior permission in writing from the publishers.

Bloomsbury Publishing Plc does not have any control over, or responsibility for, any third-party websites referred to or in this book. All internet addresses given in this book were correct at the time of going to press. The author and publisher regret any inconvenience caused if addresses have changed or sites have ceased to exist, but can accept no responsibility for any such changes.

A catalogue record for this book is available from the British Library.

A catalog record for this book is available from the Library of Congress.

ISBN: HB: 978-1-8504-3726-0
PB: 978-1-3503-5155-4
ePDF: 978-0-8577-1461-9

Typeset by Deanta Global Publishing Services, Chennai, India
Printed and bound in Great Britain

To find out more about our authors and books visit www.bloomsbury.com and sign up for our newsletters.

For my parents

Contents

Figures

Acknowledgements

The original edition of this book was first published by I.B. Tauris in 2005. It was based on a doctoral thesis completed in 2002 at the Queen's University of Belfast. I would like to thank Emily Drewe and Megan Harris at Bloomsbury Academic for the opportunity to correct, revise and add to the original text. I am grateful to the School of Humanities, University of Worcester, for covering the copyright and reproduction costs of the David Low cartoon. I am indebted to Professor Maggie Andrews, Catherine Armitstead, Professor Stuart Ball, Dr Declan Hanna, Dr Alan Heesom, Dr Fearghal Mac Bhloscaidh, Dr Lewis Mates, Mohammed Raffi, Professor Diane Urquhart and Carwen Vaughan for their advice and assistance. Sadly, since 2005, several of those who provided invaluable help with the original edition are no longer with us, including Professor George Boyce, Dr Alan O'Day, Charles Villiers and Lady Mairi Bury. I met Lady Mairi, the youngest daughter of the seventh Marquess of Londonderry, on several occasions at Mount Stewart in the early 2000s, to discuss her father's politics and ministerial career. She granted me full access to his papers held at the Public Record Office of Northern Ireland. After publication, Lady Mairi expressed a number of reservations about my interpretation or presentation of events which I have noted in this revised text when relevant. Ownership of the papers has since transferred to the Public Record Office of Northern Ireland.

Introduction

Viewed in its entirety the political life of the seventh Marquess of Londonderry is unique. Although not one of the great men of history, he played an active part in events that shaped the destinies of Ireland, Great Britain and Europe. No other signatory of Ulster's Solemn League and Covenant would subsequently sit at the World Disarmament Conference determining the future of aerial warfare. No other delegate to the Irish Convention at Dublin would discuss international relations with the head of German National Socialism, Adolf Hitler. No other minister in the government of Northern Ireland had been driven through the streets of late-Victorian Dublin amid the pomp and splendour of a vice-regal parade, and no other would join the cabinet of a British prime minister. Easily dismissed as the epitome of a decadent and increasingly anachronistic aristocracy, Londonderry's personal commitment to the technological development of aviation went far beyond that of a hobbyist, and the bulk of his family's enormous wealth was derived from the ownership of minerals that fuelled industry and transport across the United Kingdom and beyond. These contrasting aspects of Londonderry's background, life and career have led to contradictory assessments of his personality and ministerial record. Therefore, the founder of non-sectarian education in Northern Ireland is remembered often for bigotry, particularly anti-Semitism. Although a consistent defender of the continued existence of the Royal Air Force (RAF), he has been found guilty of napping on the job by underestimating the strength of the Luftwaffe. And labelled a warmonger by the Labour party for resisting the abolition of aerial bombing, many more recall him as an advocate for peace at all costs through the appeasement of Nazi Germany.

It is Londonderry's aristocratic background, his deeply held conviction that he belonged to a governing caste, that bound together and gave coherence to his political outlook and his ministerial career. Rather than being motivated by an inflexible sense of national identity or political philosophy, Londonderry was by instinct, method and temperament an aristocrat. In 1908 the political correspondent of the *Sunday Chronicle* described him as 'an aristocrat to the very tips of his fingers'.[1] The Countess of Oxford and Asquith noted that he was one of seven aristocrats who 'had the finest manners of any men that I have ever known'.[2] To Harold Nicolson he 'looked more like Lord Londonderry than any Lord Londonderry had looked before'.[3] The diarist Lady Spender similarly observed in 1921 that 'he apes his ancestor the great Lord Castlereagh, wears a high black stock over his collar and a very tightly fitting frock coat, and doesn't look as if he belongs to this century at all'.[4] For the political diarist Sir Henry Channon, he 'was a good friend and grand seigneur of the old school; even his appearance was almost theatrically 18th century. Slim, with an elegant figure and pointed features he was red in the face and dressed with distinction. He was always gay and amiable and completely sure of himself'.[5] Another diarist, the Conservative MP for Newcastle North, Cuthbert Headlam, similarly regarded Londonderry as 'very affable' and 'at heart such a good fellow', but he also wished 'that he could even for a few moments forget that he is Lord Londonderry . . . it is a pity he can never relax – a greater pity still that he should imagine that just because he happens to be a very rich nobleman he is more important and intelligent than he really is!'[6]

Recalling her grandfather as an elderly man, Annabel Goldsmith, née Vane-Tempest-Stewart, described him as 'tall, thin and very bony, with an oddly high forehead'. She recollected 'his long blue fingers, which we used to imitate, rigid as they hit the piano keys. I wondered if he was ever able to unbend and I now find it difficult to understand how this stiff, formal man was able to justify his reputation as a great lover'.[7] Londonderry's distinctive appearance was a gift to *Punch*, in which cartoonists depicted him with his nose tilted high and eyes closed. He appeared in the satirical weekly publication in various guises, as a frog, fly and stork, and as an Eton schoolboy. During his tenure as Secretary of State for Air, illustrations featured him flying in a balloon and riding a magic carpet en route to Baghdad.[8] The surviving footage of Londonderry in British Pathé newsreels bears out the contemporary descriptions of him as impeccably elegant, tall and stiff in his movements. In the delivery of his speeches, Londonderry's head would alternate from looking just above his audience, before plunging down to look at the text from which he drew his words. Yet, it is also possible to discern from these flickering images a nobleman whose assured self-confidence could on occasion render him affable and relaxed, at least in the company of fellow airmen.

Londonderry was well regarded by his contemporaries, yet his ministerial career was replete with misunderstandings and disagreements with colleagues and observers. His demonstrative belief in the necessity of a governing caste could not disguise the fact that he depended almost entirely on the patronage of a succession of leaders whose political accomplishments were forged by democratic forces. Yet, even though Londonderry relied on Sir Edward Carson, Winston Churchill, Sir James Craig, Stanley Baldwin and Ramsay MacDonald, he never became one of their acolytes, nor indeed did he attempt to develop, or join, a group of like-minded politicians. He was of course a member of the Carlton Club, but there is little evidence to suggest that he spent much time there let alone that he conducted political business within its walls.[9] What need had he for clubs, after all, when Park Lane's Londonderry House attracted scores of leading society, political and diplomatic figures to its grand receptions? These functions, it must be noted, were a mixed blessing, bringing Londonderry into regular contact with the great and good, but also attracting a fair measure of criticism for their opulence and self-seeking opportunism. Even so, the Londonderrys' use of salon politics into the era of the great depression should not obscure the fact that Lord Londonderry had learnt to trim his sails politically. First in Ireland, and subsequently in County Durham, he demonstrated a flexibility in outlook and approach that identified him to leading Conservatives as a potential candidate for ministerial office. Once appointed, however, Londonderry tended to place the interests of his ministry above political considerations and calculations, much to the frustration of his ministerial and party colleagues.

Londonderry's lack of charisma, his lack of a strong power base in the Conservative party and, in office, his habit of supporting unwelcome opinions, all help to account for why his ministerial career was not as successful as that of other contemporary aristocrat-politicians, such as Winston Churchill, his second cousin and four years his elder, or his contemporary at Eton, the third Viscount Halifax. Yet, Londonderry's career, albeit in the second rank, was more durable than those of several grandee aristocrat-politicians of the first rank, such as the seventeenth Earl of Derby and Lord Robert Cecil, afterwards the first Viscount Cecil of Chelwood.[10] Among those of the second rank, an instructive comparison can be made with the fifth Duke of Sutherland, who, like Londonderry, held the post of Under Secretary of State for Air, but whose ministerial career remained at the junior level. As these comparisons suggest, individual agency was still a factor even in the context of aristocratic decline. But it still leaves the question of how and why Londonderry was able to succeed in achieving ministerial office, culminating in his appointment to the cabinet in 1928 and again in 1931, when many had written off both the man and his social order. The answer, rather surprisingly, is that Londonderry, often helped by his talented and formidable wife, Edith, and assisted by his immense wealth, consistently acted as if aristocratic status, and the attendant influence that it carried, was an appropriate and effective means of obtaining high public office. Indeed, it was this attitude that made Londonderry such an individualistic politician, one reluctant to give up the traits that defined his very existence. That the Londonderrys' approach succeeded, at least in securing a succession of ministerial and other appointments for Lord Londonderry, highlights that even in a period of declining fortunes for the aristocracy, the adaptation of aristocrat-politicians to this trend could vary considerably.

Aristocratic decline undoubtedly became a marked feature of British politics in the late nineteenth century. It was the cause of considerable gloom and pessimism among titled nobles and large landowners, but historians now recognize that the practical effects of this were often exaggerated at the time.[11] It is probably more instructive to regard the period between the 1880s and the 1940s as one of transition, for the traditional authority once invoked and exercised by the aristocracy did not collapse suddenly. According to Max Weber, it gradually gave way, not always willingly, to the seemingly unstoppable march of democratic forces.[12] From a different angle, Ross McKibbin highlights that despite franchise reforms in 1918 and 1928, the outward forms of the British state remained 'semi-feudal', and that 'large numbers of people . . . freely abdicated any active political role of judgement in favour of elites who were still largely Edwardian'.[13] Whichever way it is viewed, a family's possession of noble rank and wealth still proved to be a useful entrée to the House of Commons. At the general election of 1935, the peerage alone returned thirty of its sons to the House of Commons.[14] And although the House of Lords had its powers blunted by the 1911 Parliament Act, peers continued to be a conspicuous presence in the Conservative cabinets of Andrew Bonar Law and Stanley Baldwin.

Many of Londonderry's political and ministerial appointments, as well as his successes and failures in office, were either because of, or facilitated by, his aristocratic background. The influence of his father, a former cabinet minister, was instrumental in his selection as the Conservative candidate for Maidstone in 1906. After years of obscurity on the backbenches, Londonderry's moderate and patrician performance at the Irish Convention of 1917–18 led Churchill and Walter Long to insist that he receive junior ministerial office in the post-war coalition government. Londonderry's commitment to Ulster unionism, coupled with his aristocratic aloofness from its powerful populist strain, made him a credible Minister of Education and Leader of the Senate in the first government of Northern Ireland. The general strike and miners' strike of 1926 should have ended any hopes that Londonderry, an immensely wealthy colliery owner, might have had for a ministerial career at Westminster. Instead, he gained a reputation, among Conservatives at least, for echoing the one nation rhetoric of the party's leader, Stanley Baldwin, and he was rewarded in 1928 when Baldwin appointed him to the cabinet as First Commissioner of Works. By the time that the National Government was formed in 1931, Londonderry had already acquired a reasonable amount of experience in government on both sides of the Irish Sea. And yet his appointment to that coalition of Conservatives, National Liberals and National Labour, including soon after to the cabinet, was, and continues to be, widely attributed to Lady Londonderry's controversial friendship with the Labour leader and prime minister, Ramsay MacDonald.

Despite or perhaps because of Londonderry's wide-ranging involvement in the high politics of Great Britain and Ireland, there had been no attempt, until the original edition of this book, to chart and critically analyse the entirety of his political life.[15] Each of his political appointments, and his distinctive social and economic roles, was instead considered separately, if not always fully, in specific studies of air power, the coal industry, Ulster unionism and Anglo-German relations.[16] The last has tended to overshadow everything else that is known about Londonderry, at least outside Ireland, and the treatment of it as a discrete topic divorced from his previous experience in government has served to skew some assessments of his actions, motives and even his intelligence.[17] As this book makes plain, Londonderry's controversial actions in the late 1930s can only be fully understood when set within the context of a political career that is unexpectedly long and varied given his limitations as a politician.[18]

In his *The Londonderrys: A Family Portrait* (1979), H. Montgomery Hyde charts the history of the Londonderry dynasty and devotes a considerable portion of the book to the seventh marquess and his wife.[19] Reviewing it for a literary journal, Enoch Powell observed that aside from the wives, 'there are really only two persons of any true distinction in the whole gallery: the "great" Lord Castlereagh; and the seventh marquess'. Notwithstanding Powell's complaint that 'much of the narrative is confusing to the reader', Hyde's chronicle of the Londonderry family is reasonably comprehensive and accessible.[20] Another reviewer, commenting on Hyde's much earlier study of the second marquess, made an observation similar to Powell's, remarking that he was 'not the surest of guides by any means, nor the most competent. Dr Hyde is lost in detail and too absorbed by his aim of clearing Castlereagh of the charges made against his administration. He never sees his hero's opponents save as enemies'.[21] *The Londonderrys* might also be described as hagiographical. Hyde, to be fair, did not shy away from his personal connection to the family. Indeed, he trumpeted it, often describing himself in his publications as a former employee. Lady Mairi Bury, the youngest of Lord and Lady Londonderry's four daughters, was not impressed with this self-description, nor his skill as the family's chronicler. She described him to the present author as 'the librarian', and she claimed that he had 'made very many inaccurate statements regarding the family'.[22] Whatever his status, Hyde's close familiarity with the Londonderrys brought both privileged access and its restrictions. Those sections in *The Londonderrys* that deal with the seventh marquess often read like an apologia, though the mature Hyde cannot be described as rendering his hero's opponents as enemies. Moreover, as it is argued here (see Chapter 7), Hyde was a silent collaborator in Londonderry's short book on appeasement, *Ourselves and Germany* (1938), and he might also have assisted him with his memoirs, *Wings of Destiny* (1943). Together these two books, along with Lady Londonderry's memoir, *Retrospect* (1938), constitute much of the source material for Hyde's *The Londonderrys*, just as these publications have tended to be the source material for most other accounts that have had cause to make reference to Lord Londonderry.[23]

If he was the Londonderrys' librarian, Hyde was not inclined to comment much on Lord Londonderry's reading habits, except a comic reference to him reading the first fifteen pages of Elinor Glyn's racy novel *Did She?* and his fondness for the scholarly works of the Ulster writer, Helen Waddell.[24] In relaying the latter, Hyde repeats Waddell's story, that Londonderry had once confided to her that he had removed three pages of her historical novel, *Peter Abelard*, so that he could carry them on his person.[25] Londonderry's correspondence yields only glimpses of his reading habits. He occasionally quoted poetry including in his speeches; Arthur Hugh Clough and John Milton were both invoked to explain and defend his record as air minister. In 1932 he passed on to a government colleague Alice Ritchie's novel, *The Peacemakers*, which he described as 'beautifully written'.[26] Based on Ritchie's experiences at the League of Nations secretariat in the 1920s, and those of its largely female employees, its literary merit probably came second in Londonderry's mind to the need to advertise its message about the boredom and peculiarity of small-town Geneva hosting an isolated international community. The following year, Londonderry passed on a recently published biography of Kemal Ataturk to Great Britain's representative in Iraq.[27] As with his recommendation of *The Peacemakers*, it was presumably done with the expectation that the recipient would be influenced by its message, in this case, by learning about the 'ruthless and inhuman' behaviour of Turkey's leader.[28] For a similar reason, Londonderry passed on to Lord Halifax a copy of George Ward Price's account of meeting Adolf Hitler.[29] As for Irish history, Londonderry certainly regarded himself as better informed than Michael Collins, following his meeting with the Irish republican leader in 1922 (see Chapter 4). The claim should be treated with caution, however, given their antagonistic views of the constitutional question. There is, moreover, little to suggest that Londonderry was particularly well read in history beyond its depiction of his famous forebear, Castlereagh; much later in life, he had cause to admit that he had only recently learnt how nineteenth-century politicians and diplomats had all the faults of his own age (see Conclusion). Beyond literature, he possessed a basic conversational knowledge of German that was employed during his controversial visits to Germany in the late 1930s, though the origin and development of this linguistic skill is unclear.[30]

Unusually in political and social history, it is Lady Londonderry and not her husband who has attracted the greater amount of attention in print.[31] The source material for much of this work is Edith's memoir, mentioned above, and her private papers held at the Public Record Office of Northern Ireland.[32] The centrality of Lady Londonderry to the career of her husband is something that these writers stress and this book in no way challenges, though greater attention is given here to their differences of opinion on a number of political questions. As noted already, Edith's continuation of salon politics into the 1930s is a major theme of this study, for such activities were seen by many as outmoded, and yet functions at Londonderry House remained popular. Moreover, the role of family, past, present and future, is vital to any understanding of the aristocracy in general, and the Londonderrys' political ambitions in particular.

Given the relative scholarly neglect of Lord Londonderry's political life, it is useful to outline some explanations of why this might be the case and what benefits there are from a critical examination of the entirety of his ministerial career.[33] As has already been mentioned, Londonderry was not a great man of history, but this book does not claim that he was or that he should be regarded as such. Indeed, the tendency of political biographers to focus on the famous or infamous is typically one of the criticisms levelled at the genre, along with the elevation of the individual above all other contextual considerations.[34] As for the first, J. A. Cross contends that the 'study of the careers of second-rank politicians can reveal more of the practical detail of the governing process than the examination of the more wide-ranging and generalized concerns of those who preside over governments'.[35] And the second is answered by Ian Kershaw's call for 'modern political biography' to 'be less person-centred than traditional biography'. Reversing the usual approach, he argues that biographers should ask 'how could such and such come about *without* or even against the wishes or actions of the subject of the biography?'[36] It is a particularly useful perspective in examining Londonderry's troubled tenures at the Air Ministry and Northern Ireland's Ministry of Education, and also his personal promotion of Anglo-German understanding.

The tendency of political biographers to overlook the second rank has left Londonderry a shadowy but definite presence in the interwar high politics of Great Britain and Ireland. It is reasonably well known that he played a part in some of the great controversies of the period, but little has been said, with the notable exception of his public position on Nazi Germany, on what that involved in practice. Perhaps the explanation lies, in part, on the reluctance of historians based in Great Britain to consult the Londonderry papers held at the Public Record Office of Northern Ireland, especially during the thirty-year period of political violence known as the Troubles. As a result, most scholars have tended to utilize instead *Ourselves and Germany* and *Wings of Destiny*. As noted already, these two books present a distorted picture. It is only through the rigorous use of the large archive that constitutes the Londonderry papers, alongside the relevant papers held at other archives, that the actions and significance of Londonderry's political life can be more fully examined and understood. It is worth noting here that Londonderry was aware that *Ourselves and Germany* had implicated him as one of the foremost appeasers of Nazi Germany, and he was deeply frustrated that the restrictions imposed by the government on his memoirs had the effect of curtailing his efforts at vindication. Given this, Londonderry expressed his hope that his private papers would exonerate him.[37] This book does not seek to fulfil his wish, but it is important, at the outset, to acknowledge the subject's opinion that such a study would rescue his reputation. Its purpose, rather, is twofold: to remove the shadow that has partially obscured what is a remarkably long and revealing career in governments on both sides of the Irish Sea, and to examine the relationship between aristocracy and democracy at a time when the former was increasingly questioned and considered outmoded. These are overlapping aims, for Londonderry, while not representative of the aristocracy per se, did represent in his ministerial career the diminishing continuation of the traditional authority long associated with large landowners. At the same time, to fully understand his example of aristocratic tenacity, we must, as Jonathan Powis observes, approach Londonderry's political life by discarding 'anachronistic assumptions about the inevitability of decline'.[38]

I

Why should the Londonderry family, and the seventh marquess in particular, have felt that it was worth expending so much time and effort in the pursuit of ministerial office, especially at a time when aristocratic claims on government patronage were in decline? To answer this, it is necessary to appreciate the centrality of power and political influence to the history of aristocracy. However, given the inherent difficulty of defining the nature of power, even aristocratic power, themes relevant to this topic will be examined through an outline history of the Londonderry family.

In his survey of constitutions, Aristotle defines *aristokratia*, or aristocracy, to mean rule by the best, and although this includes oligarchies, the definition is not restricted to them.[39] Writing in the early twenty-first century, Peregrine Worsthorne's *In Defence of Aristocracy* claims that 'classical republican ideals' still activate the British aristocracy, in particular, the insistence 'that the highest purpose of man was to sacrifice himself, and his family, on the altar of the common weal', and that aristocracy, 'in this tradition, was much more a burden to be taken up than a privilege to be enjoyed, much more a sacrifice than an indulgence, being born with a silver spoon in your mouth meant keeping your nose to the grindstone for life'.[40] Such ideas were certainly instilled in the seventh Marquess of Londonderry from a young age. But the silver spoon cannot be ignored. Regardless of the 'sacrifice' made by aristocrats, their status was more often than not tied to privileges that left them open to accusations of pursuing the very opposite: self-interest and self-aggrandisement. Whatever its classical origins, the term aristocracy was by the eighteenth century applied to a stratum of society that, to varying degrees, inherited wealth, rank and political power: a class of people who were literally born to rule. In the localities in which aristocratic families owned land, their authority was significant, although this often depended on the proximity and size of rival landowners. For this authority to translate into a prominent role on the national stage, aristocratic families needed to possess greater wealth, rank or input into the state, through some combination of marriage, inheritance and a will to power.[41] But before any of this could happen, aspiring families had to traverse the long and complex path to becoming part of the landowning elite. According to J. V. Beckett, 'land alone was not enough' for acceptance. 'Considerable stress was laid upon pedigree', and since 'this disbarred first generation wealth the second had to be prepared for entrance by means of an acceptable education and marriage into the elite'. This is exemplified by the rise of the Stewarts, as is Beckett's further observation that promotion through the ranks of the nobility depended on 'a variety of considerations including land ownership, state service and general acceptability'.[42]

John Stewart was one of a significant number of Presbyterian Scottish settlers who occupied land in west Ulster granted by King James I in the early seventeenth century. Stewart's property was relatively small and his pedigree questionable, so when his great-great grandson, Alexander Stewart (1700–1781), sought to extend the family's resources, he had to venture into business and commerce, first in Belfast, and later in London. Alexander's fortunes were improved when he served a term as the MP for Londonderry City in the House of Commons at Dublin, an assembly dominated by the sons and agents of Ireland's landowners. Stewart's most lasting success was his marriage to Mary Cowan, the daughter of Sir Robert Cowan, onetime Governor of Bombay. It helped to consolidate and extend the resources of both families, Mary having inherited the fortune that her father had amassed during his time in India. Their combined wealth allowed the Stewarts to purchase in 1744 the adjoining manors of Newtownards and Comber, both in County Down. The family then moved from their original home at Ballylawn, near Moville in County Donegal, to a demesne near Newtownards on the Ards Peninsula, originally called Mount Pleasant, but later renamed Mount Stewart. The onward march of Alexander Stewart was halted, however, when he failed to secure the local political interest, it being retained within the family of the former owner of the property. Nor was he successful in being elected the MP for Belfast due to his disagreements with the local magnate, the first Marquess of Donegall.

If Alexander's progress was arrested then his son Robert (1739–1821) took the family to new heights.[43] Robert successfully sought the hand of Lady Sarah Seymour-Conway, the daughter of the first Marquess of Hertford, a wealthy landowner in County Down who in 1765 was appointed Lord Lieutenant of Ireland. Hertford, not surprisingly, was keen to look after his son-in-law and solicited him a peerage, but Stewart preferred instead to represent County Down as an independent in the House of Commons. In this he succeeded, and five years after Sarah's death in 1770, Robert married Lady Frances Pratt, daughter of the first Earl Camden, Lord Chancellor of Great Britain. 'It is difficult to think of another aristocratic Irish family', Anthony Malcomson observes, 'which played the marriage market by making great tangible sacrifices for great non-financial gains'.[44] Just as Hertford had helped Robert, so too with Camden. Robert's sons were sent to Eton and Cambridge, and after Robert lost his seat in the Dublin parliament, Camden secured him an Irish peerage in 1789 as Baron Londonderry, with a seat in the Irish House of Lords. In 1795 the second Earl Camden, as Lord Lieutenant of Ireland, had Londonderry raised in the peerage as Viscount Castlereagh.

The following year Robert was raised yet again, to the earldom of Londonderry, enabling his son, also called Robert, to be styled Viscount Castlereagh (1769–1822).[45] It was for the younger Robert's services to the state that his father's title was raised finally in 1816 from an earldom to a marquessate. The famous political career of Viscount

Castlereagh – he was only Marquess of Londonderry from 1821 until his death the following year – need not be dealt with here. But it is important to observe that he was the first of his family to hold a truly significant place at the centre of the state, first in Ireland and then in Great Britain. It was to Castlereagh that future generations of the family looked back with pride, even if his legacy was not altogether positive, for Castlereagh's suicide had the effect of fuelling gossip that the family shared his mental instability.[46] Nor were Castlereagh's significant political legacies, the Irish Act of Union (1800) and the Congress of Vienna (1815), beyond controversy, although at the time and ever since these have been acknowledged as personal triumphs.

Alongside the accumulation of political capital, Castlereagh married Lady Amelia Anne Hobart, daughter of the second Earl of Buckinghamshire and heiress to her mother's fortune. Impressive as this match was, it was as nothing compared to that engineered by Charles Stewart (1778–1854), Castlereagh's half-brother and successor as the third Marquess of Londonderry.[47] Whereas Castlereagh had been raised a Presbyterian, Charles was raised as an Anglican. He served in the army with some distinction, seeing action in the Peninsular War, before settling down, with the help of Castlereagh, to a diplomatic career in Berlin and Vienna. For these services he was in 1814 created Baron Stewart of Stewart's Court and Ballylawn in the United Kingdom peerage. Seven years after the death in 1812 of his first wife – Lady Catherine Bligh, daughter of the third Earl of Darnley – Lord Stewart married Frances Anne, daughter of the Countess of Antrim and her first husband, Sir Henry Vane-Tempest. Frances Anne was the heiress of vast estates in County Durham, including coalfields, amassed by the Vane and Tempest families, and she was to prove a dynamic force in the advancement of her family's economic and political interests.[48] The couple moved to Wynyard Park in County Durham and soon after purchased property at the coastal town of Seaham. By the time that Stewart inherited his half-brother's titles and property in 1822, Castlereagh having died without issue, the third Marquess of Londonderry was a substantial landowner on both sides of the Irish Sea. That same year he purchased a large London property, Holdernesse House, on the corner of Park Lane and Hertford Street. This building, later known as Londonderry House, was intended to impress and secure the place of the now immensely wealthy Londonderrys at the heart of London society. Lord Londonderry resigned his ambassadorship upon becoming a marquess, but he insisted that the government satisfy his claims to a generous pension, to ministerial office and to an advancement in the United Kingdom peerage. The Tory prime minister, the second Earl of Liverpool, only assented to the last of these, creating him Earl Vane and Viscount Seaham. It was not uncommon for holders of Irish peerages to seek advancement to or within the United Kingdom peerage, it being deemed to confer more status on the holder than the equivalent Irish titles. From the government's standpoint, it allowed ministers to reward or pay off followers, and to add fresh members to the House of Lords. Londonderry already possessed a United Kingdom peerage, so in his case it was an attempt to satisfy his near persistent claim on further rewards without bringing him into the government.[49] In this specific instance, the Londonderrys' unbridled ambition was not an asset in every sphere, and it hardly helped that the marquess's odd behaviour was rumoured to be connected to the mental instability that had ruined his half-brother. Not even the premiership of the first Duke of Wellington could aid his cause, the two men having served alongside each other in Spain, for it was Londonderry's implacable opposition to parliamentary reform that ultimately damaged any chance that he had of achieving ministerial office. He could, nevertheless, take some comfort from his appointment in 1842 as Lord Lieutenant of County Durham, an official recognition of the Londonderrys' relatively recent attainment of pre-eminence in the area. It proved to be a lasting achievement, as several of his successors as marquess acquired the same office, and they would also head the Conservative party in the county, through to the death of the seventh marquess.

As this suggests, the third marquess's most significant and long-lasting success was his marriage to Frances Anne. Despite her husband failing to obtain a place in the government, Frances Anne was adept in using the rituals of society to advance her family's interests. She courted highly placed politicians, such as Benjamin Disraeli, to assist the political careers of her stepson and sons. Likewise, she secured the marriage of one of her daughters to the Marquess of Blandford, later the seventh Duke of Marlborough. The offspring of that marriage included Lord Randolph Spencer Churchill, the father of Winston.[50]

Following the death of her husband in 1854, the dowager Marchioness of Londonderry followed the example of the late marquess by taking an active role in managing the Londonderry Collieries, including the new pits sunk at Seaham.[51] In her case, however, she not only broke with traditional expectations regarding women, but also the presumption that aristocratic owners of industry should leave the day-to-day running of such matters to others. Norman Gash argues that the success of the aristocracy at this time in retaining the 'substance of their traditional political power . . . was a remarkable tribute to their adaptability and good sense'.[52] No doubt this was true of many families, but in the case of the Londonderrys, it was ultimately the ownership of the Vane-Tempest mining interests that protected them from the long-term economic decline that was the fate of landowners primarily dependent on agricultural holdings. It meant that by the 1880s, the Londonderrys were among the top-twenty wealthiest families in the United Kingdom, with a gross landed income of around £110,000 (the equivalent in 2021 of £13.5 million).[53]

Like the forebears of their title, the fourth and fifth marquesses of Londonderry were expected to pursue careers in politics. As noted already, Frances Anne did her best to promote their interests, in particular, her stepson, Frederick (1805–1872), who became the fourth Marquess of Londonderry in 1854, and her son, Viscount Seaham, who inherited his father's United Kingdom peerage to become the second Earl Vane. The fourth marquess had been one of two MPs for County Down since 1822, and briefly held government offices under Wellington, as a Lord of the Admiralty, and Robert Peel, as a whip in the House of Commons. If he was an able politician, the collapse of these two ministries – in 1829 and 1834, respectively, both not long after his appointment – gave him little opportunity to demonstrate it. Like his father he had to settle instead for a lord lieutenancy, this time in County Down, although he was also made a Knight of St Patrick, the highest order of chivalry in Ireland. The fourth marquess spent the last decade of his life suffering from mental illness. He died in 1872 and was buried at Newtownards.

As the fourth marquess left no heirs, his half-brother, Lord Vane, became the fifth Marquess of Londonderry (1821–1884). Like Frederick, the fifth marquess had served as a Conservative MP, in his case for County Durham, before succeeding to the earldom. And like his father and half-brother, the political career of the fifth marquess was also unremarkable. Disraeli ensured that he received the honours then due to a man of his rank – the Order of St Patrick in 1874 and the lord lieutenancy of County Durham in 1880 – but he was not judged suitable for ministerial office. This prolonged hiatus in the political fortunes of the Londonderry family was by no means unusual in the aristocracy, but the situation might have been different had the wives of the fourth and fifth marquesses possessed the determination and talent of Frances Anne. As Diane Urquhart demonstrates, such influence could be crucial in aiding the careers of male family members.[54] The energies of Frederick's wife, however, were devoted to her Catholic faith, having converted in 1855. And far from the fifth marquess consolidating and extending his local power bases in County Down and County Durham, he preferred instead to live at Plâs Machynlleth, his wife's estate in Montgomeryshire, Wales. This addition to the family's already extensive properties meant that the Londonderrys possessed over 50,000 acres across the United Kingdom with an estimated land value in 1872 of £2,502,950 (the equivalent in 2021 of £290 million).[55] If the political careers of the third, fourth and fifth marquesses are judged as failures, at least on the national stage, it is because they were unable for various reasons to take advantage of their significant inheritances. The family, nevertheless, managed to retain its substantial wealth and status throughout the period, and it was this that the sixth marquess and his wife were able to utilize to successfully gain ministerial office for the former, albeit under more fortuitous circumstances.

The sixth Marquess of Londonderry (1852–1915) was educated at Eton, where he was Arthur Balfour's fag, the National University of Ireland, and Christ Church, Oxford, during which time he was known as Viscount Seaham.[56] Following his father's succession as fifth marquess in 1872, Seaham's courtesy title changed to Castlereagh, and it was as Viscount Castlereagh that in 1875 he married Lady Theresa Chetwynd Talbot, eldest daughter of the nineteenth Earl of Shrewsbury. Emotionally, the marriage was not a happy one, due in part to Theresa's romantic indiscretions; her behaviour even received satirical treatment in Vita Sackville-West's *The Edwardians*.[57] Politically, however, Theresa's passion for politics and her unceasing quest to advance the family proved to be crucial factors in her husband's acquisition of ministerial office.[58]

That change in the Londonderry family's political fortunes also owed something to developments in Ireland. Castlereagh had followed the family tradition by sitting in the House of Commons from 1879 until his father's death in 1884. It is significant that he represented County Down and not County Durham, for his association with Ulster was to leave a deep mark on his political outlook and career, and those of his son, the future seventh marquess. When the third Marquess of Salisbury formed his second government, in July 1886, he invited Londonderry to become Lord Lieutenant of Ireland.[59] The sheer expense of the Irish viceroyalty, its reputation for being dangerous, the need to reside for long periods in Dublin and the perception that it was not a stepping stone to higher office, all served to limit the ability of prime ministers to find suitable candidates. Londonderry had the necessary wealth and long-standing commitment to Irish affairs, including a permanent residence in Ireland. Indeed, in appointing him Salisbury claimed to be responding to calls for an Irishman to hold the post.[60]

Nevertheless, Londonderry's Irish background made him a controversial appointment. For the nationalist and land reformer Michael Davitt, the 'enmity to Irish nationhood' perpetrated by the second marquess, as Castlereagh, in 1800, rendered the sixth marquess the 'representative of the nobility thus created'.[61] More substantially, during the time that he had represented County Down in the House of Commons, Londonderry like other Ulster landowners had met the challenge of Irish nationalism by allying with pro-Union politicians and organizations in the province. This involved the future sixth marquess associating himself with the largely plebeian Orange Order and acquiescing in the development of an independently minded group of Irish Conservative MPs at Westminster.[62] It was these associations, historical and contemporary, that help to explain why the nationalist Lord Mayor of Dublin boycotted Londonderry's formal entry to the city, as Lord Lieutenant of Ireland, on 17 September 1886.[63]

Londonderry's viceroyalty was otherwise unremarkable, not least because the political work was largely in the hands of the Chief Secretary for Ireland, Sir Michael Hicks Beach, succeeded in 1887 by Arthur Balfour. But as suggested already, in merely occupying the post, Londonderry embodied the link between the Irish Unionists and the Conservative party in Great Britain. It was not a straightforward or easy position to occupy, however, even after the defeat earlier that year of William Gladstone's first Home Rule bill. This is because the Salisbury government's efforts to undermine nationalism through ameliorative legislation created anxiety among Irish Unionists. Londonderry was conscious of his status as a leading light for the latter, but he was also the member of a 'Unionist' government at Westminster concerned with ensuring the unity and survival of the Conservative party. It was a situation that, decades later, his son would also occupy when serving in the government of Northern Ireland (see Chapter 4). Londonderry's appointment was also significant in that it came at a time when the politically active peerage had responded to franchise reforms by attempting to make the House of Lords work more effectively. Salisbury was crucial to this process, balancing the vested interests of peers with the need for the upper house to appear constructive and pragmatic, and by also ensuring that peers occupied around half the number of ministerial positions.[64]

Londonderry was not only useful to Conservative ministers for his connections to Ireland, but also for his prominence in the affairs of County Durham. The need to finance politics nationally was also a factor, for the contributions of Conservative peers to central funds increased after 1885, amounting to a third or even half of all monies raised. Alloyed to Lady Londonderry's active cultivation of political patronage, Lord Londonderry's period at Dublin was followed sometime later by his appointment as Postmaster-General, from 1900 to 1902, and thereafter in Arthur Balfour's government as President of the Board of Education. From October 1903 he also served as Lord President of the Council. It is noteworthy that even at this stage the use of political patronage by Lady Londonderry, to advance her husband's career in government, attracted criticism in the press, prefiguring the negative commentary that would later be experienced by the seventh marquess and his wife.[65]

This remarkable period of aristocratic influence at the heart of government began to unravel from 1902, and it culminated in the Liberal's landslide victory at the 1906 general election. The bitter divisions over tariff reform that then convulsed the Conservative party were a significant factor. The Durham coalfield was largely bound up with the export of coal, so it is hardly surprising that Londonderry resisted the siren calls of tariff reformers to substitute imperial economic unity for free trade. Indeed, the militancy of advanced tariff reformers in the early 1900s, and growing support in Conservative ranks for their policy, led to clashes between them and the sixth marquess.[66] As a result, both he and his son became closely tied to Balfour, as the increasingly beleaguered party leader tried to meet this pressure by fashioning a compromise policy on the fiscal question. It was a period when the Londonderrys might have lost the political capital that they had gained under the premierships of Salisbury and Balfour. But after a number of difficult years, the constitutional and political crises of 1911–14 thrust the Londonderrys back on the national stage.

II

Charles Stewart Henry Vane-Tempest-Stewart was born on 13 May 1878 to Lord and Lady Castlereagh at 76 Eaton Place, London. He was the second of three children and the eldest of two boys. The poor health of his younger brother, Reginald, which led ultimately to his early death at the age of 20, meant that the enormous weight of his parents' ambitions was placed squarely on him. It would be the source of recurring tensions between Londonderry and his eldest and only surviving son. The latter's upbringing was otherwise one of seemingly unruffled financial, social and political privilege. Charles, to his friends Charley, or Viscount Castlereagh, as he was known from 1884, was initially educated at home by a governess, then at the preparatory Mortimer Vicarage School, Reading, before attending Eton College at fourteen years old. He later acknowledged that he had failed to distinguish himself at school either academically or physically.[67] In addition to his formal schooling, he received an informal education in politics through his parents' central place in London society and his father's positions in the successive governments of Salisbury and Balfour. Londonderry introduced Charles to the various institutions that he would one day inherit: the collieries, the social and political role of Londonderry House, and the family's prominent position in the local affairs of both Ulster and County Durham. His mother was particularly keen to impress upon him the reputation of the eponymous subject of her short book *Robert Stewart, Viscount Castlereagh*.[68] Charles was eight years old when his parents entered Dublin in state in 1886. As he sat in the coach with the lord lieutenant and his vicereine, Castlereagh – following the instructions given to him by his mother – tipped his hat to the cheering crowds that lined the streets.[69] His informal education also included less elevated activities, such as waiting upon tables in 1890 at a Primrose League function held at Seaham.[70] Encouraged by his parents, Castlereagh had some modest experience of addressing meetings, typically by seconding a vote of thanks to the chairman, but nothing more substantial. He later admitted that 'even when I was twenty-seven years old I didn't know how to make a good speech. I invariably lost all connexion between

Figure 1 Viscount Castlereagh in costume, 1897.

my thoughts and my words if I got up unprepared. The consequence was that I wrote out all my speeches and learned them by heart'.[71]

After Eton, Castlereagh enrolled as a cadet at Sandhurst Royal Military College; fighting, according to David Cannadine, being 'the aristocratic profession par excellence'.[72] Even here Castlereagh was an unremarkable student, but his skilled horsemanship saw him win the college's 'Saddle' prize.[73] And given his pedigree, it was almost a foregone conclusion that he would achieve a posting to a prestigious regiment; after passing out in June 1897, he duly joined the Royal Horse Guards. 'The Blues' was socially exclusive and glamorous, and it appears to have provided Castlereagh with an environment in which he could flourish, for within a few years, at the age of 22, he was appointed adjutant of the regiment.[74]

Castlereagh's skill and interest in horsemanship was not confined to the military. He would maintain the family stud at Wynyard after inheriting the property in 1915, and not long after, in 1921, he won the famous St Leger.[75] His commitment to horse racing even led him in 1917 to write to *The Times*, while serving at the Western Front, to criticize a government proposal to prohibit it for the duration of the war, and he singled out Lords Derby and Curzon for their apparent acquiescence with the idea.[76] As might be expected, Castlereagh was also a keen practitioner of field sports, including fishing, and he often indulged in the pastimes of golf, tennis and bridge.[77] He was a sailor too, later a member of the Royal Yacht Squadron at Cowes, and most often indulged this particular pastime on Strangford Lough when staying at Mount Stewart.[78]

Alongside his military duties, Castlereagh played an active role in society and at court. In this social scene he met Edith Chaplin, daughter of Henry Chaplin, a former Conservative cabinet minister, and Lady Florence Leveson-Gower, eldest daughter of the third Duke of Sutherland. Charles and Edith, aged 21 and 20, respectively, were married on 28 November 1899 at St Peter's, Eaton Square, London. As with Frances Anne and Theresa, Edith would also be an enormous asset to her husband, for like them she possessed a passion for politics and the determination to use whatever material advantages the Londonderrys possessed to aid the political ambitions of her family. It would prove to be an emotionally strong and enduring marriage, though Edith's tolerance of her husband's disposition to infidelity was tested from the very outset.[79]

The Londonderrys were so determined that Castlereagh sire an heir, and make a mark in politics, that they forbade him from seeing action in the South African War. The outbreak of hostilities in 1899, after all, had coincided with the premature death of his younger brother, Reginald. The restriction was met with great resentment, all the more because Castlereagh enjoyed the soldiering life and did not look forward with any pleasure to a life in parliament.[80] While his brother cavalry officers were overseas serving the cause of empire, Castlereagh remained at home, living the life of a soldier gentleman – the hunt, polo, horse racing and society functions – and performing the ceremonial duties associated with the Blues. Indeed, the only time that Castlereagh's military career and the Anglo-Boer conflict converged was in 1900, when he commanded Queen Victoria's escort in a parade to celebrate the relief of Ladysmith. The elderly monarch was so impressed by her escort that she afterwards asked that the Castlereaghs visit her at Windsor Castle.[81] Her death in 1901 provided Castlereagh with another opportunity at ornamental soldiering, when he was appointed aide-de-camp to the first Viscount Wolseley. Edward VII assigned the Dublin-born field marshal the task of formally announcing the succession to other monarchs. Wolseley and Castlereagh toured the courts of Europe and the Near East, visiting the masters of a world that was soon to vanish, including the Emperor Francis Joseph of Austria, the Queen of Rumania, King Alexander of Serbia and the Ottoman Sultan Abdul Hamid II.[82]

A similar fate would await the aristocratic character of government in the United Kingdom, one presided over by an aristocratic sovereign. However, before the era of popular monarchy, the royal family was content to flaunt its close connections to the higher aristocracy, including the Londonderrys.[83] In 1902 King Edward sponsored the christening of the Castlereagh's first son, Robert.[84] The following year witnessed visits by the king to both Mount Stewart and to Wynyard Hall. Not only was the latter to mark Londonderry's appointment as Lord President of the Council, but it involved convening the Privy Council at Londonderry's house, reputedly the first time that it had been performed at such a location since 1625.[85]

A considerable portion of Castlereagh's final years outside of parliament were taken up touring the British Empire, an Edwardian version of the European grand tour that had characterized earlier aristocratic travel. Accompanied by his wife, whose illness had prompted the trip, Castlereagh sailed to Bombay on the same vessel as the governor-general of India, the first Baron Curzon of Kedleston. The Castlereaghs spent Christmas 1904 with Curzon near Calcutta, and during their subsequent tour of the subcontinent they met and stayed with a number of Indian princes, including the maharajahs of Baroda, Rajputana, Jodhpur, Idar and Benares, as well as the Nizam of Hyderabad and several provincial governors.[86] Lord Castlereagh was evidently inspired by his time in India and his close proximity to the viceroy and Indian princes, for he retained the hope in later life that he might be considered as a candidate for the viceroyalty. If that ambition was never realized, India still featured in his future career, for the visit inclined him in later years to support limited plans for Indian responsible government. And his visit to the Northwest Frontier in 1905 would be repeated almost three decades later, on that occasion as Secretary of State for Air (see Chapter 6).[87] Before returning to England in the second half of 1905, the Castlereaghs travelled through Singapore and Hong Kong, and arrived in Japan immediately after the conclusion of its victorious war with Russia, before crossing the Pacific and journeying the length of Canada and on to New York.[88] In contrast to Lord Castlereagh's time in India, the Canadian leg of the tour left a mixed impression. Writing several years later, he noted that it 'is a very impressive country[,] everything so immense and progressive. The Canadians are not so attractive but they do work and even in the short time since I was here the change is stupendous'.[89] It is tempting to see this as the reason for his subsequent refusal, on three separate occasions, of the governor-generalship of Canada. Certainly, his first impressions of the dominion might have coloured his later outlook, but his repeated resistance to that appointment was chiefly to do with it being a largely ornamental office.

Towards the end of 1905 it was clear that a general election loomed in the New Year. Increasingly compromised by divisions over tariff reform, Balfour's government resigned on 4 December to be replaced by a Liberal ministry under Sir Henry Campbell-Bannerman. Londonderry was determined that the moment was right for his 26-year-old son to stand for election to the House of Commons, but Castlereagh had other ideas and did not want to leave the army. In 1904 he had managed to deflect his father's attempt to make him take up the vacant Unionist candidature for County Down.[90] But the imminence of a general election, and the threatened loss of financial help from his parents, ensured that on this occasion he succumbed to his father's will. Castlereagh later admitted that his 'father was very anxious that I should stand for Parliament . . . He even thought I was wasting my time, enjoying myself with my soldiering. All during that autumn he was constantly urging me to find a seat somewhere'.[91] Lady Castlereagh later recorded that it was with 'a heavy heart my husband agreed . . . and I cannot think that I was any help to him in this decision. I much preferred the easy going soldiering life, but the fiat had gone forth'.[92]

With many of the safer Conservative constituency nominations already allocated, including the family palatines of Down and Durham, Castlereagh haunted Conservative Central Office in search of a constituency near London. He failed to get anywhere when he attended interviews at constituency associations in the capital, at Chatham, and in Shrewsbury. It was only when Londonderry sought the help of a former cabinet colleague and fellow free trader, Aretas Akers-Douglas, that Castlereagh became a viable candidate for the constituency of Maidstone in Kent, where Akers-Douglas was a prominent landowner.[93]

Tariff reform dominated the 1906 general election, although Irish home rule and the education reforms piloted through parliament by Londonderry also featured prominently.[94] As tariff reform was such a divisive issue within the Conservative party – and even, it appears, within the Castlereaghs' marriage – Lord Castlereagh preferred to address the Maidstone association on his opposition to home rule.[95] It was a strategy recommended to him by the prominent Irish Unionist and family friend, Edward Carson, for it was an issue in which Castlereagh could claim a family interest and one on which the Conservatives were resolutely united. Carson attended Castlereagh's first meeting to help him gain the nomination. He reported back to Lady Londonderry that her son was 'very well received' and that he 'made a sensible short speech, not touching on fiscals and leaving the bulk of the evening for me. I was quite delighted with the way he met people, and he was affable and jolly with them'.[96] Castlereagh's speech also associated himself with his father's recent education reforms, a topic that like Ireland was used to promote Conservative unity. However, if Castlereagh sought to take on his father's mantle, then he had to be wary of their inescapable association.[97] For it was Londonderry who had sparked off the most recent dispute between Joseph Chamberlain and Balfour on tariff reform, when, on 1 November 1905, in an address given at Sunderland, he had warned that Chamberlain's policy might split the Conservative party.[98] Chamberlain's immediate response was to attack Londonderry, although his real target was Balfour.[99]

On Christmas Eve 1905 the Castlereaghs stayed at their marital home, Springfield, near Oakham in Rutland. Referred to as a hunting box, it was a relatively large property with four reception rooms and ten bedrooms situated on a 90-acre estate.[100] From there, Castlereagh informed his mother that his adoption for Maidstone would be a 'very near thing', that 'there was a good chance, I think, as they like a lord'.[101] It was therefore from the very outset of his career in politics that Castlereagh was convinced that his background was not a barrier to public office, and that it could even be played up in order to help his chances of success. And if he was complacent or even arrogant in thinking this, especially at a time when aristocrats were losing their confidence about remaining a force in government, then the Maidstone constituency association clearly agreed with him. Having been adopted as their candidate, Castlereagh chose to carry on with the style of politicking that had aided him thus far. This, he hoped, would help him to overcome the serious obstacles that stood in his way of winning the constituency. These not only included his recent arrival to the area and his lack of experience, but also the more serious difficulty of taking the seat from the sitting Liberal, the businessman Sir Francis Evans. Given that both men were free traders, the contest would invariably centre on the background of each candidate. Unable and unwilling to deny his high birth, or even compensate for it, Castlereagh played to the gallery, encouraging his mother to help and to give 'the Maidstone people a show' by making an appearance in the family carriage.[102] Having done so much to assist the career of her husband, Lady Londonderry had little difficulty in aiding her son with a combination of speeches, canvassing and regal tours in her coach.

Castlereagh's return to the House of Commons was very much a family affair, from his father's intervention in finding a constituency to the assistance of his wife and mother on the stump. It was in fact typical of a style of electioneering that was fast dying out, but Castlereagh's success in achieving the nomination, and afterwards the seat, did little to shake his confidence in the old order. Still, it is telling that he found the practicalities of electioneering distasteful, informing his mother that 'I shall be heartily sick of this vote cadging in a very short time'.[103] After polling day on 12 January 1906, Castlereagh received news of his slender victory over Evans by 132 votes. Given the Liberal landslide that had decimated Conservative representation throughout the country, 367 seats to 157, it is unsurprising that elements of the press viewed Castlereagh's victory as remarkable.[104]

The general election did not heal Conservative divisions over tariff reform. Indeed, the party's ranks were divided between 109 tariff reformers, 11 supporters of the status quo, 32 willing to back Balfour's efforts to achieve a compromise and 5 undecided. The subsequent period on the opposition benches would be an immensely difficult time for the party and for Conservative peers in particular. The latter, in the House of Lords, became the party's only parliamentary bulwark against a reforming House of Commons, and as a result the target of much Liberal invective, and to pressure from contending wings of the Conservative party. As if to underscore how much had been lost, fifty-three Labour MPs were also returned in 1906, alongside the now inevitable encampment of eighty-three Irish nationalists.

More immediately, Castlereagh found his return challenged a fortnight after polling. Maidstone's reputation for electoral corruption, the national swing against the Conservatives and the narrow margin of Castlereagh's victory, all probably influenced Evans' decision to contest the result.[105] Other than that, it is hard to discern if his claims of bribery had any validity. At least one of Castlereagh's local activists was sure that there had been 'elaborate care taken to prevent anything of the sort', but against this, Lady Castlereagh conceded long afterwards that 'there was probably a certain amount of "treating" by unauthorized agents'.[106] Evans' election petition contained 'ninety-seven allegations, comprising specific and general bribery by money, treating in public houses, distribution of free meat, illegal voting, and unlawful payments to voters for travelling expenses'.[107] From reports in the local press, it would appear that Castlereagh treated the challenge with a light heart. On the sixth day of the hearing in May 1906, the 26-year-old MP was 'cheered on his arrival at the Court House, while Sir Francis Evans was greeted with hisses'. Castlereagh is reported as having given 'a witty defence under cross examination' and to have fallen asleep at various times when observing the court's proceedings. Matters became more serious when the MP endured a grilling from Evans' barrister, but within a week the petition was dismissed.[108] With Castlereagh now safely in the House of Commons, the Londonderry dynasty's political ambitions appeared to be secured for another generation.

The Londonderrys were determined that their son carry on the family tradition of parliamentary representation. Several years before Castlereagh's return to the House of Commons, at his coming of age celebrations at Mount Stewart in 1899, which had been delayed for a year due to his commitment to the Blues, the sixth marquess expressed his hope that the assembled tenants 'would not deny that Lady Londonderry and he had done their best from his birth to bring up their son in the way he should go, and to realise the great responsibilities that in the future must be his. They had attempted to bring him up the way an Irish landlord should go'.[109] The Londonderrys' tutelage did indeed have a profound impact on Castlereagh, for he not only came to accept their charge, albeit reluctantly, he would later adopt the constructive and pragmatic qualities of aristocratic leadership that had been so successful during his father's period in the Salisbury government.

1

Politics and war, 1905–18

The years from Viscount Castlereagh's election to the House of Commons in 1906 to the First World War were a period of heightened political turbulence.[1] The Conservatives struggled to overcome the shock of opposition and were beset with continued infighting over tariff reform, which exacerbated the anxiety of many in their ranks about the Liberal government's radical agenda. Not even the introduction in 1912 of the third Irish Home Rule bill brought unity to their ranks, as pre-existing divisions continued to simmer and new ones emerged about the extent to which the party was committing itself to the militant posture adopted by Ulster unionism.

In these difficult circumstances, a number of recently elected Conservative MPs soon rose to prominence. They were helped by their parliamentary party's depleted ranks following the 1906 general election and the Conservatives' modest recovery at the two general elections held in 1910. Among them were the future party leader, Stanley Baldwin, and the lawyer F. E. Smith. The latter's maiden speech occurred the day after Castlereagh's, and Lady Castlereagh later recorded that her husband was fortunate 'in "getting in" before . . . Smith, the future Lord Birkenhead, who electrified the assembly with an oration of extraordinary power and wit'.[2] Castlereagh's did not rise to such heights. As he later divulged, he 'was terribly nervous', but 'was able to get through all right'.[3] In Baldwin's brief assessment of Castlereagh's time in the House of Commons, given decades later in 1936, he noted that the MP for Maidstone had failed to make an impression particularly when home rule became a vital issue.[4] It is an important appraisal that has inevitably influenced the judgement of historians, but a detailed examination of Castlereagh's time in the House of Commons presents a more nuanced picture.

That Castlereagh did not in this period rise to the first rank is clear, but that in part reflected his equivocal commitment to a career in the House of Commons, one that had been compelled by parental fiat rather than individual choice. Another important factor, seemingly overlooked by Baldwin, was that Castlereagh belonged to an increasingly embattled minority in his parliamentary party, the dwindling number that remained opposed to tariff reform.[5] Whereas an overwhelming majority of Conservative MPs had indicated their preparedness to adopt the policy as an alternative to Liberal social legislation, the Durham coalfields' reliance on the export trade kept Castlereagh, like his father, tied to free trade. Or, more accurately, it wedded them to the efforts of the party leader, Arthur Balfour, to find a policy that retained its essence while accommodating the concerns of tariff reformers.[6] In this uncertain and hostile environment it tended to be the supporters of tariff reform, such as Smith and Baldwin, and Andrew Bonar Law, Balfour's successor as party leader in 1911, that made a mark. With the more advanced tariff reformers working tirelessly against Balfour's equivocal stance, the newly elected free traders stood little chance of making similar progress. Given Baldwin's retrospective judgement, it is worth noting several contemporary press assessments of Castlereagh's early years in the House of Commons. Reporting on his maiden speech, the Liberal *Westminster Gazette* referred to him as a 'fresh talent'.[7] And two years later, the Conservative and Unionist free-trade Manchester *Sunday Chronicle* described him as 'a keen politician, and a first rate speaker . . . never gets excited, and never speaks except on subjects he knows something about. . . . There is no dash or splash about his speaking; he argues quietly, cogently, clearly'.[8] It even concluded by predicting that he would be elevated to the front bench in the next Conservative government. But a backbencher he remained, something that he later attributed to the difficulties he encountered in getting press attention. As he recalled, it 'was even more difficult to catch the eye of the Press Gallery than that of the Speaker', and it 'was the same when at the behest of [Conservative] Central Office he went round the country making speeches, which rarely found any reflex in the Press'.[9]

Castlereagh's maiden speech on 21 February 1906 was the first in the new parliament. Like his first public address in Maidstone, it dealt with the Irish question and opened with the characteristic declaration that he had a 'hereditary interest'. He went on to express his 'sympathy with the claim that Ireland should be ruled according to Irish ideas, but insisted that they should be consistent with the unity of the Empire'. It was an early if subtle indication of his flexible approach to the union, adumbrating his later performances at the Irish Convention (see Chapter 2) and in the government of Northern Ireland (see Chapter 4), though it was obfuscated at the time by the follow-up assertion that 'He very much doubted whether Nationalist views would stand that test'.[10] Ireland, of course, had been the raison d'être of the Unionist coalition of Conservatives and Liberal Unionists, and it was an issue that had shaped the political careers of the second and sixth marquesses of Londonderry. But it was not to the fore in the Conservative party when Castlereagh took his seat, nor would it be until the passing of the Parliament Act in 1911. In the meantime, the internal wrangling over tariff reform raged on, adding to the already considerable sense of disenchantment felt by Conservative MPs of all hues.

It was not uncommon during the 1906–10 parliament for the opposition benches to be largely empty, fuelling the accusations of absence made by Conservative MPs about other Conservative MPs.[11] For his part, Castlereagh quickly found the House of Commons tiresome, but he still attended debates with reasonable regularity, especially when they touched on issues of keen personal interest. During his early years as an MP he contributed to parliamentary debates on the army, coal mining, alcohol licensing, tenant law, Ireland, access to mountains, pensions, death duties, land taxation and horse breeding.[12] As suggested by his first intervention on Irish affairs, the positions that he adopted on these matters shed light on the political questions that would play a significant part in his subsequent career as a government minister on both sides of the Irish Sea.

Out of tune with the tariff reform majority in his party, Castlereagh sat below the gangway and formed political friendships with free traders and Balfourites such as his cousin Viscount Helmsley, Lord Hugh Cecil and Charles Mills, and after his election in 1911, Mark Sykes.[13] He did not, however, cut himself off from tariff reformers, as demonstrated by his friendship with the Irish peer and MP, the sixth Earl Winterton, one of the most advanced advocates of that cause.[14] Indeed, Castlereagh's brief membership of the Imperial Maritime League, a militant breakaway from the Navy League, indicates that he was not completely immune to the type of radical right politics that characterized the most zealous advocates of tariff reform.[15] What membership of that organization did not signal, however, was a sincere interest in naval affairs, about which he had little to say then and in subsequent years. In contrast, Castlereagh's parliamentary speeches in defence of laissez-faire economics were persistent, and directed as much at his own benches as the Liberal government, for he championed the status quo against those in both parties who sought to change established practice. In delivery, however, the rhetoric of his speeches was aimed squarely at the government benches; on one occasion he mocked the Liberals' steady abandonment of laissez-faire by accusing them of going against the free trade beliefs of their 'patron saint' Richard Cobden.[16] Similarly, Castlereagh's stances on issues such as changes to the army, state intervention in the coal industry and alcohol prohibition were outwardly partisan, but these also implicitly railed against a cross-party trend that saw social legislation as the solution to many of the country's ills. What therefore emerges in Castlereagh's speeches is not only an unfolding critique of the Liberals, but an attitude that seemed at this stage of his political career to take little heed of shifting opinions within his own party.[17]

I

With a background in the cavalry it is unsurprising that army reform was one of the first issues that Castlereagh took up in parliament. Early in 1907, the Secretary of State for War, Richard Haldane, sought to make financial savings and deal with the threat of a continental war by introducing a bill to amalgamate all voluntary military organizations into one territorial force. It was not a simple party issue, though it is notable that Conservative aristocrats were among the leading opponents of what became the Territorial and Reserve Forces Act 1907. For his part, Castlereagh opposed the clauses of the bill that ended the tradition of local volunteers, militia and yeomanry. Like many in his party, he suggested instead that the threat of continental war could only be met by some measure of universal military service.[18] Castlereagh had logistical concerns about Haldane's legislation, but it is clear that foremost in his mind was its further diminution of landed influence. The aristocracy had long been associated with local voluntary militias, and although legislation in the nineteenth century had curtailed the link, the measures outlined in Haldane's bill would end it completely. In this sense, the measure infringed on an old order that felt itself to be under attack in the widest sense.[19] As such, Castlereagh did not necessarily intend, in his contributions to the House of Commons, to propose 'national service', the preferred label for conscription among its advocates. Rather, he suggested that it would be more effective in raising a new reserve force than the measures proposed in Haldane's bill. Only a minority of MPs actively pressed for some form of conscription before the First World War, and Castlereagh was not among them.[20] Even so, the fact that he was prepared to air the idea is a reminder that it was not regarded by everyone as an infringement of personal liberty. If he had been pressed, it is unlikely that Castlereagh would have regarded national service as a breach of his commitment to laissez-faire, as the armed forces were viewed by many politicians, across the House of Commons, as the armed guardians of free trade and the United Kingdom's global economic interests.[21]

However he might have rationalized it, Castlereagh's disposition to at least consider national service exhibits a particular strain of authoritarianism that needs to be acknowledged and examined. Much later, in 1927, he would confide to the onetime Conservative MP, Arthur Baumann, that 'if you asked me which form of government I like best, I would at once say a benevolent dictatorship, next a very wise privy council; and as neither of these is possible in this country, I am prepared to make the very best I can of what is called democracy'.[22] It is tempting to read into these words more than was intended, given his subsequent promotion of an 'understanding' between Great Britain and Nazi Germany, and as such they need to be placed in their full context. Aristocrats in this period were never likely to be the most enthusiastic supporters of democracy given that – in their classical and ideal forms – the two concepts of government were in opposition to one another.[23]And like many in his class with links to Ireland, his experience of politics there encouraged scepticism about the universal applicability of democracy. As late as 1938 his wife would write that 'Democracy as the British know it is not for Southern Ireland. They are of a different race. They want firm, wise but powerful control, to prevent them trying to eat each other up.'[24] The couple's later call for Great Britain to reach an understanding with Nazi Germany was similarly premised on the notion that the two countries were very different, and therefore that the erosion of democracy in Germany should not be unduly criticized by British observers. They did not, however, oppose democracy in Great Britain; indeed, both of them were active in supporting women's suffrage in the 1900s and 1910s. Their support for representative institutions extended to India, for in the early 1930s Lord Castlereagh, then Marquess of Londonderry, supported the extension there of 'responsible government'.[25] In doing so he faced down the criticisms of diehard Conservatives, including their most prominent spokesman at the time, Winston Churchill. The Conservative party's success at the polls after 1918 no doubt played a part in reconciling many British aristocrats to democracy, albeit reluctantly and unenthusiastically. It is noteworthy in this respect that the conservatism that characterized British Conservative governments between the wars was qualitatively different from the authoritarian style found in other European states.[26]

All this lay in the future. For the moment, as a backbencher, Castlereagh's parliamentary interventions were notably frequent and unequivocal when it came to the series of reforms to the coal mining industry that the Liberal government hoped would appease an increasingly restless labour movement. Castlereagh began his speech on one of these measures, the Eight Hours bill, by remarking impertinently 'that if it were not regarded as an absolute crime to be connected with a coalowner, I should like to advance some reasons against this bill'. Mining magnates were still reeling from the Trade Disputes Act 1906 which had prevented them obtaining damages from trade unions for peaceful picketing. Speaking on the Eight Hours bill in April 1907, Castlereagh avoided his obvious reason for objecting to the measure – its further interference in the management and profits of colliery owners – by tailoring his objections to what he viewed as the concerns of his employees and consumers. He argued that the bill restricted the freedom of miners to work as many hours as they chose, adding that modern ventilation had reduced the risk of damage to their health. When he addressed the financial difficulties that it would involve, he pointed out that the inevitable rise in the price of coal would affect those who depended on cheap supplies, namely the working class and the struggling industrial sector.[27] Faced by an onslaught of Conservative amendments, the bill was delayed for over a year by a government cautious to secure its passage. On 9 December 1908, having become a leading opponent of the bill, Castlereagh broadened the scope of his attack, now presenting the measure as 'the first attempt made in this country to curtail the hours of adult labour'. He further claimed that 'it was not called for by the people' and that it sought to establish 'uniform legislation to meet wholly different local conditions'. He warned that 'if the principle of the Bill was once admitted it must extend to other industries and eventually control the whole of industrial life of the country'.[28]

Conservative objections in the House of Commons were ultimately overcome by the Liberal's large majority, and so attention turned to the inbuilt Conservative majority in the House of Lords. The latter, however, was wary of taking a stand against the lower house on an issue concerning labour, and as a result the measure was allowed safe passage; if a stand had to be made, it needed to be one that would command wide public sympathy. For his part, Castlereagh behaved more like a partisan MP than a Conservative peer staying his hand, as he objected to a number of related bills that his party was in broad agreement with, such as the 1909 Coal Mines (Clock Weighers) bill. On occasion, his self-interest was audacious. In a parliamentary debate on 13 July 1911, two Labour MPs objected to plans by the North Eastern Railway Company to replace a footpath on the banks of the Humber with an overhanging promenade. Castlereagh responded by questioning the two Lancashire MPs' 'authority' to speak for the people of Hull, but he declined to mention that he sat on the company's board of directors, having replaced his father in that capacity earlier in the year.[29]

It is noticeable that when discussing his industrial interests in public, Castlereagh took care to avoid appearing to criticize his employees, the very people whose representatives sought legislative reforms to the industry. Instead, he preferred to think of workers as individuals who exercised a choice, although this sat uneasily with his contention that their best interests were in placing industrial success above their own concerns. Commenting on an attempt to regulate pay, he placed his emphasis on the latter position by arguing that 'No wages board could fix a rate which would at once give the workers adequate wages and ensure plenty of work for the factory'.[30]

Against the Liberal government's expectation, its labour reforms failed to appease the trade union movement. Strikes had been a relatively rare occurrence during Balfour's premiership, but in 1907 three million working days were lost through industrial action. And despite or perhaps because of the government's movement on reform, the figure rocketed to forty-one million in 1912.[31] Towards the end of 1911 the government attempted to offset the risk of a miners' strike by introducing the Coal Mines (Regulations) bill. Given that the legislation was designed to increase pit safety, Castlereagh's objections were reduced to defensive claims that his family's interest was not solely motivated by profit, that safety was a concern of the owners and that industry-led regulations could recognize local conditions better than an act of parliament. Rather than blaming the miners, his frustration was vented instead in dismissing the activities of the trade unionists, and through the accusation that the government constantly violated the law of contract.[32]

Legislation continued to lag behind the demands of the trade unions, in particular, the call for a minimum wage. Following a breakdown in negotiations, the Miners' Federation of Great Britain (MFGB) called a strike in March 1912. Unlike the three-month strike that had been called in 1910 – which had only hit the Durham and Northumberland coalfields – the 1912 stoppage had a crippling effect on the mining industry more widely. In the face of such action, it was difficult for Castlereagh to maintain his naïve impression of the miners' interests, so he attributed the rising number of strikes to greater government interference. What emerged as the Coal Mines (Minimum Wages) Act 1912 bore little resemblance to the disaster that Castlereagh had predicted it would herald.[33] Just as he rejected national pay agreements in favour of local agreements, the Act established district conferences at which miners, owners and government representatives would negotiate local deals.[34] Coming as it did in the wake of the Parliament Act 1911, and during the period of the third home rule crisis of 1912–14, it is notable that unlike earlier mining legislation, Castlereagh adhered rigidly to the policy of his party leaders, objecting to the bill only during its second reading.[35]

The Liberal government's preoccupation with regulating the alcohol trade was another area of politics in which Castlereagh cast himself as a defender of laissez-faire and the working man. The Liberals, influenced by the nonconformist lobby within their ranks, took the line that too much money was being spent by husbands and fathers on alcohol. In April 1907 parliament debated the policy of 'local option' in Scotland, where a harsher regime of public house opening hours existed than in England.[36] Castlereagh argued against it by citing the failure of similar schemes in the United States. He claimed that prohibition would 'spread the habit of secret drinking and the consumption of bad liquor, which were so detrimental to the mental and physical conditions of all classes of the community'. He also pointed out 'that one area might be entirely a prohibited area, and another in close proximity might be doing a roaring trade'.[37] Like many Conservatives, he regarded such Liberal measures as 'class legislation', intended to harm an identifiably Conservative stronghold, that is, the producers – brewers and distillers – as well as consumers, and he met Liberal paternalism with his own, claiming in November 1908 that the closing of workmen's clubs would 'do a great deal of harm to the lives of working men'.[38] Like his defence of the mining industry, Castlereagh's objections could be camouflaged in Conservative paternalism, in a form that was likely to be more welcome among drinkers than miners; though even the former could not always be relied upon by Conservatives given organized resistance from within some working-class communities to the politicization of leisure.[39] Even so, in contrast to reforms to working hours and wages, the House of Lords was able to successfully hold off the various schemes of prohibition put forward by the Liberals, at least until the First World War, when regulation was deemed necessary for the sake of the war effort.[40]

Until the two general elections of 1910, Ireland was not the central issue that it would become in the wake of those polls. However, Castlereagh spoke regularly in parliament on the government's Irish policy, often remarking that it was motivated by partisan politics rather than economic concerns. In particular, he rounded on the Evicted Tenants (Ireland) bill, supporting what he viewed as its more practical provisions, but ultimately opposing the whole bill as being motivated by the government's need to appease the United Irish League.[41] Such criticisms were echoed in the House of Lords where the bill was amended to be less harmful to landowners. Regardless of Castlereagh's attempt to make his views on Ireland appear activated by rational economic motives, he was, like many Conservatives, especially those with Irish connections, stirred by deeper passions that found expression during heightened moments of partisanship. In February 1909, to take one instance, during a House of Commons debate on crime, Castlereagh accused the Chief Secretary for Ireland, Augustine Birrell, of being 'heart and soul' with the 'criminals' and for allowing Irish people to feel that crimes had been committed with his 'sanction and connivance'.[42]

II

In the closing months of 1909 a constitutional crisis emerged that dominated the political agenda until 1911, and which created the conditions thereafter for a crisis over Irish home rule. In an effort to rejuvenate flagging support for the government, the Chancellor of the Exchequer, David Lloyd George, introduced his people's budget. His plan to raise and create new taxes to pay for social reform and dreadnought battleships was to be borne most by the rich. It included a rise in income tax and death duties, a new supertax on the wealthy and a duty of 20 per cent on the unearned increment of land value. City bankers, merchants and businessmen were vigorously opposed to it. Yet, as David Cannadine highlights, it 'was not just a budget designed to raise money from the rich: it was the landed rich who were its principal target and victim'.[43]

Lloyd George's dislike of the aristocracy was well known. It was evident in a bitter exchange with Castlereagh, two years later, over the dukes of Sutherland, the family of Lady Castlereagh. The chancellor then accused the Sutherlands of having in the past undertaken land clearances on their Scottish estates.[44] He did so to make a highly favourable contrast with the policies recently pursued by his government in the areas concerned. In what became known as the Sutherland case, Castlereagh responded angrily to Lloyd George in *The Times*, accusing him of 'endeavouring wilfully to mislead the public'.[45] Later still, after Castlereagh inherited the marquessate in 1915, the consequences of Lloyd George's budget would touch him more directly, as he found it necessary to consider selling 'some of his outlying properties' in County Durham 'to pay death duties and heavy taxation'. He nevertheless used the opportunity to attach an element of *noblesse oblige* to this otherwise involuntary divestment, by offering Pelaw Wood to Durham City Council 'as a pleasure resort, and wished to associate with the gift the memory of the brave Durham soldiers who have sacrificed their lives in the great cause'.[46]

Given these later events, it might be assumed of Castlereagh that he was among the shrillest detractors of the people's budget. Certainly, like most landowners in parliament, he believed that it was intended as a punitive measure. But unlike the majority of his party, even those who were regarded as free traders, Castlereagh was wary of undermining a budget that many Conservatives sought to counter with tariff reform. Rather than attacking the principle of taxing the wealthy, therefore, he instead focused on questioning the proposed level of taxation.[47] It meant that he was now out of step with his beleaguered party leader, Balfour, whose belated and reluctant endorsement of tariff reform was matched by his resolution that the House of Lords should veto the bill and thus break a centuries-old precedent.[48] Faced with this stand-off, Herbert Asquith – who had replaced Henry Campbell-Bannerman as prime minister in April 1908 – dissolved parliament and went to the country to get a mandate for both the budget and House of Lords reform.

The indecisive result of the January 1910 general election ensured that a resolution to the crisis would not be arrived at quickly. A small swing to the Unionists meant that they now held 273 seats to the government's 275; Castlereagh retained Maidstone with an increased majority of 247.[49] But the Liberals were supported in parliament by eighty-two Irish nationalists and forty Labour MPs. The equivocal result of the general election added to the confusion within Conservative ranks, for it left them divided over whether tariff reform had helped or hindered their performance. Further divisions were evident over how they should react to Asquith's Parliament bill, a measure that proposed to end the vetoing power of the upper chamber. Castlereagh's response to the crisis year of 1910 was to lay the blame firmly with the Liberals and John Redmond's Irish nationalist party: 'the conduct of the Government deserved the deepest censure', Conservatives 'saw the whole fortunes of this country thrown into the melting-pot and prostituted before Mr Redmond'.[50] It was a common claim among Conservatives, but it did little to solve the divisions afflicting their own ranks.

The death of Edward VII on 7 May led to a truce of sorts during which an inter-party conference was arranged to discuss constitutional reform.[51] In the meantime, Castlereagh found another issue on which to attack the government and possibly delay the passage of legislation concerning the House of Lords: women's suffrage.[52] As suggested above, on this issue he was strongly influenced by his wife, a leading light of the constitutional suffragists in Great Britain and in Ulster.[53] In April 1910 Lord Castlereagh pressed the government to make time for the discussion of women's suffrage and attempted an amendment to stop them from conducting any more business until a bill was discussed.[54] And in November 1910, against the backdrop of the militant suffragette riots, Castlereagh attacked Asquith's opposition to suffrage reform and again demanded movement on the issue.[55] Given this odd reversal of roles, it is easy to mistake the Castlereaghs' support for Millicent Fawcett's National Union of Women's Suffrage Societies as being at odds with the Conservative party, or just a purely tactical device, especially as some suffragists regarded their movement as being more Liberal than Conservative.[56] However, suffrage was not a simple party issue, as is evident from the position of Asquith. People's views, according to Jose Harris, 'were often deeply rooted in individual psychology and so transcended the usual categories of ideology and class'.[57] This is evident even among Lady Castlereagh's own family. Whereas she was actively in favour of suffrage, her mother-in-law, Lady Londonderry, and her father, Henry Chaplin, were both opposed.

The House of Commons debate on the Accession Declaration bill, that followed the death of the king, offered a rare public glimpse into Castlereagh's religious outlook. In asking the government to clarify the term 'Protestant' in the declaration, he remarked that it was important that only true Protestants could sit on the throne as the 'meaning of the word "Protestant" might alter in years to come'.[58] It was a potentially sensitive issue among the Londonderrys' Unionist-supporting tenantry in County Down, especially as the bill sought to regulate something that had been introduced in 1688 for William III and Mary II.[59] Yet Castlereagh did not elaborate on what he thought true Protestant meant, nor did he mention Catholics. What he did refer to was the potential opportunity for atheists to take advantage of changing meanings.[60] If there is some uncertainty about his attitude to matters of religious faith, the evidence suggests that Lady Castlereagh took her Anglicanism seriously. Her granddaughter, Lady Annabel Vane-Tempest-Stewart, later recalled her childhood visits to Mount Stewart, and how the two had sat together on Edith's bed turning 'the pages of her black prayer book'; like the other grandchildren, Annabel was expected to 'learn to recite parts of the catechism by heart'.[61] Edith's Anglicanism was high church, and much later, in 1927, she supported the revision of the Church of England prayer book, a measure that was opposed by many committed Protestants within the church and outside it.[62] As Castlereagh rarely addressed religious questions in parliament, it is instructive to place his comments on the Accession Declaration bill alongside his position in the latter debate. The Ulsterman and onetime Conservative MP, Ronald McNeill, by then first Baron Cushendun, assumed in 1927, during the prayer book debates, that Charles was a committed Protestant in the sense ordinarily understood in Ulster. 'I was asked if I knew your views. . . . I said I did not, but that I could hardly imagine that you, being your Father's son an Ulster leader, could be anything but a stout Protestant.'[63] As it turned out, Charles adopted the same stance as his wife and sided with those in the House of Lords in favour of the revised prayer book.[64] In doing so he opposed not only Cushendun but other senior Ulster Unionists, including Carson, by then Baron Carson of Duncairn, and James Craig, by then first Viscount Craigavon.[65] A likely factor in his willingness to dissent from the line taken by other Ulster Unionists was his bitter experience of militant Protestantism as the Minister of Education in Northern Ireland (see Chapter 4). As he later remarked to one of his local supporters there, 'if a great many [Protestant clerics] gave up politics, speech-making, letter-writing and became pastors it would be much better for us all'.[66] Nor was his sensitivity about clerical interference limited to Northern Ireland. Writing in 1932 about British education policy, he commented on the need for the responsible minister 'to control the Christian Churches which, as we know, contain the most militant elements in the country'.[67] It was an extraordinary assessment given that he had for many years been at the sharp end of industrial tension on the coalfields.

Following the tense breakdown of the constitutional conference on 10 November 1910, another general election was arranged for the following month. Once again, the Conservatives debated the merits of advocating tariff reform, a pressing issue given the obvious unpopularity of what its Liberal and Labour opponents called food taxes. Castlereagh had nailed his colours to the mast the previous July when he opposed it on the basis that it would tax the poor.[68] Even prominent proponents of tariff reform such as Bonar Law were not immune from the realization that the cry of stomach taxes would create difficulties for the party at the December poll. Balfour took advantage of the situation by proposing that they promise a referendum on tariff reform in place of their existing policy to implement it if in government.

The Conservatives' efforts to formulate an acceptable fiscal policy could not disguise the fact that the future of the House of Lords was of greater importance at the poll.[69] Its indecisive result therefore left no one the better informed. Castlereagh was returned again for Maidstone, only this time with a majority of seventy.[70] Nationally, the Conservatives made a small advance, winning 271 seats to the Liberals' 272, but it was not enough to scupper the government's plans, especially given their promise of a third Home Rule bill in return for the continued support of Irish nationalist MPs. As before, the result fuelled Conservative divisions, as each side of the fiscal debate blamed the other for the party's failure to win a majority.

Conservatives were also divided on how they would react in the House of Lords to the government's determination to curb that chamber's powers with the Parliament bill. Castlereagh's attitude fluctuated between pragmatism and frustration. Speaking in March 1911, he highlighted a perennial problem for those who sought to reform the upper house in the name of democracy, namely, that 'the hereditary element – which was condemned on all sides – tended to maintain in the House of Lords a Second Chamber which would not attempt to compete with the House of Commons, but would be subordinate to it, in the management of public affairs'. The image that he painted was not one that Liberals would have recognized, at least in recent years, but it is noteworthy that he also signalled his family's position on the question by declaring that the 'only solution . . . was one arrived at by compromise'.[71] The following month he professed that he 'felt in a hopeless position because the Government had taken up an absolutely uncompromising attitude towards amendments, and orders had been issued to their followers to adopt a negative line'.[72] In May he echoed the complaints of other Conservatives by accusing the Liberals of 'abusing the mandate they had obtained to alter the legislative machinery of the nation', for the purpose of maintaining 'the coalition upon which the Government rested'.[73] By July his argument was even more dramatic, not only objecting to the 'unscrupulous and increasingly rigid application of the guillotine' procedure in parliament, but also threatening to use unspecified measures to stop what he regarded as a 'revolution'.[74]

The last outburst was in the wake of the revelation that the new sovereign, George V, had agreed to create a sufficient number of Liberal peers to pass the bill in the House of Lords should that chamber reject it. In spite of his recent histrionics on the question, and his mother's active sympathy for the substantial minority of Conservative peers who declared their determination to oppose the measure in the last ditch, Castlereagh did not adopt the 'ditcher' stance.[75] This was no doubt due to the continued support given by his father, Lord Londonderry, to Balfour, who felt that the upper house should allow the Parliament bill to pass. For although much of the opposition to the bill was on the basis that it would pave the way for home rule, a preponderance of Conservative peers felt that such a stand would be futile. Indeed, many in the upper house had been increasingly sceptical of their effectiveness for some time, but especially since the return of the Liberals in 1906. With their confidence sapped, and being overly cautious about using their veto, the Parliament bill offered a solution by granting the peers a statutory power to delay bills for two years.[76] When the House of Lords finally divided on 10 August 1910, a significant number of peers abstained, and so the bill was allowed passage by 131 votes to 114. Having laid the issue to rest, at least for the time being, the Conservatives squared up to the most pressing consequence of the Parliament Act, a third attempt at home rule, and did so with a new leader, the compromise choice of Bonar Law. The shift that this represented in the party leadership, from land to business, seemed to mirror the profound change ushered in by the Parliament Act. As Cannadine observes of this moment, aristocrats 'might, in some cases, retain great individual wealth, political influence, or personal prestige. But the belief in their innate superiority, in their collective political wisdom, in their unique position as the responsible and hereditary custodians of the national interest, was gone forever'.[77] What is striking about Castlereagh, therefore, is that he did not shake off these assumptions. He continued to believe that he and others like him possessed an innate right to play a role in national affairs. And it was a conviction that only increased in its intensity after he inherited his father's title and position in 1915.

III

The political turmoil surrounding the third Home Rule bill hung over British politics from 1912 until the outbreak of the First World War in 1914. It was an issue that allowed the Conservative and Unionist party to appear united, even if beneath the surface there were anxieties about the limits of opposition. Nor did it completely push aside the question of tariff reform. By March 1912 the only members of Bonar Law's shadow cabinet to oppose the retention of food taxes were the seventeenth Earl of Derby and Lord Londonderry, aristocrats with strong connections to export industries that relied on free trade. Still, senior Conservatives recognized that the fiscal question could again undermine the party at the polls. In December 1912 Bonar Law backed a compromise position that limited the number of food taxes and shifted the burden of proposing them away from the United Kingdom and onto the self-governing dominions.[78] Castlereagh signalled his support for the compromise in an address to the Ulster Women's Unionist Council, the largest female political group in Ireland, and a body that his mother would soon afterwards oversee as its president.[79] His remarks included the disingenuous claim that he 'believed in tariff reform', but in a sideswipe at the more advanced tariff reformers, he added that imperialism to him meant the union of Great Britain and Ireland.[80] His declaration was clearly not a Pauline conversion; like most Conservative free traders this would have to wait until after the 1929 Wall Street Crash.

Rather, it was an attempt, in co-ordination with the majority of the parliamentary party, to unite its ranks for the more pressing struggle against the third Home Rule bill.

That measure was introduced to the House of Commons on 11 April 1912. Edward Carson, the leader of the Irish Unionists since 1910, and James Craig, the party's leading figure in its Ulster stronghold, led the opposition attack. Following Craig, Castlereagh delivered a measured speech that argued that the bill would 'postpone indefinitely the great settlement to which the country was rapidly coming. . . . Only by the hearty co-operation of the different sections, races, and creeds in the island could real Irish prosperity be reached'.[81] Like some other Irish Unionists, including Carson, Castlereagh was sympathetic to ideas about a federal arrangement for the whole of the United Kingdom that might accommodate Irish nationalist aspirations within a larger scheme of home rule all round.[82] It was not, however, an approach that had any significant effect on the debate, and there was a lack of consensus among Conservatives about what it meant in practice.[83] Castlereagh's speech also emphasized the Londonderrys' ancestral and familial obligations to the union. This was particularly important for aristocrats with close connections to Ulster unionism, for the movement was, by 1904, largely led by an upper middle-class coterie of businessmen and professionals, and many Ulster Unionists were increasingly wary of the commitment of British supporters to their cause.[84] Their guardedness extended to local landowners with strong connections to the Conservative leadership at Westminster.[85]

Figure 2 Viscount Castlereagh, *c.* 1910s.

In June 1912 Thomas Agar-Robartes, a backbench Liberal MP, proposed to reconcile the Ulster Unionists' objections with Irish nationalist aspirations by proposing that the northeast counties of Ireland be excluded from a home rule settlement. Following a conference on the matter at Londonderry House, Unionist MPs decided to back Agar-Robartes's amendment, not through any desire for the partition of Ireland, but so that they could not be accused of avoiding a compromise. Nevertheless, in a speech to the House of Commons on 18 June, Castlereagh reflected on this development by taking on a more sectional and defensive tone than he had previously. In an implicit acknowledgement of his famous namesake's role in forging the union, Castlereagh admitted that the 'men of Ulster were not anxious to go into the Union, they were forced into it; but since they went in they had realised that the Union made for their prosperity and interest. Having prospered they wanted to remain as they were'. He also addressed the oft-made nationalist criticism of unionism, that John Dillon, the MP for East Mayo, 'was going about saying that the Protestants of Ireland would not be satisfied with anything less than a position of ascendancy. They had never asked for that and did not want it. All they desired was to be left alone'.[86]

Castlereagh's reading of Irish history was not uncommon among the Irish Unionists, but the speech also reflects how the Ulster question was a significant issue for aristocrats with connections to Ulster.[87] The establishment of the Ulster Unionist Council (UUC) in 1905 might have cemented the power of its bourgeois leadership, but the new structure was capacious enough to accommodate the landlord class that had hitherto been the dominant force at the apex of the movement. As such, while Carson was leader of the parliamentary party, Londonderry was the UUC's chairman. Titled landowners, after all, added respectability to a campaign that would become increasingly controversial and unconstitutional.[88] As a result, the partnership of landlords and the middle class was a prominent feature of Ulster unionism in this period, though it should be seen against the wider trend of co-operation between these two social classes across the industrialized regions of the United Kingdom.[89]

It was particularly evident in the political salon of Lady Londonderry. She had befriended Carson in the 1880s when her husband had been Lord Lieutenant of Ireland and Carson a promising young Dublin lawyer.[90] If this was fortuitous, then her role as political hostess for Bonar Law, a widower, was more opportunistic, especially given her initial disdain for this socially inferior successor to the noble house of Cecil.[91] In time, Carson and Bonar Law came to depend on Lady Londonderry personally as much as she and her husband depended on them politically. The Londonderrys were therefore conspicuous beneficiaries of the coalescing of British Conservative and Ulster Unionist interests. The family's resumption of a prominent role in national affairs must however be qualified. Lord Londonderry might grace political platforms with Carson, and he was counted among the most senior of leaders in Ulster, but he is notable only for his patrician presence on the UUC and at set piece rallies, and his significant financial help to the cause. As for his son and heir, Castlereagh's practical input could be likened to that of a sympathetic English MP.[92]

A series of great demonstrations was arranged throughout 1912 to impress the resolve of the Ulster Unionists' opposition to home rule upon the seemingly indifferent Liberal government. At all of them Londonderry took his place beside Carson.[93]

Display was the main function of these great rallies, at Balmoral, near Belfast, on Easter Tuesday, and in July, at Blenheim Palace, near Oxford. It was only at the grandest of these occasions, 'Ulster Day', on 28 September 1912, that Castlereagh played a prominent part, albeit one that was purely ornamental. This was the occasion of the mass signing of Ulster's Solemn League and Covenant, a defiant pledge of contractual loyalty to the crown that rejected the Home Rule bill proposed by the king's ministers.

In the lead up to that great demonstration at Belfast, Castlereagh privately expressed his resentment at not being among the inner circle of the Ulster Unionists. What he found particularly galling was looking on as prominent English MPs, such as F. E. Smith, took a more prominent role than he in the campaign. Castlereagh's long experience of being at odds with the dominant tariff-reform wing of the Conservative party, including men such as Smith and Bonar Law, only added to his sense of grievance, which was made worse by his mother's aristocratic embrace of the two politicians. Writing to his wife from Ulster, he confessed that 'It is damnable here and I am bored to tears, nothing in the world to do; I am simply loafing about; as yet I have done nothing; tomorrow evening a meeting and the same on Thursday and I sign on Saturday.' At a time when the political temperature in Ulster was rising, Castlereagh confided his resentment at occupying a purely decorative role. 'I wish I had just come over for the signing', he informed Edith, 'for all the good I have done or will do I might have been at Timbuctoo. I hate swelling the train of Carson and F.E. [Smith]; there are so many anxious to do it. I have no news, I am bored here. I played golf this morning and I do the same this afternoon.'[94]

Castlereagh's role was not as passive as this suggests. In the run up to Ulster day, he addressed a meeting at Crumlin, County Antrim, accompanied by other speakers including Colonel Hercules Arthur Pakenham, the fourth Viscount Templetown and Charles Craig, the brother of James. Like Templetown, Castlereagh made reference to his local ancestry. More ominously, he warned the government – with the vagueness characteristic of such threats – that violence could result if the Ulster Unionists' demonstrations were ignored.[95] After Crumlin, Castlereagh was summoned to County Durham by his father, in order to meet Bonar Law at Wynyard, a trip that he resented, for it was one thing for Castlereagh to toe the line for Bonar Law, but quite another for him to attend the court of a man whose leadership he resented.[96] Following his return to Belfast, on the day before the signing of the covenant, Castlereagh's frustration boiled over. 'This blasted week has put me all wrong', he confessed to Edith. 'Never again do I undertake a week like this unless I am the central figure, and I fear that it interests me less and less. The cast and the humbug of the whole thing is really sickening.'[97] On Ulster day itself, at Belfast City Hall, in what was a deliberately theatrical performance, Carson applied his name first to the covenant, followed by Londonderry and then the leaders of the six Protestant denominations. Castlereagh was next to apply his signature, a gesture that implicitly recognized and recalled his famous namesake, the Irish architect of the union, rather than a sudden promotion within the ranks of Ulster unionism.[98] In total, 471,414 signatures were collected.

Parliamentary debates about home rule took on a more heated tone following the spectacular of Ulster day. Asquith, regardless, continued to exude a cool temper and maintain his posture of wait and see. Like many Conservative and Unionist MPs,

Castlereagh was left exasperated by the prime minister's muted reaction to recent events. Speaking in parliament on 14 October, he 'attributed the docile attitude of the Government's supporters to the fact, among other things, that the Government had bribed the House of Commons'. This prompted one MP, in a reference to the parliamentary practices that facilitated the Irish Act of Union, to exclaim 'Castlereagh on bribery!' The interruption was ignored. 'As long as the Government's supporters obeyed the party Whips', Castlereagh continued, 'their £400 a year was safe; if not, they came under the ban of the caucus and out they went'.[99]

It is undoubtedly the case that opposition MPs sought to delay the passage of the third Home Rule bill with procedural devices and delaying tactics, although these were often checked by the government's use of the guillotine. It is nonetheless noteworthy that Castlereagh, like others on his side of the house, proposed amendments that seemed to accept that the bill would be passed. Amendments were, however, a conventional parliamentary method of criticizing and undermining bills, and in this instance their advancement was a useful means for Unionists to deflect charges of intransigence. In June 1912, he supported an amendment to ensure that the proposed Dublin parliament would be subservient to Westminster.[100] In October, he proposed that the bill codify the concerns that he feared might be left to a nationalist-dominated parliament. These included the enshrining of 'rigid' safeguards for Unionists and reforms to the congested district boards.[101] On 24 October, Castlereagh, supported by James Craig, proposed that the office of Lord Lieutenant of Ireland be replaced with that of a secretary of state on the basis that this would make the head of the Irish executive more accountable to Westminster. It was not unusual for Conservatives and Irish Unionists to call for the abolition of the Irish viceroyalty given that it marked Ireland out as a place apart.[102] Still, it is noteworthy that Castlereagh – in contrast to his defence of the yeomanry and militia – labelled the office once held by his father 'a complete anachronism'. As he put it, 'retaining this appointment served to accentuate the fact that England had been separated from Ireland', and he wondered aloud whether or not the prospect of a federal solution would mean viceroys for England, Lancashire, Scotland and Wales.[103]

The Unionists' frustration with Asquith's posture of wait and see could turn more threatening when goaded. This happened in the House of Commons in mid-October when the President of the Board of Agriculture, Walter Runciman, mockingly compared the fervour of feeling in Ulster with the business-like way that Conservatives and Irish Unionists behaved at Westminster. Echoing his earlier warnings of heightened militancy, Castlereagh hit back. 'Did the Government think it was all bluff and brag? . . . The people of Ulster were a minority and felt they were being treated tyrannically. When people felt like that there was no limit to what they would do in defence of their liberty.' In a melodramatic flourish he declared that 'If the Government were endeavouring to goad the people of Ulster into a frenzy (Ministerial laughter) by the irritating suggestions responsible Ministers were making in various parts of the country, then their blood be upon their own head.'[104] The dramatic end of the first reading of the bill illustrated how wrong Runciman had been about well-behaved opposition MPs. Not only did they call and win a snap division on the bill on 22 November, 228 votes to 206, but the House of Commons then witnessed an act of violence when a book was thrown at the Treasury bench following Asquith's refusal to recognize the division.[105]

The Home Rule bill was sent to the House of Lords in January 1913 where, predictably, it was rejected. The Parliament Act 1911 ensured that this meant that the bill would be delayed until the autumn of 1914. The hitherto parliamentary struggle now extended to the drilling fields of Ireland. It did not mean, however, that the political process had ended. Rather, it now ran parallel to a more militant mobilization in Ulster. In January 1913, the UUC officially sanctioned the creation of the Ulster Volunteer Force (UVF) and began to make plans for a provisional government in Ulster should home rule come to pass. The continued support of Bonar Law and his party for these developments ensured that Ulster's landowners were largely united in their support for, and in some cases, participation in, the UVF and the proposed provisional government. In addition to lending respectability to these legally dubious initiatives, the military experience of many landowners, and their substantial properties, ensured that they were particularly useful to the UVF. Montgomery Hyde claims that Carson attempted to dissuade Londonderry from involving his family in this militant phase of Ulster Unionist opposition. 'They can do little to me. . . . But you have great possessions, a great title, friendships at court, a seat in the House of Lords. You have to consider also the future of your son Charley.' With tears in his eyes, Londonderry is reputed to have replied, 'My dear Edward, if I was to lose everything in the world, I will go with you to the end.'[106]

An exact picture of the Londonderrys' involvement is not easy to discern. It is clear that their participation was quintessentially aristocratic, that is, highly placed if ornamental, while at the same time being involved with raising funds. Therefore, Londonderry, already chairman of the UUC, was appointed to the proposed provisional government. And like other wealthy men in the region and beyond, he contributed to a £10,000 indemnity fund for the UVF.[107] As for Castlereagh's involvement, the picture is more confusing. Ronald McNeill's account of the period names him as an officer in the UVF.[108] A document among the Londonderry papers identifies Castlereagh as the commanding officer of the North Belfast Regiment, although A. T. Q. Stewart claims that a Captain Malone took command of North Belfast.[109] To further confuse matters, the Mount Stewart estate had its own UVF company. In January 1914 this combined with others in the area to form the second battalion North Down Regiment.[110] In addition, Carson's official biographer, Ian Colvin, recounts how, on at least one occasion, Castlereagh accompanied the Irish Unionist leader as his aide-de-camp on a visit to the army commander in Ireland, General Sir Nevil Macready.[111] Timothy Bowman's study of the UVF brings some clarity to the matter by highlighting the widespread use of dual appointments. Castlereagh, he notes, was the 'most outrageous example of this' given his commitments on paper to the Mount Stewart contingent, the Newtownards Battalion and the North Belfast Regiment.[112] The practice was therefore not indicative of a deep commitment to the UVF but symptomatic of its weak command structure. After all, Castlereagh was often absent from Ireland in this period, and it is doubtful that his parents would have tolerated any meaningful involvement in military preparations given their refusal to allow him to serve in South Africa. What is certain is that the Londonderrys continued to fill that social and political niche that they had assiduously carved for themselves. Their closest practical involvement with the UVF, therefore, was in housing its commander, General Sir George Richardson, at Mount Stewart between 1913 and 1919.[113] Still, their contribution was important for its financial utility and symbolic value, and these were not insignificant factors in what was a potentially dangerous and unconstitutional venture.[114]

If Castlereagh was not permanently manning his volunteer posts in Ulster, his parliamentary appearances also declined in this period. A fairly regular speaker in the House of Commons during 1912, his attendance dipped the following year when he spoke on only eight separate occasions.[115] In 1914 his record improved only slightly, albeit doubling the previous year's activity.[116] The few speeches that Castlereagh did make in 1913 dealt in the main with army matters and not Ireland, whereas his speeches in 1914 protested against the possible use of the army in Ulster and complained about extravagant spending on the Palace of Westminster. His lack of parliamentary performances would tend to confirm Baldwin's later criticism that Castlereagh did not make a mark on the home rule issue; however, it is worth noting that Baldwin himself spoke on only eight different occasions in 1913 and only five the following year, none of which dealt with Ireland.[117] What is not in doubt is that after years of relative backbench obscurity, Castlereagh had become disenchanted with politics. In part it reflected his personality. Having initially been pressed by his parents into abandoning soldiering for the House of Commons, the continued expectation that he toe the line and play the political subaltern to his superiors aroused his irritation and deepened his sense of frustration. But it was more than this. Castlereagh was one of a dwindling band of free traders on the Conservative benches whose opportunities for advancement in the party had long been limited if not closed completely. And yet, Castlereagh occupied a political space in 1912 that, like his parents, he might have made his own had he possessed the charisma and will to do so. He was not, however, a creature of twentieth-century mass politics, and he struggled to move from under the shadow of his parents. As if to confirm this, he announced in March 1913 that he would not be standing at the next general election for the marginal Maidstone seat that he had held since 1906, but that he would be standing instead for one of the safest Conservative seats in the country, Kensington.[118]

The momentous events of 1914 do not need to be rehearsed here, especially as Castlereagh, like many Conservatives and Irish Unionists, was not privy to the decisions taken by his party leaders. Like the country at large, he had to wait and see what the consequences of the gunrunning at Larne in April would be, and a similar pause of breath was adopted when it came to the inter-party conference at Buckingham Palace in July. Carson and Redmond's failure to agree on the size of the area to be excluded from home rule, and the permanency of the arrangement, meant that the conference ended in deadlock. This failure only helped to increase fears about what might happen in Ireland. That the First World War would temporarily freeze the Irish question is well known. What is important here is the dramatic change that it would have on the political career of Castlereagh.

IV

On 4 August 1914 the United Kingdom declared war on Germany. The inconclusive results of the Buckingham Palace inter-party conference meant that when the Home

Rule bill was given royal assent on 18 September, it contained no special treatment for Ulster. However, the wartime emergency served to ensure that the Act would not come into force until after the conflict had been concluded. This equivocal outcome allowed both Carson and Redmond to encourage their respective supporters to enlist in the armed forces, albeit with some initial hesitation on the part of both men. Their approval, of course, was not necessary for all Irishmen. Castlereagh rejoiced at the opportunity to return to the army and fulfil one of the few remaining aristocratic duties of real practical value. As Paul Fussell explains, the war 'took place in what was, compared with ours, a static world, where the values appeared stable and where the meanings of abstractions seemed permanent and reliable. Everyone knew what Glory was, and what Honour meant'.[119] Re-enlisting held out the hope for Castlereagh that he could return to such a static world, one free of the tensions, frustrations and defeats of almost a decade on the opposition benches in parliament. Aristocratic enthusiasm for the war can be understood in this light, but it also helped them to demonstrate the practical worth of the old order. According to Cannadine, the aristocracy was 'by tradition, by training, and by temperament . . . the warrior class. They rode horses, hunted foxes, fired shot-guns. They knew how to lead, how to command, and how to look after the men in their charge'. The outbreak of war provided aristocrats with 'their chance – to demonstrate conclusively that they were not the redundant reactionaries of radical propaganda, but the patriotic class of knightly crusaders and chivalric heroes, who would defend the national honour and the national interest in the hour of its greatest trial'.[120] Lady Castlereagh too would carve out a wartime role that married aristocratic tradition with her suffrage activism, becoming in 1914 colonel-in-chief of the Women's Volunteer Reserve, and the following year establishing the Women's Legion, which by 1917 evolved to become the Women's Army Auxiliary Corps.[121]

Lord Castlereagh's hope of finding satisfaction by abandoning parliament for the army was soon to be disappointed. From the outset, his first weeks at the Western Front encouraged uncomfortable memories of his earlier spell as a cavalryman. And his hope that previous military experience might now lead to a command was quickly dashed and would continue to elude him. Not only had the 35-year-old spent over eight years outside the army, he had also missed the South African War, an essential training ground for aspiring commanders in the present conflict. He was not unaware of the obstacles that his ambition faced. It inclined him to look back with regret for having abandoned the army for politics. 'How much better I should have done if I had remained in the Army, and done the staff college instead of stagnating for eight years in the House of Commons', he wrote to his wife. It irritated him to 'see people in important positions, no better than me, and to feel that I am a sort of mixture of footman and a clerk and this I shall remain as I see no prospect of doing anything else'.[122] He referred here to his duties as the aide-de-camp to General William Pulteney, commander of the Third Corps. Lady Castlereagh, like his parents, did not want her husband to be involved in direct combat and had asked for Pulteney's help in securing a relatively safe appointment.[123] Captain Lord Castlereagh had accepted the situation reluctantly and arrived in France with the general at the end of August 1914. Removed from the front line it was not long before he grew to dislike both his job and Pulteney.

Castlereagh's frequent correspondence with his wife at this time is notable for its revealing detail, a feature facilitated by the King's Messenger system. He provided her with information on morale, troop movements and battles involving him and the army generally. Aware of the potential danger of such information, he warned her early on not to reveal the content of any of his letters.[124] Shadowing Pulteney, Castlereagh was privy to the strategy of the allied commanders but not party to its formulation, an unfortunate echo of his peripheral and ornamental role in Ulster before the war. In his letters to Lady Castlereagh, he commented upon and criticized Sir John French's top-heavy administration and the occasional visits of government ministers. 'Winston [Churchill] was at Dunkirk', he informed her on one occasion. 'Winston I suppose came over to get a medal; he is entitled to one if he sets foot on French soil I believe.'[125] By December 1914 Castlereagh was even more barbed in his comments about the First Lord of the Admiralty. 'Winston arrived here this morning looking very old and very flabby. I do not know what excuses he makes to come here, mere joyriding, and he has a destroyer to take him back again.'[126]

Some of the controversial opinions that Castlereagh would express in the 1930s are discernible in this period. His disdain for Great Britain's closest ally, for example, was apparent early on. 'The French I fancy are useless. I do not believe they ever put up a fight. The thing is they really don't care.'[127] Conversely, he like other British soldiers at the front had a grudging admiration for the opposing army. Writing to his wife in November 1914, he declared that he did not 'know how you defeat a nation which has prepared in every detail for years'.[128] Frustrated at being with staff officers and away from the front line, he was still capable of acknowledging the 'horrors of war' after visits with Pulteney to injured soldiers.[129] He lost friends too, the best man at his wedding, Harold Brassey, and his close colleague in the House of Commons, Lord Helmsley, now the second Earl of Feversham.[130]

It was in the earliest stage of the war that Castlereagh recorded his first experience of the relatively new aerial dimension to warfare. 'The thing that has most impressed me here has been the aeroplane service', he wrote in September 1914. 'A splendid lot of boys who really don't know what fear is.'[131] He described his first flight as a 'delightful sensation. I seldom enjoyed anything more'. It occurred on the same day that he made a rare visit to the trenches. Like many officers with little experience of mixing with the ranks, Castlereagh wrote in glowing terms about meeting the Irish Fusiliers. 'I only spent a few hours in the trenches . . . and got tight on rum. There was no shelling only sniping. . . . I never saw people so pleased; they say the staff never go there and don't realise what they have to go through. There were 15 inches of water in the fire trenches.'[132]

The troops under Pulteney's command were not ready for the Battle of Mons, but they did make it on time for the German retreat from the Marne and the first Battle of Ypres, the latter lasting from mid-October to November 1914.[133] Being near decision-making and not part of it, Castlereagh's correspondence grew increasingly ill tempered about what he regarded as the mismanagement of the war. He wrote of the great strain that the troops were under and expressed pity for the Belgian civilians who were victims of the constant shelling. Castlereagh's ten months with Pulteney were made more frustrating by the general's reluctance to let him transfer to his old cavalry regiment. This, and so much else, would change following the unexpected death of the sixth Marquess of Londonderry on 8 February 1915.

The seventh Marquess of Londonderry took a short period of leave from the army to attend his father's funeral, and to return the late marquess's Order of the Garter insignia to the king.[134] Despite his recent high-profile role in the UUC, the sixth marquess was buried alongside the third marquess at Long Newton Parish Church in County Durham. A large memorial to him and his wife was later installed at Durham's magnificent cathedral. The seventh marquess returned to the front soon after with a promotion to major.[135] Edith, now the Marchioness of Londonderry, pressured Pulteney to recommend her husband for a military honour, but the influence of Pulteney over the future of Charles had ended with the death of the sixth marquess.[136] The new Lord Londonderry was thus able to resign as the general's aide-de-camp and rejoin his cavalry regiment, albeit without the medal that his wife had requested. However, far from satisfying his determination to serve at the front, the War Office placed him in command of the reserves stationed at Regent's Park, London. He was far from happy with the placement, but at least it permitted him to spend more time with his wife and four children: Maureen (born 1900), Robert (born 1902), Margaret (born 1910) and Helen (born 1911). Inheriting the marquessate also meant that he afterwards started to acquire purely ornamental military appointments, as honorary colonel of the fourth battalion, Royal Irish Rifles, in April 1915, and honorary Colonel of the Durham Light Infantry, in August 1916.[137]

The seventh marquess's earliest acts of noblesse oblige and political campaigning were very much war related. Like other owners of large properties during the conflict, the Londonderrys had Londonderry House and a property at Seaham converted into army hospitals.[138] Lord Londonderry spoke at a small ceremony at the opening of the latter in October 1915, prompting his mother to observe that he emulated his father, although she claimed that her son spoke more slowly.[139] In June 1915, in what was perhaps a bout of over enthusiasm, the new owner of the Londonderry Collieries attempted to press upon the government the idea of converting his mining operations into munitions factories.[140] The army was certainly desperate for shells, but the government was determined to ensure that the equally vital mining industry was running at full capacity. As such, Londonderry's suggestion was not only ignored, but in 1917 the government extended an earlier scheme to control mines in south Wales to cover all of Great Britain.

Much more significant was Londonderry's political contribution to the war, for it introduced him to an increasingly personal and satisfying involvement in Irish affairs. In the summer of 1915, he joined the Central Council for the Organization of Recruiting in Ireland.[141] Wartime recruitment was a divisive issue there and became more so after 1916, when the threat of conscription increased support for Sinn Féin at the expense of Redmond's constitutional nationalists. Like other Irish Unionists, Londonderry was unable or unwilling to understand this, for he did not appreciate that Redmond's opposition to conscription was qualitatively different from that espoused by Sinn Féin.[142] As such, he had few qualms about advocating conscription for Ireland in 1917, on the basis of equality with the rest of the United Kingdom, arguing that without large-scale recruitment Ireland would suffer national dishonour.[143]

Around the same time, Londonderry succeeded his father as Lord Lieutenant of County Down. Inheriting this element of his father's local political interest had the effect of altering his pre-war relationship with Ulster unionism.[144] Tellingly, however, he was not the first choice of the Ulster Unionists. Richard Dawson Bates, the UUC's secretary, had written to Bonar Law only days after the death of the sixth marquess to recommend Colonel Sharman Crawford, a member of the county's gentry with close connections to the UUC.[145] Bonar Law, however, had recently led his party into a wartime coalition with the Liberals. If an Ulster Unionist had to be appointed, then the latter would have found Londonderry a more acceptable candidate than Crawford, and Bonar Law's sense of loyalty to the Londonderry family is also likely to have exerted some bearing on his recommendation.[146]

Once a powerful position in local government, the role of lord lieutenant had evolved during the nineteenth century to become almost purely ornamental, though it still had political value as its holders retained limited powers of local patronage. Not long after his appointment, Londonderry found himself involved in a potentially difficult situation over the appointment of his deputy lieutenants. The Liberal Lord Lieutenant of Ireland, the second Baron Wimborne, recommended that Londonderry should appoint his 'late political opponents' to two vacant posts.[147] The Ulster Unionists resented and resisted such directions from Dublin Castle, believing that after almost a decade of Liberal government they had lost out to nationalists in matters of local patronage. As the Liberals were now in a coalition with the Conservatives, the Ulster Unionists saw an opportunity to recover lost ground.[148] In response to the two names recommended by Wimborne, Sharman Crawford, one of Londonderry's deputy lieutenants, made clear his opposition to both men on political and social grounds.[149] Reports were solicited about both candidates, and although these took a more equivocal position than that adopted by Crawford, it was still acknowledged that their 'origins and surroundings' meant that there would be some resistance from landowners in the county.[150] In the end neither candidate was appointed, though Wimborne ensured that the candidates favoured by the Ulster Unionists were not appointed either.[151] There is no evidence to indicate how Londonderry viewed this episode at the time, but months later he echoed the Ulster Unionists' wider criticism of Dublin Castle in his complaint to Lloyd George that Wimborne was an 'abject slave of Redmond', and that all appointments were 'invariably' given to nationalists.[152]

Major Lord Londonderry's new roles in Ireland and his return to the Blues did not stop him wanting see action at the front. By the winter of 1915 he felt increasingly stuck in a rut as the War Office refused to consider a return until early 1916.[153] Londonderry later suggested that he had at this time refused an offer of command from General Sir Douglas Haig. The claim was advanced in 1918 to agitate for a good military placement, but there is nothing otherwise to indicate that Haig ever made such a proposition.[154] All the evidence suggests instead that had Londonderry received such an invitation it would have been accepted without hesitation. As the dowager Marchioness of Londonderry noted in December 1915, 'Charley threatens in every letter that he is going to the front after Christmas.'[155] She knew that she could not dissuade him given his new status, but also that she was partly responsible for his attitude given that 'the South African affair' had left its mark. 'I wish he would be content to stay in one of the reserve regiments in Regent Park [*sic*], but it is impossible that any child of mine could be content with doing nothing.'[156]

In the third week of January 1916 Londonderry was at last permitted to serve with the Blues at the front, with a promotion to second-in-command under Colonel Lord Tweedmouth. Although once again a subordinate, Londonderry felt closer to the action and no doubt hoped that this would eradicate his lack of front-line experience. His new posting coincided with the determination of British strategists to launch a major offensive, and it was thought that the cavalry would play their traditional part by following the infantry on horseback to capture the enemy's position. The carnage wrought on the first day of the Battle of the Somme, 1 July 1916, proved how outmoded that assumption had been. Even so, Londonderry complained to his friend Colonel Cyril Hankey about the recent attachment of cavalrymen to infantry units, arguing that they could be better used as a unit, and backed this up with some logistical analysis. His frustration touched a deeper chord, of course, for like so much else that he had keenly felt the demise of, the traditional functions of the cavalry struggled to meet the challenges posed by the Western Front.[157]

In September 1916 Londonderry was temporarily transferred to another cavalry battalion as its second-in-command, and soon after appointed its lieutenant colonel following the commanding officer's departure. It proved to be a thoroughly boring post for Londonderry as the troops under his command were behind the lines and

Figure 3 Lord Londonderry, *c.* 1916.

non-combative.[158] This mundane command was broken with leave to England in September and December.[159] The latter visit coincided with the formation of the second wartime coalition government, now with Lloyd George as prime minister and his Conservative backers occupying positions of greater influence. It was a government that Londonderry had no hope or expectation of joining, at least not until he had proved his worth in Irish affairs.

Londonderry returned to his old regiment in early 1917. In April the Blues participated in the Battle of Arras. During combat Londonderry temporarily took command following the death of his commanding officer, General Bulkeley Johnson.[160] But his military superiors did not think him suitable for such a post and had a replacement appointed soon afterwards.[161] Their attitude contrasted with the new disposition of the UUC leadership towards Londonderry. For around the same time, the Ulster Unionists were discussing the nomination of Londonderry as one of their delegates to the proposed Irish Convention. On top of this there were rumours that Londonderry might be appointed as British ambassador to Paris. The latter was highly unlikely given his limited political experience, so the speculation is only noteworthy for being symptomatic of the post's declining importance around this time.[162] Londonderry's involvement with the Irish Convention is examined in the following chapter, but it is instructive to note here that he viewed that assignment as only a temporary one, and that he continued to lobby for a position in the military that he felt would suit him best. Even in July 1917, when the Irish Convention had barely started its proceedings, Londonderry made efforts to join the tank corps. General John Capper was not impressed by the peer's credentials and refused to 'hold out any prospects', adding emphatically that the only scenario in which Londonderry could join would involve the decimation of existing officers.[163] A few months later Londonderry was pressuring the Secretary of State for War, Lord Derby, to allow him to join the Royal Flying Corps. The future Secretary of State for Air was advised not to pursue the matter.[164]

Londonderry's lobbying was not to seek any means of exiting the Irish Convention, but to achieve either a command or a placement in a highly technical unit such as the tank corps or the flying corps. When it looked as though he might be recalled to his post as second-in-command of the Blues in early December 1917, Londonderry protested that he was too busy with his duties in Ireland.[165] Only a week later, however, he informed his wife of rumours about a vacancy for the command of the Blues.[166] His failure to obtain that command, and his role at the Irish Convention, made him realize with some reluctance that his ambitions had to be confined to the political sphere. Following the breakdown of the Irish Convention in April 1918, Londonderry asked for Derby's advice on whether he should remain in politics. The war secretary replied unequivocally that he had done his bit, 'and I think people will quite understand your taking up politics. . . . I am quite certain of one thing: there is nothing worse for the army than that a man should be one thing one day and one thing another. He must either be a politician or a soldier'.[167]

With that Londonderry remained in politics and out of the army. His subsequent years in parliament were indelibly marked by his time in the House of Commons and his return to the army in 1914, particularly the abiding sense of frustration that he had endured throughout. If he was not among the most intellectually gifted of politicians, by the end of the war Londonderry was astute enough to realize that he needed to be more adaptable and less complacent about his right to rule. And yet he could not leave behind the expectation that he was indeed born to govern, the product of an aristocratic upbringing that filled him with confidence, but not necessarily the skills and ability to match those ambitions. With his sense of entitlement now tempered by experience, Londonderry was subsequently able to take advantage of his landed background to remould himself as a credible candidate for government patronage, and did so, paradoxically, in Irish politics, an arena more usually cast in this period as the graveyard of aristocratic ambition.

2

Ireland, 1916–18

It is remarkable that Lord Londonderry was rescued from political oblivion at a time of profound change in British and Irish politics. Before this, his period in the House of Commons was marked by frustration and failure. But the rapidly changing situation brought about by the First World War created a political environment in which he found a new role, one useful to the government at Westminster and to the Ulster Unionists. This change of political fortunes was facilitated by his succession to the Londonderry title and economic interests in February 1915. For he could now slot into the role previously carved out by his parents as useful and well-placed intermediaries between British Conservatives and Ulster Unionists, and at a time when the relationship between the two was coming under increasing strain.

Like previous marquesses of Londonderry, the seventh marquess could claim an office in the gift of the state by virtue of his title and immense wealth; this having long been used to confirm the family's status in County Down and in County Durham, and on occasion at Westminster. When their status and wealth were viewed as a political asset, as in the case of the second and sixth marquesses, a place in the government had been forthcoming. In the case of the third, fourth and fifth marquesses, it secured local and ornamental rewards such as a lord lieutenancy, a rise in the peerage and membership of the chivalric orders of the Garter or St Patrick. Until he inherited his father's title in 1915, Londonderry had not established himself as a useful asset to the Conservative front bench. After inheriting the marquessate, however, he at once became a grandee magnate at a time when that could still count for something, and as Lord Lieutenant of County Down he could potentially serve as a useful check on the increasingly self-reliant and militant Ulster Unionists. Even so, very little would have been expected of the king's representative in the county merely on account of that ornamental office. Just as it could not have been anticipated that the fluid political situation in Ireland would unfold in such a way as to give Londonderry a degree of prominence locally: out of tune with many Ulster Unionists, but very much in tune with their considerably more influential allies in Great Britain. As a result, Londonderry was not only rewarded after the war with the Garter, but also a government post at the Ministry of Air.

I

The Easter Rising of 1916 dramatically returned the Irish question to the forefront of British political concerns. Up until this point, Londonderry had adhered to the

Conservative policy of supporting the coalition government headed by Herbert Asquith, in spite of his discomfort with the trend of increasing state interference. But the insurrection led Londonderry to break his silence in a letter to *The Times* about the Liberal's record on Ireland. He began by criticizing the willingness of the coalition Conservatives to shoulder responsibility for the rebellion, and the 'understanding that any suggestion of controversy must be avoided'. He attributed the rising to 'Ten years of Radical rule' and expressed his concern about press and public reactions. 'The feelings of the relatives of those killed in the performance of their duty have not received due consideration', he claimed. 'The minds of those who cry the loudest for sympathy with the rebels seem somewhat out of focus in face of the facts and figures. Hundreds of soldiers and civilians have been murdered by men openly in league with the King's enemies.'[1] The letter made no immediate impact, aside from Londonderry receiving the support of like-minded opponents of the government's Irish policy, but it did mark him out as a potential critic of Sir Edward Carson in the lead up to a critical juncture when Irish unionism and the coalition itself looked as if they might come apart.[2]

This tense situation developed out of David Lloyd George's post-rising meetings with Carson and John Redmond, and his belief that he had been empowered by the cabinet to reach a settlement with them concerning the immediate implementation of home rule. Lloyd George had been remarkably quick in reaching an agreement with Carson and Redmond, although controversy surrounds what each man knew or desired to know about the provisions for excluding the six north-eastern counties.[3] Carson and Redmond even managed the difficult task of securing majorities in their respective parties in favour of the scheme. Londonderry played a small but important part at the two UUC meetings summoned on 6 and 12 June to decide on the proposals.[4] Speaking in favour of Carson's position, Londonderry aligned himself with the movement's leadership, which was predominantly drawn from the business and professional classes of east Ulster, and with the Conservative party leader, Andrew Bonar Law, who also supported the compromise brokered by Lloyd George. It meant overriding the objections of southern Irish Unionists, many of whom were fellow landowners, as well as Ulster Unionists in the province's three outlying counties, Cavan, Donegal and Monaghan, which would fall under the jurisdiction of the proposed parliament.[5] Londonderry wrote to his mother after the second meeting, informing her that it had been

> a very sad day for us all but there was nothing else to be done and I think our action was tactically right. The offer we got is a better offer than we have ever had before or are ever likely to get again and if there is a Bill to establish a clean cut, that places us in an impregnable position.

His position on the proposed settlement was not merely a matter of falling into line with senior figures at Belfast and Westminster. Londonderry also recognized the importance of British public opinion to the Ulster Unionists. 'It remains now to see what the Nationalists are going to do. I cannot believe that they will accept the situation and in that case we get all the credit for having taken the patriotic line and of having made a real sacrifice.'[6]

It was the southern Irish Unionists, however, not the nationalists, who moved against the proposals and left the Ulster Unionists exposed. The former's hostility to the immediate implementation of home rule was shared by their allies in the cabinet, Walter Long and the fifth Marquess of Lansdowne, and they set about a train of events that ultimately killed-off the proposed settlement.[7] Long made his objections known to Lloyd George on 29 and 30 May, after which he was said to be happy with developments. However, after almost a fortnight of public silence on the issue, Long launched a blistering series of attacks on Lloyd George and Carson in an attempt to ruin the deal and even challenge the Conservative party leadership.[8] On 1 June he wrote to Edith, Lady Londonderry, perhaps under the impression that her husband's recent letter to *The Times*, mentioned above, placed the couple against Carson and Lloyd George. Long not only sought Lady Londonderry's help to oppose the settlement, he also solicited her support in forming what he called 'a real Conservative Party. We have been betrayed. We shall save the state now but we must be prepared for the future and I want you to join the "salon". . . . I am writing Charlie. He must come out as the great Irish Gentleman'.[9]

Lady Londonderry was sympathetic to Long's argument, but her husband, who had been serving at the Western Front, was not so persuaded, and as noted above chose to support Carson at the UUC at the two crucial meetings in June. On 14 June Londonderry drafted a letter to Lloyd George in which he admitted to having 'misgivings' about the immediate implementation of home rule for the south and west of Ireland, but he expressed his hope that the stand that he took alongside Carson at the UUC would help the government at a time of crisis.[10] It was after this, on 15 June, that Long launched his attack on the settlement. The main thrust of his criticism was that Lloyd George had not been given authority by the cabinet to make the deal that he had with Carson and Redmond. Londonderry had returned to the front by this stage and was away from Westminster just as divisions deepened between cabinet Conservatives, with Arthur Balfour and Bonar Law on one side, and Long, Lansdowne and the second Earl of Selborne on the other. With Selborne's resignation on 26 June, and an angry encounter between Long and Carson three days later, the future of the Conservative party and the wartime coalition appeared uncertain. Despite her husband's support for Carson at the UUC, Lady Londonderry remained convinced of Long's critique of the settlement, and this in turn led to her own charged encounter with the Carson-loyalist Ronald McNeill, the Ulster-born MP for St Augustine's, Kent. In the combative correspondence that arose from this, Lady Londonderry gave particular emphasis to Long's argument that it was inappropriate to alter the constitution at a time of war.[11] McNeill took the opposite view, that the war made a settlement necessary, and that by agreeing to this the Ulster Unionist leadership were making a legitimate and practical sacrifice.[12]

Long wrote to Lord Londonderry at the Western Front on 2 July, the day after the opening of the Somme offensive.[13] A letter drafted subsequently by Londonderry suggests that he was confused about recent events, and that he had come to feel duped by Lloyd George. Nevertheless, he erred on the side of Carson and advised Lady Londonderry to do likewise. In his lengthy missive to her, Lord Londonderry sought to win her over to his way of thinking. At the same time, he played down his capacity to do anything when serving at the front and claimed that his position in Ireland was 'just an interested one'. And he contextualized his stance with reference to inheriting the family interest in County Down, which 'carries a certain responsibility with it'. He urged her to see Carson

> and find out exactly the position from him. I have every confidence in him and I am sure that he can explain to you what seems so obscure now. I was in full agreement with him in Ireland. I was persuaded by him that we should support that proposal ... that Home Rule should come into operation at once for the 3 provinces [*sic*] and that there should be a permanent clean cut of the six counties.

He admitted that his view had been shaken by revelations that the scheme had not been agreed by 'the United Cabinet', and he attributed the confusion to Lloyd George for having reached different agreements with Carson and Redmond. But Londonderry maintained that there 'may be other good reasons for urging the Ulstermen to accept the present policy which I gather is nearer the proposal put forward by Redmond', presumably a reference to its impermanence, and he advised his wife that he thought it 'a pity that there should be any split in our old Unionist party and it seems to me that must be avoided, but it won't be avoided if there is any bitterness and I do see great bitterness'.[14]

In an attempt to assuage the concerns of Long and Lansdowne, and the growing discontent on the Conservative backbenches, a cabinet committee was established to look at increasing the safeguards for Irish Unionists living under the proposed area of the home rule settlement. The changes recommended by the committee proved, not surprisingly, to be too much for Redmond, and his rejection of the altered settlement on 22 July dealt it the final blow. The episode had severely tested the bonds of unionism, within Ireland and between Ireland and Great Britain, but having played his cards well, Londonderry was an unintended beneficiary. He might have been a relatively unimportant if prestigious member of the UUC, but his support for Carson and Bonar Law at this crucial stage ensured that he would have a political future within both conservatism in Great Britain and unionism in the north of Ireland. An alliance with Long and the southern Irish Unionists might have been tempting, but Londonderry was never as close to them in this period as he was to Carson, Balfour and even Bonar Law, however unrewarding his relations with them had been during his years in the House of Commons.

II

If the Irish question was temporarily put on the backburner after July 1916, the demands of the first total war ensured that addressing it was of increasing strategic importance. Even politics at Westminster could not escape the stresses of war. As noted in Chapter 1, a second coalition was formed in December that year with Lloyd George as prime minister, Asquith having been manoeuvred out of office by a plot involving Carson and Lloyd George. The new administration, dominated numerically by the

Conservatives, marked an end to the pre-war era of party factionalism and ushered in a new phase of consensus that endured until 1922.[15] It was its stewardship of Irish affairs that provided Londonderry with the opportunity and position to demonstrate his own consensual approach to the Irish question, and which in turn brought him favourable government attention and patronage.

High-level discussions on the constitutional future of Ireland occurred throughout the winter of 1916–17, but it was the decision of the United States to the enter war, in April 1917, that made these more urgent for the sake of appearances.[16] On 16 May Lloyd George offered the Irish party leaders a choice of immediate home rule, excluding the six north-eastern counties, or a convention to debate a way out of the political impasse. All sides, for differing reasons, agreed to the latter; the Ulster Unionists having ensured that the convention's conclusions would be non-binding, and the nationalists having been satisfied that parliament would enact any substantial agreement reached.[17] The government hoped that this assembly of Irishmen on Irish soil discussing Irish affairs might foster good relations between the United Kingdom and the United States, and also go some way to blunting the criticisms of the Irish-American lobby.[18]

Membership of the Irish Convention was, and remains, a matter of some controversy.[19] In particular, the absence of Sinn Féin undermined the convention's claim to be representative. Still, among the hundred or so delegates who did attend were government appointees representing labour, the churches and local government. What this amounted to in practice, however, were sizeable delegations representing Irish nationalism, Ulster unionism and southern unionism. That Londonderry would be swept up in this large assembly is not that remarkable. What is of note is that he was selected because he was not a leading Unionist, and yet his actions at the Irish Convention served to enhance his standing on both sides of the Irish Sea.

The evidence suggests that Londonderry was initially reluctant to be tied to the Ulster Unionists. Not only was he slow to accept his nomination as a delegate of the UUC, but it appears that he would have favourably considered nomination as an Irish peer or as a government-appointed delegate. This is intimated in a letter from the ninth Viscount Midleton, leader of the southern Irish Unionists, in which he informed Londonderry that he would not be one of the two delegates that the Irish peers were entitled to nominate, but that 'the Government have it in mind to make you one of their representatives. It is quite clear you ought to have a seat on the Convention'.[20] The government, for its part, appears to have assumed that Londonderry would represent the Ulster Unionists, for on 22 June and again on 17 July, Downing Street notified him that he had failed to reply to the prime minister's confirmation of his nomination as a delegate of the 'Ulster Party'.[21] The assumption that Londonderry was a committed Ulster Unionist was hardly unreasonable. As he had recently remarked to the House of Lords, 'We in Ulster have always believed that our prosperity and of the position which we occupy in the world is due to the union betwixt England and Ireland.' After expressing his hope that 'there was a possibility of uniting the Irish nation', he still declared that 'there is a dividing line. We are of a different race, a different creed, and we believe that the best government of these two different races is under the British Crown'.[22] Perhaps to avoid the appearance of being irreconcilable, he also alluded to the federal solution proposed by some senior political figures at Westminster, reassuring his listeners that 'there were bound to be great extensions of government and great changes in the future, and [Ulster Unionists] were willing to go forward with Great Britain in those great extensions'.[23]

What is more certain is that Londonderry did not end up representing the UUC due to any rapid rise to the top of Ulster unionism. The UUC was wary of the convention from the outset. Moreover, its most senior figures, Carson and Craig, preferred to remain in their posts as government ministers. The UUC therefore sent a delegation of party lieutenants, which had the utility of allowing senior figures in the movement to distance it from any potentially unpopular conclusions reached by the convention. It did not mean however that Carson and Craig were uninvolved. The parliamentary party was kept in regular contact with the convention delegation and it played an important if opaque role in its deliberations about what course of action to adopt at the convention. The Scottish-born businessman and MP for North Londonderry, Hugh Thom Barrie, led the delegation as its chairman. Londonderry, nominally the delegation's honorary secretary, was Barrie's deputy, no mean achievement given that he was also one of the youngest convention delegates. The other UUC delegates included Sir George Clark, a Belfast shipbuilder and former MP; Colonel Robert Wallace, the Grand Master of Belfast Orangemen and a lawyer; and Michael Knight, a solicitor and leading Unionist from County Monaghan. Although not officially nominated by the UUC, other Ulster Unionist delegates and their supporters met with the UUC delegation, including the heads of the Anglican and Presbyterian churches, Hugh Pollock of the Belfast Chamber of Commerce, and Sir Alexander McDowell, a Belfast solicitor.[24] The UUC's secretary, Richard Dawson Bates, also a solicitor, served as the delegation's secretary.[25] More ominously, an external advisory committee was established by the UUC to ensure that its delegation remained in contact with opinion in the north, including those sceptical about the convention's chances of success.[26]

The Irish Convention first met on 25 July at Trinity College, Dublin, and continued to convene until its undignified demise on 5 April 1918. After some deliberation at its first meeting, the convention elected Sir Horace Plunkett – a former Irish Unionist now in favour of home rule – as its chairman, and Sir Francis Hopwood – subsequently created Lord Southborough – as its secretary.[27] With this and other administrative business out of the way, the delegations outlined their positions when the convention reassembled in August. Londonderry spoke first for the UUC and according to Plunkett was 'listened to with the closest attention, there being, naturally, much anxiety as to the line the Ulster Unionist groups would take'. Londonderry was keen to demonstrate that the Ulster Unionists were not intransigent, stating that they had come to the Convention in 'friendliness' and with an 'open mind' to reach 'some general kind of agreement of what is the best for the government of this country'. He took pains to explain how the Ulster Unionists believed that their economic prosperity was attributable to the union and the empire, and how they viewed the British Isles as a common unity. Plunkett recorded that the 'speech produced the best possible impression. . . . It was delivered with an obvious lack of platform practice, which he explained by three years spent in discharging the duties of a soldier in France, but its tone and temper were perfect'.[28] Plunkett had personally known Londonderry's father. He even claimed in 1893 to have extracted a pledge from the sixth marquess that he would never consent to the separation of Ulster from the rest of Ireland in a home rule settlement.[29] He had similarly lofty expectations of the seventh marquess. 'As I listened to him I felt that he had all the charm of his father and a good measure of his mother's brains. He seemed to belong a little more to the later nineteenth and early twentieth century than either of his parents.'[30] Intended primarily for his 'confidential report' to George V, it is noteworthy that Plunkett's flattering references to Londonderry were contained in material that was widely circulated among convention delegates.[31]

Barrie and Pollock also spoke for the Ulster Unionists at this initial stage of the convention's deliberations, again stressing the economic arguments against home rule. None of them, to the great frustration of the nationalist delegates, put forward a firm proposal on the future of Irish government.[32] This is not entirely surprising given that the Ulster Unionists were not at the convention to make proposals, but to safeguard what they considered to be the interests of Ulster in any settlement reached, if necessary by securing partition. Yet, Londonderry was temperamentally disposed from the outset to reach an agreement if that proved possible. This is evident from his exchange with the Ulster-born advanced nationalist, George Russell, on the first day of the convention. Russell, in his 'Thoughts for a Convention', published in May 1917, rejected Ulster Unionist claims that the economic success of Ulster depended on the union and empire.[33] It was his reiteration of this argument at the convention that prompted Londonderry to reply that the 'Unionists can be won if they can be persuaded that self-government is better than the Union'.[34] That statement, in part, was a signal that the Ulster Unionists would adopt a relatively passive posture at the convention, waiting to be convinced by its nationalist delegates of the case for home rule. At the same time, it was arguably more than this, as it represented Londonderry's sincere belief – which became more apparent in the months that followed – that a settlement might actually be within reach.

Plunkett's policy of allowing all the delegates to air their views meant that the convention did not get down to any serious negotiations until after the summer. Even then, when the convention assembled at Belfast and then at Cork, the emphasis was on getting to know one another as much as reaching an agreement. During its time in the northeast, Londonderry emulated what other aristocratic figures associated with the convention had done in Dublin by inviting delegates to Mount Stewart. Plunkett hoped that these entertainments would have a more political function by helping to forge friendships across the political divide or at least promote mutual understanding.[35] It certainly worked in the case of Londonderry.

At this early stage of the convention, Londonderry experienced a sense of political satisfaction that stood in contrast to his barren years on the backbenches of the House of Commons. On 1 September he wrote to his lifelong confidant, Lady Desborough, a society hostess over ten years his senior.[36] His 'ambitions in another sphere having failed, this does satisfy a desire to be someone and to be really filling a place somewhere which carries responsibility with it'. He was evidently charmed by the people that he met, from representatives of Irish Labour – the 'working man here does not look with such suspicion on a lord as his confrere in England does' – to the royal circle at the Viceregal Lodge, where he 'met rank and beauty in dazzling profusion'. He got on well with prominent nationalist figures, in particular, Timothy Healy, and Desborough was left in no doubt that Londonderry enjoyed 'being in Ireland very much. I really like it infinitely better than England, and I get on better with the people'.[37]

Londonderry's enjoyment of Dublin society rubbed alongside his growing frustration with the limitations placed on the UUC's convention delegation. He instinctively wanted to make the convention work, and he despaired at the lack of common ground among the delegates. In the first week of September he complained to the Secretary of State for War, Lord Derby, that the government had failed to demonstrate any concern for the convention's lack of constructive progress.[38] But it was clear that Londonderry was also frustrated by the UUC, and little wonder given how far he was prepared to go in negotiations. Writing to his mother on 23 September, he declared that 'We could govern Ireland from Belfast but I am not sure the stalwarts want to do that; they would much prefer to remain behind a six county [border] and make faces at the rest of Ireland. They have the whole thing in their own hands and I expect the verdict in a fortnight or so.'[39]

A fortnight or so later and the cumbersome size of the convention, and its inability to make any progress, was addressed from the floor by the formation of a subcommittee of nine. This cross-party rebellion against Plunkett's plodding chairmanship included nine senior delegates from the main parties and excluded the hapless chairman. Barrie, Londonderry and Pollock represented Ulster unionism on the subcommittee, which also included Midleton for the Southern Unionists. The increasingly fragmented range of nationalism was represented by Redmond and William Murphy, as well as the Ulstermen Joseph Devlin, George Russell and the Catholic Bishop of Raphoe, Patrick O'Donnell.[40] After some initial hesitation on the part of the Ulster Unionists, O'Donnell assured them that its deliberations would be non-binding, thus paving the way for all to discuss the powers and composition of a hypothetical parliament for the whole island.

The Unionist members of the committee were keen to ensure that their supporters' minority status was addressed. After some debate, the subcommittee agreed that the upper house of the new parliament would be appointed and not elected, and with representatives from the churches, the peerage, the Privy Council and organized commerce.[41] Agreement was less forthcoming when it came to the lower house. Londonderry, however, assured Midleton that the more 'satisfactory' that representation was for Unionists the more liberal they could be about the powers of the parliament.[42] In the end Barrie settled at 40 per cent, having originally demanded 50 per cent, and the nationalists also conceded to continued representation at Westminster.[43]

Having settled the question of composition, the subcommittee turned its attention to what powers the hypothetical legislature and executive would possess. In contrast to the preceding consensus, a combination of economic fears and political intransigence led to deadlock on the extent to which Ireland would be fiscally independent from Great Britain. O'Donnell proposed that Dublin should control customs and excise, but the Ulster Unionists feared that this would be detrimental to their province's economic interests. Plunkett intervened at this point, suggesting that each side write down their fears and objections about the economic policy that their opponents were proposing. The Ulster Unionist subcommittee members assumed that a Dublin parliament would prioritize the economic needs of Ireland's agricultural economy, to the detriment of industry in the northeast, and that it would shirk any financial obligations to Westminster. They were not convinced by the nationalist subcommittee members' offer to offset this with an imperial contribution from the Irish parliament and for the retention of a British Isles free trade area.[44] Plunkett suggested that the nationalists send their economic concerns to the Unionists first. But unknown to him, they did so with a covering note that revealed how their economic policy was determined by notions of nationhood and self-determination. In reply, the Unionists similarly mixed economic concerns with other considerations, claiming that an Irish parliament would evade contributing to British national debt and defence spending, and that fiscal autonomy would so separate Ireland from Great Britain that it would in effect achieve the goals of Sinn Féin.[45]

The ensuing deadlock created a mood of gloom. The subcommittee met on 15 November to prepare a negative report for the convention's grand committee, scheduled to meet a week later. With all seeming lost, Londonderry without warning offered what seemed to Plunkett to be a glimmer of hope. It became known that he was going to table a motion for a federal scheme at the final meeting of the subcommittee, scheduled for 21 November.[46] The idea of a federal United Kingdom, with Ireland as a constituent part or parts, was not new to the convention or to Londonderry (see Chapter 1). But as a backbench MP, his disposition to federalism had been of little political consequence. Now, as the Marquess of Londonderry, and an Ulster Unionist delegate to the convention, his advocacy of federalism was altogether more significant and potentially consequential. Londonderry had never carefully and systematically outlined what he meant by federalism, though he was in contact with other high-profile proponents, including Carson, the fourth Earl of Dunraven and the former Liberal foreign secretary, the first Viscount Grey.[47] Given that these men were influenced by federalism's leading exponents, Frederick Scott Oliver and Lord Selborne, it is likely that Londonderry was influenced by their vision of national assemblies with wide powers.[48]

Plunkett noted hopefully that 'Now an Ulster leader suddenly announces his intention of not only making, on behalf of his party, a constructive proposal, but of offering at any rate a certain measure of self-government, presumably for the whole of Ireland.'[49] Federalism, however, necessarily ruled out Ireland's fiscal autonomy from Great Britain, making it unlikely as a means of ending the deadlock on the subcommittee of nine. Moreover, Londonderry was still a representative of the UUC, and he had not yet won over his delegation to the policy of federalism. He was contacted at this time by Adam Duffin, a senior Ulster Unionist and linen baron. Duffin was

> fully impressed by the view held by you and Mr Barrie on the desirability of the Ulster Unionists on the convention showing readiness to consider if not to initiate some alternative constructive policy while breaking with the Nationalists on the demand for fiscal autonomy. I gather that you think this should take the shape of a federal scheme which would fit it with a wider one likely to be adopted before long for the United Kingdom.

Such a proposal, he warned, should be made in 'the most general terms. I feel that you may be launched upon a sea of fresh controversy if they are even tentatively accepted as a basis for discussion by the other side, especially as you would have to make large reservations for Ulster, including probably education and judiciary'. Duffin then revealed the gulf that separated him from Londonderry by welcoming the prospect of the convention's breakdown. 'I am more than ever convinced that it should be frankly confessed that the Convention cannot come to any agreed settlement at the present time and that its deliberations should be suspended until such times as they may be renewed at the request of the Government. This is no time to succeed in framing a constitution for Ireland'.[50] A week later, Duffin confided to his wife that 'I think I am of use . . . in . . . keeping some check on L[ondonderry].'[51]

There is no minute of a meeting between the Ulster Unionist delegates, or their advisors, in the week following Londonderry's offer.[52] But Duffin represented a point of view that could not be ignored by Ulster Unionist delegates, and on 21 November, at the final meeting of the subcommittee of nine, Barrie announced that Londonderry would not propose a federal scheme as the Ulster Unionists 'did not think that such a course would ease the situation'. Plunkett noted in response to Barrie's announcement that 'There was nothing for it but to take Lord Londonderry's will for somebody else's deed.'[53] When the grand committee met the next day, Barrie blamed the failure of the subcommittee on the distance between Unionists and nationalists on the fiscal question.

Londonderry remained open in principle to attempts at reaching a settlement, regarding federalism as a solution in waiting, even if not one for the convention. Five days after the final meeting of the subcommittee, he outlined his views in a long and defensive letter to the Countess of Fingall, with whom he had clashed after meeting her at the Theatre Royal. Fingall appears to have taken Londonderry's performance at the convention as a sign that he might come to see the wisdom of home rule. In reply, Londonderry angrily dismissed the political value of his uttering

> a few phrases to gain thunderous applause from a number of very ignorant men. Suppose I had reason to suddenly change my views, what purpose would I serve, because if that is what you intended to suggest please let me say at once that if the principles which I hold are so flimsy that Sinn Fein pressure can completely change them, those amongst whom I live are of totally different material.

He declared that there was no real difference between 'the loyal Nationalist programme' and that advocated by Sinn Féin, except for a distinction that

> lies in the attitudes of these two sections towards the Empire as explained by their leaders. Redmond so far as he expresses a definite view at all, claims that the feelings of benevolence which he undoubtedly entertains towards England and the Empire will ensure that separation will not be the result of the policy. Sinn Fein frankly states that the policy is intended to lead to complete separation.

He went on to state 'that so long as the British Empire exists Ireland must remain politically within the circle of the United Kingdom and whatever path is chosen, long or short, or through whatever intermediary stages . . . that Ireland will be politically governed in exactly the same manner as England or Scotland or Wales'. Federalism,

Londonderry went out of his way to state, was not a concession to separatism. Indeed, the recent pressure applied on him by Duffin, and no doubt others too, is evident in his declaration 'that while I am willing to proceed on the lines of Federation, I am convinced that it is folly to choose this moment to establish so far-reaching a change'. He also responded to her suggestion that Ulster was responsible for the present crisis in the strongest terms, 'One of the many causes controllable by human agency was the criminal folly of the Irish-Radical-Socialist alliance which seduced our Army, wrecked our Constitution and for wholly immoral reasons unconnected with that issue endeavoured to force on a free community a measure of Home Rule which, mark you, is now repudiated by everyone.'[54]

Fingall overlooked the tone of his letter by responding positively with the suggestion that he seek the assistance of George Bernard Shaw to promote federalism.[55] If this was fanciful, then she was not alone in regarding Londonderry as the possible broker of an agreement. It was a view shared by others, most notably Professor W. G. S. Adams of the cabinet secretariat, and also the convention's secretary and chairman, Southborough and Plunkett.[56] General Bryan Mahon, the commander-in-chief in Ireland, added his voice to the chorus. 'I believe you are the only hope of any settlement being arrived at, both parties trust you.'[57] Despite their hopes, Londonderry was not prepared to break publicly with the UUC, although this did not prevent him from making his frustrations known in private.

On 18 December, at the final meeting of the convention before it adjourned for Christmas, Midleton signalled his intention to propose a new scheme that he hoped would command wide support. The central thrust of his proposal was that Ireland should have a parliament with powers over all Irish affairs; this would be mitigated for the Unionists by the retention of customs at Westminster, and by constitutional safeguards for Ireland's Protestant minority. The Ulster Unionists – having resolved the same day that their role at the convention would be to safeguard 'the interests of Ulster' – were now faced with another test of how far this could be reconciled with the wartime pressure to reach a settlement at Dublin.[58]

III

The Irish Convention reconvened on 2 January 1918 with Midleton pressing for his scheme to be adopted. Given the recent high-level speculation about Londonderry, there was some hope among southern Irish Unionists that he might support Midleton's proposals. He had, after all, remained on reasonably good terms with them despite the widening gulf between northern and southern unionism. In an obvious effort to court Londonderry, the third Baron Oranmore and Browne suggested that the Midleton scheme might form part of a federal plan. The maverick southern Unionist, Professor J. P. Mahaffy, observed that Londonderry was not impressed by Oranmore's 'too recent' conversion.[59] Londonderry's reaction was also the product of a meeting held the day before between the Ulster Unionist delegates, their advisory committee and several Ulster Unionist MPs. The meeting confirmed that the Ulster Unionist delegates would try to amend the Midleton scheme to reserve more powers to Westminster, but that they would also propose a 'scheme for exclusion'. It was left to Barrie's discretion about when it might be introduced.[60]

Addressing the convention on 3 January, Barrie claimed that the Ulster Unionists 'had come . . . to find a compromise between the Act of 1914, which had been accepted as a final settlement of the Nationalists' demand, and the partition proposals of 1916', only to find that nationalists had enlarged their demand, 'entirely owing to outside influences', and that they had submitted proposals that 'headed for separation and nothing else'.[61] If that appeared to completely close the door to a deal, he went on to express his hope 'that it was not even now too late to find a mean between the two extremes of the Home Rule Act on the one hand and the partition of Ireland on the other', and failing that, he added that an Irish parliament could demonstrate its worthiness to the Ulster Unionists.[62] The following day the stakes were raised when Redmond gave his approval to the Midleton scheme on the proviso that the government legislate for it immediately. In response to Barrie's specific accusation, he declared that it was the Ulster Unionist delegates and not the nationalists who were 'pledge-bound to consult an outside body'.[63]

R. B. McDowell argues that 'goodwill was in the air' in the first few days of January 1918, as a large majority of Unionists and nationalists seemed to back the Midleton scheme, leaving only the extremists of either side at the margins.[64] Not unexpectedly, Londonderry regarded the scheme as a 'great opportunity', and Barrie is reputed to have assured Midleton on 3 January that he could rely on the Ulster Unionist delegates not to oppose him.[65] The momentum gathered in these first few days of the New Year was soon lost, however, following the decision of Plunkett to adjourn this debate in favour of discussion on the land question, which he claimed would also allow parliamentarians among the delegates to attend Westminster. In any case, Londonderry was unable to attend the convention at this time due to ill health.[66]

With the convention's attention diverted, and several of the Midleton scheme's backers absent, the main opponents of the proposals were able to consolidate their positions. Still determined to secure full fiscal autonomy for Ireland, O'Donnell received the support of his fellow Catholic bishops and a number of prominent nationalists. As a result, Redmond felt compelled to withdraw his support for Midleton when he returned to the convention on 15 January.[67] The parties thereafter returned to their entrenched positions. Londonderry feared that instead of grasping something positive, the UUC had allowed the convention to fail and that the Ulster Unionists would receive a large measure of the blame. As he informed his mother,

> The Leadership of Ulster is not altogether a comfortable position and a great deal will depend on what comes out of the next few weeks. I think the Ulster men have a great opportunity but I do not think they are going to take it and it certainly looks as if they would come out of the Convention as being quite *non-possumus*.[68]

A fortnight later he informed his wife that an Ulster Unionist had

> suggested that the Ulster Division should mutiny or words to that effect . . . not even to win the war is a single concession going to be made . . . the rest of Ireland

> can go to blazes . . . Belfast always disheartens me . . . and the hatred of Ireland is a thing I really resent.[69]

His 'struggle here is to make Ulster look dignified instead of foolish', he wrote on another occasion to his wife. 'To me Ulster is like a horse with no bridle; there is no one who can guide them. Carson never really did and has neither the power now nor the desire to do anything.'[70]

Lloyd George intervened at this point by offering to receive a delegation of convention representatives. Informal discussions preceded the actual meetings with the prime minister. At these preliminary meetings, Barrie discussed with Professor Adams the possibility of a vetoing Ulster committee in the Dublin parliament, and Carson mulled over the idea of an Irish parliament containing two lower houses, one representing the north and the other representing the south.[71] Lloyd George exchanged these ideas with the other parties until he finally met the whole convention delegation on 13 February.

The prime minister's hopes of creating a working consensus proved to be too ambitious. His insistence that the fiscal question be left until after the conclusion of the war, and his view that partition was a barrier to settlement, offended O'Donnell's supporters and the Ulster Unionists, respectively. Having been influenced by F. S. Oliver's most recent pamphlet on federalism, Carson now wrote to Lloyd George on 14 February to propose a settlement on federal lines.[72] To the Ulster Unionist delegates, Carson admitted that a federal solution was impractical during the war, and that they should if required propose Ulster's exclusion from a home rule settlement. Barrie expressed his frustration to Londonderry on 16 February: 'You will recall . . . the Chief's letter which I received yesterday. . . . Reading it over carefully it means an absolute refusal of the P.M's suggestions, and no doubt this is a correct interpretation of the feeling of most of our delegates.' Barrie believed this to be a tactical error on their part, as he 'had rather hoped that we should have arrived at the same end by allowing the Bishops and their friends to veto these proposals, but we must be guided by our Chief and loyally obey his instructions'.[73]

On 21 February Lloyd George wrote to Barrie putting forward a compromise position. The plan included home rule, a delay in the fiscal question until the end of the war, greater representation for Ulster in an Irish parliament and an Ulster committee with the power to veto relevant legislation. The prime minister suggested that the Ulster Unionists should consider his proposals favourably for the sake of the war effort and to appease critics in the United States.[74] Londonderry was supportive and drafted a letter to Carson on the same day.

> I never was in your confidence before my Father died and I certainly am not in it now. I believe your view is more or less the same as mine, namely that the war must take precedence of every other problem great and small and that even a temporary arrangement of our prejudices and difficulties ought to be come to if it can possibly be done.
>
> I believe also that you are satisfied that the offers suggested to be made to Ulster now eliminate those dangers which induced us in 1914 to take up arms in

> our own defence. But even holding these views . . . you feel that because Ulster opinion appears to be so strong, we should not even make an effort to induce our constituents not only to consider the desperate position of the Empire, but also to realise that from the tactical point of view we can brand the R.C. Church as really opponents to a settlement of the question.
>
> If this is so I feel very unhappy about it. You are the only man who has any real over-riding influence in Ulster – we do not count and I especially do not count, for reasons which I need not go into and as your determination seems to be to throw your weight into the scale of the strongest opposition to any settlement; then all I can say is that I wish that instead of procrastinating because we have done nothing else, we had left the Convention some months ago.[75]

Four days later, on 25 February, the Ulster Unionist delegates met with their advisory committee and MPs at Belfast.[76] The meeting fulfilled Londonderry's worst expectations. When he attempted to convey the prime minister's intentions, it drew forth the implacable opposition of Hugh de Fellenberg Montgomery. The landowner and veteran Unionist wrote the following day to explain his concern that Lloyd George had intended to give Londonderry a 'free hand . . . to consent to this proposal if you liked, which I was sure the Advisory Committee or the majority of them were not prepared to do'. Montgomery dismissed Lloyd George's intervention as 'absolute bunkum' that was intended to satisfy 'promises' given 'to the Home Rulers and possibly to the Americans and other sentimental sympathisers'. Unable to 'deliver goods', he 'wants us to enable him to do so', and 'he gives absolutely no reason for the statement that a settlement would make it easier to get on with the war'. Montgomery dismissed the possibility of reaching any such agreement in wartime, and he declared 'that the proper conclusion to draw from the state of things was that the moderate Redmondites ought to join us'. But for the sake of appearances, he asked Londonderry to present their position as a refusal to consider the prime minister's proposals until 'they are put in a clearer and more detailed form'.[77]

Londonderry blamed Carson for not having the strength to overrule the doubters on the UUC. It was a trait that he would exhibit throughout his political career, unable or unwilling to appreciate the constraints that party leaders faced on politically sensitive matters, especially when confronted with the prospect of judgement at the ballot box. 'I think Carson is quite impossible', Londonderry wrote to his mother on 27 February, 'and he thinks that he can come and go as he likes; back one day, disappear the next'.[78] In a fit of pique not dissimilar to the frustration that he had felt in September 1912, he concluded his letter by refusing to return to Ulster politics until the rebelliousness of the Ulster Unionists had waned. The dowager marchioness responded to his frustration by engaging in that long-practised art of pressuring the Conservative front bench at Westminster to have her son appointed to ministerial office. 'I am bitterly disappointed that a place has not been found for Lord Londonderry in the new Government', she informed Bonar Law. 'All his contemporaries in the House of Commons have got places and honours and it seems hard that one who was in Parliament from 1906–1914, fought for three years with his Regiment, was recalled to attend the Irish Convention, should not have been given a post.' She was convinced that familial achievements, including her own, were relevant to his case for preference. 'I will not go back to past considerations, but I think my own record, had I been a man, should have helped, but being a woman and requiring nothing, I think my work and his father's, added to his own achievements which are not small ought to have produced something.'[79]

Rather than uniting the convention, Lloyd George's intervention had the unintended effect of sealing the divisions that had been brewing for several months. Having repeatedly encountered scepticism at meetings with their advisory committee, even outright opposition, the Ulster Unionist delegates could do little else other than to offer the convention their original exclusion proposal. And although Londonderry once again touched on the possibility of a federal solution – an idea that now commanded wide support at Westminster – the Ulster Unionists were aware that it was unlikely to attract support from the nationalists.

On 6 March the convention adjourned to mark the passing of Redmond, his death seeming to symbolize both its demise and that of constitutional nationalism as a force in Irish politics. Londonderry was the only leading Ulster Unionist to attend the service held at Westminster Cathedral. On 16 March he wrote to Lady Desborough that he had 'processed behind Redmond's remains for 2¼ hours'. In reference to a subsequent riding injury, he joked that the 'stout Protestants of the north with whom I am associated look on this as a direct visitation for associating myself with Papistry. Perhaps there is something in it'. The convention was doomed, he informed her, and needed to be wound up. 'Ireland has always been a tragedy and I am at a loss to know what to do now. It is such a pity that Ireland cannot be pushed a little further out into the Atlantic. . . . I am planless now. I do not know what place to drop into.'[80]

When the convention reconvened on 12 March it began a process of voting on an extensive list of proposals. Londonderry wrote to his wife about having to make 'an impassioned speech in support of exclusion proposals formally proposed by Barrie', and how his 'heart was very heavy because as you know I hate exclusion'.[81] The Ulster Unionists also proposed that a secretary of state should be appointed for the excluded area, which was to consist of nine counties not six, a feature that must have raised some doubt about the sincerity of the proposal given that the UUC had resolved in 1916 to support six-county exclusion.[82] O'Donnell and his supporters also voted against many of the proposals. A combined majority of southern Irish Unionists and Redmondite nationalists voted in favour of the schemes put forward, but their political weight outside the convention was not nearly so strong. A final report was considered in early April and passed with a majority of 44–29. The Ulster Unionists and O'Donnell nationalists compiled their own minority reports, reciting their positions, respectively, on exclusion and fiscal autonomy. Plunkett sent all the reports to Lloyd George and wrote a covering letter citing Ulster and customs as the main obstacles to an agreement.[83]

IV

The Irish Convention's failure coincided with an increasing demand for manpower at the Western Front. Ireland had been spared the enforcement of conscription but not the constant rumour of its implementation, and it was an obvious but by now largely unwilling recruiting ground. From the end of March, the cabinet discussed the possibility of simultaneously implementing conscription and home rule. Concerns were raised about the reaction of the Ulster Unionists to the latter, and of the effect that conscription might have in increasing support for Sinn Féin, but even the likes of Bonar Law and the first Viscount Milner leaned in favour of this solution.[84]

But the government faced a problem. The convention was still drafting its final reports in the first week of April, so the home rule scheme could not be immediately adopted, whereas the army's request for more manpower needed to be addressed as a matter of urgency. On 9 April the prime minister announced to the House of Commons that legislation allowing for conscription in Ireland would be drafted. In what was surely an error, Lloyd George later recorded in his memoirs that Londonderry did not support the application of the Military Service Act to Ireland.[85] Londonderry's speech to the House of Lords on 17 April, the day before royal assent was granted, suggests otherwise, for he 'urged the conscription of Ireland as an Irishman who was jealous of the good name and honour of Ireland'.[86] A few months later, on 20 June, he demanded that conscription be implemented in Ireland on the basis of equality with the rest of the United Kingdom. He also called on the cabinet committee then considering the implementation of home rule to approach it as part of a federal scheme. This latter speech formed part of a damning critique of the coalition and its Irish policy, which was delivered not long after Londonderry had refused a very junior position in the government. Justifying this decision, he argued that 'Members of such a Government were inclined to lose their individuality, and to accept doctrines to which in pre-war times they were opposed. They had seen a policy pursued which those under whom he had served had always condemned – Ireland cajoled at one moment and dragooned at another.'[87]

These criticisms aside, Londonderry welcomed the recent appointment of the first Viscount French as Lord Lieutenant of Ireland, and he expressed his hope that the accompanying restructuring of the Irish government would allow French to govern without interference from London. Londonderry was referring to a new departure at Dublin Castle whereby the lord lieutenant took charge of Irish policy with the assistance of a fully subordinate chief secretary. Londonderry's endorsement was significant given that French was sympathetic to home rule; it was the new viceroy's tough stance on law and order that leant him, at least initially, what Eunan O'Halpin describes as 'unique crossparty appeal'.[88] Londonderry's welcome to French was not merely rhetorical. The viceroy paid two visits to Mount Stewart in 1918, occasions that required concealed sentries to be posted on the estate.[89] His support for French notwithstanding, Londonderry remained ill disposed towards the government's simultaneous policy of delaying conscription until the autumn in the expectation that it might recruit 50,000 volunteers.[90]

Whether he was aware of it or not, Londonderry might have faced the same dilemmas as French had Walter Long gotten his way. Prior to French's appointment, the colonial secretary had suggested to Lloyd George that Londonderry should be appointed as Lord Lieutenant of Ireland.[91] The idea appears to have been discussed among those closest to Lloyd George.[92] Having abandoned the hostile attitude to home rule that he had adopted in 1916, Long was increasingly disposed to a federalist settlement, and he looked to Londonderry to embody a new dispensation in Irish government. Given the contrasting positions adopted by Long and Londonderry on the proposed 1916 settlement brokered by Lloyd George, it is significant that Londonderry's aristocratic status and performance at the Irish Convention now held out the prospect of a significant political advancement. Long's endorsement of Londonderry should not be overplayed, however, for the former was determined to have a controlling hand in Irish policy, and it is likely that he envisaged a Londonderry viceroyalty as fully subordinate to him.

If not as lord lieutenant, Londonderry still became associated with the new proconsular arrangements at Dublin Castle. He had been considering a return to the army following the convention's termination on 5 April. However, as noted in Chapter 1, the war secretary, Lord Derby, encouraged him instead to continue in politics. And as noted above, the dowager marchioness had meanwhile been busy lobbying the Conservative front bench to find a post for her son. It is likely that Long's proposal to Lloyd George was at least prompted if not fully explained by her efforts.[93] On 28 February Arthur Balfour reported to Bonar Law that she had 'written me an impassioned appeal to get Office for her son', that he would in reply 'tell her that this is no affair of mine, and that I never thrust in my advice on such matters', but that he would 'add that I have communicated with you!' Significantly, Balfour signalled to Bonar Law that Londonderry 'is a very good fellow, really appears to have done very well in the Irish Convention, and to have won golden opinions from all Parties'.[94] Bonar Law replied that

> I think myself that Londonderry is well entitled to get an appointment and if he had not gone to the House of Lords I am sure he would have got it long ago. As it is we are all anxious to find something for him and the first vacancy there is of any kind for which a Peer is suitable will, I hope, be of such a kind as to make it possible to offer it to him.[95]

As for the coalition Liberals, the junior minister, Ian MacPherson, after consulting Derby, reported to Lloyd George around the same time 'that Londonderry is regarded by his friends as a man of courage and ability'.[96] The slippage of government posts from the House of Lords to the House of Commons was not new in 1918 – Londonderry even addressed the upper house on this matter in July 1918 – so the first suitable vacancy to arise would come out of a diminishing pool.[97] In early June Londonderry was offered the post of whip. Whips in the Conservative-dominated upper house had more powers than their equivalents in the House of Commons, particularly in the management of government business.[98] But Londonderry was not entirely reconciled to the coalition, and with the support of Derby, he came to the conclusion that the role was not enough to 'muzzle' him on Irish affairs.[99] It was in the wake of this rejection that he went on to launch his stinging public attack on the coalition, provoking the resentment of Lord Curzon that he should 'be called upon to answer these questions'.[100]

If Londonderry had previously enjoyed an uneasy relationship with fellow Ulster Unionists, then the more aggressive posture that he adopted towards the coalition government was well received among their number, including his onetime critic, Adam

Duffin.[101] Not long afterwards, Londonderry made his first appearance at two twelfth of July Orange demonstrations in County Antrim, at Finaghy and at Lambeg. The senior Orangeman, Colonel Wallace, who had served with Londonderry on the convention, introduced the peer to those assembled as the man who had initiated the debate that had led Lloyd George to delay home rule (see below); a selective presentation, to say the least, of Londonderry's commitment to Ulster unionism.[102] Londonderry went on to use his platform speech to attack the government's military recruitment policy. On 13 July he accompanied Carson to a meeting at Belfast of the newly formed Ulster Unionist Labour Association. The appearance of a marquess before this organization seems out of place, but the association was deferential, socially conservative, strongly loyalist and ultimately a failure.[103] Addressing the meeting, Londonderry summarized his views on the convention in a way that failed to acknowledge how close he had been to promoting a deal with Redmond and Midleton. As 'a member of the Convention he was convinced that there was nothing between the maintenance of the union and separation', *The Times* reported. 'There was no separate nationality in Ireland any more than in Scotland or Wales, and for military and commercial reasons as well as for social progress it was absolutely necessary to maintain the essential unity of the United Kingdom.'[104] Londonderry was being recast, with his connivance, as a staunch east Ulster loyalist. The convention's breakdown and failure appears to have convinced him that the safest public course lay in consolidating and deepening his identification with Ulster unionism, especially given the waning political fortunes of southern Irish unionism and constitutional nationalism.

Others still held out hope that he might emerge as a leading advocate of federalism. The issue had become increasingly popular among pockets of support across the political spectrum, a reflection of the growing feeling that the Irish question had to be settled for the good of the war effort. Londonderry identified himself as a proponent of Oliver and Selborne's most recent pamphlet on federalism, *Suggestions for the Better Government of the United Kingdom*, a tract that also influenced leading members of the cabinet committee charged with looking at home rule.[105] However, the announcement by Lloyd George on 25 June that home rule would, like Irish conscription, be delayed, effectively killed-off the need for the government to consider a federal solution. A delegation of federalists that included Selborne met with Lloyd George the following day, and although the prime minister gave them a sympathetic hearing, he made it clear that there would be no radical reform to the United Kingdom for the duration of the war. Not included in the delegation was the MP Moreton Frewen, a member of the Irish gentry with business interests in the United States and a keen champion of landlord rights.[106] Responding to Londonderry's disappointment that the delay of home rule meant that federalism was off the agenda, Frewen suggested that the peer might head a campaign to bring it back. We 'have been had', Frewen claimed, 'I should value a quiet talk with you . . . a talk on the wider subject of Federal Govt [*sic*] than merely one's hopes as to Ireland'. He questioned Selborne's handling of the issue and declared that this is the 'moment for you & Carson to take hold. . . . We others who have been working it will drop out & help as best we can, with our knowledge, in the background'. He even suggested that Londonderry 'come out and advocate a "League of Federals" & be the first President. I could not only steer a lot of good fellows in, but

I think send over a lot of funds from the US'. It was a job that 'wants a young man & a brand new man, all of us who have hunted in that line were too "previous" & previosity [*sic*] in a matter of this kind is never forgiven'. He went on to advise that Londonderry would

> have to advocate two States for Ireland & if you do this, bear in mind *en revanche* every Irishman will do his utmost to break up England . . . But if you advocate Two Statehood [*sic*] for Ireland & make all sorts of good tempered alluring speeches 'that when the right time comes Ulster will join at Dublin' – play that sort of hose on them & you will create a good federal atmosphere.[107]

By the end of June, however, Frewen's enthusiasm was dampened by the meeting between Selborne and Lloyd George, 'a deplorable mess', but he still suggested that Londonderry could 'do something' as long as it was 'along safe lines'.[108]

With even such a long-time enthusiast for federalism having given up hope, it is not surprising that Londonderry did not jeopardize his increasing political capital by heading a futile 'League of Federals'. It did not mean, however, that he had abandoned the idea of promoting a federal solution behind the scenes, especially when he was told that his 'views on the Irish situation . . . carry great weight'.[109] On 13 August Londonderry wrote to the prime minister to complain about the home rule sympathies of the Chief Secretary for Ireland, Edward Shortt, the Liberal MP for Newcastle, and to use the opportunity to again press for a federal scheme. Having warned Lloyd George against raising hopes, Londonderry encouraged him to definitely rule out dominion-style home rule in order to make Ireland 'peaceful and contented'. He claimed that 'conflict in the Convention' had 'raged round Dominion Home Rule', and despite having no following it gained strength from 'the fact that utterances like Mr Shortt's were taken to mean that some time or other Dominion Home Rule will be granted'. Londonderry concluded by noting that he welcomed the recent change at Dublin Castle which meant that 'Lord French was the actual Governor of Ireland', and that while he had 'willingly done what I could to strengthen the administration which you have set up in Ireland[,]. . . by remaining silent now I run the risk of appearing to endorse Mr Shortt's views and this is a situation I am not prepared to accept'.[110]

Irish conscription had been delayed until September 1918 to give French more time to raise 50,000 recruits. On 18 August, with the deadline in sight, and only around 8,000 men recruited, Londonderry took the extraordinary step of informing the lord lieutenant that he was prepared to raise his own Irish brigade to go to the front.[111] French refused the offer on the basis that the War Office would reject it, but the letter might have brought the Ulster nobleman to the viceroy's attention just as he was looking for candidates for his new Advisory Council, or perhaps even confirmed Londonderry's suitability for such an appointment.[112] Either way, the government chose to drop their plans for conscription.

On 23 August Londonderry was one of seven men formally invited to join the viceroy's Advisory Council.[113] It was one of a series of military and civil committees that were created under French to assist this quasi-military governor in the administration of Ireland, but it would prove to be the most significant, even despite its untimely demise in December 1918. The council was intended to represent 'men of position and standing in different parts of the country', but, as O'Halpin observes, 'a less representative collection of Irishmen it would have been hard to find: they were simply rich men who were afraid of Sinn Féin. Apart from Londonderry'.[114] Other members of the patrician consultative body included the fourth Earl of Dunraven and the eighth Earl of Granard, both southern Irish Unionists; the nationalist Walter MacMorrough Kavanagh; Frank Brooke, of Ulster gentry stock; Sir Stanley Harrington, a bank director and railway chairman; and Sir Thomas Stafford, a medical doctor and government official. Those like Londonderry who were not already Irish privy councillors were sworn in and thereby given access to Irish government files. And although the council did not meet until October, Londonderry's new position meant that he was quickly drawn into a heated row between the Ulster Unionists and Dublin Castle.

The draconian measures implemented by French's administration proved to be reasonably effective in meeting the challenge of militant republicanism, but it struggled to stem increasing public support for Sinn Féin. In line with Dublin Castle's crackdown on violent groups, Shortt issued orders in August that the weapons of the UVF – like those of the National Volunteers – should be seized and placed in military custody. Carson and Dawson Bates agreed that Londonderry, given his new association with the viceroy, should be engaged to press their objections.[115] Their position vis-à-vis the authorities in Dublin was aided by the lord lieutenant's private secretary, Edward Saunderson, second son and namesake of the onetime parliamentary leader of the Ulster Unionists. Initially, the Ulster Unionists' protests to Shortt were met with a stony resolution. Dawson Bates argued that the seizure of UVF arms would drive young Belfast men into the ranks of the 'Bolsheviks' and other left-wing groups, a far-fetched claim that was perhaps calculated to play on French's strong dislike of Irish trade unionism.[116] When the lord lieutenant intervened to allow UVF weapons to be gathered at its own armouries, and to be placed thereafter under military control, with permits granted to those who handed in weapons, Shortt halted the planned movement. The orders of Shortt were in turn rescinded by a furious French, following a request from Londonderry.[117] French and Saunderson now personally arranged for the storage of UVF weapons, thus ensuring that the Ulster Unionists' concerns were assuaged.[118] In subsequent correspondence with Carson, Londonderry referred to the question of UVF arms as a 'nuisance', but one that he felt needed to be addressed.[119]

French viewed the deteriorating political situation in the country as proof that, for the present, Ireland was incapable of governing itself. He confidently declared the problem to be one of insufficient infrastructure and wanted his new Advisory Council to focus on development.[120] The council met for the first time on 10 October. Contrary to the wishes of French, Shortt arrived at the first meeting and suggested that it was a 'body in the nature of a Cabinet'.[121] Walter Long, who acted as a conduit between the coalition government and Dublin Castle, also indicated that he wanted to see the council turn into 'a sort of Irish Cabinet'.[122] Londonderry took a more cautious approach, stating that while he hoped that the council would 'develop into something more substantial and responsible', he disagreed with the term cabinet, for it implied 'one conviction, one idea, one thought'.[123] He was similarly cautious about how the council's activities would be made known to the public and was successful in having publicity about it delayed for a few weeks after the first meeting.[124]

As Londonderry wished, collective responsibility was not imposed upon the Advisory Council, but in the few months that it sat its members were still not aware of the exact nature of their posts: Were they advisors or governors? Its main and stated purpose was to look at economic matters, but this was a capacious remit as evidenced by the agenda for its second meeting, which included politically sensitive questions such as examining the general condition of the country, election precautions and a scheme for granting land to soldiers.[125] In addition, the evidence suggests that individual members were given portfolios. Londonderry became involved with agricultural matters, a topic that he had only the slightest association with since his election to the House of Commons in 1906.[126] For his part, Frank Brooke appears to have been dealing with the council's fears about the possibility of Sinn Féin-controlled county councils mistreating returning soldiers.[127] He was later killed by the Irish Republican Army (IRA) on 30 July 1920.

It was the question of what the Advisory Council constituted, or more properly, what it might become, that framed its very public collapse in the second week of December. Long and French had been discussing the possibility of turning the council into something more like a government, one that might replace a scheme for home rule. The cabinet then considered giving the council new legal powers to aid its reconstruction. Fearing the intentions of Long and French, Shortt protested, and in the resulting confusion *The Times* on 13 December described the council as being in a 'muddle'.[128] With that, no extra powers were granted to the Advisory Council and French quickly lost interest in it. No further meetings were convened.

Despite the failures of the Irish Convention and the Advisory Council, Londonderry had emerged from both with his reputation enhanced. He had developed in Ireland a political persona that was characterized by moderation. To British observers, he was someone who put the war above Irish matters, including the concerns of the Ulster Unionists. To the latter, he was someone who had remained loyal to them even after a tense period in their ranks. Londonderry's reward was the satisfaction of his mother's claim for a place in the post-war coalition government, and soon after, his admission to the Order of the Garter.[129] His outwardly steadfast association with the Ulster Unionists also gave him the opportunity, several years later, to join the first government of Northern Ireland, and thus have a career in government in both Great Britain and Ireland.

It is ironic that Londonderry's political career started to progress at a time when the various species of unionism with which he was associated, directly or by temperament, began to unravel and part company. It was the culmination of what Alvin Jackson describes as Ulster unionism's simplification, retreat and retrenchment to its northeast core.[130] Yet, this dynamic was at the heart of why Londonderry's authority was enhanced in Ulster and at Westminster at this very moment. Contrary to what Michael Farrell suggests, Londonderry was not a typical example of the Ulster Unionists' 'close political and personal ties with the British upper-class establishment and the Conservative Party'.[131] His embodiment of these two facets was in fact relatively rare after 1918 and became rarer still in the years that followed. Rather, it was his exceptionalism in this regard that made him useful to both. Westminster viewed him as a conduit between Belfast and London, a reliable and safe pair of hands in an increasingly unreliable Ulster Unionist movement. For the Ulster Unionists he provided a highly placed political and social link with the Conservative front bench at Westminster. At a time when the United Kingdom's great landowners were feeling the effects of almost forty years of decline, Londonderry had survived marginality, earned positive prominence through his work in Ireland and begun a ministerial career that would last, intermittently, into the mid-1930s.

3

Coalition government, 1919–21

If the scope of Lord Londonderry's political ambitions had once seemed constrained by his aristocratic background, then, paradoxically, his inheritance of the Londonderry title and vast fortune in February 1915 had helped to loosen those constraints. Political ability, or the perceived lack of it, still counted, but so did opportunity. As an immensely wealthy grandee peer, Londonderry could not realistically imagine himself as prime minister, but his upbringing had inculcated him with a belief in his right to govern, and the social and economic structures to potentially realize his ambition. His family background also afforded him territorial bases on both sides of the Irish Sea, and the consequent opportunities for political influence in Ulster, northeast England, and nationally, as the landed aristocracy was still able to transcend localism and provincialism.[1] Individual agency, of course, was still important in forging a successful political career. Had Londonderry sided with the southern Irish Unionists in the summer of 1916, or at the subsequent Irish Convention, the Ulster Unionists would not have invited him in 1921 to join the first government of Northern Ireland. And it hardly needs to be stated that he would not have been found a comparable place in the executive of the emerging Irish Free State. Throughout the post-war 'Troubles', or war of independence, the large landowners in that new state were often subject to harassment and violence, including attacks on their property, which led many to abandon Ireland altogether.[2] Individual agency would also play a role in Londonderry's ability to gain, remain and return to the heart of power at Westminster, for no matter how wealthy he was or how grand his title, his political outlook had to acknowledge the greater emphasis given after the war to consensus and appeasement.

Londonderry's period in the post-war Liberal–Conservative coalition government was relatively brief, but it was significant for several reasons. First, as mentioned in Chapter 2, it demonstrates that his recent performance in Irish affairs made him a more visible and viable candidate for government office at Westminster, and that the political spheres of Ireland and Great Britain were not wholly separate, especially for aristocrats. Second, it is significant for what he did in office. Londonderry learned to trim his sails and accept political realities, especially the renewed emphasis on Liberal–Conservative co-operation, to oppose the threat of Labour, which was espoused by the prime minister, David Lloyd George, and the cabinet Conservatives who supported him. In Londonderry's particular case, it meant reducing government expenditure by overseeing the decimation of the nascent RAF, and his raising no public protest at the increasing role of the state. Last, his reasonably competent handling of this relatively short spell in office provided Londonderry with valuable experience that was not only useful for the ministerial portfolios that he would later hold, in Belfast and London, but also for providing him with a more sustainable claim on those offices.

I

Londonderry's attitude to the Liberal–Conservative coalition had fluctuated significantly in recent years, spanning hostility and unease through to acquiescence and support (see Chapter 2). In June 1918 he was offered and turned down the post of whip in the coalition government. Months later, he was invited to sit on the Irish viceroy's Advisory Council and having accepted he was made an Irish privy councillor. The latter in no way bound him to the coalition government, or the survival of it after the war, but it must have impressed upon him the potential rewards awaiting those who swam with the tide of Conservative opinion at Westminster, specifically, the acceptance of Lloyd George as the premier of a Conservative-dominated coalition government. Conservatives of all hues realized that the post-war years would be very challenging and highly uncertain, especially with the introduction of universal male suffrage, new women voters and the expected rise of Labour as a political force. Most of the party's MPs were therefore prepared to keep Lloyd George at the helm of the government, at least for the time being.[3]

This is not to suggest that opportunism was Londonderry's underlying motivation for adhering to the coalition's notion of political consensus. He had already demonstrated in the Irish context a marked disposition to achieving consensus. Signs of the approach in other areas had been evident during his time in the House of Commons, albeit obscured by his unimportance and his lack of opportunities to develop the theme. If he was biased against reforms to taxation and parliament, and biased in favour of the colliery owners, he could still employ rhetoric that foregrounded the need for co-operation and moderation on these sensitive questions. In part, his approach represented the futility of his position on the opposition backbenches and the need to make the Liberals' legislative reforms as palatable as possible. At the same time, his estrangement from many in his party meant that he had some room for manoeuvre. Before the First World War, this was largely the result of his being on the wrong side of the tariff reform row. By the end of that conflict, Londonderry's disenchantment with many Conservative parliamentarians was also influenced by the pessimism and sense of betrayal felt by all Irish Unionists. As he informed the government's chief whip, Lord Edmund Talbot, in August 1918, 'Speaking for myself, I shall never forget their attitude to Home Rule, and when I look up Bonar Law's speeches in Belfast before the war I see that his convictions are somewhat easily adjusted.'[4] Disappointment with his party did not equate to disillusionment with conservatism, just as his eventual support for the coalition did not mean that he accepted the ascendancy of certain Liberal policies. Both wings of the coalition had to make adjustments, and that included the prime minister. As Avner Offer observes, it 'fell to Lloyd George, who had invested so much political and emotional capital in his budget and land campaigns, to preside over the programme's demise' in response to the 'anti-Radical backlash' that attended the tenure of the post-war coalition.[5]

Londonderry's support for the coalition could not be confined to rhetoric. The armistice called on 11 November 1918 necessitated the first general election since December 1910. Like his forebears he was the head of the Conservative and Unionist party in County Durham and an influential voice in the selection of its candidates for the county's parliamentary constituencies. The Reform Act 1884 had done much to erode such influence, but according to David Cannadine, determined landowners could still exert themselves as local political leaders.[6] One prospective candidate for the Conservative constituency of Stockton-on-Tees, Captain O. L. Martin, assumed that the dowager Marchioness of Londonderry continued to perform this function in the county, even after her husband's death, for it was she and not her son who occupied Wynyard Hall during the First World War. Lady Londonderry in reply informed Martin that her son now took care of these affairs, and soon after the captain's case was impressed upon Lord Londonderry.[7] By the end of August 1918, he was also contacted by a local Conservative organizer in County Durham, Major Stanley Appleby, who advocated an alternative candidate for Stockton, a Mr Watson. But Londonderry had already decided in favour of Martin, and in response to the pronounced anti-coalition rhetoric of Appleby, he added that despite being 'diametrically opposed' to Lloyd George, 'I feel that at this Election it is our duty to support him as Prime Minister'.[8] Appleby in reply again promoted Watson as the Conservative candidate. He added that it was necessary to 'clear out of this country all the alien blood and let the national characteristics of Englishmen carry their full weight in the government of the country'. In doing so, he claimed, 'we shall find the greater portion of Labour coming out on the right side in favour of order and common sense'.[9]

Such attitudes had grown in prominence during and after the First World War, and within the Conservative party these were most readily associated with its right wing, often referred to as the diehards.[10] Outside the party, Appleby's concerns were expressed by a number of small political groups that campaigned to restrict the presence of aliens, and which made the organization of a patriotic working men's movement the focus of their activities.[11] Aware of these critics of the government, Londonderry attempted to assuage Appleby's frustration by agreeing 'with what you say about English Bolshevists, but I will ask you to remember that party politics and party organisations have been in existence for too long to establish anything in a moment in direct opposition to them'. He suggested instead that it 'is far better to capture the old organisations then to infuse those same organisations with the principles in which we believe'.[12] It is tempting to read into his words an endorsement of the diehard outlook. But as Stuart Ball observes, the diehards typified 'something fundamental which the party could not afford to dispense with . . . the impulses of its heart, even if the head decided to face another way'.[13] In practise, in the periodic clashes between the Conservative front bench and the diehards, before and after this period, Londonderry stood consistently with the former.

A total of 533 seats were won by the coalition Liberals and coalition Conservatives at the December 1918 general election, the latter taking 339 seats. Lloyd George remained as prime minister, and Bonar Law acted as his deputy and guardian of the

Conservative and Unionist interest. Winston Churchill, a coalition Liberal, was in 1919 appointed Secretary of State for War and Air, and he ensured that his second cousin, Londonderry, was appointed to the Air Council as its Finance Member.[14] The latter noted that 'friend Winston has come to the rescue just when I was going to turn into a "Local Magnate"'.[15] As it turned out, Londonderry's association with Churchill proved to be a mixed blessing during his period at the Air Ministry. Moreover, it is likely that even without Churchill's patronage Londonderry would have received some minor office, albeit in another department, given that he had other significant supporters, including his mother's close friends, Walter Long and Arthur Balfour.[16] Still, in the longer-term, Londonderry's relationship with Churchill continued to be of importance, helping him back into office in the late 1920s, and ensuring the very opposite in the 1940s.[17]

II

It is noteworthy that the case for Londonderry entering the government was not outweighed by his ownership of collieries. The future of the coal industry, which employed around 1,250,000 men at this time, was not just an economic question but a political matter. From 1913 its root problem had been its chronically excess capacity and the resulting extreme stagnation in demand. But its difficulties were exacerbated by the attitudes, habits and prejudices of the owners and managers, and the blame for its problems was more often than not laid at their door.[18] The owners' tendency to cut wages during temporary slumps was a particular source of tension with the highly unionized workforce. The safety record of coal mining also left a lot to be desired. In the period between 1922 and 1924, industrial accidents resulted in the deaths of 3,603 miners and 597,193 injured, figures that do not take account of the diseases caused by coal dust.[19] Admittedly, when Londonderry joined the Air Council, the coal trade was experiencing a temporary post-war boom. It was also still subject to wartime controls, and so it was to the coalition government that the MFGB made their demands for higher wages, and for the industry to be made more efficient through nationalization. To see off the risk of a strike, the government established in February 1919 a royal commission under Sir John Sankey to examine the future of the industry. It was made up of three colliery owners, three miners' leaders, three industrialists and three economists. The timing of Londonderry's entry to the government was fortunate, for the Sankey commission's hearings in the months that followed shook the public and government ministers alike, as it drew attention to the dire living conditions of miners and their families. It also detailed the highly fragmented and scattered structure of the industry that resulted in around 3,000 pits being owned by 1,500 companies or individuals, and more controversially, the payment of royalties to 4,000 landowners for coal brought to the surface.

Londonderry was attending the international aeronautical commission at Paris in May when he was summoned to give his evidence to the commission on the 8th. Under cross-examination, he revealed that he was 'the owner of minerals already proved to exist under about 5,808 acres in the County of Durham'. Aside from four shares of

£100 each, he was the sole shareholder of the Londonderry Collieries Limited, which included three collieries in and around Seaham: Seaham itself, purchased by Frances Anne, Marchioness of Londonderry in 1849; Dawdon, sunk by the sixth marquess between 1900 and 1906 and Silksworth, sunk by the fifth marquess in 1872 and now held under a lease. At these pits a total of 7,000 men and boys were employed. The average annual output of his collieries was 546,720 tons, around half of which was worked by lessee companies. The royalties paid to him were fixed to tonnage, the average being 4½ d. per ton, totalling £9,608 annually (the equivalent in 2021 of £508,000). A further £5,726 was paid each year to Londonderry for way-leaves (the equivalent in 2021 of £302,000). When it was his turn to question Londonderry, Frank Hodges, general secretary of the MFGB, wrested from him the acknowledgement that nationalization during the war had benefited 'the community at large'. When Hodges asked about ownership of the air above his estate, Londonderry evaded the allusion to royalties by remarking that he had just been discussing that very question at Paris and that he 'did not feel at liberty to state the results'. He could nevertheless be direct in his answers to other questions, such as the admission that he would use his membership of the House of Lords to block reforms to the mining industry if he felt that it was in his interests. His position in the government appears not to have been raised during the hearing, but it was clear from Londonderry's evidence that he was not prepared in all circumstances to submerge his private responsibilities beneath the lofty idea of public duty.[20]

The attitude adopted by Londonderry before the Sankey commission highlights that there was little to distinguish him at this point from the position adopted by the Mining Association of Great Britain (MAGB), the colliery owners' representative body. Notwithstanding the considerable range and variety of mining enterprises, there was a general tendency among the owners to assume that the great prosperity enjoyed by the industry between 1873 and 1913 could be repeated if they were freed from the shackles of government interference, especially concerning wages and hours of work. Recent drops in output, according to this outlook, were the result of state controls and interference, as well as a malign strategy by the mining unions to restrict the amount of coal brought to the surface.[21] The MAGB was remarkably successful in containing differences of opinion within its ranks, typically the product of regional factors and differences in scale and markets. Nevertheless, it is possible to discern by the end of 1919 that Londonderry was becoming uneasy with MAGB's truculent posture.

Sankey was disturbed by the testimonies of the coal owners. His commission recommended wage rises and 7-hour working days, but on the question of nationalization the commissioners were divided. All of them agreed that coal should be nationalized, but it was only through Sankey's casting vote that a majority favoured nationalization of the collieries. This allowed the coalition government to rule out nationalization altogether, which in any case had become less appealing as the industry began to operate at a loss. The government's reaction had the effect of undermining the influence of moderate trade union leaders, and it paved the way for further industrial strife on the coalfields that reached its dramatic climax in 1926 (see Chapter 5).[22] Londonderry personally experienced the heightening tension in August 1919, when he visited the Easington Colliery in County Durham to present the venue for a memorial club to the local branch of the Comrades of the Great War. The inclusion in his speech of a call to increase production would have been provocative in less testing times, but in the wake of the government's limp response to Sankey it caused Londonderry's audience to make constant interruptions, obliging him, according to press coverage, 'to resume his seat for some time'.[23] There were no similar reports of disturbances a week later, when he entertained about 10,000 invited miners from his collieries, and their wives, in the grounds of Seaham Hall. The stated purpose of the gathering – to celebrate 'the peace' and to present a number of ex-soldier employees with decorations for gallantry – probably helped to prevent a repeat of the previous week's protests.[24]

In the period between the Sankey Commission and 1 April 1921, when the government planned to hand back control of the collieries to the owners, Londonderry attempted to adopt a more moderate and consensual tone in public. Addressing the Seaham Colliery Conservative Club on 19 December 1919, he declared that 'the ideas actuating employers and employed were now very much greater than they were. The employers realized that the first consideration was the welfare of the workers. Cooperation for the benefit of all concerned was now the idea'. He warmed to his theme: 'The drawback to any industry was the element of suspicion. There were some people who thought that between employer and employed there was a chasm which it was impossible to bridge. He thought that that chasm did not exist, and that if it did the great majority of our people were anxious and willing to bridge it.'[25] In this transitional period, Londonderry also reduced his financial exposure to the industry's problems. The Durham coalfield's reliance on export markets meant that it would experience protracted decline in the 1920s.[26] Early on, in September 1920, the Londonderry Collieries sold Silksworth Colliery to another County Durham concern, the Lambton and Hetton Collieries, transferring with it responsibility for the colliery's 2,000 employees and their houses in the village of Silksworth.[27]

The owners' determination to impose wage reductions on 1 April 1921, following the government's withdrawal from the industry, led the MFGB to mark the occasion with a national strike. A state of emergency was declared and all leave in the armed forces was cancelled. The miners remained on strike for three months, despite losing the support of the other major unions on 15 April. In the meantime, Londonderry made a public intervention that signalled his willingness to depart from MAGB orthodoxy. Writing to *The Times*, he urged everyone to reach a solution in the national interest. 'It must be obvious to all that our present methods of production and distribution in the coal industry are antiquated and require thorough revision, and it is quite impossible that such a revision can take place without the sympathetic cooperation of all concerned.' After ruling out nationalization, he argued that the 'whole trend of modern commercial development is towards amalgamation and unification, and I can see no reason whatsoever why such a policy should not be adopted in the coal trade'. He hoped that 'all those interested in the coal trade are prepared to review the situation with minds untrammelled by antiquated prejudices', otherwise 'we shall very soon find ourselves, as a nation, in a hopeless and irretrievable position'. He concluded by claiming that most members of the MFGB were simply anxious about wages. The federation's resolutions, in contrast, were the result of unrepresentative 'extremists'. There could be no 'free expression of opinion of the miners', he reasoned, unless ballots were conducted in secret.[28] Londonderry sought the aid of the newspaper's owner, Lord Northcliffe, and he responded favourably after conducting his own extensive investigation into the matter.[29]

Nothing came of the two men's efforts, however. The government had no intention of forcing amalgamations and owners tended to prize the independence of their own enterprises. Moreover, amalgamation was viewed by many of them as a potentially costly option that did not necessarily bring about the more efficient organization of the industry, given the potential for confused lines of managerial authority and expanded boards of directors.[30] The first Baron Gainford, a former Liberal MP and government minister, and a neighbouring coal owner in County Durham, dismissed Londonderry's support for amalgamation as inapplicable to 'the present situation' as it would take time to reduce the production costs. In any case, he admitted, 'I have a strong personal dislike to all efforts made to secure in any trade a combine or trust.'[31] The MAGB's ability to subsume divergences of opinion among its members had the effect of ensuring that the conservatism espoused by Gainford trumped Londonderry.[32] When the stand-off with the miners came to an end on 1 July, the owners as a body triumphed again as the miners returned to work on lower wages based on district agreements. Thereafter, the severe slump of that year had the effect of reducing unrest and even led to some improvement in industrial relations, to the extent that the owners agreed in 1924 to wage rises.[33]

III

The Ministry of Air might have been under the control of the Secretary of State for War, but Churchill was committed to the RAF's independence, and the Air Ministry maintained its own structures and bureaucracy. Its ruling Air Council, which was analogous to the Board of Admiralty, was one of the few emergency bodies established during the First World War to outlive that conflict.[34] Churchill was its president, and the Under Secretary of State for Air, John Seely, his deputy. The Air Council also contained other members with responsibilities for the RAF and civil aviation, including Sir Hugh Trenchard, Chief of the Air Staff; Sir Frederick Sykes, Controller-General of Civil Aviation; Edward Ellington, Director-General of Supply and Research; Sir John Hunter, Administrator of Works and Buildings; Sir Arthur Robinson, Secretary to the Council and several additional members including Sir James Stevenson, Sir Arthur Duckham and William Alexander. As Finance Member, Londonderry was responsible for decreasing the RAF's post-war funding and for encouraging private enterprise in civil aviation. Against expectation, his membership of the House of Lords served to enhance his limited authority within the ministry, for it designated him its spokesman in the upper house.[35] Even so, that role could not disguise the fact that as Finance Member he held a very junior post. That it received no remuneration troubled his mother, for reasons of status rather than income, leading her to conclude that Londonderry had 'never had the luck of the race'.[36] The dowager marchioness did not live to see him promoted to Under Secretary of State for Air in April 1920, for she died on 16 March 1919.

It was inevitable that the end of the war would necessitate demobilization and drastic cuts to expenditure on the armed forces. The transformation was reinforced by the ten-year rule, agreed by the cabinet in August 1919, which declared optimistically that Great Britain and its empire would not be engaged in another great war for a decade.[37] Reductions to the RAF so soon after its foundation raised questions about the desirability and viability of maintaining an independent air force. And in the context of inter-service rivalry for reduced resources, it was a subject raised most frequently by the army and Royal Navy. As a result, Londonderry's two years at the Air Ministry as Finance Member, then Under Secretary of State, were dominated by the need to balance the reduction of RAF expenditure with the preservation of its existence.[38]

Much of Londonderry's time was spent terminating government contracts for aircraft and selling off equipment and land. Another member of the Air Council, James Stevenson, warned him that the task might arouse public concern about the process being subsidized by the state. 'I should get down to these contracts as soon as possible', he advised. 'There are innumerable difficulties ahead and the sooner most of them are cleared away the less likelihood there is of anything bordering on public scandal. You won't sleep comfortably in your bed until these difficulties have been settled.'[39] The need to sell or dispose of aircraft for what amounted to very little, such as transferring over fifty aeroplanes to Canada in February 1919, was deemed necessary as buyers would cover the immense costs of disposal.[40] At home, a consortium fronted by Frederick Handley Page and Godfrey Isaacs – the younger brother of the first Earl of Reading, a favourite of Lloyd George – agreed to purchase most of the former air force stock for one million pounds, paid in yearly instalments with the Air Ministry receiving half the profits from further sales. As the whole value had been estimated at roughly 100 million pounds, Stevenson's warning was substantiated in so far as there were accusations that these actions created a monopoly.[41] H. Montgomery Hyde's history of air policy takes a more benign view of the Air Ministry's handling of the matter, noting that 'in the end . . . the taxpayers got back several millions of pounds from what, but for the skilful handling of sales, would have been scrap metal and timber'.[42] By the time that Londonderry left the Air Ministry in the spring of 1921, he had completed this 'grim' task without arousing any scandal, no small achievement given the cry of 'anti-waste' then gaining ground in the press and within the Conservative party.[43]

A potential opening for Londonderry emerged in December 1919 when John Seely resigned as Under Secretary of State. A former Secretary of State for War, he had become increasingly unhappy about his subordinate position at the Air Ministry, and he had failed to persuade Lloyd George to decouple it from the War Office. Having attempted to assuage the frustrations of Seely, Londonderry emerged from the episode with some credit, but when Churchill recommended that his cousin replace the outgoing minister, Lloyd George chose instead the Conservative MP, George Tyron.[44] In his memoirs, Londonderry claimed that Lord Curzon had blocked his first opportunity of promotion, and he also recorded Churchill's response, 'What can I do? . . . your own people are against you.'[45] As to why Curzon should be so hostile to his ambitions, Londonderry attributed this to poor relations between the two of them, in particular, his recent refusal to grant early demobilization to Curzon's footman.[46] Londonderry could certainly be strict in enforcing his ministry's writ; much later, in 1934, when he was Secretary of State for Air, he had the Air Ministry formally reprimand his daughter, Margaret, for flying too low over Windsor Castle, though in this instance it can equally be considered an act of mischief on his part.[47] If the former viceroy of India was an obstacle to Londonderry's promotion, then the decisive factor is more likely to have been the latter's close association with Churchill, for Curzon, recently appointed foreign secretary, found himself at this time in near constant disagreement with the war secretary.[48] Another possible explanation for Londonderry's failure to be appointed in Seely's stead lies in his status as a colliery owner. As noted above, his and other mine owners' testimonies to the Sankey Commission had attracted considerable adverse publicity.[49] It is possible that Lloyd George, and even some Conservatives, considered it prudent to avoid promoting a colliery owner with the revelations of that inquiry still fresh in people's memories.

Not even Londonderry's investiture as a knight of the Garter on 18 December 1919 could lift him out of his despair at having been passed over. It seemed not to matter that the same honour had only been granted to his father after serving two demanding years as Lord Lieutenant of Ireland.[50] Churchill wrote to his cousin on Christmas day to remind him that he had been bestowed a great mark of respect, and he advised him to 'be entirely good tempered and apparently indifferent', to be 'guided' by him. '[T]hen I am sure that your public career will open out satisfactorily; whereas quarrelling with the present regime will only strand you on the mud flats.'[51] The Garter was indeed a prestigious honour for any aristocrat, and its award to Londonderry led Curzon to express his misgivings to other ministers.[52] What appears to have troubled Londonderry, however, was that it was meant to satisfy his claim on being appointed to a higher ministerial office, and that it might herald the end of a short-lived period of progress in the government. After all, the third, fourth and fifth marquesses of Londonderry had received similar honours as an alternative to giving them ministerial rank.

Unsatisfied, Londonderry lobbied Bonar Law hard for a promotion, with help also from his wife and Churchill. Their efforts finally paid off on 2 April 1920, following Tyron's move to the Ministry of Pensions, when Londonderry was appointed Under Secretary of State for Air, Curzon's opposition now having evaporated.[53] In its coverage of the appointment, *The Times* expressed concern about its impact on Irish affairs – 'comment will no doubt be caused by the promotion of two of the leaders of Ulster Unionism, Sir James Craig and Lord Londonderry' – and also the appropriateness of Londonderry being in the upper house. 'He has given good service as Finance Member', it conceded, 'But the House of Commons will assuredly object to an arrangement by which, with the Under-Secretary in the House of Lords, it can only secure information on air policy from Mr Churchill, whose predominant interest is in the Army.'[54]

If Londonderry had to struggle to gain even this modest promotion, it did not stop him from having greater ambitions. With a declining number of government posts for peers to occupy at home, the ambitious in their number looked to the empire for satisfaction. The 'British Empire provided secure, comfortable, well-paid, and essentially ornamental employment opportunities in quite unprecedented numbers', Cannadine observes, 'And as a result was a system of outdoor relief for the upper classes.'[55] Londonderry felt that he too deserved a place in the sun. Not a mere

Figure 4 Lord Londonderry, 1920.

ornamental office, however, but India, the pre-eminent viceroyalty and one that also carried political weight.[56] On 3 May, only a month after becoming an under secretary of state, Londonderry wrote to the colonial secretary, Lord Milner. He intended the letter to end recent speculation that he might accept the post of governor-general of Canada, as he claimed that he would not give up his place in the government and his commitments to Ireland for a purely ornamental role.[57] The intended implication of the letter was that he might do so for India, though in fact the prospect of a move there would have to overcome the opposition of his wife.[58] Milner was clearly unimpressed by Londonderry's claim on the viceroyalty and appalled by his dismissal of the Canadian post, the training ground of several Indian viceroys. The grand old man of the British proconsular service therefore avoided mentioning the subcontinent in his reply and accepted Londonderry's refusal of Canada, adding that he for one thought more of Rideau Hall than the Under Secretary of State for Air.[59] In the end, Lord Reading was appointed to the post, and Londonderry continued to entertain the notion that he too might one day be considered.[60]

In contrast to his uneasy relationships with some senior ministers, Londonderry got along very well with the Chief of the Air Staff, Hugh Trenchard. This was not without significance. In the weeks that followed the establishment of the RAF on 1 April 1918, Trenchard's repeated clashes with the first Secretary of State for Air, the first Baron Rothermere, led first to his own resignation followed by Rothermere's.[61] Afterwards reinstalled as head of the RAF, he found in Londonderry an agreeable minister who shared his passion for promoting the service's independence and survival in straitened times.[62] Londonderry later fondly recalled their first meeting in his memoirs, noting how he ignored protocol by visiting Trenchard at his office and not insisting that the Chief of the Air Staff come to see him:

> after a formal greeting, [Trenchard] began to tell me what he intended to do with this and that. He delved among piles of papers and found the one he wanted immediately. Then he went on with his short, decisive phrases with so much energy that I was a little taken aback. After listening for a while I ventured to remark, 'But what if I don't agree with you?' He looked up in doubt: there was a moment of silence: then he laughed as energetically as he had been talking. From that moment there was a complete understanding between us.[63]

With Churchill preoccupied at the War Office, Londonderry looked more like the head of his own department, albeit not a particularly important ministry. It was Trenchard, of course, who was decisive in forging a post-war role for the RAF. But it helped that the two men agreed on air policy almost instinctively; it was not unusual for Trenchard to assign his proxy at meetings to Londonderry.[64] Nor was the relationship all one-way in the matter of influence. When the First Sea Lord, Admiral of the Fleet Lord Beatty, called for the Royal Naval Air Service to be re-established, Trenchard was angered by his implication that the RAF was inadequate. Londonderry assuaged him by asserting the very opposite, claiming that the Royal Navy feared losing major responsibilities to the RAF, and of being in 'dread that an air officer might one day be Commander-in-Chief'.[65] The two men became close friends, they shared confidences, and in the summer of 1920, Londonderry became godfather to Trenchard's newly born son.[66] It is not inconceivable that Trenchard, the déclassé son of a bankrupt provincial lawyer, was delighted by the prospect of a marquess being his son's godfather. Likewise, Londonderry brought a touch of aristocratic grandeur to the belittled RAF. This was most obvious in the use of Londonderry House as a venue for formal and informal Air Ministry functions, an accompaniment to its recently acquired role hosting political receptions for the coalition government. That development was first marked in 1919 by the Conservatives' eve of parliament reception taking place there instead of Lansdowne House.[67]

It is tempting to see Londonderry as a mere ornament adorning Trenchard's air force. But in his role as Under Secretary of State, he established public positions that were in later life to take on greater consequence. As he noted in his memoirs, Trenchard 'gave me that sense of the air and the Air Force so that when the Service was threatened with extinction, about a decade later, I was already aware of the air possibilities whereas many of my colleagues were not'.[68] Similarly, his later response to alarmist speculation about the scale of the Luftwaffe's expansion in the 1930s was adumbrated at the sixth Aeronautical Exhibition at Olympia, held in July 1920, when he used the opportunity of his address to criticize rumours of covert rearmament by Germany. Just as he would in the late 1930s, he reassured the military and civil dignitaries in his audience that the Air Ministry had matters in hand, in this instance, through a commission of control that would ensure that any new German machines would be of no military use.[69]

Londonderry's audience would have been just as if not more anxious about French intentions and capabilities in this period, an important factor in securing the RAF's survival and independence after 1918. But the main reason that the air force persisted in these otherwise difficult years was the imperial role that Trenchard cultivated for it, first in Afghanistan and the Northwest Frontier, then Egypt, the Punjab, Yemen, British Somaliland and, above all, in Mesopotamia. The RAF quickly demonstrated its usefulness in 'policing' remote and often inhospitable regions in these territories, or, as David Omissi puts it, the air force helped to 'extend the limits of government action in marginal areas which had hitherto resisted the encroachments of the state'.[70] The resulting asymmetrical combat, involving unilateral strikes against poorly armed targets, could not have been further removed from the fanciful notions of knights of the sky and chivalry that are often supposed to explain the enthusiasm of aristocrats for aeroplanes and aerial combat, especially as its victims were not always confined to combatants. As noted in Chapter 1, Londonderry's admiration for military aeroplanes had begun during his time at the Western Front. But his desire then was to achieve a command, and if that was not possible, he was just as interested in joining a tank regiment as aeroplanes. As such, the metaphor of huntsman is more pertinent than knight when it comes to the supposed aristocratic enthusiasm for aerial combat.[71] It was one that had an obvious relevance to Londonderry, but its bearing on his behaviour at the Air Ministry is open to question given that he was largely confined to committees and parliament. At most, it might explain his admiration for RAF pilots, and his instinctive defence of the service, but it was his enthusiasm for flight itself, rather than aerial combat specifically, which is most apparent at this time and indeed for the remainder of his life.

Cutbacks to spending and greater imperial commitments had an undoubted impact on the RAF, especially as the economy began to falter in the winter of 1920–1. Indeed, it was these seemingly contradictory demands that provided the context which allowed the air force to survive. Great Britain had emerged from the Paris peace conferences of 1919 with an enlarged empire that now included a string of League of Nations mandates in the Middle East, from Palestine through to Mesopotamia. With the army already stretched, the Air Ministry was able to take on a higher profile in the affairs of Mesopotamia, as the RAF offered a fast and cheap form of policing over a large amount of difficult terrain.[72] The air force was used alongside ground forces in the revolt that erupted there between July and September 1920, and although doubts were raised about its effectiveness on this occasion, the RAF's relative cheapness meant that the following year it was given control of policing operations in the renamed mandate of Iraq.[73] The role, which continued into the 1930s, would become one of the main planks of Londonderry's defence of aerial bombing at the World Disarmament Conference that convened in 1932.

Churchill and Trenchard were the key individuals in securing the RAF's responsibilities in Mesopotamia, though the Under Secretary of State was kept appraised.[74] Indeed, the link between the Air Ministry and the Middle East became so strong that Londonderry acted as the government's spokesman in the House of Lords on the mandate of Palestine. On 20 April 1921 he dealt with questions from peers hostile to continued Jewish immigration there, and who pressed for the details of a recent US report on the subject to be released. Londonderry did not have any strong views on the Palestinian question and therefore unhesitatingly adopted the government line on the importance of the 1917 Balfour declaration, that it was a precondition of the mandate, and he denied that he could reveal the results of a foreign report.[75]

IV

Civil aviation was still in its very early stages during Londonderry's time as Under Secretary of State. One of his notable achievements was the introduction and passage of the Air Navigation bill in May 1920, as this became the basis of the international law of the air. Londonderry was also involved in the provision of grants and subsidies to aircraft companies in an attempt to boost private enterprise in air transport.[76] His role was enhanced in March 1921 when Churchill appointed him chairman of the Cross-Channel Subsidies Committee, following press criticism about the poor performance of British air transport companies in comparison to their generously subsidized French rivals.[77]

Londonderry was all too aware that his appointment did not signal that the increasingly stringent Treasury was willing to part with more money for the sake of national pride, especially against the backdrop of the anti-waste discontent. When he held the first conference between his committee and representatives of the aircraft industry on 10 March, he warned the latter that while the Air Ministry wanted to increase investment, they would have the considerable task of constructing a good case for the government to agree to this.[78] A week later he announced to the press that the conference had agreed on two broad schemes: that the ministry should purchase British aircraft and then rent these to private companies, or give them guarantees against losses. Londonderry ruled out any underwriting of private companies, but he promised that subsidies would be provided at least until the end of the summer season so as to prevent French companies from eclipsing their British counterparts.[79] It was a patchy solution to a long-term problem, and it signalled Londonderry's acquiescence with the idea that government intervention could be required to assist private enterprise. It did not amount to a wholesale conversion, however, as he remained hostile to the concept of nationalization, and beyond the question of civil aviation, he was still largely unconvinced about the value of state intervention when it came to social reform. But given that the government's initially enthusiastic programme of social legislation was by 1921 under significant pressure from the anti-waste lobby, Londonderry's position, by default, appeared more in harmony with Conservative opinion in the coalition government than at any time before.

The recent criticism of British civil aviation led the prime minister on 1 April 1921 to separate the ministries of War and Air by appointing the Liberal MP, Freddie Guest, as Secretary of State for Air. Churchill had recommended Londonderry for the post, but the appointment of a peer would have risked further hostility from the press at a time when the government was coming under mounting criticism from several directions. Londonderry had until then been able to make a virtue of his background, in certain favourable circumstances, but his membership of an unelected chamber now appeared as an impassable barrier to further progress at Westminster. For Londonderry, the blame also lay with Bonar Law and other leading Conservatives for failing to support his promotion.[80] Curzon, it seems likely, would have objected to Londonderry's appointment, for the foreign secretary remained on guard against any further increase in the already considerable influence in external affairs of Churchill, now colonial secretary.[81]

There is, however, another reason, already highlighted, that would have made Londonderry a controversial choice for promotion, one that he never acknowledged: his status as a prominent colliery owner. Londonderry's initial failure to replace Seely as under secretary of state, only to achieve the appointment the following year, suggests that the source of his wealth and his controversial contribution to the Sankey commission had not completely hindered his modest progress within the government. Yet, it is probably no coincidence that his failure to receive promotion on 1 April occurred on the same day that control of the mines was handed back to the owners, an event, as noted above, that was accompanied by the first post-war national miners' strike and the declaration of a state of emergency.

If Londonderry's background had finally caught up with him and halted his steady progress in the government, it still afforded him the option of returning to Irish politics. As *The Times* had earlier suggested, with more than a hint of disapproval, Londonderry had retained his close links with Ulster unionism throughout his time at the Air Ministry; indeed, Carson had encouraged this with the assurance that it would lead to a post in the newly established government of Northern Ireland.[82] And like the coal situation, Londonderry's association with Ulster unionism might have played a part in checking his hopes for promotion, for several prominent figures associated with the movement, including Edward Carson and Ronald McNeill, were counted as diehards and prominent critics of the coalition.[83]

On 31 May, Bonar Law became aware that Londonderry was shortly to take up the combined post of Minister of Education and Leader of the Senate in the devolved government recently established at Belfast. It prompted him to write to Londonderry, assuring him that he could find him another post at Westminster.[84] But the peer had made up his mind, and probably felt that there was little that Bonar Law could do since the former leader of the Conservative party had already resigned from the government on the grounds of ill health.

Londonderry left the Air Ministry on relatively good terms with its civilian and air force personnel.[85] He had successfully steered through several of its more controversial measures at a time when the government was coming under greater pressure to cut back on waste and lessen its military commitments. He had also managed to avoid the bitter controversies that were to severely test the coalition government, particularly the debate about fusing the two coalition parties into one, and the even more divisive issue of social policy. Nor had he dabbled in the government's increasingly controversial handling of foreign affairs, except to dampen down some of the wilder rumours about German rearmament.[86] But his close associations with Churchill, the Ulster Unionists and the coal industry, and his membership of an unelected chamber, all worked against his hopes of steady promotion. Moreover, he had shown himself to be rather too keen on advancement, particularly in his dealings with the respected Milner. These were hardly matters that could decide the mortality of a political career, but they were relevant when the coalition government had a considerable pool of experience from which to choose ministers.

In time Londonderry too would have more experience, and he would be offered the post of Secretary of State for Air in 1922 and again in 1931. More immediately, his experience in a Whitehall department made him an invaluable asset in the turbulent and troubled context of Northern Ireland. Londonderry had resigned from the Westminster government because of his failure to be promoted, not because of any significant difference in political outlook. This is notable in itself, for it demonstrated how far he had come from his many years of sniping from the sidelines. It was a lesson that he had learnt remarkably quickly while at the Air Ministry and under the tutelage of Churchill, one that would help him to regain office at Westminster in 1928, and to enter the cabinet in 1931.

4

Northern Ireland, 1921–6

In contrast to his peripheral and ornamental involvement with Ulster unionism before the First World War, Lord Londonderry steadily achieved an increasingly prominent position in the provincial hierarchy that culminated in 1921 with his appointment to the first government of Northern Ireland. Like the five other ministers in the devolved administration, Londonderry was faced with the task of establishing Northern Ireland at a time when its very existence and legitimacy were being challenged by politicians, British and Irish, and when it was plagued by the violence of republican opponents and loyalist supporters. Yet, his reaction to these difficult circumstances tended to distinguish him from his colleagues. As Minister of Education, he was the only member of the cabinet charged with implementing a significant measure of social reform that required support from both Protestants and Catholics. As leader of the Senate, he was the only government minister among the upper house's twenty-six senators; conversely, he was the only cabinet minister not returned to the new parliament by the electorate. Londonderry was the wealthiest member of a cabinet almost entirely made up of wealthy men, and although not the only landowner, he was the only titled nobleman. With the exception of Sir James Craig, the first prime minister of Northern Ireland, Londonderry was the only other minister with experience of office at Westminster. Unlike Craig, Londonderry's career and political outlook had not been grounded in the travails of Edwardian Ulster unionism.[1] Along with the Minister of Finance, Hugh Pollock, Londonderry had served on the Irish Convention, though the two men had taken contrasting positions on the possibility of reaching a compromise settlement.

The distinctiveness of Londonderry's presence in the government of Northern Ireland is captured in an oft-repeated story that on one occasion he turned up for work dressed for a hunt and was observed to emphasize the points that he made to his staff with a riding crop.[2] As noted already, Londonderry was not the only landowner in the government, indeed, landowners would continue to be a conspicuous presence in successive Northern Ireland governments through to the early 1970s.[3] He was nevertheless an immensely wealthy grandee peer with strong attachments to County Durham and London, and the humorous anecdote has often served to highlight the supposed exoticism of a marquess at the heart of the new provincial government. It follows that Londonderry's appointment is described as 'an anomaly', that his lack of conventionality guaranteed the emasculation of his progressive education reforms in 1925.[4] This is overly deterministic, for there was in the very first years of the new devolved administration, as Patrick Buckland argues, a fragile willingness to govern for everyone.[5] Donald Akenson likewise avers that until the mid-1920s there was a 'determined effort to govern in a non-sectarian manner'.[6]

No less a figure than Sir Edward Carson had impressed upon the Ulster Unionists the importance of this approach in his farewell address as party leader in February 1921.

> [I]f you are in the majority that part carries with it grave responsibilities. We used to say that we could not trust an Irish Parliament at Dublin to do justice to the Protestant minority. Let us take care that that reproach can no longer be made against your Parliament, and from the outset let them see that the Catholic minority have nothing to fear from a Protestant majority.[7]

It is too simplistic, therefore, to write-off Londonderry, and his successor at the Ministry of Education, the eighth Viscount Charlemont, as anomalous Ulster Unionists. Rather, they were manifestations of a strain of constructive unionism that coexisted with the more vocal and dominant populist strain.[8] Londonderry's strong connections to England, his sense of Irish patriotism and his belief that Ireland could only prosper under the union were the typical features of constructive unionists.[9] Originating in the 1890s with attempts by Conservative ministers at Dublin Castle to kill home rule with 'kindness', Andrew Gailey argues that constructive unionism is unintentionally destructive, raising nationalist expectations without being able to carry the support of most Unionists.[10] This too, if not qualified, can be overly deterministic, for it tended

Figure 5 Richard Dawson Bates, Londonderry, James Craig, Hugh Pollock, Edward Archdale and John Andrews, *c.* 1921.

to be at times of acute crisis that constructive Unionists found themselves sidelined by populists in the movement.[11]

In his memoirs, Londonderry described his move from the Air Ministry to Northern Ireland as

> a real call of the blood . . . for my family had been so long associated with Ulster. My father always sought to persuade me to make the Irish Question the main theme of my political activities, and when he died in 1915 I was expected to take his place, and if I had turned my back on the offer which James Craig had made to me, I should never have forgiven myself, or been forgiven by those with whom I had been associated for so many years.

Even so, his memoirs do not evade the other explanation, his lack of promotion at Westminster, so that the move to Belfast is ultimately justified on the basis that he 'could do more useful work in Ulster'.[12]

Akenson quips that Londonderry was a 'peer of long Irish ancestry and of too-long residence in England'.[13] But this overlooks his association with Ulster unionism before 1921, especially since inheriting the marquessate. Even after his difficulties representing Ulster unionism at the Irish Convention, Londonderry continued to support the movement's interests, on the viceroy's Advisory Council, at the Air Ministry, and in a private capacity. Days after the Armistice of 11 November 1918, for example, he wrote to David Lloyd George to protest about George V not visiting Belfast as part of the victory celebrations.[14] And exactly a year later, at the Air Ministry, Londonderry lobbied for contracts awarded by the Ministry of Munitions to be given to Ulster businesses.[15] His continued friendship with the Lord Lieutenant of Ireland, Lord French, long after the untimely dissolution of his Advisory Council, also allowed him to carry on articulating the Ulster Unionist viewpoint in that quarter.[16] And Londonderry's continuing association with the province was formally recognized on 8 April 1920, when he was awarded the freedom of Belfast, along with Field Marshal Sir Henry Wilson and the Marchioness of Dufferin and Ava.[17] Looking back from the vantage of 1927, Londonderry confided to an audience at Belfast

> that one of his British friends said to him a few days ago that he had made a very grave mistake in not staying in England. He . . . assured him that he was absolutely wrong, and added that when his own people made a call upon him his first duty was to be with them. . . . That was the reason of his existence, and that was the only value he could be to any community, whether in England or Ireland.[18]

Londonderry's increasing prominence in post-war Ulster unionism did not mean that he conformed completely to the expectations of his party managers. Unlike Craig's outward indifference to the fate of south and west Ireland, Londonderry, as a member of the British government, a period when he rarely spoke publicly on Irish affairs, used those occasions when he did to address the increasingly dire situation that faced the entire island.[19] Speaking at Belfast in January 1921, he referred to the imminent establishment of Northern Ireland's parliament as an opportunity for 'Ulstermen to show how the other portions of Ireland should be governed, and that by their example the rest of Ireland would realize that they should follow suit'.[20] Nor was his concern for all of Ireland restricted to ministerial rhetoric. Only days before he was given the freedom of Belfast, Londonderry had offered to rescue George Russell's journal, the *Irish Statesman*, from financial difficulties. Having recently been appointed a director of the Provincial Bank of Ireland, Londonderry had a vested interest in the island's stability and prosperity, and in an organ that purported to promote these aims.[21] But it is unlikely that many Ulster Unionists would have understood or sympathized with his desire to help a Dublin periodical edited by a prominent advanced nationalist.[22] For this reason it was perhaps fortunate for Londonderry that his offer was declined and not made public. Nevertheless, his interpretation of Ulster unionism was far from being a secret, as the readers of the *Belfast News-Letter* would have discovered on Christmas Eve 1920. 'The setting up of two Parliaments', he declared, 'gives the best chance of ultimate unity. Those acute points of difference may disappear in the discharge of duties common to the whole of Ireland. . . . I do venture to hope that every Irishman, whether he be of the North or of the South, will . . . give his wholehearted co-operation towards achieving success'.[23] Similarly, in an interview several months later with the *Observer*, he echoed Carson's recent farewell speech to the Ulster Unionists by arguing that the party must take a 'very tolerant attitude towards the minority'.[24] These public declarations would not have escaped Craig's notice, and it is surely no coincidence that he appointed Londonderry to the only ministry that was expected to engage meaningfully with the Catholic minority.[25] Far from being an anomaly, therefore, Londonderry can be regarded as the most appropriate of Craig's ministers to take charge of the Ministry of Education. His appointment might have seemed all the more fitting given that the sixth Marquess of Londonderry had served as President of the Board of Education, and in that capacity he had introduced the principle of local control to English schools.[26] If so, the fact that those earlier reforms encountered a storm of controversy about denominational schools appears not to have deterred Craig from expecting that the seventh marquess could oversee similar legislation in an effort to maintain parity with Great Britain.

I

On 29 April 1921, four weeks after Londonderry had been passed over for promotion at the Air Ministry, Craig formally asked him to accept nomination to the Senate of Northern Ireland.[27] Winston Churchill expressed his misgivings upon hearing about the move, hardly an unreasonable reaction given how much help he had given Londonderry in recent years.[28] Beyond his personal feelings, it is not hard to see why Churchill thought it ill judged. Throughout Londonderry's tenure at the Air Ministry, Ireland had slipped into a routine of bloody tit-for-tat violence with the IRA on one side and the Royal Irish Constabulary (RIC), its auxiliaries and regular troops on the other. Constitutionally, only the Ulster Unionists were prepared to work the Government of Ireland Act 1920, which had created parliaments in Northern Ireland and Southern Ireland; Sinn Féin boycotted the latter and its MPs elected to Westminster sat instead in Dublin as Dáil Éireann. The only certainty was that the Irish question remained unresolved.

The king's speech at the state opening of the Northern Ireland parliament at Belfast City Hall, on 22 June, was the first public indication that Lloyd George had decided to seek an agreement with Sinn Féin on Ireland's constitutional status. Hostilities between the IRA and crown forces ceased within weeks, followed by months of protracted discussions, before the formal negotiations between delegations representing Sinn Féin and the government finally began on 10 October. It was agreed beforehand that the latter would negotiate only with Sinn Féin and that the government of Northern Ireland would attend the talks in London as consultants. This arrangement suited all sides including the Ulster Unionists, for it allowed them to avoid responsibility for the negotiations and went some way to meeting the criticism from their own supporters that they should not parley with Sinn Féin. Addressing these critics from the floor of the Senate on 20 September, Londonderry defended his government's decision to attend on the basis that to have refused would have placed them in the wrong before the British people and risked a settlement being made behind their backs.[29]

In private, Londonderry had little faith in his former Conservative colleagues in the coalition government, a feeling that was exacerbated by the difficulties that his own government faced in establishing itself in Northern Ireland. He outlined his thoughts to the fourth Marquess of Salisbury, one of the coalition's most prominent critics:

> our position as a Government is being hopelessly prejudiced. I don't know if you are aware that, although we are called the Cabinet of Northern Ireland, we have no power whatsoever. The offices are not yet transferred . . . the police and the military are under the control of the British Government. Consequently, you will see that whereas everybody here looks upon us as the Government, we have no power to do anything on our initiative. If it were the Machiavellian plan to make the Northern Parliament a failure, this is by far the best way to do it.[30]

It would be another five months before Londonderry's ministry finally possessed the authority that had previously been exercised by the Irish administration at Dublin.[31]

Londonderry was one of the Ulster Unionist consultants to the negotiations.[32] With Craig firmly in control of the party's delegation, there was little for the Leader of the Senate to do other than play host at Londonderry House, though even this could be potentially useful. From 1915, Lady Londonderry had made herself and Londonderry House the centre of a small group of politicians and artists known as the Ark (see Chapter 5). It was through this group, specifically the artist Sir John Lavery and his wife Hazel, that the Londonderrys were able to have some indirect communication with senior Sinn Féin figures during the negotiations.[33] As a nationalist, Lady Lavery felt that progress might be made if Lord Londonderry could meet directly with Michael Collins.[34] She was not the only one who thought that such an encounter might be productive. Churchill, one of the British negotiators, also considered the potential usefulness of a meeting between the two men. On this occasion, however, Londonderry declined to meet with Collins, claiming that the IRA leader had been party to the murder of his fellow officers and friends.[35] He must also have realized that such a meeting would produce very little, for even Craig had almost no room for manoeuvre had he wished to be more flexible.[36]

The relationship between Ulster unionism and British conservatism, never straightforward, once again came into focus during the negotiations. Austen Chamberlain, one of the British negotiators, had succeeded Andrew Bonar Law as Conservative party leader in March 1921. Chamberlain was prepared to press the Ulster Unionists to submit the Northern Ireland parliament to the authority of a Dublin parliament if it could produce a satisfactory settlement with Sinn Féin.[37] Chamberlain's outlook was not unique among Conservatives. Many of those who had supported Ulster Unionist militancy before the war were now prepared to consider the dissolution of Northern Ireland as a bargaining device with Sinn Féin on the question of sovereignty, the desired outcome being that Ireland become a self-governing dominion within the British Empire.[38] Given Londonderry's performance at the Irish Convention (see Chapter 2), it is possible that had he remained in the coalition government he too might have shared the view that the Ulster Unionists had gone from being defenders of imperial unity to its greatest obstacle. But in the event, Londonderry took the Ulster Unionist position that his former colleagues were reacting to IRA violence, and that sections of the Conservative press had betrayed them by advocating their surrender.[39] Not all Conservatives agreed with Chamberlain, of course, and it is from this quarter that the Ulster Unionists were thrown a lifeline. The so-called diehards were bitter critics of their party's continued participation in the coalition, and they threatened to use their party conference at Liverpool in November to provoke a rebellion on the question of Northern Ireland.[40] Chamberlain's immediate predecessor, Bonar Law, effectively endorsed the diehards' threat by indicating that he would publicly intervene if he felt that Northern Ireland's constitutional position was under threat due to the negotiations with Sinn Féin. The reassurances given in response to Bonar Law, and thereafter to the party conference, proved to be decisive. On 28 November, Craig confidently informed his cabinet that they no longer needed to quarrel with London as 'the Government was changing its attitude towards Ulster'.[41]

The articles of agreement for a treaty between Great Britain and Ireland were signed on 6 December. The treaty, as it was popularly known, conceded to Sinn Féin the essential unity of Ireland, but it also allowed the Northern Ireland parliament to opt out of the new dominion, the Irish Free State. If it took that decision, which was entirely expected, a Boundary commission would be established to adjust the border in accordance with local considerations. This aside, the Ulster Unionists had emerged from the negotiations with the most favourable result. Sinn Féin's representatives, in contrast, had failed to achieve either recognition of their republic or Irish unity.

That outcome did not stop the Ulster Unionists from expressing frustration about what had happened. For his part, Londonderry not only attacked the government's conciliatory attitude to Sinn Féin, he joined the growing chorus of backbench Conservative unease with Chamberlain's leadership.[42] As the leading Ulster Unionist in the House of Lords, Londonderry led the opposition there when it debated the treaty on 15 December. In doing so he risked associating himself and the Ulster Unionists with the diehards.[43] However, rather than adopt their narrow perspective, he dismissed the ability of the treaty to deliver lasting peace. With allusions to his famous forebear,

Viscount Castlereagh, he condemned the misuse of the Act of Union ever since it had come into effect in 1801, arguing that the present situation had arisen because Ireland had not been governed properly or allowed to enjoy a long period of prosperity. He went even further by stating – in a formula that he had used since before the First World War – that the Dublin parliament only needed to prove itself worthy for the Ulster Unionists to consider participating in it, as they had 'never expressed a determination to remain outside for all time'.[44]

The speech was in marked contrast to the 'brilliantly vulgar' tirade of Edward Carson, now Lord Carson of Duncairn.[45] It was probably for this reason that the Lord Chancellor and treaty signatory, F. E. Smith, now first Viscount Birkenhead, remarked that Londonderry had shown 'statesmanship' in his contribution.[46] As this suggests, Londonderry, in contrast to Carson, emerged from the treaty debate with some credit at Westminster, which would serve him well in the coming years when he sought a return to government there. In the short term, however, his formal opposition to the treaty might have been a factor in the decision to divest him of responsibility for carrying the Cap of Maintenance at the next state opening of the Westminster parliament, although court officials claimed that the decision had been taken in the light of new constitutional arrangements. Londonderry, they reasoned, was now associated with the Senate and government of Northern Ireland, and he had acted as the Minister in Attendance when George V opened the parliament at Belfast earlier in the year. It is uncertain if the king had any part in the decision, but he certainly made up for it when he and the queen dined at Londonderry House a few months later, on 10 March 1922.[47]

To a section of Ulster unionism, Londonderry's displays of 'statesmanship' portended his suspect loyalty to their cause. He had previously alarmed some in the movement by expressing similar platitudes at the Irish Convention, but he was now the guardian of a parliament that many of them felt to be their best line of defence against the hostility of Dublin and the caprice of London. Writing in September 1922, Londonderry acknowledged that he had 'always been criticised in Ulster and I always will be, because I am sometimes half a length in front of local ideas and this makes me suspect . . . Somebody has got to tell the truth instead of agreeing with everybody, and I fancy it is a duty of mine'. And not for the first or last time, he went on to confess his weariness with local politics. 'Belfast has always disappointed me a little . . . Craig is so splendid about raising the whole thing out of the slough of parochialism, and I see so many agents doing their best to drag it down again.'[48]

In a newly devolved jurisdiction that had struggled to survive political intrigue and bloody violence, it is not surprising that Londonderry's constructive approach to governing Northern Ireland aroused disapproval in certain quarters. For the practitioners of constructive unionism, heavy policing could only be one part of a broader strategy to secure the future of the union with Great Britain; a pragmatic and understanding attitude towards the significant nationalist minority was also necessary. This inevitably meant that constructive Unionists like Londonderry were suspected by some of being unduly lenient towards the Ulster Unionists' political opponents.

At the same time, it also made him appear to be a benign figure to those in Dublin and London who resented the apparent truculence of Craig's administration. In April 1923, it was to Londonderry that the then premier of the Irish Free State, W. T.

Cosgrave, wrote to successfully seek the release of a southern prisoner in Northern Ireland.[49] It was also to Londonderry that the British government turned when faced with deadlocks in inter-Irish and British–Irish relations, as in December 1921, outlined above, and later in August 1924, examined below. Conversely, the British government's regard for Londonderry could be useful to the government of Northern Ireland, lending it a friendly face when it tried to secure assistance from Whitehall.

The importance of this should not be underestimated. The violence that engulfed Northern Ireland before, during and immediately after its creation in June 1921 worsened sectarian animosities in the six counties and across Ireland. Between June 1920 and June 1922, 1,766 people were wounded and 428 killed as a result of the violence, including two Ulster Unionist MPs. The majority of those killed were Catholics.[50] In one of the more notorious outrages, in February 1922, a bomb in Belfast was thrown among Catholic schoolchildren resulting in five deaths.[51] It was widely believed that Collins, the first premier of the Irish Free State, had a hand in the IRA's attacks on Northern Ireland, and the British government feared that the effectiveness of the treaty settlement might be damaged as a result. To help ease tensions, Churchill hosted a conference between Craig and Collins at the Colonial Office in the third week of January 1922. The two Irishmen agreed on a series of measures, but their commitment to deal with the boundary question bilaterally was fatally compromised by the lack of consensus on how much territory might be transferred from the north to the south.[52]

Continuing unrest in Northern Ireland necessitated a further meeting between the two heads of government at the end of March 1922.[53] Once again the talks faltered on the possible size of territorial transfers from north to south. There was, however, some agreement on other matters, such as the Free State's boycott of northern goods and police reforms in Northern Ireland. If some Ulster Unionists felt that Craig had conceded too much, they would have been furious had they known about Londonderry's informal meeting with Collins during the second attempt at a pact. Both men had emerged from it praising the other. Collins informed 'Lady L.' that 'I contrast myself with him, my uncouthness with his distinction, my rough speech with his unconscious breeding and the worst of it is I like and admire him, and feel that he is brave and honest.' He concluded cryptically 'On one point alone I believe myself his superior', a possible reference to Collins's patriotism or his political authority, or perhaps something more intimate.[54] Londonderry recollected that he had

> spent three of the most delightful hours that I have ever spent in my life . . . [Collins'] enthusiasm was delightful as he unfolded his plans for the future in stirring phraseology. Perhaps I knew history a little better than he did and perhaps also I knew the power which he had over his followers and also the power which I had over mine when he entreated me to join with him in a really big conception.[55]

Writing later to the prominent advocate of imperial federation, Lionel Curtis, Londonderry claimed that Collins had told him how he wanted to turn Ireland into a loyal portion of the empire as an inducement to the Ulster Unionists.[56] The claim is hard to verify given that it was made shortly after Collins had been killed in an ambush by the anti-treaty faction of the IRA, though some of Collins's political successors certainly echoed this type of reasoning. Another claim that arose from the meeting between Londonderry and Collins was that Lady Londonderry, or 'Lady L.', and Collins had had an affair; 'Lady L.', however, referred to Lady Lavery not Lady Londonderry.[57]

Also in March 1922, Craig announced the appointment of Sir Henry Wilson – the recently retired chief of the Imperial General Staff – as his government's security advisor.[58] Wilson was a staunch supporter of the Ulster Unionists, and with the help of the Londonderrys he had been elected MP for North Down at the start of the year.[59] Like them, he had a stake in developments at Westminster, and he was keen to talk with them about the possibility of pulling the Conservatives out of the coalition government, a view that was no longer just synonymous with the diehards given that it had achieved a wider appeal in the party.[60] Lady Londonderry was responsive to such calls, just as she had been in 1916 (see Chapter 2).[61] At first glance, it appears that her husband agreed, for he added his name to a public statement of Conservative and Unionist principles published in *The Times* on 8 March, a gesture organized by the diehards with the intention of embarrassing Chamberlain.[62] But subsequent events demonstrated that Lord Londonderry held back from fully embracing the party's right wing. On 16 April, when he accompanied Wilson to address a meeting of Ulster Unionists at Newtownards, he urged his audience not to blame the British government for the failure of the Craig–Collins pacts to deliver peace.[63] And when the diehards published their manifesto in June, Londonderry's name was absent.[64] On 2 September, as the head of the Conservative and Unionist party in County Durham, he delivered a speech at Wynyard Park that called for continued co-operation between Conservatives and coalition Liberals to defeat the challenge of Labour.[65] The contrasting positions adopted by Lord and Lady Londonderry on the future of the coalition are an example of their differing attitudes to conservatism. As in 1916, Lord Londonderry disagreed with his wife and remained fixed in that outlook. Stanley Baldwin's later recollection that Lady Londonderry was not 'a very happy influence on [Lord Londonderry] in politics', that her judgement was 'unsound and she is much too stubborn ever to admit a mistake', is therefore too sweeping an assessment of her influence on him given that it clearly did not pertain in all circumstances.[66]

Not long after Wilson and Londonderry addressed the meeting at Newtownards, the former wrote to Craig requesting that Londonderry replace the party apparatchik, Richard Dawson Bates, as Minister of Home Affairs, whose responsibilities included security policy.[67] Both Londonderry and Wilson were critical of Dawson Bates's lack of experience, in particular, his handling of relations between the police and the army.[68] Wilson argued that Londonderry would make a more suitable Minister of Home Affairs because of his experience as a soldier and service minister, his relationship with Churchill and his influence at Westminster.[69] Wilson's advice was not acted on and two months later he was assassinated by the IRA outside his home in London. In any case, Londonderry's appointment to Home Affairs was an unlikely prospect. Craig and Dawson Bates had become almost solely responsible for security matters. Employing a double standard that discriminated against nationalists and in favour of their own supporters, they were able to make on the spot decisions without dissent from the other.[70] It would not have been possible to replicate this dynamic had Londonderry replaced Dawson Bates at Home Affairs. On 14 March, a month before Wilson's suggestion, and a week after signing the statement of Conservative and Unionist principles published in *The Times*, Londonderry became the first Ulster Unionist minister to publicly indicate his discontent with the security policy of his own government. Admittedly, it was a gentle intervention befitting the atmosphere of the Senate, but it was nonetheless a significant departure from government rhetoric: 'a section of those who see eye to eye with us on the present political situation are implicated in outrages that are as reprehensible as those committed by Sinn Féin'.[71] The behaviour of District Inspector John Nixon of the Royal Ulster Constabulary (RUC) was perhaps an example of what Londonderry had in mind, for he had been implicated in some of the most notorious reprisals against the Catholic minority. Two years after Londonderry's intervention on the floor of the Senate, Nixon caused further controversy by establishing an Orange Lodge exclusively for members of the police. Londonderry warned his colleagues about the damaging impact of not handling Nixon properly during what were then difficult negotiations with the Labour government about the Boundary commission (see below).[72] The inspector was soon after suspended then dismissed from the RUC. Rooting out bad apples made it easier for Londonderry, in his dealings with Labour ministers, to defend the size and controversial powers given to the RUC and Special Constabulary.[73] The Irish army mutiny of March 1924 provided him with a more solid reason. '[S]o long as the danger from disaffected elements existed', he informed the Senate, 'so long did they feel it was incumbent upon their Government to maintain the Constabulary about the present strength'.[74]

Craig did act on at least part of Wilson's advice, that concerning Londonderry's relationship with Churchill. Initially at least, Craig had tended to deal personally with the Colonial Office, demanding and more often than not receiving continued financial assistance from London for a range of services, from unemployment insurance to the Special Constabulary. However, in May and June 1922, Londonderry was also involved, perhaps to soften what were sometimes tense meetings between the Ulster premier and the colonial secretary.[75] As the only Northern Ireland minister with a seat in the House of Lords, Londonderry was also able to use that platform to advance the interests of his government at Westminster. His parliamentary intervention on the restrictions imposed on Irish cattle imported to Great Britain – arising from an outbreak of foot-and-mouth disease – is particularly notable, given that it was 'a matter which affects Ireland, both in the North and in the South', and on which he ventured 'to speak for the whole of Ireland in this connection'. It was a speech that anticipated debates a century later, about the internal trade frontier between Northern Ireland and Great Britain, or Irish Sea border, that was established in 2021 as a consequence of the United Kingdom's withdrawal from the European Union. As he reasoned in February 1923, the restrictions could not be relaxed only for cattle from Northern Ireland as it 'would mean the establishment of a strict surveillance of the frontier between Northern and Southern Ireland, and entail great expense'. He then invoked a long-standing Irish nationalist critique of the union to call for a remedy:

> It will be well within your Lordships' recollection that one of the most serious of Irish indictments against this country is contained in a grievance which is centuries old – and this grievance has been repeated with, I might say, wearisome reiteration – that England in her own interests has always disregarded and even destroyed Irish trade. I have spent a great deal of my time in combating this suggestion as imaginary and illusory, but in this case I have no weapon with which to continue that argument, and I feel that this country . . . is doing an injury, a very great injury, to a trade on which Ireland so essentially depends.[76]

The idiosyncrasies of Londonderry's Ulster unionism notwithstanding, he was from the British perspective the acceptable face of a regime that continued to give London cause for concern, not only as a drain on finances at a time when retrenchment was the order of the day, but also for its controversial use of the Special Constabulary.[77] In the early summer of 1922, Stephen Tallents was dispatched by the Colonial Office to report on security policy in Northern Ireland. It is telling that his report makes no mention of the Minister of Education, unlike his colleagues, except to say that Tallents had enjoyed the hospitality of the Londonderrys at Mount Stewart.[78]

The eruption of civil war in the Irish Free State at the end of June 1922 served to ease Northern Ireland's security difficulties a little, although border attacks did not entirely cease due to Collins's concern for the fate of the nationalist minority in the six counties. For their part, the Londonderrys had a guard of Special Constabulary at Mount Stewart, and like other ministers in the Northern Ireland government, Lord Londonderry had the benefit of personal security protection. On one occasion, when Lady Londonderry made a trip to a friend living at Rostrevor, near the new border, the threat to her life was deemed to be sufficiently high as to require the protection of an armoured escort car.[79]

II

Growing unease among Conservative backbenchers and junior ministers led to the collapse of the coalition government on 19 October 1922. Within days Bonar Law replaced Lloyd George as prime minister of a wholly Conservative government, the first since 1905. The new premier took the opportunity to offer Londonderry the post of Secretary of State for Air.[80] Londonderry had certainly maintained his interest in aerial matters, having initiated a debate in the House of Lords on 27 July 1922 on 'the alleged deficiencies of the Air Service in all its branches', in which he restated the need for an independent RAF.[81] He also had other marks in his favour, including not being associated with the more unpopular policies of the post-war coalition government, and for having echoed the diehards' concerns about the direction of that administration without joining their ranks.[82] Londonderry's father-in-law, Henry Chaplin, now first Viscount Chaplin, played his part by lobbying Bonar Law to offer Londonderry a post.[83] More significantly, Lord Salisbury, the only parliamentarian associated with the diehards to receive high office in the new government, also pressed Londonderry's case to the prime minister: 'He represents the North of England and, what is far more important his appointment would be a witness to the world of your respect for Ulster. And yet he is a reasonable and moderate man.'[84]

The possibility of returning to the Air Ministry must have been tempting, especially in the wake of criticism directed at Londonderry in the pages of Belfast's *Northern Whig*. His dual commitment to the Conservatives and the Ulster Unionists had unquestionably provided Londonderry with opportunities at both Westminster and Belfast, but it could on occasion expose him to misunderstanding and disapproval. This happened following his speech in September 1922 to Conservatives at Wynyard Park, mentioned above, in which he called for coalition unity. The *Northern Whig* responded by attacking him as a supporter of Lloyd George. It led Londonderry to complain to his parliamentary secretary, Robert McKeown, about the 'narrow and selfish Belfast spirit which . . . is in my judgement fundamentally destructive, and I find myself always up against it'. He felt that there existed 'an element of jealousy and a desire to decry and destroy me, which exists in fairly influential circles'. Nevertheless, he believed that he had a 'mission, and the moment that mission is in my judgement fulfilled, I shall return to where I came from and leave Belfast to run the Six Counties'.

> This brings me to the dual position which I occupy. First and foremost an Ulster Minister, as such negotiating with the British Government, it is not likely that I am going deliberately to wound the hand that feeds us, for the reason that if the British Government withdrew supplies, I do not see Belfast repairing the deficiency by voluntary subscription, or submitting to extra taxation. It is very easy to criticise the British Government, and as I said in my speech no one can do it better than I can, but if I do that I include Winston Churchill who I know has fought our battle courageously from beginning to end, and he is a real personal friend to me too.
>
> Secondly, I am President of the Unionist organisation controlling 19 seats in Durham, and my speech was expressly directed to this point. I know well what the menace is there and elsewhere. The menace is that if the Conservatives and Coalitionists fight each other on the old Conservative and Liberal prejudices, Labour slips in and wins all the seats.[85]

Londonderry was clearly not at ease in the government of Northern Ireland, but he was determined to see through his Education bill and play his part in putting the devolved administration on a firm footing. Declining Bonar Law's offer, he said that he felt 'pledged' to help Craig.[86] He also wrote to his confidant, Lady Desborough, acknowledging that he had 'made a sacrifice this time', one that might 'destroy my prospects . . . But judging dispassionately at this moment, as I have done, I have followed the right course. I came here to help deal with a crisis; that crisis is not over and it amounts to running away if I follow the path of my personal ambition'. Alluding to his supporters within the Ministry of Education and beyond, he added that 'I knew I was of a certain value here, that I filled a place which no one at the moment could fill, but I did not realise that my suggested departure would really create consternation'.[87] To Bonar Law he made it clear how tempting the offer had been, but 'I am driven by the feeling that my duty is to give up what makes so strong an appeal to my personal feelings, and play my part here for a while longer. I believe you will understand the struggle in my heart far better even than I can explain it.'[88] His sense of mission, or unfinished business, is conveyed in a letter that he wrote to the editor of the *Spectator*, John Strachey:

> It is very difficult to know at this stage of Irish history, how far magnanimous concessions and the broad minded view are really operative. Some will say that anything in the nature of a conciliation is merely taken as a sign of cowardice and ineptitude. However, that may be, I have always got my eye on doing anything I can to remove the bitterness of feeling which exists at the present moment although I am restrained by the determination which [I] have fixed in my mind to do nothing, if I can help it to change our attitude of straight and fair dealing with everyone in the Six Counties.[89]

An additional factor that might have had a bearing on his decision was a possible plan by Bonar Law to scrap the RAF and wind-up the Air Ministry. There is no evidence to suggest that Londonderry knew about such a proposal, but if it was a possibility and he did know, his loyalty to Sir Hugh Trenchard and the RAF would have made the position very unappealing.[90] Declining Bonar Law's offer did not, of course, mean that Londonderry had severed his connection with the Conservatives at Westminster. As noted above, he remained a relatively active figurehead for the party in County Durham, and Londonderry House remained at the disposal of Bonar Law. Lady Londonderry underscored the latter point when she wrote to the prime minister about her husband's 'sense of duty' to Craig, making it clear that the Park Lane mansion was his to 'command'.[91] Her ulterior motive is revealed in an earlier letter to her husband, in which she suggested that hosting at least one large function every year for the Conservative government at Londonderry House 'would always keep you in touch with them and at a time of year I presume you will not be needed here [in Northern Ireland]'.[92] Bonar Law responded to Lord Londonderry's decision with sympathy. 'I was really very sorry that Charlie could not take the post', he informed Lady Londonderry, 'but from the first I felt that it would hardly be possible for him to leave Craig at the present'.[93] As for Lady Londonderry's offer of Londonderry House, Bonar Law did not remain in good health long enough to properly take advantage of it, but his three successors as prime minister would certainly do so.

It is possible that Lord Londonderry's commitment to Northern Ireland would have been more severely tested had he been offered a more distinguished office. At the start of November 1922, he responded favourably to a rumour that he might be offered the ambassadorship to Paris, only to learn that his public commitment to remaining in Ulster had ruled him out of the running.[94] To add insult to injury, Londonderry was at the same time being discussed as a candidate for the ornamental post of Governor of Northern Ireland. Needless to say, he was no more inclined to accept it than the governor-generalship of Canada.[95] These disappointments led him to complain that his October sacrifice had not been acknowledged properly in the pages of the *Spectator*. It was all well and good remarking privately on his 'self-sacrifice', Londonderry wrote to Strachey, but why did this not appear in print?[96]

Had Londonderry accepted office at Westminster then he would not have remained at the Air Ministry for very long. Stanley Baldwin, who had replaced Bonar Law as prime minister in May 1923, called a snap general election for 6 December in the hope that his definite pledge to implement tariff reform might unite the Conservatives and win them another victory at the polls. Instead, the number of its MPs fell from the 483 returned the previous year – Bonar Law had called a general election after the collapse of the coalition – to 258. With 191 Labour MPs, and the tacit support of 159 Liberals, Ramsay MacDonald was able to form the first Labour government on 22 January 1924. If some Conservatives were sufficiently hostile to this outcome to favour an arrangement with the Liberals, Londonderry had signalled in advance, to the Seaham Harbour Conservative Club, that a 'policy to manoeuvre the Socialist Party so as to prevent them taking office would have no support from him, and he strongly deprecated any coalition with this object in view'.[97] Not long after, when the Londonderrys attended a dinner hosted by the king for his new prime minister at Buckingham Palace, Lady Londonderry struck up a friendship with MacDonald, based in part on their shared background in the Scottish Highlands. MacDonald invited the Londonderrys to Chequers the following month, and he corresponded with them on the boundary crisis that dominated British–Irish relations throughout the year. In the longer term, their relationship was to reap rewards that not even Edith could have foreseen.

III

The boundary crisis was slow to emerge and took even longer to resolve. The Northern Ireland parliament voted itself out of the Irish Free State without hesitation, but there remained uncertainty about what adjustments to the frontier would mean in practice, and the Boundary commission's formation was delayed by the civil war in Southern Ireland, Baldwin's decision to call a general election at the end of 1923 and the formation of the minority Labour government in January 1924. When the mechanisms for the commission's establishment were finally being put in place by London and Dublin, in May 1924, Belfast threw a spanner in the works by refusing to nominate its commissioner.[98]

The boundary question gave Londonderry the opportunity to present himself as a steadfast Ulster Unionist in the face of growing unease in the party that its leaders might back down to pressure by appointing a commissioner. He duly defended in public his government's position, including on 13 May, when he directly refuted rumours to the contrary on the floor of the Senate.[99] He also delivered a series of speeches in the spring of 1924 that defended the principle of partition. The 'great clash between North and South was not some petty idiosyncrasy of the Ulsterman as opposed to that of an inhabitant of the South of Ireland', he informed an Ulster Association luncheon at the Criterion Restaurant, London. 'It was the clash of ideals. Ulster would never agree with the South as long as the latter were looking at themselves and considering their own grievances and difficulties while Ulstermen were thinking of the Empire and keeping their eyes fixed on the Imperial ideal.'[100] He returned to the theme in a speech delivered shortly afterwards to the North Down Unionist Association, in which he referred to the Free State's 'grudging acceptance of the Imperial idea. So long as the South was actuated by those motives, it was no use for them to suggest any union with the North'. He repeated the argument the following month at a dinner given at the Ulster Reform Club, for British members of parliament then touring Northern Ireland.[101]

Londonderry's approach on these occasions tends to confirm Alvin Jackson's observation that leading Ulster Unionists exploited 'the vision and vocabulary of Empire to divert attention from some of the more miserable realities of life in the new partition state'.[102] They were not alone, however, in utilizing imperial topes to suit their specific needs. Bernard Porter argues that such 'value systems . . . governed people's perceptions of their empire'. He adds that aside from 'fanatics', most imperialists 'saw it as merely tangential to their lives, or their philosophies and value-systems, which were still mainly rooted in domestic considerations that had nothing to do with the empire at all'. In this specific sense, there was little to differentiate Londonderry from his colleagues in the government of Northern Ireland, especially as his rhetoric on these occasions was mainly directed at winning over sympathetic listeners in Great Britain. Moreover, his bitter experience of parochialism in Northern Ireland did not remove his conviction that the separatist strain of Irish nationalism was even more parochial, and dangerously so, in so far as it sought to reduce or even eliminate Ireland's place in the empire. Londonderry might not have shared the zealous imperialist outlook of advanced tariff reformers or diehard Conservatives, but, as Porter also remarks, there were 'wide and important differences between sorts and degrees of imperialists'.[103] That being said, Londonderry's imperialism was itself wide-ranging, varied and flexible, encompassing the outlook of Irish and Ulster unionism, the defence of aerial policing in Iraq and the need for constitutional reform in India. Domestically, as the boundary crisis rumbled on, it included his provision of funds to schoolchildren from Seaham and Northern Ireland to visit the British Empire Exhibition at Wembley.[104]

Londonderry's handling of the boundary question was soon tested when it became clear that Craig's refusal to appoint a commissioner not only risked a constitutional crisis between London and Belfast, but that the result of this might threaten the electoral prospects of the Conservative party in Great Britain. Pulled once again in two directions, Londonderry came to adopt a more emollient stance than other Ulster Unionists on the boundary question. This added to his problems in Northern Ireland, for he was also on the receiving end of growing criticism about his Education Act. The fact that Londonderry at this time frequently deputized for Craig – the latter suffered from repeated bouts of ill health – only added to the strain. It was Londonderry who represented Northern Ireland at the intergovernmental conference held at London at the start of August. It was hoped that this meeting of ministers representing London, Dublin and Belfast might finally resolve the impasse.[105] But Londonderry could do little other than echo the view that Craig had expressed at similar conferences and discussions held throughout that year, that Belfast would not nominate a commissioner. Thomas Jones, who as deputy cabinet secretary was heavily involved in the discussions, noted in his diary for 2 August that Londonderry was 'the only reasonable negotiator', but 'too weak to bring along the rest of his party'.[106]

Two days later Londonderry received a delegation of MPs at Londonderry House. The Conservative MP for Canterbury, Ronald McNeill, an Ulsterman and prominent diehard, acted as their spokesman. He made it clear to their host that he had to stick to the 'not an inch' position that Craig had promised his supporters in Northern Ireland. Afterwards, a 'largely attended' meeting of Ulster Unionist MPs and their allies at Westminster was held to press home the posture of defiance.[107] This public embarrassment for Londonderry was followed days later by another, as he was again obliged to give public assurances that he had not made any agreement behind the back of Craig.[108]

The suspicions of McNeill and his accomplices were not entirely unfounded. As Thomas Jones also noted in his diary, Londonderry felt that having made a display of defiance, the Belfast government should make a concession, but that such a move would depend on Craig's health. He also reassured Jones that there would be no violent resistance to the bill.[109] Writing the following day to MacDonald, Londonderry vented his frustration by complaining that the prime minister did not include the Ulster Unionists when he spoke of owing a debt of honour to the Irish, and he confessed that the best way to govern Ireland was through 'ordinary local administration under the British Parliament'.[110] It was a judgement that he applied to all of Ireland and not just the six counties, but it was still a damning assessment of devolved government in Northern Ireland by one of its senior figures.

Londonderry's frustration at this time was not just the product of his precarious position in the Ulster Unionist hierarchy; it also reflected his anxiety about the electoral fortunes of the Conservative party. At the end of July 1924, the Judicial Committee of the Privy Council had ruled that new legislation would be required if the British government wanted to appoint Northern Ireland's boundary commissioner. When MacDonald decided to press ahead with this legislation in August, Baldwin feared that the diehards would throw in their lot with the Ulster Unionists and foment a wider revolt. This would not only risk a party split and undermine Baldwin's project to replace territorial unionism with one nation conservatism, but also, if the House of Lords blocked the bill, a general election in which the rallying call would be, like 1910, peers versus the people.[111]

On 27 August Londonderry wrote to Baldwin to inform him that he had made some progress in persuading Salisbury to avoid a constitutional showdown in the House of Lords, although the Conservative leader in the upper house insisted that 'the Bill can only be allowed to pass through the House of Lords on a direct intimation being received from Northern Ireland that there will be no misunderstanding between the Conservative Party and Ulster on this particular point'. Londonderry added that 'I feel sure you will see the force of this argument and it appears to me that this had better be done in the form of a public letter from James Craig to yourself.'[112]

When Londonderry wrote the letter, Northern Ireland's prime minister was on a three-week sea cruise to help mend his ill health. By the time of Craig's return in mid-September, he and his cabinet agreed that they would not encourage peers to oppose the bill, but that they would instead urge Baldwin to ensure that Conservative parliamentarians propose amendments in favour of the Ulster Unionist position.[113] Londonderry remained anxious about what amounted to a change of emphasis rather than effect. 'Our people are very headstrong', he wrote to Salisbury on 18 September, 'and they can only think for themselves. They cannot take the long view of British politics which might be that an election on this point would not serve the interests of the Conservative Party'.[114]

Not long afterwards a rumour surfaced that Lord Carson might be willing to represent Northern Ireland on the Boundary Commission. Londonderry reported to his wife that when the idea was discussed at a cabinet meeting on 30 September, Craig initially 'jumped' at the suggestion, but that other ministers rejected it on the basis that once the commission was recognized by the Belfast government it would be bound by its decisions.[115] Craig and Londonderry had been opposed by their colleagues on the boundary question before, back in February, when they favoured a solution involving the Council of Ireland.[116] But now the situation seemed so tense that Londonderry wondered if he might be called upon to replace Craig should his leader be removed by discontented elements in the party. Unlikely as it seems, others considered it a possibility; the nationalist *Irish News* later speculated that he had an agreement with Craig to succeed him as premier.[117] Craig, for his part, later referred to Londonderry as his 'right hand man'.[118] Wisely, as it turned out, Londonderry dismissed the idea and set his sights on returning to office at Westminster. As Stephen Tallents noted in his 1922 report, should Craig ever be forced to resign he would be replaced by a hardliner.

If Londonderry was unable to steer Ulster unionism as he would have liked, he played an almost imperceptible part in the Conservative victory at the general election held on 29 October 1924. Earlier that month, Conservatives in the House of Commons gave up in their attempt to amend the Boundary commission bill. But it was feared that the House of Lords would not be so passive, especially as Craig had failed to give a clear indication of what he expected Conservative peers to do. The situation was saved by Londonderry's ally in the upper house, Salisbury, who on 8 October reluctantly warned his colleagues of the electoral consequences that would face the Conservative party should it block or otherwise attempt to amend the bill. The victory for common sense was not fully achieved, however, until Carson and Londonderry added their voices to Salisbury's, albeit in the same reluctant tones.[119] The bill passed, leaving the Labour government's policy towards the Soviet Union as the major focus of the October general election.

Londonderry played his part in the Conservatives' efforts to whip up a red scare ahead of that poll. The 'issue of the general election', he informed an audience at Durham, 'was whether the Union Jack or the Red Flag should wave over the country'.[120] Addressing another meeting in northwest County Durham, he caused 'pandemonium' by comparing his right to own coal royalties with MacDonald's shares in the biscuit firm, McVitie and Price, an issue used often at this time by Labour's opponents to tar the party leader.[121] There were further 'frequent interruptions' when Londonderry referred to the Labour government's relationship with the Soviet Union.[122] Notwithstanding this reaction, the strategy was not ineffectual everywhere, for the Conservatives were returned with a massive majority, 419 MPs in total. In County Durham, the party gained three seats to return seven MPs. Londonderry celebrated their success by hosting a social gathering for local party officers. Reflecting on the need for younger members to sustain the Conservatives' 'overwhelming victory', he observed in his remarks to the gathering that the 'Conservative creed was almost unknown in some parts of the county', and he drew laughter when he followed this by claiming that 'At some meetings he attended he was looked upon as a curiosity'.[123]

Londonderry's troubled handling of the boundary crisis, the increasingly vocal opposition to his Education Act (see below), his campaigning on behalf of the

Conservative Party in County Durham and the brewing crisis in the mining industry (see Chapter 5) ensured that he was on the lookout for an opportunity to leave the cockpit of Ulster politics. The appointment of his ally, Churchill, as Chancellor of the Exchequer, provided a further incentive.[124] As if to signal his wider field of interests, Londonderry gave a speech at the Seaham Harbour Constitutional Club on 4 January 1925 that addressed British party politics, unemployment, industrial relations, housing and education.[125] In the short term, however, he remained bound to his responsibilities at Belfast. Rather than lobby overtly for a post at Westminster, he confined himself to reminding Baldwin of his contributions to the defeat of 'the Socialist menace in one of the reddest portions of the Kingdom' at three successive general elections. He also pressed, unsuccessfully as it turned out, for the MP for Sunderland, Walter Raine, to receive one of the minor ministerial posts still outstanding.[126] It is possible that Craig too wanted his Minister of Education to consider a return to British politics. It was the Ulster premier who recommended that Londonderry be made a British Privy Councillor, although seeking the appointment can also be viewed as a means of formalizing Londonderry's usefulness as an intermediary with London. He was duly sworn in on 6 February 1925.[127] The announcement prompted one reader of *The Times* to point out that Londonderry was the only person to hold three such offices, in Ireland, Northern Ireland and Great Britain.[128] Whatever the motivation, it is clear that Craig had become increasingly estranged from Londonderry, especially as Protestant opposition mounted to the 1923 Education Act. It even threatened the unity of Ulster unionism at the snap election called by Craig for 3 April 1925 on the boundary question. Addressing an election meeting at Newtownards, Londonderry presented the Ulster Unionists' willingness to work the Government of Ireland Act 1920 as a sacrifice that was now being betrayed: 'when the people of Ulster accepted the Act of 1920, if they believed anything was fixed or certain, they believed their boundaries were. If they had been told it was possible that there could be any revision of these boundaries they would in no circumstances have accepted the Act of 1920'.[129]

In these trying circumstances, Londonderry became more willing to lobby for a post at Westminster and to solicit the help of Churchill for this purpose, but nothing was available.[130] Yet his desire to leave Belfast was not unbounded, for he still ruled out Canada when it was again suggested that he might become its governor-general.[131] Matters were soon brought to a head by his deteriorating relationship with Craig. Despite denying it to Londonderry, the prime minister was being kept secretly informed of the Boundary commission's deliberations.[132] It is not possible to determine whether Londonderry found out that this was happening, but had he been presented with evidence that contradicted Craig's personal assurance then he would certainly have taken it as a personal slight and an insult to the office of Leader of the Senate. What is more certain is that when the commission's findings were leaked to the *Morning Post* and published on 7 November, Craig took a senior civil servant, Charles Blackmore, not Londonderry, to the hastily arranged meetings in London with Baldwin and Cosgrave. The three premiers agreed to suppress the commission's report and thereby leave the frontier unchanged. Upset at having been sidelined in favour of a civil servant, Londonderry took care not to resign until the following January. This way he could demonstrate that he was not the sort of person to resign in a fit of pique, an important consideration for someone seeking ministerial office at Westminster. The timing also put some distance between his departure and the emasculation of his Education Act.

IV

The Education Act 1923, also known as the Londonderry Act, was one of the most significant pieces of legislation in the embryonic years of Northern Ireland. Not because of what it achieved, some of its most important provisions were ultimately reversed, but for its original intention: the attempt to establish local control of education instead of clerical control, and as a result of this, to dismantle the denominational segregation of children in a society deeply divided by sectarianism. Much ink has been spilled in examining education policy in the early years of Northern Ireland, although little of substance has been said about the role of Londonderry.[133]

The government of Northern Ireland set out to reform education following the lead but not the example of England.[134] The most significant difference was that whereas the sixth Marquess of Londonderry had helped to usher through increased financial support for denominational schools, the seventh marquess set about achieving the opposite. The central plank of his proposals involved the transfer of clerical-controlled elementary schools to the Ministry of Education and their oversight by local education authorities. Prior to the creation of the Northern Ireland parliament, Ulster Unionist MPs at Westminster had supported attempts at similar reforms as a means of addressing underfunded schools, especially in Belfast. However, the opposition of the Catholic hierarchy and Irish nationalist MPs ensured that these measures were not passed. With Ulster unionism now the master of its own house, two further factors determined that the new government would address education reform in the manner outlined above: the constitutional prohibition against funding religious bodies, and the willingness of key personnel in the government to pursue this object.

Section 5 of the Government of Ireland Act 1920 prohibited the Northern Ireland parliament from passing legislation that directly or indirectly endowed, preferred or prejudiced any denomination or religious group. It was interpreted by Londonderry and his supporters to include elementary schools under the management of clerics. Later, when the government of Northern Ireland came under increasing criticism for Londonderry's Education Act, its ministers initially defended the legislation on the basis that anything else would be unconstitutional. As their adherence to this position began to waver, it became clear that Londonderry's commitment to the idea of non-denominational schools went beyond merely observing section five. Like constructive Unionists before and after, the Minister of Education believed that nationalists had to have an investment in Northern Ireland. Controversially, he believed that this could be achieved by removing clerical influence in education and schooling children together regardless of their denominational background. He was not alone in seeing merit in this object; Craig's biographer claims that he also believed that clerical control had to be ended.[135] Furthermore, Londonderry was assisted at the Ministry of Education by a group of talented and like-minded civil servants who held both him and his agenda in high regard. Akenson, writing in the early 1970s, learnt at first hand from Londonderry's assistant private secretary, James Scott, that although the minister had treated the civil servants 'like domestic staff', they were 'unswervingly loyal to him, even adulatory'.[136]

On 23 June 1921, at the first sitting of the Senate, Londonderry signalled his desire for reform, taking care to acknowledge that there would be many difficulties ahead.[137] At this stage he was not so much thinking of possible organized opposition to his plans, but the structural and political difficulties of governing Northern Ireland at a time of violence and political instability. Delivering his speech to senators in the temporary home of the new parliament, the Presbyterian Church's Union Theological College, Belfast, Londonderry had little inkling that some of the fiercest opposition he would encounter would come from representatives of that denomination. As noted above, the Ministry of Education, like other departments, was seriously hampered by the delays in transferring powers and personnel from London and Dublin.[138] It had to build itself up from almost nothing, and as a result it relied on the previous ministerial experience and self-confidence of its minister.

In September 1921 Londonderry paved the way for legislative reform by establishing a committee under the chairmanship of Robert Lynn, a journalist and Ulster Unionist MP.[139] Those involved in education, including clerics, were invited to make submissions. Londonderry hoped that Catholic representatives would sit on the committee or at least make submissions. The previous month, he had suggested to the Catholic Archbishop of Armagh, Michael Logue, that his forthcoming visit to Armagh provided an opportunity for the two men to meet. After some delay, Logue claimed that the letter had been mislaid.[140] Londonderry then wrote to the cardinal requesting the co-operation of Catholic representatives.[141] The appeal was never likely to succeed. The head of Ireland's Catholics supported a general boycott of Northern Ireland and was certainly not prepared to allow Catholic priests or teachers to engage with its Ministry of Education. With the politeness of a prince of the church addressing a marquess, he informed Londonderry that he did not doubt his personal intentions, but that the Lynn committee was the 'pretext' for an attack on Catholic schools.[142] Before replying to Logue, Londonderry wrote to Lord French's successor as Lord Lieutenant of Ireland, the first Viscount FitzAlan, in the hope that this scion of the Catholic Howard family might make a positive intervention. He stressed that if Catholics sat on the committee, they would be allowed to frame a minority report if they so wished.[143] Nothing happened and Londonderry called a meeting of the cabinet to discuss the situation. At this he took a bullish attitude, claiming that Logue was making a 'direct challenge' to the government, but his colleagues felt that the matter should simply be dropped.[144] Londonderry wrote to Logue regretting his decision, and although he avoided directly asking him to reconsider his position, he made it clear that an opportunity was being missed.[145]

The Lynn committee issued an interim report in June 1922; most of its structural recommendations found their way into the 1923 Act. These included the means by which elementary schools would be transferred to local control: the matter of control resting in the appointment of school managers. In those schools fully transferred to the state, the local education authority would appoint all school managers and the school receive full funding. Schools that wished to remain independent were to receive minimal funding – though this included the most significant financial outlay, the salaries of teachers – and retain their power to appoint managers. A third class of school would act as a bridge for those hesitant about full transfer. Known as four-and-two schools, the local education authorities were to appoint two managers, with the remaining four appointed by the existing school managers. It was hoped that under this system denominationally controlled schools might be induced to transfer totally, or at least partially, to local authority control. Months later, in a statement published in *The Times*, Londonderry acknowledged that his proposals 'will entail considerable sacrifice on the part of the people of Northern Ireland. The measure of the confidence of a State in the permanence of its institutions lies in the extent to which each generation is prepared to sacrifice itself for the welfare of posterity'. The 'cordial reception' given to the interim report, he claimed, 'convinced me that I shall have the people behind me in effecting the necessary changes'.[146]

That last observation was untenable given the position taken by the Catholic hierarchy. The acquiescence of Protestant vested interests at this stage also turned out to be provisional, and it is probably explained by the interim report's recommendation that the curriculum include a programme of simple Bible instruction – a reflection of the Lynn committee's exclusively Protestant make-up and the involvement of Protestant clerics. But in his determination to devise a system that complied with Section 5 of the 1920 Act, Londonderry omitted this particular recommendation from the 1923 bill. He also forbade managers at transferred schools from requiring teachers to come from a particular denomination. It was on these two issues, Bible instruction and teacher appointments, that Protestant opposition would later focus, especially when it became clear that only Protestant-controlled schools were willing to consider transferring to the new system. For its part, the Catholic hierarchy had its own battle with the Ministry of Education on the question of teacher training.

Even before the bill became law, Londonderry had to persuade his ministerial colleagues that it was the correct course to pursue. When the cabinet met on 15 December 1922, with Londonderry in the chair due to Craig's absence, Pollock 'expressed the view that the province generally demanded religious education'. After some discussion, the Minister of Finance signalled his satisfaction that 'provided the right of entry is given, the Protestant clergy generally will welcome the opportunity to transfer'.[147] A further challenge came weeks later, when the cabinet rejected Londonderry's proposal to establish small local education authorities that bore no relation to local government boundaries.[148]

These initial skirmishes in the cabinet were intimations of what was to come. The first potentially serious attack came from the Lynn committee's chairman, Robert Lynn. After he read the draft bill and Londonderry's cover note in February 1923, Lynn attacked the proposed legislation and Londonderry's handling of it, and he threatened to mount an opposition campaign.[149] Londonderry had reason to be concerned, for it was Lynn, as editor of the *Northern Whig*, who the previous year had attacked Londonderry's speech to Conservatives in County Durham (see above). It is not clear how, but within a month Lynn had been talked out of his opposition, to the extent that he became one of the bill's leading advocates.[150] Whatever the cause, it should be noted that Londonderry reluctantly contributed to Lynn's election expenses in 1924.[151]

Londonderry introduced his measure in the lower house of the Northern Ireland parliament on 14 March 1923, a procedure that was permitted to a government minister based in the Senate. He addressed the denominational question directly by invoking ecumenism not secularism:

> The State, as does the individual, looks to the Churches to give the lead in Christian idealism, and I feel we need not look in vain. Do not let it be said that these same Churches, all possessing a proud history of good deeds, responsible as they have been for almost all the education in past years, are now, with all the opportunities that the community can possibly give, the stumbling-block in the way of an ideal system by a determination to segregate their flocks and create from birth a division when union is so essential to the well-being of the province. There are schools in existence where children of different denominations work together and play together, and who will assert that this association is anything but beneficial for all concerned?
>
> The State itself can do but little in this direction. It can afford, and under this Bill it does afford, opportunities, and I look with confidence to the future believing that in the new spirit of the new era dawning before our eyes, tolerance and a mutual respect will replace prejudice and jealous mistrust. But beyond giving opportunities for denominational instruction the State cannot go.[152]

Having seen off Lynn's threat of an opposition campaign, it was not long before Londonderry faced another rumbling of dissent, and this time within the cabinet. On 16 April Craig suggested that the bill be amended to allow for religious education, but that the burden for it be placed on local authorities and not the government. Londonderry admitted that at this stage he was coming under pressure from some clergymen to adopt this course, but that his own opinion was 'unchanged', adding that the bill allowed for 'moral instruction' of a non-denominational character within school hours. The Minister of Labour, John Andrews, and the Parliamentary Secretary to the Ministry of Education, Robert McKeown, added their voices in support of Londonderry. Their interventions ensured that he won this round, but at a price. The cabinet resolved that the bill would not be altered unless 'the course of debate made it clear that further concession was demanded', in which case 'the scheme advocated by the Prime Minister would be adopted'.[153] The way was now clear for the Northern Ireland parliament to pass Londonderry's Education bill into law on 2 June.

The Education Act 1923 repealed seventeen earlier pieces of legislation and introduced structural changes affecting the ownership, management and financing of elementary schools. Londonderry was keen to emphasize its provisions for local accountability, the democratic 'keystone of the arch of our new system of education'.[154] At this stage the level of Protestant hostility to the Act remained minimal, indeed Londonderry received the support of Orangemen from the staunchly loyalist Sandy Row district of Belfast.[155] It is noteworthy too that elementary school teachers, Catholics and Protestants, were among the measure's most enthusiastic supporters.[156]

Yet, Protestant anxiety was perceptible from the outset, particularly among a vocal number of Presbyterian clerics. Long before it reached its peak in 1925, it found an early vessel in the most powerful Presbyterian in the land: the prime minister. On 27 September Craig again called for an amendment that would satisfy the Protestant critics, on this occasion, the lifting of the prohibition on transferred schools from employing a denominational test in teacher appointments.[157] Londonderry had been absent at this meeting, and so it was decided to await his return. At the next meeting of the cabinet, on 2 October, Londonderry dismissed the proposal as unconstitutional, and for being 'against the general principle of a Secular Education Bill'. As for the risk that opposition might become widespread, Londonderry claimed that it was not 'of a serious character', that 'it was largely manufactured by certain interested ecclesiastics'.[158]

Craig was only troubled by the opposition of Protestants, not the Catholic boycott, for the former threatened to damage the image of Unionist unity that he had cultivated over many years to see off threats from within and without. As he had warned Londonderry in January 1923, while being 'satisfied that sticking to the strict letter of the law always pays in the end; in any event it is better to have trouble with enemies rather than with friends'.[159] The following month he asked Londonderry in cabinet 'whether any particular denomination could, in his opinion, with justice assert that it had been penalised'. Charles Hendriks, Londonderry's private secretary, stepped in to suggest that it would be the Catholic sector that would feel penalized due to reduced funding. On the basis of this answer the cabinet concluded, revealingly, that 'the proposals of the Bill are impartial in their dealings with the denominations'.[160]

The Protestant clerical opponents of the Act set about harnessing the Orange Order to lend their campaign an element of popular support. The Catholic hierarchy's refusal to transfer schools to local authority control had enabled the legislation's Protestant critics to argue that it was only the Protestant denominations that were obliged to end religious instruction. It was a disingenuous position, for the Protestant denominations could retain full control like the Catholic schools by becoming independent, but that would mean accepting reduced funding.

The responses of the main denominations to the 1923 Act, which ranged from unenthusiastic to outright hostility, meant that its social and ecumenical benefits could not be fully realized, which in turn led to new and separate grievances among its Protestant and Catholic opponents. Nowhere was this clearer than in the area of teacher appointments. Protestant critics focused on the ability of Catholic teachers to be allowed to teach at 'Protestant' schools, but not vice versa. Given that the Ministry of Education's newly established teacher training college at Stranmillis had managed to enrol a significant number of Catholic students in 1923, it was not an altogether paranoid claim, especially as the Catholic hierarchy appeared to rule out employing the students at Catholic schools.[161]

Protestant opposition grew throughout 1924, with the Ministry of Education having to deal with frequent letters of complaint and deputations seeking to persuade its minister to change his mind. Their concerns were echoed on the floor of the House of Commons by Hugh Morrison, MP for the Queen's University of Belfast. In colourful language, Dr Morrison denounced Londonderry's 'revolutionary attitude' and likened his Education Act to Sir Robert Peel repealing the Corn Laws and Benjamin Disraeli expanding the electoral franchise.[162] Londonderry in response adopted an aloof attitude towards his critics, but he still took care to appeal over their heads to the people. In one such instance, on 1 April 1924, he boldly asserted that the government had not endangered the moral upbringing of children by entrusting it to their parents and teachers.[163] The following day a deputation of Protestant clerics met with Londonderry to demand an amendment. He refused outright to consent to any element of compulsion on teachers to give religious instruction. As the minutes record, 'their desire for immediate amendment could not be met with if he were to continue in office'. He 'pointed out that circumstances had radically changed with self-government in Ulster, that the decentralization in education under the Education Act was a necessary corollary to the new position, and that the Churches must be prepared to surrender their privileged position in education'. In reply, the clerics said that they would surrender the teaching of religious instruction if teachers were compelled to take it. Londonderry declined to accept their demand.[164] Opposition to Londonderry's reforms gathered momentum in the months that followed, and by December it took on a more organized form with the formation of the United Education Committee of the Protestant Churches (UEC).

The early months of 1925 witnessed further clashes between Londonderry and his opponents. Moderate members of the higher clergy and senior Orangemen now began to call on the Minister of Education to make a gesture to temper the opposition, not least because the agitation threatened their own authority.[165] It was particularly notable in the case of the Orange Order. On 4 February the Grand Orange Lodge of Belfast informed Londonderry that while it appreciated the many 'popular benefits' contained in the 1923 Act, it opposed the absence of religious instruction and the prohibition of a denominational test for teachers.[166] Hendriks subsequently informed Londonderry that Sir Edward Archdale – the Minister of Agriculture and Commerce, and the recently appointed Grand Master of the Grand Orange Lodge of Ireland – had responded to this by dismissing the Belfast Orangemen as 'riff-raff'.[167] Hendriks then met with the grand secretary of Belfast and was informed that both he and Sir Joseph Davidson, the grand master of Belfast, 'had the greatest difficulty in restraining the hot-heads amongst the Orangemen, who are being persuaded by the clergy that the Bible is in danger'.[168] With this knowledge Londonderry felt that he could deal personally with the 'malcontents'. At his meeting with them on 23 February, the grand master of Belfast asked Londonderry if any amendment might be possible, only to receive the reply that the Orange Order's objections were simply too late.[169]

On 5 March the UEC held a demonstration at the Presbyterian Assembly Hall in Belfast. As was intended, Londonderry's contention that their cause was unrepresentative began to appear untenable. Worse still, the meeting coincided with Craig's decision, noted above, to call a snap general election on the boundary question for 3 April. Having called the poll in order to demonstrate Ulster Unionist unity on the territorial integrity of Northern Ireland, Craig was not about to allow the education row to overshadow his campaign. With Londonderry absent due to ill health, Craig met with a UEC deputation on 6 March. The next day, with Londonderry still absent, the cabinet agreed that the Education Act would be amended to remove the prohibitions on Bible instruction and teacher selection on the basis of denomination.[170]

When Londonderry moved the second reading of the amendment bill on 12 March, he emphasized that the measure only sought to clarify existing law. He claimed that although the legislation would lift the prohibition on religious instruction in schools, it remained voluntary for both teachers and pupils. Furthermore, school management committees would only have an advisory role in teacher appointments, not the determining one that the UEC had demanded.[171] The 'short and non-contentious measure', as Londonderry described it in the Senate, was speedily dispatched before parliament was prorogued in advance of the snap general election.[172]

As Londonderry's remarks suggest, it became apparent to the UEC that Craig had misled them about the effect of the Amendment Act.[173] This only fuelled the wider discontent within unionism that led a significant number of independent Unionists to stand in the 1925 general election.[174] The consequent fall in the number of Ulster Unionists returned to the Northern Ireland House of Commons, from forty to thirty-two, did not directly threaten the party's control of that chamber. But the return of four independent Unionists, three Labour and one farmers' representative – ten nationalists and two Sinn Féin were also elected – was an uncomfortable reminder that Unionist unity could not be taken for granted. Craig's reaction was twofold. First, he set about establishing a more favourable electoral system, by replacing the 1920 Act's provisions for multi-seat constituency proportional representation with the method used in elections to the Westminster parliament. Second, the prime minister came down in favour of applying pressure on Londonderry to satisfy the UEC's demands, but only after some initial hesitation.

A fortnight after the general election, on 17 April, Londonderry gave an address to the annual congress of the mainly Catholic Irish National Teachers' Organization, on how his reforms had 'entrenched' the position of teachers.[175] A week later, the UEC again demanded that the Ministry of Education allow transferred schools to compel their teachers to give religious instruction. Londonderry refused, just as he continued to deny their call for a denominational test for teachers. The agitation continued throughout May and June.

At the start of June, lawyers for the UEC challenged the government's interpretation of Section 5 of the Government of Ireland Act 1920. Despite the advice of the Attorney General that the UEC were incorrect, Craig suggested on the 4th that the cabinet seek a ruling on the matter from the Judicial Committee of the Privy Council. Londonderry successfully countered this by arguing that it would create 'an awkward situation' for the government if the United Kingdom's highest court agreed with the UEC.[176] On 12 June the Presbyterian general assembly upped the stakes by calling on local councillors to withdraw levies to the Ministry of Education if further amendments were not made. With the situation getting worse, it seemed that Londonderry was incapable of dealing with it effectively, at least to the satisfaction of his cabinet colleagues. In response to the general assembly, he announced that the government

> are in fullest sympathy with their desire and their determination to secure the continuance of religious instruction in transferred schools. But we wish to make it clear beyond any possibility of misapprehension that if, as appears to be the case, the method proposed for securing this object in such schools involves any

> compulsion – direct or indirect – on the teachers, it can receive no support from the Government.

He went further, adopting a position that could only have infuriated his opponents, by declaring that the government would adhere to this view 'even if it could be established that no actual legal bar exists to the application of such compulsion'.[177]

Against expectation, Craig backed Londonderry at this point and agreed in cabinet that nothing further should be conceded.[178] His ministerial colleagues, however, were not so sure. Andrews, hitherto a supporter of Londonderry, complained of being subjected to pulpit harangues at his local church about the loss of Protestant rights.[179] Other ministers feared that they too would be verbally attacked at the upcoming annual twelfth of July Orange demonstrations, and that this would undermine the authority of the government in advance of the Boundary commission's report. Tallents had almost forecast such an outcome in his 1922 report: 'Ministers are too close to their community and cannot treat their supporters as from a distance'.[180] After 'exhaustive conversations' between Craig and Londonderry in the third week of June, the latter was persuaded to meet with the UEC and reach an agreement.[181] At the ill-tempered meeting, the Minister of Education refused to give in to the UEC's demands concerning the appointment of teachers, but he did offer to allow local authorities to permit non-denominational Bible instruction. He also agreed to compulsory religious instruction for teachers if it met with the approval of their unions.[182] On 23 June he informed Craig that he would resign if teachers refused to comply with the proposed changes. Londonderry went on to admit that he had 'handled all this controversy very badly . . . I never have understood Orangemen and Presbyterians and it is always difficult to know under the shouting and the threats what the people really want and what is best for them to have'.[183] In what was a sympathetic response, Craig urged his Minister of Education not to resign.[184]

On 24 June Londonderry met with the teachers' representatives and secured their consent to compulsion. The following day he met again with the UEC and the row was resolved. On the same day, in a letter to the Ulster Unionist chief whip, Herbert Dixon, Craig remarked that Londonderry had 'very cleverly handled the Education question'.[185] Weeks later, on 10 July, in what appears to have been a gesture of goodwill, Londonderry held a garden party at Mount Stewart. Press reports claimed that 5,000 people attended the event, mostly from the UUC and the Orange Order. Craig was a notable absence.[186]

V

If Londonderry's difficulties with the Protestant opponents to his reforms ultimately ended in 'surrender', then his relations with the Catholic hierarchy followed a different course.[187] At the end of 1922 all teachers in Catholic schools in Northern Ireland came under the authority of its Ministry of Education, the Irish Free State having stopped its payments to the minority of Catholic teachers who had held out in the hope that Northern Ireland might cease to exist or that parts of it might be ceded to the south. Londonderry had appealed directly to Michael Collins to bring about this outcome, writing that it would assist their broader efforts to develop north–south co-operation.[188] The north's Minister of Education nevertheless took a tough line. He refused to backdate the pay that these teachers had lost until their transfer to Belfast; it would be unfair, he reasoned, to the Catholic teachers who had not boycotted the ministry.[189] This aside, Londonderry had a relatively benign attitude to Catholic educational concerns. On 1 December 1922, in a letter to his British counterpart, Edward Wood, later first Viscount Halifax, Londonderry acknowledged that many Catholics regarded 'the present system of government in Northern Ireland as an attempt at Protestant domination and, consequently, as part of the long-standing feud between the Protestants and themselves'.[190] At a cabinet meeting on 29 October 1923, he unsuccessfully opposed Craig's decision to include all teachers paid by the state in a scheme to compel civil servants to give an oath of allegiance to the crown. Londonderry informed his colleagues that the Christian Brothers teaching order had asked him not to impose it for religious and political reasons, and that he 'had a certain amount of sympathy with the representations made by those who were merely influenced by their desire to advocate a union with the South on constitutional lines'.[191] Londonderry probably heard such views articulated most effectively by the leader of constitutional nationalism in Ulster, Joseph Devlin, an occasional guest at receptions organized by Lady Londonderry.[192]

Londonderry's sympathies should not be overstated. He did not, for example, permit the use of the Irish language in examinations other than those specifically designed to test that subject, and he also abolished the post of organizer of Irish language instruction.[193] In part, these actions reflected his assumption that the language should be treated like any other non-English or European language. But Londonderry also shared the belief common among Unionists, north and south, that the promotion of the language by education authorities in the Free State was ultimately harmful to the place of Ireland in the world, that it would make the country what he called a 'little Irish speaking island'.[194] As Fionntán de Brún observes, this outlook was rooted in utilitarian assumptions about the usefulness of minority languages, as well as the growing perception among Unionists that the promotion of the Irish language was a manifestation of Irish nationalism.[195] In any case, the sustained tension between the Catholic hierarchy and Londonderry was not about language but teacher training, and in the end it was handled successfully.

In January 1922 the cabinet agreed to implement new teacher training arrangements in place of the existing system of sending students to institutions that were now in the southern state.[196] As noted above, the government established Stranmillis College in south Belfast for this purpose, but the Catholic bishops refused to allow their male student teachers to attend, insisting instead that they continue to attend training colleges across the border. As these colleges refused to teach the Northern Ireland curriculum, and the Irish language was a compulsory element in the training provided, the Ministry of Education in Northern Ireland felt that it had to find some compromise. St Mary's College in Belfast already trained Catholic women, but it refused to admit men. In June 1924 Londonderry dispatched Andrew Bonaparte Wyse, a senior civil servant and Catholic, to negotiate with representatives of the Catholic hierarchy. Some progress was made with proposals for separate lectures, grounds and halls of residence at Stranmillis. But the government was concerned about the extra costs that this would impose, and further progress appeared to be blocked by Cardinal Logue. Londonderry then attempted to break the logjam by writing to his old adversary at the Irish Convention, Patrick O'Donnell, now coadjutor Archbishop of Armagh, but he too refused to join a government committee.[197] Several months later, however, O'Donnell succeeded Logue as Archbishop of Armagh and in this office he initiated a more co-operative attitude to the Ministry of Education.[198] Not long after, an agreement was reached to send male Catholic students to the Catholic teacher training college at Strawberry Hill in Twickenham, west London. Not only did this outcome allow Londonderry to quell Unionist discontent about funding the building of a third teacher training college, it also meant that Catholic students from Northern Ireland would be trained in England in place of the Free State.[199]

VI

The seemingly benign image of Londonderry that emerges from his efforts to engage the Catholic hierarchy, alongside his dealings with Protestant agitators, makes him appear a relatively attractive figure in an otherwise unattractive Ulster Unionist government. But his contribution to the embryonic years of Northern Ireland was more complex than this suggests. After all, he played a significant personal role in securing the financial support of the Colonial Office for the highly controversial Special Constabulary.[200] And despite his bruising experience of the flawed system of government that emerged in these years, Londonderry's public commitment to Ulster unionism and the continued existence of devolution in Northern Ireland remained unwavering. In a radio broadcast on 21 January 1925, he celebrated that 'Ulstermen now held a unique position in the Empire. Ulster had a Parliament of her own competent to deal with her local problems, but still sent her representatives to the Imperial Parliament, and made the financial sacrifices which the privilege of holding and directing the Empire entailed'.[201] Carson had impressed such an outlook on him in June 1921, 'always remember that the provincial status was forced upon us and our loyalty alone compels the working of it'.[202] Soon after, Londonderry echoed these words in the House of Lords. 'The British Government had fashioned a scheme and are endeavouring to cause Ireland to accept that scheme. We in the North are proposing to accept it and to do what they could to make it a success.'[203] This understanding of devolution, framed positively as an act of loyalty to Great Britain, was primarily for audiences there, for the negative justification accepted by most leading Ulster Unionists was unlikely to achieve the same effect. As Graham Walker observes, 'within the context created by the Government of Ireland Act [Ulster unionism] identified preservation with control of its affairs'.[204] In private, Londonderry was more obviously uneasy with devolution in Northern Ireland. Looking back from the vantage of 1928, he confided to Lynn:

> I was the only person who ever stood up to the Presbyterians and I should have done more in that direction if I had felt that my colleagues would have (I won't say

> supported me) not worked against me. There is no democratic feeling and very little religion amongst a good many of the well known Churchmen. . . . I never think Ulster is democratic and that the battle here is for some sort of ascendancy. Craig has established quite a good ascendancy for himself: now the Presbyterians want the ascendancy on the so-called democratic Education Committees. I wanted this province governed in quite a different way; but I was a voice crying in the wilderness. . . . Somebody has got to capture ascendancy here and each one gains support by coming forward as the Champion of some sort of ascendancy. I am not very happy about the future.[205]

Compared to his ministerial colleagues, Londonderry was undoubtedly a force for progress. Beyond education policy, he successfully opposed those in the cabinet who supported a bill that would have prevented women from being jurors.[206] Likewise, when in August 1925 the Belfast Corporation voted 30–12 against a proposal to permit band-playing in public parks on Sundays, Londonderry challenged the claim that it was 'the thin edge of wedge'. Such music, he argued, would be 'ennobling', a reflection, perhaps, of his involvement with the National Opera Trust and its campaign to promote music throughout the United Kingdom.[207] Yet he was not in all matters progressive. In a flurry of correspondence with the Minister of Home Affairs, Londonderry expressed concern about legislation that would grant rights of inheritance to illegitimate children; he only relented when Craig backed Dawson Bates in cabinet.[208]

Londonderry's attitude to Northern Ireland politics was fundamentally paternalistic, a reflection of his landed background and unelected seat in its parliament. As the *Irish Statesman* commented, 'if the principle underlying the [Education] Act had been carried into effect, it would have done more to destroy sectarian divisions in Northern Ireland than anything which has been said or done for the last century'. The journal reflected its editor's nationalist outlook by placing the blame firmly with the Protestant critics rather than the Catholic boycott:

> Lord Londonderry must have read with a wry smile Sir James Craig's assurance in his valedictory letter of the gratitude of the people of Ulster for all that their late Minister of Education has done for them. For while the Protestant Ministers were destroying his work, and largely succeeding in their object, the laity either followed their lead or did nothing to support him.[209]

The last claim was not entirely true. The teaching unions, no less, had expressed their support for the 1923 Act. It is clear that Londonderry valued these important representative bodies, but he could have exploited them more effectively to create a broad-based alliance of support. Instead, he tended to ignore or face down the concerns of his Protestant critics, which only fuelled their anger and determination to emasculate those elements of his legislation that dealt with Bible instruction and teacher appointments.

To his opponents within Ulster unionism, it appeared as if Londonderry was trying to undermine its raison d'être. With the creation of Northern Ireland, the Ulster Unionists had developed from an 'ethnic association' – in which the members develop common interests and political organizations – into an 'ethnic community', possessing a permanent, physically bounded territory over and above its political organizations.[210] Having played only a marginal part in the mobilization of Ulster unionism before the First World War, Londonderry's link with it as an ethnic association was not as strong as that of his fellow ministers, so it is unsurprising that he should have found it difficult to fully understand or empathize with the internal dynamics of Ulster Unionist governance after 1921. As Jennifer Todd explains, 'Northern Ireland . . . was founded on an exclusivist legitimating principle, which was impervious to more generalized and universalistic pleas for justice and democracy if these were to conflict with unionists' basic interest in the survival of the state and the union.'[211] Unlike Londonderry, the UEC understood this and exploited it to the full.

This is not to suggest that the outcome was certain. Constructive unionism had achieved some successes in the past, and in the person of Londonderry it had helped in Northern Ireland to defrost relations with the Catholic hierarchy. This endeavour, alongside the Catholic Church's determination to maintain control over Catholic schools, must surely qualify Brendan O'Leary's contention about Unionist policy in the newly created Northern Ireland. This, he hypothesizes, was an outgrowth of seventeenth-century settler colonialism which sought to implement a 'control system' intended to disorganize the minority community.[212] In the end, the understandable if ultimately futile boycott of the new polity by the Catholic bishops and nationalist politicians, Northern Ireland's violent birth and the Ulster Unionists' fear of the Boundary commission, all combined to undermine efforts at constructive unionism and even Londonderry's position in the devolved government. Indeed, far from being peculiar to Northern Ireland, the situation that Londonderry faced there was replicated across the British world. As far apart as Canada and Australia, tension existed between independent-minded Catholic school managers and the governments of these dominions, and there were also parallel campaigns to strengthen the place of Protestantism in state schools.[213] Judged in this unfavourable context, Londonderry can be credited with having had some success as a government minister in Northern Ireland. He provided at a critical stage in its development an experienced pair of hands and a helpful and trusted conduit to Westminster. He established through legislation a set of educational structures that remained in place until after the Second World War; what the Labour senator, Robert Dorman, called the 'foundations of a lasting blessing to the people'.[214] And last but not least, his efforts to resist the worst excesses of the new government at Belfast met with the approval of Conservative opinion in Great Britain.

5

Catering his way to the cabinet? 1926–31

Assessments of Lord Londonderry's political career typically neglect the years between his departure from the government of Northern Ireland in January 1926 and his appointment to the British cabinet in October 1928, and again in November 1931. Without acknowledging his political activities in this period, historians have been content to echo Lord Birkenhead's witty observation that Londonderry was engaged in 'catering his way to the Cabinet', a barbed reference to the famous political functions held at Londonderry House.[1] More specifically, many point to the close friendship between Lady Londonderry and Ramsay MacDonald as the reason for her husband's two appointments in 1931 to the National Government that he led. It is true that these factors played a part in Londonderry's return to government at Westminster, and that in contrast to her famous contemporaries – Lady Cunard, Lady Astor, Mrs Laura Corrigan and Lady Colefax – Lady Londonderry had more success as a political hostess. However, it should be borne in mind, as Martin Pugh observes, that the influence exerted by political hostesses tended to be 'exaggerated by frustrated rivals'.[2] Birkenhead's relationship with the Londonderry family is also worth noting given his pithy appraisal of their methods. In the earlier part of his political career, he had been befriended by Lord Londonderry's mother, Theresa. The young, talented and ambitious F. E. Smith readily accepted the marchioness's political patronage and the entrée offered by receptions at Londonderry House.[3] Through her he had what his biographer describes as a 'directly personal element' to 'his already strong attachment to the cause of Ulster', staying often at Mount Stewart when visiting Ireland.[4] Birkenhead's initial and flamboyant support for Ulster unionism waned considerably after the First World War. He could nevertheless still admire the statesmanlike response of Theresa's son, Lord Londonderry, to the treaty that established the Irish Free State (see Chapter 4). In the years that followed, however, relations between the two men turned sour. 'The real truth is that you in Belfast are far too sensitive', Birkenhead wrote to Londonderry in 1927. 'Even you, who are so largely in touch with Imperial affairs and with English political society, the moment you go back to Belfast become parochialised.'[5] None of this invalidates Birkenhead's suggestion that Londonderry catered his way to the cabinet, but it provides some context that is often lacking when it is regurgitated by others.

What then are the additional and often overlooked explanations for Londonderry's return to ministerial office at Westminster? It is argued above (see Introduction) that grandee aristocrats could still utilize their status and wealth in pursuit of a diminishing pool of government offices. The periodic but hitherto limited satisfaction of Londonderry's political aspirations demonstrates that this increasingly anachronistic aspect of British political culture still had some influence in the first half of the twentieth century. But this is not to say that he just slipped into high office by virtue of his noble birth, enormous wealth and his wife's pre-eminence as a political hostess. He was, to some extent, the master of his own destiny. Irish politics, both during the First World War and after, had cast Londonderry as a conciliatory figure willing to rise above narrow party interest. His association with Ulster unionism also meant that he was on the right side of a divided Conservative party when the post-war coalition government fell in October 1922.[6] Its reinstalled leader, Andrew Bonar Law, offered Londonderry the non-cabinet post of Secretary of State for Air. Londonderry chose to remain in Northern Ireland, but he remained a figure of significance to senior Conservatives, actively ensuring through his role in the 1924 boundary crisis that the party would not be sacrificed on the altar of old fidelities. Indeed, far from his association with Ulster unionism being a liability, it is possible that leading Conservatives thought it useful, on occasion, to consider Londonderry for ministerial office as a means of acknowledging their party's working relationship with the small phalanx of Ulster Unionist MPs regularly returned to Westminster, for there was no wish or expectation that any of them would be brought into the government.[7]

The most conspicuous oversight in Birkenhead's assessment of Londonderry's path to the cabinet is his ownership of the Londonderry Collieries Limited. He was the fourth generation of his family to have benefitted from the company's enormous industrial wealth.[8] But his status as a colliery owner also made him a hate figure for the Labour movement and a potential liability to Stanley Baldwin's one nation approach to Conservative statecraft. As such, the great industrial disputes of 1926 and their bitter legacy should have ended Londonderry's ambitions to re-enter the British government. But during the general strike, if not the miners' strike that continued for months afterwards, he applied the lesson from Northern Ireland that active attempts at conciliation, or appeasement, could go some way to solving difficult disputes. Such efforts also had the additional benefit of enhancing the standing of those who espoused this form of politics, at least among senior figures at Westminster and beyond.

To the surprise of his contemporaries, Londonderry reacted to these circumstances by coming out as a prominent advocate of industrial peace. Instead of a liability, he became a potentially useful figure to Baldwin's government, during the general strike of 1926, again in late 1927 and again in 1928–9, during the latter period as an active contributor to an industrial co-operation initiative that helped to create a new atmosphere nationally in industrial relations. Throughout, party functions at Londonderry House served to remind senior Conservatives that he was available for work. He was not disappointed. In 1927, Londonderry was given the chairmanship of a royal commission. He was then asked, as a colliery owner and peer, to help quell unrest in the Conservative party at its annual conference later that year. In 1928, he was appointed Lord Lieutenant of County Durham.[9] And later that year, following a cabinet reshuffle, he was appointed First Commissioner of Works – the lowest ranking cabinet office – and reappointed to the same post in the emergency National Government of August–October 1931, this time outside the cabinet. Commenting on

Londonderry's suitability for office at this time, the former cabinet minister, William Bridgeman, a close ally of Baldwin, observed that 'as far as I could tell his judgement was sound on most points of dispute. He is not strong in debate, but very willing and ready to do anything he is asked to take up'.[10] In short, Lady Londonderry's role as a leading political hostess undoubtedly played a part in securing ministerial office for her husband in 1928 and again in 1931, but he still had to possess other qualities, including a political record that did not raise serious doubts about his credibility and suitability.

I

Londonderry's resignation letter to the prime minister of Northern Ireland, James Craig, was published in the press on 9 January 1926.[11] It spelt out his wish to devote more time to his mining interests in County Durham, a plausible reason given the coal industry's continuing difficulties, and one that extricated him from a troubled and frustrating period as a minister in the government of Northern Ireland. 'I am rather liking the free lance complex and expect to continue in that state altogether', he informed his confidant, Lady Desborough. 'I have time now to do all sorts of things I have always wanted to do without trammels and collective responsibility which is in one scale, whilst the honour and prestige and importance of being a member of the Government are in the other.' As if to persuade himself, he added that he did not 'care about the [Conservative] Government either and I am sure I should not agree [with them]. They have all served together for years and are a sort of executive of a Trade Union speaking a language which I don't understand and should never learn'.[12] It was in fact the analysis of a disappointed man, for no leading figures in London seemed to be interested in his having left Northern Ireland to concentrate on the coal industry.[13] The one exception, at least initially, was the press baron Lord Beaverbrook, though his interest appears to have evaporated following an ill-advised request from Lady Londonderry that he help her and her husband publicize an 'Anti Socialist Propaganda Ball' at the Kit Kat Club.[14]

Notwithstanding the impression that he sought to convey to Desborough, Lord Londonderry could not accept as consolation the numerous honorary and ornamental offices that he had been given by virtue of his aristocratic background. The local status and ceremony attached to some of these certainly appealed to him, such as his role as chancellor of the Queen's University of Belfast, but he regarded them as accompaniments and not alternatives to ministerial office.[15] His wariness of getting stuck in largely decorative appointments had prevented him in 1920 and 1925 from agreeing to his nomination as Canada's governor-general, and he would turn down the post again in 1931. It is likely that he would have responded the same way to a suggestion aired in November 1926 at the Imperial Conference hosted by Baldwin in London. In an attempt to revise Ireland's relationship with Great Britain, and at the same time forge a 'Commonwealth of Northern and Southern Ireland', the vice-president of the Irish Free State's executive council, Kevin O'Higgins, put forward a plan for dual monarchy that included a viceroy-type figure, with Londonderry as a possible candidate.[16] A new Irish viceroyalty, if it had achieved that status as it was commonly understood – on par with the Indian viceroyalty – would likely have had a greater appeal to Londonderry than Canada, given that his father had occupied the original viceroyalty. But it is doubtful that O'Higgins used the term viceroy in this sense, or that his executive council would have consented to a constitutional arrangement that diminished its hard-won authority to the benefit of such an office. O'Higgins's inclination to mention Londonderry in this regard nevertheless demonstrates that his record in Ireland and his grandee status were still perceived by some there as being potentially useful, and that his record in the government of Northern Ireland had earned him plaudits in certain quarters of Southern Ireland as well as at Westminster. He was an especially apposite candidate given his Irish and British titles and his previous government appointments in Dublin, London and Belfast. On a less exalted scale, he was deemed suitable for the presidency of the Benevolent Society of St Patrick, an organization that assisted destitute Irish people living in London. Indeed, his appointment to that position in 1931 made him 'the fourth member of his family to hold that office since 1825'.[17]

Some aristocratic appointments, of course, retained a degree of political influence. He was after all a member of the House of Lords, and he remained a Northern Ireland senator until 1929. He had also retained his presidency of the Conservative and Unionist party in County Durham. With many of the area's male voters rallying to the Labour banner, Pauline Lynn highlights how the female vote was cultivated by the Londonderrys through their patronage of ostensibly non-political organizations, such the Women's Institute, which promoted values that indirectly aided the Conservatives.[18] Even so, the erosion of Lord Londonderry's political authority in the county was not just observable in the popular vote for Labour, but also in the attitude and expectations of its leading Conservatives. If middle-class party members enjoyed the garden parties held in the grounds of Wynyard Hall, others resented the continued political pretensions of an aristocratic family that they viewed as anachronistic, and constituency chairmen and MPs were particularly exercised by the fact that the rising Labour vote was feeding off discontent among Londonderry's employees.[19] Moreover, if the influence of landowners in provincial politics had for several decades been bound up with their contributions to Conservative party funds, then a marked decline in contributions added to the tension already existing between the aristocracy and their political inheritors. It led the Conservative MP for Barnard Castle, Cuthbert Headlam, to complain in October 1926 that the local party's finances were in a dire state because of lords Durham and Londonderry.[20] It made Headlam all the more resentful of their families' continued involvement in the management of the local party, going so far as to blame them personally for its defeat, including his own, at the general election of May 1929.[21]

As it happened, Londonderry's heir, Lord Castlereagh, also failed at that poll to win Darlington for the Conservative interest. In an effort to turn the Londonderrys' wealth into an electoral liability, Castlereagh's candidature drew the stinging criticism of Sir Charles Trevelyan, Labour MP for Newcastle Central, that they 'only take part in political work to save their swag'.[22] In contrast to Headlam, Lady Londonderry took the view that the local party's poor showing in 1929 was due to her family's lack of influence, namely, the recent decision by Central Office in London to subsume County Durham into the larger 'Northern Area'.[23] Another factor that probably had a bearing on the result was the two-month-old lockout of over 2,000 miners at Londonderry's Dawdon Colliery, south of Seaham, an industrial dispute that would last until November and which was the subject of criticism in parliament in advance of the general election.[24] Whatever the causes, Londonderry still managed to maintain his attenuated status in the newly designated Northern Area, as he was elected its president in 1930 and remained in the role until his death.

II

Industrial relations improved at pits across the country after the tumult of the April–July 1921 national miners' strike.[25] It helped that economic conditions were more favourable, but it was a situation that could not last given that the problems of excess capacity had not been overcome. As a coalfield geared towards exports, County Durham was particularly vulnerable. And with trade unionism in the area the best organized and most politically significant in the country, its colliery owners had to contend with formidable organization on the ground.[26] Throughout Londonderry's lifetime, the Durham Miners' Association had gone some way to unbinding the bonds of paternalism in pit village life, stripping the employer–employee relationship to its economic core. The union was also instrumental in developing the local Labour party whose main objective, according to Lynn, was 'to limit the Londonderry influence within the community', and by 1923 the Seaham constituency had become a Labour stronghold.[27] The declining profitability of the Durham coalfield inevitably tested industrial relations and challenged the legitimacy and practicality of the remaining forms of paternalism. Just as Londonderry had divested himself of the Silksworth Colliery in 1920, it was announced two years later that Seaham Hall – which had been acquired by his family a hundred years previously – would be closed and its contents sold, though the public would continue to have free use of the grounds.[28] These were financial decisions, of course, the latter explained as the result of 'heavy taxation and cost of upkeep', and he followed them in 1923 with the sale of his first home, Springfield, near Oakham in Rutland.[29] Whatever might be said of his motivations, Londonderry had not repudiated the paternalistic role that he was expected to play in his employees' lives and communities.

In the decades that followed the death of the third Marquess of Londonderry, County Durham's pit villages experienced considerable change, as their residents' dependence on the patronage of the employer, and the ubiquitous presence of the chapel, was supplemented by co-operative stores, reading rooms and social clubs. Even so, the last of these, as Huw Beynon and Terry Austrin highlight, actually helped to extend the influence of paternalistic employers due to the 'deeply masculine nature of club culture'. They cite the example of the Londonderry family, which 'continued to fuse its relationship with the miners through a deep sense of nationhood and populist ideals of democracy'. This was achieved through their involvement, and that of their agents, in the local associational culture of political, religious and secular organizations, including the working men's clubs.[30] Only months after the announcement about

Seaham Hall, Lord Londonderry unveiled the war memorial erected at Seaham Harbour on 20 August 1922, and nearby, a week later, a statue of his late father.[31] In December that year, he opened a new parish hall and institute at Dawdon Colliery.[32] The following July, he unveiled the war memorial at New Seaham, erected by the miners of Seaham Colliery to the 165 local men who fell in the First World War. As an active supporter of the local branch of the Comrades of the Great War, established to counter the influence of socialist ex-servicemen's organizations, he remarked that the monument would serve as 'a reminder to generations to come that the real function of life was to be found in the selfless devotion of every one of them to the cause of duty, of humanity, and of the belief in Christian ethics'.[33] Weeks later, he opened a new pavilion at Dawdon Recreation Grounds at Seaham Harbour, which was presented to the miners of Dawdon Colliery.[34]

The bonds of paternalism between Londonderry and his employees were not confined to ceremonial unveilings and openings. In March 1920 Londonderry gifted a new stand, designed by his surveyor, to Seaham Harbour Football Club.[35] More significantly, in January 1923, he held out the possibility of a new pit being sunk in Seaham Harbour, informing a meeting there that he hoped it 'would see a large addition to the community in a few years, with Seaham growing into one of the most influential towns in the North of England'.[36] Later in the year, he announced that he would build twenty houses – 'of the three-roomed type, with scullery and bath-room' – at Dawdon and twenty at Seaham, for the purpose of selling to employees through hire purchase. In what was described as 'an experiment', the purchaser would pay a deposit of five pounds and would receive the benefit of a government subsidy which was calculated at about £75 per house.[37] On 6 September, Londonderry descended the mines at both Dawdon and Seaham, accompanied by his wife and son; it was reported that lords Londonderry and Castlereagh wore pit suits and that Lady Londonderry had a mackintosh over her dress.[38] In May 1924 Lord Londonderry donated the land, bricks and £100 towards the construction of twelve homes for aged miners at Dawdon, the bulk of the money having already been raised by the miners.[39] In November that year, he gifted twelve 'Castlereagh Aged Miners' Homes' to mark the recent coming of age of his son; each of the occupants also received what was reported as 'a substantial sum' from Londonderry's sister, the Countess of Ilchester.[40]

These acts of *noblesse oblige* aside, the more peaceable conditions in the mining industry, and the prosperity that briefly returned in 1923, appear to have disinclined Londonderry from dissenting from the intransigent line adopted by the owners' representative organization, the MAGB, in the way that he had in 1921, and he would again in 1926 and 1929. It followed that he was not only opposed to the trade unions' call for nationalization but also its touted alternative, 'unification', because it meant that successful districts would have to bail out those where the coal had been worked 'to such an extent that it is no longer profitable to produce'.[41] On 1 December 1924, in an address to the Coal Trade Benevolent Fund attended by 400 dinner guests, he offered the limp observation that if 'owners had freedom from interference and a continuance of friendly relations with their men he was sanguine that they would surmount those difficulties and that the British coal trade would flourish'.[42] At that point, as he acknowledged in his speech, the period of favourable conditions was coming to an end, largely as a result of the increased competition from Germany; its coal now being exported free in fulfilment of war reparations. As the crisis began to bite in the early months of 1925, many collieries began running at a loss resulting in closures and rising unemployment. Londonderry now recalled his earlier rhetoric by appealing for everyone to pull together and 'face the odds which they were up against'.[43] The crisis confronted by the coal industry was compounded in April 1925 by the government's decision to return to the gold standard, thereby making British exports more expensive and less competitive. Predictably, the MAGB insisted on wage cuts and longer hours without offering a commensurate diminution in the owners' rate of profit.[44] In response, the MFGB, supported by the Trades Union Congress (TUC), rejected the owners' demands and called for nationalization. Fears grew of another national strike until the prime minister, Stanley Baldwin, intervened at the end of July with a nine-month subsidy and the establishment of a royal commission under Sir Herbert Samuel.

Speaking at Plâs Machynlleth on 13 August, Londonderry praised Baldwin's 'high statesmanlike attitude' and contrasted it with the unions, 'to which they owed debts of gratitude for many reasons', but which 'had become dominated by minorities, who, with the machinery and weapons they had at their disposal, were setting themselves up as the tyrants of the British race'. Referring to the MFGB's general secretary, A. J. Cook, he added 'that if it became an issue between Mr Cook and the British Government and the British nation they would find every right-thinking Labour man – and a great majority were right-thinking men – ranged on the side of the Government – not the Conservative Government, not the Liberal Government, but the Government of the country under his Majesty the King'.[45] Cook responded in kind. 'I notice that Lord Londonderry has joined with some of the Press in the country in its attack upon myself', he informed a meeting in Montgomeryshire.

> Surely this man should be the last to charge our people with fomenting revolution. A close examination of his history, especially with regard to Ireland, will prove that Lord Londonderry has been the greatest fomentor of revolution in Great Britain, and, instead of him warning me, the British public will know what a danger he is to peace and security and happiness for the British working classes.[46]

Speaking afterwards at Durham, Londonderry addressed a demonstration of the Junior Imperial League on Baldwin's 'statesmanship' and 'courage', contrasting it with the 'arrogant and impudent assertion of power by what was a minority of the community – and, let them remember, a minority of the minority, because Mr Cook and his friends did not represent the great mass of trade unionism in this country . . . They represented Communists and Bolshevists'.[47]

These interventions aside, Londonderry chose not to comment publicly on the proceedings of the Samuel commission. He was nevertheless unhappy with its progress. Building on the relatively moderate position that he had adopted in 1921, he now signalled to Baldwin his dissent from the intransigent posture adopted by most other owners, which had barely moved in the years since. That is, they maintained that the industry's prosperity between 1873 and 1913 provided an adequate rebuttal to calls for nationalization, and that its problems were due to syndicalism and the deliberate restriction of output by miners.[48] As Londonderry put it, with reference to the evidence given to the Samuel commission by his fellow County Durham coal owner, the eighth Duke of Northumberland, the MAGB line was 'very advantageous to Socialism'. 'The question which must be answered soon', Londonderry insisted to the prime minister,

> is how the cost of the production of coal can be reduced and the way it can be reduced is by a greater freedom from restrictions and by a larger output. In my opinion, there is no need to reduce wages, in fact I should be very sorry to see that happen. It would merely mean a reduction of purchasing capacity throughout a large section of the community.[49]

In public, however, he did not appear at first to dissent from the MAGB. In an address to the Seaham Harbour Constitutional Club, published in the press on 9 January 1926 – the same day as it published his resignation letter from the Northern Ireland government – Londonderry said that the owners were better able to run their industry than 'politicians', and that 'their desires were to do everything in their power to make the industry a success, and he knew perfectly well that nine-tenths of the workmen were actuated by the same ideals'.[50] The following evening, however, he betrayed a little of his private frustrations with fellow owners in an address to the annual dinner of the Dawdon Colliery Officials' Association. After remarking on his being able to spend 'more time among those with whom he was associated in the North of England . . . among whom he hoped to carry out the responsibilities which had fallen on his shoulders', Londonderry waxed on the erosion of 'individuality' that had accompanied the transformation of small businesses into 'corporations', and on the need to 'march towards idealism' rather than 'towards materialism'; that 'it was the duty of those who were in authority, whether as owners or officials, to realize that they were dealing with human beings and not machines, and to extend to them that sympathy and understanding of their point of view and outlook to which they were justly entitled'.[51] He was considerably more forthcoming, in contrast, about his dislike of Cook. On 11 January he rounded on the former syndicalist's recent assertion that the owners had exploited the miners during the war and that they continued to do so. 'A more discreditable misstatement was never made', he informed a meeting at New Seaham Conservative Club. 'It was Mr Cook and his friends who exploited the nation, because, whenever our Army was in a tight corner during the war, they held the country up to ransom by threats of strikes and cessation of supplies of coal.'[52]

It was only in the weeks that followed that Londonderry and other moderates emerged publicly from the ranks of the coal owners in an effort to diffuse the growing tension in industrial relations. Addressing a social gathering at Dawdon Working Men's Club on 22 January, he called for 'mutual understanding', and 'speaking for himself and many others he declared that owners did not believe that the prosperity of the industry depended on reducing wages or lengthening hours. At the present time America paid high wages and gave reasonable hours to those engaged in the coal industry, and the industry thrived'. At the same time, he warned against the idea that the restriction of output – it is not entirely clear from the press coverage whether he referred to the alleged behaviour of miners or as a policy solution – 'would secure more work for others . . . because what was wanted in this country was an abundance of output . . . in order to reduce working expenses'.[53] It was this speech that led Beaverbrook to welcome Londonderry's departure from the government of Northern Ireland, noted above:

> I am glad of it because the heads of the Coal Industry will want all the wise advice and statesmanship which they can get if they are to weather the storm. I hope that a year from now I may be able to congratulate you on having done as much for them as you did for the Northern Irish Government.[54]

The Times's labour correspondent was similarly positive. He observed that Londonderry's suggestions for a settlement 'although tentative in character, are arousing a good deal of interest'. He had 'gone beyond the proposals of the Mining Association by suggesting that district negotiations and settlements might be subject to national agreements, and that if piece rates depended on district settlements it would not necessarily follow that earnings would be reduced'. It was reported that:

> At first Mr A.J. Cook . . . was disposed to welcome Lord Londonderry's intervention as signifying a weakening of the forces represented by the Mining Association; but now – as if it were a family quarrel and a third party's endeavours to square a settlement were the last thing to be tolerated – Mr Cook refers Lord Londonderry to the Mining Association . . . that if Lord Londonderry has anything to put forward he should do it through that body.[55]

On 27 January Baldwin addressed a 10,000 strong crowd at Sunderland Stadium. That Londonderry presided at the meeting is unremarkable given that he was the head of the party in the county, yet his recent actions ensured that this did not compromise the prime minister or his one nation approach to handling the brewing crisis. Introducing Baldwin, Londonderry addressed his own recent intervention.

> I have taken this decided step in the past few days because I feel that we are bound to follow the example which the prime minister gives us, and to do every single thing we can to stimulate the spirit and feeling of sympathy, fellowship and cooperation . . . they had seen in Europe the challenging trumpets of strife playing in unison the tune of sympathy and cooperation. They had seen the same phenomenon in Ireland.

Baldwin in his speech explicitly endorsed what Londonderry had said, and appealed 'to those who have the destinies of that great trade in their hands not to play fast and loose with the employment of men in dependent trades'.[56] Castlereagh, who was dispatched to the United States to study its mining industry, can be forgiven for noting that his 'father has now come out as the coal King and at the moment is the central figure in the picture'.[57]

Londonderry was given an advanced copy of the Samuel commission's report before its publication on 10 March.[58] It recommended amalgamations, for the purpose of making the industry more efficient, and for the nationalization of royalties. It called for wages to be bargained on a national not district basis, and that the working day should be 7 hours. The report further recommended the construction of pithead baths and of decent houses at new collieries. It was a clear repudiation of the intransigent position long adopted by most owners, but it disappointed the miners too with its refusal to support the industry's nationalization and its call for wage cuts as an immediate solution to its difficulties.

The Samuel report did little to encourage compromise between the MAGB and the MFGB, even with the nine-month subsidy due to expire at the end of April. It did not help that the former took little heed of the moderate owners in its ranks. In fact, with the notable exception of Sir Alfred Mond, the association succeeded in pressing moderates into public silence. Nor was Baldwin prepared to coerce the owners. Londonderry was not involved directly in the negotiations between the association and the federation, but he felt that deadlock between the two obliged the prime minister to intervene. 'I put this to you with all respect and humility', he informed Baldwin on 13 April,

> because we collectively, owners and men, have failed to do what I earnestly hoped and prayed we could do, which was to join together and work out a solution to the problem. If our failure is due to deeper reasons than those which appear on the surface, it is for those outside the industry to diagnose the causes which are nullifying the best elements in the representatives of each side.[59]

The leading trade unionist and former colonial secretary, James Thomas, wrote to Londonderry the following day.

> The situation is very black at the moment – the breakdown has taken place on the question of National v. Local arrangements. Of course behind it all is the mistrust of each side for the other. Nothing can be done for the next two days, but we are meeting this afternoon and I will write you again later. I think you ought to . . . take a hand.[60]

Londonderry, however, was not yet prepared to break ranks decisively with his fellow colliery owners.

The negotiations having broken down, the owners expected the miners to accept lower wages and longer hours. The federation refused and its members were locked out on 30 April. As a result, the government declared a state of emergency and the TUC's general council pledged its support for the miners and made plans for a general strike, or as it preferred, a national strike, to include the railwaymen, dockers, road transport workers, printers, and gas and electricity workers. The combined action was scheduled to begin at 1 minute past midnight on 4 May. Last minute negotiations between senior government ministers and the TUC – which had been given responsibility for the conduct of the dispute by the MFGB – were broken off by Baldwin in the early hours of the morning, in response to the news that unauthorized industrial action had been called by the printers at the *Daily Mail*.

The result was that one million striking miners were joined by two and a half million workers. This impressive display of solidarity – some eighty unions were involved – belied the TUC general council's lack of enthusiasm for the general strike and its unpreparedness for its consequences. Divisions quickly emerged between moderates on the general council, such as Thomas, and the miners' leaders. On the other side of the dispute, disagreements about strategy emerged between a section of moderate owners, including Londonderry, and the prime minister, who, in spite of his inclination to reach a settlement, did not want to appear to be negotiating during the strike. Nor did he want to press a particular settlement, and so he instead continued to appeal to the public for trust. As a result of this, Baldwin declined to inform his cabinet colleagues that Londonderry and one of Mond's managers had contacted him to express their unhappiness about the hard-line position of the MAGB.[61] On the first day of the strike, Londonderry was one of several prominent politicians and churchmen to visit the Archbishop of Canterbury, Randall Davidson, who was known to sympathize with the plight of the strikers. Baldwin and even MacDonald discouraged Davidson from making an immediate overture to end the strike, but he was persuaded to do otherwise by Londonderry, 'the one mine owner whom I have found to possess suggestiveness or resource is Londonderry, of whom I myself should hardly have expected it'.[62] However, the archbishop's appeal for a negotiated settlement was not as effective as it might have been, for the British Broadcasting Company refused to air it after coming under pressure from the government, and when it was published in the provincial and national press, it received a mixed reaction from politicians and clerics alike.[63] Londonderry was also part of a deputation of ten major colliery owners, which included Mond, that met with Baldwin in secret on 7 May, with the purpose of promoting a compromise that was based on the report of the Samuel commission.

The TUC called off the general strike on 12 May after Thomas was contacted by Herbert Samuel and the two men discussed possible solutions, including an extension of the subsidy. Samuel, however, did not speak for the government and so the miners remained locked out while members of the other trade unions returned to work. Londonderry wrote to Baldwin on 15 May to congratulate the prime minister on his 'wonderful achievement', and to welcome the fact that he had 'taken the coal dispute over'. Londonderry continued to support a compromise and advised that pressure would be needed if all sides were to give ground, and he offered his assistance should it be required.[64] It appears that his offer was accepted, for he was afterwards in consultation with the deputy cabinet secretary, Thomas Jones, and the result was a new settlement under Londonderry's name, published in the *Colliery Guardian* in mid-June.[65] As well as a national wages board and better conditions for the miners, Londonderry argued that the industry could only be returned to profitability if local pits were organized so that 'co-partnership and cooperation' existed between miners and owners. He suggested that the government could legislate to establish a national wages board, as well as pithead baths and pit committees, the latter to be made up of 'owners and representatives of the men . . . which would go fully into the question of the reorganization of each particular undertaking'. He nevertheless cautioned that under present conditions, mines that were not profitable could not be reopened as 'no one expected the miners to accept a lower standard of living'.[66] The Bishop of Durham, Herbert Henson, privately expressed to Londonderry his reluctance to take sides, 'But certainly what I understand to be your general position as a mine owner commends itself very strongly to me.' He urged Londonderry to get the miners' backing.[67]

Contrary to the spirit of the bishop's advice, Londonderry did little to enamour himself with the MFGB. 'I have endeavoured to do whatever has lain in my power to bring about peace and to get the industry as a whole to understand in which direction lies ours and the nation's ultimate prosperity', he informed an audience at Belfast, shortly after the appearance of his proposed settlement in the *Colliery Guardian*, 'but I have been checkmated at every turn by the foolish utterances of Mr Cook'.[68] His frustration was not only directed at the miners' leader. In private, he clashed with Beaverbrook over the *Daily Express*'s lack of sympathy for his own position and that of the owners generally.[69]

Locally, the experience endured by Londonderry's employees and their families was not as hard as it was in west Durham, where a greater incidence of strikes and unemployment meant that people had fewer savings to draw upon. Indeed, the Londonderry Collieries were among the first in the area to recommence, on 7 May, the supply of free weekly loads of coal to its workmen.[70] But the circumstances and hardships of the strike still provided fertile ground for controversy. In particular, Londonderry's preparedness to financially support the wives and children of miners became the subject of a bitter public row with Joseph Batey, Labour MP for the Spennymoor division of Durham and a former official in the Durham Miners' Association.[71] In like manner, Londonderry took to the press in August after learning that MacDonald had been seeking aid in the United States for distressed mining families. He attacked this as propaganda and invited the Labour leader to inspect conditions at the Londonderry Collieries.[72] In a follow-up letter to *The Times*, Londonderry listed what the miners' children ate in their two meals a day, advertised his company's welfare schemes and reminded readers that his employees lived rent free in colliery houses and that they received a coal allowance.[73] Hester Barron highlights that local miners were aware that Londonderry provided relief to their families, that he was more enthusiastic and forthcoming in doing so than the Labour MP for Seaham, Sidney Webb, and that an anonymous interviewee even described him to a journalist as 'the ideal coal owner'.[74] Yet, the publication of Londonderry's defensive letter, which coincided with the MFGB's decision to enter negotiations unconditionally, was unfortunate in so far as it was the worsening circumstances of miners and their families that brought the strike to an end. And in response, they were informed that the owners would accept nothing other than complete surrender.

This and other missteps should not obscure the fact that the industrial unrest of 1926 had endowed Londonderry with new political significance. The Mining Industry Act passed that year gave legislative expression to elements of the Samuel report, just as Londonderry and other moderate owners had demanded. Speaking on the measure when it came before the House of Lords, he described it as 'a permissive and temporary Bill' that 'only holds the ground so long as any one else has no better suggestion'.[75] When Winston Churchill invited representatives of the colliery owners to meet with him at his house, Chartwell, in early September, he could be heard by Thomas Jones discussing the crisis 'from every conceivable angle . . . walking the grounds with "Charley" Londonderry and owing to the echo his voice can be heard a quarter of a mile away'.[76]

Up until this point, the actions of the Chancellor of the Exchequer had tended to worsen the crisis in the coal industry, from his decision to return to the gold standard in 1925, to the notoriously bellicose posture that he adopted during the general strike.[77] Even so, Churchill was coming round to the view that it was the MAGB that was the real obstacle to a settlement.[78] He hoped that his cousin might persuade the owners to compromise or at least offer information on their thinking. After their meeting at Chartwell, Londonderry wrote to the chancellor about his dealings with the MAGB. He had been able to carry it with him in accepting

> the Federation as a body which in some form was bound to be in existence, and we agreed that our district arrangement should be subject to the acceptance or rejection of the Federation, but not if we could help it to variation by the Federation. That means that wages, loans and conditions of working should be district arrangements and that other matters should be for the Federation to discuss and arrange with the Association.

Londonderry then addressed the question of nationalization, 'they could accept a national agreement which allowed for the working at a profit of the poorest district. . . . The great point for the district settlements which is being lost sight of is that a trivial local dispute would not have the effect of holding the country up to ransom'. He counselled Churchill that 'if the Federation . . . are judiciously handled' then its leaders

> will be only too glad to climb out on the bare recognition of the Miners Federation, but if you give them the smallest inkling that your mind is moving from the equilibrium away from the owners' side of the table even by a hair's breadth then they will fight like tigers for the National agreement and nothing but the National agreement.[79]

As his advice suggests, Londonderry feared that Churchill was indeed tilting away from the owners. He complained to the prime minister on 12 September that the chancellor's

> efforts appeared in my judgement to follow on the lines of Cook['s] desires. . . . I am fearful of any buttressing of [him] even in the earnest desire of paying that price to end the strike. I know Winston has gone strenuously and whole heartedly and loyally to put an end to this deadlock, but Winston has never been a good doctor: he has all the attributes of the Quack and his training under L[loyd]G[eorge] was disastrous.

In the same letter, Londonderry acknowledged that the 'strategy of the owners has not been very good and rightly I suppose they are very jealous of interference, and like running their own show'. But he offered an explicitly political justification for the government to support them that was meant to buttress his position, even though it tended to repudiate his repeated calls for sacrifices on all sides:

> The principle on which their contentions are based is a sound one from our political point of view as the Federation is dead against us politically and always will be and while it is the duty of the Government to hold the scales evenly between capital and labour when the one endeavours to exploit the other, any support for the Federation is ammunition for those forces which are being used to destroy our party and our policy.[80]

Tellingly, Baldwin's private office sent only the briefest acknowledgement in reply.[81]

Publicly, Londonderry still maintained his call for 'mutual respect and understanding between employers and employed', as he informed an audience at Belfast on 15 October, and he insisted that he was still 'convinced that there was a prevailing desire on the part of parties to come together'.[82] But the partisanship evident in his letter to Baldwin also became more apparent in his public interventions. He made known on 26 October his letter to the MP for Seaham, Sidney Webb, which claimed that a Dawdon miner had been denied financial assistance for his sick child out of a relief fund,

> on the grounds that the applicant and his wife had both voted for the Conservative candidate at the last General Election . . . I am bringing this case before you as a real example of the tyranny which the Labour Party practises throughout the country, a tyranny which is mainly responsible for the continuance of the strike, and by which, through this and other forms of intimidation, it is hoped to secure unwilling support at the next election.[83]

He addressed the Cambridge Union on 23 November, speaking against the motion 'That only by the adoption of Socialist principles in her government can Britain ensure the happiness and prosperity of her people.' After declaring that he 'did not wish to approach the question at all in a party spirit', he went on to do just that, expressing his belief that if Labour came to power it would quickly explode 'All the Socialistic fallacies' and 'we should then go back to Conservatism and Liberalism, with Socialism a thing of the past'. He warned that to 'hand over all interests to the State would simply mean stagnation and decay', and 'he questioned the House whether during the past few months Government interference had been a benefit to anyone – coalowners, miners, or public'.[84] Around this time he wrote to Churchill, defending the owners in the same manner that he had to Baldwin, that they were 'fighting socialism . . . one of the most powerful army corps in the field against us'.[85] Unlike the prime minister, Churchill did respond, writing on 3 November that it

> is not the business of Coal Owners as Coal Owners to fight Socialism. If they declare it their duty, how can they blame the Miners' Federation for pursuing political ends? The business of the Coal Owners is to manage their industry successfully, to

> insist upon sound economic conditions as regards hours and wages, and to fight Socialism as citizens and not as owners of a particular class of property.[86]

Speaking at Jarrow on 3 December, Londonderry initially appeared in his opening remarks to return to the more emollient language that he had employed earlier in the year, with the claim that he was 'a strong believer in trade unions and he saw a great future for them'. But his animus towards the MFGB quickly manifested itself, and it was accompanied by the barbed observation that the government and the churches had been 'used by Mr Cook for the purpose of prolonging the struggle'.[87] On 16 December, by which point most of the miners had returned to work, thoroughly beaten and considerably poorer, he informed the Seaham Harbour Constitutional Club

> that he claimed no victory at all. He had been a very heavy loser. The funds which he had hoped to utilize in extending enterprises at Seaham, and in schemes which would have benefited the district, had been dissipated in useless idleness instead of being used in profitable production. Work on his new colliery had been delayed for seven months, and the employment which it would have found for thousands of workers had been proportionately delayed.

Only Cook, Londonderry averred, 'had gained a victory . . . The miners had been pawns in the game, and he had won nearly all his objectives. He had caused enormous loss to the mining industry and to the country'.[88] Two days later he delivered a similar message at a ceremony to open the new premises of the Royal Antediluvian Order of Buffaloes at Seaham Harbour, which was built on a site cleared of undesirable slum property. 'He had built more than 200 houses during the past two or three years', *The Times* reported him as saying, 'and, but for the effects of the coal stoppage on financial resources, he would have been continuing to build'.[89] On 8 January 1927 he devoted much of his address to the annual dinner of the Dawdon Colliery Officials' Association to attacking Cook, alluding to the general secretary's former membership of the Communist Party of Great Britain in the claim that he 'talked gaily to his Moscow friends about a revolution in this country'.[90] The occasion was otherwise notable for the exhibition, on the dinner table, of the first piece of coal drawn from the new colliery at Seaham Harbour. Three days later, when he addressed several thousand people gathered at Sunderland in support of the Industrial Peace Union, established by the veteran trade unionist, Havelock Wilson, and organized locally by Lord Castlereagh among others, Londonderry's speech in support of the organization's purported aim was peppered with attacks on Cook and his 'wicked and insane ideals'.[91]

These two messages were coherent in so far as Londonderry regarded Cook, not the miners, as the root of the problem. He in effect turned the popular view of the owners on its head, presenting Cook as the real exploiter of the miners' predicament. Cook had his critics, of course, on the left as well as the right, but the interpretation advanced by Londonderry was an exercise in wishful thinking if he felt that the grievances that Cook articulated could be separated from the ordinary business of industrial relations.[92] Yet, he was not alone among Conservatives in regarding Cook's influence over the miners as something demonic. Londonderry's attacks on the MFGB were part of a wider rhetorical strategy among Conservatives after 1918 that attempted to draw a distinction between ordinary working-class men and women and a sectional labour movement that challenged the moderation of the Conservatives.[93] The strategy was given institutional expression in some parts of the country, including County Durham, through the formation of the National Conservative League, an ancillary working-class movement outside the formal party organization.[94] Londonderry presided over his county's grand lodge on 11 April, which met to pass a resolution in support of the government's new trade union legislation.[95] The controversial bill went some way to addressing calls on the right of the Conservative party for a punitive measure, as it prohibited strikes that were interpreted as inflicting hardship on the community, provided a wide definition of intimidation during strikes and made trade unionists contract in rather than contract out of the political levy paid to the Labour party.[96] Writing to *The Times* shortly after the grand lodge meeting, Londonderry claimed that the bill gave expression to 'certain principles with which every one is in agreement', and he rounded on 'the so-called moderate Labour leaders' for failing to support the measure, of endeavouring 'to run with the hare of public opinion, which in theory accepts the proposals, and hunt with the hounds of the extremists, who reject those same proposals as curbing the political activities of the executives'.[97] On 30 April, he went further, describing the bill to Conservatives at Durham as the 'Charter of the Working Man' as 'it gave him liberty which he did not now possess'.[98] Londonderry spoke on three occasions during the bill's passage through the House of Lords, on 30 June, 12 July and 13 July. In addition to revisiting the themes of his recent speeches – acknowledging the good work of trade unions but warning that they could be used by malign forces, and condemning Labour moderates for failing to join the government in framing a suitable measure of trade union reform – he took an active part in shaping the legislation, and he was frequently referred to in the speeches of opposition peers.[99] In spite of the legislation and the other notable victories over the miners, Londonderry was moved in August to contribute a letter to *The Times* criticizing 'the miners' representatives' for thinking that the coal industry could resume the status quo ante because 'the coal export trade of this country has been destroyed as a result of a seven-months' strike which they themselves brought about'.[100]

The relative moderation displayed by Londonderry in the lead up to and during the general strike, which at the time encountered resistance from Baldwin, had given way in the months that followed to a protracted posture of hostility to Cook and his union, and in due course to a sharper critique of trade unionism and the Labour party. If Londonderry's direction of travel put him at odds with Baldwin and Churchill, who emerged from the general strike hoping for a more conciliatory response from the owners, he was still broadly in tune with the temper of the Conservative party. It is a curiosity that his trajectory appeared, at least on the surface, to follow that of his great grandfather. The third marquess had been involved in various charitable and far-sighted initiatives in County Durham, and in 1831 he had successfully played a personal role in settling a strike.[101] But his forceful and often successful actions against trade union influence tended to overshadow anything that might have redeemed his reputation in local folklore. Little wonder that in certain quarters, the seventh marquess now appeared to fulfil the widespread mythology in the county that had long cast the

Figure 6 Lord Londonderry, 1927.

Londonderrys as villains. Fortunately for him, others took a different view. Whereas the negative reputation of the third marquess reinforced the tendency of front bench Tories to keep him at arm's length, the seventh marquess's hostility towards the MFGB did not prevent his appointment to the chairmanship of a royal commission in July 1927, and his appointment to the cabinet the following year.

That progression was not necessarily by design. It is even possible that by offering Londonderry the chairmanship of the Royal Commission on London Squares, the government hoped to extricate itself from having to consider his return to ministerial office.[102] Alternatively, the appointment might have been intended to test him after several years spent as a minister in the peculiar context of Northern Ireland. The reason might have been even more straightforward. The chairmanships of royal commissions were often given to noblemen, and the charge handed to Londonderry was relatively benign, straightforward and in its subject matter, highly appropriate for the owner of a large property on Park Lane. As David Cannadine notes, government ministers tended to regard aristocrats as well suited to chairing royal commissions, as they were deemed to possess 'those attributes of leisure, dignity, a broad view, and a disinterested tone' necessary for the task and were 'less inclined to be controversial or acrimonious'.[103] The two other royal commissions appointed in 1927 were also chaired by aristocrats, of whom one was a junior minister in the government, and the other a leading diplomatist. Whatever the reason, it was surely fitting that as First

Commissioner of Works Londonderry would later implement the royal commission's report that he had prepared in 1927; it recommended that all but five squares should be permanently preserved as open spaces.[104] If in fact the royal commission was meant to test Londonderry's suitability for a return to ministerial office, the prime minister soon found another, one that had emerged from the recent period of industrial unrest and the resulting political backlash on the right.

The Trade Disputes Act 1927 was widely regarded on the left as a punitive measure. Yet it failed to satiate the desire of reactionary Conservatives to press home the advantage over the Labour movement. Between the Conservative party's annual conference in 1927 and the gathering planned for Cardiff the following year, large numbers of grassroots members rallied behind calls for the powers of the House of Lords to be restored or at least strengthened as a constitutional safeguard against a future Labour government. Baldwin was determined to see off this threat to his one nation approach to party policy.[105] On the recommendation of the MP for Stockton-on-Tees, Harold Macmillan, the prime minister asked Londonderry to move the leadership's amendment to a conference motion on the House of Lords.[106] It is possible that Baldwin recalled the small role that Londonderry had played in 1924 in helping to quell the diehard revolt in the House of Lords over the Irish boundary bill (see Chapter 4). But the colliery owner's selection had a more obvious and immediate utility given that he had both a record of pragmatism in industrial relations and of attacking militant trade unionism. In his speech to the conference, Londonderry advanced the argument that there was no need to amend the constitution as it had been vindicated during the general strike. He claimed that the proposal would 'change the whole poise and balance of our constitution', and that it would 'establish a suspicion in this country that the free exercise of the vote can be controlled, altered and thwarted'. The press reported several protests of 'no, no' from the floor, an indication, as it turned out, that he was out of step with the majority gathered in Cardiff.[107] As the *Manchester Guardian* commented, it was 'too liberal a speech to find much acceptance here'.[108] Even so, his contribution went down well in sections of the party. The MP for Ripon, John Hills, remarked that 'you were right and history will justify you'.[109] The most noteworthy praise came from Churchill. 'I certainly do not think you should regard the upshot as a political failure or disaster', he reassured his cousin. 'It is nothing of the sort and will not be of the slightest injury to your political influence. On the contrary, I have no doubt it will be seen that the course you advocated will in the main be borne out by events.'[110]

Significant though the speech was, Londonderry could not afford to take his eye off the Londonderry Collieries if he wanted to follow through and make himself a viable candidate for ministerial office.[111] As one of this Conservative critics, J. C. C. Davidson, later remarked, 'as a mine-owner in Durham [Londonderry] had quite a good reputation, but the people who were his agents were regarded as a pretty hard lot'.[112] Fortunately, despite Londonderry's recent fulminating that precious resources had been wasted during the miners' strike, he had not abandoned the principle of paternalism or the motivation to invest in his collieries.

On 28 May 1927, the annual meeting of the Durham County Aged Mineworkers' Association reported that 'despite the strike, the contributions to the association from miners, owners, and private subscribers totalled £37,610', and it noted in particular

Londonderry's earlier gift of the Castlereagh Aged Miners' Homes, at a cost of £6,000, his handing over £1,693 for maintenance and his granting 'the inmates free coal for all time'.[113] On 3 March 1928, Londonderry presented prizes at the final of the Durham, Westmoreland and Cumberland Mines Inspection District Ambulance League, a competition made up of sixty teams of volunteers trained to rescue injured and trapped miners.[114] Several months later, on 18 June, he held a ceremony at his new colliery at Seaham Harbour to celebrate reaching the bottom of the Vane shaft, informing the gathered miners that

> he was told by numbers of people that he was engaged on what they almost called a foolish venture at the present time, but he was determined to take the risk, because he felt it his duty, if he had the opportunity, to develop industry . . . not only for the benefit of himself and his family, but to increase the wealth and prosperity of the district and the country, which was of far greater importance.[115]

On 13 September he reversed a decision to terminate the employment of 2,700 men and boys at his loss-making colliery at Seaham. The oldest pit operated by the Londonderry Collieries, it was inevitably more expensive to maintain than the newer pit at Seaham Harbour, and it had for some time only operated one or two days a week. Londonderry's original notice of termination came as a devastating blow to the 7,000 residents of New Seaham, who depended almost entirely on the colliery. It was after meeting with a deputation representing the miners on 11 September that Londonderry agreed to keep the pit open for a further period.[116]

That decision in the autumn of 1928, and the method of arriving at it, put into practice a recent initiative in industrial co-operation that came to be known as the Mond–Turner talks, named after the industrialist and colliery owner, Alfred Mond, and the TUC's chairman, Ben Turner. Mond chose thirty-nine leading industrialists to participate alongside him, selected not as representatives of their industries or employers' associations, but for their progressive outlook. As noted above, Mond had worked with Londonderry during the general strike and he now sought to do so again.[117] In spite of his hostile rhetoric about Cook and the MFGB, Londonderry had remained open to important elements of the Samuel commission's report, including the principle of amalgamations – when these advantaged owners, miners and consumers – and its proposal for an element of co-operation in the retailing of coal.[118] When news of the initiative emerged in December 1927, Londonderry informed Conservatives at Dawdon that 'He thought they owed Sir Alfred a deep debt of gratitude for rendering possible a meeting between employers and employed and tribute should be paid to the leaders of the Trades Union Congress for the manner in which they had accepted the invitation.'[119] In an understandable if selective reading of his record in the period since 1926, Londonderry now sought to project the image of himself as an established and consistent advocate of industrial peace.[120] In doing so he was unwittingly assisted by Cook's persistent hostility to the Mond–Turner talks which he derided as 'Mond moonshine'.[121]

Londonderry was present for the first meeting of the talks at Burlington House, Mayfair, on 12 January 1928. He was then selected as one of Mond's seven-man subcommittee charged with carrying on detailed discussions with the TUC's subcommittee. The two subcommittees met throughout the spring and summer, preparing an interim report that was agreed on 4 July.[122] Londonderry's warmth towards the men sitting across the table was obvious from his public statements. 'It was comparatively easy for employers to consent to this discussion', he informed the Industrial Co-partnership Association in March, 'but all would agree that the TUC had had a more difficult task. He was willing and anxious to pay a great tribute to the leaders of the TUC for having come so willingly and showing themselves anxious to arrive at some satisfactory conclusion with the employers'.[123] Addressing Conservatives at Durham on 13 May, he referred to his being 'engaged with conferences with leaders of the TUC and whenever those meetings came round he welcomed them more and more'. It was 'no use sweating workmen and calling upon them to work long hours for low wages', he informed the same meeting, 'for the simple reason that when the human element was destroyed discontent was created in industry'.[124] In a speech to Conservatives at Kendal on 16 June, he described the Mond–Turner talks as an attempt 'to devise a means of establishing complete harmony in relations between capital and labour'. He reflected that 'While in the last century this country had the foremost place in commercial prosperity, it had lagged behind in humanitarian principles, on which every nation should base its activities.'[125] Two days later, he assured a gathering of employees at his new colliery at Seaham Harbour 'that the employers were beginning to see that cooperation was the real factor which was desired'.[126] Addressing a garden fete at Bishop Auckland on 4 July, he looked forward to the publication of the interim report, which, he assured his audience, 'would do much to bring about a spirit of conciliation and cooperation' through the establishment of a National Industrial Council consisting of representatives of the TUC and the Federation of Employers.[127] The resulting report recommended recognition of the trade unions as the most effective and appropriate representatives of the workers, it called for the rationalization of industries, it opposed the 'victimization' of trade unionists and, as Londonderry highlighted before its publication, it devised permanent machinery for industrial co-operation. The TUC was easily able to see off Cook's opposition to the report. However, the emphatic hostility of many employers and their representative organizations proved to be much harder to overcome, as they sought to resist any perceived attempts to restrain or direct their business practices, including relations with their workforces.

Regardless of this outcome, the Mond–Turner talks had done much to boost Londonderry's reputation. On 17 October, at a time when employer hostility to the interim report was beyond doubt, it was announced that Londonderry had been appointed to the cabinet as First Commissioner of Works.[128] The *Aberdeen Journal*'s editorial speculated that his appointment, 'instead of one of the younger members of the Unionist Party', and the 'decision that the post should carry Cabinet rank, is a very emphatic commentary on the intellectual gifts of the new Minister'. 'Because of the man Mr Baldwin had chosen', it went on, 'the inference seemed obvious . . . The post of First Commissioner of Works is not a very onerous one . . . Since Lord Londonderry takes such a deep interest in the campaign for industrial co-operation . . . it is taken for granted that Mr Baldwin in this selection had a very definite purpose'.[129] Notwithstanding the newspaper's speculation, the appointment actually obliged

Londonderry to withdraw from the Mond–Turner process that continued after the report's publication. Speaking at Darlington shortly afterwards, he again spoke warmly of the TUC and described the report as an attempt 'to create a new spirit throughout the country . . . so that they might in future be saved from those disastrous deadlocks which had hampered their activities, not only in this country, but in the competition with the rest of the world'.[130]

Even after his appointment to the cabinet, Londonderry still had to contend with his pits and the men who worked them, and at a time when the great depression continued to hinder the full recovery of coal exports.[131] On 26 November he presided over a public dinner to celebrate the centenary of the construction of Seaham Harbour's dock. The celebration occurred just two months after Londonderry had issued then reversed notices of termination at the oldest of his three pits, Seaham, so it is not entirely surprising that he only referred to the new pit at Seaham Harbour when claiming that he was an 'incorrigible optimist' about the future.[132] In a follow-up article on Seaham's history, published in *The Times*, Londonderry also gave a positive assessment of his colliery at Dawdon, which he claimed 'has been developed to a remarkable degree of perfection, and now gives employment to 3,700 men and boys' with an output of 4,000 tonnes a day.[133] Within six months, however, Dawdon became the scene of a major dispute between managers and miners following the decision of the former to reduce piece work rates. As noted above, the resulting stand-off resulted in a lock out that lasted fifteen weeks.

In contrast to his handling of Seaham the previous September, Londonderry declined to meet with a deputation of the miners at Dawdon. 'I am quite conversant with the terms offered to you', he informed them, 'which are fair and reasonable, and, as you must be aware, will merely bring the colliery more into line with the customs and conditions prevailing in other collieries in the county'.[134] Londonderry had previously enjoyed relatively cordial relations with his employees at Dawdon, attending social functions at its working men's club on a number of occasions.[135] But far from repudiating the spirit of Mond–Turner, his stance on this occasion was effectively endorsed by the Durham Miners' Association, which itself had declined to support the Dawdon miners. Seizing the opportunity, the Communist Party of Great Britain took a greater role in the dispute and ensured its escalation.[136] On learning that the prime minister was to receive a deputation from the MFGB, the First Commissioner of Works wrote to him on 5 March to explain the situation at Dawdon,

> the best pit in the North of England and because I have asked the miners to accept the rates of pay which are the custom throughout the whole country, the pit in consequence is idle. I should like to point out that the notices were given over a fortnight ago but the men have kept on postponing their meeting and now, when the notices have expired, I receive a letter saying that they want to have an interview with me.

But rather than blame the Communists, he attributed responsibility to the MFGB, 'the moment the Federation representatives come in, there is always trouble because it is the main policy of the Federation to misrepresent the Owners'.[137] Baldwin was already aware of his cabinet colleague's sensitivity about the reputation of his collieries; the publicity generated by the Prince of Wales's recent visit to pit villages in Northumberland and County Durham had provoked the First Commissioner of Works to complain to the prime minister about the future king's reference to 'appalling conditions'.[138]

Apathy among Conservative supporters ahead of the general election, eventually called for 30 May 1929, along with Londonderry's dual role as a government minister and colliery owner, saw his public statements on the labour movement return to the dualism – commending the TUC's moderation and attacking the Labour party and MFGB's extremism – that had characterized his interventions before joining the Mond–Turner talks. On hearing that both the leader of the Labour party, MacDonald, and the leader of the Communist Party, Harry Pollitt, intended to stand in the Seaham constituency, Londonderry quipped to a meeting of Seaham Conservatives that 'On a great many issues, I believe, they see eye to eye, but it is characteristic of our opponents that they are always quarrelling'.[139] On 25 March, he responded in the House of Lords to criticisms of the government's unemployment policy by remarking that 'a great deal of the unemployment which now exists was due to the general strike of 1926'.[140] At an election meeting at Putney on 7 May, he contended that 'the Socialist Party was not a national party; it was a party of the trade unions. If Mr MacDonald was returned to power they would find the country governed by the executives of the trade unions. The Socialist Party was a party governed by extremists'. Yet, in the same speech, he also acknowledged that 'influences on both sides' still sought industrial peace, and that it was the Communist Party that stood opposed, and even here he admitted that 'their voices did not carry the influence they did a few years ago'.[141] He subsequently wrote to MacDonald, following the latter's election as the MP for Seaham, on how Communist activity at Dawdon had 'reduced a splendid colliery. My family have done every single thing we have been able to do, but this class propaganda has beaten us'.[142] In an address to Seaham Conservatives on 21 October, Londonderry complained that the MFGB's leaders were responsible for 'nine-tenths of the difficulties [that] the coal trade is labouring under at the present moment', and he attributed the recent problems at Dawdon to 'the example of Mr Cook . . . who spreads his revolution in our midst . . . And here we are, after this dispute, not one iota better'. At the same time, he also effectively endorsed efforts by MacDonald's second Labour government to facilitate negotiations between representatives of the coal owners and the miners, and he held out the hope that 'if we can work in a spirit of cooperation these difficulties which we have experienced recently will be a thing of the past never to return'.[143] Similarly, in an address the following month to Sunderland's Chamber of Commerce, he outlined 'three new elements which appeared to . . . hamper the development of prosperity in industry. The first was the attitude of extremist Labour; the second the interference of the Government in trade concerns; and the third the excessive taxation imposed on them'. But he went on to remark that 'it was encouraging to see the support given to the movement for cooperation by the Trades Union Congress', and he looked forward to the outcome of negotiations carried on between the government, trade unions and coal owners. He now recognized more explicitly that Cook dissented from the course taken by the TUC, and although he continued to insist that the MFGB's general secretary 'was responsible for the present difficulties', he was just as clear about the other cause, the 'world-wide factors which it was their duty to meet as best they could'.[144]

The outcome of the government's negotiations with owners and miners was the Coal Mines bill that was introduced to parliament in 1929 and passed the following year. In many respects it was a bill that was in keeping with Mond–Turner and broadly favourable to the owners; a reflection of the fact that when Labour was in power, government influence on industrial relations remained relatively weak, with even the trade unions desiring the formal neutrality of the state.[145] The bill, as such, did not compel amalgamations but facilitated them, and mineral rights were left untouched. The working day would be reduced from 8 hours but only by a mere 30 minutes. It also made provisions to set prices and production quotas for the home market. Having long deprecated government interference, the failure of price cuts to deal with declining consumption convinced the majority of owners to support these measures.[146]

It is perhaps surprising then that Londonderry, contrary to what he had said at Sunderland, and in contrast to his earlier involvement in the Mond–Turner talks, was greatly troubled by the legislation. Political opportunism cannot be discounted; the minority Labour government had experienced considerable difficulty with the bill in the House of Commons, through its efforts to secure Liberal support, which made it easier to pick apart and question the coherence of the resulting legislation.[147] Early on, Londonderry signalled that 'he deprecated strongly any Government interference'.[148] Speaking at Seaham Harbour Conservative Club on 5 January 1930, he described the measure as 'a very bad Bill indeed'. Like other Conservative critics, he argued that it would increase the price of coal to the consumer. What was required was 'an abundance' of the 'cheapest possible fuel', though he acknowledged that industries which were 'sheltered' from foreign competition could pay more.[149] He again rounded on the bill when addressing a meeting of Conservatives at Penarth, near Cardiff, on 27 March. The reduction in the working day meant a reduction in wages, 'It was necessary that the industry should make both ends meet.' Amalgamations should not be compelled, he went on, and quotas 'implied a reduction of production, and that necessarily, in his judgement, meant an increase in the price of coal'. It might be assumed that Londonderry, like other coal exporters in County Durham, would object to the bill's provisions for marketing coal.[150] Yet, in contrast to his misgivings about most of the legislation's important provisions, he referred to its proposed selling schemes as the 'one bright spot in the Bill'.[151] He justified this with reference to the recent tendency of export districts to turn to the domestic market. This had resulted in increased competition and reduced prices for consumers, the latter giving rise to unwelcome consequences for both the owners' profits and miners' wages.[152] 'At the present stage of industry cutthroat competition among themselves was not calculated to operate in their interests or in the interest of the community, and he felt that a marketing association would give them an economic price for their coal.'[153]

Having previously consulted with his party leader in the House of Lords, Lord Salisbury, Londonderry indicated that he would not oppose the legislation when it was debated on the floor of that chamber in April.[154] He still referred to it as 'a stepping-stone' towards nationalization, and he claimed that while he was not opposed to all the proposals in the bill, he was opposed to their being enacted in statute. But as most senior Conservatives recognized, rejecting the bill, or passing an amendment that rejected one of its fundamental purposes, or passing a number of amendments that amounted to a rejection, all risked a confrontation between the unelected peers and the House of Commons. It would, as Londonderry conceded, create 'chaos and confusion'.[155] In May and June, when the bill reached its committee stage in the House of Lords, Londonderry's contributions effectively deferred to Salisbury and Mond – now first Baron Melchett – who took the lead in advancing amendments that were broadly in keeping with the legislation, albeit with the purpose of limiting or eliminating any risk of compulsion on the coal owners.[156] The effectiveness of the Coal Mines Act 1930 has been the subject of scholarly debate.[157] The self-assurance with which Londonderry addressed a gathering of the Institute of Fuel later in the year, on how he was 'an optimist', his pride in the pit that he had sunk at Seaham Harbour – 'it was going to be the greatest success in the world' – and his confidence that 'notwithstanding all the devices which individuals endeavoured to put into practice, they would always find that economic laws would come through in the end', all suggest that he regarded the legislation as largely innocuous to his perceived self-interest.[158]

Londonderry's confidence on that occasion might also have been bolstered by developments at Dawdon Colliery. The Communist Party had since the previous year's lockout retained its significant influence in the local lodge of the Durham Miners' Association, but it had failed to gain the local hegemony that it had achieved in certain South Wales pit villages.[159] In February 1930 Londonderry publicized in the press what he described as the Dawdon lodge's 'victimization' of William Wharton, a miner. Wharton had during the lockout obtained work elsewhere and returned to Dawdon at its conclusion, only to find that he was put under 'undesirable pressure' to vacate his house.[160] In a separate development, it was reported five months later that Londonderry had won an arbitration dispute arising from the lockout. Awarded £535 in back money, he agreed to accept £100 and donated it to the Dawdon Aged Miners' Homes.[161] If these incidents suggest that he remained adversarial in his approach to the situation at Dawdon, his private appeal to the prime minister paints a more complex picture. In a letter that enclosed a copy of the *Lamp*, the Dawdon Communists' newssheet, he highlighted that the publication attacked not only him but also local officials of the Durham Miners' Association, and that as a result, 'I do feel that in opposition to Communism and everything else that this newspaper stands for, the Dawdon Lodge, yourself and myself, must be at one.' He also informed MacDonald that he and Lord Castlereagh had recently met with the executive of the Dawdon lodge, at which they had 'a very interesting and amicable conversation . . . and whilst I was able to do something for them, I found myself compelled to refuse some of the requests which they made'.

> I am wondering if there is any possibility of our working together publicly as well as we seem to be able to work together privately, because I feel very strongly that as time goes on, if the management and the executive of the Lodge are continually at logger heads, that we shall entrench the Communists in a far stronger position than they are in at the present moment. Whenever you go to Seaham in the near future, I wonder if you would have a talk to your friends on these lines. I do not

> know if you are aware of it, but the Urban District Council is the Dawdon Lodge, and the Dawdon Lodge is the Urban District Council, and the result is that all sorts of jobs are being found for the friends of one or the other.[162]

The two men's common disposition to oppose the local activities and influence of Communists, along with the close friendship established between Lady Londonderry and MacDonald (see below), meant that the request was entirely plausible. These important considerations aside, party politics could still divide Seaham's MP and the local colliery owner. On 3 January 1931 Londonderry delivered a highly partisan speech to the Seaham Harbour Conservative Association, in which he spoke at length on why the Labour party was 'unfit to govern'. Among his list of reasons, he revisited his earlier accusations by claiming that the party 'is dominated by militant political members of the trade unions'.[163] Days later, MacDonald also spoke at Seaham Harbour and referred pointedly to Londonderry's speech to question the fitness of colliery owners to run their industry. 'I am sorry', the prime minister was reported as saying, 'he is not disappointed with us as much as I am disappointed with him'.[164]

If this was the knock about of party politics, then the run up to the general election held later in the year, on 27 October, could not have been more different. Now fronting up both the National Labour party and a coalition government that included the National Liberals and Conservatives, MacDonald endured a torrid time campaigning in his Seaham constituency. The practical help that he received from local Conservatives, including Londonderry, only inflamed the anger of Labour supporters.[165] Little wonder, then, that 'One of the questions most frequently asked Mr MacDonald at his meetings', *The Times* reported,

> is why a post in the [Emergency National] Government was given to Lord Londonderry who has mining interests in the constituency. Mr MacDonald's answer to the question is that he is not responsible for the individual Conservative and Liberal representatives in the Government. He allotted the number of seats to each party, but the individuals to fill them were selected by the respective leaders.[166]

Londonderry took this response badly, which required the prime minister to reassure him that he had not meant to repudiate him, and that another remark by him on the campaign trail, about hauling Londonderry 'over the coals', was merely his attempt at humour.[167] Ever sensitive to perceived slights by ministerial colleagues, Londonderry appears to have overlooked MacDonald's real purpose in attributing responsibility for his appointment to ministerial office to Baldwin: to reject the widespread criticism that it was a consequence of Lady Londonderry's close friendship with the prime minister.

III

It has already been noted that wealthy territorial magnates could still claim an office in the gift of the state, and although the incidences of this had been diminishing from the 1880s, it remained a feature of British public life during the first half of the twentieth century. There was, of course, a serious qualitative decline in what they could receive. While many titled aristocrats could easily claim a deputy lieutenancy in their county, far fewer could ever hope to enter the government, let alone the cabinet. But even here their decline was far from sudden. When Londonderry's father had entered Salisbury's second government in 1886, he was one of ten aristocrats in a cabinet of fifteen men. In Balfour's cabinet he was one of nine in a cabinet of nineteen men. When Bonar Law asked the seventh marquess to join his government in 1922, half of his sixteen-man cabinet hailed from the aristocracy. And when Baldwin formed a cabinet of twenty-one in 1924, it included nine aristocrats. But it was not so much the existence of Londonderry's claim on office in the late 1920s and early 1930s that aroused criticism, as the way that it appeared in the eyes of many to have manifested itself. At a time when aristocrat-politicians had largely abandoned the more overt and extravagant methods of gaining political patronage, the Londonderrys continued as if nothing had changed.[168] '[W]hy cannot these foolish people behave like ordinary citizens', Headlam confided to his diary in 1927, 'and not ape at being Royalty'.[169]

Commenting on Lady Londonderry's role as a leading political hostess, Diane Urquhart observes that 'whilst some aristocrats entered a post-war retreat, the Londonderrys dug in'.[170] In 1935, the MP and socialite Henry Channon noted in his diary that Lady Londonderry was 'the only political hostess left'.[171] Two years later *The Times* observed that 'Londonderry House has carried on well into the twentieth century the tradition of the great political houses of the Victorian age. It now stands almost alone.'[172] Writing in the 1950s, Robert Vansittart recalled that Londonderry House was 'the last great house in London'.[173] In 1936, Baldwin informed Lord Castlereagh that his parents had played 'politics in the old style. They proceeded to entertain politically on a vast scale with of course the set purpose of political advancement'. After reciting the well-known quotation from Birkenhead that opens this chapter, Baldwin went on to inform Castlereagh that it 'was very magnificent and beautifully done but to me it was out of date and at times in dubious taste. It did not fit in with my idea of Tory democracy. Central Office of course loved it. These methods were not calculated to make your Father popular with his colleagues'.[174]

When Lord Londonderry inherited his father's title and property in 1915, his wife also inherited the role of leading political hostess that her mother-in-law had cultivated from the 1880s.[175] It meant carrying on the tradition of holding grand receptions at Londonderry House, with its army of servants, reputedly including twenty-eight in the kitchen and sixteen in the stewards' room.[176] It also meant hosting royalty, British and foreign, such as the dinner given to George V and Queen Mary in March 1927.[177] Edith's assumption of the role nevertheless led to some innovations. Shortly before her death, Theresa regretted that the new marquess and marchioness 'do not mix with the servants as we used to'.[178] More consequentially for the Londonderrys' political influence, Edith distinguished herself from previous form in two other notable ways. First, in addition to the formal receptions held for the Conservative party, including the famous eve of parliament reception, Londonderry House hosted evening parties of the type that characterized 1920s London, with live music and guest lists that included politicians, ambassadors, writers and artists. Second, Edith formed a dining club in 1915 which she called the Ark, with an exclusive but varied membership of leading figures from politics, society and the arts. This divergence from previous socializing was an adaptation to changing times with the purpose of ensuring continuity, but, as Ross McKibbin highlights, it also hastened the 'Americanization' of London society, a process that Lady Londonderry later lamented but by her own actions had encouraged.[179]

The Ark was outwardly superficial, its Wednesday suppers at Londonderry House often involving frivolity and general entertainment.[180] Members of the Ark – around 200 in the two decades of its existence – were given pet names: Lady Londonderry was 'Circe the Sorceress', her husband, 'Charley the Cheetah'.[181] But the Ark also allowed the Londonderrys to have a more intimate relationship with leading political figures and members of the royal family. The Ark's members included Churchill, Lord Halifax, Samuel Hoare, Edward Carson, Arthur Balfour, Harold Macmillan, Stanley Baldwin and Neville Chamberlain. The more artistic of its members reflected the Londonderrys' familial connections to Ireland and Scotland, with the likes of Sir William Orpen, Sean O'Casey, Sir John Lavery, St John Gogarty, George Bernard Shaw, John Buchan and W. B. Yeats gracing the Ark's gatherings at Londonderry House.[182]

The Ark also included Ramsay MacDonald, who as 'Hamish the Hart' became a member in 1929 after being appointed prime minister for the second time. Although correspondence between Lady Londonderry and MacDonald had lapsed by the time that the latter had left office at the end of 1924, it was rejuvenated again in 1926 just after Lord Londonderry's departure from the government of Northern Ireland.[183] The friendship became even more intense and controversial when MacDonald succeeded Webb as the MP for Seaham in 1929, followed soon after by his return to Downing Street. As a result, the spotlight intensified on the Londonderrys' social activities. Gossip columnists made frequent reference to Lady Londonderry and MacDonald, and Labour MPs expressed unease about the high society company that their leader was keeping.[184] The relationship was even fictionalized by Howard Spring in his 1940 political novel, *Fame is the Spur*, the satirical account of a MacDonald-like Labour politician who befriends a 'Lady Lostwithiel', the wife of a wealthy mine owner. It was later released in 1947 as a motion picture starring Michael Redgrave and Rosamund John, and in 1982 it was broadcast as a television series on the BBC.[185] When in August 1931 MacDonald broke with the majority of his Labour party colleagues by agreeing to head a Conservative-dominated emergency National Government, his relationship with the Londonderrys inevitably came into sharper relief. Not only was a place found for Lord Londonderry in the emergency administration, but he was promoted to the cabinet three months later. Beatrice Webb, whose husband preceded MacDonald as the MP for Seaham, declared to the Women' Section of the Seaham Labour party that 'Evil communications corrupt good manners'.[186] Even Headlam noted in his diary that Lady Londonderry had been playing her cards well.[187]

Feeling angry and betrayed, it is hardly surprising that Labour critics rounded on MacDonald's relationship with Lady Londonderry and her husband's return to office as symptomatic of his treachery. The grand receptions held thereafter at Londonderry House cemented the link in people's minds, particularly the image of MacDonald in full evening dress standing atop its grand staircase alongside a diamond bedecked Lady Londonderry, greeting the guests as they arrived.[188] As such, few considered

Lord Londonderry's previous ministerial experience, or the appointment of five other aristocrats to the cabinet, or that he had been appointed to Baldwin's wholly Conservative government in 1928. The two ministerial appointments in 1931 just seemed less justifiable than previous appointments, even though the essence of the criticism was nothing new. Little wonder that Londonderry privately regretted his wife's eagerness to advance his career, though the utility of her methods is likely to have meant that he hid any such frustration to all but his close confidante, Lady Desborough.[189]

Throughout the 1920s popular daily newspapers were keen to give their readers news of the social activities of London's bright young things. The decadence and frivolity of the interwar period captured the public imagination, but not always in a flattering light.[190] The upper classes were often portrayed as grotesquely extravagant at a time when the country struggled economically, especially during the great depression. On 30 December 1930, Headlam referred to Lady Londonderry as 'that wretched woman . . . she really is about the silliest and most conceited donkey that ever lived. She is a perfectly valueless person politically . . . except that she is only too willing to entertain the Party in London'.[191] He was somewhat less hostile three years later, when he found himself invited to Londonderry House by Castlereagh, and there introduced to the prime minister and other leading figures of the day.[192] The presence

Figure 7 Lady Helen Vane-Tempest-Stewart, Lady Londonderry, and Lady Margaret Vane-Tempest-Stewart, 1927.

of Headlam and senior politicians on this occasion is a reminder that whatever its detractors said, Londonderry House remained popular among its exclusive set well into the 1930s. This did not mean that Lord Londonderry was ignorant of the criticism. As he admitted to Baldwin on 11 October 1930, 'I am always glad to give the party, as you know, if it is necessary . . . My difficulty is . . . when the newspapers write us up as the perpetrators of Bacchanalian orgies.' In 1936, again to Baldwin, Londonderry referred to the 'traditional eve of parliament reception' as 'expensive and not much fun but does a lot of good'.[193] Consciously or otherwise, he was keen to present these occasions as fulfilling the requests of others. 'I hope Neville [Chamberlain] is right when he thinks these parties do a great deal of good', he informed Baldwin in October 1930. 'We get the smug-faced citizens of London with their wives and daughters who vote Conservative anyway. I always wish that we could touch the other strata where the bulk of the votes lie: but please rest assured that we are always delighted to do anything that gives you the smallest assistance.'[194] His own post hoc reservations aside, Baldwin was a frequent guest at Londonderry House, and he readily conceded the usefulness of its social functions to the Conservative party, both in satisfying its hierarchy and also in helping to replenish its coffers through the aristocratic embrace of wealthy businessmen and other potential donors.[195] It was perhaps to address their critics, and to 'touch the other strata', that the owners of Londonderry House also attempted to host more worthy events, such as the reception in May 1935 for the 'largest conference of probation officers so far held in this country', which was attended by 500 guests.[196]

Lady Londonderry later wrote that the 'Upper Class' that had emerged from the First World War had effectively encouraged the press 'limelight on their doings', something that she described as an 'American importation'.[197] And it is not hard to see how newspaper reports of these occasions made the Londonderrys appear extravagant and associated them with the vacuous social world captured by Evelyn Waugh in his 1930 novel, *Vile Bodies*. Indeed, attentive readers might perhaps have associated the Londonderrys with the characters of Lord and Lady Anchorage of Anchorage House.[198] Lord Londonderry's unease intensified after his appointment to the National Government in August 1931. By January 1932 he had had enough and wrote to the proprietor of the *Daily Express*, Lord Beaverbrook, to explain how reports of lavish functions at Londonderry House showed little consideration for his employees and friends in County Durham and Northern Ireland. He had been obliged to cut back on socializing at his provincial bases, he informed the press baron, but he could not avoid the duties expected of him at London. Beaverbrook was unimpressed and replied with the tongue-in-cheek suggestion that Londonderry's lavish spending was an ideal cure for the ailing economy. He in return accused Beaverbrook of espionage.[199] Before denying the charge, Beaverbrook contributed a leader to the *Sunday Express* on 10 January 1932 in which he defended lavish spending on entertainments.[200] When Londonderry demanded to know why no society reports on Beaverbrook were printed, he received a curt reply: 'I am not in Society. I spring from the working classes and belong to them. I don't go to parties. I never dine outside my own house or go to restaurants.'[201] With this Londonderry ended their correspondence, at least for the time being, effectively passing to his wife the responsibility for taking issue with coverage in the Beaverbrook press.[202] Given the intensity of the clash, it is noteworthy that two years later Beaverbrook accepted an invitation to attend the eve of parliament reception held at Londonderry House. A contemporary press report conjures something of the spectacle of these occasions:

> Jack Harris's band played. The hall and staircases were decorated with yucca flowers and foliage, berries, and pampas grass, and the rooms were massed with shaded chrysanthemums and mixed roses, all sent over from Mount Stewart.
>
> The Marchioness of Londonderry, who received her guests at the head of the double staircase, wore a gown of black paillettes trimmed with drapery of black pleated georgette and a cluster of multicoloured flowers at the shoulders. She had a diamond tiara and wore diamond ornaments.[203]

A more intimate account is found in Headlam's diary. 'The crush at Londonderry House was bigger than ever', he recorded on 20 November 1933.

> I saw a lot of people and Robin [Castlereagh] was very civil to me – he invited me to 'the private bar' at the end of the proceedings and I found myself among the select few – a curiously assorted party including the Baldwins, the Hailshams, the Readings, some of Charley's lady friends, the Macmillans, some foreigners, the family [Vane-Tempest-]Stewart, and a few others.[204]

It was no oversight that Londonderry did not mention his provincial base in Wales when complaining to Beaverbrook. He had inherited the 10,000-acre estate from his uncle, Lord Herbert Vane-Tempest, following the latter's death in the Abermule train collision of January 1921, in which sixteen others were also killed. Nine years later Londonderry set about disposing of 5,500 acres through the sale of thirty-four farms. There was some opposition to the sale among the tenantry.[205] He attempted to address the concerns raised with the assurance that he would not sell his family's residence, Plâs Machynlleth, and he granted the existing tenants the first offer on their farms.[206] Yet, Londonderry's connection to the area, never particularly strong, inevitably became attenuated in subsequent years and was completely severed following the Second World War. His relationship with Welsh life would be undermined in another significant way too. Londonderry offered Plâs Machynlleth for the 1937 National Eisteddfod and was duly appointed one of its presidents along with Churchill. But he decided to resign his presidency in February 1937, following the resignation of eight eisteddfod adjudicators in protest against 'too much English'. The preceding months had witnessed growing controversy in Wales over the trial of three Plaid Cymru members implicated in the burning of a RAF school at Pen-y-Berth, on the Llyn Peninsula. It is likely that Londonderry's recent tenure at the helm of the Air Ministry made his presidency of the forthcoming eisteddfod at Machynlleth even less welcome in certain quarters.[207] His public reply mentioned only that his appointment had 'not met with universal approval in Wales', but he pointedly referred to his 'purely Welsh' grandmother and his pride in his Welsh descent. As 'one who honours and reveres the Eisteddfod', he did not want to 'be the cause of creating a breach, however small, in the traditional harmony which has always attended and should attend these historical gatherings'.[208]

IV

It was Birkenhead's resignation from the cabinet in 1928 that provided the first opportunity for Londonderry to enter Baldwin's second government, following a reshuffle that left a vacancy at the Office of Works. According to Headlam, the prime minister had no choice: 'One can't use a man's hospitality and not give him a job if he wants it.'[209] Given such comments, it is noteworthy that Baldwin appeared to court further criticism by choosing to visit Londonderry House when making the formal offer of the Office of Works to its owner, rather than summon him to Downing Street.[210]

In fact, the decision to appoint Londonderry to the government owed much to Churchill, who had assured him in 1927 that his party conference speech would serve him well.[211] The new First Commissioner, however, was under the impression that he owed his gratitude to the prime minister of Northern Ireland, James Craig, now first Viscount Craigavon.[212] The mistake probably arose from the fact that Churchill and Londonderry had just emerged from a tense period in their relationship. In March 1926, when Londonderry conferred an honorary degree on Churchill at Queen's University, all had seemed well between the two.[213] However, by the end of the year, as noted above, the miners' strike created tensions between them that lasted well into the following year. In August 1927, Londonderry complained to the Chancellor of the Exchequer about increases in company tax. Churchill denied that he had done this and asked bluntly that his friends do not write to him on public issues unless they had suggestions of their own.[214] When Londonderry replied that his cousin was being 'unfriendly', Churchill accused him of giving him 'a lecture on my public misdeeds and short comings'. He went on:

> Then you say in effect 'aren't we friends after all'? Of course we are; but it is not part of friendship to neglect to reply to criticism. I take criticism in good heart, but not if I am to be gagged. Even in the House of Commons I am allowed to reply and if any member had used your tone of arguments to me there I should have tried to answer them suitably. But that would have had nothing to do with personal relations.[215]

Within a few months familial bonds were revitalized and their relationship improved, and, as noted above, Churchill praised Londonderry's contribution to the 1927 Conservative party conference and offered the assurance that it would serve him well. The following year Londonderry joined his cousin around the cabinet table.

Londonderry's re-entry to the government was marked in ceremonial style when the new First Commissioner was allowed to carry the Cap of Maintenance at the opening of parliament in November 1928.[216] Otherwise, it was difficult for Londonderry to do anything remarkable during his first period at the Office of Works. Not only because it lasted just under nine months, but also because the department dealt mainly with the mundane task of maintaining government buildings at home and abroad.[217] As his ministerial post aroused almost no controversy and yet still provided him with a seat in the cabinet, Londonderry enjoyed his time as First Commissioner. If he did little of note, several decisions that he took in office are worthy of record. In February 1929 he refused to support a proposal to create national parks through the transfer of Forestry commission land to the Office of Works, arguing that the costs involved did not justify it.[218] It was Londonderry who approved the statue in Whitehall of Field Marshal the Earl Haig. It had been criticized on ascetic grounds by Lady Haig, and on moral grounds by the king, who desired that its site be moved further away from the cenotaph.[219]

If Londonderry's portfolio was not of itself demanding, then as one of six peers in the cabinet he found himself representing the government on a wide range of matters in the House of Lords, from unemployment to electricity supply. He played a small part in curtailing the first Viscount Cecil of Chelwood's attempt to introduce a bill that would have established tests for both motor car drivers and their vehicles.[220] Despite the rising number of road fatalities and injuries, the road lobby's resistance to such measures was readily supported by government ministers. It is perhaps no coincidence that Londonderry, in keeping with the typically upper- and middle-class profile of most offenders, had been convicted of speeding in 1920.[221]

It was as First Commissioner that Londonderry presided over the North of England Education Conference when it met at Newcastle in January 1929. His local connection, and his previous tenure as Northern Ireland's Minister of Education, made it an obvious if largely ornamental appointment, but Londonderry used the opportunity of his presidential address to focus on the necessity of encouraging the fullest participation of children in education 'in the midst of industrial depression and trade gloom'. He went as far as calling for it to continue beyond the period of compulsory attendance at the age of fourteen: 'Central, secondary, and technical schools must be kept running at full pressure.' He warned that the 'temptation was especially strong just now for parents to snatch at the earliest chance of employment that presented itself to their children. Nothing could be more fatal to this country than that we should lose ground as an educated people under the stress of industrial and trade depression'. He believed that it 'was largely with the masters of industry that the eventual success of our educational system would lie. Into their hands would pass the vast majority of the children from the public elementary schools, and he appealed to them to assist the nation generally and the local education authorities in particular'. The teaching of science, he highlighted, was important because modern production processes

> necessitated a greater use of the intelligence of the worker and smaller demand upon him for actual manual dexterity. . . . The so-called machine-minder of to-day had under his charge engines and tools of the most delicate and intricate nature and of enormous cost. It was more than ever necessary to-day that the worker should proceed not by rule of thumb but by rule of reason.[222]

Notwithstanding his remarks at Newcastle, Londonderry subsequently opposed a Labour bill that would have raised the school-leaving age to 15. 'I feel in the circumstances in which we find ourselves at the present moment', he informed the House of Lords on 18 February 1931,

> that by establishing a rigid system of education up to fifteen you are going to waste a certain sum of money on an enormous number of children who would

> derive far more benefit by being released at the age of fourteen, and brought into education in conjunction with industry and also with the technical classes and night schools by which a combination of useful education can be inculcated in these children.[223]

There is a measure of consistency between these remarks and his speech at Newcastle two years previously, but his stance on this occasion was at root partisan, part of a Conservative attack on the bill that utilized the party's majority in the upper house to inflict a defeat on MacDonald's second Labour government.

The Conservatives' relatively brief spell in opposition during that period arose out of the May 1929 general election. Baldwin's policy of moderation had for some time caused unease in the party and fears in certain quarters that he was pushing through semi-socialist measures.[224] As noted above, Londonderry's efforts to address the resulting apathy among party members disposed him to attack Labour and trade unionism in a way that sat uneasily with his record in the Mond–Turner talks. The results of the general election revealed that the Conservatives polled around the same number of votes as they had in 1924, but that the Labour party went from around five and half million votes to almost eight and a half million, giving it 288 seats to the Conservatives' 260. The second Labour government, nevertheless, was like the first a minority administration, and no one expected it to last long, especially after the Wall Street Crash in the final week of October 1929.[225] Observing the now established convention when Conservatives sat as his majesty's loyal opposition, Londonderry was summoned by Baldwin as a member of the shadow cabinet.[226]

Consigned to the opposition benches, the deteriorating international economic situation led Conservatives to once again consider their position on tariff reform.[227] Baldwin did not want to repeat his defeat at the 1923 general election and so opposed those in the party who called on him to advocate imperial preference. Above all, he was concerned that Labour would use the scare of food taxes to take more seats from the Conservatives in the industrial north. However, with most countries opting to raise tariffs to meet the challenge of the great depression, Londonderry's cautious acquiescence in the policy before the First World War, following the lead of Balfour, became gradually more full-throated in response to the troubled economic climate of the 1920s, a modification that probably owed something to the troubled coal export trade. Addressing an 'Empire bazaar' at Sunderland in October 1923, in the lead-up to the general election of that year, Londonderry spoke of the need to reconsider 'proposals which from time to time had been put forward but which had been rejected because they appeared to infringe the traditional financial policy of this country'. In particular, 'the time had arrived when the Government, in conjunction with their colleagues from the Dominions, should inaugurate a policy which would remove the necessity of the "dole" and place the Empire in a position of commercial security'.[228] Six years later, he gave cautious support to Beaverbrook's increasingly popular campaign for tariff reform. On 16 December 1929, not long after Londonderry had arranged for Baldwin to stay at Mount Stewart, he offered his car for Beaverbrook's tour of County Durham, though he subsequently declined the press baron's invitation to join him on the campaign trail.[229] In February 1930 Beaverbrook moved his campaign up a gear by forming the Empire Crusade party. On the 14th of that month, Londonderry chaired a meeting of the UUC at Belfast at which Baldwin was the guest speaker. As the presiding officer, Londonderry used his opening remarks to welcome Baldwin's statement on the need for the liberal use of safeguarding – the targeted protection of struggling industries as opposed to general tariffs – delivered to a meeting the previous night. Londonderry then proceeded to outline the problems faced by the Irish linen industry in dealing with international competition. It appears that Baldwin avoided the implicit invitation to recommend that Irish linen be safeguarded and instead focused on the loyalty of Ulster to the empire.[230]

Like many Conservatives, Londonderry's attitude to Baldwin and Beaverbrook remained equivocal throughout 1930. At a meeting of the shadow cabinet on 3 March, he expressed his objection to doing any deals with Beaverbrook.[231] Yet, a few months later, on 16 July, Londonderry informed an audience at Rothbury, Northumberland, that the 'country owed a debt of gratitude to Lord Beaverbrook for bringing forward his great policy of Empire free trade, which must form the main plank in the Conservative platform'. But he took care to deny that 'there were two camps in the Conservative Party . . . There was only one', and he assured his audience that 'he was not prepared to go as far as Lord Beaverbrook and go to the country on the question of food taxes until he knew what business-like arrangement could be made for the mutual benefit of the country and the Dominions'.[232] He repeated these statements to Beaverbrook three days later, adding that he could not agree with him using his newspapers and 'crusade' to harm the Conservative party leadership.[233] By August Londonderry was further trimming his sails, informing an audience at the Ulster Reform Club, Belfast, that 'Empire Free Trade was an inspiring ideal which they hoped one day to attain, the sooner the better', but that safeguarding 'was a practical policy, gaining fresh supporters from all parties every day. He had no patience with any one, whoever he might be, who sought to create dissensions [*sic*] in their ranks on matters of pure detail. On great principles they were clearly and obviously united'.[234]

On 8 October, during the Imperial Conference at London, Baldwin took the wind out of Beaverbrook's sails by welcoming the offer of a reciprocity agreement from the Canadian prime minister, Richard Bennett. Londonderry, who hosted a reception for the conference at Londonderry House, was privately apprehensive about the success or otherwise of Baldwin's position, informing his party leader that safeguarding would be a mere palliative until an international trade agreement could be reached.[235] In public, however, he displayed no such doubts, informing Conservatives at Norwich that the 'great policy upon which the Conservative Party was desirous of educating the country was an extension of safeguarding which would enable them to place in healthy and remunerative work a great many of the unemployed. On the other side of their policy was Imperial preference, a policy with which he had always been associated'.[236] He later made a similar claim as a government minister, in February 1932, when he moved a bill on import duties, informing the House of Lords that he had always had 'little sympathy' with free trade; an untruth, but one that earned him the praise of the Scottish MP and writer, John Buchan.[237] In fact, like many politicians, it was political expediency that helped to determine his public position at any given time. Campaigning during the 1923 general election – the snap poll called by Baldwin on a platform of tariff reform

– he had claimed that 'I never was a protectionist and never was a free-trader'.[238] Yet, in February 1929, he informed an audience at Birmingham, of all places, that 'protection meant a tax on food and there was no party in the State that was prepared to tax the food of the people'.[239] His actual view on tariffs is clear in a letter that he later wrote to Leo Amery in June 1936:

> I remember at Londonderry House you said that neither my father nor I were thoroughly in accord with the policy which [Joseph Chamberlain] propounded and that of course, is quite true. I have always looked on Protection as an evil in itself but rendered absolutely necessary by events. I am quite convinced however that unless tariffs can be lowered all round, we shall have to make up our minds to a very bleak and unpromising future.[240]

At a crucial party meeting on 30 October 1930, Baldwin received the support of members for a free hand in trade negotiations with the dominions. Londonderry wrote afterwards to congratulate him on his 'victory'.[241] Like many others in the party Londonderry now felt that he could back Baldwin without equivocation. On 22 November he informed an audience at Gateshead that Baldwin's leadership was 'strong', though his appeal for Baldwin to have 'a free hand . . . in negotiations with the Dominions' suggested otherwise.[242] The final crisis on this issue for Baldwin occurred on 1 March 1931, when his shadow cabinet came close to asking him to resign. Within a fortnight however Baldwin had recaptured his party's support. In the intervening period, Londonderry wrote to Beaverbrook on 5 March to declare that the Conservatives were now united, and that their previous divisions had only helped the Labour party remain in office. On 8 March Beaverbrook disbanded his Empire Crusade party in the belief that Baldwin had given in to his demands. He wrote to Londonderry the following day to say that he had decided to back down as his campaign was destroying the only party that could deliver what he wanted.[243] After that there was only a transient reactivation of Empire Crusade in the spring of 1931 – attracting the covert support of many Conservatives including Londonderry – but for Baldwin's leadership the crisis had effectively ended.[244]

V

Londonderry's engagement with and attitude to the party crisis over tariff reform demonstrated his desire to re-enter a Conservative government. Out of office he had only part-time and ornamental roles to fulfil, as a lord lieutenant twice over, as a colliery owner, a director on the boards of Sun Life and the North East Railway Company and the chancellor of two universities, Belfast and Durham.[245] In January 1931 the king, acting on the advice of the prime minister of Canada, offered Londonderry the governor-generalship of that dominion.[246] For the third and final time, Londonderry declined it in the belief that he would be in the next Conservative government, visiting Buckingham Palace personally to deliver his refusal.[247]

It proved to be a sagacious decision. The increasingly dire state of the British and international economy had been fuelling divisions in the Labour government and its collapse seemed inevitable; yet unpopular economic decisions would have to be taken by whichever government replaced it. On 24 August, with the king's blessing, the three main party leaders formed an emergency National Government to take these decisions and thus avoid a divisive general election. Like most other Conservatives, Londonderry supported Baldwin's decision to enter a coalition with the Liberals and the minority of Labour MPs who remained with MacDonald. It was also agreed that the Labour leader would continue as prime minister; indeed, Lady Londonderry had recently been a vocal proponent of 'national government' and keenly pushed MacDonald to accept such an outcome.[248] Lord Londonderry was rewarded with his reappointment to the Office of Works, albeit without a seat in the cabinet.[249] MacDonald telephoned him with the offer; Londonderry declined to reply until he had consulted the first Viscount Hailsham, whom he increasingly regarded as one of his closest friends in parliament, and whose family also had an ancestral connection to Ulster. With all the formal expressions of self-effacement that might be expected in his response to Baldwin, Londonderry made the otherwise incredible claim that 'It never entered my head that I should be fortunate enough to be in this Gov[ernmen]t: in fact I never thought about it [at] all'.[250]

Having taken some preliminary measures to avert further economic disaster, the Emergency National Government sought a doctor's mandate to continue in office and a general election was scheduled for 27 October. In his campaigning, Londonderry endorsed tariff reform and asked the people to do their duty to the country by supporting the 'National' parties.[251] The general election returned 554 MPs supporting the National Government, a staggering majority that completely eclipsed those who refused to join it. Within a week it was announced that Londonderry had been appointed to the cabinet as the Secretary of State for Air.[252] On this occasion, the appointment is more likely to have been down to MacDonald rather than Baldwin. As the new head of the Air Ministry later noted, he was from this time marked out as 'Ramsay's man'.[253] Subsequent events also played a part in fostering the belief that it was MacDonald and not Baldwin who appointed Londonderry. For the latter two had an increasingly poor relationship in the years that followed which led Baldwin to remove Londonderry from the Air Ministry in June 1935, at which point MacDonald intervened to ensure that Londonderry was given another post. The truth is probably less straightforward. If it was MacDonald's decision, he still needed Baldwin's approval. Londonderry's claim on office in 1931 did not therefore rest entirely on his wife's friendship with the leader of the Labour party. And even if it was a major factor, his appointment to the cabinet was rendered more plausible by his handling of a number of sensitive issues that were crucial to the future electoral success of Baldwin and the Conservative party. Indeed, Londonderry's appointment as Air Minister – never a prestigious or important office before the mid-1930s – was more credible than his assignment to the Office of Works. Not only had Londonderry previously served as Under Secretary of State for Air, he had been offered, and turned down, the post of Secretary of State in 1922 (see Chapter 4). Moreover, Londonderry had remained interested in air policy since departing the Air Ministry in 1921. In 1924 he spoke in the House of Lords in support of the Labour government's Air Force Reserve and Auxiliary Air Force bill, albeit teasing the then air minister, the first Baron Thomson, by speculating whether he had 'great difficulty with his pacifist colleagues in connection with this measure'.[254] And in 1930, Thomson's predecessor, Sir Samuel Hoare, solicited Londonderry's help in shoring up Sir Hugh, now first Viscount Trenchard, against diehard critics in a House of Lords debate on the RAF.[255] If Londonderry catered his way to the cabinet, his reputation for moderation in Ulster, his political choices in sensitive debates about Conservative policy, his previous ministerial experience at the Air Ministry and continued interest in the RAF, and his association with industrial co-operation, all combined to make his three successive appointments to government, in 1928 and twice in 1931, entirely plausible.

6

Secretary of State for Air, 1931–5

As the Secretary of State for Air with a seat in the cabinet, Londonderry had reached the pinnacle of his ministerial career. At the time of his appointment, however, no one expected that it would, in the words of Winston Churchill, 'become one of the most important offices in the State'.[1] That retrospective assessment arose from the fact that Londonderry's tenure at the Air Ministry coincided with an increasingly tense period in international relations. As a result of this, it was also a time of heightening anxiety about the destructive potential of air power, leading first to diplomatic efforts to prohibit it, and when that did not work, to an arms race. The greater significance attached to the Air Ministry in these circumstances meant that Londonderry's position at its helm came under the spotlight. The controversy surrounding his appointment to the National Government (see Chapter 5) assumed new relevance as critics questioned his competence. But it was his deteriorating relationship with Stanley Baldwin over aerial armaments that ultimately sealed his fate. Their differences of opinion, caused by Londonderry's unwillingness to forsake air force dogma, provided Baldwin with the opportunity in 1935 to remove him from the Air Ministry, and several months later from the government altogether. Londonderry's close relationship with the Air Staff was not unusual for a service minister. In the case of the Air Ministry, the tendency was reinforced by the existential uncertainty that hung over both it and the service that it oversaw, which meant that air ministers and RAF chiefs alike jealously guarded the independence of both.[2] What is especially noteworthy is that it repeated Londonderry's experience in Northern Ireland (see Chapter 4). In both instances he believed himself to be in the right as the defender of ministry wisdom, and in both posts he disregarded the need to appease the perceived concerns of the electorate, no matter how much these conflicted with his own potential for remaining in office.[3]

I

The continuing international economic crisis ensured that the temporary National Government of August 1931 evolved into a permanent one. The 'National' parties went to the polls as a unified body in October 1931 and won an overwhelming mandate to continue in office. The Conservatives now dominated the House of Commons, with Ramsay MacDonald's Labour supporters winning a dozen seats and the official Labour party only retaining fifty-two. MacDonald retained the premiership, but the locus of power in the cabinet lay with the Lord President of the Council, Baldwin, the leader of the largest party in the coalition. Aside from the two Liberals occupying the Foreign Office and the Home Office, respectively, the Conservatives and the four MacDonald-Labour members received between them the remaining sixteen posts – six of which went to aristocrats.

Londonderry made his first formal policy announcement in the House of Lords on 17 November 1931.[4] It dealt with the question of air routes, a policy that gave preference in some instances to foreign states over British possessions. Londonderry was not entirely comfortable with the policy. Like other imperial-minded advocates of air travel, he believed that aviation might potentially reverse the centrifugal forces of dominion assertiveness and Indian nationalism. But the policy would be the first of many examples of how the Air portfolio and collective cabinet responsibility demanded a measure of flexibility on his part.[5] Indeed, membership of the coalition government compelled him, like other Conservative ministers, to advocate policies that he had once attacked. Therefore, when Londonderry moved the second reading of the Finance bill in 1932, he referred to it as a necessary sacrifice despite the damaging cutbacks that it inflicted on the Air Ministry.[6] On another occasion, he defended British trade with the Soviet Union, a state whose Communist system he both feared and despised. He informed the House of Lords that although he sympathized with critics of the policy – notably on this occasion these included two men later synonymous with appeasement, the first Baron Mount Temple and the eleventh Marquess of Lothian – trade between the two countries would prevent further hostilities, promote domestic employment and positively affect the development of the Soviet Union.[7] On yet another occasion, Londonderry responded to accusations that the Soviet Union was interfering in Indian affairs by reminding peers that the market afforded by 180,000,000 people was not one that could be lightly ignored.[8]

As one of four peers in the cabinet, Londonderry took his responsibilities in the House of Lords very seriously. It was, of course, the basis of his right to sit in parliament, and it was perhaps for this reason that he could chide peers for their low attendance in the upper house, and yet defend the chamber against those who sought to introduce life peerages. If reform had to occur, he reasoned, then it had to be substantial and not a dilution of the institution that he cherished.[9] Among his range of responsibilities in the upper house, Londonderry dealt with matters concerning the Ministry of Transport, including the 1933 London Passenger Transport bill.[10] Aware of unrest among Conservatives with the direction of transport policy, he reassured peers that the bill had been 'purged of any Socialist character'.[11] Such reassurances were deemed necessary by Conservative ministers in the National Government. After Londonderry addressed the House of Lords on the Petroleum (Production) bill 1934, which vested the crown with the ownership of petrol and natural gas found in Great Britain, the Conservative MP, Cuthbert Headlam, described it in his diary as 'a very socialistic measure'.[12] In defending that legislation, Londonderry also appeared to cast aside his earlier concern about large business corporations eroding 'individualism' (see Chapter 5) by advancing the argument that these were part of the 'development of modern civilisation', that they 'imposed upon us all a certain measure of surrender of individual and private rights'.[13] Similarly, addressing the upper house in 1935, Londonderry defended the

'National' aspect of the government by arguing that people recognized the increasing need for the state to control certain activities, 'they had been willing to surrender part of their personal sovereignty in the belief that this control . . . was beneficial to the community'.[14] He again demonstrated how much he had shifted ground politically when he moved the Lotteries bill on 30 May 1934. In contrast to his attitude before the First World War, when he opposed government restrictions on the lifestyle of 'working men', Londonderry now agreed with the finding of a royal commission that deplored 'the general detriment to the character of young persons in poor neighbourhoods due to the excitement of day-to-day betting on greyhound tracks'.[15] As a long-serving president of the Chelsea Hospital for Women, he also expressed his strong opposition to any attempt to emulate the Irish Hospital Sweepstakes.[16]

Londonderry's advocacy of limited interventionism and concomitant defensiveness against accusations of socialism should not exaggerate the political distance that he had travelled. Like other Conservatives, he sought to preserve the National Government by appealing to national unity through measures that sometimes owed more to state interventionism than Conservative orthodoxy. But this was a calculated precaution against the growth of an increasingly doctrinaire Labour opposition and the extremist ideals of fascism and communism.[17] As he and most other Conservative parliamentarians knew only too well, the Cecilian conservatism of the late Victorian period was incompatible with the universal franchise inaugurated in 1918–28. In a speech to the Carlton Club, Oxford, delivered in February 1933, he acknowledged this to make several remarkable claims about conservatism, and its political opponents, that were intended to reassure his audience of the Conservative character of the government:

> Conservative principles in the circumstances of the present day could find adequate expression in the policies of the National Government. Conservatism was not reactionary. It stood for evolution, not revolution. It was essentially national in character, scope, and outlook, embracing all classes of the people.
>
> Liberalism or Radicalism had been called into existence in this country in the middle of the nineteenth century to oppose privilege, and now that privilege had disappeared their *raison de'ètre* had vanished, and they were merely striving to retain their separate identity without any essential difference in policy and outlook from that of the National Government . . . The first test of every policy before its adoption would be its reaction upon unemployment.[18]

The Import Duties Act 1932 was another decisive policy shift, at least for lifelong free traders like Londonderry. He had to actively support it given that he was charged with the responsibility for moving the bill in the House of Lords. The National Labour peer and opponent of tariffs, the first Viscount Snowden, observed that Londonderry did so by 'praising it with faint damns'.[19] In the later 1930s, when he was out of office, Londonderry felt able to assume a more honest position, warning that 'Tariffs, with the benefits which they certainly confer, if pursued entirely from a national point of view, are definite hindrances' to international trade and economic recovery.[20] For all his preparedness to toe the National Government line on tariffs and the role of the state, Londonderry still took care as a minister to defend certain libertarian beliefs, in particular, the commercial freedom of the City of London and press freedom.[21] But that fundamental belief could also lead him to support international regulations that facilitated commercial activity, not only in air travel but other fields too. Addressing the Incorporated Society of Authors in November 1934, alongside the Archbishop of Canterbury, Cosmo Gordon Laing, and the novelist, H. G. Wells, Londonderry expressed his support for what would become the Brussels copyright convention of 1936.[22]

II

Air policy in the early 1930s might have been dominated by strategic and diplomatic concerns, but Londonderry's office at Gwydyr House in Whitehall also dealt with the expanding civil aviation industry. However, with even the RAF's budget curtailed by spending limits, there was little of significance that the Air Ministry could do to actively support civil aviation other than through influence and encouragement.[23] In performing that task, Londonderry used newspaper coverage of the many conferences and functions that he attended as air minister to champion civil aviation. This aspect of the ministry's work took on more importance towards the end of 1933, as the World Disarmament Conference teetered on the brink of collapse. As detailed below, the conference had witnessed attempts to internationalize civil aviation as a means of effectively prohibiting the use of aerial bombing; indeed, the difficulty of trying to bring such an idea into being rendered Londonderry a sceptic of any possible disarmament agreement. But it also reinforced his conviction that aviation should be presented as a force for peace not war. The 'discovery of the means of flight had too often lately been represented as a misfortune rather than as a blessing to mankind', he declared in his opening address to the thirtieth session of the International Air Traffic Association, held at Lincoln's Inn, London. Yet the 'aeroplane . . . was destined to be a more potent instrument for peace in the world and for union among the nations than any other which at present they possessed'.[24]

Limited in what he could spend, and with his attention concentrated on the RAF, Londonderry did what he could to advocate and celebrate developments in civil aviation such as the internationalization of aerial law and the Air League of the British Empire's scheme to provide funding to assist 'the young men of this country' to train as pilots.[25] Likewise, he encouraged the construction of airports by local authorities, though he and the government drew the line at local authorities establishing their own air services.[26] And if Imperial Airways was the Air Ministry's preferred instrument for international air routes, Londonderry also encouraged private companies to put forward viable proposals and thus open the market.[27] He soon took up the task personally with the construction of an aerodrome at his Newtownards estate, to be operated by Airwork, the company responsible for Heston near London.[28] Within a year the first civil airport in Northern Ireland was opened in dramatic fashion. Following the usual formal proceedings that attended such events, Lord and Lady Londonderry, accompanied by their daughters, boarded an aeroplane. After taking off, Lord Londonderry attempted to address the assembled crowd using a wireless set, from a distance of 15 miles, but as his voice could hardly be heard the crowd overheard the wireless operator request that the aeroplane come nearer. After a few minutes it was reported that his voice 'could be heard fairly distinctly over quite a large area'. 'I am talking to you from a height of 3,000 feet, and am at present flying through the clouds', he broadcast to those below. 'This experiment shows the great progress made by wireless for aviation in the past few years. I am sure that within the next few years there will be even greater and more valuable developments.'[29] Having learnt to fly in 1932, and having opened his own airport in 1934, Londonderry was thus devoted not only to the Air Ministry but also to aviation itself.[30]

Unfortunately for the air minister, growing recognition of the importance of civil aviation had the unintended effect of undermining his control of it. Against the backdrop of the World Disarmament Conference, there were concerns that the Air Ministry was too preoccupied with the RAF. The Gorell committee's report of July 1934 failed to abate this unease with its recommendation, on financial and structural grounds, that civil aviation remain the responsibility of the Air Ministry. Clearly rattled that the issue was being discussed, Londonderry urged the chief whip two months later to ensure that no parliamentary debate took place on the Gorell report.[31] But he could not escape the mounting criticisms of the United Kingdom's relatively poor record in civil aviation in comparison to other powers.[32] By the second week of December 1934, a serious disagreement on the issue led to a row between the air minister and his permanent secretary, Sir Christopher Bullock.[33] The result of this was the appointment of a Director General of Civil Aviation to reassure critics of a new dispensation for civil aviation. The episode also heightened tensions between Londonderry and the Under Secretary of State, Philip Sassoon, who along with Baldwin was appropriating more Air Ministry business for the House of Commons.[34] It would be the first of several incidences that undermined incrementally Londonderry's position at the Air Ministry.

III

As the Secretary of State for Air Londonderry found himself embroiled in one of the most controversial issues of the early 1930s: the attempt to reach a multilateral agreement to abolish aerial bombing.[35] Within days of his appointment, he accompanied the prime minister to the Lord Mayor of London's banquet at the Guildhall, and delivered a speech in which he relayed his belief that 'under the influences of democratic educational systems, of which previous empires and nations knew practically nothing, increasingly enlightened communities must incline more and more towards the logical understanding of the blessings and the benefits of peace and recede further and further in their political outlook from a method so barbarous and so antiquated as the arbitrament of force'. He nevertheless cautioned against the complete abandonment of armed forces. 'To some, but fortunately not to any considerable number, our forces mean nothing but the embodiment of aggression, of weapons to maintain our world position, but this is a fallacy which needs no refutation from me.'[36] The Labour MP, Sir Stafford Cripps, did not agree. Addressing the House of Commons on 12 November, Cripps quoted Londonderry's Guildhall speech, and, as he did so, he pointedly observed that the cheers which greeted his recitation did not include the Treasury bench. It 'seems to be an unfortunate attitude to adopt when you are about to enter upon a Disarmament Conference', Cripps quipped, 'and I hope that the Prime Minister, or some other Member of the Government Front Bench, will tell us whether that is a statement made with full Governmental responsibility'.[37] The government did not respond to his invitation. It was in any case not an easy question for this government of individuals to answer, and it was one that would continue to trouble Londonderry's relationship with his colleagues. It also led to policies that were not always easily reconciled, such as the abandonment of the ten-year rule in March 1932, shortly after the opening of the World Disarmament Conference.[38]

If the air minister's opening shot in the public debate on disarmament attempted to focus on pacifism in the Labour party, he had good reason to worry more about the economic crisis that had brought the National Government into existence. In particular, how the country's finances might play a determining role in shaping the development of Great Britain's overseas commitments, and related to this, the thorny question of disarmament. Paul Kennedy argues that the economy was 'the most critical conditioning element in the formulation of the country's external policy'.[39] Yet, as others highlight, political choices could still be made regardless of financial considerations.[40] Londonderry would later lament that the choices that he believed to be correct were never effectively made because of the economic policy of the Chancellor of the Exchequer, Neville Chamberlain. Other political choices would also come to be seen by Londonderry as inimical to the interests of the air force, especially the attempt by senior ministers to interpret public opinion against a shifting backdrop in international relations.[41]

Londonderry set out his stall to cabinet colleagues within weeks of taking office. The thrust of his message was that the RAF was weak, that it had unilaterally disarmed and that as a result it had fallen to fifth among the world powers for aviation spending.[42] It chimed with the messages emanating from the Admiralty and War Office about their respective services. In fact, like them, the RAF was one of the best funded air forces in the world, even if its resources did not keep pace with the Air Staff's ambitions.[43] That Londonderry and his service thought otherwise owes much to years of inter-service rivalry, the periodic questioning of the RAF's independence and the imminence of the World Disarmament Conference. To pre-empt the likely challenges that would arise from the conference, Londonderry highlighted to cabinet colleagues the importance of the air force in any potential European conflict, as well as its existing strategic roles in the Middle East, East Africa and the Northwest Frontier.

As the use of aerial bombing was highly controversial, its advocates tended to utilize the liberal-sounding rhetoric that was employed to celebrate civil aviation. In his commentary on the disarmament conference, Squadron Leader C. G. Burge, founder and editor of the *Air Annual of the British Empire*, remarked, 'The progress of civilization is more likely to be hastened and the risk of war actually made less by allowing aviation to develop and to take its rightful position among the defence forces of the country'.[44] His observation applied to Europe, where the possibility of aerial bombardment, the air men held, would serve to prevent its utilization. In Europe's overseas empires, however, 'peace' in troublesome outlying areas was enforced in the opposite way, through bombing and the threat of bombing.[45] Similarly, the claim that the RAF was a relatively inexpensive alternative to using the army drew on a liberal militarist rationale, one that thought of war in economic terms, and which attached great importance to technology and the role of the private sector in its development. Thus, according to David Edgerton, 'The liberal emphasis on cheapness in defence combined in unexpected ways with anti-liberal sentiments.'[46]

The air force typically worked alongside land forces, but in the Middle East it had achieved pre-eminence in Aden and Iraq. In the former, the RAF had been given primary responsibility for its defence in 1927 and quickly went on to prove its worth in the years that followed.[47] But it was in the League of Nations mandate of Iraq, formerly Mesopotamia, that its presence was deemed to be most vital. The threat and periodic use of aerial bombing there had proved to be the most financially prudent means of controlling unrest in its outlying areas. The air force went on to assume overall control of Iraq's defence, maintaining its pre-eminence even after the United Kingdom surrendered the mandate in October 1932.[48] As Londonderry and the Air Staff presented it, the prohibition of aerial bombing represented nothing less than the demise of British influence in the Middle East.

Countering this were the powerful humanitarian objections to aerial bombing, and the related fear that Great Britain itself would be subject to a devastating aerial attack.[49] In addition, what might be labelled the imperial case for the RAF was weakened by two factors. First, inter-service rivalry ensured that doubt persisted about the effectiveness of air policing. After a decade of chalking up successes in Somaliland, Transjordan and Iraq, the RAF experienced a significant setback in August 1929 when it failed to contain growing communal conflict in the mandate of Palestine. The resignation shortly afterwards of Lord Trenchard as Chief of the Air Staff added to its difficulties by depriving the service of its most able champion.[50] Second, the colonial secretary, Philip Cunliffe-Lister, had long been an opponent of the British presence in Iraq, and he would soon emerge as one of those in the cabinet opposed to the retention of aerial bombing.[51]

On 2 February 1932 the World Disarmament Conference held its first session at Geneva. Sixty-one delegations were represented including the United States and the Soviet Union. Londonderry was uneasy about the idealistic aims of the conference from the outset. He disliked the venue and later argued that it was too removed from the real world, that Geneva was 'full of old women and sentimental cranks'.[52] His cynicism about its likely success was hardly unique among British ministers, although others were more guarded. It was quickly substantiated by several factors that were identified by critics of the conference from the outset: the competing interests of so many delegations, hostile relations between France and Germany, and the crusade to formulate a ban on aerial bombing that was motivated more by understandable public anxiety and the need for a diplomatic breakthrough than the practical considerations of what it involved, and which was given an extra impetus by the recent Japanese invasion of Manchuria.[53] In this sense, the disarmament conference, like the League of Nations, sustained what several scholars identify as the tension between myth and reality that undermined the interwar international state system. As Zara Steiner puts it, of adhering to 'the illusion of an alternative [League] system of preserving the peace while using the methods of the past to settle interstate disputes'.[54] Or, as a contemporary observer of British politics and diplomacy noted, 'the Conservatives would have been ruined electorally if they had denounced the League'.[55]

The United Kingdom's delegates to the disarmament conference, like the government itself, were divided on the prohibition of aerial bombing. Some agreed with the view of the Air Ministry and the RAF, and others felt under political pressure to abandon it. The main difficulty for the opponents of aerial bombing lay in the fact that although the foreign secretary, Sir John Simon, and most other cabinet ministers disagreed with Londonderry, he was still the Secretary of State for Air and responsible for the air force. Moreover, he was supported by the Secretary of State for India, Sir Samuel Hoare, as well as the Government of India, and he often received the more cautious support of MacDonald, who was also, at least officially, the chief British delegate to the disarmament conference. The prime minister had 'a very soft place for the Air Force', Sir Maurice Hankey, the cabinet secretary, noted in his diary. 'He loves flying . . . Lord Londonderry . . . and Lady Londonderry are now the best friends of that rather lonely man, and have shown him innumerable kindnesses.'[56] But MacDonald's ill health meant that he rarely attended the conference, leaving representation to Simon, Londonderry and the other two service ministers.[57] Back in London, the Committee of Imperial Defence (CID) struggled through its subcommittees to mediate between the three services, the Foreign Office, and what it perceived as public opinion.[58]

After only two weeks Londonderry assumed that the conference would never succeed in its aims.[59] He was aware, however, that the expectations of the country demanded that he ignore his own doubts and pursue a policy with which he disagreed, although this did not stop him from fighting his case in private.[60] The air minister had little choice. With the exception of Simon, Londonderry was more involved with the conference than any other minister. And as the sole British member of the disarmament conference's general committee, he also reported directly to MacDonald, Baldwin and even to the king.[61] On 22 February he sent his early impressions of the conference to Baldwin:

> This is the most terrible place. It is bitterly cold outside, and the hotels inside are like furnaces. . . . I find the complete League of Nations atmosphere very interesting, but I am fully conscious that it is quite a different atmosphere to any other . . . I am sure, however, that it is of the highest importance that we should maintain the League of Nations, and it depends on Great Britain whether the League will develop or whether it will languish. . . . If it receives no more than favourable acquiescence from us it may not be worth while to go on spending money that we do in this connection, but on the other hand if we are determined to maintain the position which we now hold, then I am inclined to think we shall have to take a more active participation in its activities.[62]

Londonderry also pressed Baldwin to make Simon a permanent delegate to the conference, an indication, given Simon's reluctance to safeguard the RAF, that Londonderry knew that the real power lay not with the delegates but with the CID's disarmament subcommittee back in London. It was an echo of his uncomfortable experience years before as an Ulster Unionist delegate to the Irish Convention (see Chapter 2). The request also represented his frustration at being, very often, the sole British representative at Geneva, giving an opinion with which he did not always concur.[63]

The ongoing Sino-Japanese crisis overshadowed the first meetings of the conference. Londonderry argued – in reasoning similar to the attitude that he would adopt with Nazi Germany in the late 1930s – that once the damaged prestige of the Japanese was alleviated then a settlement would be easier to reach. Referring to the League of Nations' decision to reprimand Japan, Londonderry, temporarily taking the place of Simon at Geneva, informed Baldwin of his meeting with the Japanese delegate, Koto Matsudaira. 'I did my best to point out to him that there was no indictment and no criticism but an appeal to Japan as a strong power', he relayed to the Lord President. 'I especially made this point in the few remarks I had to make at the public meeting of the Council, that we had made an appeal to the strength of the honour of Japan, but I see there was no mention of that in *The Times*.'[64] The press reports of Londonderry's efforts were indeed mixed. On 17 February the *Daily Express* recorded that he had 'objected strongly to the dispatch of a drastic warning to Tokyo' but was 'outnumbered and overruled' by the smaller powers without Far Eastern interests, who 'clamoured for a sharply worded Note to placate China'.[65] The correspondents of the *Manchester Guardian* and the *Daily Telegraph* contradicted one another by reporting, respectively, that he had been 'particularly firm' and conciliatory.[66]

By 10 March Londonderry was worried about the prevalence of anti-Japanese sentiment at Geneva. He warned Baldwin that 'the smaller States are hoping to establish some League of Nations doctrine which will safeguard their own boundaries no matter what crime they may have committed'.[67] MacDonald agreed with a line of appeasement towards the Japanese and informed Londonderry that he should privately let them know the British position, that the affair must be straightened out without conflict and that British prestige in the Far East should be maintained.[68] Accordingly, Londonderry encouraged Japan and China to avoid further incidents without condemning the former, a position that irritated the United States.[69] The episode is interesting in itself, but it also demonstrates that Londonderry's rationale for appeasement was not restricted to Germany. He had accepted in 1932 the principle that the British Empire was incapable of prosecuting a successful war against another power in the Far East due to the neglect of its armed forces. And although he attempted in private to blame the crisis on British and American arms suppliers, he never condemned the ultimate source of the problem, Japanese aggression.[70]

In spite of its private disagreements, the British delegation gave the impression of unity at the start of the disarmament conference. It pressed for the limitation of air forces and claimed to take the lead by ending the Air Ministry's post-war programme for fifty-two squadrons, a measure that Londonderry announced on 3 March 1932. Posturing aside, British calls for limitation were not entirely selfless given that the RAF was only fourth in the world in first-line strength. But it also meant that the strategy was a gamble, one that Londonderry admitted publicly was a 'direct and inevitable result of the current financial crisis'.[71] The Foreign Office, however, wanted to go further, even at this early stage. Its opening shot came on 19 March, when Simon circulated a memo to cabinet colleagues that called for the curtailment of aerial bombing.

Londonderry had been aware of Simon's views from late January and had acted at the end of that month to try to delay the conference's procedures by using his position on the general council.[72] Following the foreign secretary's memorandum to the cabinet, Londonderry registered his opposition at Baldwin's Cabinet Disarmament Committee – the CID subcommittee that oversaw the British position at Geneva – of which the air minister was a member.[73] He took exception to Simon's deviation from the original policy and argued that while the foreign secretary's proposal allowed the RAF to continue its policing duties in the Middle East, it prevented its use against enemy warships outside territorial waters on course to attack British possessions. The air minister also felt strongly that such an agreement would be ignored in a war scenario. In spite of Simon gaining the support of the Admiralty and the Chief of the Imperial General Staff, the cabinet and its Disarmament Committee agreed with the Air Ministry that a counteroffensive was necessary.[74] However, Baldwin and the disarmament committee did differ with the Air Ministry on what the desired end should be, for the Lord President believed that the best solution would not be a mere limitation of aerial bombing but its outright abolition.[75] He raised it at cabinet on 4 May while Londonderry was making his way back from the conference to address Conservatives in Cumbria on the need for 'realism' at Geneva.[76] With the support of the Admiralty, War Office and the cabinet, Simon and Hankey devised a draft proposal to ban military and naval air forces and to internationalize civil aviation; the last was deemed necessary to prevent states from using civil aircraft for military purposes.[77]

The Air Staff, and consequently the Air Ministry, was indignant about the proposal despite friendly overtures from Simon.[78] The Chief of the Air Staff, Sir John Salmond, warned Londonderry on 8 June that the proposal would mean the end of the RAF and suggested that the air minister press both MacDonald and the king to intervene.[79] Londonderry informed MacDonald on 9 June that his ministry was furious and that he needed to be persuaded that their fears were unnecessary.[80] Following an audience with George V on 10 June, Londonderry informed the prime minister that the sovereign was 'very indignant with any attempt to do away with the Air Force'. The king was sufficiently convinced of Londonderry's case that shortly afterwards he had heated words with Hankey, who insisted in reply that something had to be done to protect Great Britain from an aerial attack.[81] Emboldened by royal patronage, Londonderry expressed to MacDonald his dissatisfaction with the government's handling of aerial disarmament: 'I cannot become reconciled to acquiescing in the abolition of military aviation except under the remote possibility of an international agreement to abolish all weapons of war.'[82]

Londonderry's opposition was sufficient, according to Hankey, to make MacDonald and Simon unenthusiastic in their attempts to woo the disinterested French and German governments. However, it was not Londonderry who was the decisive factor, but those who supported his position, including the viceroy of India, the first Earl of Willingdon, and as noted already, the king. As Londonderry readily admitted the following month to the king's private secretary, the sovereign's 'views were very valuable at that particular moment'.[83] The Simon proposal was scrapped and British

Figure 8 Londonderry and Ramsay MacDonald, 1932.

officials began anew to examine ways of dealing with aerial bombing. Londonderry's own solution to the tense international situation, delivered to his Cumbrian audience on 4 May, was that success could only come through security and that could only be achieved by removing the fear and mistrust that bedevilled Franco-German relations. He went further, warning that unless this was addressed, German support for the Nazi party would increase. He concluded his address by calling for immediate disarmament, at the same time maintaining that Great Britain could not take the lead in case it jeopardized imperial security.[84]

Two months later a compromise between the positions of the Foreign Office and the Air Ministry was embodied in a government white paper dated 7 July. Prompted by the need to respond constructively to a recent initiative by the President of the United States, Herbert Hoover, it prohibited aerial bombing on civilians with further limits to be laid down by an international convention. Given its purpose, it gave more ground than Londonderry and the Air Staff felt necessary and was published while the air minister was at Geneva supporting the admission of Turkey to the League of Nations: 'a further step towards the completion of the League'.[85] Salmond reassured him that the Air Ministry would fight this latest attack from those he called the 'anti-Christs'.[86] The British delegation at Geneva, however, went even further than the new proposal by agreeing to the collective resolution proposed by the Czech foreign minister, Edvard Beneš, which called for the abolition of aerial bombing subject to an agreement on how it could be made effective. Londonderry was angered by the departure and wrote to MacDonald blaming the Foreign Office for surrendering 'all along the line', adding that he would be more anxious about the Beneš resolution had he thought that such a solution could be found. Londonderry felt that they should have 'brushed aside' the 'unreal' suggestion of a ban but not restrictions, and that the British could find support for such a position from France, Japan and Argentina. 'Surrendering to Americans is usually very bad for them', he informed MacDonald, 'and I do not think that this case will be an exception to the rule'.[87] He also took the opportunity, not long afterwards, to remind the prime minister that air cover was an integral part of highly secret plans for dealing with threats in Ireland to the strategic interests of Great Britain.[88]

These anxious missives aside, Londonderry could take some comfort from the fact that MacDonald shared his view that the involvement of the smaller countries hindered the prospect of a more effective agreement between the great powers, one that could repeat the success of the 1922 Washington Naval Treaty.[89] Encouraged by this, and MacDonald's antipathy to the French, Londonderry wrote optimistically to Hankey requesting that the prime minister direct foreign policy and not the Foreign Office.[90] But any influence that Londonderry had on MacDonald was by this stage waning. Days after his suggestion, MacDonald met Hankey and discussed what was perceived to be the main weakness of the air minister's position: that the maintenance of aerial bombing would allow other countries to attack the United Kingdom.[91]

Londonderry's dislike of Simon did not prevent him from maintaining a good working relationship with the Foreign Office officials that he dealt with at Geneva.[92] But this could bring only modest comfort given that he was now isolated from the majority of his cabinet colleagues. Moreover, he found it increasingly hard to deal with his own party leader, and his attempts to get around this difficulty by corresponding with MacDonald and the king could not override the wishes of the cabinet. Writing to the king's private secretary, Londonderry expressed his unease about representing a government policy with which he did not agree. Air power, he maintained, despite what was being attempted at Geneva, 'will play the leading part in any future war should we be faced with such a dreadful calamity'.[93]

In response to Londonderry's continuing opposition, the Cabinet Disarmament Committee asked him to submit a draft proposal. Duly submitted in September, the air minister advocated limitation on both the use and size of air forces and on the weight of individual aeroplanes. He also recommended that the French air force be cut by a third and that all other forces be fixed in relation to it, and that aerial bombing be confined to military purposes and not be used against civilians. But events conspired to make his proposals inoperable. Throughout the summer, the German government of Franz von Papen had been repeating its calls for equal treatment with the other powers. Londonderry was sympathetic to their demands, and he had warned publicly about the growth of 'Hitlerism' if Germany's concerns were not appeased.[94] Finally, its government cited the continued opposition of France to explain its decision to leave the disarmament conference in September. Londonderry's prediction of failure appeared to be fulfilled. The following month, as president of the County Durham Scout Association, he signalled his lack of faith in the conference to an audience that included the first Baron Baden-Powell. 'The world is sighing for security', he declared. 'But, however far the nations may disarm materially, they cannot make war impossible without a disarmament of the spirit and the mind to war. Weapons once cast away can be reforged. It is the will to make use of weapons that makes weapons dangerous, and the spirit of aggression that makes wars possible.'[95] It was a line of reasoning that was rational if contested, and it was shared by others in the government, but Londonderry was unusual in being so frank about it in public. The contrasting tendency among other ministers was to publicly acquiesce in the assumption that the possession of arms made war inevitable.[96]

In the wake of Germany's withdrawal, the British attempted to forge a new policy, but it was delayed by continued disagreements between the Air Ministry and the Foreign Office over the abolition of military and naval aircraft.[97] With only days to go before Baldwin was scheduled to give an announcement on 10 November, Salmond and Bullock pressed Londonderry to present their view to the cabinet. As a result, the cabinet agreed on 8 November to propose only an inquiry into abolition.[98] Even so, MacDonald warned Londonderry afterwards that 'some gesture has got to be made if our influence in the world is not to be completely lost'.[99] Baldwin outlined the new policy to the House of Commons on 10 November. Famously, the Lord President expressed his preference for abolition as 'the bomber will always get through', but he admitted that an offensive capability was still needed, especially as peacetime rules could be abandoned under wartime conditions.[100] Salmond afterwards wrote to Londonderry, 'You must have had a great battle yesterday to induce the cabinet to shift the ground as far as they have done.'[101]

The following week Simon submitted new draft proposals to the disarmament conference. He stated that Great Britain wanted to abolish aerial bombing and air forces except for police purposes in outlying places, and he called for an international civil aviation scheme. He also proposed weight limitations for aircraft and the reduction of all air forces to a level equal to the RAF, which would be followed by a further reduction of one-third. The proposals went some way to restoring confidence in the conference proceedings. Further progress was made in December when, in an effort to re-engage Germany, a formula of words was agreed upon by the United States, Great Britain, France and Italy that acknowledged the right of Germany to 'equality of rights in a system which would provide security for all nations'.[102]

The air minister followed this in January 1933 with an inspection tour of RAF bases in the Middle East. Lasting three weeks and covering 8,000 miles, he stopped at Rome, Athens, Cairo, Jerusalem and Baghdad, travelling the route 'all by air, except for the passage through the Alps and across Italy on the outward journey'. He spent over a week in Iraq, taking flights over Barzan and Diana, the districts in the north of the country where the RAF had been actively policing during his tenure at the Air Ministry. He visited the Kurdish villages inhabited by Iraq's beleaguered Christian refugee minority, the Assyrians, 'a particularly fine lot of men', from whose small population the RAF recruited its aerodrome guards or 'levies'. He met with the Patriarch of the Assyrian Church of the East, the Mar Shimun, and claimed that 'the Assyrian difficulty was now on the way to settlement on the lines agreed upon after the recent discussion at Geneva'.[103]

It proved to be a premature assessment given that the Mar Shimun was subsequently detained by the Iraqi authorities in May, and in August there were deadly clashes between the Iraqi army and a party of armed Assyrians.[104] During that period of heightening tension, which occurred after Londonderry had returned home, he entertained Iraq's king, Faisal I, at Londonderry House. 'I am afraid the Iraqis are difficult people to deal with and I feel our control over this strange race of people is going to be no easy task', he wrote afterwards to MacDonald. 'Faisal like all these Eastern Potentates is no use at all. They only prospered, when they did prosper, by the exercise of powers which our civilisation derives to them', Londonderry added, against the backdrop of the bloody encounter between Assyrians and the Iraqi army.[105] The prime minister replied with the assurance that he would be handling the Assyrian crisis.[106] Despite this, the Assyrians' situation remained precarious, a product, in no short measure, of British policy during the mandate period, which had shored up the large Sunni Arab minority at the expense of Iraq's smaller minorities.[107]

It was on the return leg of his Middle East tour that Londonderry had his first brush with the theatrics of fascism. Stopping at Rome on 30 January, he took the opportunity to meet with General Italo Balbo, the Italian air minister. By coincidence it was the same day that Adolf Hitler assumed power in Germany. In addition to the usual series of diplomatic meetings, Londonderry was taken to see an exhibition on the 'Fascist revolution', and when leaving Rome his hosts organized for the train carrying him to be accompanied by a formation of aeroplanes.[108]

Notwithstanding the recent progress made at the disarmament conference in November 1932, and the installation two months later of Hitler as Germany's chancellor, the British remained divided in their attitude to aerial bombing when the conference reconvened in February 1933. On the first of that month, Londonderry used his recent tour of the Middle East to champion the role of his service in that region. 'Once the boundary of Asia is crossed the RAF becomes the symbol of British power and the world's policeman', he informed the press. 'In fact, it plays here a part corresponding with that which the British Navy has played for so many years on the seas.'[109] A week later, however, his visible efforts at highlighting the role of the RAF appeared to crumble when Anthony Eden, deputizing for Simon at Geneva, used the opportunity to omit the reservation of police bombing. His diary entry for the 9th records the response from his superior and Londonderry:

> John Simon dragged me to telephone box & tried to dictate sentences of my speech re air disarmament. I said I had no one to take 'em down. No pencil, speech already typed. He was not pleased & turned me to Charlie [Londonderry] who was more reasonable although his own service is at stake. They both wanted to make explicitly a statement about bombing for police purposes. . . . Simon unhelpful, but I eventually convinced Charlie far enough for him to ring off. On return to hotel foyer telephone message that I 'must' specifically mention police bombing. Decided not to. Furious with Simon for making no attempt to defend me against service dep[artment]ts. He was worse than they.[110]

Londonderry was able to correct the omission when he presented the compromise British position to the conference's air committee on 20 February.[111] The following week, however, that committee agreed to the abolition of military and naval aircraft provided that a subcommittee discussed schemes for the internationalization of civil aircraft. Fortunately for the air minister, nothing was done and the momentum was lost. Londonderry returned to London to brief his fellow ministers and the king.[112]

Motivated by both financial constraints and the need to make a gesture, the cabinet decided upon a slight reduction to the 1933 air estimates, thereby maintaining the RAF at 75 formations. The Air Ministry published the estimates on 8 March.[113] On the same day, Londonderry addressed his objections privately to the war minister, Hailsham, who was similarly sceptical about the possibilities of a successful outcome at the disarmament conference.[114] The estimates, Londonderry confided, were an attempt to 'destroy the independent Air Force' that was becoming the country's first line of defence.[115] Without doubt, the cabinet's decision was in sharp contrast to the substantial increases implemented by the other leading air powers. A clear indication that the gesture would in the longer run damage the government came when Churchill publicly attacked the move. It was an intervention that Londonderry privately welcomed, even though his ministry inevitably became the target of his cousin's complaints.[116]

On 16 March, following Japan's withdrawal from the disarmament conference, the chief British delegate made a rare appearance to address it on the importance of reaching an agreement. The prime minister brought with him the British draft convention, or MacDonald plan, which embodied the proposals that Eden and MacDonald felt would be most acceptable to the conference. These included the limitation of armaments and

Figure 9 Lord Hailsham, Ramsay MacDonald, and Londonderry, in the gardens of Mount Stewart, 1933.

the abolition of aerial bombing except for police purposes. The plan, which did not specifically mention Germany, envisaged that an international commission would oversee disarmament and that the air forces of major countries would be reduced to 500 aircraft, with a decreasing scale for lesser powers. Londonderry later recalled that this definite agenda 'set Geneva by the ears'.[117] MacDonald's delivery of the plan in person certainly helped to ensure that it was well received, even if it was the clearest indication so far of his government's scepticism about the possibility of reaching a practical agreement. As a Foreign Office official noted in his diary, the prime minister 'doesn't want to disarm – particularly in the air (Londonderry air)'.[118]

During a subsequent break in the conference proceedings, Londonderry spent the week beginning 15 May undertaking a series of flying visits to domestic units of the RAF: the Central Flying School at Wittering; the Armament Training Camp at North Coates, Lincolnshire; the RAF College at Cranwell; then north to Scotland and stops at Donibristle, Leuchars and Novar.[119] Like his Middle East tour, this circuit of home-based units had the utility of courting press attention as well as providing an opportunity to boost the morale of servicemen amid the testing circumstances of the disarmament conference.

When the conference met again the same month, it used the MacDonald plan as the basis for discussion, but it was by no means universally accepted. At home, Churchill raised new fears by claiming that Hitler was rearming, while at Geneva a majority of the delegates still hoped for the abolition of aerial bombing and air forces; the United States and France in particular criticized MacDonald's reservation of police bombing.[120] This led Londonderry to fear that the British would bend under pressure. He reminded Baldwin that both he and MacDonald had promised that this would not happen. Fearing a decision in his absence, especially as he was to replace Simon as the head of the British delegation, Londonderry wrote to Baldwin on 29 May to ask the Lord President not to dispatch him to Geneva and to express his misgivings about Eden's reliability on the police bombing reservation.[121] The air minister was compelled to go regardless, not to avoid a decision on the reservation but rather, as was well publicized, to explain it.[122] Basil Liddell Hart, a contemporary observer at Geneva, recalled that 'contrary to expectation' the air minister 'succeeded wonderfully well in restoring Britain's shaken prestige. He achieved this by combining a maximum of "presence" with a minimum of words, playing his role with such gracious dignity and apparent sincerity as to evoke from many foreign observers admiring comments about "*le grand seigneur*" and references to the guidance of his great ancestor, Castlereagh'. Liddell Hart was so impressed that he later confessed in his memoirs that despite feeling that the defects of the hereditary system outweigh its advantages, he was 'glad to record a case where its value was manifest'.[123]

As a result of further deliberations at Geneva, an agreement was reached on 7 June that the MacDonald plan would be the basis of a future international convention to be drawn up following the summer adjournment.[124] This was immediately followed with further talks between the British, represented by Londonderry and Eden, and the French and Americans, but little progress was made and these soon broke up.[125] The cabinet then agreed that the MacDonald plan would be the furthest that Great Britain would go. Londonderry had succeeded in retaining police bombing, although he remained unhappy with and unnerved by Eden's lack of enthusiasm for the compromise.[126]

The air minister's temporary victory did nothing to increase his standing in the cabinet or in parliament; if anything, it only served to exacerbate existing tensions. In June 1933, the former foreign secretary, Sir Austen Chamberlain, expressed his opposition to the retention of aerial bombing for police purposes at a meeting of the League of Nations Union at Edinburgh.[127] Londonderry had previously enjoyed cordial relations with Chamberlain.[128] But he resented the elder statesman's intervention and he attempted at length to explain the difficulties through which he had laboured at Geneva. A British withdrawal of the reservation would have little effect, he conveyed to Chamberlain, until Germany and France sorted out their differences; the 'French are terrified' and 'Germany does next to nothing to dissipate their fears.'[129] Chamberlain in reply said that he had spoken 'on the spur of the moment' and that he had 'felt great difficulty in coming to a decision on the subject'. He recognized 'to the full that in the circumstances in which we have used it on the North West Frontier, Irak [*sic*] and, I think, in the Sudan it is a humane method', but he could not avoid the conclusion that if Great Britain retained it then so would France and Italy, and with their bases in north Africa 'they would be readily available for use in Europe'. He urged Londonderry to give it up if there was a risk of the disarmament conference breaking down on this specific point, 'you have a very large body of opinion in the Churches strongly ranged against you'.[130]

Chamberlain repeated his views in the House of Commons on 5 July when Eden was at the dispatch box. The latter's reply seemed to suggest that the reservation might indeed be dropped though he did not have the cabinet's approval for such a move.[131] In the absence of a definite lead, Londonderry resigned himself to making his case to anyone who would listen. Several weeks before, he had been scheduled to deliver the Royal Central Asian Society's annual lecture. He intended to use the platform to address 'Air power in the Middle East', though the loss of his voice meant that it was his deputy, Philip Sassoon, who delivered it in his stead.[132] Subsequently, on 24 July, Londonderry addressed a well-attended meeting of the parliamentary Air Committee on Disarmament, using the occasion to question the likelihood of any agreement being reached to internationalize civil aviation. He also 'reminded the committee that only about 12 of the nations represented at the Disarmament Conference had air forces of their own, and it was therefore easy for them to support proposals for complete abolition'.[133] The following month he informed MacDonald that the British Empire's strategic interest in the newly independent client state of Iraq depended on the RAF, 'we make a great mistake apologizing for the manner in which we police the world'.[134]

In the meantime, Londonderry spent most of June and July at Mount Stewart from where he engaged in various social events connected with the Air Ministry. Although his connection with the ministry was not merely social, as some were apt to remark, he did bring it social prestige.[135] In addition to the overseas and domestic RAF tours mentioned above, Londonderry made individual visits to various units throughout the country and he gave addresses regularly on air matters.[136] Indeed, public relations were an important element of the air minister's responsibilities given his difficulties holding the line against his cabinet colleagues and their reading of public opinion.

It was therefore a happy coincidence that 24 May 1934 was not only 'Empire Day', but also the date for the annual pageant of 'Empire Air Day'. The latter involved the Air Ministry overseeing the organization of motor coaches and trains in London, Birmingham, Cardiff, Glasgow, Leicester, Hull and Portsmouth, so that the public could attend specially organized events in or near those cities.[137] Londonderry's public appearances at occasions connected with the RAF were given an added touch of flair the following month when he was made an Honorary Air Commodore of No. 607 (County of Durham) (Bomber) Squadron, Auxiliary Air Force, a position that entitled him to wear an air force uniform.[138] Two previous air ministers, F. E. Guest and Samuel Hoare, had likewise been appointed to the same rank in the Auxiliary Air Force.

Londonderry House also played its role. In April 1932 it had hosted a meeting between MacDonald and the French air minister, and the following June between British representatives and General Balbo.[139] There was the dinner for the King of Iraq, mentioned above, on 22 June 1933, attended also by Faisal's former prime minister, Nuri al-Said, as well as the British prime minister, foreign secretary, Lord Chancellor and the former viceroy of India, Lord Irwin. RAF officers and others with connections to Iraq were also in attendance.[140] Londonderry hosted another function the following month, this time for the Air Council, that was attended by dominion and imperial representatives, including Canada's prime minister, R. B. Bennett; the Indian high commissioner to London, Sir Bhupendra Nath Mitra; the Indian administrator, Sir C. P. Ramaswami Iyer and the former prime minister of South Africa, Jan Smuts.[141] On 2 July Londonderry opened Liverpool Municipal Airport alongside MacDonald, using the occasion to declare that it would 'be idle to pretend that armaments could in fact be abolished at the end of the existing Conference'.[142] The following day he flew to Derry city in Northern Ireland where he met Balbo; Italy's air minister was en route to the United States to demonstrate the skills and abilities of the Italian air force.[143] Londonderry felt privately that the stunt reflected the Italians' 'inferiority complex', but he used the opportunity provided by the meeting to help smooth relations between the two countries.[144] When asked afterwards in the House of Lords why the RAF did not engage in such feats, or attempt to break speed records, the air minister admitted that it would be too expensive.[145]

IV

The failure of Paris and London to reach an agreement with Berlin led Germany to withdraw from the conference and the League of Nations on 14 October 1933. By this action the World Disarmament Conference was effectively terminated. Hitler's withdrawal led inevitably to mounting fears of another war, one that would involve aerial bombing, and this in turn led to a discernible shift of opinion in the United Kingdom. Regardless of the mixed benefits that it would bring to the Air Ministry, Londonderry not only failed to capitalize on the change of outlook, but he was perceived to be actively against it. He had become fixed on the need for peace through the limitation of armaments and felt that German grievances had been exacerbated by France and ignored by his own countrymen.[146] Therefore, when many on the right were calling for increased armaments, Londonderry was calling for the peaceful resolution of differences through the League of Nations.[147] At first glance, this suggests that Londonderry was now closer to Labour than many in his own party, or that he was responding to the Labour party's by-election victory at East Fulham on 25 October, which was viewed by many at the time as an expression of pacifism and one that threatened moves towards rearmament.[148] Londonderry certainly complained that he was subject to journalistic 'attacks' that suggested he was a 'pacifist', and that he was 'anxious to see the Royal Air Force abolished and the defensive forces disappear'.[149] And whatever his private his reservations, he like most senior Conservatives defended the purpose and maintenance of the League of Nations. But he was equally clear on his concerns about the disarmament conference, and these were hardly new or calculated to satisfy the perceived meaning of the East Fulham result. Speaking days afterwards to Conservatives at Newcastle upon Tyne, he stated that expectations of the disarmament conference had been too high:

> At the beginning of the Conference it was believed that you could eliminate definite weapons of war. I am not sure that it is possible for anyone to do that. Every country was pressed to use every means and scientific invention placed to their hand to preserve their people. If you can get people to agree to diminish their armaments I believe we shall have gone a long way in the direction of postponing and perhaps eliminating war.
>
> I believe in time we may get rid of the warlike spirit. But so long as the warlike spirit exists and is on the increase, as some people tell us, we shall find great stagnation and every country unwilling to make experiments in the development of their trade, which is essential to the prosperity and welfare of mankind.[150]

The following week, at Newtownards, Londonderry described as an 'election lie' the Labour party's claim that the government had never been in earnest about disarmament. Ministers, he went on, 'would exert every effort to secure the continuance of international co-operation towards securing that atmosphere of appeasement, mutual trust, and security without which a general measure of disarmament was impossible'.[151] In the House of Lords, he was careful to make it clear that although he viewed disarmament as a solution to international tensions, no further steps would be taken in this direction.[152] Not long after, in contrast, he was also obliged to deny press speculation that the government was about to announce a new policy of rapid expansion.[153]

After hosting on 20 November 1,500 guests at the Londonderrys' now regular eve of parliament reception at Londonderry House, Lord Londonderry prepared for a second tour of overseas RAF units during the parliamentary recess.[154] He took the precaution beforehand of arranging for Hailsham to keep him in touch with any relevant government business.[155] The second tour was considerably more ambitious and better publicized than his first, covering 16,000 miles and lasting from December 1933 to February 1934. He was accompanied by his wife and three daughters – Margaret, Helen and Mairi – on the first leg, flying from Croydon to Cairo on the regular Imperial Airways service, and staying at the Egyptian capital's famous Mena House Hotel, where the guests' view took in the Giza pyramid complex.[156] After spending Christmas together, Londonderry bade farewell to his family and travelled south to the Sudan, arriving in Wady Halfa on 27 December, before flying the following day to Khartoum where he and his companion, Air Vice Marshal Cyril Newall, were the guests of the acting governor-general, Gawain Bell.[157] From there Londonderry flew to Amman in Transjordan, and on New Year's Day on to Baghdad.[158] On this visit to Iraq he stayed for only two nights, during which time he met Faisal's successor, King Ghazi, and he inspected the Assyrian levies that continued to guard the country's RAF bases.[159] The alacrity of that visit was to make space for the tour's main destination, the subcontinent, where the 55-year-old air minister was to visit 'every RAF unit in India'.[160]

Arriving first at Karachi, Londonderry was photographed by the press wearing his jumpsuit, and he remarked on how his Imperial Airways flight 'might be accelerated in order to compete with the French and Dutch'.[161] Stopping briefly at New Delhi, he arrived at Calcutta on 7 January to spend several days as a guest of the viceroy, Lord Willingdon, at Belvedere House.[162] There he informed the press that he 'was in India as a student, learning and making useful contacts with business men, officials, and flying men'. He also returned to the theme of speed, remarking 'that wherever he went the desirability of getting mails through as quickly as possible was impressed on him by business men'.[163] From Calcutta he returned briefly to Delhi before flying north to Lahore, and from there, accompanied by Air Marshall Sir John Steel, Londonderry embarked on a tour of the Northwest Frontier.[164] The political purpose of this part of his trip was unmistakable. The RAF's role in policing India's border with Afghanistan had grown gradually since the mid-1920s, and although the Government of India had refused to transfer operational control from the army, Willingdon, a National Liberal, and Hoare, the India secretary and a former air minister, were both keen to safeguard the air force's role on the frontier.[165] Londonderry duly visited Peshawar, Malakand and the Khajuri plain.[166] As intended, the visit attracted publicity, though Londonderry's memoirs barely touch on his time there.[167] His wife's memoirs, in contrast, are more forthcoming, expanding on an incident reported in the press in which Lord Londonderry's flight over the mountains near Quetta encountered a pocket of air that caused his aeroplane to drop 2,000 feet.[168] Several of Lady Londonderry's other observations on the visit are worth quoting:

> This was a unique experience not only for a Secretary of State, but also for anyone even in these days, for he flew all over [the Northwest Frontier], and his pilot pointed out to him the tribes in that neighbourhood. He motored up the Malakand and also up the Khyber Pass again, going through Jamrud and Ali Musjid. He went on to Landikotal [*sic*] and looked over the Afghan frontier towards Kabul. He also motored through the Kohat Pass, and on his way back saw a rifle factory which is in the hands of the Pathans . . . They are very warlike but very fine people . . . My husband was presented with a rifle made at the rifle factory, and a large fierce looking dagger.

Lady Londonderry then offered a frank assessment of the RAF's role in the area using phrasing that was typically employed by air power advocates. 'The Air Force have done a great work in the North-West Frontier Province, and have maintained order with the minimum loss of life and the minimum of expenditure. The threat of a village being bombed, which is only carried out after due notice, causes recalcitrant tribes to think better of breaking the law.'[169]

On the return journey from Karachi to London, Lord Londonderry stopped at Rome on 29 January to meet with his Italian counterpart. On this occasion, it was not Balbo but Benito Mussolini, the country's dictator, who had the previous year transferred Italy's three service ministries to himself in preparation for an eventual colonial war.[170] Along with the Air Ministry's Director of Civil Aviation, Colonel Francis Shelmerdine, and a representative of Imperial Airways, Londonderry hoped in his discussions to end the practice of British air routes to the east having to travel by train from Paris to Brindisi, so that the entire journey could be accomplished by air.[171] Londonderry was received by Mussolini on 30 January, after which it was announced that a provisional agreement had been reached allowing British civil aircraft on the England–India and England–South Africa routes to fly over Italy.[172] At their meeting, Mussolini also signalled that he would support a convention to control German rearmament.[173]

If Londonderry's two winter tours of overseas RAF units, in 1933 and 1933–4, were intended to highlight the necessity of retaining the air force's overseas commitments, the debate about aerial bombing had moved on considerably during the second tour as a result of the failure of the disarmament conference, a report produced by the Defence Requirements Committee, and growing evidence that Germany was rearming illegally. As a result, on 2 March 1934, the air minister announced a modest expansion to the RAF, justifying it on the basis that the other powers had failed to reduce their air forces in line with the MacDonald plan.[174] However, in welcoming the 'definite statement' from Baldwin on RAF expansion, Londonderry failed to appreciate fully at this point that the perceived public demand that had initiated the policy reversal could also dictate its pace.[175] This blind spot, which grew more pronounced in the weeks and months that followed, would lead some Conservatives to hope for a cabinet reshuffle that might remove Londonderry, Simon and other 'dead wood'.[176]

The disarmament conference's demise was hugely significant, and not only for ushering in a period of rearmament. It represented what David French describes as the final crumbling away of the liberal international order that Great Britain had helped to fashion in 1918 and to reshape in their own interests in the years that followed.[177] Londonderry's determined defence of the RAF might have been blamed by some for playing its part in this outcome, but it was not his intention nor was it a development that he welcomed. As such, he along with Simon became associated with Sir Evelyn Wrench's All Peoples' Association, which sought to promote international dialogue through a global network of branches. Londonderry, as chairman of the Committee of International Understanding and Co-operation, addressed the official opening of its London branch by praising Wrench's 'internationalism' in front of an audience of ambassadors and ministers representing other countries.[178]

In the early months of 1934, it appeared on the surface as if Londonderry and his cabinet colleagues were in harmony. Therefore, when further schemes for an international disarmament agreement were circulated among the cabinet in April, both Londonderry and Baldwin were pessimistic about such a move, especially with increasing rumours of significant German rearmament.[179] On 17 May the Cabinet Disarmament Committee, which had hitherto been reluctant to approve the Air Ministry's views, now ratified its plans for expansion. A week later, on Empire Day, in a speech to the Royal Empire Society that was broadcast on the radio, Londonderry argued that the government had earnestly pursued disarmament but as others had refused to follow its lead the National Government had no choice but to rebuild the country's armaments.[180] He relayed the same message at a garden party the following month in Lanarkshire, given by the Marquess of Clydesdale, MP for Renfrew East and a noted aviator, on that occasion also invoking the 'wishes of our own people' to reinforce his case.[181] Unavoidably, the government's new policy encouraged rumours of another war. At a graduation ceremony in July at Queen's University, and at a dinner at Sunderland the following month, Londonderry attributed the rumours to the rising generation which lacked direct personal experience of the 'catastrophe' of war.[182]

Toeing the line, and defending the government's record, did not stem the criticisms directed at its air armaments policy from the right or the left. Churchill attacked the government for not arming fast enough, and the Labour party condemned it for risking the destruction of another war through its failure at Geneva. Confined to the upper house, Londonderry could not address Churchill directly, or for that matter, Clement Attlee, the rising star of the Labour Party and by now one of his most vociferous critics.[183] Attlee, to be sure, was consistent in his criticism of aerial bombing: 'I doubt very much whether bombing in outlying regions is justifiable. I do not see a nice point of ethics between bombing an Indian village or an Arab encampment and dropping bombs on a great Western city', he had informed the House of Commons in June 1933.[184] But his own position inevitably raised the question of why Labour had not abolished the practice during its two periods in office. A plausible explanation is that the purported 'moral effect' of air policing underwent a change in 1924, corresponding with the first Labour government. Originally, the expression had been used by the RAF to refer to killing and maiming those resisting lawful authority and threats of the same. But from 1924, the emphasis was placed instead on the air force's capacity to disrupt everyday life. This was accompanied by the removal of references to deaths in published RAF reports and the use of euphemisms in their stead, a practice that took on a new importance during the disarmament conference. Attlee's concerns aside, Labour in office appears to have been convinced by this shift in emphasis, so that the National Government only had to worry about how the opposition presented aerial bombing as an obstacle to peace in Europe.[185]

In advance of a question from Attlee scheduled for 19 July, which Baldwin would likely have to answer, Londonderry wrote to the Lord President to argue that although there was no total protection for the country against aerial bombing, this should be a reason for rearmament and not another fruitless quest for the abolition of aerial bombing. No one would suggest, he insisted, that because the Royal Navy could not provide complete protection against an attack 'it is useless to maintain a navy'. In the House of Commons, Baldwin took a less confrontational approach that was intended to neutralize Attlee's attack, announcing that the RAF's expansion did not diminish the National Government's goal of working towards international disarmament.[186] In contrast to Baldwin, Londonderry confidently asserted in the House of Lords that the proposed expansion would be a deterrent, not merely to war, but also to an armaments race. He was careful to couch this in terms similar to Baldwin,

> although we still ought not to abandon all hope of something materialising at Geneva, the idea of parity in the air with any Power within striking distance must be a cardinal principal of policy. If this new policy was effectively carried it would strengthen our influence for peace, and, far from inaugurating a new race in armaments, might effectively stop one.[187]

In his memoirs, Londonderry attributed his colleagues' change of heart at this time to his own efforts.[188] He received some sympathetic support for this assumption from others, including the Chief of the Air Staff, Sir Edward Ellington.[189] But Londonderry's stalwart defence of the existence and independence of the air force, his efforts at Geneva to prevent the abolition of aerial bombing and his disquiet about the 1933 air estimates were not the reasons for Baldwin's change of tack. The explanation lies instead with the Lord President's reading of shifting public opinion, the total collapse of the disarmament conference, the hectoring of Churchill and backbench pressure. The thread which actually ran throughout, as far as Londonderry's critics were concerned, was the air minister's lack of sensitivity to these wider factors.

At root, it was fear of German rearmament during the second half of 1934 that transformed the debate about RAF expansion from whether it should happen to the rate and size of the increase. The result was that the careful steps taken in the summer of 1934 to reorient the National Government's aerial armaments policy transformed within a year into a panicked dash. The Air Ministry's sources recorded that Germany was steadily expanding its air strength, but Churchill attacked its assessment for failing to take account of the potential for enlarged production. Londonderry, however, was determined to avoid the implications of Churchill's scaremongering. Speaking at Darlington on 22 October, he attempted to reassure his audience that the new policy 'had no element of panic'. He went on, somewhat belatedly, to address Churchill's concerns, which were now amplified by another former air minister, the press baron Lord Rothermere. 'From those who were crying out for a vast armament of aeroplanes immediately, he would ask first to what purpose they were to be put and for what immediate crisis they were intended. Then he would inquire where they were to be housed, and how they were to be manned.' Londonderry remarked pointedly that demands 'of this kind might be inspired by patriotism, but they were certainly not inspired by statesmanship. We obviously had no need of an enormous fleet of aeroplanes of this kind now'.[190]

On 9 November Londonderry gave an address to the Lord Mayor of London's banquet at the Guildhall, three years after his first controversial address to the same city function. In many ways the two speeches were the same, but the first was made at a time of expectation, prior to the World Disarmament Conference, whereas the latter was delivered in its ruins. Addressing his critics in the Labour Party, Londonderry defended the RAF's expansion on the basis that the United Kingdom required protection as other states had failed to limit their air forces. He went on to argue that 'No armaments which we might provide for our defences would ever be regarded by the rest of the world as containing a menace to the world's peace.' Instead, 'they would minister to the cause of peace, for they would aid the establishment of a general sense of security and greatly diminish that fatal fever of suspicion and the international tension to which it gave rise'.[191]

Londonderry's underlying rationale was that strengthening the armed forces in a responsible manner would put pressure on the German government to reach a limitation agreement. He was motivated by respect for Germany not hostility, for his experience at Geneva had reinforced his sympathies for that country and filled him with contempt for France, whose leaders he blamed for ruining any possible agreement.[192] He was not, however, on the cabinet subcommittee now charged with considering German rearmament. He therefore encouraged his daughter Maureen, and her husband Oliver Stanley, the Minister of Labour, to use their forthcoming trip to Berlin in October 1934 to meet the German air minister, Hermann Göring. The meeting was duly arranged for the evening of the 4th. Sitting with Göring in the palace of the Reichstag president, the Stanleys were assured by their host that he desired an air force that would present no threat to the British.[193] That response prompted Londonderry to write to Hailsham, as his friend was a member of the subcommittee then considering German rearmament. The air minister used his letter to advocate the readmission of Germany into the League. He argued that this could have three alternative outcomes.

> The first is that we should be successful in converting them into helpful partners in the scheme of the world; the second is that if the first fails we should be in a position, by knowing what the Germans are doing, to immobilize their hostile activities; and the third is that if the Germans are determined . . . to be wholly aggressive and unwilling to join in a peaceful comity of nations, then they will stand arraigned in their true colours before the world.[194]

Londonderry's hope that Germany's readmission to the League might bring clarity about its intentions is understandable given Berlin's inconsistent policies since the Nazi accession to power; such as Hitler's apparent support for the MacDonald plan when it was presented to the disarmament conference, only to be followed by Germany's withdrawal from the conference and the League; and the stark contrast between Germany's non-aggression pact with Poland and the aggressive attitude that it adopted towards Austria.[195]

Readmitting Germany to the League, he pointed out to Hailsham, would not be surrendering to them. It would, rather, re-establish their lost prestige and help to bring about a limitation agreement that would enable the world to be certain of what the Germans possessed:

> If I am entirely wrong, I do not see that the situation is rendered more difficult than it is at the present moment. The practical view which appeals to me at this moment is that whereas we may move some distance along the road of idealism by reason of the Germans not being in a position to challenge the world, this situation will be entirely altered in a comparatively short space of time, and we shall then

> find ourselves up against ultimatums from Germany and a power behind those ultimatums which will plunge the world once more into the catastrophe of war.[196]

Hailsham later noted that Baldwin adjourned the subcommittee considering German rearmament after Londonderry's letter was read, having decided to wait for the Saar plebiscite on rejoining Germany before making a decision on its content.[197] Baldwin and Simon subsequently decided that something had to be done and so began months of diplomatic efforts to secure Italian and French backing for an arrangement with Germany, culminating in the defence white paper of 1935 and Simon and Eden's meeting with Hitler in March that year.[198] Although Londonderry had encouraged this process, he would later attach a different importance to his letters to Hailsham.[199] Privately and in print, he argued that the letters justified his later promotion of Anglo-German understanding; that had his advice been adopted in 1934, Germany would not have become as powerful or uncontrollable as it became in the late 1930s (see Chapter 7).

In anticipation of Churchill questioning British assessments of Germany's air strength, the cabinet arranged to meet on 28 November to agree on Baldwin's statement. Still hoping for a limitation agreement, Londonderry warned MacDonald beforehand that any announcement would reveal that the government had known all along about German rearmament and that it had only the policy of an arms race to counter it.[200] Londonderry, like the Air Staff, was wary of the consequences of making definite statements. In cabinet, he advised that specific figures should be avoided and assured his colleagues that his ministry, contrary to the claims of Churchill, was monitoring German expansion accurately. For its part, the Foreign Office regarded the French claim of over 1,000 first-line aircraft to be excessive, preferring instead the figure of 600. Londonderry in contrast stated that the figure stood at 1,000 military aircraft, including first line and training aeroplanes, with an estimated production rate of between 160 and 180 aircraft per month.[201]

In spite of Londonderry's concerns about stating figures, Baldwin wanted his House of Commons statement to be a warning that the British government was aware of German rearmament. During the course of the debate Churchill asserted that by 1936 the Luftwaffe would overtake the RAF, and that it would double its size the following year. Baldwin in reply accused him of exaggerating, arguing that it was impossible to predict beyond two years. He then countered Churchill's claims by citing the figures given in cabinet: that Germany possessed between 600 and 1,000 aircraft in total, that this was not its first-line strength and that, however rapidly it might try to rearm, Germany lacked the infrastructure possessed by the British. His statement, based largely on Air Ministry advice, was correct in as much as it referred to first-line aircraft. On this basis, the Lord President assured the House of Commons and the country that aircraft production would keep a position 'not inferior' to the Germans.[202]

It appeared that Londonderry's views were once again in line with those of his colleagues. His figures were used to challenge a volatile and potentially destabilizing attack from Churchill, and his hopes of a rapprochement with Germany were shared by Baldwin and the Foreign Office. However, he remained outside the formal diplomatic efforts to pursue this policy and could only exercise influence from the sidelines. In December he wrote to Simon to blame the French for the breakdown of the disarmament conference and to promote the recognition of equal treatment for Germany within a limitation agreement.[203] It is noteworthy that by this stage even Simon had moved to a more pro-German attitude, one that compelled Baldwin to exercise restraint over him during his discussions with the French.[204] Not long after, Londonderry's attention was drawn to the unofficial meeting between Hitler and the Liberal peer, Lord Lothian, in January 1935; the two marquesses subsequently exchanged positive views on the German chancellor.[205] The following month, on 24 February, Londonderry's peculiar usefulness to the government was utilized again when Londonderry House hosted a dinner for the beleaguered chancellor of Austria, Kurt Schuschnigg.[206]

V

Superficially at least, Londonderry's position appeared to be secure in the early months of 1935. He had spent the Christmas break relaxing at Mount Stewart, from where he reminisced with Lord Craigavon, and then at County Durham, where he echoed the views of others in the National Government by giving a cautious welcome to David Lloyd George's plans for national recovery.[207] More significantly, Londonderry rose to the challenge of defending the government's legislative scheme to extend Indian responsible government, siding with Baldwin on an issue that had provoked diehard Conservative MPs to launch a sustained campaign of opposition.[208]

Londonderry's support for Indian reform was not, however, like his matter-of-fact statements on the Soviet Union, a mere affirmation of government policy. Addressing a large meeting of Conservatives at Torquay on 16 March 1933, he had defended the government's India white paper against accusations that it was socialist in origin and inspiration. In comments directed at the diehards, whose number now included Churchill, he remarked, 'Those who were pulling this scheme to pieces were supplying no alternative for the solution of the problem, which every day was increasing in its magnitude. In every attack which was made on any progressive policy there was always one section which advocated doing nothing.' Conscious of the considerable unease in his party about appeasing Indian nationalism, Londonderry claimed that he 'understood the critics', but that 'they were telling us nothing new. The Government fully recognized that they were taking risks, and they had weighed them. But they were conscious also of the fact that no great thing was ever done on safety first or "do nothing" principles. Little minds and great empires went ill together'.[209] Again in October 1934, in advance of the India bill's long and tortuous passage through parliament, he argued before an audience at the Mechanics Institute, Darlington, that the reforms were 'progressive' and in the tradition of constitutional developments across the empire: 'Why should we make so great an exception in the case of India, by seeking to maintain an old-fashioned method of Government and giving as our reason that we were fearful that the numerous communities in India were incapable of exercising those powers of self-government which had proved so beneficial to all other portions of the Empire?'[210] A month later, at Maidstone, he returned to the theme of historical development:

> For a century . . . we had been extending the principle of responsible government throughout the Empire. The case of South Africa and the case of the American Colonies, each in its own way, proved the wisdom of this policy and the folly of anything else. Therefore in the case of India it was the course both of honour and of interest to concede as much of responsible government as the circumstances permitted.

He acknowledged that some remained to be convinced, but he noted that 'the impressive fact [is] . . . that so many had expanded their ideas as they came more and more into contact with the living facts'. He supported the government's policy 'as a Conservative supporter of the National Government, who wished to preserve the unity of the great traditions of the Conservative Party, to keep India a contented member of the British Commonwealth, to do justice to our Indian fellow subjects, to safeguard our own interests, and, above all, to discharge our obligations'.[211] In January 1935, at Seaham Harbour, he took aim again at the diehards for denying the Indian people the 'advantages of democratic government', and for the impact of their agitation on the Conservative Party.

> If they can achieve the split which they seem in the process of making . . . there is a great danger of finding ourselves at the next election in a position of, I do not say defeat, but in such a position that the majority in the House of Commons will not be one which will be able to give that strength necessary to the National Government.[212]

On 19 February he hosted a talk at Londonderry House on the India bill that was addressed by the former viceroy, Lord Halifax, arguably the instigator of the most recent British push to extend Indian responsible government.[213] As such, Baldwin could not fault Londonderry when it came to the crisis over India that rocked the Conservative party in the early months of 1935, but this would not be enough to save his position at the Air Ministry in the months that followed.

On 4 March the government published its defence white paper. It dealt among other things with the increased investment in aerial defence and the conditions for German rearmament. The RAF's expansion was outlined the following day when Londonderry released the Air Ministry's estimates for 1935.[214] However, on 8 March, the day before the House of Commons was due to discuss the white paper, Göring admitted publicly that his country possessed an air force. Londonderry attempted to ease fears by assuring the parliamentary Air Committee on 13 March that 'nearly twice as many machines would be ordered' for the RAF in the coming year.[215] Growing public unease prompted Baldwin to seek further assurances from Londonderry that measures were being developed to counter an air attack; he was informed that progress was being made.[216] Then, on 16 March, Hitler announced the introduction of conscription to raise his army to 500,000 men.

The cabinet met two days later to agree that Simon and Eden would visit Hitler as previously arranged, but that they would convey their government's protest about Germany's breach of the Versailles treaty. When they met with Hitler on 25 and 26 March, Simon and Eden failed to persuade the chancellor of the need for limitation, and worse still, they came away with something fatal to diplomatic efforts up to that point. When asked about the Luftwaffe, Hitler declared that it had already reached parity with the RAF and would soon reach it with the French air force. Although Londonderry maintained at the time, and subsequently, that Hitler's statement was incorrect, and was, after the fact, judged to be correct in his assessment of its veracity, the anxiety it created ensured that the air minister's view was set aside and his credibility badly damaged.

With the cabinet, the press and the country at large in a state of panic, Londonderry was summoned to Buckingham Palace to explain himself.[217] Rothermere's newspapers singled him out for blame, though the proprietor claimed in a letter to Londonderry that he had 'not the remotest intention of criticising you personally'. '[T]he figure, viz. nearly 11,000 given to me by Hitler as the present strength of the German air force is likely to be accurate', he went on. 'I have German relatives and travel a great deal in Germany so I really know what goes on better than almost any Englishman.'[218] The government was thus faced with two contradictory claims, Londonderry's and Hitler's, and as noted by the Chancellor of the Duchy of Lancaster, J. C. C. Davidson, the resulting dilemma meant that it was compelled to prepare for the worst-case scenario.[219] A contributing factor was the weakness of British intelligence gathering and analysis. The Foreign Office and the three service ministries each had their own intelligence departments, with their own specialist officers charged with assessing the significance of the intelligence gathered. It was always possible, even probable, that their respective assessments of German armaments would be different. The winding up of the Inter-Allied Control commission in 1927 had deprived analysts of reliable information, and it made them even more reliant on journalists, diplomats and the Secret Intelligence Service. Information gathering became still more difficult under the Nazis, in what was now a police state, a problem that was exacerbated by Hitler's tendency to make policy without proper thought or preparation.[220] The chief mandarin at the Foreign Office, Robert Vansittart, was moved to use his own intelligence gathering, and as a consequence he entered what Wesley Wark calls 'a vigorous battle of half truths' with Londonderry on the German figures.[221] Simon panicked and like Vansittart he believed Hitler rather than the Air Ministry.[222] The foreign secretary then circulated a letter to his cabinet colleagues declaring that the Germans had no motive to exaggerate the size of the Luftwaffe and that they had indeed reached parity. Convinced that Hitler had deceived Simon, Londonderry denied the claim and on that basis the Air Ministry made preparations for a comparatively modest expansion of the RAF.[223]

Given its possession of reasonably accurate figures for the composition of the Luftwaffe, the Air Ministry's confidence in its own response was based on the assumption that German expansion would be as efficiently executed as the RAF's, and that as a result the Luftwaffe could not realistically achieve parity in the near future. In an already febrile atmosphere, it was this assumption that the alarmists rounded on in the weeks that followed. When the Air Ministry conceded that German aircraft output might be greater than that in the United Kingdom, but that RAF expansion must proceed carefully as the Air Staff regarded efficiency, resources, training and industrial organization as more important, its critics had all the ammunition they required. The Air Ministry protested that it could do little else after years of neglect, and that any scheme of expansion needed to be done in consultation with aircraft manufacturers.[224] By taking this line Londonderry no doubt felt that he was doing the best thing for the air force; it was after all a view shared by the first Baron Weir of Eastwood, the widely respected Scottish industrialist who had for many years worked closely with officials at the Air Ministry.[225] The alternative response, which was implicitly accepted by some air power enthusiasts, would have required Londonderry to work with the shift in public opinion in the hope of producing a more desirable outcome.[226] That, of course, would have risked riding roughshod over the understandable concerns of RAF personnel and the aircraft industry. It would also have meant accepting the fact that several trying years defending the RAF's role in the Middle East had little or no bearing on the service's expansion, and that this was instead the result of an off-the-cuff remark by a foreign dictator.

With the pressure for rapid expansion coming from all quarters, Londonderry's scheme for expansion was sidelined. Even Neville Chamberlain joined the clamour, calculating that it would be easier to get air force expansion through parliament than proposals to expand the army or navy.[227] Consequently, a new subcommittee of the Cabinet Disarmament Committee was established on 30 April under Cunliffe-Lister, the colonial secretary. In consultation with the Air Ministry, it discussed schemes for an accelerated expansion of the RAF. The subcommittee undermined Londonderry not only by its very existence, but also by treating him, along with Ellington and various intelligence officers, as if they were witnesses to be cross-examined. The colonial secretary afterwards reported to Baldwin on 10 May that Hitler's assertion was correct.[228] J. C. C. Davidson's conclusion was closer to the truth, 'Although it was clear that the Air Ministry was absolutely right . . . there seemed to be a certain lack of drive in their programme. I know that SB [Baldwin] attributed the responsibility to Londonderry personally.' Davidson, a former Conservative party chairman, had a poor opinion of the air minister's political abilities:

> Londonderry had the reputation of being a rather soft, Regency-beau type of man. Although he had a certain amount of cunning and capacity, he was not really equipped for thinking . . . He was never really fit for Cabinet rank, and his association with the Air Force was, although keen, rather on the social than the technical side. Amongst the politicians of the Party – people like [Viscount] Bridgeman and [Edward] Wood and Sam Hoare, he was regarded as a lightweight and only fit for an under-secretaryship . . . He hadn't got the capacity to deal with his Air Council or to give them a positive lead, and their intelligence department was always regarded by the two other fighting departments and by the Foreign Office as extremely weak. But Londonderry took himself very seriously.[229]

Even before the establishment of Cunliffe-Lister's subcommittee, Londonderry's authority as air minister had been undermined from another quarter. Countering charges that Great Britain had no air defences, thereby leaving it with only bombers as a deterrent, Londonderry had in January 1935 established a committee of scientists under Henry Tizard that, from its first meeting, helped to bring about the development of radar detection. It also attracted the critical attention of Professor F. A. Lindemann, supported by Austen Chamberlain and Churchill, who pressed MacDonald for a new interdepartmental committee to be formed that would be independent of the Air Ministry. Londonderry mounted a successful defence of Tizard's committee by claiming that it was making progress and that the Air Ministry was able to supply it promptly with funds whenever it was necessary.[230] Nevertheless, while the Air Ministry's committee continued its vital work, Cunliffe-Lister was tasked with also examining the question of air defences.[231]

Attending a royal banquet on 9 May, Londonderry later recalled that Churchill had warned him about 'intrigues' to remove him from the Air Ministry, that 'there was very strong opposition' to his remaining in post, 'they are going to kick you out. I should resign if I were you'.[232] Reflecting back on this period, Londonderry liked to claim that Churchill wanted him to resign so that the two could tour the country campaigning for rapid rearmament, and that it was his loyalty to the government that prevented him from taking this course. At the time, however, the air minister knew that an alliance with Churchill – who had resigned from Baldwin's front bench in 1931 over the latter's support for Indian constitutional reform – would consign him to the political wilderness alongside his cousin. More importantly, he did not agree with Churchill's assessment of German air strength or his calls for rapid rearmament.

Far more serious for Londonderry's future prospects was the attitude and waning influence of MacDonald. Baldwin had been taking over many of the ailing prime minister's duties, and without his political patron Londonderry despaired that his ministerial career was indeed at an end. He wrote to his wife on 27 April, 'I have several enemies and now the [general] election approaches there are one or two who would like to have my place. If I survive I think it will be on your merits. I am sure the P.M. would never sponsor me again and SB has always resented (I think) our support of the P.M.' On the assumption that his 'present post is already allotted', Londonderry offered the bittersweet claim that his successor would 'reap the harvest' that he had sown.[233]

As if reconciled to his fate, Londonderry used his remaining time in office to disagree behind closed doors with the government's new air policy. He also criticized his cabinet colleagues for failing to defend him against press attacks and for their failure to invest in the RAF at an earlier date.[234] As a result, even his relationship with MacDonald worsened. In response to warnings from the prime minister that the Conservatives were against him remaining in office, Londonderry turned on him by attributing the inability of the Air Ministry to defend itself to MacDonald's lack of 'dictator spirit', that while he himself had it, he lacked the power to enforce it.[235]

Cunliffe-Lister produced his report at a full meeting of the Cabinet Disarmament Committee on 12 May. Londonderry was present and claimed that there were 4,000 trained pilots in Germany, despite knowing beforehand that Cunliffe-Lister had estimated it at double that figure. The committee inevitably preferred to work on the basis of the figure given by Cunliffe-Lister.[236] On 20 May Londonderry protested at a cabinet meeting that he had been criticized at Geneva for maintaining the RAF and that he was now being criticized for not rearming at a speed satisfactory to his critics, when 'all he had done was to warn his colleagues of the consequence of an attempt to expand very rapidly'.[237] The cabinet ignored the air minister and formally approved its scheme for rapid expansion.

On 22 May Churchill informed the House of Commons that the Luftwaffe had achieved superiority to the RAF and that by the end of 1935 it would be three to four times as great. In reply, Baldwin admitted that although he was sure that his previous figures for current strength were accurate, he had been misled about future estimates and that the only facts came from Hitler himself. He added that no one minister was responsible and that the government as a whole was at fault.[238] As Davidson noted, Baldwin 'knew it was no longer practicable politics to try to argue in defence of the [Air Ministry] figures. The only practicable and right course was to assume the worst and prepare for it'.[239]

The apologetic tone of Baldwin's speech earned him cheers from the Conservative backbenches. In contrast, Londonderry's contribution in the House of Lords was neither contrite nor well received. The debate in the upper house was opened by the first Baron Lloyd, a leading diehard and a prominent figure in the campaign for rapid rearmament.[240] Londonderry's contribution was ostensibly in response to Lloyd, but he knew that his statement might be his last as air minister, and so he delivered what amounted to a valedictory speech. It included a survey of the development of air policy since the First World War, and he took the opportunity to cast doubt on the veracity of Hitler's claim about Germany's air power. Londonderry suggested that criticisms of the apparently slow rate of the RAF's expansion failed to appreciate an important difference between the two countries:

> In a country under a dictatorship the organisation of industry, the mobilisation of all the various manufacturing activities connected with the output of aircraft and aero engines and the munitions of war from the air, is a matter of comparative simplicity. The people of these islands, on the other hand, are a free people, who will tolerate neither dictators nor the semblance of autocracy. But we can and shall discover our own answer to this particular problem. In our own way we shall set about the immediate organisation of our industrial resources and, by the sacrifices willingly self-imposed of a free people, we shall possess ourselves of the means of self-protection in the unhappy event of war.

Londonderry's patriotic faith in democracy seemed to abandon him, however, when he also expressed his disdain for the 'strange changes in public opinion and public policy in regard to the air arm, which must depend ultimately upon that opinion in a democracy like ours'. But it was his defiant declaration about his efforts to preserve 'the bombing aeroplane' at the World Disarmament Conference that really stood out in the speech, and which handed the Labour Party a weapon to repeatedly attack the National Government:

> Through that period, difficult for any Air Minister and particularly for one who, like myself, has always been convinced of the prime importance of the maintenance

> of an effective air arm to the security of this country, I kept impressing upon my colleagues and upon the country generally the vital nature and place of the Royal Air Force in the scheme of our defences. I had the utmost difficulty at that time, amid the public outcry, in preserving the use of the bombing aeroplane even on the frontiers of the Middle East and India, where it is only owing to the presence of the Air Force that we have controlled these territories without the old and heavy cost in blood and treasure. I felt certain that when the ideals of abolition of Air Forces were examined practically they would be discovered to be inapplicable in the state of the world to-day. We could not put the clock back. Limitation, not abolition, was all we could really hope for. Limitation, I foresaw, was the ultimate policy; the policy which I continually urged; the policy for which I and my advisers at the Air Ministry were constantly preparing; and I am indeed gratified to find in Herr Hitler's words a definite acceptance of this doctrine.

The speech concluded with a quotation from John Milton's *Areopagitica*: 'Methinks I see in my mind a noble and puissant nation rousing herself like a strong man after sleep and shaking her invincible locks. Methinks I see her as an eagle mewing her mighty youth and kindling her undazzled eyes in the midday beam.'[241]

A normally unapologetic Londonderry later realized how misjudged, even vindictive, his speech had been. In November that year he admitted to a sympathetic Labour peer, the tenth Baron Strabolgi:

> [that] my phraseology in the House of Lords was unfortunate, to say the least of it. I really was telling their Lordships that I had the greatest difficulty in maintaining an Air Force because I really accomplished this almost single-handed and my way of explaining this with a certain amount of vindictiveness in my mind was by saying how difficult it had been for me to retain an Air Force at all, and that I was only able to keep the policing of outlying districts, which really is the smallest part of Air Force activities . . . Of course the words 'bomb' and 'bombing' are the authors of the mischief.[242]

Later still he recorded in his memoirs,

> My name became forthwith associated with air bombing and all its attendant horrors . . . It was soon made clear to me that my statement of fact had been unfortunate, however much it was justified. It was not calculated to catch votes, and after all a General Election was in the offing. From a purely political point of view my statement of fact had made me an embarrassment.[243]

On the day following the speech, he was at the centre of another and related storm of controversy. News of the recent shooting down of an RAF aeroplane in Iraq obliged him to publicly revisit the policy of retaining aerial bombing, as well as its controversial role in that supposedly independent country. It 'appears that the machine was not shot down in flames, but that it was set on fire by the tribesmen after the dead bodies of the occupants had been taken out', he informed peers. 'I am very happy to be able to give . . .

the assurance that the aircraft was carrying out a reconnaissance in the course of its duty and was not taking part, in any way in any operations against the rebels.'[244] At the same time, Londonderry also found himself having to respond to the criticism from Berlin that he had singled out Germany as the justification for expanding the RAF. In a follow-up radio broadcast, he tried to correct this by saying that 'Our programme is aimed at no country in particular. It is solely directed towards the maintenance of this country in security against an attack from whatever quarter it might come.'[245]

Londonderry, accompanied by Ellington, marked Empire Air Day with a one-day tour of RAF stations including Upper Heyford, Worthy Down and Gosport.[246] A fortnight later he was out of the Air Ministry. A combination of factors compelled Londonderry's removal in the first week of June 1935. His uneasy relationship with cabinet colleagues, his aloofness from the need to court public opinion and the controversial House of Lords speech that was symptomatic of both. As Churchill put it in his history of the period, the 'Air Ministry did not realise that a new inheritance awaited them. The Treasury's fetters were broken. They had but to ask for more', but instead it 'led its chief into an elaborate vindication of their own past conduct, and in consequence were entirely out of harmony with the new mood of a genuinely alarmed Government and public'.[247]

Not unexpectedly, it was assumed that Londonderry would be removed from the government altogether. Baldwin had indicated as much as far back as 30 April, when he informed MacDonald that Londonderry and Simon had to go – the latter for his handling of the disarmament conference – along with the former's son-in-law, Oliver Stanley.[248] That Londonderry actually remained in the cabinet, as Lord Privy Seal and

Figure 10 David Low, *Evening Standard*, 3 June 1935.

Leader of the House of Lords, is all the more remarkable in view of the quality and range of opposition to him. Still, he had some supporters. Hailsham for one impressed on Baldwin the view that Londonderry 'had worked very hard and loyally for four years', and that he should be retained.[249] On learning that Londonderry was in fact to remain in the cabinet, the Conservative MP, Henry Channon, ascribed this 'surprise' to Lady Londonderry's hold over MacDonald. Perhaps their relationship was a factor, but it had been deteriorating in the run-up to the cabinet reshuffle.[250] The transport minister, Leslie Hore-Belisha, later offered an alternative explanation. He cited Londonderry's retention to highlight an unwelcome feature of British political culture, the 'trouble . . . in all this Cabinet making was that "claims" counted for so much. Meat was all right for the Bar and journalism; if a man did badly at the Bar he failed, while if he did badly at journalism he lost his job, but in politics "claims" counted enormously'. Citing Londonderry as an example of the practice, Hore-Belisha condemned him as 'a second-rate man, not capable at all and really ignorant, yet when they got him out of the Air Ministry he was made Lord Privy Seal'.[251]

After swapping offices with MacDonald to become prime minister, Baldwin informed Londonderry that Cunliffe-Lister would replace him as Secretary of State for Air, explaining that the holder of such an important office needed to be in the House of Commons. It was obvious to Londonderry's wife, among others, that his sinecure as Lord Privy Seal was merely a staggered dismissal, but Londonderry was too keen on office to relinquish the temporary reprieve. Accepting Baldwin's offer, he admitted his disappointment in giving up 'at this point the work of development which after a long struggle is now decided upon, to say nothing of leaving those in the Ministry who have never spared themselves all the years to help me in what at times . . . has been a desperate work'.[252]

Temperamentally, Cunliffe-Lister was very different to Londonderry, and it was the former's hard-headedness, reputation for bluntness and eye for detail which commended him as the man to take charge of the troubled Air Ministry. Even so, Londonderry took exception to Baldwin's suggestion that his successor would succeed better at 'hustling' in the House of Commons: 'I think I can claim to be as capable of that as any one . . . and the record of my work here, especially when as recently the occasion demanded it, will prove what I say'.[253] In his friendly reply Baldwin was 'relieved' with Londonderry's response and reassured him that his cabinet colleagues wanted him to remain among their number.[254] But bereft of a department, Londonderry knew he had 'been got rid off'.[255] The reshuffle was announced on 8 June and on the 17th Londonderry gave his farewell message to the RAF.[256] His departure coincided with the conclusion of the so-called peace ballot, which had been conducted by the League of Nations Union since November 1934. It revealed that almost 90 per cent of its 11.5 million respondents favoured the abolition of military aircraft.[257]

VI

As Leader of the House of Lords and Lord Privy Seal, Londonderry was responsible for managing government business in the upper chamber. Maurice Cowling caustically observes that in this role he was a 'makeweight to Salisbury among peers', but even Londonderry had few illusions about his new position.[258] Not only had he lost his own department, but Baldwin refused to accede to his requests to join the CID and the Defence Requirements Committee. He found little consolation in being allowed to retain his presidency of the Oil Board.[259] In office but not in power, Londonderry considered resigning, but he was persuaded by Hailsham that it was important for the government to stay united at a delicate moment in international relations.[260]

Baldwin's resistance to appointing Londonderry to any committee connected with armaments made political sense even if it disregarded the former air minister's experience and knowledge. Londonderry, however, was not so easily persuaded to abandon his active interest in his former department, and he soon made himself a nuisance to his successor when his interest became bound up with his sense of loyalty to Northern Ireland. His attachment had not abated in the years since his departure from its government in January 1926. Indeed, having initially offered to resign his seat in the Senate, only to be persuaded by Craig to wait until his term expired in 1929, he later attempted without success to be renominated.[261] In February 1926, in the wake of his resignation as Minister of Education, a luncheon in his honour was given by the Lord Mayor of Belfast, Sir William Turner. The mayor remarked 'that though Lord Londonderry was no longer a member of their Government, he remained, if not actually an ambassador for them in England, at any rate their firm and faithful friend, to whom they could always turn in times of difficulty and of whose powerful assistance they could all feel assured'.[262] Londonderry certainly rose to meet this expectation. In July 1932, he discussed with MacDonald the range of possible British reactions to the formation of the first Fianna Fáil government in the Irish Free State, among them, military intervention.[263] The installation of that party in power meant that he was from time to time contacted by former ministerial colleagues at Belfast to exercise his influence on Great Britain's relations with the Irish Free State.[264] Baldwin's infrequent visits to Northern Ireland invariably brought him into contact there with Londonderry, such as in October 1933, when the then Lord President was conferred an honorary degree by the then air minister, in his role as chancellor of Queen's University.[265] And of course Londonderry's son, Lord Castlereagh, continued to sit as the MP for County Down.

When Londonderry heard in the autumn of 1935 that British-led discussions to establish a transatlantic air route to Canada favoured the Irish Free State in preference to Northern Ireland, he registered his opposition to the plan with cabinet colleagues.[266] On this occasion, however, he did so without any prompting or support from the government of Northern Ireland. Already sensitive to being excluded from interfering in the affairs of his former department, Londonderry was informed by his private secretary in late September that the air route was being kept off the cabinet's agenda.[267] He subsequently wrote to Craigavon, who had agreed to the Air Ministry's proposal, to express his misgivings that 'the over-riding principle is that if we do not make this concession to the South of Ireland, we shall find that some foreign nation or nations will jump in to our disadvantage'. He also took issue with Craigavon dissociating himself 'entirely from the political point' in favour of the 'technical point', that is, proximity to North America, describing the outcome as a 'grave injury . . . to British interests and particularly to Northern Ireland'.[268] Writing to Baldwin the following day, Londonderry asserted that 'I ought to be fully aware of the question of the Atlantic Flight from which I have been definitely and deliberately excluded.' It led him to complain that his position as leader of the House of Lords was impossible unless he had close contact with the prime minister and 'those who control policy'. Referring to Baldwin's recent decision to call a general election, he added, 'You asked me if I should be happy in a different kind of life. Happy is a relative term. I am happy in all work, the more strenuous the better: but I am uneasy in the position in which I stand now because I bear full responsibility and have neither power or knowledge.'[269]

At odds with the prime ministers of Great Britain and Northern Ireland over the proposed transatlantic flight, Londonderry was at the same time on the receiving end of criticism from the Labour benches over his record at the World Disarmament Conference. This was given a sharper edge by Italy's use of aerial bombing in its recent invasion of Abyssinia. Labour's attacks invariably undermined Baldwin's effort to draw a line under Londonderry's tenure at the Air Ministry, and the latter compounded the situation by rushing to his defence. Addressing a Conservative fete at Southampton on 27 July, Londonderry offered a relatively novel interpretation of the distinction between Conservative and 'socialist' views of the League of Nations. The former, he argued, did not view the League as a superstate controlling its members, but as the embodiment of collective responsibility for the maintenance of peace. The socialist view, he claimed, in an effort to exploit Labour's internal tensions over the League, 'was nothing more or less than the employment in the last resort of compulsion by force of arms'.[270] Days later, Attlee, Labour's chief spokesman on defence, used the speech to embarrass Baldwin in the House of Commons by pressing the government to clarify its position on the League. Had Londonderry, he asked, challenged the power of its council to recommend what forces each state should contribute to protect the League of Nations' covenants? Baldwin responded by attempting to focus on the Lord Privy Seal's reference to collective security. Attlee, however, continued to press him on why Londonderry had made a distinction between Conservative and socialist views, leaving the prime minister little option but to duck the question by remarking that the press coverage of the speech was 'considerably truncated'. When Baldwin suggested that Attlee look at the speech again with this in mind, and forgetting that Londonderry is 'a colleague', the House of Commons erupted in laughter.[271]

The Abyssinian crisis that rumbled on in the months that followed descended into armed conflict by October. On the 22nd of that month, Londonderry gave his final parliamentary statement as a cabinet minister; it defended the government's support for collective sanctions against Italy in preference to taking unilateral action.[272] Baldwin afterwards had parliament dissolved in preparation for the general election to be held on 14 November. As in 1931, Londonderry became an election issue. In the Seaham constituency, MacDonald's official Labour opponent, Emanuel 'Manny' Shinwell, made much of the former prime minister's friendship with the Londonderrys.[273] But his attacks paled in comparison to Attlee's. In a short cinema newsreel made for the general election, the recently installed Labour leader juxtaposed Baldwin's admission that the 'bomber will always get through' with 'his colleague, Lord Londonderry', who 'boasts at having prevented air disarmament'.[274] The former air minister also featured prominently in the Labour party's manifesto. 'The Government has a terrible responsibility for the present international situation . . . It has wrecked the Disarmament Conference by resisting all the constructive proposals made by other States. As regards air armaments, in particular, Lord Londonderry has boasted that he succeeded, though with great difficulty, in preventing an agreement for the abolition of all national air forces.'[275]

Prevented by his lord lieutenancy from campaigning in County Durham – a predicament that he disliked, though it was not a prohibition that extended to his wife – Londonderry unintentionally assisted Labour's efforts by using the few occasions that he was invited to address Conservatives elsewhere to defend his record as air minister.[276] 'What right had I to accept a doctrine of abolition, however soothing to an anxious people', he informed a meeting at Barnstaple on 5 November, 'and certain though I might have been of receiving the gratitude and applause of Mr Attlee and his friends, when I know that the menace we want to destroy must still exist by reason of Civil machines which, in the absence of Service machines, and without some form of international control, could drop bombs and fire machine-guns with impunity?'[277] Days later, speaking in support of the 'National Government candidates' at Southampton, he declared that 'They tell you that it is our fault that the Disarmament Conference failed, and that I personally am responsible for the breakdown over air disarmament. It is in their manifesto. I have heard Mr Attlee say so on the wireless and on the films. I have read it all over again in the *Daily Herald*. It is all fantastic nonsense.'[278] On 13 November, at Wallasey, he complained that Attlee had 'travestied' his speech on 22 May to the House of Lords, that 'it was to the Socialists and the ultra pacifists at home who were making my task so difficult that I alluded in the passage from my speech in the House of Lords with which Mr Attlee has made so much play during the Election campaign'.[279] On the day before polling, he addressed a meeting in his former Maidstone constituency on the Labour party's deliberate use of 'rowdyism' during the general election campaign.[280] It was a tried and tested method employed by Conservatives to question their opponents' suitability for office, though on this occasion he was probably moved to make the remarks in response to MacDonald's often heckled and ultimately unsuccessful campaign to retain Seaham.[281]

As expected, Baldwin remained in power with a decreased majority. Free of MacDonald's influence and with his own mandate for government, Baldwin wrote to Londonderry on 21 November. The prime minister expressed his profound distress 'that I find myself unable to offer you a place in the new Government . . . I have more men than places'. He went on,

> You remember our talk in the House: you know what I feel. You have ever been a loyal and trusted friend; I think I know what you will feel. Yet I have faith to believe that our friendship is too firmly based to be broken by a cruel political necessity which obliges a PM – and none have escaped it – to inflict pain on those they hold not only in regard but in affection.[282]

Castlereagh came across his father in Londonderry House after he had received the letter. 'He was a tragic sight . . . I never really knew before the meaning of the phrase

"A broken man." He was sitting sideways in his chair with his legs dangling over the arm. Holding a letter in his hand and with the tears running down his cheeks, he kept muttering: "I've been sacked – kicked out."'[283] Baldwin and the Londonderrys subsequently agreed not to hold the customary eve of parliament reception at Londonderry House, and a press statement was released to this effect.[284] Lord Londonderry later recalled that the prime minister had reached this decision 'because of a threatened coal strike which I told you would not materialize . . . It was not the real reason and just that we were speaking in different languages'.[285]

Londonderry was never able to fully reconcile himself with Baldwin's decision to remove him from the Air Ministry and subsequently the government. 'I recollect that you very expressly said that if I joined your Government in June [1935] I might retain the leadership of the House of Lords as long as I wished to do so', he wrote in November. 'This hardly corresponds with your present decisions.'[286] This missive was followed by more letters of bitter complaint – Baldwin had 'destroyed him' – that lasted for years, much of which Baldwin chose to ignore. If Londonderry's grievance with the prime minister was personal, it happened to coincide with the decline of Baldwin's popularity from its earlier peaks. As Austen Chamberlain observed in June 1936, his 'moral reputation, which was his strength, seems gone. There is no man now to praise him . . . Now he has Duff Cooper and Londonderry on his hands. He will not spend a happy weekend I fear'.[287] But Londonderry never posed a serious threat to Baldwin, nor did he ever try to do so. If anything, he felt that the worsening international situation bound him to avoid doing anything that might be perceived as a calculated attack on the National Government. He therefore had nothing to do with Churchill's famous challenge to Baldwin's authority in this period, the putative 'King's Party', that rallied to the cause of Edward VIII during the abdication crisis.[288]

Londonderry nevertheless sought to vindicate his record at the Air Ministry. The first attempt, a lengthy letter to *The Times*, 'now that the election is over', was published on 30 December.[289] It drew a sharp response from Attlee in the same newspaper. He accused Londonderry of focusing at Geneva on preserving the RAF rather than taking the lead in devising the means to achieving an end to aerial bombing: 'he never really believed in abolition or in the internationalization of civil aviation. He pinned his faith to limitation, and above all desired the continuance of national air forces'. The Labour party's leader juxtaposed Baldwin's famous admission that there was no security against aerial attack with Londonderry's preference for 'individual' over 'collective' security. 'The fact is that Lord Londonderry belongs to a past age. He does not believe in international action to remove the air menace, or in an effective League of Nations. He stands for old fashioned national defence and Power politics.'[290] Londonderry's determination to correct Attlee, and rebut the very different criticisms of air policy articulated by Rothermere and Churchill, contributed in the longer run to the publication in 1938 of *Ourselves and Germany*, an article on aerial bombing the following year, and his memoirs, *Wings of Destiny*, published in 1943.[291]

More immediately, the hurt felt by Londonderry was deepened in May 1936 when his successor at the Air Ministry, Cunliffe-Lister, was created Viscount Swinton, with a seat in the House of Lords. 'The reason you gave me for taking the Air Ministry away from me was that it was an Office which must be held by a member of the House of Commons', he wrote to Baldwin in the wake of Swinton's elevation.[292] He found little comfort in the years that followed, as public anxiety about air armaments refused to abate under Swinton's stewardship of the Air Ministry, or from the fact that Swinton, like his predecessor, would in April 1938 be sidelined – from an Air Council inquiry on rearmament – and then replaced the following month as air minister by Sir Kingsley Wood.[293]

VII

Londonderry's dismissal from the National Government led him in the months that followed to search for issues through which he could make his voice heard. Inevitably, his determination to counter Labour's criticisms that he was a warmonger, which led him to promote the cause of Anglo-German understanding (see Chapter 7), overshadowed everything else. But for a moment, in December 1935, it looked as if he might re-emerge as a prominent advocate of industrial co-operation in the coal industry. In contrast to earlier periods of economic instability, miners' wages in the early 1930s had been remarkably stable against the backdrop of the great depression.[294] At the same time, the Coal Mines Act 1930 encouraged a discernible shift in the attitude of most colliery owners.[295] In particular, the reduction of the working day to 7½ hours disposed them to lessen their attachment to district arrangements in favour of collective or national discussions about wages, in the spirit of what Londonderry had advocated in 1926 (see Chapter 5).

The changed mood was observable at Dawdon. At a ceremony held on 9 January 1932, almost three years after Londonderry had locked out his employees for fifteen weeks, he and Castlereagh formally opened new pit head baths at the colliery, designed to accommodate 2,500 men, at a cost of £32,000. 'Some of you – and I believe you do it more good-naturedly than otherwise – are inclined to express your criticism not only of me but of my forebears in very forcible language (Laughter)', he was reported as saying to the gathered miners.

> Whatever condemnation you pass on my forebears it is not correct. They have always tried to inculcate in those of us who came after them a sense of our responsibilities, and I sincerely hope that I have been able to carry out with some success those duties . . . My sympathies and my hopes are with the people in this neighbourhood to which I am proud to belong.

In his vote of thanks, James Gilliland, a senior official in the Durham Miners' Association, made the remarkable declaration that

> if the question of the ownership of Dawdon Colliery was put to the vote of the workers, 90 per cent would vote in favour of the continued ownership of Lord Londonderry (Cheers). He knew of some collieries that had passed out of the hands of Lord Londonderry, and, if the workmen were given an opportunity to ballot, they would come back again.[296]

Given such praise, it is little wonder that colliery owners in the area were disinclined to support the Non-Political Union, to the considerable frustration of local Conservatives.[297] When Havelock Wilson requested that Londonderry contribute towards the £30,000 required to establish the organization, he gave it only £50 and asked that it should not be publicized as it would antagonize the Durham Miners' Association.

Developments at Dawdon vindicated Londonderry's efforts to maintain what remained of the paternalism practised by his forebears. In this spirit, he responded to a request from Seaham Urban District Council for the sale or lease of his land at Dawdon Dene, for the purpose of creating a public park, by announcing in July 1933 that he would transfer 21 acres as a gift.[298] In December that year, against the backdrop of rising unemployment on the Durham coalfield, it was announced that he would gift half a ton of coal to each unemployed workman of the Londonderry Collieries in the Seaham district.[299] It has been suggested that these actions were part of a strategy by Londonderry to use his 'extremely influential' and 'tremendously powerful' position locally to assist MacDonald's popularity in the area, as a means of breaking the Labour movement on his doorstep.[300] Undoubtedly, paternalism was a means of promoting bonds that had been placed under strain for several decades by the Durham Miners' Association, and that it therefore stood in the way of the latter fully realizing its goals. But it is hard to credit the individual acts mentioned above with the specific purpose of assisting MacDonald, or the notion that MacDonald's candidature, and his representing Seaham in the National Government interest from 1931, is something that Londonderry had a hand in engineering for his own specific local and industrial purposes.

For her part, Lady Londonderry encouraged philanthropic work in distressed areas through the establishment of the Personal Service League in March 1932. This non-political and non-denominational charity was run, according to Susan Williams, 'by very rich ladies to distribute clothing to the unemployed'.[301] At an early stage of its development, the league recruited Queen Mary as its patron, and by the mid-1930s it had grown into a significant organization.[302] Its local depot for distributing aid to 'worthy' recipients was based at the south Tyneside town of Jarrow.[303] The district was also the site of an analogous counterpart to the Londonderrys' paternalism, in the form of the Special Areas Act 1934, which introduced an element of state support for severely depressed areas. In an effort to highlight that legislation, Lord Londonderry made an official visit to Jarrow on 20 October 1934. Although undertaking the visit on behalf of the government, he did so as a well-known industrialist in the area, and as president of the North Eastern Development Board, a position that he had held since December 1932. Londonderry was conducted by the Mayor of Jarrow on a tour of the recently closed Palmers' shipyard and works, as well as projects to 'alleviate the effects of the depression', including an occupational centre for the unemployed and the local corporation's housing estate. The resulting press coverage was meant to advertise Jarrow's latent potential to private investors as well as its economic plight.[304]

As this suggests, in both his private and public roles, Londonderry's belief in the paramountcy of private enterprise easily survived and accommodated the modest inroads established by the Coal Mines Act 1930 and the Special Areas Act 1934. Another resilient trait was his sensitivity about the reputation of his collieries. The passages on industrial distress in east County Durham in J. B. Priestley's *English Journey*, published by Victor Gollancz in 1934, particularly displeased him.[305] Priestley, like Londonderry, made much of the prevailing ignorance of most people about life and working practices in remote pit villages. Priestley, however, sought to enlighten the general public, whereas Londonderry invoked it to deflect criticism. As noted in Chapter 5, Londonderry took pride in his family's role in creating and building up Seaham Harbour over the preceding century. Priestley, in contrast, described it as a place that looks 'as weird as a cart-horse with scales and fins'; 'it seemed drearier than the ordinary inland mining towns, perhaps because the coast itself there has a dirty and depressing look'. He also observed that 'its citizens are all being shockingly underpaid', but that 'the ground landlords and royalty owners had not done badly out of it'.[306] Priestley's publisher subsequently issued George Orwell's *The Road to Wigan Pier*, which also provided a vivid and widely read insight into the life and work of a miner that, needless to say, bore little relation to how Londonderry perceived the lives and welfare of his workforce.[307] There is a noteworthy coda to Londonderry's reaction to *English Journey*. The book recounts Priestley's visit to an education settlement at Seaham run by Miss Jowitt at Rock House. In the face of opposition from his chief agent and manager of the Londonderry Collieries, Malcolm Dillon, Londonderry made sure that the land on which Rock House stood was subsequently gifted to Jowitt's settlement.[308]

The coal trade's revival in the mid-1930s did not at first lead to any significant increase in wages.[309] As a result, a national miners' strike was in the offing around the time that Londonderry departed from the National Government: a possibility alluded to in the letter quoted above, from Londonderry to Baldwin, about not holding the traditional eve of parliament reception at Londonderry House. But instead of responding negatively to the national wage claim put forward by the MFGB, the MAGB responded by approaching the industry's largest customers to secure an increase in what they paid for coal, so that it could be passed on to the miners. Barry Supple describes the association's response as a new interpretation of self-interest that recognized that most miners could be 'weaned away from their more radical representatives'.[310] It was the type of response that Londonderry had been advocating for almost a decade, and on 11 December 1935 he gave his full backing to the arrangement in the House of Lords:

> I may appear to be an optimist, but I am certain that this is a most favourable moment . . . to begin a new chapter in the history of the coal industry of this country . . . The relations which exist between owners and men in the districts are of the friendliest possible description, and I know that I am not speaking only for myself as I am not unique . . . One does feel that, if it only depended on those friendly relations, we ought definitely and forcibly to resent any interference from an outside quarter; but I know quite well that the problem is of such widespread importance that it must pass into the political arena, and that all those who are considering other problems, and how they correlate to each other, feel they must take some part in settling those differences of opinion that are put forward in this industry . . . but I venture to say at the same time that I hope to see the question

> put in its proper perspective, and this great industry not sacrificed entirely to what I might call political exigencies.

He then turned to the past and future organization of the coal trade:

> We had the enterprising pioneer, who in the hope of success was prepared to accept the failure which might be his lot – and if we study the history of the coal trade there are many such failures which are entirely forgotten at the moment, although their contribution to the industry has been of no mean order – but I would say that at this moment the era of the individual playing a lone hand in industry is passed. He must link up with his friends, and his policy must be one of co-operation, a policy in which organised labour, for obvious reasons, has led the way . . . I am not suggesting this organisation for the purpose of the owners' organisation waging war upon the miners' organisation. I want to see the two sides united and co-operating to establish the proper economic prices for the sale of the commodity.

The ultimate rationale for co-operation was the 'cutthroat competition' that he had referred to four years previously (see Chapter 5).

> Each owner was desirous of obtaining markets. If he took the markets from his colleague he was not always averse from that activity, but he did it with one main object in his mind . . . to ensure the continuous working of his pits . . . When demand exceeded supply that policy could be successfully pursued, but the fact that Durham County has presented coal to the consumer at a loss of the best part of £2,000,000 in the last five years shows that that policy requires reconsideration.

What he proposed, he assured peers, was not an arrangement that disadvantaged individual consumers, but which called on 'the actual users, the great companies . . . to play their part in gaining for the miner the living and adequate wage to which he is justly entitled'.

> What is it, then, that we require? First of all, we require the elimination of competition which exists between pits and between districts . . . Secondly, we require a price for coal which will ensure a just return to the owner and a proper wage to the worker, and I shall hope that these two great fundamental principles can be rapidly brought about by the industry itself without the interference of Parliament. Central selling, to be set up forthwith, goes a long way in the direction that I have indicated.

In closing, he cautioned that his suggestions 'will create tremendous changes throughout the industry and throughout the country', as the principle of correlating supplies with demand, alongside the established movement for amalgamations, would inevitably lead to pit closures, derelict districts and unemployment. '[B]ut I venture to put forward my humble opinion, for what it may be worth, that in this age of organisation we cannot afford to follow any haphazard line of policy, or we shall fail in the mission which Great Britain has to fulfil as the leader in the world of progressive development.'[311]

Shortly afterwards, Londonderry approached Beaverbrook about the possibility of the two men working together to promote a scheme along the lines that he had pressed for in parliament. 'The Coal business is not a possibility for me' the proprietor wrote in reply. 'My newspaper business has grown to be very big. And my ambitions have grown to be very small.'[312] As a consequence, the more constructive attitude of coal owners that emerged in this period did so without Londonderry assuming the high profile that he had in previous years. Indeed, aside from addressing the House of Lords on the National Government's Coal bill in 1938, his public interventions on the industry's future decreased markedly in the late 1930s (see Conclusion). His energy was instead consumed by his determination to vindicate his record as air minister, and his related efforts to promote Anglo-German understanding.

VIII

The disarmament campaigner and Nobel Peace Prize winner, Philip Noel-Baker, recounts in his 1979 study of the World Disarmament Conference that Londonderry was a 'hawk' and that he and other British ministers were responsible for its failure.[313] Others have been more sympathetic to Londonderry's difficult role at Geneva, although in contrast to Noel-Baker, there is an accompanying tendency to dismiss him as ineffective. As noted above, J. C. C. Davidson wrote him off as a regency beau. To Vansittart he lacked the strength to impress parliament.[314] Londonderry himself would later lament that he did not have 'the force of personality or, perhaps, the presence' needed for the job.[315] However, not all his contemporaries were so dismissive. There were of course the usual letters of sympathy from close friends.[316] He also received a letter from Baldwin's cousin, Rudyard Kipling, two months before the writer's death: 'I am writing to you to say how sorry I am that after your courageous stand and speech on Re-Armament you are not to lead the debates in the Upper House on this vital matter . . . at any rate, you have put yourself on record, and we shall not forget it.'[317]

In his contemporary analysis of the period, John F. Kennedy, then a student at the University of London, argued that if Londonderry and other ministers had underestimated Germany's rearmament, the British public were equally to blame for the situation by being hostile to rearmament.[318] Robert Sencourt's biography of Churchill, also published in 1940, presented its subject and Londonderry as being in agreement on air force expansion.[319] Similarly, the Oxford historian, R. B. McCallum, speculated in his 1944 study of public opinion that had there been a House of Commons 'Air Force committee' scrutinizing the work of the Air Ministry, 'which contained Mr Churchill, and which Lord Londonderry would have attended as Minister', then it 'might well have brought about a speed-up in rearmament'.[320] In his history of British air power, also published in 1944, Hilary St George Saunders depicted Londonderry as 'an energetic and maligned Secretary of State for Air'.[321] Londonderry's replacement at the Air Ministry, Lord Swinton, provided a similarly positive if more insightful assessment in his memoirs: 'Londonderry had a thankless and impossible task' and 'had no opportunity to give the [aircraft] industry either orders or encouragement. He and his colleagues deserve credit for having maintained the spirit, the tradition and the training of our small Air Force in those disappointing days'.[322]

In *The Gathering Storm*, published after the Second World War, Churchill offered the charitable if patronizing assessment recounted above, that Londonderry had only misled Baldwin about German air estimates because the Air Ministry had misinformed him. After noting that Londonderry had lacked the political potency of Swinton, he still claimed that the great achievement of his 'kinsman . . . was the designing and promotion of the ever-famous Hurricane and Spitfire fighters', something which he correctly claimed that Londonderry had not mentioned in his own defence, at least in print.[323] Similarly, Vansittart later admitted that he was 'sorry' to have embarrassed Londonderry in the wake of Hitler's statement, regarding him as having all the good intentions and vagueness of MacDonald.[324]

Notwithstanding Noel-Baker's assessment, and the Labour party's 1935 general election manifesto, publications by other Labour figures and supporters are remarkably reluctant to heap on criticism. Michael Foot et al. omit him from the 'cast' of their famous critique of appeasement, *Guilty Men*; he is mentioned only in passing, to express what was a conventional view among service ministers: that there was no need for a single co-ordinating defence minister responsible for the three services.[325] The journalist Malcolm Muggeridge took a benign view on his record at Geneva, though it still contained a sting in its tail with the suggestion that if 'Lord Londonderry's reservation' for aerial bombing had not prevented an agreement at the World Disarmament Conference, 'it is highly improbable that, in view of subsequent developments, such an agreement would ever have become operative. At most, Lord Londonderry's guilt may be compared to that of a small boy who, seeing a gang of men bent on setting fire to a house, allowed them to strike a match on the sole of his shoe'.[326]

Without naming Londonderry, the military historian and theorist, Basil Liddell Hart, effectively endorsed his positions on both disarmament and rearmament in *Europe in Arms*, published in 1937. On the former, Liddell Hart observed that 'The cause of peace has suffered much from idealists who, in their enthusiasm, put forward airy solutions that can be easily pricked by technical objectives . . . There is often more restraining power in the cumulative effect of a number of small but practicable checks than in a single sweeping measure formulated in vague terms.' On the need to rapidly rearm, he likewise echoed Londonderry by claiming that 'The creation and expansion of the German Air Force has been carried out in such a haze of secrecy as to foster exaggerated assumptions', and that its rapid expansion was checked by 'the difficulty of training personnel and organizing units as fast as the manufacture of machines, which has been proceeding at a rate that was probably in excess of the capacity to absorb them'.[327] In his memoirs, Hart recalled that 'Londonderry's influence with [MacDonald] enabled him to be more helpful to the RAF than expected, and he served it well in many ways.' But like Churchill, Hart felt that 'it was not in him to take a strong lead in urging radical changes'.[328]

Those historians who have dealt with Londonderry's period at the Air Ministry, typically with a brief synopsis, have for the most part tended to emphasize the constraints under which he operated rather than his perceived shortcomings. Echoing Londonderry's assessment of the disarmament conference, A. J. P. Taylor avers that its failure 'had little to do' with Londonderry's defence of police bombing as the 'real deadlock' was between France and Germany.[329] This is echoed in Andrew Webster's study of interwar disarmament, in which he argues that it was not technical issues such as aerial bombing that determined the fate of the disarmament conference, but the different priorities of Great Britain and France as maritime and land powers, respectively.[330] In his biography of Anthony Eden, David Carlton suggests that Londonderry's stance on the police reservation for the RAF made Baldwin and Eden appear more 'progressive' than they 'wholly deserved'; it could be similarly argued that their priorities made Londonderry appear more intransigent than he actually was.[331] Robert Shay, in his study of the economics of rearmament, highlights the overriding restraint placed on Londonderry by the Treasury.[332] Conversely, Martin Gilbert and Richard Gott view Londonderry's period at the Air Ministry as typical of an appeasement tendency, and one that was effectively instrumentalized for that purpose. 'If the spiritual home of the appeasers was at Cliveden', they write, then 'their happiest working hours were spent at the Air Ministry. From here poured forth the facts and figures that made war seem impossible; the true opiate of the appeasers'.[333] For Robert Rhodes James, Londonderry's eventual downfall was attributable to many factors, his role as a society host, his pro-German views, his ownership of mines and his role as a 'bomber' in the disarmament debate.[334]

Many of the above assessments are reductive in so far as they are not primarily concerned with Londonderry or in fully examining his record at the Air Ministry. The result is that these tend to telescope almost four years into a brief summary that invariably distorts his actions and intentions. Londonderry arrived at the Air Ministry in 1931 having previously served his ministerial apprenticeship there in 1919–21. As he had then, he continued to work closely with the Air Staff, and his personal interest in the potential of aircraft grew considerably. His attachment to his portfolio meant running up against the Treasury's policy responses to the great depression, and the desire of his colleagues in government to sacrifice the practise of aerial bombing for the sake of a diplomatic breakthrough at Geneva. When these same ministers perceived a change in public opinion, following the collapse of the disarmament conference, and especially after Hitler's claim that the Luftwaffe had reached parity with the RAF, Londonderry's determination to explain and implement his ministry's cautious approach to rearmament ran against his colleagues' demand for acceleration. There were thus two highly contrasting contexts in which Londonderry served as air minister. His fidelity to the Air Ministry was a constant. That led to another, the assumption by ministerial colleagues that he was insensitive to the need for political calculations and diplomatic gestures, and that as a result he was unsuited to manage his increasingly demanding and controversial ministerial portfolio.

It is hard not to compare Londonderry's tenure at the Air Ministry with his earlier period at Northern Ireland's Ministry of Education. In both cases, the unelected peer and senator approached ministerial office as a solemn charge. In Northern Ireland, he consistently opposed those seeking to amend his Education Act until it became clear that the prime minister would no longer support him. At the Air Ministry, his persistent adherence to the outlook and working assumptions of the Air Staff ultimately brought about his removal from that department. In an observation that could be made of Craig's government at Belfast a decade earlier, David French remarks that the National Government 'cannot be absolved entirely from the charge that when they were considering how to make good the worst deficiencies of the three services they placed electoral considerations before those of imperial defence'.[335]

It is important, however, not to let these curiously similar trajectories obscure what was actually a more complex record in each office. The first is considered in Chapter 4. As a member of the coalition National Government, Londonderry overcame his own prejudices to support better relations with the Soviet Union and to give his support to tariff reform. He accepted as inevitable some encroachment on individual freedom by the state and large corporations. He actively supported Indian constitutional reform. He consistently addressed Conservative and other meetings across the country, despite or perhaps because he was unelected, including in the politically inhospitable territory of his collieries. Indeed, it is worth noting that despite Rhodes James's assessment, Londonderry's record as a colliery owner was the dog that did not bark, at least on the national stage. What is beyond doubt is that Londonderry became a liability to the National Government in 1935, attacked from the left for not disarming in the air and from the right for not rearming fast enough. It cost him the Air Ministry, and when he persisted in defending his record there, and in trying to involve himself in its business, his place in the National Government. He was hardly the first or last minister to leave office under a cloud. But his time at the Air Ministry would take on a new importance in the years that followed, as Great Britain looked over the precipice at the prospect of another war against Germany.

7

Ourselves and Germany, 1936–49

The years following Lord Londonderry's removal from the cabinet in 1935 are the most infamous portion of his political life. Like the general strike in 1926, he attempted to influence public policy as a private citizen outside of the government. His motivation stemmed from his troubled period at the Air Ministry, but in choosing the avoidance of war through the promotion of Anglo-German understanding, he attracted the criticism, then and ever since, that he was a 'pure pro-Nazi apologist'.[1] Those adopting this interpretation have rarely if ever acknowledged the relevance of his period at the Air Ministry or his approach to interwar politics. When it is noted that he was a former cabinet minister, it is only to boost the significance of his visits to Germany. As a result, he is typically reduced to an effete, out-of-touch aristocrat, a reactionary or simple-minded Conservative wilfully blind to the horrors of Nazism, much like the fictional character of Lord Darlington in Kazuo Ishiguro's 1989 novel, *The Remains of the Day*.[2] The caricature is explicit in the 1981 television series, *Winston Churchill: The Wilderness Years*. In episode 6, Lord and Lady Londonderry – played by David Langton and Patricia Hodge – appear in only one scene, a dinner party, at which the latter holds forth about visiting Nazi Germany and the virtues of Adolf Hitler, with Langton playing the role of a diffident and agreeable husband.[3]

To fully understand the man and his actions, and the significance of both, it is necessary to acknowledge Londonderry's sometimes contradictory public and private statements, his underlying personal motives and that he played a role, often an unwitting part, in events that were out of his control. As Basil Liddell Hart observed in 1937, 'It is easier for men to see the ways in which war may come than how it might be avoided. The hopes that they express have no firm ring of confidence.'[4] It is also important that Londonderry's attitude to Germany in the 1930s is not viewed in isolation. Not only can the seeds of his outlook be detected during the First World War (see Chapter 1), but he had adopted similarly conciliatory positions at the Irish Convention in the late 1910s (see Chapter 2), as a minister in the government of Northern Ireland in the early 1920s (see Chapter 4), during the 1926 general strike and in the latter part of that decade through his participation in the Mond–Turner talks (see Chapter 5). Moreover, his rationale for appeasement extended beyond Germany. In a rare public pronouncement on Japan, delivered in February 1938 to a dinner hosted by the Japan Society at Claridge's, he stated that he

> was one of those who regretted that the Anglo-Japanese alliance no longer existed. He felt sure that the difficulties with which they were confronted and the problems which had to be resolved could be approached in a much easier frame of mind if they had that bond of understanding and unity which was comprised in what was called by the old-fashioned word alliance.[5]

In response to Italy's demands in the early part of 1939 for increased influence in East Africa, which Londonderry described as being 'put forward in a most objectionable and truculent manner', he still maintained that the Italian government should be given a seat on the board of the Suez Canal Company and some interest in the railway to Djibouti, and that these matters should be settled, along with the revision of borders, on the back of an agreement on the reduction of armaments.[6]

In contrast to the period since the Second World War, the term appeasement before then could have a positive connotation. David Dutton observes that it had long been used to describe 'the attempt to diffuse conflict through the pacific settlement of disputes'.[7] As Londonderry wrote to a correspondent in 1937, 'We beat the Germans and I am very glad we did, and it is just because I don't want to have to do it again that I have gone all out to capture the Germans another way.'[8] After 1945, Dutton goes on, it 'took on the more sinister connotation of granting unwarranted concessions and sacrificing the interests of the weak in order to purchase peace at the expense of a third party'.[9] The existence of widespread support in the 1930s for appeasement, or 'the redress of German grievances', on the left and the right, receded afterwards in popular memory as it became synonymous with the 'guilty men' in charge of the National Government, and above all, Neville Chamberlain.[10] The later revisionism that to some extent rescued his reputation, and that of Stanley Baldwin, has eluded Londonderry. In part, the explanation lies with his relative lack of importance when compared to two former premiers. Another significant difference is that Londonderry was out of the government after 1935 and under no compulsion to reckon publicly with the dilemma of how to deal with Germany. Like the former Liberal prime minister, David Lloyd George, and the former Labour party leader, George Lansbury, Londonderry took it upon himself to indulge in amateur diplomacy by travelling to Germany to meet with Hitler. Again, these two men are considerably better-known politicians whose visits to Nazi Germany are readily squared with their internationalism and judged accordingly.[11]

Londonderry was like them guided by what might be described as ideological assumptions. In his case, however, his approach to appeasement was fundamentally Conservative. Geoffrey Hicks observes that Conservative foreign policy had from the mid-nineteenth century followed a basic sequence, beginning with the assumption of minimal engagement with European affairs; then, if peace was threatened, to be willing to consider intervention by dealing with other states, even if repugnant; then to make concessions if necessary; and if these steps failed, to make a definite commitment to deter a would-be aggressor.[12] This approach is evident in Londonderry's two letters to Lord Hailsham written in November 1934, on the options that he believed were available to British ministers in their handling of Germany (see Chapter 6). Londonderry's support for appeasement was therefore rooted in his time at the

Western Front, it was in line with a wide spectrum of opinion in the country, it was not confined to Germany but extended to other revisionist powers and it was grounded in a traditionally Conservative approach to foreign policy. All the same, there is an additional factor that requires consideration.

It is a popular perception that the British aristocracy were leading proponents of appeasement. There is an accompanying belief that many were inclined to fascism, and even that they harboured a desire to establish a fascist government in the United Kingdom. The evidence suggests that most aristocrats were indeed favourable towards appeasement and that some even played a prominent role in promoting better Anglo-German relations. However, it should be remembered that aristocrats tended to be in a better position than most to engage in public work outside the government, and that support for appeasement, as noted already, was by no means exclusive to wealthy nobles. As far as it can be ascertained, and for a variety of reasons, the bulk of the British people appear to have supported the government's rationale for appeasing Germany, at least until after the 1938 Munich agreement. Few wanted to live through another conflict between the European powers, with all its attendant horrors, and now with the significantly enhanced risk that civilian populations would be bombed from the air. In this respect the aristocracy's disposition to appeasement can be understood as being in line with broader attitudes to the possibility of a second world war.

It does not necessarily follow, however, that all were agreed on what appeasement meant in practice, or that they shared a view of international relations. Indeed, in a society noted for its class divisions, the motive of Conservative-supporting aristocrats for promoting the redress of German grievances, following the Nazis' assumption of power, differed significantly from the rationale of its enthusiasts on the Labour benches.[13] Even so, it is noteworthy that Londonderry's efforts elicited the approval of several Labour figures, including the first Baron Noel-Buxton, the first Baron Arnold and the first Baron Allen of Hurtwood.[14] Moreover, Conservative aristocrats could still perceive Nazi Germany to be a threat, but regard Communism as a greater threat, challenging as it did the social order on which everything rested.[15] By the 1930s, British aristocrats had endured half a century of political and economic decline. The most prominent aristocratic appeasers – the second Duke of Westminster, the eighth Duke of Buccleuch and the marquesses of Lothian and Londonderry – were all outside the government, at least from 1936. What they did possess in abundance was status and wealth, two attributes that Joachim von Ribbentrop, the Nazis' foreign affairs expert, confused with political power.[16] In reality, aristocratic interference in the conduct of British foreign policy had to compete with that of government ministers, as well as backbench parliamentarians, the civil service, the armed forces, various interest groups and the press.[17]

David Cannadine observes, 'For many disaffected patricians, [their] outward admiration of fascism was made easier because it seemed as if the regimes of such dictators were merely recreating in a national setting the benevolent paternalism of the landed estate.' This is not a generalization but his assessment of the 'déclassé and marginal', the 'mavericks and rebels . . . vainly struggling to recover their position, and find their bearings, in a new and increasingly hostile world'. As Cannadine goes on to argue, aristocratic decline did not produce a uniformity of responses given the varied economic and social circumstances of landed families.[18] In stark contrast to Londonderry, Sir Oswald Mosley was the heir of a broken up and sold estate. In a rare public pronouncement on Mosley's British Union of Fascists, made in response to the disturbances at its infamous Olympia meeting in June 1934, the then Secretary of State for Air remarked that 'steps must be taken to put a stop to such clashes and to make it clear that the country was to be governed by a constitutional Government and not by a faction. He believed the country was solid behind the determination not to tolerate violence and dictation from any quarter'.[19] It might be added that right-wing disaffection was not confined to déclassé and marginal landowners. The sons of trade and industry were just as conspicuous in the small and negligible coterie of Roman Catholic and Anglo-Catholic intellectuals who in this period advocated neo-feudalism as the solution to England's ills.[20] Notwithstanding the outlook of all these marginal men, the old order had not been completely swept aside after the First World War as it had elsewhere in Europe. The majority of British aristocrats therefore had little incentive to support a fascist revolution at home given that they still possessed social and economic privileges that bound them to the status quo.[21] If the fiction of Ishiguro offers Lord Darlington, then P. G. Wodehouse gives us Roderick Spode, leader of the 'Black Shorts'. This 'amateur dictator' is presented as a political oddity and figure of fun, and he drops his movement after unexpectedly inheriting from his uncle the earldom of Sidcup.[22] Disdaining fascism at home could therefore sit alongside accepting that it had taken root in other European countries. The long-established Westphalian system provided an additional rationale for ignoring or playing down the controversial internal policies of fascist states. And the existential threat posed by the Soviet Union served as a reminder about what was at stake should the Communists gain the upper hand.

I

Londonderry's amateur diplomacy was, on the surface, unnecessary for a former cabinet minister in his late fifties with enormous wealth and leisure at his disposal, but he was animated by several factors originating from his recent spell in office. Indeed, far from being what the silent collaborator in his memoirs, *Wings of Destiny*, called an 'incidental' part of his life, Londonderry's interaction with the Nazi leadership can be regarded as the summation of his career in politics, one that he sometimes thought might place him in the pantheon of outstanding diplomatists alongside his famous ancestor Viscount Castlereagh.[23] Londonderry had always been disposed to highlight his familial connection to Castlereagh, whether in Irish matters or those of European diplomacy. In 1925 he had loaned Sir Thomas Lawrence's full-length portrait of Castlereagh to the Foreign Office, so that it could be hung in its reception room at the signing of the treaty of Locarno. The following year he donated a copy of the Lawrence portrait to hang in the Foreign Office's old cabinet room.[24] Castlereagh was of course a controversial figure, but the appearance in the interwar years of four volumes by three historians, Charles Webster, Montgomery Hyde and Sir John Marriott, had gone some way to revising his reputation.[25] Londonderry contributed to this process in 1937, when he publicly corrected the diplomatic historian, Harold Temperley, for failing to recognize that the policy of non-interference in the affairs of another state, which the professor had attributed to George Canning, was in fact inherited from his predecessor at the Foreign Office, Castlereagh.[26] As noted in the Introduction and Chapter 1, it was the sixth Marquess of Londonderry and his wife who had pressed their son into politics and initially guided him. But it was the reputation of the second marquess, known to posterity as Castlereagh, who activated the seventh marquess to a greater extent in the years that followed. From his childhood he was tutored to admire the famous foreign secretary. In adulthood, his ministerial career, like that of Castlereagh, followed a similar progression, from Irish, to British, and finally European affairs, albeit on a less spectacular scale.

Londonderry not only looked back and admired the work of his forebear in Europe, he sought to apply it to the 1930s. *Ourselves and Germany* opens by quoting part of a letter, dated 17 August 1815, from Castlereagh to the then prime minister, the second Earl of Liverpool: 'It is not our business to collect trophies, but to try if we can bring back the world to peaceful habits.' Londonderry's proposed solution to international tensions was also inspired by Castlereagh, namely that the great powers of Western Europe had to collaborate to find a solution to the political crisis.[27] The means by which an agreement could be reached – as he wrote to Lord Halifax in December 1936 – was through a forum that 'resembled' the Congress of Vienna.[28] Londonderry could not avoid seeing direct parallels between 1815 and 1918. Writing in January 1938 he admitted, 'I have always been guided by the doctrines of Castlereagh and the Duke of Wellington who recognised that as soon as the indemnity . . . was paid by France after the Napoleonic Wars, occupation should come to an end and France should have the full opportunity of regaining her equilibrium and playing her part in international affairs.'[29] Following Castlereagh's example also satisfied a more contemporary prejudice, one that had caused Londonderry considerable frustration at the World Disarmament Conference. 'Tories respect size', observed R. B. McCallum in his *Public Opinion and the Last Peace*, published in 1944. 'In international politics they are power-snobs. They think of international diplomacy as a concern of the great powers round which the smaller states are to revolve like satellites. But this, although true to a considerable extent of nineteenth-century Europe, had become a different problem in terms of magnitude in the twentieth century.' There were now, he observed, many more 'second-class powers', their 'relative magnitudes had altered considerably', and to 'dismiss them as small states and leave it at that was both arrogant and ignorant'.[30]

Although Londonderry never stated it explicitly, it is evident from his words and deeds that he believed that he might replicate Castlereagh's success by advocating détente. As such, his repeated invocation of Castlereagh was not only a personal preoccupation, a template that he felt could still be applied to achieve diplomatic success, but also an attempt to associate with and inherit a great man's reputation at a time of personal political isolation. It is certainly the impression that he sought to give to Hitler in 1938 when he sent a copy of a book on the Congress of Vienna to the dictator's translator; Londonderry had already encouraged the author to publish it in German.[31] Inevitably, therefore, the eventual failure of his personal efforts to promote Anglo-German understanding weighed heavily on his sense of family duty.

As he admitted in private, 'I sometimes feel rather sham faced vis-à-vis my ancestors. I feel that they are murmuring: "Well, he might have done better than that," and with the motto I have always had graven on my heart: "Luck is the superstition of the incompetent", I find I have no answer to make.'[32]

Castlereagh was not Londonderry's only source of inspiration. A more immediate role model was Lord Lothian, whose amateur diplomacy paved the way to Hitler's door that Londonderry and others would follow.[33] Londonderry nevertheless acted alone and outside of official channels. Temperamentally inclined to treat his personal crusade for Anglo-German understanding as if it was one of his ministerial appointments, adhering with stubborn determination to the perceived rationality of his lofty goals, it followed that his subsequent complaints of non-recognition by senior government figures echoed his earlier grievances when serving under MacDonald and Baldwin. A character trait, certainly, but this should not obscure the profound connection that existed in Londonderry's mind between his period at the Air Ministry and his actions afterwards. His bitter reaction to his removal from the National Government has been considered already (see Chapter 6). The deep and lasting sense of grievance that he nurtured towards Baldwin was fuelled by a belief that he had not been treated fairly and that his reputation as air minister had been badly tarnished. He resented, in particular, Baldwin's claim about being misled over the strength of the Luftwaffe, and he informed him of this in a voluminous correspondence that carried on even after Baldwin had retired from the premiership in 1937.[34] Londonderry was prepared to discuss in public this particular detail from his time in office, as in June 1936 when it was the subject of his address to the northern branch of the National Society of Conservative and Unionist Agents at Newcastle upon Tyne.[35] But a sense of duty to his former ministerial colleagues prevented him from saying more about the reasons behind his removal from the government. This in turn fuelled another grievance. As he often reminded Baldwin, and other correspondents, there had been no official exchange of letters between the two men when Londonderry had been moved out of the Air Ministry. As a result, Londonderry felt 'impotent rage' that he had been hung out to dry and that his silence had gone unnoticed. Worse still, he felt that this was a significant factor in why his promotion of Anglo-German understanding was not being given the attention that it deserved.[36]

Londonderry's experience in the National Government also haunted him in another way. The charge levelled by Labour in 1935 that he was a warmonger had cut deep. His sensitivity was periodically provoked in the years that followed when Labour MPs, most notably Hugh Dalton and Herbert Morrison, repeated the charge.[37] 'Was it not Lord Londonderry himself who boasted that he had preserved the use of the bombing airplane?' Dalton asked the Labour party conference at Edinburgh in October 1936. 'He had preserved it! He has preserved it for Hitler and Mussolini. Bombers over Abyssinia yesterday. Bombers over Spain today. Will it be bombers over Britain tomorrow? That will be a proud day for Lord Londonderry if it comes.'[38] 'My speech in the House of Lords I agree, was a very unfortunate one', he wrote to Clement Attlee the following year, 'but it really was a technical one as bombing in outlying districts has really a meaning of its own'.[39] Londonderry's decision to engage in amateur diplomacy was therefore a very public reaction to the deafening silence of his former Conservative colleagues and the strident attacks on his reputation by Labour. He believed that by engaging in the promotion of Anglo-German understanding he might demonstrate his credentials as a practitioner of great power diplomacy and in the cause of peace.

In his influential study of 'British enthusiasts for Nazi Germany', Richard Griffiths argues that Londonderry's promotion of Anglo-German understanding only began after his removal from office in 1935, that 'No such views were in evidence up to that time'.[40] The statement is incorrect. Rather, the evidence is clear that he was, for personal, political and strategic reasons, sympathetic towards Germany from the early 1920s. In August 1923, after opening a new bathing pool, tennis courts and putting greens at Hartlepool, he gave an address in which he called into question the French government's determined pursuance of reparations from Germany.[41] He returned to the reparations question, and the 'destruction of Germany', two months later at an event at Sunderland. 'No one would say, in view of the sin against humanity committed by the Germans in 1914, that any punishment was too severe', Londonderry remarked, before cautioning that it was also 'necessary to consider the future of the world and the best basis on which peace could be established . . . No one could look on a Balkanised Central Europe without feelings of grave anxiety'.[42] The following year, in an Armistice Day radio broadcast for the British Broadcasting Company, he called on the country not to harbour animosities when remembering the war.[43] In 1929, as a cabinet minister, he praised the Locarno treaty for bringing Germany into the League of Nations, and he informed an audience of Conservatives at Birmingham that he hoped that it would establish 'for all time and understanding throughout the world that there was a desire for peace'.[44] Addressing Essex Conservatives at Orsett Hall in 1931, prior to his appointment to the emergency National Government, he praised the decision of the President of the United States to postpone Germany's payments of international debts as 'brave', that 'by giving a breathing space to Germany Mr [Herbert] Hoover had done a great national and international service'.[45] And the following year, in a talk given to Conservatives at Keswick, he warned that the failure to address Germany's grievances would encourage the growth of 'Hitlerism, which is openly threatening to dominate German politics and whose object is declared to be the overthrow of the Peace Treaties'.[46]

Ideologically, Londonderry viewed Germany as a physical barrier against the expansion of the Soviet Union. Eighteen months before Hitler's appointment as chancellor, he informed an audience at St Helens that the

> world's danger was a German collapse. The Communists would welcome it. They were out to destroy everything in which this country believed. If there were not a satisfactory end to the deliberations of the nations Germany would be driven into the hands of the Communists, with consequent rebellion and the country torn from top to bottom by dissensions. That would have a grave repercussion on the whole civilized world, and it was our duty to give all the assistance we could to prevent it.[47]

Londonderry's sympathy for Germany when serving in the National Government was constrained by the difficulties and deliberations of the League of Nations and the World Disarmament Conference, although in private he made known his dislike for the French and their policy towards Germany. Londonderry's plea to cabinet colleagues – via his November 1934 letters to Hailsham – that Germany should be readmitted to the League in order to reach a new settlement was yet another manifestation of his pro-German leanings, more notable than on previous occasions because the Nazis had by this point established a dictatorship. As noted in Chapter 6, his two letters to Hailsham also influenced his justification of later appeasement activities by allowing him to argue that when he had pressed for an Anglo-German agreement in 1934, it was because Great Britain was in a position of strength and could direct the settlement.[48] Such a diagnosis was not without merit, but it also became a useful moral prop for Londonderry to air when accused of wanting to make peace at all costs. It is noteworthy that he did not draw a similar lesson from Sir John Simon and Anthony Eden's meeting with Hitler in March 1935. The Führer's false claim about the Luftwaffe clearly demonstrated that he could not be trusted, yet after leaving office Londonderry called on British ministers to have direct meetings with their German counterparts. Hitler's deceit was hardly an incidental matter for Londonderry given that Simon and Eden's 'unfortunate visit to Berlin had a good deal to do with my place at the Air Ministry being taken by someone else'.[49] But as this remark suggests, Londonderry attached any fault arising from the encounter exclusively to his former colleagues. He went further, arguing that their gullibility created an 'inferiority complex' that explained the failure of British foreign policy in the 1930s.[50] Again, this specific claim has merit, for British policymakers did indeed overestimate German strength and reach pessimistic conclusions as a result, but it suited Londonderry to draw only this lesson from the episode rather than his personal experience of Hitler's unreliability.[51]

An important explanation for Londonderry's wilful blindness to the above inconsistencies is the fact that his amateur diplomacy was actively encouraged by the Nazis. As noted above, Ribbentrop initially assumed that the British aristocracy still wielded authority. He relied on those like Londonderry to influence the British government, to spread propaganda in the United Kingdom and to provide the Germans with general information on British opinion. Hitler after all was initially anxious to avoid a war with the former enemy, so amateur diplomats such as Londonderry were welcomed and encouraged by Berlin. As he had little regard for normal diplomacy, the Führer sought relations with foreign interests outside the orthodox channels of the Wilhelmstrasse.[52] Ribbentrop was given his own foreign affairs bureau in 1934, the Dienststelle Ribbentrop, which reported directly to Hitler. It engaged in a policy of influencing prominent people in Great Britain and exploiting the sympathies of those who were already pro-German and anti-Communist. It arranged visits with a number of British peers in order to prepare the ground for direct meetings between Hitler and British ministers, in the hope that such encounters would repeat the success of the Anglo-German Naval Agreement of June 1935. The work of the bureau had begun prior to Londonderry's visits, and many of the rhetorical devices that Londonderry would later utter had been well practised on Lothian, including Hitler's desire for Anglo-German friendship and the need for direct contacts between British and German statesmen to quickly seize the vital issues. These two points framed Londonderry's calls on British ministers to deal with Hitler directly, and as a result, like others, he actively promoted Hitler's claim that he did not want to go to war.

Through the work of the Dienststelle Ribbentrop the former air minister was injected with a new sense of purpose, encouraged to believe that he had a vital role to play on the international stage. The refusal of the Foreign Office to act on his advice inevitably frustrated him and led him to conclude – as he had done throughout the early 1930s – that it was ignorant of European affairs. It was, after all, preferable to believe the ministers and diplomats of Germany when they assured him of the importance of his role as an intermediary than it was to support a government department with which he had a history of bad blood. With hindsight, however, it is clear that it was Londonderry, like so many others, who was blind to Hitler's intentions. 'I know Hitler does not want to fight', he informed a correspondent in March 1937, 'in fact, he dreads it'.[53] In the context of Nazi Germany's early and calculated breaches of the Versailles treaty, this statement had a ring of plausibility, at least among those yearning for it to be true. In reality, Hitler believed in the necessity of waging war, to create 'living space' for the German race.[54] Even Germany's commercial policy, William Carr observes, was subordinate to the Führer's territorial policy, in fulfilment of a 'solemn duty to preserve the racial group'.[55] It was not until June 1939, following the German invasion of what remained of Czechoslovakia, that Londonderry appears to have come to fully appreciate Hitler's world view. Expressing his bitter sense of disappointment to the former German chancellor, Franz von Papen, he lamented that 'War is glorified; material strength appears to be the only object in view, and we feel that if we wish to understand the Chancellor's policy, we can find the full interpretation of it in *Mein Kampf*'.[56] As a contemporary student of Nazi propaganda observed, many of its accomplices in Great Britain had too long failed to understand that its 'deliberate purpose' was 'not to *tell* people anything, but to make them *do* something'.[57]

Nazi duplicity was to some extent recognized at the Foreign Office, or at least by its permanent secretary, Robert Vansittart, with whom Londonderry had clashed during his time as air minister. Vansittart felt that Londonderry and Lothian were dupes being used for the purpose of driving a wedge between Great Britain and France. But far from stopping diplomatic tourists, the Foreign Office was without the authority to prevent their contacts and the subsequent promotion of Anglo-German understanding in the press. This was despite the fact that amateur diplomats unintentionally damaged relations between the two countries by encouraging Hitler to believe that an exclusive deal could be reached with the British, whereas the Foreign Office preferred instead to push Germany into agreeing a general settlement. As for the Nazis, these visits – in addition to their diplomatic goals – had some benefit domestically. As Gerwin Strobl observes, photographs in the German press of Nazi leaders enjoying country pursuits with British politicians suggested to their readers 'a reassuring symmetry in British and German national lives'.[58] Even after 1937, when Ribbentrop and Hitler no longer looked upon Great Britain as a likely ally, at least in the near future, their change of heart was helpfully and unwittingly camouflaged by the continued pleas of amateur diplomats for Anglo-German understanding. As a result, the Dienststelle Ribbentrop and Londonderry benefited from and fed off each other's existence, caring little for the delusions of either party to the arrangement.

II

Londonderry initiated his new career as an amateur diplomat with a private trip to Germany at the end of January 1936. His stated purpose was to visit the German air minister, Hermann Göring, and to ascertain German opinion. Londonderry subsequently noted the 'lavish' treatment and hospitality that he received during a seven-week tour that concluded with his attendance at the Winter Olympics in Bavaria.[59] In keeping with the policy of Ribbentrop's bureau, Londonderry had access to leading politicians in addition to Göring, including Hitler; the foreign minister, Baron von Neurath; and the deputy führer, Rudolf Hess. He was also permitted to visit aircraft factories and Luftwaffe training facilities.

At his meeting on 1 February with Hess and Ribbentrop, Londonderry was repeatedly informed of the 'danger of Bolshevism' and the need for the British Empire and Germany to forge an anti-Communist alliance. Their discussion also dealt with the restitution of the colonies that Germany had lost after the First World War, something that Londonderry felt reflected his hosts' 'inferiority complex'. Ribbentrop continued conversing with Londonderry in this vein for the remainder of the day, drumming into him the need for a French-backed 'Anglo-German arrangement of all the complex problems surrounding present-day international affairs'.[60]

Several days later, on 4 February, Londonderry had a 2-hour audience with Hitler, accompanied by Hess and Ribbentrop. In response to Londonderry's appreciation that he was treated like an official representative, Hitler replied that he welcomed unofficial visits. Like his lieutenants, the Führer was keen to press for an anti-Communist alliance and gave a long tirade on the threat of the Soviet Union. For the remainder of the meeting, questions from Londonderry on rearmament, German aims and the League of Nations were ignored or deflected with veiled threats about the failure of Anglo-German understanding, especially in relation to Hitler's desire to recover former colonies. Despite Londonderry's inability to receive clear answers, he would use much of what his hosts told him to justify the German position in *Ourselves and Germany*. Before returning home, he along with his wife and their youngest daughter, Mairi, enjoyed the hospitality of several pro-Nazi aristocrats, including the Prince of Hesse, the Duke and Duchess of Brunswick and the Duke of Saxe-Coburg.[61] As with their British counterparts, Hitler also used the German aristocracy for tactical purposes; he was otherwise contemptuous of them and sought to establish a new racial and meritocratic élite. As he remarked in 1938, the upper class were 'in reality no more than the scum produced by societal mutation gone haywire from having had its blood and thinking infected by cosmopolitanism'.[62]

After they returned home, the Londonderrys were effusive in expressing gratitude to their German hosts. Lord Londonderry wrote to Ribbentrop and to Göring, lavishing praise yet also raising a number of sensitive issues – anti-Semitism and German trade with the Soviet Union – in the hope that these could be addressed for the sake of Anglo-German understanding.[63] Lady Londonderry's letter to Hitler was unalloyed by such concerns:

> It was a very great pleasure to meet you and to have seen all that you have done in Germany in the last three years. To say that I was deeply impressed is not

Figure 11 Lord Londonderry, Adolf Hitler and Joachim von Ribbentrop, 4 February 1936.

> adequate. I am amazed. You and Germany remind me of the book of Genesis in the Bible. Nothing else describes the position accurately. The beauty of the buildings is something that I shall not forget, their strength and simplicity are I feel symbolic of their creator . . . Neither my husband or myself will forget your kindness, and to the best of our abilities, in our different ways, we will do our best to help towards a better understanding of our two countries.[64]

Hitler was initially too busy to reply personally, but he thanked her in April 'for sending me the picture and the charming collection of songs with the beautiful old melodies. I was particularly overjoyed to learn from your accompanying letter how much you and your husband sympathise with my efforts to bring about a genuine Peace'.[65] To Göring, Lady Londonderry declared that 'I would prefer to call you "Siegfried" as you are my conception of a Siegfried of modern times!' She then listed those in Great Britain opposed to the German government: trade unionists, the press – 'controlled to a great extent by Jews' – and 'many nice people here, who have been led by the Government in the past, to pin their entire faith on the Geneva policy, in order, as they imagine, to create a more humane world'.[66]

The announcement in the German press that Lord Londonderry had met with Hitler inevitably attracted the attention of British newspapers.[67] Londonderry hoped that this would happen and to some extent courted it. Addressing a meeting at Durham on 22 February, he made some remarks on the expansion of the Luftwaffe that gave way to an account of his meeting with Hitler.[68] But contrary to Londonderry's expectation, only one of his former cabinet colleagues, Oliver Stanley, expressed any immediate interest following his return from Germany, and Stanley was married to his daughter, Lady Maureen.[69] Neither Baldwin nor Vansittart were initially interested in or concerned about Londonderry's self-declared mission, except in so far as giving him encouragement might do harm. Nevertheless, there was some interest. *The Times* had followed his tour. The cabinet secretary, Sir Maurice Hankey, also took note of his findings. Leopold Amery wrote to share his belief that he too felt that Hitler desired peace.[70] And on 29 June, ninety backbench Conservative MPs attended the 1922 Committee to hear Londonderry's findings. As its secretary recorded:

> The Marquis of Londonderry . . . thought that the [German] people and the Government were anxious for the friendship of Britain. There was considerable expenditure upon armaments but the figures had to be taken with reserve. The German organisation was so powerful that it could be switched into dangerous channels. Hitler appeared to want peace and the Government would favour an understanding with both Britain and France. Germany feared the possibility of encirclement and Hitler had a genuine obsession with regard to the Bolshevist character of Russia. He would like the Colonies back but was not prepared to fight for them.[71]

Just as Lothian's amateur diplomacy had attracted messages of support as well as angry criticism, the Londonderrys' visit to Germany was met with a similar range of responses in the society and political salons in which they had played a leading part.[72] Harold Nicolson wrote to his wife, Vita Sackville-West, that his

> new pal Maureen Stanley asked me to come round and meet her father who is just back from hob-nobbing with Hitler. Now I admire Londonderry in a way, since it is fine to remain 1760 in 1936; besides he is a real gent. But I do deeply disapprove of ex-Cabinet ministers trotting across to Germany at this moment. It gives the impression of secret negotiations.[73]

Londonderry was aware of such hostility. He warned his wife in March that 'we shall be left out of everything and it will be a trifle galling, but if you understand it, and are ready for it, and I have got you, I feel I don't mind'.[74] Yet, it would be wrong to conclude that the Londonderrys were now social pariahs. Shortly afterwards, Amery asked Londonderry to host a reception for his Empire Unity Campaign. Amery's diary records that in response Londonderry 'was gratifyingly keen . . . but a little doubtful whether Londonderry House would be quite appropriate just now, or be misunderstood as an attempt to get back on Baldwin for having turned him out'.[75]

As noted in Chapter 6, Baldwin and Londonderry had agreed in the wake of the latter's removal from the government not to hold the eve of parliament reception at Londonderry House. Its disappearance from the political calendar prompted the cartoonist David Low, in the *Evening Standard*, to publish 'The Eve-of-the-Session reception at Londonderry House'. It depicts Lord and Lady Londonderry in a vast and empty room, with only one guest, Churchill, announced by a chorus of servants.[76] Brilliant satire, to be sure, but it was wide of the mark. In May 1937 the Londonderrys' Park Lane mansion held a reception for 'overseas visitors', the guest list of which took up two columns in *The Times*.[77] It included the prime ministers of Great Britain, Canada, Australia, New Zealand, South Africa and Northern Ireland; almost two dozen sultans and Indian princes; as well as foreign diplomats, British government ministers, royalty, aristocrats, parliamentarians and senior officers in the armed forces. It also included a number of people who might be expected to have taken a dim view of the Londonderrys' promotion of Anglo-German understanding, including Churchill and Lloyd George's daughter, Megan. An equally impressive guest list for Londonderry House was published months later, on this occasion taking up three columns of *The Times*, when it hosted a reception to meet Baldwin's successor as prime minister, Neville Chamberlain.[78] Londonderry hinted that year, in the foreword to Montgomery Hyde's *Londonderry House and Its Pictures*, that the property's tradition of serving as a great political house was coming towards its end, and the reception for Chamberlain would indeed be the last of its kind before the Second World War.[79] But the status of Londonderry House and its occupants continued on occasion to be affirmed in this period, as in July 1938 and May 1939, when, as the court circular phrased it, the dowager Queen Mary honoured the Londonderrys with her presence at dinner, and in March 1939, when the couple were invited to attend a dinner at Downing Street for George VI and Queen Elizabeth.[80]

What makes the willingness of so many eminent people to associate with the Londonderrys all the more noteworthy is the controversy that surrounded the hospitality that the latter extended simultaneously to their German hosts. In February 1937, on inquiring if Göring was to be his country's representative at the coronation of King George, Londonderry indicated that the German air minister could stay at his Park Lane property. The prospect of a senior Nazi attending the coronation inevitably aroused criticism in the press and in parliament, and it further placed Londonderry in an unfavourable light, including with Göring, who was angered by the now organized opposition to the visit.[81] But the episode did not prevent hundreds of eminent persons attending the two functions at Londonderry House mentioned above.

Ribbentrop was the only senior Nazi able to avail himself of the famous Londonderry hospitality, and this started even before his appointment as the German ambassador to London in October 1936.[82] The Londonderrys had attempted to cultivate his predecessor in that post, the career diplomat, Leopold von Hoesch.[83] But it was the spectacle of Ribbentrop, a senior Nazi, spending weekends at the Londonderrys' estates in Northern Ireland and northeast England that aroused considerable press attention at the time. The Swastika tailfins of the aeroplanes that in May 1936 carried Ribbentrop and his entourage to Newtownards, the game of golf that he played with Lord Londonderry at nearby Scrabo and the porcelain statuette of an SS man that he gave in appreciation for his stay – which continued to grace the mantelpiece of Londonderry's study at Mount Stewart after it opened to the public as a National Trust property – all entered local folklore. In contrast, few if any remember the great demonstration of RAF aeroplanes that accompanied Ribbentrop's visit to County Down, and which added a quasi-official element to the proceedings. Likewise, Ribbentrop's weekend at Wynyard in November 1936, on this occasion as the German ambassador, is still remembered for an alleged incident at Durham cathedral. During a religious service which Londonderry attended as the Mayor of Durham, the visiting German dignitary is said to have stood and given a fascist salute in response to the German national anthem, only for Londonderry, seated beside him, to quickly intervene by lowering his guest's arm.[84] Ribbentrop became so associated with Londonderry through these visits and other social engagements that he earned the humorous sobriquet, 'the Londonderry Herr'.[85] Londonderry would later claim that he did not like Ribbentrop, but at the time he was a perfect host to the ambassador, and he in turn repaid him with further visits to Germany and a sense of playing an important part in a great endeavour. Ribbentrop did not entirely deceive Londonderry, at least initially, for both men shared a nineteenth-century view of European power politics. It was Hitler who did not hold this view, preferring instead to see the world in ideological and racial terms.[86]

On 6 March, two months after Londonderry's trip to Germany, the Wehrmacht occupied the demilitarized Rhineland. In what would prove to be a recurring strategy, Hitler accompanied this with calls for a new peace settlement. In contrast to the majority of British Conservatives who outwardly showed restraint, Londonderry defended the occupation in a letter to *The Times*. Repeating the German government's grievances with the Versailles treaty and France, he advocated the right of Germans to run their country as they pleased.[87] The letter created a poor reaction and firmly placed him among the most notable of active appeasers. That in turn made him question whether he should continue in his new self-appointed role, but his sense of mission was emboldened by his wife's enthusiasm. For her part, she continued to enjoy her own, more informal, correspondence with Hitler and Göring.[88] Londonderry also received encouragement from Lord Beaverbrook, who praised his *Times* letter as 'brilliantly done'.[89] In reply, Londonderry admitted that he was 'megalomaniac enough to think that we can dominate the whole situation but Baldwin can't do it. Neville is too parochial, in fact I see no one who can fill my bill'. Confessing that he would 'like to do it myself', he went on to acknowledge that his 'record is not good enough. I could not carry the people. Whilst I know what ought to be done I have too many gaps in my intelligence to do it. Whether a democracy could do what I want I am not quite sure. So I am looking on'.[90] Beaverbrook replied with words of encouragement, 'It is your duty to go back into public life. And, if you will allow me to say so, you should go without the slightest feeling against Baldwin.'[91]

If the bulk of the Conservative party was more restrained than Londonderry in its response to the Rhineland crisis, it was a rude awakening that compelled its parliamentarians to re-evaluate their varied expectations.[92] The government, for its part, was reluctant to use sanctions in case these drove Germany into an alliance with Italy. The possibility of an embarrassing split among Conservative parliamentarians was avoided by a number of changes in foreign policy, including the recognition of Italian rule in Abyssinia, further diplomatic efforts with Germany and increased rearmament. Londonderry supported rearmament, but as with his time at the Air Ministry, he grew concerned that it was not being balanced with diplomatic initiatives.[93] In April he repeated in the House of Lords his earlier call for a settlement with Hitler.[94]

There was at the same time growing concern among Conservative MPs that a possible deal with Hitler could involve the restitution of Germany's former colonies, which were now administered on behalf of the League of Nations by a number of Allied powers, including Great Britain and the British dominions.[95] Like Chamberlain and other senior Conservatives, Londonderry's attitude to this possibility reflected what Richard Whiting describes as the 'superiority of "international relations" over "empire"', that it was deemed to be 'an acceptable sacrifice for peace in Europe'.[96] To Amery, a leading opponent of colonial restitution, Londonderry relayed his belief that although 'the Germans are making claims to Colonies in relation to raw materials and population . . . their real object is a question of prestige'.[97] In public, having advocated a new settlement with Germany, with the implication that it would mean addressing the colonial question, Londonderry sat out the subsequent party crisis in silence knowing that he could not win by adopting any position. If he spoke against the return of colonies then he would damage his relationship with the Nazis, if in favour he would alienate himself from a significant number of backbench Conservatives. Caught in the middle he privately urged Göring to avoid policies that created anxiety in Great Britain.[98] To Churchill, Londonderry suggested that he 'go easy with Baldwin otherwise you will give him renewed strength as the British are very sentimental and sympathetic'. He also tried to reassure his second cousin that while he felt 'a certain admiration' for regimes that created 'efficient organisation', such as those of 'Hitler, Mussolini and Stalin', he 'should not like to live under these regimes myself because they are the negation of the freedom which we have learnt through the ages to claim and to enjoy'. Still, he went on, 'I feel that if the Nazi regime in Germany is destroyed, Germany will go Communist and we shall find a lining up of Communism between France, Germany and Russia.'[99]

By July the government began to take some interest in Londonderry's visit. It followed a temporary improvement in his relations with Baldwin.[100] Earlier, on 21 May, Londonderry had written yet another letter to the prime minister complaining about his removal from the cabinet, but of more interest to Baldwin he added, 'I have had a most interesting letter from Göring to-day. It is meant for propaganda but it has a value and I wish our F.O. could get out of their straight waistcoat.'[101] Londonderry followed the letter with a press statement denying that he had misled Baldwin in 1935 about air parity with Germany. Baldwin had no political reason to assuage his former air minister, so it is entirely possible that it was his curiosity about the Göring letter that led the prime minister, on 2 July, to announce to the House of Commons that he had not meant anyone to think that Londonderry had misled him.[102]

The way was thus paved for Halifax to meet with Londonderry and discuss his findings, followed by correspondence on the latter's proposals for better Anglo-German relations.[103] The rapprochement was short lived, however. Londonderry echoed Hitler's suggestion at their first meeting by pressing the Lord Privy Seal to adopt an anti-Communist policy that would be the basis of further understandings between the two states.[104] Halifax stressed instead the need for a general settlement and cautioned against the alienation of the Soviet Union.[105] In turn, Londonderry suggested that extending the hand of friendship to Germany would give Hitler a 'get-out'. 'I have no doubt', he professed, 'that as we get stronger and as our prestige increases', Hitler 'will be only too glad when he finds a policy of his not working out exactly as he desires to have an excuse of going back on it by saying that he is determined to preserve the good opinion of Great Britain'. The general tenor of Londonderry's letter, however, was negative; he criticized the 'drift' in foreign policy, accused the government of 'misunderstanding' him and warned that war loomed if they merely rearmed and avoided talking to Hitler.[106]

In reacting badly to Halifax, Londonderry not only misjudged British foreign policy and his own ability to steer it in a different direction, but he recklessly damaged his already low standing among former colleagues. The government was not so much interested in Londonderry's personal opinion, but rather what Hitler and other senior Nazis were communicating through him. Therefore, the Lord Privy Seal, renowned for his good nature, overlooked his predecessor's outburst and assured him that he had no intention of alienating Germany.[107]

Londonderry's very public advocacy of a deal with Germany made him increasingly defensive about accusations that he was pro-Nazi.[108] In September he wrote to Halifax to condemn the speeches given at the Nazis' recent Nuremberg rally.[109] He also dropped his initial emphasis on reaching direct agreements between London and Berlin in favour of a conference of the great powers, to include Great Britain, France, Germany and Italy, but not the Soviet Union.[110] 'My desire is to pin Hitler down to peace under all circumstances for a period of time if necessary', he informed Halifax. '[I]f the four great powers of Europe with no reservations took this line, there can be no war . . . it is no use crediting the smaller nations with any actual power in this issue.' In a line of reasoning similar to his 1934 letters to Hailsham, he went on to proclaim that

> In default of a definite reply from Hitler in a conference of actual plenipotentiaries, which on the lines I suggest has a resemblance to Vienna . . . we should announce at once that we were proposing to take the definite line of power politics and give up for the time being the doctrines which we have sought to develop.[111]

At the end of October, after a tour of Eastern Europe that included an audience with Romania's King Carol II and Prince Bibesco, Londonderry met with Göring and Hitler for the second time.[112] He did not record what was said at the meetings, or if the Nazis approved, or indeed acknowledged his four power proposal, but it is likely from Londonderry's subsequent correspondence with Halifax that the meeting dealt with the colonial question, the eastward expansion of the Reich and Hitler's dislike of the foreign secretary, Eden. It is also clear from what Londonderry would afterwards pass on to Halifax, that Hitler had informed his guest of Germany's next move a year in advance of the Czech crisis: 'it appears to me that German policy is moving in the direction of Danzig and Polish interests, and also Czechoslovakia, and it would not surprise me if the next sudden demarche were not some movement in that direction'.[113] Londonderry's only notable public intervention in the months that followed was an address at Seaham Harbour, in which he urged the acceptance of Hitler's 'tremendous offer' of an air pact between Great Britain, France and Germany, on the basis that such co-operation was essential to the maintenance of peace.[114]

The foreign policy drift that had characterized Baldwin's premiership came to an end in May 1937, following his retirement and the succession of his heir apparent,

Neville Chamberlain. Under the latter's stewardship, the government went on to pursue a policy of active appeasement and rearmament. Londonderry had long held a grudge against Chamberlain, but he welcomed the end of drift, and as noted above, in October that year Londonderry House held a reception 'to meet the Prime Minister' that in many respects resembled those once given to mark the eve of parliament.[115] Londonderry shared with Chamberlain a belief in the sincerity of Hitler's requests for a peace settlement, and both men argued that this could be brought about by an agreement between the great powers. Londonderry did not, however, share Chamberlain's emphasis on economic appeasement, preferring instead to focus on the balance of power and anti-Communism. This aside, it is noteworthy that despite other ideas in common, most notably the four-power pact, and Londonderry's public support for Chamberlain, the two men rarely corresponded or met.

In the month prior to the Londonderry House reception for Chamberlain, Anglo-German relations had been severely tested by Hitler's demand for the return of Germany's colonies, delivered at his party's rally at Nuremberg. It was more than a rhetorical outburst, for Ribbentrop had belatedly come to the bitter realization – influenced at least in part by Londonderry – that his efforts to cultivate British opinion had come to nought, and that the British aristocracy were not in fact as influential as he had believed. Hitler was now determined to seek other allies and the usefulness of Londonderry and others to the Nazis was significantly diminished and altered as a result. Altered because Ribbentrop continued to use advocates of Anglo-German understanding to disseminate misleading words of reassurance and goodwill in Great Britain.

Alongside prominent individuals such as Londonderry, Ribbentrop's deception was assisted by the 900 strong Anglo-German Fellowship.[116] Londonderry had been a member of the fellowship since February 1936, following the conclusion of his first foray into amateur diplomacy. Its mere existence, in contrast to the mythical 'Cliveden Set', was important given what it signified, an organized lobby of the great and good.[117] An elite body, certainly, but the fellowship was not exclusively aristocratic. Rather, it was, as Charles Spicer describes, the 'child of business and finance'.[118] Londonderry attended a number of functions hosted by the fellowship, but as noted above, he was driven by a very personal sense of mission and did not come to regard it as a vehicle that might be harnessed to his ends. Nor was he always comfortable with the untempered enthusiasm of others in the organization. Contacted by a member in March 1938, with the suggestion that the fellowship praise Hitler's handling of the *Anschluss* with Austria, Londonderry replied that it should instead send 'a deputation . . . to the German Embassy, or to Berlin itself, stating very categorically that if Germany desires to join the comity of nations she will have to conform to some international phraseology and demeanour which will inspire confidence rather than create fear and despondency'.[119] That said, his view on this occasion was in tune with the fellowship's ruling council, which decided to condemn the manner of the *Anschluss* in a letter to Ribbentrop.[120] As for the claim sometimes made that the Londonderrys were members of the so-called Cliveden Set, Norman Rose observes that the two most famous society salons of their day, the Astors and Londonderrys, had little regard for the other.[121] If Lady Astor was a member of Lady Londonderry's Ark, it was not that remarkable or significant given her prominence as the first woman MP to take her seat, not to mention her famous parliamentary performances.[122] And the exchange of letters in December 1938 between Lord Londonderry and the second Viscount Astor's heir, on their respective visits to Germany, was remarkably brief and inconsequential.[123]

Londonderry made his third visit to Nazi Germany in September 1937, the same month that Hitler hosted Mussolini for a state visit. Having accepted Göring's invitation to join him for a hunt, Londonderry found his host 'less conciliatory', defensive about Germany's newly acquired Italian and Japanese allies and condemnatory of Great Britain's refusal to engage in friendly relations with Germany.[124] Londonderry afterwards informed Ribbentrop that the meeting was unsatisfactory and put the blame for this on the arrival of the Italian dictator.[125] Unwittingly, in his subsequent correspondence with Göring, Londonderry affirmed the new direction in Nazi foreign policy by protesting that he had barely any influence over his former ministerial colleagues. He recommended instead that they deal with the new British ambassador in Berlin, Nevile Henderson, a keen advocate of appeasement.[126]

It is possible that it was Londonderry's insistence that he had no influence over British ministers that finally persuaded Ribbentrop to change his mind on Anglo-German rapprochement, that and the former ambassador's inability to find acceptance in London society. As Hugh Dalton commented in his diary in September 1938, 'All really depends on Hitler, whom it is very difficult to reach. In so far as he is reached by Ribbentrop he is misled, for Ribbentrop saw too much of Londonderry and Mayfair and too little of England.'[127] When the German ambassador to London made his final report to Berlin in January 1938, prior to taking up the post of foreign minister, he cited a letter from Londonderry to justify his reassessment. Without the possibility of an agreement on the lines that he and his British allies had been advocating, Great Britain, he concluded, was the Reich's main enemy.[128]

III

Just as the Nazis were downgrading Londonderry's value as a man of influence, British ministers, contrary to his later complaints, renewed their interest in his recent findings, as worsening relations between London and Berlin made informal contacts more valuable. Following his hunting trip with Göring, Londonderry met with Chamberlain in October 1937, and even Baldwin asked for a meeting.[129] The latter had earlier in the year asked Londonderry to be his sponsor upon taking his seat in the House of Lords, but neither that nor their meeting after Londonderry's return from Germany amounted to a reconciliation. That, according to Baldwin's son, would have to wait until the occasion when Londonderry was in hospital, 'not very long before the death of both of them'.[130] As for Chamberlain, Londonderry was unhappy with the prime minister's poker face during their meeting, but Halifax, now Lord President, compensated through his increased interest.[131] In any case, the meeting with Chamberlain seemed to herald a partial rehabilitation of Londonderry, at least in the eyes of some senior Conservatives. It occurred the same month that Londonderry House hosted the reception to meet the prime minister, noted above, and it was around this time that Londonderry was nominated as the incoming president of the National Union of Conservatives and Unionists. The 'loud cheers' from the conference floor – the last Conservative party conference held before the Second World War – that greeted his nomination must have brought some comfort to Londonderry; he was even nominated again the following year.[132] Still, it was a purely ornamental role that rotated between the party's large area organizations.[133] It did not signal that Chamberlain valued Londonderry's counsel or even that it was sought. Many years later, in 1946, Londonderry recalled that 'although Chamberlain spent a week fishing with me in the spring of 1938, we never once mentioned the German situation. I led up to it on various occasions, but the conversation was always turned off in other directions both by Neville and his wife.'[134]

It is likely that the reason for Londonderry's new-found favour can be traced to Chamberlain's desire to arrange a meeting between Halifax and Hitler in the aftermath of Germany's pacts with Italy and Japan. Londonderry was secretly given prior knowledge of the proposed visit and discussed the idea at length with Halifax.[135] At the time, Eden noted that Halifax's ideas for the visit included advocating a 'Four-Power Pact', which is suggestive of Londonderry's imprint, though the idea was hardly novel.[136] Officially, it was announced that the visit was in response to an invitation to an international exhibition on hunting, an event that Londonderry himself attended during a brief overnight trip to Berlin.[137]

The Halifax–Hitler meeting on 19 November inevitably heightened tensions within the National Government. Against the wishes of Eden and Vansittart, Chamberlain and his emissary were keen to inform Hitler that any revision to Germany's eastern borders should come through the course of peaceful evolution. More controversially, it was Halifax and not Hitler who first named the areas where the Versailles treaty might be revised. Halifax has often been criticized for allowing Hitler to know, without prompting, that the British would consent to German expansion in Eastern Europe. However, it was Halifax who had been prompted, albeit indirectly, as Hitler likely assumed that his conversations with Londonderry were being passed on to the British government. It is also possible that Londonderry would have informed Hitler of this, not least to highlight his utility as an unofficial conduit between the two governments. He was disappointed afterwards that Halifax and Hitler did not lay the groundwork for a settlement. Characteristically, Londonderry placed the blame on the former. As he later recalled to the journalist, Colin Brooks, Halifax had not made 'a first-class occasion of it'. He instead 'went with a single valet, whom he lost on the train, and apparently presented himself to Hitler as a rather vague person who wanted to talk generalities.'[138]

Notwithstanding his criticisms of Halifax, Londonderry recognized that the Nazis no longer seemed to be responsive to British concerns. As a consequence, his letters to Ribbentrop continued to hope for a four-power conference, but now more readily added his concern for the damage being done to British opinion by Nazi policies.[139] Yet, to the British public, Londonderry's New Year message for 1938, published in the *Newcastle Journal*, devoted considerable attention instead to the 'foolish' treatment of Germany since 1918.[140] Indeed, to his lasting misfortune, the cooling of Anglo-German relations led Londonderry to conclude that it was necessary for him to expand considerably upon that New Year message. At a time when more pamphlets and books on foreign affairs were published than ever before, his contribution was *Ourselves and Germany*. A short book, it was first published in March 1938 by Robert Hale and serialized in the *Evening Standard*, before a revised version was published later in the year as a Penguin Special. It had two purposes, he informed the veteran journalist, J. L. Garvin, 'One is to try and guide public opinion, and the other is to vindicate my own position.'[141] *Ourselves and Germany* would cement his reputation as an apologist for the Nazi regime.

Londonderry was selectively clandestine about his visits to Germany. Much of what was said between the author and the Nazi leadership during his first visit was included in the book; what was not we know through his correspondence with Halifax. *Ourselves and Germany* elicited some praise from readers; the Penguin edition reprinted supportive correspondence from several Labour peers, lords Arnold and Allen, as well as Hitler and Göring, and Italy's ambassador, Dino Grandi, on behalf of Mussolini.[142] A review in *The Times* remarked that the 'principal interest of his short book naturally attaches to Lord Londonderry's record of the conversations which he had', and it noted the 'honesty which distinguishes the book'.[143] But in one particular instance that honesty would immediately backfire. *Ourselves and Germany* contained correspondence with Ribbentrop in which Londonderry addressed the Jewish question. Intended as a warning, it was also unthinkingly offensive to a section of his readership:

> I should be wrong if I minimized in any way the anxiety which is felt here in relation to your policy towards the Jews, for there is the feeling that we do not like persecution, but in addition to this there is the material feeling that you are taking on a tremendous force which is capable of having repercussions all over the world.

Then came the reassuring admission that he had 'no great affection for the Jews. It is possible to trace their participation in most of those international disturbances . . . on the other hand, one can find many Jews strongly ranged on the other side who have done their best . . . to counteract those malevolent and mischievous activities of fellow Jews'.[144] Gladys Hirsch, née Wilenski, wrote to Londonderry to ask on what foundation he based his assertions. Replying through his private secretary, he expressed regret that his words caused pain to those he looked upon as friends. Hirsch responded that private regret was not enough and that he should make a public apology.[145] When he received similar criticism from Anthony de Rothschild, Londonderry replied personally, but his clumsy attempt to assuage the former's concerns led to the further criticism that he promoted myths about the international influence of the Jews.[146] Given the purposes of *Ourselves and Germany*, Londonderry was not prepared to publicly apologize for his remarks, though he did attempt, unsuccessfully, to persuade Rothschild to agree to the publication of their correspondence.[147]

Londonderry, like many other British people, did not regard his prejudices about the Jews as anti-Semitic. He had learned to tame his initially strong dislike for his Jewish son-in-law, the second Baron Jessel, and the brutality of Nazi anti-Semitism disinclined him from questioning the seeming harmlessness of his own prejudices.[148]

Moreover, on several occasions, including in a letter to Hitler, Londonderry protested about the treatment of Jews in Germany.[149] But it is clear that Londonderry held anti-Semitic opinions, such as his conflation of Jews with Communism, and his repeated belief in the supposed global influence of Jews that consciously or otherwise echoed the notorious forgery, endorsed initially in 1920 by *The Times*, *The Protocols of the Learned Elders of Zion*.[150] Ultimately, however, the Jewish question only mattered to appeasers like Londonderry in as much as it harmed their hopes for Anglo-German understanding.[151] In this sense, there was a general tendency among them to treat the Jews of Germany, like the new states of Eastern Europe, as expendable for the sake of achieving their goal.[152] Londonderry's inclusion of the offending letter in *Ourselves and Germany* exemplified this attitude. It had at least one salutary effect, however, for it encouraged – along with lobbying by British religious groups – Londonderry to raise the issue of persecution more frequently in correspondence with his German contacts. Even so, the riskiest example of this, his aforementioned letter to the Führer, sent in April 1938, was based on the incorrect assumption that Hitler cared.[153]

The publication of *Ourselves and Germany* coincided with, and perhaps even prompted, a number of requests for Londonderry's help in securing the release of political prisoners in the Reich, notably in the wake of the *Anschluss* on 13 March. The writer and educationalist Belle Rennie raised the case of the psychologist Professor Karl Bühler, an 'Aryan', she remarked, with a half-Jewish wife; he had been imprisoned in Vienna.[154] Dr Sonia Wachstein's brother, Max, a physiologist, was likewise arrested in the Austrian capital and taken to Buchenwald. She begged Londonderry 'with all my heart to help me . . . to save an innocent highly respectable human being whose life and health are being ruined, it was a life devoted to help the suffering, a life that could be extremely useful in the future'.[155] Another Austrian, Paul Müller, who had previously met Londonderry in Italy, asked for his help in securing residence in Great Britain or the dominions.[156] It is not clear if Londonderry responded to every request, or what personal influence he exerted in each instance, but the German embassy's first secretary, Edwart von Selzam, subsequently reassured him that Bühler would be released, along with others identified by Londonderry, including the Austrian politician, Count Rudolf Hoyos.[157] For their own part, the Londonderrys sheltered the Austrian diplomat, Baron Franckenstein, his posting to London having been terminated as a result of the *Anschluss*.[158]

The German government's unpredictable actions troubled advocates of appeasement, but for many including Londonderry these tended to strengthen their resolve. When Halifax replaced Eden as foreign secretary in February 1938, the appeasers were dismayed that it was followed by the Führer's announcement of a more militant foreign policy. Fearing that a solution was slipping away, Londonderry wrote a conciliatory letter to Ribbentrop, and in parliament he called on Chamberlain not to allow the two countries' differences to stand in the way of an agreement.[159] By way of contrast, he privately informed a colleague in the Anglo-German Fellowship that he 'condemned the methods employed' by Hitler and predicted a bleak future.[160] Publicly, Londonderry criticized the suddenness of the *Anschluss*, but he also warned of the risk of war unless there was a better understanding of German aspirations.[161] In private, he admitted to a German correspondent that he neither knew of nor understood Hitler's recent actions, including his continued persecution of the Jews.[162] For her part, Lady Londonderry complained to her Nazi contacts about the arrest of two Austrians – ski instructors and friends of the family who were subsequently released – and ended her flattering correspondence with Göring and Ribbentrop.[163] Indeed, her enthusiasm for promoting Anglo-German understanding dimmed as the year progressed, as is evident from a series of public interventions from this time onward that were critical of the Nazi regime.[164]

Having written *Ourselves and Germany* to improve Anglo-German understanding, Lord Londonderry now believed that it was having the opposite effect in Germany. In the above-mentioned letter to Hitler, he defended its content on the basis that he needed to address issues that aroused concern among British readers. As noted already, he also used the opportunity to emphasize the damage being done to Anglo-German relations by the persecution of Jews, as well as the *Anschluss*. Appealing to sentiments expressed by the dictator at their first meeting in 1936, Londonderry claimed that if an agreement could be reached between them, Great Britain and Germany could rule the world.[165] There was no accompanying explanation of what this meant in practice, or whether such an arrangement should be reached bilaterally or through a four-power pact, and it is the only correspondence in which this dramatic scenario is touted by Londonderry. Given his obvious inability to deliver such a development, it was more a desperate attempt to replenish the almost non-existent understanding between the two men than a serious proposition. Hitler sent a curt acknowledgement thanking Londonderry for a copy of *Ourselves and Germany*. The book was subsequently refused publication in Germany until its author leant on Göring.[166]

It was around this time that Londonderry crossed swords with Beaverbrook over claims in the *Daily Express* that he was 'pro-Nazi'. The newspaper's proprietor had initially encouraged his activities, but far from acknowledging this, he retorted that the *Express* reflected public opinion.[167] Londonderry's reply relayed his deep sense of frustration:

> I have had a pretty difficult time since I left the Government. I have a friendship and an understanding with Neville [Chamberlain], because he knows I don't want anything; but he and his colleagues are just a little frightened of me and just a little jealous. I am beginning to think of throwing my hand in altogether. Why should I bother about public life? I find the Socialists proclaiming me a Nazi and Fascist in my judgement two insulting terms and contrary to the whole of my point of view. Now the *Daily Express* joins in and I feel that if after all these years I can't get it across, then I am disposed to leave it all alone and fly aeroplanes, travel, play Bridge . . . I can't go on saying I am not a Nazi, but have pleaded for justice for Germany.[168]

Subsequently, when the *Express* reported that the 'pro-Nazi' Londonderrys had sheltered Baron Franckenstein, Lord Londonderry asked Beaverbrook 'if you would do me the great favour of omitting my name altogether from your publications. I really am not well known enough to stand up against the pin-pricks and silly innuendos which are continually being made by your correspondents'.[169] Beaverbrook afterwards reassured him, perhaps with tongue-in-cheek, that 'Great care is taken to see that nothing is printed of which you disapprove and the editors are all asked to give special consideration to everything that comes into the office concerning you.'[170]

Londonderry paid a short visit to Germany at the end of June 1938. Contrary to his claim in the second postscript of *Ourselves and Germany*, the visit was not of an entirely private character. Although attending a conference of the Fédération Aéronautique Internationale, as its vice-president, he had also arranged a meeting with Göring.[171] Halifax had briefed Londonderry before his departure. His private secretary, Oliver Harvey, noted on 14 June that he had learnt 'that Londonderry is off shortly to Berlin to see Hitler and Goering and it is strongly rumoured that he will bear some sort of "appeal" from the P.M. to Hitler. H[alfiax] has asked him to come and see him before he goes, as I hope, to stiffen him up a bit'.[172]

In his subsequent report to the foreign secretary, Londonderry noted a change in the German leadership's attitude to Great Britain, especially Göring, who he felt was less truculent, a Nazi with whom business could be done. The German air minister had informed his guest that the Reich's final demands would be satisfied by the settlement of the Sudeten question. Conversely, Ribbentrop and Heinrich Himmler had spoken as though they had 'rehearsed parts'.[173] Once again Londonderry was left with the impression that a solution was within reach. Little wonder, for Göring's suggestion had been deliberately designed to encourage British appeasers and to counter French opposition to any alteration of Czechoslovakia. And although Chamberlain was prepared to reach an accommodation with Hitler on the issue, Halifax appears not to have taken kindly to Londonderry's conclusion that Prague was to blame for the crisis and that Czechoslovakia was 'one of the unfortunate post-war developments'.[174] It was, nevertheless, an attitude widely shared among Conservatives, at least in private. As noted by a contemporary observer, the historian R. B. McCallum,

> both the League [of Nations] and the doctrine of self-determination were conceived as Wilsonian Liberal fads, academic and intellectual notions divorced from the facts . . . The Conservative mind was irritated by having to become accustomed to this new and improbable looking map of Europe. Those who set store by aristocratic tradition noted that they were states ruled very much by peasants and small bourgeois. Some were only republics, others had monarchies, but not of ancient vintage.[175]

As the crisis intensified Chamberlain flew to Germany for a meeting with Hitler at Berchtesgaden on 15 September. Londonderry had a brief meeting with the prime minister before his aeroplane departed from Heston; he was naturally pleased that his hoped-for summit between the two leaders was finally happening.[176] The eventual outcome was the four-power conference convened at Munich on 29 September. The resulting agreement gave Germany the Sudeten territories and guaranteed, through an agreement with France and Italy, the remainder of Czechoslovakia. The following day Chamberlain had Hitler sign the famous letter declaring their intention never to go to war. As Churchill admitted, the conference and subsequent agreement were almost exactly what Londonderry had advocated: 'Your policy is certainly being tried.'[177]

Londonderry was in Munich during the four-power conference. He had no involvement with the negotiations, but he conversed with local people as well as Nazis and journalists, including the editor of the *Deutsche Allgemeine Zeitung*, Dr Karl Silex.[178] Not unexpectedly, Londonderry sought afterwards to associate himself with what appeared to be a victory for peace. In a letter published in *The Times* on 3 October, he drew attention to an excerpt from the concluding chapter of *Ourselves and Germany* to claim that Chamberlain had fulfilled his hopes of reaching an understanding between Great Britain and Germany.[179] Likewise, in the House of Lords, he accompanied a tribute to Chamberlain by reminding peers of his advocacy of direct contacts between the powers: 'I can say quite honestly that what has happened has been the fulfilment of the hopes which I have had in my mind.'[180] However, far from basking in Chamberlain's reflected glory, the only public attention that Londonderry received after returning home was from left-wing critics, and rather than ignoring their taunts he characteristically rushed to his own defence. Addressing a meeting at Sunderland, he sought to answer their disapproval by denying that he was 'pro-Nazi', and he stressed that his visit to Munich was to meet ordinary Germans and not their leaders. As he presented it, 'it happened that the German and French delegations came to the hotel at which I was staying, and I could not avoid meeting with some of the Germans whom I knew personally. I did not go over to see any of them'.[181] He further tarnished his name after adding it to a letter in *The Times* from the pro-Nazi lobby group, the Link, which heaped praise on the Munich agreement.[182] He was not the only non-member to add his name, but his status as an ex-cabinet minister and the group's reputed connections to Berlin made it scandalous. He paid for it with what he called a 'conspiracy of silence'.[183]

The satisfaction with Munich felt by advocates of appeasement did not last long. On 8 October Hitler delivered a speech at Saarbrücken that attacked Chamberlain and his government's condescending and hypocritical policy towards Germany. A month later, on 9–10 November, the murderous outrage against Germany's Jews that came to be known as *Kristallnacht* left most of the active appeasers with little choice but to outwardly abandon the cause. Londonderry retained his belief in the necessity of mutual understanding, but as he wrote to one of his corresponding supporters, 'at this time, we should condemn what is being done in the name of the German people by the German Government'.[184] On 24 November Londonderry wrote a frank letter to Göring in which he made a number of complaints. The common theme was that he felt let down by the German government, that on each occasion that he had acted for Germany, Hitler had embarked on a sudden action or policy that he could not explain. He also protested about the persecution of Germany's Jews, and about the Nazis' continued complaints about reports in the British press, something, he said, that was 'unbecoming for a great nation'.[185] Göring's secretary sent a brief reply that included a German newspaper clipping that addressed the violence of the British military in Palestine.[186] As Hitler had recently indicated, senior Nazis were in no mood to be lectured on morality by the champions of British imperialism.[187] Addressing the House of Lords on 30 November, Londonderry referred to

> the most detestable persecution of a portion of their people that the world has ever seen, a persecution which we must condemn to the fullest degree. While that

> persecution continues and unless we can convert them to our way of thinking, and cause them to give up that persecution, one feels that all those desires which are in the minds of every one of your Lordships of bringing nations closer together, are rendered more and more difficult.

Still, he expressed his hope that 'even on that count I would not feel that any of us are justified in feeling that all our efforts at co-operation and at bringing peoples together have been brought to naught and that we should try some other line of policy'.[188] Speaking at the Over-Seas League a fortnight later, on the German government's demand for colonial restitution, he remarked that

> these matters were complicated in view of the terrible persecution of the Jews . . . a persecution which appeared to be so medieval in its ferocity, so unjustified by any information we could obtain, and so antagonistic to that friendly international understanding without which all efforts towards a higher standard of living and cultural material progress must inevitably come to a standstill.[189]

Notwithstanding his comments to the House of Lords, Londonderry's personal contacts with the Nazi leadership appear to have largely dried up at this time. As he informed an administrator at Oxford University, who sought his help in securing the release of a lecturer from a German prison camp:

> I have written to the German authorities in more than one instance, but I am rather unwilling to do so just now. As you know, I have tried for some years now to establish better relations between this country and Germany, but by reason of the fact that I could not receive any support, the influence which I may have had with the German leaders has really diminished to vanishing point. I am at the present moment, rather anxious to have no communication whatsoever with the German authorities.[190]

Yet, as his recent speeches suggested, the brutality of the Nazi regime did not lead Londonderry to completely abandon his belief in the need to avoid war through the promotion of Anglo-German understanding.[191] To several of his correspondents he even laid part of the blame for the present difficulties between the two countries at the door of the press, for giving undue attention to Germany when similar incidents were taking place in Spain and Russia.[192]

Speaking at Belfast on 20 January 1939, Londonderry returned to a more familiar refrain: 'Germany has received but little understanding and sympathy from us . . . It was Hitler who offered the naval limitation which was grudgingly accepted; it was Hitler who proposed a limitation of the German Air Force, which was not accepted . . . Germany had not been given her legitimate rights by the peace treaties'.[193] His intervention on this occasion prompted some of the most enthusiastic advocates of appeasement to seek his patronage, with invitations to assume the presidency of the Link and a new Anglo-German friendship league, respectively.[194] Londonderry declined, though it is noteworthy that his response to the Link did not contain any principled objection to the group, merely that he was 'President of so many different undertakings that I really feel I cannot add to their number'.[195] Perhaps in response to such unwelcome approaches, he addressed the Primrose League days later, juxtaposing 'the difficulties in which Germany was placed' with 'the great material assets of the British Empire'. Allied with 'the great democracies of the United States and France . . . there was no force in the world which need give them cause for anxiety'.[196]

International tension increased in the early months of 1939, signalled by General Francisco Franco's victory in Spain. The Londonderrys had a close and well-publicized friendship with the country's deposed king, Alfonso XIII. Before the First World War, Alfonso's engagement to Princess Ena of Battenberg had been tacitly agreed, according to Lady Londonderry, at a ball held at Londonderry House. The Castlereaghs, as they were then, had attended the subsequent royal wedding at Madrid, witnessing at first hand the failed assassination attempt on the newly married couple. Later, as the Marquess and Marchioness of Londonderry, they often hosted the controversial king during his annual trips to Great Britain, accompanied by his wife and other members of the Spanish royal family.[197] Just as Lord Londonderry was sensitive to reports about Londonderry House in the *Daily Express* (see Chapter 5), so Lady Londonderry complained to Beaverbrook about its coverage of Alfonso.[198] After the king had fled his country, following republican successes in its municipal elections held on 12 April 1931, he was three months later standing next to Lord Londonderry on a platform at Paddington station, awaiting the arrival of the Infante Don Juan on a special train bringing cadets from the Royal Naval College, Dartmouth. Londonderry addressed the assembled press on behalf of the king, denying reports that he had renounced his claim to the Spanish crown in favour of the infante.[199] Given the Londonderrys' relationship with the Spanish king and queen, and their undoubted hostility to republicanism in that country, it is not surprising that they are reputed to have belonged to the Friends of National Spain.[200] However, there is little evidence to suggest that their royalism translated into Francoism, certainly nothing that compares to their efforts in promoting Anglo-German understanding.

In March 1939 the Londonderrys stayed in Stockholm as guests of the British Legation, from where they attended a number of events hosted by members of the Swedish royal family.[201] The visit had its light-hearted moments. At the Royal Swedish Aero Club, at a meeting presided over by Prince Gustaf Adolf, which Lord Londonderry addressed on British civil aviation, both he and his wife were presented with genealogies that purported to show how they were descendants – twenty-fifth and twenty-seventh generation, respectively – of the twelfth-century Swedish king, Erik the Saint.[202] More serious was Londonderry's meeting with the German minister to Stockholm, Prince Victor of Wied, which appears to have been planned in advance, but about which nothing is recorded.[203] Whatever was said, events took a turn for the worse during the Londonderrys' visit to Sweden when Germany repudiated the Munich agreement by invading Prague and carving up the remainder of Czechoslovakia with Poland and Hungary. As Londonderry informed the famous Swedish explorer, Sven Hedin, after meeting him in Stockholm, 'the German Chancellor has, I regret to say, overstepped all limits'. In response to Dr Hedin's enthusiastic reading of *Ourselves and*

Germany, Londonderry insisted that 'I see no possibility of any confidence ever again being placed in [Hitler's] statements and undertakings.'[204]

On the surface, Londonderry appeared to be in tune with the outrage felt by many British people at Hitler's breach of the Munich agreement. Addressing the Devizes Women's Unionist Association on 19 April, he remarked that the British Empire 'had one purpose, and that was to establish independence of thought and freedom throughout the world. The policy of the dictatorship countries was the reverse'.[205] He was also keen to impress on his German correspondents that Hitler had gone too far. Writing to Göring, after a break of five months, Londonderry declared that he had little choice but to support Chamberlain's tougher stance towards Germany, announced on 17 March, which included the guarantee given to Poland that would ultimately trigger the Second World War. Nobody would listen to his calls for better understanding, Londonderry claimed, because Hitler had 'destroyed' all his efforts.[206] On 9 June, he informed Franz von Papen, now his country's ambassador to Turkey, that he regretted that it had taken the invasion of Prague for him to change his mind about Hitler.[207]

In private, however, like Chamberlain and other enthusiastic appeasers, Londonderry could not altogether abandon his hopes that war could still be averted through renewed dialogue. In an unsent letter to the journalist Ward Price, dated 28 March, he confessed, 'I still think that our proper line is to accept Germany as the strongest military power in Europe.'[208] Tellingly, he took the trouble to keep a close eye on German public opinion, especially in the wake of the guarantee to Poland.[209] And on 17 June, he wrote to the German ambassador to London, Herbert von Dirksen, asking him to stem the decline in Anglo-German relations by challenging press reports about Nazi brutality.[210]

Around this time Londonderry assured Halifax that he had left politics, that he would even leave the Conservative party once his term as president of its National Union came to an end.[211] But his belief in the necessity of an Anglo-German agreement meant that it was not long before he broke cover and made public his true disposition. In a letter to *The Times*, published on 22 June, ostensibly in response to Sir Norman Angell's advocacy of collective opposition to Germany through the League of Nations, Londonderry reviewed his record on Anglo-German relations and concluded that it 'would be unfortunate to sink back into the delusion that collective security can be achieved by certain Great Powers securing the sympathy and support of many smaller nations when other Great Powers refuse to enter that organization'. Instead, he maintained his position that 'the question of peace throughout the world and the arrangement of a new order of understanding between nations can only be brought about by the Great Powers themselves agreeing, either at a conference or through diplomatic agencies . . . to abide by the decisions which might be arrived at by those methods of discussion'.[212]

If Londonderry now threw his weight behind a new four-power agreement that would include Germany, he had abandoned his efforts to explain away the policies of its Nazi government. In early July, the secretary of the Anglo-German Fellowship, Philip Conwell-Evans, now an anti-appeaser with links to German opposition groups, arranged for Londonderry to meet the 'moderate' Lieutenant-Colonel Schwerin of the German general staff.[213] Schwerin was one of a number of aristocratic senior officers who regarded Hitler's military plans as disastrous. Following the meeting Londonderry dutifully renewed contact with Halifax and relayed Schwerin's desire for British military assistance.

> He . . . conveyed that Hitler, being a soldier, would only be impressed by arguments given to him by soldiers, and that the political points made very little impression upon him. I, of course, retorted that if he wanted a soldier's answer the only way that that could be given was in war, which I was quite certain all peoples . . . were longing to avoid.[214]

Halifax in reply expressed his appreciation for the information.[215] The episode appears to have rekindled Londonderry's interest in making another visit to Hitler, though in his memoirs he claimed instead that the idea was in response to a request from the sixth Earl Winterton.[216]

As soon as Halifax was informed of Londonderry's proposed mission, at the start of August, he made moves to prevent it. Londonderry had overinflated his own usefulness at what was a highly delicate moment in international relations. The prime minister had his own preferred unofficial intermediaries, such as the former MP, Henry Drummond-Wolff, just as Hitler had his, including the press magnate, the first Baron Kemsley.[217] Initially, Londonderry was defensive, arguing that he had unique contacts with the German leadership that would allow him to declare that he had been betrayed by Nazi assurances and that he 'represented the spirit of the British Government and people in being determined to resist any further aggression'.[218] It was Hitler's style to leave his British visitors with the impression that they mattered. As Harold Macmillan later noted, the emphasis placed by the Nazis on private audiences with their important visitors was 'dangerous'. 'It is no mean feat to have charmed such varied and distinguished men as Lansbury, Lothian, Rothermere, Arnold Toynbee, Londonderry, Allen, Tom Jones, and Lloyd George.'[219] Halifax, himself a victim of this, replied to Londonderry that the visit would betray British anxiety and look too much like a negotiation.[220] With that Londonderry's amateur diplomacy was at an end. He responded with chagrin, bitterly attacking the prime minister for the failures of the National Government.[221] His anger was also a response to the Nazi-Soviet Pact of 23 August, for that agreement further demonstrated how badly he and other appeasers had misjudged Hitler. Frozen out by his former ministerial colleagues, Londonderry moved to his Ulster estate a few weeks prior to Chamberlain's announcement on 3 September that the United Kingdom was at war with Germany.[222]

IV

The outbreak of the Second World War did not subdue Londonderry for long. Not only did he still hanker after a role in the affairs of state, but the war also provided its own necessities and opportunities. Chief among his priorities throughout the conflict was the need to vindicate his actions as Secretary of State for Air and his prominent role in promoting Anglo-German understanding. Not unrelated to this were his other concerns: the removal of Chamberlain from the premiership, the political and military defence of Northern Ireland and scrutinizing the performance of the Air Ministry.

Londonderry disliked Chamberlain for a number of reasons, ranging from the clash between their fathers over tariff reform through to the prime minister's reluctance to take a personal interest in his amateur diplomacy. His main line of criticism, however, focused on Chamberlain's stringent control of defence spending in the early 1930s, a policy that Londonderry adhered to reluctantly at the time, and which he used subsequently, with some justification, to absolve himself from any responsibility for the country's relatively weak strategic capability in the air. Indeed, it was Londonderry's need to vindicate his ministerial record that prompted his most bitter falling out with Chamberlain.

As noted already, Londonderry believed that his two 1934 letters to Hailsham demonstrated that he had called for the British government to deal with Germany from a position of strength.[223] It was in preparing the manuscript for *Ourselves and Germany* that he first sought the government's permission to reprint the letters, only to be told that he could not as Hailsham's bringing them to the attention of the cabinet rendered them confidential cabinet papers.[224] Rebuffed on this occasion, Londonderry persisted with his requests to make them public. Even the prime minister was obliged, several weeks into the war, to take the time to reaffirm the government's position to Londonderry.[225] It is unlikely that publication of the letters would have changed public perceptions of the former air minister; after all, his actions subsequent to 1934 demonstrated that he had wanted to negotiate with Germany regardless of Great Britain's strength. Nevertheless, he took Chamberlain's response as a personal blow and an obstacle to the vindication of his name, if not in the short term, then in the judgement of posterity. On 1 October he replied to Chamberlain, lamenting that the destruction of his reputation was 'only a matter of importance to myself and my family'.[226]

If Londonderry felt bitterness towards the government, did he belong to a 'peace lobby', as some have suggested, even after the start of the war?[227] That Londonderry should be considered an opponent of the war, even a potential traitor, is not that surprising given his prominent campaign for Anglo-German understanding. It had been announced in the court circular of 16 August, over a fortnight before war was declared, that he and his wife would remain in Northern Ireland 'until the end of the year'.[228] Shortly after the outbreak of hostilities, a rumour circulated that far from being a voluntary arrangement, he had in fact been interned at Mount Stewart. Londonderry publicly acknowledged the claim in order to deny its veracity.[229] A subsequent court circular, dated 4 October, announced that he was returning to London from Mount Stewart.[230] On the 14th of that month, he gave a speech at Luton that attempted to clarify his views on the enemy. 'The Germans are a very nice people so long as they are in a subordinate position', he informed his audience. However, 'Once you allow them to get the mastery the whole of that character disappears, and they become what is inherent in them – of a very arrogant and domineering disposition'. He added his 'sincere' hope 'that no doctrines would be put forward for making terms with Germany. There were no terms to be made'.[231]

In private, however, he still could not completely shake off his rationale for appeasement and even his hope, at this stage of the so-called bore war, that terms could be reached with Germany. In one of a number of lengthy and wide-ranging letters to Halifax on how the war should be conducted, Londonderry made it clear in December 1939 that he still harboured fears of Communist expansion following the conflict between Great Britain and Germany, and that for this reason, alongside the widespread apathy towards the war, he thought that the government, during what he described as a 'pause' in the conflict, should give favourable consideration to the offer of mediation made by the Dutch and Belgian governments, and other similar peace initiatives should these be forthcoming.[232] It is possible that he was aware that the foreign secretary was the regular recipient of peace feelers from various quarters in Germany, and indeed that Halifax was privately disposed to a genuine and suitable offer.[233] Londonderry nevertheless took care to admit that he lacked the government's knowledge of events and Hitler's intentions, and that going down the path of negotiations would require 'some complete change in the German attitude'.[234]

Londonderry was not part of any 'peace party'. He was not among the handful of prominent pro-German aristocrats calling for peace, notably the dukes of Bedford and Buccleuch, nor had he endorsed the calls for a negotiated peace made by Lloyd George and some Conservative MPs in early October.[235] Admittedly, his reputation was not helped by his principled resistance to disassociating himself from other autocratic but neutral regimes. He had been president of the Anglo-Hungarian Society since its establishment in May 1930.[236] It was a small – 296 members in 1939 – and relatively uncontroversial organization compared to the Anglo-German Fellowship. The involvement of Hungary's ambassador to London, and Great Britain's ambassador to Budapest, even leant it a measure of official approval in both countries.[237] But Londonderry's long association with it came to an end in August 1940 when he and a number of other senior figures tendered their resignations. This was in response to the news that Budapest had congratulated Mussolini on his conquest of British Somalia. The society's secretary, Sir William Goode, tried his best to dissuade Londonderry, claiming that 'in the opinion of the Foreign Office it would be a great pity if the Anglo-Hungarian Society, which up till now has done really useful work, were dissolved as suggested . . . Its dissolution would place the British Minister in Budapest in an extremely awkward position'.[238] Londonderry's hostility to the Foreign Office, as he confessed in reply to Goode, meant that such an appeal was never likely to succeed.[239] The multiple resignations from the society were not without impact, for these obliged the Foreign Office, against its own inclinations, to give its attention to the otherwise relatively trivial incident.[240]

A potentially more damning indictment concerning Londonderry's loyalty came on board the aeroplane flown by Rudolf Hess to Scotland in May 1941. In what was a truly remarkable episode shrouded in mystery, the deputy führer carried with him a list of British peers whom he believed had constituted a peace party. As noted already, some peers did indeed favour a truce. But the episode only revealed how deluded some Nazis continued to be about the influence of the British aristocracy and the possibilities that would arise out of direct contact between the leading figures of both countries.[241]

If anything, Londonderry aligned himself in early 1940 with the 'war party', albeit with a deep sense of regret that could make him appear equivocal. This claim is not based on the occasional anti-German speech that he made, or his family's patronage of war measures in County Down and County Durham, but his actions beyond the public gaze.[242] In October 1939, for example, he wrote to the then Secretary of State for Air, Sir Kingsley Wood, asking if he might be able to join the RAF. He cited the example of Sir Arthur Wilson, a former Iraq hand six years his junior, who in 1940 became the first serving MP to die in the Second World War. Wood politely turned down the 61-year-old's request.[243] Far more significant was Londonderry's association with Lord Salisbury's self-styled 'Watching Committee'. Even before the formation of the group in April 1940, Londonderry had been a keen behind-the-scenes critic of the government's handling of the war. To this end, he had expressed concern in the House of Lords that without the facility for convening secret sessions, peers would 'feel themselves muzzled and controlled by reason of the fact that some of their speeches might savour of criticism of the Government'.[244] He believed that war did not suspend the duty of parliamentarians to hold ministers to account, but it is hard not to suspect that he also sought to discredit Chamberlain. His supportive letters to Churchill – brought into the cabinet by popular demand – were in this spirit, and these had the additional utility of potentially ingratiating himself with a leading voice in the war cabinet.[245] The First Lord of the Admiralty did not reciprocate his cousin's efforts, but Londonderry continued to back Churchill in the knowledge that it was an indirect method of attacking Chamberlain. Likewise, Londonderry continued to correspond with Halifax. In one of his many letters to the foreign secretary, Londonderry informed him that Churchill was the only member of the war cabinet qualified to 'carry us through these difficulties', and that he was by far the most inspiring minister, especially in his radio broadcasts.[246]

With his credentials as an anti-Chamberlainite well established, it is still remarkable that a committed anti-appeaser such as Salisbury should choose to welcome Londonderry into the Watching Committee, notwithstanding the two men's longstanding friendship.[247] Still, Londonderry was a former air minister, and it was his experience in that area that he contrived to bring to the attention of Chamberlain's growing number of critics. In the same month that Salisbury formed his Watching Committee, Londonderry wrote to his immediate successor at the Air Ministry, Lord Swinton, now out of office, to advocate the reformation of the 'Independent Peers', a Conservative party ginger group once led by Salisbury that had pressed for the unrelenting prosecution of the First World War. For good measure he also suggested that it should scrutinize the government through a private committee.[248] Having in effect described Salisbury's Watching Committee, he was invited to join it on 1 April.[249] Mere membership of the committee boosted Londonderry's self-esteem, and he was not the only one. As Larry Witherell observes, 'the Watching Committee unleashed a thrust of constructive assessment and encouraged the dissidents to believe that they had a vehicle with which to influence government reform, shape policy, and make a positive contribution to the administration of the war'.[250]

Londonderry did not have a good record of attendance at meetings of the Watching Committee, mainly because he had thrown himself into the role of wartime landlord in counties Down and Durham.[251] He was nevertheless active in the committee's deliberations about how the RAF might be better used, working alongside his old friend and fellow committee member, Lord Trenchard.[252] Londonderry also added his concern about the need to improve the role of women in the services, a reflection of his wife's lifelong campaign for women's participation in the armed forces.[253] He made his dissatisfaction with Chamberlain's leadership clear to Salisbury, but Londonderry's poor attendance at meetings of the Watching Committee, and the inability of peers on the committee to intervene directly during the Norway debate of 7–8 May, meant that he was only associated by implication with the subsequent replacement of Chamberlain with Churchill as prime minister.[254] The following month, in a transparent attempt to curry favour with the new premier, Londonderry wrote to *The Times* to highlight and criticize those who cast 'aspersions on those of the previous Administration whom the Prime Minister in his wisdom has invited to share with him the overwhelming burden of the Government'. In the same letter, he reversed his earlier stance on the importance of parliamentary secret sessions, arguing that the 'whole situation is now entirely altered' as a result of 'the brutal determination of Germany to achieve victory at all costs'.[255] A positive gesture, to be sure, but the continuity in personnel that he at first praised soon after began to trouble him, and it was not long before Londonderry emerged as a critic of Churchill's government, especially its handling of Northern Ireland and air matters.

V

Londonderry had not abandoned his interest in Northern Ireland after resigning from its government in January 1926. This was clear during his time as a cabinet minister in the National Government (see Chapter 6), and it continued in the years that followed. Despite sharing much of Chamberlain's rationale for appeasing Germany, he took exception to the prime minister's related overtures to the Fianna Fáil premier, Eamon de Valera.[256] He communicated with Samuel Hoare to this end, pressing the Northern Ireland government's position in the run up to what became the 1938 Anglo-Irish Trade Agreement.[257] When the IRA launched its 1939 campaign, Londonderry successfully pressed Chamberlain to give him guarantees that the government would not cave into its demands.[258] He was less effective in getting ministers in London to publicly disavow and resist any attempt by de Valera's government to pressure them on partition.[259] Even so, Londonderry's status as a champion for Northern Ireland was recognized by his former colleagues there. He was the principal speaker at a luncheon held at the UUC's annual conference in March 1939.[260] In July that year, it was announced that Craigavon had asked Londonderry to visit the United States and Canada in the autumn on behalf of Northern Ireland and to pay a special visit to the Irish Linen Guild section at the World's Fair at New York.[261]

That trip was prevented by the outbreak of war. As the conflict developed, and the question of partition re-emerged as part of British efforts to secure the co-operation of the Irish government, it became clear that Londonderry's reluctant support for partition at the Irish Convention had hardened since into steadfast support. His stance at this juncture is all the more noteworthy given that several other Ulster nobles, including the fourth Marquess of Dufferin and the eighth Earl of Antrim, were now open to an all-Ireland settlement if it helped the war effort, applying a rationale that Londonderry had once articulated, albeit in private, during the deliberations of the Irish Convention.[262]

If he was not interned at Mount Stewart, the Londonderrys nevertheless spent much of the war at their County Down estate, carrying out the various charitable and war-related activities that were expected of them. Their son, Lord Castlereagh, remained the MP for County Down through to his retirement from the House of Commons in June 1945, but he was largely absent having obtained leave from his parliamentary duties to join the Royal Artillery and serve in the Middle East.[263] Lord Londonderry remained in post as both Lord Lieutenant of County Down and chancellor of the Queen's University of Belfast. Indeed, he had become something of a veteran figure in Northern Ireland. In July 1933 he had delivered a speech at the unveiling of Lord Carson's statue outside the new Parliament Buildings at Stormont. On this occasion he dutifully waxed lyrical about the pre-war response of the Ulster Unionists to the third home rule crisis, despite having personally experienced it at the time as a tiresome chore.[264] Both the statue and Londonderry's speech are indicative of how the earlier period had, by the early 1930s, achieved mythic status among Ulster Unionists.[265]

It should not be inferred that Londonderry had completely abandoned Wynyard and his duties in that part of the world. Certainly, the house was commandeered by Durham County Council as a teacher training college, having initially been offered by Londonderry as a home for evacuated children.[266] But the Londonderrys still patronized local organizations associated with the county's war effort. As with County Down, Londonderry remained in post as both Lord Lieutenant of County Durham and chancellor of Durham University. In the former role, he took an interest throughout the war in the appointment of the county's magistrates, just as he and Lady Londonderry continued to grace Conservative party functions in the area.[267] These were not belated acts calculated to obfuscate their several years promoting Anglo-German understanding. As noted above, Lord Londonderry had recently served a term as Mayor of Durham, in 1936–7, to coincide with the coronation. And in March 1939, against the backdrop of Germany's invasion of Prague, he had been appointed the president of a committee to promote national service in the northeast of England.[268]

Against expectation, Londonderry found it harder to assume a similar role in Northern Ireland. His former cabinet colleague, John Andrews, now Minister of Finance, had been supportive of Londonderry's efforts to promote Anglo-German understanding.[269] But when Londonderry offered his services to the Northern Ireland government on 8 September 1939, only one minister, Sir Basil Brooke, Minister of Agriculture, took practical steps to use the former Minister of Education and Leader of the Senate, and this was because he made the same request of all county lords lieutenant. In any case, Londonderry found himself, as in the First World War, promoting voluntary recruitment to the armed forces, as conscription had once again been effectively ruled out by Irish nationalist objections.[270] It was, by coincidence, an issue that Londonderry had raised earlier in the year with the air minister, Kingsley

Wood. 'There are many reasons' why it would be difficult to recruit in Northern Ireland, he warned Wood on 12 July,

> and they are all associated with the unfortunately artificial position which Ulster has to maintain in the British Isles . . . we are in a transition stage now of which I certainly cannot prophesy the outcome. The psychological effect which this has had on Northern Ireland is to destroy all confidence in themselves, and to make them feel that they must get whatever they can out of the British Government.[271]

This and similar missives on Ulster affairs had the effect of further souring relations between him and his former ministerial colleagues at Westminster. In particular, he became convinced, like a number of others, that a German fifth column might attempt to take control of Éire.[272] He passed on his concerns to Churchill's new war cabinet in May 1940, along with his opposition to the possibility that de Valera might be offered an end to partition in return for his state's participation in the war. Eden, the Secretary of State for War, responded politely if evasively by saying that he had the situation under control.[273] This was followed by further complaints in June about the inadequate protection of Belfast's dockyards against an aerial attack; his warning was given less than a year before the Luftwaffe's blitz on the city killed over 900 people and injured twice that number.[274] Londonderry also criticized Eden's decision to accept Craigavon's use of the Ulster Special Constabulary for anti-parachute defence duties.[275] Indeed, the policy led Londonderry to despair about his former colleague's ability to govern Northern Ireland during the wartime emergency, and to go as far as suggesting to Eden that he appoint a military governor to take charge of Northern Ireland's defence.[276] Exasperated with the situation, Londonderry eventually went over Eden's head by writing directly to Churchill on 21 June.[277] Whereas Halifax had for several months indulged Londonderry's disposition to pass on his lengthy assessments of war policy, the new prime minister had no such inclination. In reply, Churchill sent a terse and angry rebuke that effectively ended any meaningful communication between the two cousins.[278]

Londonderry then unsuccessfully attempted to press Salisbury to take up his concerns.[279] When his ally of so many previous occasions politely rebuffed his efforts, Londonderry responded by blaming Eden and others for a disastrous foreign policy that he felt had led the country to its present difficulties.[280] This was followed in August with accusations that his correspondence to and from England was being opened. Replying to the charge, Eden justified it on the basis that Northern Ireland did not censor its mail with Éire.[281] It is likely that the war minister also had in mind an incident earlier in the year, recorded in the diary of Henry Channon, when a celebratory service at St Paul's Cathedral on 19 May had to be moved from noon to six o'clock, after the censor intercepted a telegram from Londonderry's butler at Mount Stewart that mentioned the original time. Channon records that the authorities took the precaution of changing the time in case the Luftwaffe targeted a building full of 'all the notabilities of England'.[282] Craigavon's death in office several months later, to be succeeded by Andrews, at least addressed one element of Londonderry's immediate concerns, though in practice the limited changing of the guard at Stormont did little to address his anxiety about Northern Ireland's defences.

VI

The affairs of Northern Ireland were not the only interest that Londonderry maintained after leaving the cabinet in 1935. He had also sustained his close links to aviation, the air force and the Air Ministry. As a former air minister, he was occasionally invited to perform ceremonial duties, such as opening the new RAF drill hall at Usworth, near Sunderland, in October 1936, and opening Charles Winn's private aerodrome at Nostell Priory, near Wakefield, in July 1938.[283] In September 1937 he was elected Master of the Guild of Air Pilots and Air Navigators of the British Empire, the professional association for aeroplane pilots.[284] In addition to these ceremonial functions, he also intervened publicly in air debates, such as when he wrote to *The Times* in January 1937 to complain about a proposal by the Air Ministry to site an aircraft factory at Maidenhead rather than one of the government's designated special areas. 'I am at a loss to understand why it is necessary to plant a new community of 20,000 people in a rural area, and in the vicinity of London', he protested.

> I should have thought that when the question of the Special Areas is of such vital importance, and when it is realized that in these Special Areas there exist many of those requirements which will all have to be set up *de novo* in this agricultural area, a scheme could have been put forward for utilising these areas which, at this moment, owing to reasons of which we are aware, are making no contribution to the economic life of the country.[285]

Such interventions, alongside his contacts in the aviation industry, and even some of his ceremonial duties, inevitably brought him into contact with the Air Ministry.[286] There were also more direct exchanges with his former department. In May 1938 an official at the ministry sent Londonderry material to assist his forthcoming contribution to a House of Lords debate.[287] The following month, Londonderry gave advance notice to Kingsley Wood of his attendance, noted above, at the Fédération Aéronautique Internationale in Germany, perhaps in the hope that the air minister might give the visit an official sanction.[288] It led officials at the Air Ministry to draft a memorandum that confirmed Londonderry's connection to the federation, as well as his membership of the Aerodrome Owners' Association and the Guild of Air Pilots.[289] Wood afterwards added to these appointments by making Londonderry the chairman of the Air Guard Commissioners, which had recently been established to encourage civilian training for the purpose of quickly supplementing the RAF should the country go to war.[290] Within months it reported the enrolment of over 20,000 members.[291] Londonderry responded in kind, praising Wood in a letter to *The Times* for overseeing the completion of the empire air mail service.[292] Weeks later, Londonderry was appointed Honorary Air Commodore of No. 602 (Ulster) (Bomber) Squadron, Auxiliary Air Force.[293] The following year, he spoke in the House of Lords in favour of the government's policy to merge Imperial Airways and British Airways to form the state-owned British Overseas Airways Company.[294] In 1942 he was made Regional Commandant of Northern Ireland's Air Training Corps.[295]

Londonderry's new-found favour with the Air Ministry in 1938 was a significant development given that it is often supposed that he was ostracized by ministers in the late 1930s. It should not, however, be taken to indicate that he held any residual influence over his former colleagues. Even during his brief spell as Lord Privy Seal in 1935, he had failed to change the government's preferred transatlantic air route (see Chapter 6). Now out of office, he was even more powerless. Despite his protests, therefore, he was unable to prevent the Air Ministry preferring Sydenham, near Belfast, to his own airfield near Newtownards, when it came to channelling state support for civil aviation in Northern Ireland.[296] The same fate awaited his efforts to secure the new location for the province's Auxiliary Air Force squadron.[297] The ministry's consistent preference for Sydenham even led Londonderry afterwards to complain to Wood that he was no longer permitted to stop aeroplanes and airliners at request at Newtownards.[298] His other criticisms and grievances with the ministry included its failure to promote the women's section of the RAF; that it failed to treat properly the Air Guard Commissioners; and he even revisited the transatlantic flight.[299] The last prompted Wood to request that Londonderry desist from putting down a parliamentary question as the matter was bound up with the promotion of good relations with the Canadian and Irish governments.[300] If Wood was discomfited by his predecessor's interventions, he still renewed Londonderry's chairmanship of the Air Guard Commissioners when it came up in August 1939, thus extending it to August 1942.[301]

The outbreak of war did little to stem Londonderry's inclination to comment on air matters. Early on, his high regard for Trenchard was evident in a request made to Wood that the marshal be brought back into the RAF. Trenchard's return, he felt, would boost morale in the service.[302] It was also expressed through a complaint made to his son-in-law, Oliver Stanley, now war minister, that Trenchard was being prevented from visiting his old regiment and air force units.[303] In October 1940, at the concluding stage of the Battle of Britain, Trenchard and Londonderry addressed a debate on the air force in the House of Lords. Both men celebrated its achievements and argued in time-honoured fashion that it needed to remain an independent service.[304]

Having upset Churchill and Salisbury in June 1940, there were almost no ministers left in the wartime government prepared to listen to Londonderry. A notable and surprising exception was Beaverbrook. Between May 1940 and June 1945, the newspaper proprietor held a succession of posts, including Minister of Aircraft Production, Minister of State, Minister of Supply, Minister of War Production and Lord Privy Seal. In contrast to his newspapers' earlier coverage of lavish functions at Londonderry House and Londonderry being 'pro-Nazi', the *Daily Express* praised the former air minister in January 1940 for having preserved the RAF: 'the nation knows that Londonderry was right'.[305] Londonderry's letter of appreciation in response to the article appears to have amused Beaverbrook, for he attached to it a note that it should be returned to Londonderry should he complain again about his name appearing in the *Express*.[306] Londonderry seems to have assumed that it was his criticisms of government policy that led to Beaverbrook being drafted into the wartime government. Writing in

Figure 12 Lord Londonderry in RAF uniform, 1943.

February 1942, Londonderry informed him that he was the only independent voice in the cabinet who could counter Churchill's dominating style of leadership.[307] Two years later, he wanted to let Beaverbrook know that he had paid Churchill an 'undeserved compliment in attributing the success of the Battle of Britain to him. I am sure the drive and energy which you put into your work when you were Minister of Aircraft Production has to a very large extent been responsible for much of the success of the RAF during these five desperate years'.[308]

If these and similar missives had any effect, it is likely to have shored-up Beaverbrook in his subterranean marshalling of wider Conservative discontent about Churchill and his stewardship of both the Conservative party and the war. But in practical terms, Beaverbrook confined himself to only periodically consulting the former air minister, such as in the early months of 1944 when he passed on confidential government documents in the hope that it might help him defend legislation intended to reform civil aviation.[309] Through activities such as this, Londonderry felt that he was playing a valuable role, although it is clear from a later declaration – that he would not serve in a government under Churchill – that he overestimated his importance.[310] In the end, Beaverbrook's polite solicitations to a former air minister could not hide the fact that, for all purposes, Londonderry was a finished politician with an obvious sense of grievance towards those in office.[311] Outside of his early communications with Beaverbrook, Londonderry's political interventions and outlook had become wholly negative. Even his other political concern of the mid-1940s, Foreign Office reform, was motivated by his bitter experience of that department in the 1930s. Still, his efforts in this area achieved some impact in so far as these contributed to the critique of the Foreign Office advanced by a number of its former luminaries, including Sir Eric Phipps, Sir Victor Wellesley and Sir Walford Selby.[312]

VII

Out of office, out of favour and unwilling to remain silent, Londonderry again considered how he might vindicate his ministerial record.[313] His more recent dealings with the Nazis made the task of justification all the more necessary. Assurances to the contrary from his circle of close friends and supporters counted for little; for in the midst of a war against foes that he had once courted, Londonderry was compelled to place his version of history on record.[314] Further incentives were supplied by the periodic attacks on his reputation that appeared in print. Two volumes published by the Left Book Club, in 1938 and 1939, respectively, singled him out for criticism. The first, by F. Elwyn Jones, described Londonderry as 'a frank supporter of Hitler'. *Ourselves and Germany*, he went on, 'contains a long *apologia* for the outrages committed by the Nazis since 1933'.[315] The second, by 'Simon Haxey', the pseudonym used by Arthur and Margaret Wynn, made several references to Londonderry's association with the Anglo-German Fellowship, 'a platform in this country from which various Nazi leaders can plead their cause and gain sympathy for their methods'.[316]

Wickham Steed's *The Fifth Arm*, published in 1940, expanded on the criticisms made by Jones and the Wynns. It recommended *Ourselves and Germany* as 'proof of the receptivity of British public men who were eager to sit at Hitler's feet', and noted, suggestively, that as Air Minister Londonderry had been 'primarily responsible for keeping an eye on Germany's air force and its huge expansion in 1933 and 1934 after Hitler came into power'.[317] Despite not having read the book, Londonderry complained to Steed 'that those of us who did our best to keep the peace should meet with criticism from a large number of people who have probably never read anything that we have written, or listen[ed] to anything that we have said, but simply gone by newspaper announcements that we went to Germany and became acquainted with leading men in Germany'.[318] Steed's reply was unflinching. 'I am quite unable to understand how any Minister of the Crown, with all the resources of Government information at his disposal, can have been unacquainted with the real purposes of German policy before and under Hitler.' He went further, revealing that in 1934 he had been willing to share information on Hitler's intentions with the Foreign Office and the War Office, but not the Air Ministry, then under Londonderry, as

> one of my informants had learned on unimpeachable authority from Berlin that the relations between our Air Ministry and the German Air Force were so close that it would not be safe to put the full text of a document of this kind in the

> hands of Air Ministry officials. On enquiry in London I found a similar impression prevailed in some very 'inside' quarters here.[319]

Stung by Steed's claims, Londonderry persisted in defending his record and that of his former department, with the telling confession that 'My only object in continuing this correspondence is to have on record amongst my papers the replies to those half truths which may create so many misunderstandings if not explained.'[320]

According to Montgomery Hyde, Londonderry decided to start writing *Wings of Destiny* in 1942 as a means of distracting his mind from the untimely death of his daughter, Maureen Stanley.[321] It is an inaccurate statement on two points, authorship and date. An undated memorandum among the Londonderry papers indicates that Londonderry was assisted in writing *Wings of Destiny*. The anonymous author suggested that as Londonderry's visits to Hitler were 'incidental', and had already been dealt with in *Ourselves and Germany*, *Wings of Destiny* should concentrate on Londonderry's time at the Air Ministry.[322] Hyde, a barrister and historian, had collaborated with Londonderry in the writing of *Ourselves and Germany*, and it is possible that he was the ghost writer hired for *Wings of Destiny*.[323] Rather than Maureen's death serving as the catalyst for the book, the evidence suggests that Londonderry was making preparations a year beforehand, in the summer of 1941, as he then boasted to Beaverbrook that his November 1934 letters to Hailsham would soon 'see the light of day', and he subsequently received permission from the war cabinet to consult cabinet papers for his research.[324]

In fact, the proofs of *Wings of Destiny* were ready by the end of 1941. Instead of writing the book, the following year was taken up in negotiations with the war cabinet for permission to publish particular documents, and in undertaking several reworkings of the manuscript following government objections to certain passages. Londonderry even enlisted the help of the prime minister's wife, Clementine Churchill, who duly proofread the manuscript. She was assured afterwards by her husband's personal assistant, Desmond Morton, that it contained nothing that would infringe the Official Secrets Act.[325] The permanent secretary at the Foreign Office, Alexander Cadogan, likewise found that there was no security risk in publishing the manuscript.[326] Even Buckingham Palace was involved. It relayed its objections to a number of passages, including one that referred to the late king, George V, wanting the equestrian statue of the first Earl Haig in Whitehall to be moved further away from the cenotaph.[327] When Londonderry complained about the length of time that it was taking to review the manuscript, the Minister of Information, Brendan Bracken, sent a frank reply:

> I can well understand your feelings about the unfair criticisms which have been directed against you. But I fear that you have written your book in a very bad temper and I do not think it will do you any good. But of course you must judge for yourself. [Sir Edward] Bridges is not 'taking his time about the book because it is not connected with the war'. The truth is that it contained certain passages which I am told must be referred to the War Cabinet.[328]

Bridges, the cabinet secretary, advised Churchill that 'To put the matter bluntly, the book will damage its author, but, I think, no-one else.' He noted, however, that it included text from a lot of state documents and that publication of these should be prevented.[329] Replying to Bridges, Churchill was dismissive of Londonderry's 'twaddle' and 'tale-telling', but he still took the precaution of forming a cabinet committee to examine the potentially compromising manuscript.[330]

Unknown to Londonderry, the task was assigned to the Lord Privy Seal and Labour MP, Sir Stafford Cripps.[331] The Treasury solicitor, Sir Thomas Barnes, thought that some of the criticisms made of ministers 'may be thought to be in bad taste or to be undesirable at the present time', but, as there was no 'objection on legal grounds', he felt 'that the best hope of stopping the book altogether or getting it revised in acceptable form is for some responsible Minister to ask Lord Londonderry to come and discuss the matter with him'.[332] A memorandum prepared by Bridges on 11 November noted that although Londonderry had toned down derogatory remarks about former colleagues, he still left some in the manuscript.[333] Several days later, Cripps recommended to the cabinet that if Londonderry amended passages that referred to the content of government documents, he should be allowed to publish the resulting manuscript.[334] When Bridges informed Londonderry of this outcome, the latter expressed only bitterness and disappointment in response. The delay, he retorted, meant that he could not make the Christmas book list. 'I am afraid the deletions and my desire to hurt no one's feelings have really spoilt this book', he went on, 'but I shall have to wait and see'.[335]

The setbacks that Londonderry faced in trying to publish his book unredacted further embittered him towards the wartime government. Through correspondence and in the House of Lords, he continued his 'watching', openly questioning the management of the war, from issues as varied as coal mining to the surrender of Singapore, and periodically initiating parliamentary debates on air matters.[336] Speaking in the House of Lords in February 1942, he opened a debate on the conduct of the war with a sweeping assessment of the government's 'lack of appreciation of the magnitude of the issues involved, and I feel that one can say there has also been a lack of planning and foresight'.[337] His persistent keenness to appraise and critique the government later earned him a gentle reprimand from the former foreign secretary, Lord Halifax.[338]

Londonderry's near constant grumbling did not serve him well. But as noted already, it did chime with wider discontent in the Conservative party about Churchill's leadership. After lunch with Henry Channon in December 1943, the latter recorded that 'Charlie held forth about his cousin Winston, who, he maintains, has few Churchillian qualities'.[339] As Channon was aware, Londonderry at this stage attributed his almost non-existent relationship with Churchill to a dinner party given by Lady Cunard before the war, at which Londonderry purportedly remarked on the unreliability of the French as allies, as well as the strength of Jewish influence in Great Britain, the United States and France. If there is any truth in the story, it was more than a mere disagreement as it touched on deeper political divisions between the two men. As Clementine Churchill suggested in January 1942, holding out the hope of personal reconciliation, the cousins' estrangement was 'purely in the field of public affairs'.[340] The prime minister, for his part, did not have the time or inclination to reply to Londonderry. On one of the few occasions that he did, it was to reject the former air minister's advocacy of a posthumous Victoria Cross for the flying ace, Group Captain Charles Pickard, killed in an operation to assist the escape of French

Resistance prisoners at Amiens.[341] The incident ensured that Londonderry remained hostile towards Churchill long after the tide of the war had turned in the Allies' favour, and Churchill's position in parliament became unassailable. In time, Churchill would make amends, just prior to Londonderry's death. As noted in Chapter 6, the first volume of Churchill's war memoirs, *The Gathering Storm*, was more generous than might be expected in its appraisal of Londonderry as air minister. Perhaps for this reason, he was able several years later to gain Lady Londonderry's permission to wear her late husband's diamond garter star for the coronation of Elizabeth II.[342]

Lord Londonderry was without doubt presumptive and on occasion arrogant in the way that he expected his former colleagues to treat him. But he was not ignorant of his failings. In 1943 he wrote to his lifetime confidant Lady Desborough:

> When Baldwin removed me I instinctively knew that I was finished, that my active life was over and that I had to fall back on resources which it is difficult to cultivate when you have been in the middle of politics as I had been since the end of the [First World W]ar. In your last letter you say so kindly, 'The swing of the pendulum will come.' But of course I know it won't be for me and I confess that knowing this, as I have known it, I have touched almost the lowest depths of despair . . . So the war, the crisis of our lives, finds me completely isolated and under a sort of shadow which I cannot get away from. Politicians burn their boats . . . I want you to know that I have no illusions about it and that I am bitterly disappointed. I had great chances and I missed them by not being good enough and that really sums up the whole thing . . . It all has worked out badly and I know it is some inherent fault in myself. However I know I have got to carry on and I am doing my best.[343]

In November 1945 Londonderry was injured in a gliding accident. He had suffered similar mishaps in the past. In April 1938 he had fractured his collar bone after tripping over wire during a game of golf at Brora in Sutherland.[344] In November that year, on a flight from Durham, he was forced down at Halton, Buckinghamshire, causing damage to the aeroplane, though neither he or his two passengers, Lady Londonderry and Lady Mairi, was injured.[345] The incident in November 1945 was altogether more serious, though it was reported at the time as 'a slight accident in which he injured his back'.[346] 'I had a mishap gliding, which I will not seek to explain to you', he afterwards informed Walford Selby, 'because I doubt if you would understand these mysteries. I will tell you that I did nothing foolish and that I did not harm the machine at all, but that the cable on which the glider does depend to a certain extent broke at the wrong moment'.[347] Two months later, he reported to Selby that he was still wearing a plaster of Paris jacket that cramped his movements.[348] Hyde implies, without explanation, that the accident was somehow linked with the series of strokes that Londonderry suffered in the final years of his life, which had the effect eventually of impeding his power of speech.[349] It is impossible at this distance to pronounce on the cause or causes of his strokes, but he had clearly been suffering from an all-consuming sense of grievance that probably took its toll. His family at this time were also the cause of considerable heartache. Maureen's death in 1942, at the age of 41, has already been noted. Cuthbert Headlam, on hearing the news, recorded in his diary that he was 'terribly sorry . . . for Charley Londonderry who was so fond and proud of her'.[350] Londonderry's relationship with his son, on the other hand, was poor and had been deteriorating for some time. Dynastic tensions between fathers and sons are hardly unusual, but Robin's lack of interest in a parliamentary career reflected and fortified differences of opinion in other areas too. Their drifting apart was further exacerbated by Robin's alcoholism.[351]

As Londonderry's physical condition worsened in the spring of 1948, the doctors informed Castlereagh that his father 'will never be able to speak again or think consecutively'. The former confided to Headlam that he believed 'his father is really happier as he is than he was before his breakdown, because he worried and repined so dreadfully – there may be something in this though it is not easy to understand'.[352] Londonderry had good reason to worry and repine in what were his final years. In a striking coincidence, his gliding accident had been reported in the press on the same day that news emerged from the Nuremberg International Military Tribunal that Ribbentrop's lawyers intended to call him as a witness.[353] They were subsequently granted the court's permission to send interrogatories to Londonderry, Beaverbrook, Halifax and the first Baron Vansittart, among others, in lieu of appearing at the trial in person.[354] Ribbentrop's representatives sought to establish that their client had wanted peaceful relations between Germany and Great Britain. Londonderry's answers to the interrogatory duly acknowledged that Ribbentrop had expressed such ideas in the past, but he added that he had not been convinced of the Nazi's sincerity. It is hard to square this assessment with Londonderry's attitude to Ribbentrop during his ambassadorship to London, but the souring of their relationship in the years that followed probably convinced Londonderry of its veracity.[355] The interrogatories returned by Londonderry and others did little to help Ribbentrop, who under cross-examination remained loyal to his dead Führer.[356] The man once dubbed the Londonderry Herr was hanged on 16 October 1946, principally for having conspired to wage an aggressive war.

Earlier that year, Londonderry had revived his correspondence with Bridges over the content of *Wings of Destiny*. He was goaded by the appearance of Samuel Hoare's recollection of his time as wartime ambassador to Madrid, which freely reprinted official correspondence between Hoare – now first Viscount Templewood – and government ministers.[357] Not unreasonably, Londonderry asked the cabinet secretary why Templewood was able to include government letters and even publish these in the accompanying newspaper serialization.[358] In private, it prompted Bridges to suggest to the Foreign Office that some mechanism needed to be put in place for the publication of ministerial memoirs.[359] To Londonderry, however, Bridges offered the unconvincing explanation that there was a difference between a former cabinet minister publishing official correspondence and a former ambassador.[360] Londonderry's lengthy response revisited the grievances that he had raised over many years. On the specific issue of publishing official documents, he pointedly made the claim that Churchill had sold a story to the American press about a meeting that was supposed to be secret. 'I think Winston would have liked the war earlier', he added for good measure, 'and he would have been disappointed had there been no war'.[361] The hypocritical position adopted by the Cabinet Office encouraged Londonderry to consider a further effort at vindication. At first, he asked the Labour government's air minister, the first Viscount Stansgate, if his ministry could publish the figures for the RAF and the Luftwaffe 'from 1933, until say 1941'.[362] As it was not possible, he sought permission in February 1947 to access official papers for the purpose of writing a comparative history of the British and German air forces before the war.[363] When Bridges heard about this development, he noted that the former air minister 'is more a controversialist than an historian'; he had no more right to access official documents outside his period of office than a member of the public.[364] Stansgate's successor at the Air Ministry, Philip Noel-Baker, offered a potential solution by suggesting that Londonderry use parliamentary privilege to ask questions in the House of Lords on matters contained in the closed papers.[365] Knowing how impractical this would be – consistent questions in the public arena on pre-war policies that implied criticisms of Churchill – Londonderry dismissed the idea and regretted what he viewed as the inevitable development of a pro-Churchill historiography.[366] He had some modest success several months later, however, when the editor of the *Belfast Telegraph*, Jack Sayers, agreed to publish correspondence between Londonderry and Papen.[367] Now in his late 60s, Londonderry's unabated desire to rescue his reputation, and the knock-backs that he continued to receive along the way, did little to relieve him from the deterioration in his health. Castlereagh's matter-of-fact observation the following year, that his mute and confused father was now happier, can be understood in this light.

VIII

Londonderry could not help but see his amateur diplomacy as an inevitable sequel to his time as air minister. His justification of one bled easily into the other, and the resulting overarching story that he sought to convey in print prioritized autobiography over context. Londonderry's support for the appeasement of Nazi Germany was not unusual; indeed, it was typical of many British observers of foreign affairs. More interestingly, he closely resembled Chamberlain in his application of appeasement and was even given a hearing by the normally solitary prime minister, just as he was permitted to keep up correspondence with Halifax. And like Chamberlain, Londonderry's commitment to appeasement after 1938, largely hidden from the public, barely wavered even after the invasion of Prague. Both men were compelled to avoid war, holding that it was not only futile, but that it would leave Europe vulnerable to Communist expansion. They hoped that a benign, gentlemanly approach to diplomacy could somehow tame Hitler, who encouraged such notions, and in doing so they spectacularly underestimated the dictator's ambitions. The main distinction between Londonderry and Chamberlain was that it had become the accepted role of a prime minister to engage in diplomacy. Londonderry took it upon himself to play the amateur diplomat, encouraged by the Nazis, and in doing so overestimated his usefulness to both London and Berlin. Nevertheless, he had limited if unintended uses for both governments, as evidenced by Ribbentrop's memorandum and Halifax's consultations, but Londonderry on occasion mistook the latter for the possession of high-level influence. By making himself an arch proponent of appeasement through his speeches, books and visits to Germany, Londonderry suffered the fate of those other guilty men whose reputations suffered after the Second World War. In the end, Hitler destroyed the nineteenth-century world of the great powers that Londonderry and others had hoped to save. The appeasers had grossly misjudged the Nazi leader, but in their prediction that the war would end Western European hegemony and lead to Soviet expansion, they were proven to be correct.

Conclusion

On the evening of 8 May 1945, 'Victory in Europe Day', Harold Nicholson was walking through Belgrave Square when he was hailed by the man he called 'Hitler's friend'.[1] Nicolson, a former diplomat turned National Labour MP, was the author of a Penguin Special, *Why Britain Is at War*, published in 1940, in which he expounded on his hostility to appeasement and looked forward to a new and stronger League of Nations that would control all civil and military aviation.[2] As he walked with Londonderry in the direction of Londonderry House, its owner explained to Nicolson

> how he had warned the Government about Hitler; how they would not listen to him; how, but for him, we should not have had Spitfires and 'all this', waving a thin arm at the glow above a floodlit Buckingham Palace, at the sound of cheering in the park, and at the cone of searchlights which joined each other like a Maypole above our heads.

Nicolson was not impressed. 'Enraged by this, I left him in Park Lane and walked back through the happy but quite sober crowds to Trafalgar Square.'[3]

It is a curiosity that Londonderry persistently maintained this self-righteous posture to parliamentary colleagues. To his closest confidant, Lady Desborough, he could be contrastingly frank about his faults and weaknesses. He reviewed his political life to her in a long letter written in 1943, his difficulties in recent years evidently causing him to be nostalgic about all that went before:

> Whatever I touched seemed to turn to gold. I seemed to succeed in everything, not brilliantly or exceptionally, but still everything went well, everyone helped me, and I seemed to have so many friends and well wishers, and then suddenly it all came to an end. I tried loyally to carry on outside, then I dabbled in diplomacy with an idea which I know was correct but I could not somehow work it with anyone who counted. Then I did a lot of flying. I made speeches which people seemed to want to hear; we went on entertaining and everyone seemed to want to come.

Yet even to Desborough he remained unapologetic for his beliefs and actions:

> Then I had some bitter exchanges with [Stanley] Baldwin and [Neville] Chamberlain whom I knew were wrong although I commended Chamberlain for Munich but regretted everything he subsequently did. Then I fell out with Winston [Churchill] because I wanted to achieve by what I thought was statesmanship

> what he wanted to achieve by war. That quarrel I think originated sometime before because I was never really fond of F.E. [Smith] who completely absorbed Winston to the exclusion of W's allies like myself, and I disagreed with both and rightly disagreed over their Irish policy which has had such fatal results. So I really planned a bad crash and was not strong enough or clever enough to strike out on my own.

His outlook was similarly bleak as he looked to the future. 'I get so impatient about the attitude towards me in books and articles with reference to my German activities and I hate special pleading, and if I do write retorts . . . no one seems to read them or notice them.' He then returned to Churchill:

> Winston has been distinctly unfriendly and I often wonder why he never would take the trouble to find out what I was at. W. did suggest to me to resign when Chamberlain at last consented to re-arm and I wish I had done so because my loyalty to my old colleagues afterwards precluded me from joining Winston which I would like to have done.

He concluded by confessing his frustration at lacking a public role of significance:

> I am intensely lucky. But for this cussed war I am quite happy at home and I pray that will go on. A politician who has missed is really terribly out of a job. You are not wanted for the big things and there is really no place in the smaller things. All the many figure head duties were very good accompaniments to the central and dominating duty, but they are uninteresting by themselves and it is so difficult to keep oneself up to the mark . . . I was always so sorry for Hailsham, because the moment he took off his harness he became an old man.[4]

He wrote in a similar vein in his final letter to Desborough, dated 21 September 1947:

> I really am not bothering about politics. I think all the politicians are quite useless. I have been reading the histories of the last century and all the politicians were actually the most terrible liars, foreign affairs was a game, and no one ever wrote a letter or a dispatch without his tongue in his cheek. I now see why I failed to understand the very second-class people I had to deal with and how glad they must have been to get me out of the way. I am sorry I failed to handle Winston because he really could have saved the war instead of gaining the credit which he fully deserves for winning it, and we are now paying the price . . . If only someone had been powerful enough to combine Chamberlain with his passion for peace with Winston . . . we need never have had the war with its ghastly results as the price for Winston gaining an everlasting historical name . . . I am getting much interest from letters I am getting from a few people, who think I was right and everyone else wrong, who come across my books at libraries, but that the historian will deal with in years to come I think.[5]

Londonderry's final years were largely spent at Mount Stewart. His granddaughter, Lady Annabel Vane-Tempest-Stewart, later recalled the last occasion on which she met him there.

> Once, during the final summer before his death when I was about thirteen, he asked me to take him by boat across the lake. I had just learned to row and to please me he asked me to show off my new skill. The oars were so large and heavy that I could only steer a very rocky and uncomfortable course, catching endless 'crabs', but he managed to sit serenely all the way across. He had made a great effort during that holiday and I had felt particularly close to him. On the day we left he kissed me goodbye and surprised me by putting one of those enormous old five-pound notes into my hand.[6]

Londonderry's reluctant retirement from public life coincided with the ascendancy of the Soviet Union in Eastern Europe. It was an outcome of the war with Germany that he and others had feared, and it led him to observe to the BBC's Asher Lee that 'we are following with Russia the same course as was followed in connection with Germany'.[7] Another outcome of the conflict, closer to home, was Labour's landslide victory at the 1945 general election. Clement Attlee, the man who had so effectively pilloried Londonderry's record at the World Disarmament Conference, now set about as prime minister delivering what the miners' trade union representatives had been demanding for decades: nationalization of the coal industry.

The enlightened self-interest of the coal owners in the late 1930s had gone some way to fulfilling what Londonderry had called for the previous decade (see Chapters 5 and 6). He could have associated himself more prominently with that development, with consequences for his reputation that can only be guessed, but as noted already he was distracted and absorbed by vindicating his record as air minister and the related task of promoting Anglo-German understanding. Not that he altogether ignored the trade that provided his family with enormous if declining wealth. Locally, Londonderry's relationship with his employees had continued to benefit from the relatively benign economic conditions of the late 1930s. On 27 May 1936 he and other members of his family were entertained 'by the townspeople of Seaham Harbour'. The rector of the local Catholic church, Father Heggarty, paid effusive tribute to his 'work in Parliament and as soldier, Cabinet Minister, coalowner, and employer'. His generosity 'had been lavish to all sections. No peer or commoner in the land had done more for his people'.[8] Heggarty's hyperbolic praise probably owed something to the generous terms that Londonderry as landlord offered to his parish church, in the face of long-standing opposition from Anglicans and Nonconformists in the area.[9] Even so, it was not entirely without foundation given Londonderry's record in maintaining the bonds of paternalism at his pits. On 11 December 1937 he opened new pithead baths at Seaham Harbour to accommodate 1,600 miners. The £16,000 required to build the baths was raised by the Miners' Welfare Fund, but Londonderry committed to give 50 per cent of the annual maintenance charges.[10] Further local recognition came in October 1938 when he was given the freedom of the city of Durham.[11]

The relatively improved industrial relations of the mid- to-late 1930s had a discernible impact on Londonderry's outlook. Responding in May 1937 to news of the London Omnibus Strike, he informed a gathering of the Society of British Gas Industries, of which he was president, that he did not 'feel panicky nor did he believe what he had been told that all sorts of insidious forces were at work'.[12] And in contrast to his vocal hostility to the Labour government's 1929–30 Coal Mines bill, his response to the National Government's 1938 Coal bill was more muted. The legislation addressed what even the MAGB now held to be the main reason standing in the way of amalgamations and general structural change, the fragmented system of royalty payments, by nationalizing royalties and increasing the role of the state in the industry through the Coal commission.[13] In his contributions in the House of Lords, Londonderry suggested that the bill was the result of the MFGB's propaganda, he questioned how the government intended to calculate the value of the royalties for the purpose of compensating the owners, he defended the record of the owners' capacity to organize their industry and he argued for amalgamation through evolution not compulsion. But aside from a minor amendment to the wording of one section, he offered no real challenge to the bill, alluding to the growing international crisis to justify his attitude:

> I feel that the position of the Government at the present moment is one in which they require all our support, and I should not like a debate of an acrimonious character to be published in the newspapers here or abroad and so give an entirely false impression of the real situation in this country, which is that we are prepared to support the Prime Minister whatever may happen.[14]

The various inconsistencies that arose from the Coal Act 1938 gave its critics plenty to attack in the years that followed. Londonderry, however, largely confined himself to challenging the prevailing wisdom, enshrined in the 1930 and 1938 Acts, which held that amalgamations would make the industry more efficient. The 'more closely' the question is examined, he wrote to *The Times* in June 1939, 'the more apparent does it become that the [Coal] Commission itself is growing increasingly aware of the difficulties involved . . . difficulties inherent in the nature of the industry and not arising from an obstructive habit of mind on the part of the colliery owners'.[15] His observation chimes with a leading authority on the history of the coal industry in this period. 'It is easy, then, to *envisage* a restructured and better integrated industry, consisting of larger, better capitalized mines and companies using up-to-date machinery', Barry Supple writes. 'But this did not necessarily mean that such a system, even if the money and will had been available to introduce it in wholesale fashion, could have produced results sufficiently remunerative to justify the necessary expenditures.'[16]

In contrast to his earlier assumption that shortcomings in the productivity of miners were politically motivated, Londonderry during the war defended them against 'unjust' criticisms of absenteeism. 'There is no body of men more determined to do their utmost to win the war than the miners', he wrote to *The Times* in August 1941. 'The shortage of rations has been responsible to a very large extent for this absenteeism by reason of the fact that it is impossible for the hewer to give of his best in sustained effort when he is not receiving the nourishment to which he has been accustomed.'[17] The problem, of course, was more complex than the individual physical capacity of the miners. The prevalence of older pits and the failure to fully mechanize the coal industry in the 1930s were important factors, along with the reduction in the workforce during the same period.[18] Output nevertheless remained a significant problem throughout the war, and so another investigation of the industry's problems was established in 1944, under the chairmanship of Sir Charles Reid. The Reid commission's report damned the status quo and called for parliament to establish an authority to take control of and refinance the industry. With even many Conservatives coming round to the view that the coal trade required significant overhaul, the owners still failed to use this last opportunity to fend off nationalization by establishing a voluntary trust that might have sought government finance.[19]

On 26 January 1946, after the Labour government had published its bill to nationalize the coal industry, Londonderry sent a message to the annual dinner of his colliery officials in which he defended free enterprise as the best means of managing the pits. He nevertheless acknowledged that the owners might have handled things better in the past with reference to his own efforts. 'I wish I had been forceful enough to get my plan across', he said in reference to his intervention in 1926 (see Chapter 5).

> Instead of that the colliery owners as a whole have taken for granted that the coal industry will be nationalised and have taken steps accordingly. The Mining Association have spoken for the coal trade, but I have not found myself in agreement with the attitude they took up, beyond full agreement with the undertaking to do everything in their power to increase production.[20]

Nationalization ensured that the colliery owners were compensated for the transfer of their pits to the newly established National Coal Board. Nothing, however, could compensate Londonderry for the decision of his son to stand down at the 1945 general election. Castlereagh's decision not only severed his family's long cultivated political connection to County Down, it abruptly brought to a close the Londonderrys' dynastic ambitions. After Robin inherited the marquessate in 1949, his son and heir, Alistair, highlighted how far the family had fallen from its own pedestal when he publicly criticized the royal family. The dowager marchioness, Edith, who outlived her husband by a decade, forced her grandson to publicly apologize.[21] Later, as the ninth Marquess of Londonderry, Alistair declined to take his seat in the House of Lords. Even had he been inclined to do so, he lost the privilege in 1999 along with most of the other hereditary peers. If the lens is widened beyond the marquessate, however, it is possible to observe dynastic survival. Lady Annabel had three children with her second husband, Sir James Goldsmith, the billionaire financier, founder of two political parties – L'Autre Europe in France and the Referendum Party in the United Kingdom – and Member of the European Parliament for France. Their first-born son, Zacharias, or 'Zac', sat as the Conservative MP for Richmond Park in 2010–16 and 2017–19, and he was created Baron Goldsmith of Richmond Park in 2020. In both the House of Commons and the House of Lords, he served as a government minister under three successive prime ministers, Boris Johnson, Liz Truss and Rishi Sunak. His older sister, Jemima, although primarily occupied with her career in the media, has been involved in a number of political campaigns and was for a period married to the Pakistan cricketer and future prime minister of that country, Imran Khan. Annabel herself came to symbolize another noteworthy legacy of her forebears. The Mayfair club, Annabel's, was opened by her first husband, Mark Birley, in 1963, and like Edith's Ark it became famous for attracting an elite clientele that transcended the worlds of politics and the arts.

The seventh Marquess of Londonderry died at Mount Stewart at the age of seventy on the night of 10–11 February 1949.[22] On St Valentine's Day, he was laid to rest in the family graveyard, *Tír na nÓg* – the land of the forever young – surrounded by the statues of four Irish saints. On 16 February a memorial service was held at St Anne's Cathedral, Belfast, and another the following day at Westminster Abbey.[23] At his death, Londonderry's wealth was valued at £1,021,754 (the equivalent today of £37 million). Both Mount Stewart and Wynyard Hall – the latter continued to house a teacher training college into the 1950s – were retained by the family. However, the two properties were split, the former going to his wife and their youngest daughter, Lady Mairi, and the latter to Robin. The eighth marquess, who retained his own living quarters at Wynyard, relayed to Headlam his displeasure with this outcome, especially as most of the family's wealth went to Edith and Mairi. The diarist was not entirely sympathetic, 'he will be terribly hard up . . . Of course Robin has only himself to blame – for he was a rotten son'.[24] Years later, Mount Stewart was transferred to the National Trust and Wynyard Hall sold to a local business tycoon. Two properties at Seaham Harbour that had been used as hospitals during the Second World War remained so after it. The Royal Aero Club took on Londonderry House as its headquarters before the building was eventually pulled down to make way for a hotel. What remained of the Welsh estate, Plâs Machynlleth, was given to the local people.[25]

Londonderry's final years had been spent in relative obscurity. Outside Northern Ireland, his pre-war political preoccupations were of little concern to a nation that had endured the Second World War and its immediate aftermath. More than ever before he seemed to belong to a bygone age. His obituary in *The Times* gave a comprehensive overview of his political life and concluded that his promotion of Anglo-German understanding had lost him a lot in public esteem.[26] Lord Trenchard was moved to write a further obituary, in which he emphasized Londonderry's role alongside him in preserving the RAF. Another in the same newspaper, by an anonymous 'old friend', compared him to his forebear, Lord Castlereagh: 'In spite of his obvious advantages he was curiously diffident about himself . . . he possessed the moral courage which enabled him to take the course which he believed to be right and to hold his road, deeply distressed, but outwardly indifferent to misrepresentation and abuse.'[27]

Historiography has not been altogether kind to Londonderry. As outlined in the Introduction, a significant factor is that assessments of him tend to be partial and disjointed. Thus, a study of Lady Londonderry's role as a political hostess makes the brusque assertion that her creation of the Personal Service League (see Chapter 6) demonstrated 'charitable intentions which were markedly absent from her husband's approach to the poor'.[28] Not only does this statement overlook Lord Londonderry's presidencies of the Chelsea Hospital for Women, which provided treatment to women of limited means, and the Benevolent Society of St Patrick, an organization that assisted destitute Irish people living in London (see Chapter 5), it fails to acknowledge Londonderry's relatively benign record as a colliery owner. Even his granddaughter, Annabel Goldsmith, makes a similar error of judgement by claiming that her father, the eighth marquess, 'distinguished himself by bothering to take time down the mines himself, something that many previous Castlereaghs and Londonderrys, including his own father, had failed to do'.[29] In fact, as noted in Chapter 5, her father, as a young man, had accompanied his father and mother when they descended the pits at Seaham and Dawdon on 6 September 1923. In both cases, a simplistic caricature of the seventh marquess is employed to boost the reputations of his wife and son, respectively.

More significantly, Londonderry's political and ministerial record has suffered from its partial coverage in the distinct historiographies of Ireland and Great Britain. An accomplished practitioner of the former observes that Londonderry was a 'peer of long Irish ancestry and of too-long residence in England'.[30] Yet, an important study of Conservative politics in County Durham claims that he was 'preoccupied with Irish affairs and his role in the government of Northern Ireland'.[31] As these contrasting assessments suggest, historians have tended not to connect Londonderry's experiences at Dublin and Belfast with his record at Westminster and Geneva, let alone Berlin. A surprising and hostile exception is the December 1935 number of the *Catholic Bulletin*, which did so to condemn Londonderry's actions at the World Disarmament Conference.

> The performer-in-chief concerning [John] Bull as International Air-Bully and as Advocate of Bombing from Aeroplanes is, we make haste to say, that champion of Ascendancy in Ireland, the Most Noble the Marquis of Londonderry . . . A clumsy champion, this ex-Minister of the [James] Craig Compound, the man who planned the iniquitous Belfast Education Act of 1923, the heir of the title given to Castlereagh.[32]

Notwithstanding the *Catholic Bulletin*, it is not entirely unexpected that historical assessments of Londonderry have been partial and disjointed. He was a second rank politician, and related to this, the significant setbacks and problems that he encountered in his various government offices prevented him from leaving an indelible mark on government policy on either side of the Irish Sea. But this has led to a tendency to focus only on failure. Therefore, his role in creating a new education system in Northern Ireland, which lasted through to the post–Second World War expansion of schooling across the United Kingdom, tends to be overshadowed by failure in one particular area: non-denominationalism. Similarly, his determined preservation of the RAF, against significant opposition within the cabinet as well as at the disarmament conference, was crucial to its preservation, but his achievement was quickly eclipsed by the scramble to build up the air service in the wake of Hitler's false claims about the Luftwaffe.

Biography is a genre of limited utility if it is to be restricted to so-called great men. Looking beyond the first rank is not only revealing in itself, but in this case, it demonstrates how an aspiring aristocrat-politician was able to defy the trend of aristocratic decline and use supposedly antiquated claims on office to secure a succession of government appointments from the 1910s through to the 1930s. Lord and Lady

Londonderry are therefore a striking example of how the aristocratic political culture of the nineteenth century survived the growth of democracy. This is not to suggest that all aspirant aristocrat-politicians were like Londonderry. Rather, he was a living relic of an era when they regarded themselves as born to rule, and he practised with some notable success aristocratic methods of political advancement. Knowing that everyone loves a lord, and playing up to it, won him election to the House of Commons in 1906. It also, through his continued role alongside his wife as prominent political hosts, made him useful to Baldwin and the Conservatives in the late 1920s, and it charmed the Labour leader Ramsay MacDonald into a close friendship that aided Lord Londonderry's entry and survival in the National Government the following decade. His patrician distance from the electorate also allowed him to play a paternalistic and relatively moderate role in Irish affairs, especially at the Irish Convention and during the crucial early years of Northern Ireland. In Ireland, at least, his reputation was such that he was mentioned by a senior minister in the Cumann na nGaedheal government as a possible candidate for a viceroy-type figure at the apex of a Commonwealth of Northern and Southern Ireland (see Chapter 5).

Londonderry's unapologetically senatorial outlook also served to limit his impact as a politician. As an aristocrat brought up to have an active role in parliament, and if possible, the government too, it is unsurprising that he found it hard to shake off the class assumptions with which he was imbued. Whereas many others in his caste retreated to their estates, or found some satisfaction in business, the professions or the empire, Londonderry held fast to his belief in belonging to the United Kingdom's governing elite. The fundamental weakness of this outlook, of course, was that he depended almost completely on the patronage of a succession of leading politicians – Edward Carson, Winston Churchill, James Craig, Stanley Baldwin and Ramsay MacDonald – whose respective mandates came from the people and who had worked hard to carve out and cultivate a broad constituency of supporters. As Londonderry admitted in his memoir, *Wings of Destiny*, he had in the early 1920s been 'Winston's man', and the following decade he 'was marked down as "Ramsay's man" . . . It would have made the world of difference had I simply been a "party man"'.[33] Other aristocrat-politicians, such as Churchill and Halifax, were considerably more willing and adept at employing their talents to insinuate themselves into the norms and expectations of post-war democracy. For his part, Lord Derby was able to draw on his illustrious family history, and his unofficial status as the 'King of Lancashire', where the Conservatives attracted significant working-class support, to secure the War Office during and after the First World War, and in between these two appointments he served as ambassador to Paris. Indeed, Derby's fiefdom in northwest England meant that he remained an important figure there and in the Conservative party nationally well into the 1930s.[34] In their contrasting ways, each of these men was regarded as useful, talented and charismatic, and widely respected as such, so that their relationship with the Conservative front bench was in important respects different from that of Londonderry. He often addressed party meetings, but he lacked personal magnetism or a political stronghold of consequence to his party, and his old-fashioned claims on office appeared to many observers to be his only viable means of climbing the greasy pole.

Londonderry might have claimed that he admired those who had 'started from nowhere' in contrast to his 'pampered life', but he could on occasion exhibit the unabashed prejudice of his class.[35] In a grandiloquent and admittedly angry letter to Churchill written after the Second World War, he condemned his cousin's predecessors in office as a 'wretched Government of shop-keepers . . . a collection of pusillanimous representatives of the middle class, or if they were not of the middle class, had middle-class minds, which have never made any contribution to statesmanship'.[36] When surveying the political landscape, Londonderry looked to the summit for legitimacy and authority, but not, like most of his contemporaries in politics, also to the parliamentary party, the voluntary party and the electorate. On the face of it, his 1939 declaration that 'Democracy requires leading, otherwise it must become anarchy', appears reasonable enough.[37] However, these words were directed at Baldwin and were the latest in a long line of complaints about his removal from the cabinet in 1935. In this context, the statement revealed his indifference to the challenges of democratic leadership, and it can be placed alongside the frustrations he exhibited towards Carson in the 1910s and Craig in the 1920s. Baldwin's handling of foreign affairs and defence questions in the 1930s might be, and has been, criticized on many grounds, but his sensitivity to perceived shifts in public opinion was the key to his success and his party's electoral hegemony between the wars. And in contrast to Londonderry's experience in Northern Ireland, where one of the central tenants of his Education Act 1923 was undermined by his own government, Baldwin actually moved in the direction of the air minister's policy of maintaining the RAF. Yet, instead of embracing Baldwin's leadership on this area of policy as it aligned, however awkwardly, with his own, Londonderry remained wedded to Air Ministry dogma and openly expressed his bewilderment with the 'strange changes in public opinion'.[38]

This should not imply that Londonderry was totally inflexible, for he had demonstrated moderation since his time in the House of Commons. Whereas most of his fellow Conservative and Unionist MPs were either free traders or tariff reformers before the First World War, Londonderry adopted the *via media* of supporting fiscal reform. In 1916 he supported excluding six counties from immediate home rule and continued to do so when hard-line Unionists in Southern Ireland and at Westminster, seeking his aid, conspired successfully against their party leaders. Indeed, Londonderry's pragmatism in Irish affairs, notably at the Irish Convention, earned him the admiration of a number of Conservative grandees. Coupled with his active support for the Lloyd George coalition, after years of hostility towards the Liberal leader, Londonderry was rewarded with a junior government post in 1919. In office he supported state interference in civil aviation after years of vocal opposition to such measures as an MP. In the government of Northern Ireland his diplomatic handling of the Catholic hierarchy facilitated their qualified participation in its new system of education. Londonderry dissented from the line taken by most colliery owners during the general strike of 1926, and he stood up to diehard Conservatives at the 1927 party conference and several years later on the question of Indian constitutional reform. He supported tariff reform in the interwar period for the sake of party unity, and he toed the government line at the World Disarmament Conference despite resenting the severe limitations that it put on the RAF. As an amateur diplomat in the late 1930s, he attempted to persuade both the British and German governments to moderate their attitude to one another.

Alongside these significant examples of flexibility and pragmatism, it is important to acknowledge Londonderry's equally characteristic stubbornness, single-mindedness and acute touchiness. His reluctance to come over to the tariff reformers before the First World War hindered his early career in the House of Commons. His attitude to Protestant critics in Northern Ireland made it almost impossible for him to remain as Minister of Education. His conflicts with fellow cabinet ministers in the National Government, and his resentment at their attempts to follow perceived shifts in public opinion, made him appear intransigent and beholden to his service chiefs. His continued public spats with the Labour opposition in the run up to the 1935 general election – when the Conservatives had hoped to minimize any negative attention about rearmament – left Baldwin with little choice but to remove him completely from his government. Most fatally of all, Londonderry's continued and enthusiastic advocacy of Anglo-German understanding, even after almost all others had abandoned the crusade, caused lasting damage to his reputation.

What made Londonderry pragmatic in some instances and immovable in others was his fundamental motivation for continuing in politics against the odds and in the face of more legitimate competition and opposition. He believed that he had a right to be in the government, and a duty in that role to call for paternalist moderation in certain circumstances and in others to take a more principled stance. He was fundamentally an aristocrat in practice, temperament and outlook. But unlike others of his social rank who ascended the greasy poll in the first half of the twentieth century, he did not adjust fully to the priorities of the mass democracy that had come to underpin and legitimize the practise of statecraft. But to write him off as a failure ignores the less tangible qualities and legacies of his political career. In the first government of Northern Ireland, he criticized and tried to withstand some of its worst excesses, and in his role as Minister of Education he helped to partly reconcile an ambivalent Catholic hierarchy to a largely uninterested government of Protestants. He brought social prestige to an otherwise belittled air force after the First World War and again in the 1930s. His defence of the RAF also ensured that no premature disarmament took place in the early 1930s, and that Great Britain maintained the core of a fully trained air force that would go on to repel the Luftwaffe in what was later called Britain's finest hour.[39] As Lord Winterton put it, 'he deserves more credit than he has received for fighting against formidable odds in the Cabinet in favour of this policy'.[40] As air minister, Londonderry also oversaw the investment that led eventually to the development of radar detection, and the Spitfire and Hurricane fighters, at a time when others had demanded disinvestment. He had of course challenged the lack of defence spending upon taking office in 1931, precipitating Churchill's campaign by two years, and his caution in building up the RAF, even in 1935, ensured that priority was not given recklessly to the building of bombers.

Londonderry's approach to his own career also reveals a degree of sagacity. His move to Northern Ireland in 1921 did not, as Churchill suggested at the time, end his hopes of office at Westminster. His decision to avoid the fate of other aristocrats by refusing, on three separate occasions, the governor-generalship of Canada, allowed him to take a seat in the cabinet until 1935. His amateur appeasement led to some rapprochement with Chamberlain and Halifax who, like Hitler and Ribbentrop, initially demonstrated their willingness to use Londonderry's self-proclaimed role as a go-between. His determination to fight for the future of the RAF ensured that he was not subjected after the war to the criticism meted out to Baldwin and Chamberlain for inadequately preparing the country for conflict; indeed, Londonderry pre-empted such attacks.

None of this means that Londonderry was necessarily always correct or even a good politician. When it mattered his view was often sidelined and undermined by his own failure to communicate effectively. In public speeches, his delivery was old fashioned and his message often unpopular. He could impress people with his presence but not necessarily his presentation. The former MP for Bernard Castle, Cuthbert Headlam, described 'a very poor speech' given by Londonderry in July 1938, to the Northern Area's annual agents and women organizers' luncheon. Londonderry, Headlam recorded in his diary, seemed 'not to attempt to prepare his orations and he is not clever enough or a well-informed enough man to do this – the result is a dull rambling speech with constant repetitions and nothing to catch hold of'.[41] Months later, Headlam observed that Londonderry 'grows, I think, if possible more stupid and vain every day and more entirely self-centred – and yet one can't help liking the man – he really does try to be a good citizen!'[42] In a similar vein, it is not hard to see how Londonderry's calm and aloof demeanour led the journalist, A. L. Kennedy, to record in his diary that he was 'Really slow on the uptake sometimes'.[43] And as noted throughout, Londonderry was a consistent critic of his own intellectual ability.

Scholarly assessments of Londonderry's intelligence tend to rely on two isolated opinions expressed by Churchill and Amery that are taken out of their specific contexts. Churchill's reputed reference in 1934 to that 'half-wit Charlie Londonderry' is recorded in the diary of Frances Stephenson, the personal secretary and future second wife of Lloyd George.[44] If true, it undoubtedly reflected Churchill's frustration that his figures on German rearmament were being challenged by Londonderry's Air Ministry, correctly as it turned out. Churchill, it should be remembered, had pulled strings in 1919 to get his cousin into the government, he tried to dissuade him from leaving it in 1921 and he helped to get him office again at Westminster in 1928. Amery's observation, made in his diary in September 1941, that Londonderry was not 'quite intelligent enough' to be considered for the Indian viceroyalty also needs to be placed in its context. It reflects the heightened importance of the post in wartime, and more importantly for Amery, his need, as India secretary, to have a suitably strong, able and agreeable ally at New Delhi given his difficult dealings with the prime minister, Churchill, on India policy.[45] Still, Churchill and Amery's comments chime with those of Headlam and Kennedy. And if such assessments are ultimately subjective, a contributing factor is probably that Londonderry's cultivated antiquation in behaviour and dress carried over into his speech. Kennedy, a critic of his style of delivery – '[he] is to [*sic*] rambly to be impressive in what he says. He flits lightly from point to point' – was a noted communicator, as was Churchill. Yet, as a journalist, Kennedy still acknowledged that some of Londonderry's remarks and opinions – on his meetings with Nazi leaders – were 'interesting'.[46]

This touches on a related matter, highlighted elsewhere by Peter Mandler and David Cannadine. The interwar intelligentsia, to say nothing of most intellectuals, exhibited little enthusiasm for arresting or reversing aristocratic decline.[47] Aristocrats were easily labelled stupid by the younger men who rejected ideas about being born to rule, who resented aristocrats clinging to senior positions and who had striven to enter parliament and the government despite lacking all the privileges of the landowning elite.[48] Headlam's above observation about Londonderry's stupidity and vanity is made in an entry that details how they met on a train, the latter accompanied by Lady Mairi, on board which 'a compartment was reserved for them and the Station Master escorted them to it – the same ceremony at York where we changed!'[49] His other observation, on Londonderry's address to a party meeting, also noted that it 'seemed to please the Agents and Organizers who all slobbered over him'.[50] It might be added that on another occasion, in April 1940, Headlam could note that Londonderry 'made quite a good speech' at a meeting of around 200 Conservatives at Newcastle.[51] Indeed, for all his evident frustration with Londonderry, Headlam could on occasion demonstrate sensitivity towards his role as head of the party's Northern Area, such as in January 1938, when he declined the offer to become grand master of County Durham's National Conservative League, 'seeing that I did all the work . . . [but] fancy Charley's feelings if he had been deposed for me'.[52] Again, in April 1940, Headlam recorded in his diary that he 'felt quite embarrassed' when a Newcastle delegate at the party's National Union described him as "our leader in the north', with Charley Londonderry sitting just behind her.'[53]

Baldwin evidently knew of the frustrations felt by the likes of Headlam, who, as it happened, was only ever offered junior ministerial positions. As Baldwin informed Lord Castlereagh in 1936, 'As an individual your Father was popular enough but as a politician it was different. He had travelled the easy road in the House of Lords whereas his colleagues had gone the hard way – back bencher, under secretary and eventually cabinet minister in the Commons. He had escaped the searching test of a young minister at question time'.[54] As this suggests, political resentment with Londonderry did not prevent him from being well regarded personally, and many contemporaries commented on his charm, manners and friendliness. On the day that Londonderry died, even Headlam was moved to record in his diary that it was

> a merciful release, I suppose – but none the less one deeply regrets his death. I was very fond of him and looked upon him as a real friend – a man who one could have gone to in difficulties and who one knew would do all he could to help one. He was extraordinarily conscientious – modest and unassuming – and is a real loss to the community – he was often misunderstood and never rightly appreciated.[55]

On the same day, Henry Channon recorded in his diary that Londonderry would one day 'be proven right politically; he always maintained that there were only two possible courses for us: either to make friends with Germany, or, if this was impossible, to re-arm. We did neither, and war was the result. But he was unpopular and much criticized at the time for his views'.[56] The maverick Conservative MP, Robert Boothby, referred to this as Londonderry's 'simple but irrefutable logic'.[57] Following the memorial service at Westminster Abbey, Arthur Henderson, the former Labour foreign secretary and onetime chairman of the World Disarmament Conference, turned to Channon and is said to have remarked that 'possibly Londonderry was right all the time'. Channon replied 'of course he was'.[58] Writing many years later, the poet Tom Paulin also raised the question, fusing Londonderry's reputation with that of his famous ancestor, Viscount Castlereagh, and concluding that both were 'sheer bad luck'.[59] Londonderry certainly came to believe in later life that he had suffered repeated misfortunes. Had he not been instilled at an early age with the importance of emulating his great forebear, he might have had many good reasons to think otherwise.

Notes

Introduction

1 *Sunday Chronicle*, 13 December 1908.
2 Margot Oxford, *More Memories* (London, 1933), p. 78.
3 James Lees-Milne, *Harold Nicolson: A Biography, 1886–1929* (London, 1980), p. 366.
4 Lady Spender, diary, 24 June 1921 (D. H. Akenson, *Education and Enmity: The Control of Schooling in Northern Ireland, 1920–50* (London, 1973), p. 41).
5 Channon, diary, 11 February 1949 (Robert Rhodes James, *'Chips': The Diaries of Sir Henry Channon* (rep. edn., London, 1999), p. 434).
6 Headlam, diary, 5 December 1937 (Stuart Ball (ed.), *Parliament and Politics in the Age of Churchill and Attlee: The Headlam Diaries 1935–1951* (Cambridge, 1999), p. 120).
7 Annabel Goldsmith, *Annabel, An Unconventional Life: The Memoirs of Lady Annabel Goldsmith* (London, 2004), pp. 15–17.
8 *Punch*, 22 June 1932, p. 689; *Punch*, 25 January 1933, p. 92; *Punch*, 4 April 1934, p. 38; *Punch*, 27 June 1934, p. 715; *Punch*, 20 June 1934, p. 689; *Punch*, 1 August 1934, p. 129; *Punch*, 17 April 1935, p. 437.
9 Stuart Ball, *Portrait of a Party: The Conservative Party in Britain 1918–1945* (Oxford, 2013), p. 336.
10 Randolph S. Churchill, *Lord Derby 'King of Lancashire': The Official Life of Edward, Seventeenth Earl of Derby 1865–1948* (London, 1959); Gaynor Johnson, *Lord Robert Cecil: Politician and Internationalist* (Farnham, 2013).
11 David Cannadine, *The Decline and Fall of the British Aristocracy* (rev. edn., London, 1996), p. 31; Peter Mandler, *The Fall and Rise of the Stately Home* (London, 1997), pp. 2–3; Lawrence James, *Aristocrats: Power, Grace and Decadence: Britain's Great Ruling Classes from 1066 to the Present* (London, 2009), pp. 325–87.
12 Max Weber, *The Theory of Social and Economic Organization*, ed. Talcott Parsons (rep. edn.; New York, 1964), pp. 324–58.
13 Ross McKibbin, *Parties and People: England 1914–1951* (Oxford, 2010), p. 195. For critique of McKibbin's thesis, see Helen McCarthy, 'Whose Democracy? Histories of British Political Culture between the Wars', *Historical Journal*, 55, no. 1 (2012): 221–38.
14 Ross McKibbin, *Class and Cultures: England 1918–1951* (Oxford, 1998), p. 20.
15 N. C. Fleming, 'The Marquess of Londonderry: A Political Life', PhD thesis (The Queen's University of Belfast, 2002). See also Alvin Jackson, 'Stewart, Charles Stewart Henry Vane-Tempest-, Seventh Marquess of Londonderry (1878–1949)', *Oxford Dictionary of National Biography* (Oxford, 2004).
16 Ian Kershaw's *Making Friends with Hitler*, published shortly before the original edition of this book, generously acknowledges the unpublished manuscript on which this book is based, and he makes it clear that his is not a biographical study (Ian Kershaw, *Making Friends with Hitler: Lord Londonderry and Britain's Road to War* (London, 2004), p. 376).

17 See Neal Ascherson, 'The Other Man Who Tried to Appease Hitler', *Observer*, 21 November 2004; Alex Danchev, 'Lord Londonderry, the Aristo Dodo', *Times Literary Supplement*, 25 November 2004; Jeremy Paxman, *Black Gold: The History of How Coal Made Britain* (London, 2021), p. 43. For rare example of contrasting assessment, see Robert Skidelsky, 'In the Führer's Face', *New York Review of Books*, 24 February 2005.
18 Karina Urbach, 'Flirting with Hitler: Biographies of the German and British Nobility in the Interwar Years', *German Historical Institute Bulletin*, 29, no. 1 (2007): 64–74.
19 H. Montgomery Hyde, *The Londonderrys: A Family Portrait* (London, 1979).
20 Enoch Powell, 'The Londonderry Papers', *Books and Bookmen* (September 1979): 10–11.
21 H. Montgomery Hyde, *The Rise of Castlereagh* (London, 1933); Philip Hughes, 'Castlereagh', *Studies: An Irish Quarterly Review*, 26, no. 102 (1937): 266.
22 Lady Mairi Bury to the author, 6 July 2005.
23 Marquess of Londonderry, *Ourselves and Germany* (London, 1938); Marquess of Londonderry, *Wings of Destiny* (London, 1943); Marchioness of Londonderry, *Retrospect* (London, 1938).
24 Hyde, *Londonderrys*, pp. 210, 263.
25 Monica Blackett, *The Mark of the Maker: A Portrait of Helen Waddell* (London, 1973), p. 110.
26 Alice Ritchie, *The Peacemakers* (London, 1928); Londonderry to Maurice Hankey, 24 July 1932 (PRONI, D3099/2/16/1/31).
27 H. C. Armstrong, *Grey Wolf: Mustafa Kemal: An Intimate Study of a Dictator* (London, 1932).
28 Francis Humphrys to Londonderry, 4 March 1933 (PRONI, D3099/2/16/2/4).
29 Londonderry to Lord Halifax, 13 November 1937 (PRONI, D3099/2/18/3/8); G. Ward Price, *I Know these Dictators* (London, 1937).
30 For former, see 'Northern Counties Area Political School: Notes for a Lecture' (followed by discussion) by the Marquess of Londonderry, K.G., on Wednesday, 4 May [1932], at 8 pm. The Lecture Room, Albion Institute, Keswick (PRONI, D3099/2/16/5/3).
31 Anne de Courcy, *Circe: The Life of Edith, Marchioness of Londonderry* (London, 1993); J. A. Pauley, 'The Social and Political Roles of Edith, Marchioness of Londonderry, 1878–1959', PhD thesis (University of Ulster, 1994); A. Susan Williams, *Ladies of Influence: Women of the Elite in Interwar Britain* (London, 2000), pp. 13–38; Diane Urquhart, 'Peeresses, Patronage and Power: The Politics of Ladies Frances Anne, Theresa and Edith Londonderry, 1800–1959', in *Irish Women's History*, eds Alan Hayes and Diane Urquhart (Dublin, 2004), pp. 43–59; Diane Urquhart, *The Ladies of Londonderry: Women and Political Patronage* (London, 2007), pp. 136–210; Annabel Goldsmith, *No Invitation Required: The Pelham Cottage Years* (London, 2010), pp. 91–104. The attempt to redress this in the original edition of this book led one historian to label it 'androcentric' (Julie V. Gottlieb, *'Guilty Women', Foreign Policy, and Appeasement in Inter-War Britain* (Basingstoke, 2015), p. 85).
32 Edith's other publications include *Henry Chaplin: A Memoir* (London, 1926); *Character and Tradition* (London, 1934); *Mount Stewart* (privately printed, 1956); *Frances Anne. The Life and Times of Frances Anne, Marchioness of Londonderry and Her Husband Charles, Third Marquess of Londonderry* (London, 1958).

33 For an exemplary example of a scholarly and analytical approach to political biography, see Philip Williamson, *Stanley Baldwin: Conservative Leadership and National Values* (Cambridge, 1999), pp. 1–20.
34 Patrick O'Brien, 'Is Political Biography a Good Thing', *Contemporary British History*, 10, no. 4 (1996): 60; Friedrich Nietzsche, 'On the Uses and Disadvantages of History for Life', in *Untimely Meditations* (Cambridge, 1983), pp. 57–123.
35 J. A. Cross, *Lord Swinton* (Oxford, 1982), p. 296.
36 Ian Kershaw, 'Personality and Power: The Individual's Role in the History of Twentieth-Century Europe', *The Historian*, 83 (2004): 8–19.
37 Londonderry to Wickham Steed, 1 August 1940 (PRONI, D3099/2/21/A/246).
38 Jonathan Powis, *Aristocracy* (Oxford, 1984), p. 3.
39 Aristotle, *The Politics* (trans. T. A. Sinclair) (rep. edn., London, 1992), pp. 256–60.
40 Peregrine Worsthorne, *In Defence of Aristocracy* (London, 2004), p. 35.
41 Cannadine, *Decline*, pp. 17–18.
42 J. V. Beckett, *The Aristocracy in England, 1660–1914* (Oxford, 1988), p. 3.
43 J. A. Hamilton, *revised by* Roland Thorne, 'Stewart, Robert, first Marquess of Londonderry', *Oxford Dictionary of National Biography* (Oxford, 2004).
44 A. P. W. Malcomson, *The Pursuit of the Heiress: Aristocratic Marriage in Ireland, 1740–1840* (Belfast, 2006), p. 52.
45 Roland Thorne, 'Stewart, Robert, Viscount Castlereagh and Second Marquess of Londonderry (1769–1822)', *Oxford Dictionary of National Biography* (Oxford, 2004).
46 H. Montgomery Hyde, *The Strange Death of Lord Castlereagh* (London, 1959).
47 E. M. Lloyd, *revised by* A. J. Heesom, 'Vane [formerly Stewart], Charles William, Third Marquess of Londonderry (1778–1854)', *Oxford Dictionary of National Biography* (Oxford, 2004); Trevor Parkhill, '"Chivalrous rather than Administrative": The Career of the Third Marquess of Londonderry, Soldier, Diplomat, Landlord', in *Politics and Political Culture in Britain and Ireland 1750–1850: Essays in Tribute to Peter Jupp*, eds Allan Blackstock and Eoin Magennis (Belfast, 2007), pp. 157–75.
48 Urquhart, *Ladies*, pp. 9–69.
49 F. M. L. Thompson, *English Landed Society in the Nineteenth Century* (London, 1963), pp. 9–11.
50 Urquhart, 'Peeresses', pp. 44–50.
51 A. J. Heesom, 'Entrepreneurial Paternalism: The Third Lord Londonderry (1778–1854) and the Coal Trade', *Durham University Journal*, 66 (1973–4): 238–56; A. J. Heesom, 'The Northern Coal Miners and the Opposition to the Coal Mines Act of 1842', *International Review of Social History*, 25, no. 2 (1980): 236–71.
52 Norman Gash, *Aristocracy and People: Britain 1815–1865* (Cambridge, MA, 1979), p. 8.
53 W. D. Rubinstein, *Men of Property: The Very Wealthy in Britain since the Industrial Revolution* (London, 1981), pp. 194, 209; Anne Casement, 'The Management of the Londonderry Estates in Ulster during the Great Famine', *Familia: Ulster Genealogical Review*, 21 (2005): 56–68.
54 Urquhart, 'Peeresses', pp. 43–59.
55 This included 23,554 acres in County Down, 12,823 in County Durham and 7,399 in Montgomeryshire; see Kevin Cahill, *Who Owns Britain: The Hidden Facts behind Landownership in the UK and Ireland* (Edinburgh, 2001), pp. 236, 315, 322, 363. In 1929 Londonderry took issue with the claim made in a 'nondescript publication' that 'he was the owner of 50,000 acres in the North of England and 30,000 in Ireland, and that he derived from these two sources an income of £150,000 per

annum'. To show his audience at Seaham Constitutional Club 'how wild the statement was, he could tell them that he owned only about one tenth of the land in question and that, instead of receiving an income of £150,000 per annum, he was actually out of pocket after he had paid taxes, repairs, and other outgoings' (*The Times*, 3 January 1929).

56 Alvin Jackson, 'Stewart, Charles Stewart Vane-Tempest-, Sixth Marquess of Londonderry (1852–1915)', *Oxford Dictionary of National Biography* (Oxford, 2004); David Gilmour, *Curzon* (London, 1994), p. 233.

57 The Londonderrys were depicted as the characters of Lord and Lady Roehampton (Vita Sackville-West), *The Edwardians* (London, 1930).

58 Urquhart, *Ladies*, pp. 76–135.

59 Joseph Robins, *Champagne and Silver Buckles: The Viceregal Court at Dublin Castle 1700–1922* (Dublin, 2001), pp. 138, 147.

60 K. Theodore Hoppen, 'A Question None Could Answer: "What Was the Irish Viceroyalty For?"', in *The Irish Lord Lieutenancy c. 1541–1922*, eds Peter Gray and Olwen Purdue (Dublin, 2012), p. 138.

61 Michael Davitt, *The Fall of Feudalism in Ireland, or, The Story of the Land League Revolution* (London, 1904), p. 31.

62 Alvin Jackson, *Colonel Edward Saunderson: Land and Loyalty in Victorian Ireland* (Oxford, 1995), p. 47.

63 James H. Murphy, *Abject Loyalty: Nationalism and Monarchy in Ireland during the Reign of Queen Victoria* (Washington, DC, 2001), p. 253.

64 Andrew Adonis, *Making Aristocracy Work: The Peerage and the Political System in Britain, 1884–1914* (Oxford, 1993); Corrine C. Weston, *The House of Lords and Ideological Politics: Lord Salisbury's Referendal Theory and the Conservative Party, 1846–1922* (Philadelphia, 1995).

65 Urquhart, *Ladies*, p. 81.

66 Larry L. Witherell, *Rebel on the Right: Henry Page Croft and the Crisis of Conservatism, 1903–1914* (London, 1997), p. 134.

67 Marquess of Londonderry, 'In the Days of My Youth', *T.P.'s & Cassell's Weekly*, 21 March 1925.

68 Marchioness of Londonderry, *Robert Stewart, Viscount Castlereagh* (London, 1904); Pauley, 'Edith', pp. 22–3.

69 Londonderry, 'My Youth'.

70 Martin Pugh, *The Tories and the People 1880–1935* (London, 1985), p. 144.

71 Londonderry, 'My Youth'.

72 David Cannadine, *Aspects of Aristocracy: Grandeur and Decline in Modern Britain* (London, 1994), p. 22.

73 Lady Mairi Bury to the author, 6 July 2005.

74 Cannadine, *Aspects*, p. 55; Castlereagh to Theresa, Lady Londonderry, n.d. (DCRO, D/Lo/C/682).

75 Hyde, *Londonderrys*, p. 156.

76 Londonderry, *Retrospect*, pp. 182–4.

77 Hyde, *Londonderrys*, pp. 111, 169, 189, 231; Londonderry, *Retrospect*, p. 181.

78 Londonderry, *Retrospect*, p. 33.

79 De Courcy, *Circe*, pp. 53–8, 245–7.

80 Political notes by Theresa, Lady Londonderry, 29 November 1915 (PRONI, D3084/C/C/B/1/7).

81 Londonderry, *Retrospect*, pp. 28–9.

82 Londonderry, 'My Youth'; Castlereagh to Theresa, Lady Londonderry, 9, 13 and 18 April 1901 (DCRO, D/Lo/C/682 (20–3)); Londonderry, *Retrospect*, pp. 30–2.
83 Roger Fulford, 'The King', in *Edwardian England 1901–1914*, ed. Simon Nowell-Smith (London, 1964), p. 39.
84 The Castlereaghs' children included Maureen (1900–42), Robert (1902–55), Margaret (1910–68), Helen (1911–86) and Mairi (1921–2009). In the same year as Maureen's birth, Charles is also reputed to have had an illegitimate daughter, Dorothé, with the American actress Fannie Ward (de Courcy, *Circe*, pp. 55–7).
85 Londonderry, *Retrospect*, pp. 40, 43, 45.
86 Londonderry, *Retrospect*, pp. 47–71.
87 Castlereagh to Theresa, Lady Londonderry, 12 August 1905 (DCRO, D/Lo/C/682 (47)).
88 Londonderry, *Retrospect*, pp. 67–71.
89 Castlereagh to Theresa, Lady Londonderry, 21 September 1911 (DCRO D/Lo/C/682 (78)).
90 Urquhart, *Ladies*, p. 139.
91 Londonderry, 'My Youth'.
92 Londonderry, *Retrospect*, p. 73.
93 Viscount Chilston, *Chief Whip: The Political Life and Times of Aretas Akers-Douglas, 1st Viscount Chilston* (London, 1961), p. 4.
94 A. K. Russell, *Liberal Landslide: The General Election of 1906* (Newton Abbot, 1973), pp. 66, 83.
95 Londonderry, *Retrospect*, p. 72.
96 *Kent Times*, 16 December 1905; Edward Carson to Theresa, Lady Londonderry, 17 December 1905 (PRONI, D3099/12). For a more cynical report of the meeting, see the *Northampton Mercury*, 13 June 1908.
97 Austin Chamberlain to Balfour, 12 September 1904 (Charles Petrie (ed.), *The Life and Letters of the Right Hon. Sir Austin Chamberlain KG, PC, MP* (London, 1939), pp. 152–5).
98 Richard A. Rempel, *Unionists Divided: Arthur Balfour, Joseph Chamberlain and the Unionist Free Traders* (Newton Abbot, 1972), pp. 132–3; Alan Sykes, *Tariff Reform in British Politics 1903–1913* (Oxford, 1979), p. 95.
99 Blanche E. C. Dugdale, *Arthur James Balfour, First Earl of Balfour, KG, OM, FRS, etc* (2 vols., London, 1936), vol. 1, p. 127.
100 Details outlined in notice of sale published in *The Times*, 4 January 1923.
101 Castlereagh to Theresa, Lady Londonderry, 24 December 1905 (DCRO, D/Lo/C/682 (51)).
102 Castlereagh to Theresa, Lady Londonderry, 24 December 1905 (DCRO, D/Lo/C 682 (50)); Castlereagh to Theresa, Lady Londonderry, 28 December 1905 (DCRO, D/Lo/C 682 (52)).
103 Castlereagh to Theresa, Lady Londonderry, 28 December 1905 (DCRO, D/Lo/C 682 (52)).
104 *World*, 23 January 1906.
105 'Maidstone's reputation in regard to political morals is not a good one. The present petition is probably the ninth, or possibly the tenth, since 1800' (*South Eastern Gazette*, 13 February 1906).
106 G. Gordon to Castlereagh, 13 February 1906 (D3099/2/4/2); Londonderry, *Retrospect*, p. 80.
107 Londonderry, *Retrospect*, p. 78.

108 *South Eastern Gazette*, 17 May 1906; *Tribune*, 10 May 1906.
109 *Newtownards Chronicle*, 29 July 1899.

Chapter 1

1 George Dangerfield, *The Strange Death of Liberal England* (rep. edn., London, 1966), pp. 90–1, 137, 291; Edward Pearce, *Lines of Most Resistance: The Lords, the Tories and Ireland, 1886–1914* (London, 1999), pp. 129, 167, 240–1, 276, 386, 393. For assessment of Dangerfield thesis, see Alan O'Day, 'Introduction', in *The Edwardian Age: Conflict and Stability 1900–1914*, ed. Alan O'Day (London, 1979), pp. 1–12.
2 Marchioness of Londonderry, *Retrospect* (London, 1938), p. 77.
3 Marquess of Londonderry, 'In the Days of My Youth', *T.P.'s & Cassell's Weekly*, 21 March 1925.
4 Viscount Castlereagh, 'Memorandum', August 1936, in *Baldwin Papers: A Conservative Statesman, 1908–1947*, eds Philip Williamson and Edward Baldwin (Cambridge, 2005), p. 369.
5 See E. H. H. Green, *The Crisis of Conservatism: The Politics, Economics and Ideology of the British Conservative Party, 1880–1914* (London, 1995).
6 Larry L. Witherell, *Rebel on the Right: Henry Page Croft and the Crisis of Conservatism, 1903–1914* (London, 1997), p. 134.
7 *Westminster Gazette*, 22 February 1906.
8 *Sunday Chronicle*, 13 December 1908.
9 *The Times*, 21 April 1934.
10 *House of Commons Debates*, 21 February 1906, vol. 152, col. 400; *Morning Post*, 22 February 1906. See Alan O'Day, 'Ireland and the United Kingdom', in *Problems and Perspectives in Irish History since 1800: Essays in Honour of Patrick Buckland*, eds D. George Boyce and Roger Swift (Dublin, 2004), pp. 13–31; K. Theodore Hoppen, 'Gladstone, Salisbury and the End of Irish Assimilationism', in *Gladstone: Ireland and Beyond*, eds Mary E. Daly and K. Theodore Hoppen (Dublin, 2011), pp. 45–63.
11 *The Standard*, 17 July 1908.
12 Castlereagh to Theresa, Lady Londonderry, 25 October 1906 (DCRO, D/Lo/C 682 (53)).
13 Londonderry, 'My Youth'; Lord Croft, *My Life of Strife* (London, 1948), p. 51; Londonderry, *Retrospect*, p. 81.
14 Earl Winterton, *Pre-War* (London, 1932), pp. 59, 268; Earl Winterton, *Orders of the Day* (London, 1953), p. 44.
15 Harold Frazer Wyatt and L. Graham H. Horton-Smith, *The Passing of the Great Fleet* (London, 1909), p. 368. Castlereagh appears to have quickly returned to the Navy League, see *Navy League Journal* (June 1908): 166. See Alan Sykes, 'The Radical Right and the Crisis of Conservatism before the First World War', *Historical Journal*, 26, no. 3 (1983): 661–76; David Thackeray, 'Rethinking the Edwardian Crisis of Conservatism', *Historical Journal*, 54, no. 1 (2011): 191–213; N. C. Fleming, 'The Imperial Maritime League: British Navalism, Conflict and the Radical Right, c. 1907–1920', *War in History*, 23, no. 3 (2016): 296–322.
16 *House of Commons Debates*, 14 December 1908, vol. 198, col. 1303.
17 See, for example, *House of Commons Debates*, 20 May 1908, vol. 189, cols 386–68.

18 *House of Commons Debates*, 9 April 1907, vol. 172, cols 147–52. See also *House of Commons Debates*, 29 May 1907, vol. 174, cols 1727, 1730–1; *House of Commons Debates*, 17 June 1907, vol. 176, cols 227–30, 240; *House of Commons Debates*, 18 June 1907, vol. 176, cols 391, 397, 417.
19 David Cannadine, *Decline and Fall of the British Aristocracy* (rep. edn., London, 1992), pp. 277–8.
20 Colin Nicholson, 'Edwardian England and the Coming of the First World War', in *Edwardian Age*, ed. O'Day, p. 153.
21 See Arthur Marwick, *The Deluge: British Society and the First World War* (rep. edn., London, 1978), pp. 155–6; Matthew Johnson, *Militarism and the British Left, 1902–1914* (Basingstoke, 2013).
22 Londonderry to Arthur Baumann, 13 October 1927 (D. H. Akenson, *Education and Enmity: The Control of Schooling in Northern Ireland, 1920–50* (London, 1973), p. 42).
23 N. C. Fleming, 'Political Extremes and Extremist Politics', *Political Studies Review*, 12, no. 3 (2014): 395–401.
24 Londonderry, *Retrospect*, p. 189.
25 N. C. Fleming, *Britannia's Zealots, vol. 1: Tradition, Empire and the Forging of the Conservative Right* (London, 2019), pp. 155–6.
26 Ross McKibbin, *Parties and People: England 1914–1951* (Oxford, 2010), pp. 62–3, 195; Brian Girvin, 'The Party in Comparative and International Context', in *Conservative Century: The Conservative Party since 1900*, eds Anthony Seldon and Stuart Ball (Oxford, 1990), pp. 695–725.
27 *House of Commons Debates*, 12 April 1907, vol. 172, cols 528–31.
28 *The Times*, 10 December 1908; *House of Commons Debates*, 9 December 1908, vol. 198, col. 520; *Sunday Chronicle*, 13 December 1908.
29 *House of Commons Debates*, 13 July 1911, vol. 28, cols 577–95; *The Times*, 9 May 1911. See also *The Times*, 26 July 1929.
30 *House of Commons Debates*, 26 March 1909, vol. 2, col. 2075.
31 Robert Pearce, *Britain: Industrial Relations and the Economy, 1900–39* (London, 1993), p. 19.
32 *House of Commons Debates*, 24 November 1911, vol. 31, col. 1552; *House of Commons Debates*, 5 December 1911, vol. 32, cols 1290–3.
33 *House of Commons Debates*, 22 March 1912, vol. 35, cols 2244–5.
34 *House of Commons Debates*, 26 March 1912, vol. 36, col. 245.
35 *House of Commons Debates*, 26 March 1912, vol. 36, cols 397–409.
36 Stephen Koss, *Nonconformity in Modern British Politics* (London, 1975), pp. 16–17.
37 *House of Commons Debates*, 26 April 1907, vol. 173, cols 403–6.
38 *House of Commons Debates*, 4 November 1908, vol. 195, col. 1322.
39 Jon Lawrence, 'Class and Gender in the Making of Urban Toryism, 1880–1914', *English Historical Review*, 108, no. 428 (1993): 648–9.
40 Gwylmor Prys Williams and George Thompson Brake, *Drink in Great Britain 1900–1979* (London, 1980), p. 42.
41 *House of Commons Debates*, 23 July 1907, vol. 178, cols 1388, 1397, 1425, 1429; *House of Commons Debates*, 2 August 1907, vol. 179, cols 1385–92.
42 *House of Commons Debates*, 23 February 1909, vol. 1, col. 666.
43 Bruce K. Murray, *The People's Budget 1909/10: Lloyd George and Liberal Politics* (Oxford, 1980), pp. 178–9; Cannadine, *Decline*, p. 48.
44 See Annie Tindley, *The Sutherland Estate, 1850–1920: Aristocratic Decline, Estate Management and Land Reform* (Edinburgh, 2010).

45 *The Times*, 14 March 1914.
46 *The Times*, 8 November 1917.
47 *The Times*, 20 July 1909.
48 David Dutton, *'His Majesty's Loyal Opposition': The Unionist Party in Opposition, 1905–1915* (Liverpool, 1992), pp. 69–77.
49 *The Times*, 8 January 1910.
50 *The Times*, 16 April 1910.
51 John D. Fair, *British Interparty Conferences: A Study of the Procedure of Conciliation in British Politics, 1867–1921* (Oxford, 1980), pp. 77–102.
52 At this time Lord Castlereagh, through his wife's involvement with promoting women's healthcare, became president of the Chelsea Hospital for Sick Women, a position he held for most of his life (*The Times*, 19 April 1910).
53 J. A. Pauley, 'The Social and Political Roles of Edith, Marchioness of Londonderry, 1878–1959', PhD thesis (University of Ulster, 1994), chapters 2 and 3; Diane Urquhart, *The Ladies of Londonderry: Women and Political Patronage* (London, 2007), pp. 137–9.
54 *The Times*, 19 April 1910. See also *House of Commons Debates*, 5 November 1912, vol. 43, cols 1083–4.
55 David R. Morgan, *Suffragists and Liberals: The Politics of Woman Suffrage in England* (Oxford, 1975), p. 71.
56 Brian Harrison, *Separate Spheres: The Opposition to Women's Suffrage in Britain* (London, 1978), p. 33.
57 Jose Harris, *Private Lives, Public Spirit: Britain 1870–1914* (London, 1994), pp. 29–32.
58 *House of Commons Debates*, 28 July 1910, vol. 19, col. 2488.
59 Vernon Bogdanor, *The Monarchy and the Constitution* (Oxford, 1997), p. 43.
60 *House of Commons Debates*, 28 July 1910, vol. 19, col. 2488.
61 Annabel Goldsmith, *Annabel, An Unconventional Life: The Memoirs of Lady Annabel Goldsmith* (London, 2004), pp. 7, 258.
62 H. Montgomery Hyde, *The Londonderrys: A Family Portrait* (London, 1979), p. 243; Pauley, 'Edith', p. 61. See Ulster Women's Unionist Council Executive Committee, minutes, 5 April 1927 (Diane Urquhart (ed.), *The Minutes of the Ulster Women's Unionist Council and Executive Committee 1911–40* (Dublin, 2001), pp. 148–9).
63 Cushendun to Londonderry, 22 November 1927 (PRONI, D3099/8/4).
64 *House of Lords Debates*, 14 December 1927, vol. 69, cols 923–90.
65 Lord Hanworth [Master of the Rolls] to Londonderry, 26 November 1927 (PRONI, D3099/2/4/43); Charles D'Arcy [Archbishop of Armagh] to Londonderry, 4 December 1927 (PRONI, D3099/2/7/118).
66 Londonderry to Robert Lynn, 9 January 1928 (PRONI, D3480/59/68).
67 Londonderry to Ramsay MacDonald, 19 July 1932 (PRONI, D3099/2/12/1/16).
68 *House of Commons Debates*, 25 July 1910, vol. 19, cols 1793–6.
69 Neal Blewett, *The Peers, the Parties and the People: The General Elections of 1910* (London, 1972), pp. 93–4.
70 *The Times*, 5 December 1910.
71 *The Times*, 2 March 1911.
72 *House of Commons Debates*, 4 April 1911, vol. 23, col. 2075.
73 *House of Commons Debates*, 2 May 1911, vol. 25, col. 238.
74 *The Times*, 28 July 1911.
75 See Gregory D. Phillips, *The Diehards: Aristocratic Society and Politics in Edwardian England* (London, 1979); Urquhart, *Ladies*, pp. 95–7.

76 Andrew Adonis, *Making Aristocracy Work: The Peerage and the Political System in Britain, 1884–1914* (rep. edn., Oxford, 2002), pp. 157–61.
77 Cannadine, *Decline*, p. 53.
78 Dutton, '*Opposition*', pp. 183–8; Anthony Howe, *Free Trade and Liberal England 1846–1946* (Oxford, 1997), pp. 237–9; David Dutton, *Austen Chamberlain: Gentleman in Politics* (Bolton, 1985), p. 42.
79 Urquhart, *Ulster*, p. xi.
80 *The Times*, 8 January 1913; Castlereagh to Theresa, Lady Londonderry, 29 January 1912 (DCRO, D/Lo/C/682 (86)).
81 *House of Commons Debates*, 11 April 1912, vol. 36, cols 1459–66.
82 Jeremy Smith, 'Sir Edward Carson and the Myth of Partition', in *Politics and Power in Victorian Ireland*, eds Roger Swift and Christine Kinealy (Dublin, 2006), pp. 178–91.
83 Alvin Jackson, *Home Rule: An Irish History, 1800–2000* (London, 2003), p. 187.
84 Jackson, *Home*, p. 116.
85 N. C. Fleming, 'The Landed Elite, Power and Ulster Unionism', in *The Ulster Crisis 1885–1921*, eds D. George Boyce and Alan O'Day (Basingstoke, 2006), pp. 86–104.
86 *House of Commons Debates*, 18 June 1912, vol. 39, cols 1536–7.
87 Jennifer Todd, 'Unionist Political thought, 1920–72', in *Political Thought in Ireland since the Seventeenth Century*, eds D. George Boyce, Robert Eccleshall and Vincent Geoghegan (London, 1993), p. 192.
88 D. George Boyce, 'Respectable Rebels: Ulster Unionist Resistance to the Third Home Rule Bill, 1912–14', in *Conflicts in the North of Ireland, 1900–2000: Flashpoints and Fracture Zones*, eds Alan F. Parkinson and Éamon Phoenix (Dublin, 2010), pp. 28–39.
89 F. M. L. Thompson, 'Britain', in *European Landed Elites in the Nineteenth Century*, ed. David Spring (London, 1977), pp. 22–3.
90 Edward Marjoribanks, *The Life of Lord Carson, vol. 1* (3rd edn., London, 1932), pp. 115, 163.
91 R. J. Q. Adams, *Bonar Law* (London, 1999), p. 65; Diane Urquhart, 'Peeresses, Patronage and Power: The Politics of Ladies Frances Anne, Theresa and Edith Londonderry, 1800–1959', in *Irish Women's History*, eds Alan Hayes and Diane Urquhart (Dublin, 2004), p. 52.
92 A. T. Q. Stewart, *The Ulster Crisis: Resistance to Home Rule 1912–1914* (rep. edn., Belfast, 1999), pp. 50–2, 76–7; Paul Bew, *Ideology and the Irish Question: Ulster Unionism and Irish Nationalism, 1912–1916* (Oxford, 1998), p. 92.
93 For example, see *The Ulster Unionist Demonstration of 1912: In Royal Agricultural Show grounds, Balmoral, Belfast*, 9 April 1912 (PRONI, D/1507/A/3/14).
94 Castlereagh to Edith, Lady Castlereagh, 23 September 1912 (PRONI, D3099/13).
95 *The Times*, 26 September 1912.
96 Castlereagh to Theresa, Lady Londonderry, 24 September 1912 (DCRO, D/Lo/C 682 (93)); Castlereagh to Bonar Law, 7 December 1911 (HLRO, BL/24/5/114); Bonar Law to Castlereagh, 8 December 1911 (HLRO, BL/33/3/30); Marquess of Londonderry, *Wings of Destiny* (London, 1943), p. 29.
97 Castlereagh to Edith, Lady Castlereagh, 25 September 1912 (PRONI, D3099/13).
98 Ronald McNeill, *Ulster's Stand for the Union* (London, 1922), p. 121; Andrew Gailey, 'King Carson: An Essay on the Invention of Leadership', *Irish Historical Studies*, 30, no. 117 (1996): 66–87.
99 *House of Commons Debates*, 14 October 1912, vol. 42, cols 845–6. See James Quinn, 'Dublin Castle and the Act of Union', in *The Irish Act of Union: Bicentennial Essays*,

eds Michael Brown, Patrick M. Geoghegan and James Kelly (Dublin, 2003), pp. 95–107.

100 *House of Commons Debates*, 19 June 1912, vol. 39, cols 1760–3.

101 *House of Commons Debates*, 16 October 1912, vol. 42, cols 1347–51; *The Times*, 24 October 1912.

102 See, for example, Hugh O'Neill, 'Ireland', in *The New Order: Studies in Unionist Policy*, ed. Earl of Malmesbury (London, 1908), pp. 47–68; Peter Gray and Olwen Purdue, 'Introduction: The Irish Lord Lieutenancy, *c.* 1541–1922', in *The Irish Lord Lieutenancy c. 1541–1922*, eds Peter Gray and Olwen Purdue (Dublin, 2012), pp. 2–4.

103 *House of Commons Debates*, 24 October 1912, vol. 42, cols 2483–6.

104 *The Times*, 29 October 1912; *House of Commons Debates*, 28 October 1912, vol. 43, cols 201–4.

105 Stewart, *Ulster*, pp. 67–8.

106 H. Montgomery Hyde, *Carson: The Life of Sir Edward Carson, Lord Carson of Duncairn* (London, 1953), pp. 340–1.

107 Stewart, *Ulster*, p. 77.

108 McNeill, *Ulster's*, p. 230.

109 Copy notes detailing personnel and logistics of 'the North Belfast Regiment' (PRONI, D3099/8/1); Stewart, *Ulster*, p. 122. See Records of the Ulster Volunteer Force (Ulster Unionist Council papers, PRONI, D/1327/4).

110 Trevor McCavery, *Newtown: A History of Newtownards* (Belfast, 1994), p. 181.

111 Ian Colvin, *The Life of Lord Carson, vol. 2* (London, 1934), p. 349.

112 Timothy Bowman, *Carson's Army: The Ulster Volunteer Force, 1910–22* (Manchester, 2007), pp. 47, 97.

113 Richardson to Londonderry, 29 April 1919 (PRONI, D3099/2/7/41).

114 The family's role was marked in 1915 by naming a wing of the UVF Hospital at Belfast after them (Theresa, Lady Londonderry, 29 September 1915 (PRONI, D3084/C/C/B/1/5)).

115 Ill health indisposed him during May 1913 (*The Times*, 1–3 May 1913; *The Times*, 5 May 1913; *The Times*, 10 May 1913; *The Times*, 23 May 1913).

116 *House of Commons Debates (General Index for 1913 Session)*, vol. 57, pp. 79–80 (*General index for 1914 session*), vol. 67, pp. 110–11.

117 *House of Commons Debates (General Index for 1913 Session)*, vol. 57, p. 27; *House of Commons Debates (General Index for 1914 Session)*, vol. 67, pp. 44–5.

118 *The Times*, 19 April 1913. This followed an earlier denial that he was leaving Maidstone (*The Times*, 30 March 1913).

119 Paul Fussell, *The Great War and Modern Memory* (London, 1977), p. 21.

120 Cannadine, *Decline*, pp. 73–4.

121 Urquhart, *Ladies*, pp. 140–1.

122 Castlereagh to Lady Castlereagh, 26 September 1914 (PRONI, D3099/13).

123 Hyde, *Londonderrys*, p. 115.

124 Castlereagh to Lady Castlereagh, 2 September 1914 (PRONI, D3099/13).

125 Castlereagh to Lady Castlereagh, 24 September 1914 (PRONI, D3099/13).

126 Castlereagh to Lady Castlereagh, 7 December 1914 (PRONI, D3099/13). Castlereagh also expressed anger about Churchill's influence following the promotion of his political contemporary F. E. Smith to the rank of major and general-staff officer, second grade (Castlereagh to Lady Castlereagh, 8 October 1914 (PRONI, D3099/13)).

127 Castlereagh to Lady Castlereagh, 5 September 1914 (PRONI, D3099/13).
128 Castlereagh to Lady Castlereagh, 8 November 1914 (PRONI, D3099/13).
129 Castlereagh to Lady Castlereagh, 16 September 1914 (PRONI, D3099/13).
130 Hyde, *Londonderrys*, pp. 126–7.
131 Castlereagh to Lady Castlereagh, 24 September 1914 (PRONI, D3099/13).
132 Castlereagh to Lady Castlereagh, 22 December 1914 (PRONI, D3099/13).
133 Hyde, *Londonderrys*, p. 116.
134 *The Times*, 26 February 1915; Pulteney to Edith, Lady Londonderry, February 1915 (PRONI, D3099/3).
135 *The Times*, 17 February 1915.
136 Pulteney to Edith, Lady Londonderry, February 1915 (PRONI, D3099/13).
137 *The Times*, 14 April 1915; *The Times*, 13 August 1916.
138 Londonderry, *Retrospect*, p. 156.
139 Theresa, Lady Londonderry, 15 September 1915 (PRONI, D3084/C/C/B/1/4).
140 Londonderry to Blumenfeld, 22 June 1915 (HLRO, Blu/Lon/3).
141 E. A. Aston to Londonderry, 23 June 1915 (PRONI, D3099/8/1); Aston to Londonderry, 1 July 1916 (PRONI, D3099/2/7/1).
142 Londonderry to Lady Fingall, 26 November 1917 (PRONI, D3099/2/7/15). See Thomas Hennessey, *Dividing Ireland: World War I and Partition* (London, 1998), pp. 114–23.
143 *The Times*, 14 December 1917.
144 *The Times*, 11 August 1915.
145 Bates to Law, 12 February 1915 (HLRO, BL/36/3/33).
146 Londonderry to Law, 18 February 1915 (HLRO, BL/36/4/52).
147 Wimborne to Londonderry, 22 September 1915 (PRONI, D3099/8/2A).
148 Lawrence W. McBride, *The Greening of Dublin Castle: The Transformation of Bureaucratic and Judicial Personnel in Ireland, 1892–1922* (Washington, DC, 1991), pp. 223–4.
149 Crawford to Londonderry, 8 October 1915 (PRONI, D3099/8/2).
150 Philip Cambray to Londonderry, 12 October 1915 (PRONI, D3099/8/2E, F); Cambray to Londonderry, 13 October 1915 (PRONI, D3099/8/2G).
151 Lord Bangor to Londonderry, 9 October 1915 (PRONI, D3099/8/2C); Bates to Londonderry, 23 October 1915 (PRONI, D3099/8/2I). Bates even tried to persuade Londonderry to overturn the government's recommendation (Bates to Londonderry, 20 November 1915 (PRONI, D3099/8/2J); T. G. G. Mackintosh to D. W. Macklejohn [Wynyard estate office], 13 October 1915 (PRONI, D3099/8/2H).
152 Londonderry to Lloyd George, 14 June 1916 (PRONI, D3099/2/7/6).
153 Theresa, Lady Londonderry, 20 October 1915 (PRONI, D3084/C/C/B/1/6).
154 Londonderry to Lord French, 18 August 1918 (PRONI, D3099/8/3).
155 Theresa, Lady Londonderry, 13 December 1915 (PRONI, D3084/C/C/B/1/9).
156 Theresa, Lady Londonderry, 29 November 1915 (PRONI, D3084/C/C/B/1/7); Theresa, Lady Londonderry, 20 December 1915 (D3084/C/C/B/1/10).
157 Londonderry to Hankey, 16 July 1916 (D3099/2/4/7). See Gervase Phillips, '"Who Shall Say that the Days of Cavalry Are Over?" The Revival of the Mounted Arm in Europe, 1853–1914', *War in History*, 18, no. 1 (2011): 5–32.
158 Hyde, *Londonderrys*, p. 128.
159 Theresa, Lady Londonderry, 3 September 1916 (PRONI, D3084/C/C/B/1/13).
160 Herbert Buckmaster, *Buck's Book: Ventures-Adventures and Misadventures* (London, 1933), pp. 134, 162. According to his daughter, Londonderry was mentioned in dispatches (Lady Mairi Bury to the author, 6 July 2005).

161 Londonderry's military records were destroyed along with many others during a Luftwaffe raid on London (PRO, WO/374/70388).
162 Charles à Court Repington to Lloyd George, 17 July 1917 (HLRO, LG/F/43/4/2); John W. Young, 'Introduction', in *The Paris Embassy: British Ambassadors and Anglo-French Relations*, eds Rogelia Pastor-Castro and John W. Young (Basingstoke, 2013), p. 3.
163 Capper to Londonderry, 25 July 1917 (PRONI, D3099/2/4/13).
164 Derby to Londonderry, 10 October 1917 (PRONI, D3099/2/8/4).
165 Derby to Londonderry, 7 December 1917 (PRONI, D3099/2/8/5).
166 Londonderry to Edith, Lady Londonderry, 6 December 1917 (PRONI, D3099/2/8/13).
167 Derby to Londonderry, 31 May 1918 (PRONI, D3099/2/8/10).

Chapter 2

1 *The Times*, 16 May 1916.
2 A. R. Preston to Londonderry, 17 May 1916 (PRONI, D3099/2/7/3A); Rev. Dr Francis Knight to Londonderry, 19 May 1916 (PRONI, D3099/2/7/3B); William Buchan to Londonderry, 24 May 1916 (PRONI, D3099/2/7/4). See also Col. Rowan Hamilton to Londonderry, 14 May 1916 (PRONI, D3099/2/7/2).
3 John D. Fair, *British Interparty Conferences: A Study of the Procedure of Conciliation in British Politics, 1867–1921* (Oxford, 1980), pp. 125–6.
4 Theresa, Lady Londonderry, 10 August 1916 (PRONI, D3084/C/C/B/1/11).
5 Timothy G. McMahon, '"It does not Matter What the Authors Meant": Covenanters in Conflict, 1916–1920', in *Ireland and Partition: Context and Consequences*, eds N. C. Fleming and James H. Murphy (Clemson, 2021), pp. 267–82.
6 Londonderry to Theresa, Lady Londonderry, 13 June 1916 (DCRO, D/Lo/C/682). See D. George Boyce, *Englishmen and Irish Troubles: British Public Opinion and the Making of Irish Policy, 1918–1922* (Boston, 1972).
7 Patrick Buckland, *Irish Unionism: One: The Anglo-Irish and the New Ireland 1885–1922* (Dublin, 1972), p. 60.
8 Alvin Jackson, *Home Rule: An Irish History, 1800–2000* (London, 2003), pp. 155–74.
9 Long to Edith, Lady Londonderry, 1 June 1916 (PRONI, D3099/8/3).
10 Londonderry to Lloyd George, 14 June 1916 (PRONI, D3099/2/7/6).
11 Edith, Lady Londonderry to McNeill, 3 July 1916 (PRONI, D3099/8/3).
12 McNeill to Edith, Lady Londonderry, 1 July 1916 (PRONI, D3099/8/3).
13 Long to Londonderry, 2 July 1916 (PRONI, D3099/8/3).
14 Londonderry, notes for a letter to Edith, Lady Londonderry, n.d. (PRONI, D3099/8/3).
15 Kenneth O. Morgan, *Consensus and Disunity: The Lloyd George Coalition Government, 1918–1922* (Oxford, 1979), p. 14.
16 Alan J. Ward, *Ireland and Anglo-American Relations 1899–1921* (London, 1969), pp. 149–50; Nicholas Mansergh, *The Unresolved Question: The Anglo-Irish Settlement and its Undoing 1912–72* (London, 1991), p. 103. See also Alan O'Day, *Irish Home Rule 1867–1921* (Manchester, 1998), p. 278.
17 R. B. McDowell, *Irish Convention, 1917–18* (London, 1970), pp. 77–8; Carson to Richard Dawson Bates, 23 May 1917 (PRONI, D3099/2/7/7).
18 Stephen Hartley, *The Irish Question as a Problem in British Foreign Policy, 1914–18* (Basingstoke, 1987), pp. 151–73.

19 H. C. Plunkett, *The Irish Convention: Confidential Report to His Majesty the King by the Chairman* (Dublin, 1918), p. 5.
20 Midleton to Londonderry, 15 June 1917 (PRONI, D3099/2/7/8).
21 Lloyd George to Londonderry, 22 June 1917 (PRONI, D3099/2/7/9); William Sutherland to Londonderry, 17 July 1917 (PRONI, D3099/2/7/10A).
22 *House of Lords Debates*, 21 May 1917, vol. 25, cols 224–5. Londonderry had an audience with King George V the following day.
23 *The Times*, 22 May 1917.
24 See Andrew Scholes, *The Church of Ireland and the Third Home Rule Bill* (Dublin, 2010), pp. 132–47.
25 'Minutes of the Ulster Unionist Delegation to the Irish Convention' (PRONI, D1327/3/17).
26 Ulster delegation minutes, 21 July 1917; Ulster delegation minutes, 7 August 1917 (PRONI, D1327/3/17).
27 H. C. Plunkett, *Report of the Proceedings of the Irish Convention* (Dublin, 1918), pp. 9–10; Carla King, 'Defenders of the Union: Sir Horace Plunkett', in *Defenders of the Union: A Survey of British and Irish Unionism since 1801*, eds D. George Boyce and Alan O'Day (London, 2001), pp. 137–54.
28 Plunkett, *Confidential*, pp. 11–12.
29 Trevor West, *Horace Plunkett, Co-operation and Politics: An Irish Biography* (Gerrards Cross, 1986), p. 111.
30 Plunkett, *Confidential*, pp. 11–12.
31 Londonderry to Theresa, Lady Londonderry, 29 August 1917 (DCRO, D/Lo/C/682 (241)); Jackson, *Home*, p. 185.
32 Plunkett, *Confidential*, p. 13.
33 Nicholas Allen, 'National Reconstruction: George Russell (Æ) and the Irish Convention', in *Ireland in Transition, 1867–1921*, eds D. George Boyce and Alan O'Day (London, 2004), p. 132.
34 Plunkett, *Confidential*, p. 18.
35 McDowell, *Irish*, p. 112.
36 Max Egremont, *Balfour: A Life of Arthur James Balfour* (London, 1998), p. 109.
37 Londonderry to Desborough, 1 September 1917 (PRONI, T/3201/29).
38 Derby to Londonderry, 3 September 1917 (PRONI, D3099/2/8/2).
39 Londonderry to Theresa, Lady Londonderry, 23 September 1917 (DCRO, D/Lo/C/682 (245)).
40 Plunkett, *Confidential*, pp. 7–8. Pollock had replaced Alexander McDowell due to the latter's illness.
41 Four representatives of labour were also permitted seats (Plunkett, *Confidential*, p. 42).
42 Midleton to Londonderry, 25 October 1917 (PRONI, D3099/2/7/14).
43 McDowell, *Irish*, pp. 121–2.
44 Plunkett, *Report*, p. 16.
45 Barrie and Londonderry to Plunkett, 14 November 1917 (Plunkett, *Report*, pp. 68–9).
46 Plunkett, *Confidential*, p. 51.
47 John Kendle, *Ireland and the Federal Solution: The Debate over the United Kingdom Constitution, 1870–1921* (Kingston and Montreal, 1989), p. 188; Grey to Dunraven, August, 1917 (PRONI, D3099/2/7/12).
48 John Turner, *Lloyd George's Secretariat* (Cambridge, 1980), p. 103. See John D. Fair, 'F.S. Oliver, *Alexander Hamilton*, and the "American Plan" for Resolving Britain's

Constitutional Crises, 1903–1921', *Twentieth Century British History*, 10, no. 1 (1999): 1–26.

49 Plunkett, *Confidential*, p. 51.

50 Duffin to Londonderry, 16 November 1917 (Patrick Buckland (ed.), *Irish Unionism 1885–1923: A Documentary History* (Belfast, 1973), pp. 422–3).

51 Duffin to Mrs Duffin, 28 November 1917 (Buckland, *Irish Unionism*, p. 423).

52 The Ulster delegation minutes jump from 12 November to the 17 December 1917 (PRONI, D/1327/3/17).

53 Plunkett, *Confidential*, p. 52.

54 Londonderry to Fingall, 26 November 1917 (PRONI, D3099/2/7/15); Countess of Fingall, *Seventy Years Young: Memories of Elizabeth, Countess of Fingall* (rep. edn., Dublin, 1991), pp. 379–83.

55 Fingall to Londonderry, 28 November 1917 (PRONI, D3099/2/7/16).

56 Adams to Lloyd George, 10 December 1917 (Turner, *Lloyd George's Secretariat*, p. 104); Southborough to Adams, 17 December 1917 (McDowell, *Irish*, p. 136); Plunkett to Londonderry, 21 December 1917 (McDowell, *Irish*, p. 136).

57 Mahon to Londonderry, 3 December 1917 (PRONI, D3099/2/7/17).

58 Plunkett, *Report*, p. 18; Ulster delegation minutes, 18 December 1917 (PRONI, D/1327/3/17).

59 McDowell, *Irish*, p. 143.

60 Ulster delegation minutes, 1 January 1918 (PRONI, D/1327/3/17).

61 Ulster delegation minutes, 3 January 1918 (PRONI, D/1327/3/17); Plunkett, *Confidential*, p. 62.

62 Plunkett, *Confidential*, p. 62.

63 McDowell, *Irish*, p. 146.

64 McDowell, *Irish*, p. 146.

65 Londonderry to Theresa, Lady Londonderry, 21 January 1918 (DCRO, D/Lo/C/682 (258)); Earl of Midleton, *Records and Reactions, 1856–1939* (New York, 1939), p. 242.

66 *The Times*, 12 January 1918; *The Times*, 25 January 1918.

67 Plunkett, *Confidential*, p. 67.

68 Londonderry to Theresa, Lady Londonderry, 21 January 1918 (DCRO, D/Lo/C/682 (258)).

69 Londonderry to Edith, Lady Londonderry, 3 February 1918 (PRONI, D3099/13/1/886).

70 Londonderry to Edith, Lady Londonderry, 18 November 1918 (PRONI, D3099/13/1/866).

71 McDowell, *Irish*, p. 156.

72 Jackson, *Home*, p. 191.

73 Barrie to Londonderry, 16 February 1918 (PRONI, D3099/8/3).

74 Lloyd George to Barrie, 21 February 1918 (McDowell, *Irish*, p. 163).

75 Londonderry to Carson, 21 February 1918 (PRONI, D3099/8/3).

76 Ulster delegation minutes, 25 February 1918 (PRONI, D1327/3/17).

77 Montgomery to Londonderry, 26 February 1918 (Buckland, *Irish Unionism*, pp. 425–6).

78 Londonderry to Theresa, Lady Londonderry, 27 February 1918 (DCRO, D/Lo/C/682 (99)).

79 Theresa, Lady Londonderry to Law, 13 January 1918 (HLRO, BL/102/1/22); Balfour to Law, 28 February 1918 (HLRO, BL/82/9/20).

80 Londonderry to Lady Desborough, 16 March 1918 (PRONI, T/3201/31).

81 Londonderry to Edith, Lady Londonderry, 14 March 1918 (J. A. Pauley, 'The Social and Political Roles of Edith, Marchioness of Londonderry, 1878–1959' (PhD thesis, University of Ulster, 1994), p. 242).
82 Plunkett, *Report*, p. 116.
83 Plunkett, *Report*, pp. 30–4; Plunkett, *Confidential*, pp. 134–7.
84 McDowell, *Irish*, p. 188.
85 David Lloyd George, *War Memoirs of David Lloyd George, vol. 2* (London, 1938), p. 1600.
86 *The Times*, 18 April 1918.
87 *The Times*, 21 June 1918.
88 Eunan O'Halpin, *The Decline of the Union: British Government in Ireland, 1892–1920* (Dublin, 1997), p. 159.
89 Marchioness of Londonderry, *Retrospect* (London, 1938), p. 170.
90 *House of Lords Debates*, 20 June 1918, vol. 30, cols 289–99.
91 Long to Lloyd George, 4 March 1918 (HLRO, LG/ F/32/5/10).
92 Cecil Bisshop Harmsworth, diary, 20 November 1917 (Andrew Thorpe and Richard Toye (eds), *Parliament and Politics in the Age of Asquith and Lloyd George: The Diaries of Cecil Harmsworth MP, 1909–22* (Cambridge, 2016), p. 259).
93 Theresa, Lady Londonderry to Law, 13 January 1918 (HLRO, BL/102/1/22).
94 Balfour to Law, 28 February 1918 (HLRO, BL/82/9/20).
95 Law to Balfour, 1 March 1918 (HLRO, BL/84/7/8).
96 MacPherson to Lloyd George, 6 March 1918 (HRLO LG/F/14/5/12).
97 *The Times*, 31 July 1918.
98 Andrew Adonis, *Making Aristocracy Work: The Peerage and the Political System in Britain, 1884–1914* (rep. edn., Oxford, 2002), pp. 35–40.
99 Londonderry to Derby, 12 May 1918 (John Turner, *British Politics and the Great War: Coalition and Conflict, 1915–1918* (New Haven, 1992), p. 300); Derby to Londonderry, 14 June 1918 (PRONI, D3099/2/8/11).
100 Curzon to Bonar Law, 17 June 1918 (HRLO BL/83/4/12).
101 Duffin to Londonderry, 23 June 1918 (PRONI, D3099/2/7/26).
102 *Belfast News-Letter*, 13 July 1918. The sixth marquess had attended a 'Twelfth' demonstration at Finaghy in 1911, remarking that it was the first occasion that a former viceroy had done so (H. Montgomery Hyde, *Carson: The Life of Sir Edward Carson, Lord Carson of Duncairn* (London, 1953), p. 286); the seventh marquess later spoke at a 'Twelfth' demonstration at Ballymanoch (*The Times*, 14 July 1919).
103 Austen Morgan, *Labour and Partition: The Belfast Working Class, 1905–23* (London, 1991), pp. 215–28.
104 *The Times*, 15 July 1918.
105 Barrie to Londonderry, 24 April 1918 (PRONI, D3099/8/3).
106 Kendle, *Federal*, pp. 110, 187.
107 Frewen to Londonderry, 26 June 1918 (PRONI, D3099/8/3).
108 Frewen to Londonderry, 30 June 1918 (PRONI, D3099/8/3).
109 Literary editor of *National News* to A. D. Mayhew [Londonderry House], 30 July 1918 (PRONI, D3099/8/3).
110 Londonderry to Lloyd George, 13 August 1918 (PRONI, D3099/2/7/27).
111 Londonderry to French, 18 August 1918 (PRONI, D3099/8/3).
112 French to Londonderry, 19 August 1918 (PRONI, D3099/2/7/29).
113 Saunderson to Londonderry, 23 August 1918 (PRONI, D3099/2/7/30).
114 O'Halpin, *Decline*, p. 171.

115 Londonderry to Carson, 4 September 1918 (PRONI, D1507/A/19/1).
116 Bates, memorandum, 31 August 1918 (PRONI, D3099/8/3); O'Halpin, *Decline*, p. 168.
117 Bates to Carson, 26 August 1918 (PRONI, D3099/8/3), Bates to Londonderry, 26 August 1918 (PRONI, D3099/8/3); Londonderry to Saunderson, 27 August 1918 (PRONI, D3099/8/3).
118 Bates to Londonderry, 3 September 1918 (PRONI, D3099/8/3).
119 Londonderry to Carson, 4 September 1918 (PRONI, D1507/A/19/1).
120 O'Halpin, *Decline*, p. 171.
121 Council minutes, 10 October 1918 (PRONI, D3099/8/3).
122 Long, memorandum, 9 October 1918 (PRONI, D3099/8/3).
123 Council minutes, 10 October 1918 (PRONI, D3099/8/3).
124 Council minutes, 10 October 1918 (PRONI, D3099/8/3); *The Times*, 24 October 1918; *The Times*, 29 November 1918.
125 Viceroy's advisory council notice, October 1918 (PRONI, D3099/8/3).
126 *Maidstone Journal*, 14 December 1905. See series of letters from T.P. Gill to Londonderry, 1918 (PRONI, D3099/8/3); P. J. McAndrew to Londonderry, 19 December 1918 (PRONI, D3099/2/7/36)). Londonderry exhibited an interest in Irish agriculture when he served in the Northern Ireland government (see Salisbury to Law, 22 February 1923 (HLRO, BL/111/29/145); *The Times*, 23 February 1923).
127 Saunderson to Londonderry, enclosing a series of letters on the issue from Frank Brooke and others, 2 November 1918 (PRONI, D3099/8/3).
128 *The Times*, 13 December 1918.
129 *The Times*, 6 December 1919.
130 Alvin Jackson, 'Irish Unionism, 1870–1922', in *Defenders of the Union: A Survey of British and Irish Unionism Since 1801*, eds D. George Boyce and Alan O'Day (London, 2001), p. 115.
131 Michael Farrell, *Arming the Protestants: The Formation of the Ulster Special Constabulary and the Royal Ulster Constabulary, 1920–7* (London, 1983), p. 4.

Chapter 3

1 David Cannadine, *Aspects of Aristocracy: Grandeur and Decline in Modern Britain* (London, 1994), pp. 9–36. See Linda Colley, *Britons: Forging the Nation, 1707–1837* (London, 1992), pp. 155–9; Olwen Purdue, *The Big House in the North of Ireland: Land, Power and Social Elites, 1878–1960* (Dublin, 2009), pp. 152–212. For dissenting view, see Ellis Wasson, *Born to Rule: British Political Elites* (London, 2000), p. 146.
2 Terence Dooley, *The Decline of the Big House in Ireland* (Dublin, 2001), pp. 208–70; Peter Martin, 'Unionism: The Irish Nobility and Revolution, 1919–23', in *The Irish Revolution, 1913–1923*, ed. Joost Augusteijn (Basingstoke, 2002), pp. 151–67.
3 Nigel Keohane, *The Party of Patriotism: The Conservative Party and the First World War* (Aldershot, 2010), pp. 209–16; Kenneth O. Morgan, *Consensus and Disunity: The Lloyd George Coalition Government, 1918–1922* (Oxford, 1979), pp. 13–25.
4 Londonderry to Talbot, 28 August 1918 (PRONI, D3099/7/1).
5 Avner Offer, *Property and Politics 1870–1914: Landownership, Law, Ideology and Urban Development in England* (Cambridge, 1981), p. 403.

6 David Cannadine, *Decline and Fall of the British Aristocracy* (rev. edn., London, 1996), p. 143.
7 Martin to Londonderry, 31 August 1918 (PRONI, D3099/7/1).
8 Londonderry to Appleby, 28 August 1918 (PRONI, D3099/7/1); Londonderry to Martin, 10 September 1918 (PRONI, D3099/7/1).
9 Appleby to Londonderry, 2 September 1918 (PRONI, D3099/7/1).
10 Adrian Gregory, *The Last Great War: British Society and the First World War* (Cambridge, 2008), pp. 234–5; N. C. Fleming, *Britannia's Zealots, vol. 1: Tradition, Empire and the Forging of the Conservative Right* (London, 2019), p. 100.
11 John Stubbs, 'Lord Milner and Patriotic Labour, 1914–1918', *English Historical Review*, 87, no. 345 (1972): 717–54; William D. Rubenstein, 'Henry Page Croft and the National Party 1917–22', *Journal of Contemporary History*, 9, no. 1 (1974): 129–48.
12 Londonderry to Appleby, 7 September 1918 (PRONI, D3099/7/1).
13 Stuart Ball, *Portrait of a Party: The Conservative Party in Britain 1918–1945* (Oxford, 2013), p. 79.
14 John Grigg, 'Churchill and Lloyd George', in *Churchill*, eds Robert Blake and Wm. Roger Louis (Oxford, 1996), p. 104.
15 Londonderry to Theresa, Lady Londonderry, 13 January 1919 (DCRO, D/Lo/C 682 (256)).
16 Long to Lloyd George, n.d. [1918] (HLRO, LG/F/33/2/5).
17 Paul Bew, *Churchill and Ireland* (Oxford, 2016), p. 5.
18 Barry Supple, *The History of the British Coal Industry: vol. 4: 1913–1946: The Political Economy of Decline* (Oxford, 1987), pp. 3, 5.
19 Robert Pearce, *Britain: Industrial Relations and the Economy 1900–39* (London, 1993), p. 75.
20 *Coal Industry Commission: Report and Minutes of Evidence*, vol. 2 (Cmd. 360), *Parliamentary Papers* (1919), XII, pp. 631–3; *Aberdeen Journal*, 9 May 1919.
21 Richard B. Simons, 'The British Coal Industry-A Failure of Private Enterprise', *The Historian*, 16, no. 1 (1953): 5–7.
22 John Davies, *A History of Wales* (rev. edn., London, 2007), p. 516.
23 *The Times*, 18 August 1919.
24 *The Times*, 25 August 1919.
25 *The Times*, 22 December 1919.
26 Supple, *British*, pp. 20, 25.
27 *The Times*, 2 September 1920; *The Times*, 20 September 1920.
28 *The Times*, 23 April 1921.
29 J. Lee Thompson, *Northcliffe: Press Baron in Politics, 1865–1922* (London, 2000), pp. 349–53.
30 Supple, *British*, pp. 400, 410.
31 *Aberdeen Journal*, 19 May 1921.
32 Supple, *British*, p. 411.
33 Pearce, *Industrial*, p. 74.
34 Kathleen Burk, 'The Treasury: From Impotence to Power', in *War and the State: The Transformation of Government, 1914–1919*, ed. Kathleen Burk (London, 1982), p. 97.
35 *The Times*, 16 January 1919; *The Times*, 12 February 1919.
36 Theresa, Lady Londonderry, 5 December 1918 (PRONI, D3084/C/C/B/1/14); Theresa, Lady Londonderry, 23 December 1918 (PRONI, D3084/C/C/B/1/15).

37 H. Montgomery Hyde, *British Air Policy between the Wars, 1918–1939* (London, 1976), p. 59.
38 See Sophy Gardner, 'Whitehall Warriors: The Political Fight for the Royal Air Force, 1917–1929' (PhD thesis, University of Exeter, 2019).
39 Marquess of Londonderry, *Wings of Destiny* (London, 1943), p. 14.
40 *The Times*, 5 February 1919.
41 Londonderry, *Wings*, p. 17.
42 Hyde, *Air*, p. 74.
43 Londonderry, *Wings*, p. 14.
44 Seely to Londonderry, 4 April 1920 (PRONI, D3099/2/9/7).
45 Londonderry, *Wings*, p. 18. The sixth Marquess of Londonderry had helped Curzon to acquire his Irish peerage (David Gilmour, *Curzon* (London, 1994), p. 375).
46 Curzon to Law, 17 June 1918 (HLRO, BL/83/4/12). Hyde repeats the story along with Curzon's complaint about an occasion when Londonderry was not on the government front bench in the House of Lords, when, according to Hyde, he should have known that Londonderry was attending to business at the Air Ministry (H. Montgomery Hyde, *The Londonderrys: A Family Portrait* (London, 1979), p. 139).
47 Londonderry to Francis Humphrys, 13 March 1934 (PRONI, D3099/2/16/34).
48 Gilmour, *Curzon*, p. 534.
49 Supple, *British*, p. 414.
50 *The Times*, 19 December 1919. He had the king and queen to dinner in Londonderry House the following year (*The Times*, 24 June 1920).
51 Churchill to Londonderry, 25 December 1919 (PRONI, D3099/2/5/5).
52 Curzon to Lloyd George, 27 November 1919 (HLRO, LG/F/12/2/6).
53 Londonderry to Law, 28 January 1920 (HLRO, BL/100/1/46); Edith, Lady Londonderry to Law, 29 January 1920 (HLRO, BL/100/1/47); Law to Tyron, 31 March 1920 (HLRO, BL/101/4/22); Londonderry, *Wings*, p. 19; Churchill to Londonderry, 7 April 1920 (D3099/2/5/6); Seely to Londonderry, 4 April 1920 (PRONI, D3099/2/9/7).
54 *The Times*, 3 April 1920.
55 Cannadine, *Decline*, p. 588. See Annie Tindley, *Lord Dufferin, Ireland and the British Empire, c. 1820–1900: Rule by the Best?* (London, 2021).
56 David Cannadine, *Ornamentalism: How the British saw their Empire* (London, 2002), pp. 45–6.
57 Londonderry to Milner, 3 May 1920 (PRONI, D3099/2/7/52). See *The Times*, 13 September 1911; Castlereagh to Lord Robin Vane-Tempest-Stewart, 21 September 1911 (DCRO, D/Lo/C/682 (77)).
58 J. A. Pauley, 'The Social and Political Roles of Edith, Marchioness of Londonderry, 1878–1959', PhD thesis (University of Ulster, 1994), p. 254.
59 Milner to Londonderry, 5 May 1920 (PRONI, D3099/2/4/24). Londonderry's youngest daughter, Lady Mairi, claims that he was offered the viceroyalty of India in 1933 and declined 'because he didn't want his family brought up in India' (Bury to the author, 6 July 2005).
60 Hyde, *Londonderrys*, p. 165.
61 Hyde, *Air*, pp. 35–6.
62 John Robert Ferris, *Men, Money, and Diplomacy: The Evolution of British Strategic Policy, 1919–26* (New York, 1989), p. 68.
63 Londonderry, *Wings*, p. 9.

64 Trenchard to Londonderry, 26 September 1919 (PRONI, D3099/2/9/4).
65 Londonderry to Trenchard, n.d. (Hyde, *Air*, pp. 99–100).
66 Trenchard to Londonderry, June 1920 (PRONI, D3099/2/9/11); Trenchard to Londonderry, 16 June 1920 (PRONI, D3099/2/9/6).
67 Marchioness of Londonderry, *Retrospect* (London, 1938), p. 173; Diane Urquhart, *The Ladies of Londonderry: Women and Political Patronage* (London, 2007), p. 149.
68 Londonderry, *Wings*, p. 14.
69 *The Times*, 10 July 1920. See also *The Times*, 22 April 1920.
70 David E. Omissi, *Air Power and Colonial Control: The Royal Air Force, 1919–1939* (Manchester, 1990), pp. 9–13, 106.
71 Thomas Hippler, *Governing from the Skies: A Global History of Aerial Bombing* (London, 2017), pp. xxi–xxii, 38.
72 G. H. Bennett, *British Foreign Policy during the Curzon Period, 1919–24* (New York, 1995), p. 107.
73 Omissi, *Air*, pp. 23–7.
74 Trenchard to Londonderry, 26 August 1920 (PRONI, D3099/2/9/8).
75 *House of Lords Debates*, 20 April 1921, vol. 44, cols 1064–71; Glen Balfour-Paul, 'Britain's Informal Empire in the Middle East', in *The Oxford History of the British Empire, vol. iv: The Twentieth Century*, eds Judith M. Brown and W. Roger Louis (Oxford, 1999), p. 498.
76 *House of Lords Debates*, 11 May 1920, vol. 40, cols 223–33. He later proposed that the City of London be allowed to have an aerodrome despite the obvious lack of space: 'developments might take place in aviation which would change the position in that respect' (*The Times*, 10 June 1920).
77 *The Times*, 8 March 1921.
78 *The Times*, 11 March 1921.
79 *The Times*, 19 March 1921.
80 Londonderry, *Wings*, p. 19.
81 Morgan, *Consensus*, p. 115.
82 Carson to Londonderry, 5 December 1920 (PRONI, D3099/2/7/54); *House of Lords Debates*, 24 November 1920, vol. 42, cols 541–9.
83 Carson to Londonderry, 8 January 1921 (PRONI, D3099/2/7/56); Carson to Londonderry, 6 June 1921 (PRONI, D3099/2/7/59).
84 *The Times*, 31 May 1921; Law to Londonderry, 31 May 1921 (HLRO, BL/101/5/30).
85 Guest to Londonderry, 23 July 1921 (Londonderry, *Wings*, p. 20).
86 He was given a permit to fly to the Paris peace conferences on 11 March 1919, but there is little to otherwise indicate that he had any involvement with the negotiations (Air Ministry permit, 10 March 1919 (PRONI, D3099/2/9/3)).

Chapter 4

1 T. P. Daly, 'James Craig and Orangeism, 1903–10', *Irish Historical Studies*, 34, no. 136 (2005): 431–48.
2 D. H. Akenson, *Education and Enmity: The Control of Schooling in Northern Ireland, 1920–50* (London, 1973), p. 41.
3 N. C. Fleming, 'The Landed Elite, Power and Ulster Unionism', in *The Ulster Crisis 1885–1921*, eds D. George Boyce and Alan O'Day (Basingstoke, 2006), pp. 86–104.

4 Mary Harris, *The Catholic Church and the Foundation of the Northern Irish State* (Cork, 1993), p. 197.
5 Patrick Buckland, *Irish Unionism: Two: Ulster Unionism and the Origins of Northern Ireland, 1886–1922* (Dublin, 1973), pp. 127–46.
6 Akenson, *Education*, p. 53.
7 *The Times*, 5 February 1921.
8 Paul Bew, Peter Gibbon and Henry Patterson, *Northern Ireland 1921/2001: Political Forces and Social Classes* (London, 2002), p. 60; Duke of Abercorn to Home Secretary, 13 January 1926 (PRO, HO/276/195).
9 See, for example, his call for Northern Ireland to become an agent of rapprochement between England and Ireland (*The Times*, 18 October 1923).
10 Andrew Gailey, 'The Destructiveness of Constructive Unionism: Theories and Practice, 1890s–1960s', in *Defenders of the Union: A Survey of British and Irish Unionism since 1801*, eds D. George Boyce and Alan O'Day (London, 2001), pp. 227–46.
11 Jennifer Todd, 'Unionist Political thought, 1920–72', in *Political thought in Ireland since the Seventeenth Century*, eds D. George Boyce, Robert Eccleshall and Vincent Geoghegan (London, 1993), p. 191.
12 Marquess of Londonderry, *Wings of Destiny* (London, 1943), pp. 20–1.
13 D. H. Akenson, *Small Differences: Irish Catholics and Irish Protestants, 1815–1922: An International Perspective* (Kingston and Montreal, 1988), p. 125.
14 Londonderry to Lloyd George, 17 November 1918 (HLRO, KG/F/29/2/65).
15 Londonderry to F. G. Kellaway [Ministry of Munitions], 21 November 1919 (PRO, MUN/4/5847); Kellaway to Londonderry, 22 November 1919 (PRO, MUN/4/5847).
16 Michael Hopkinson, *The Irish War of Independence* (Dublin, 2004), p. 31.
17 *The Times*, 8 April 1920. Londonderry would join Wilson and Lady Dufferin again the following year at a ceremony to open the memorial tower to the Ulster Division at Thiepval (H. Montgomery Hyde, *The Londonderrys: A Family Portrait* (London, 1979), p. 149).
18 *The Times*, 21 April 1927.
19 *The Times*, 17 June 1921; *The Times*, 24 June 1921; D. George Boyce, 'Conservative Opinion, the Ulster Question, and the Partition of Ireland, 1912–21', *Irish Historical Studies*, 17, no. 65 (1970): 103.
20 *The Times*, 25 January 1921.
21 *The Times*, 5 March 1920.
22 George Russell to Londonderry, 2 April [1920] (PRONI, D3099/2/7/58); F. S. L. Lyons, *Culture and Anarchy in Ireland, 1890–1939* (Oxford, 1979), p. 111.
23 *Belfast News-Letter*, 24 December 1920.
24 *Observer*, 20 February 1921.
25 Londonderry successfully proposed in 1924 that one of the government's four nominations to the Senate of Queen's University should go to Sir Denis Henry, Northern Ireland's first lord chief justice and a Catholic (A. D. McDonnell, *The Life of Sir Denis Henry: Catholic Unionist* (Belfast, 2000), p. 115).
26 Blanche E. C. Dugdale, *Arthur James Balfour, First Earl of Balfour, KG, OM, FRS, etc, vol. 1* (London, 1936), pp. 324–5; Tony Taylor, *The Politics of Reaction: The Ideology of the Cecils and the Challenge of Secular Education, 1889–1902* (Leeds, 1997), *passim*.
27 Craig to Londonderry, 29 April 1921 (PRONI, D3099/2/10/1); *The Times*, 31 May 1921; *The Times*, 8 June 1921; Hugh O'Neill to Londonderry, 11 June 1921 (DCRO, D/Lo/F/593 (2)).
28 Churchill to Londonderry, 20 May 1921 (PRONI, D3099/2/5/14).

29 *Hansard N.I. (Senate)*, 1, 30–8, 42–3 (20 September 1921). Londonderry had been hostile to direct talks between Sinn Féin and the government earlier in the year (Cabinet Conclusions, 16 July 1921 (PRONI, CAB/4/8/3)).
30 Londonderry to Salisbury, 1 September 1921 (PRONI, D3099/8/1); Londonderry to Salisbury, 2 September 1921 (PRONI, D3099/8/1).
31 Akenson, *Education*, p. 42.
32 *The Times*, 7 December 1921.
33 Sinead McCoole, *Hazel: A Life of Lady Lavery 1880–1935* (Dublin, 1996), pp. 77–82.
34 Lavery to Collins, undated but probably 14 December 1921 (Leon Ó Bróin (ed.), *In Great Haste: The Letters of Michael Collins and Kitty Kiernan* (Dublin, 1996), p. 90).
35 Hyde, *Londonderrys*, p. 150.
36 Londonderry later dismissed the idea of a Londonderry-Collins pact as a 'complete fallacy' (Londonderry to Churchill, 5 August 1922 (DCRO, D/Lo/C/242 (6))).
37 David Dutton, *Austen Chamberlain: Gentleman in Politics* (Bolton, 1985), p. 169.
38 Boyce, 'Conservative', p. 107.
39 *The Times*, 16 December 1921; Londonderry to R.D. Blumenfeld [editor of *Daily Express*], 12 November 1921 (HLRO, Blu/Lon/6).
40 N. C. Fleming, *Britannia's Zealots, vol. 1: Tradition, Empire and the Forging of the Conservative Right* (London, 2019), pp. 110–14.
41 Cabinet Conclusions, 28 November 1921 (PRONI, CAB/4/27/4).
42 Maurice Cowling, *The Impact of Labour 1920–40: The Beginning of Modern British Politics* (Cambridge, 1971), p. 143.
43 See N. C. Fleming, 'The Conservative Right, Ulster Unionism, and the Partition of Ireland', in *Ireland and Partition: Contexts and Consequences*, eds N. C. Fleming and James H. Murphy (Clemson, 2021), pp. 283–303.
44 *House of Lords Debates*, 15 December 1921, vol. 48, cols 58–70.
45 Alvin Jackson, *Sir Edward Carson* (Dundalk, 1993), pp. 61–2.
46 J. Mulhall to Londonderry, 16 December 1921 (PRONI, D3099/2/7/65); John Ross to Londonderry, 19 December 1921 (PRONI, D3099/2/7/66).
47 *The Times*, 24 June 1921; Lord Fitz-Alan to Londonderry, 10 December 1921 (PRONI, D3099/2/4/28); Lord Stamfordham to Londonderry, 10 December 1921 (PRONI, D3099/2/4/29); *The Times*, 10 March 1922.
48 Londonderry to McKeown, 11 September 1922 (PRONI, D3099/2/7/77).
49 Bates to Londonderry, 20 April 1923 (PRONI, D3099/2/7/82); Cosgrave to Londonderry, 1 May 1923 (PRONI, D3099/2/7/83).
50 Buckland, *Irish Unionism: Two*, p. 176. See also Brian Follis, *A State under Siege: The Establishment of Northern Ireland, 1920–1925* (Oxford, 1995).
51 Robert Lynch, *The Partition of Ireland 1918–1925* (Cambridge, 2019), pp. 102, 140.
52 Craig addressed the cabinet on his meetings with Collins, and implied that he could see a united Ireland in '10, 20 or 50 years', see Cabinet Conclusions, 26 January 1922 (PRONI, CAB/4/30/1).
53 Cabinet Conclusions, 13 March 1922 (PRONI, CAB/4/35/16).
54 Collins to Lady L., n.d. (Hyde, *Londonderrys*, p. 152).
55 Londonderry to Pakenham, 30 October 1935 (Hyde, *Londonderrys*, pp. 151–2).
56 Londonderry to Curtis, 5 October 1922 (DCRO, D/Lo/C/242 (2)).
57 Anne de Courcy, *Circe: The Life of Edith, Marchioness of Londonderry* (London, 1993), pp. 166–7; McCoole, *Hazel*, pp. 86–8.
58 Keith Jeffery, *Field Marshal Sir Henry Wilson: A Political Soldier* (Oxford, 2006), pp. 279–80.

59 Hyde, *Londonderrys*, p. 150.
60 Wilson, diary, 14 January 1922 (C. E. Callwell (ed.), *Field Marshal Sir Henry Wilson: His Life and Diaries* (London, 1927), p. 320); Fleming, *Britannia's*, pp. 97–124.
61 Diane Urquhart, 'Peeresses, Patronage and Power: The Politics of Ladies Frances Anne, Theresa and Edith Londonderry, 1800–1959', in *Irish Women's History*, eds Alan Hayes and Diane Urquhart (Dublin, 2004), p. 56.
62 *The Times*, 8 March 1922.
63 *The Times*, 17 April 1922.
64 *The Times*, 3 June 1922; Fleming, *Britannia's*, pp. 248–9.
65 *The Times*, 4 September 1922; Stuart Ball, *The Conservative Party and British Politics, 1902–1951* (London, 1995), p. 76.
66 Viscount Castlereagh, 'Memorandum', August 1936, in *Baldwin Papers: A Conservative Statesman, 1908–1947*, eds Philip Williamson and Edward Baldwin (Cambridge, 2005), p. 370.
67 Londonderry to Strachey, 15 April 1922 (HLRO, STR/9/15/8).
68 Londonderry to Strachey, 31 December 1922 (HLRO, STR/9/15/9).
69 Wilson to Craig, 19 April 1922 (PRONI, T/3775/17/2); Londonderry to Churchill, 2 April 1922 (DCRO, D/Lo/C/242(16)).
70 Patrick Buckland, *The Factory of Grievances: Devolved Government in Northern Ireland, 1921–39* (Dublin, 1979), p. 206.
71 *Hansard N.I. (Senate)*, 2, 10 (14 March 1922); Michael Farrell, *Northern Ireland: The Orange State* (rep. edn., London, 1992), p. 51.
72 Michael Farrell, *Arming the Protestants: The Formation of the Ulster Special Constabulary and the Royal Ulster Constabulary, 1920–7* (London, 1983), pp. 212, 225.
73 Londonderry to Henderson, 26 March 1924 (PRO, PREM/1/43); Londonderry to Henderson, 11 March 1924 (PRO, PREM/1/43).
74 *The Times*, 12 March 1924.
75 Cabinet Conclusions, 23 May 1922 (PRONI, CAB/4/44); *The Times*, 14 July 1922; Paul Canning, *British Policy Towards Ireland 1921–1941* (Oxford, 1985), p. 61.
76 *House of Lords Debates*, 22 February 1923, vol. 53, cols 113–19.
77 See Strachey to Londonderry, 10 April 1922 (HLRO, STR/9/15/8).
78 Bew, Gibbon and Patterson, *Northern Ireland*, pp. 24–6; Tallents' report to the British Cabinet and diary, June 1922 (PRO, PRO/CO/906/24).
79 Marchioness of Londonderry, *Retrospect* (London, 1938), pp. 212, 215.
80 R. J. Q. Adams, *Bonar Law* (London, 1999), pp. 350–2; Londonderry, *Wings*, pp. 28–9.
81 *House of Lords Debates*, 27 July 1922, vol. 51, cols 902–9.
82 Londonderry to Law, 1 December 1921 (HLRO, BL/107/1/82).
83 Chaplin to Law, 20 October 1922 (HLRO, BL/109/1/19).
84 Salisbury to Law, 22 October 1922 (HLRO, BL/109/2/32).
85 Londonderry to McKeown, 9 September 1922 (PRONI, D3099/2/7/76).
86 Londonderry to Law, 24 October 1922 (HLRO, BL/109/2/27a).
87 Londonderry to Desborough, 25 October 1922 (PRONI, T/3201/33).
88 Londonderry to Law, 25 October 1922 (HLRO, BL/109/2/27b).
89 Londonderry to Strachey, 31 December 1922 (HLRO, STR/9/15/9).
90 David E. Omissi, *Air Power and Colonial Control: The Royal Air Force, 1919–1939* (Manchester, 1990), p. 31.
91 Lady Londonderry to Law, 26 October 1922 (HLRO, BL/109/2/13a).

92 Lady Londonderry to Londonderry, 12 July 1922 (PRONI, D3099/13/2/756).
93 Law to Lady Londonderry, 2 November 1922 (HLRO, BL/109/2/13b).
94 Ralph Lambton to Londonderry, 6 November 1922 (PRONI, D3099/2/7/79); *The Times*, 25 October 1922; Sir William Tyrrell to H.A. Gwynne, 4 November 1922 (Keith M. Wilson, *A Study in the History and Politics of the Morning Post 1905–1926* (Lampeter, 1990), p. 198).
95 Archbishop D'Arcy to Craig, 8 November 1922 (PRONI, CAB/9T/3/1); Londonderry to Churchill, n.d. [1940s] (D3099/2/17/78).
96 Strachey to Londonderry, 2 January 1923 (HLRO, STR/9/15/9); Londonderry to Strachey, 3 January 1923 (HLRO, STR/9/15/9). It was not the only occasion that Londonderry complained about reports of his work in *The Spectator* (Strachey to Londonderry, 21 May 1919 (HLRO, STR/9/15/9); Strachey to Londonderry, 14 March 1923 (HLRO, STR/9/15/9)).
97 Fleming, *Britannia's*, pp. 140–1; *The Times*, 5 January 1924.
98 Cabinet Conclusions, 7 May 1924 (PRONI, CAB/4/113/9).
99 *Hansard N.I. (Senate)*, 4, 17 (11 March 1924), 4, 117 (13 May 1924); *The Times*, 12 June, 25 August 1924.
100 *The Times*, 2 May 1924.
101 *The Times*, 12 May 1924; *The Times*, 12 June 1924.
102 Alvin Jackson, 'Ireland, the Union, and the Empire, 1800–1960', in *Ireland and the British Empire*, ed. Kevin Kenny (Oxford, 2004), p. 145.
103 Bernard Porter, *The Absent-Minded Imperialists: Empire, Society and Culture in Britain* (Oxford, 2004), p. 227.
104 *The Times*, 4 July 1924; *The Times*, 17 June 1924.
105 *The Times*, 4 August 1924.
106 Thomas Jones, diary, 2 August 1924 (Keith Middlemas (ed.), *Thomas Jones Whitehall Diary, vol. 3: Ireland, 1918–1925* (London, 1971), p. 226).
107 *The Times*, 5 August 1924.
108 *The Times*, 8 August 1924.
109 Jones, 8 August 1924 (Middlemas, *Jones Whitehall Diary, vol. 3*, p. 235).
110 Londonderry to MacDonald, 9 August 1924 (PRONI, D3099/2/7/93).
111 See Stephen Evans, 'The Conservatives and the Redefinition of Unionism, 1912–21', *Twentieth Century British History*, 9, no. 1 (1998): 1–27.
112 Londonderry to Baldwin, 27 August 1924 (CUL, Baldwin 99, ff. 128–9).
113 Cabinet Conclusions, 16 September 1924 (PRONI, CAB/4/121).
114 Londonderry to Salisbury, 18 September 1924 (Kevin Matthews, *Fatal Influence: The Impact of Ireland on British Politics, 1920–1925* (Dublin, 2004), p. 177).
115 Londonderry to Lady Londonderry, 2 October 1924 (Hyde, *Londonderrys*, p. 162).
116 Matthews, *Fatal Influence*, p. 140.
117 *Irish News*, 9 January 1926.
118 *The Times*, 26 January 1926.
119 Matthews, *Fatal Influence*, pp. 189–90.
120 *The Times*, 18 October 1924.
121 David Marquand, *Ramsay MacDonald* (London, 1977), pp. 358–61.
122 *Aberdeen Journal*, 25 October 1924.
123 *The Times*, 22 December 1924.
124 For personal views of campaign, see Londonderry to Blumenfeld, 2 November 1924 (HLRO, Blu/Lon/7); Londonderry to Churchill, 7 October 1924 (PRONI, D3084/C/C/3/1).

125 *The Times*, 5 January 1925.
126 Londonderry to Baldwin, 7 November 1924 (CUL, Baldwin 42 f. 263).
127 *The Times*, 7 February 1925.
128 *The Times*, 1 January 1925; *The Times*, 3 January 1925.
129 *The Times*, 26 March 1925.
130 Londonderry to Churchill, 26 October 1925 (PRONI, D3084/C/C/3/6A–D); Churchill to Londonderry, 30 October 1925 (PRONI, D3099/2/5/16); Londonderry to Churchill, 2 November 1925 (PRONI, D3084/C/C/3/7A–B); Londonderry to Desborough, 21 November 1926 (PRONI, T/3201/48).
131 Lynn to Londonderry, 3 October 1925 (PRONI, D3099/2/11/8).
132 Alvin Jackson, *Home Rule: An Irish History, 1800–2000* (London, 2003), p. 211.
133 Buckland, *Factory*, pp. 247–65; Harris, *Catholic*, pp. 196–255; Sean Farren, 'Unionist-Protestant Reaction to Educational Reform in Northern Ireland 1923–1930', *History of Education*, 14, no. 3 (1985): 227–36; Sean Farren, 'Nationalist-Catholic Reaction to Educational Reform in Northern Ireland, 1920–30', *History of Education*, 15, no. 1 (1986): 19–30; Sean Farren, *The Politics of Irish Education, 1920–65* (Belfast, 1995), pp. 59–105; Michael McGrath, *The Catholic Church and Catholic Schools in Northern Ireland: The Price of Faith* (Dublin, 2000), pp. 15–66; Cecilia Biaggi, 'Reforming Education in Post-partition Northern Ireland: State Control and Churches' Interference', *History of Education*, 49, no. 3 (2020): 379–97. For exceptions, see Akenson, *Education*, pp. 19–88; N. C. Fleming, 'The First Government of Northern Ireland, Education Reform and the Failure of Anti-populist Unionism, 1921–1925', *Twentieth Century British History*, 18, no. 2 (2007): 146–69.
134 N. C. Fleming, 'Education since the Late Eighteenth Century', in *Ulster since 1600: Politics, Economy and Society*, eds Liam Kennedy and Philip Ollerenshaw (Oxford, 2013), pp. 211–27.
135 St John Ervine, *Craigavon: Ulsterman* (London, 1949), p. 119.
136 Akenson, *Education*, p. 41.
137 *Hansard N.I. (Senate)*, 1, 24 (23 June 1921). See *The Times*, 6 December 1922; *Teacher's World*, 1 (10 January 1923).
138 Delays in transfer stretched into 1922 (Lewis McQuibban's notes), 10 May 1922 (PRONI, D3099/5/1).
139 Londonderry to Lynn, 30 August 1921 (PRONI, D3480/59/42).
140 Logue to Londonderry, August 1921 (PRONI, D3099/2/7/62).
141 Londonderry to Logue, 29 August 1921 (PRONI, CAB/4/18/1).
142 Logue to Londonderry, 2 September 1921 (PRONI, D3099/2/7/61).
143 Londonderry to Fitz-Alan, 4 September 1921 (PRONI, CAB/4/18/13).
144 Cabinet Conclusions, 9 September 1921 (PRONI, CAB/4/18/21).
145 Londonderry to Logue, 10 September 1921 (PRONI, CAB/4/18/19).
146 *The Times*, 5 December 1922.
147 Cabinet Conclusions, 15 December 1922 (PRONI, CAB/4/61/12); Bates to Londonderry, 28 November 1922 (PRONI, D3099/5/5).
148 Cabinet Conclusions, 11 January 1923 (PRONI, CAB/4/66/21).
149 Londonderry to Lynn, 8 February 1923 (PRONI, D3480/59/44); Lynn to Londonderry, 19 February 1923 (PRONI, D3480/59/44).
150 Lynn to Senator Sam Cunningham, 16 March 1923 (PRONI, D3099/2/4/19B); Londonderry to Lynn, 10 June 1923 (PRONI, D3480/59/46); Londonderry to Lynn, 21 February 1923 (PRONI, D3480/59/44).

151 Lynn to Londonderry, 6 October 1924 (PRONI, D3099/2/11/3); Lynn to Londonderry, 9 October 1924 (PRONI, D3099/2/11/4).
152 *Hansard N.I. (Commons)*, 3, 125–6 (14 March 1923). See *The Times*, 15 March 1923.
153 Cabinet Conclusions, 16 April 1923 (PRONI, CAB/4/77/15).
154 Address by Londonderry to members of the Ulster Reform Club, Belfast, 9 November 1923 (PRONI, CAB/9D/1/4).
155 *Belfast Evening Telegraph*, 24 November 1922.
156 Akenson, *Education*, p. 79.
157 Cabinet Conclusions, 27 September 1923 (PRONI, CAB/4/86).
158 Cabinet Conclusions, 2 October 1923 (PRONI, CAB/4/88).
159 Craig to Londonderry, 2 January 1923 (PRONI, D3099/2/10/2).
160 Cabinet Conclusions, 28 February 1923 (PRONI, CAB/4/72/16).
161 *Hansard N.I. (Commons)*, 3, 356 (17 April 1923).
162 *Hansard N.I. (Commons)*, 4, 343 (26 March 1924).
163 *The Times*, 2 April 1924. See also Marquess of Londonderry, 'Public Education in Northern Ireland: The New System', *Nineteenth Century and After*, 95 (March 1924): 328–34.
164 Minute of proceedings at the reception of a deputation from the Protestant churches by the Minister of Education on Wednesday, 2 April [1924], at Parliament Buildings (PRONI, D3099/5/9).
165 D'Arcy to Londonderry, 9 March 1925 (PRONI, D3099/5/14/2); D'Arcy to Londonderry, 10 March 1925 (PRONI, D3099/5/14/2).
166 Secretary of Grand Orange Lodge of Belfast to Londonderry, 4 February 1925 (PRONI, D3099/5/9).
167 Hendriks to Londonderry, 3 February 1925 (PRONI, D3099/5/9).
168 Hendriks to Londonderry, 4 February 1925 (PRONI, D3099/5/9).
169 Minutes of the meeting between the Minister of Education and a delegation from the Grand Orange Lodge of Belfast, 23 February 1925 (PRONI, D3099/5/9).
170 Cabinet Conclusions, 7 March 1925 (PRONI, CAB/4/137/10).
171 *The Times*, 13 March 1925; *Hansard N.I. (Senate)*, 5, 29–31 (12 March 1925). See D'Arcy to Londonderry, 10 March 1925 (PRONI, D3099/5/14/2).
172 *The Times*, 14 March 1925.
173 Buckland, *Factory*, pp. 254–5; Craig to Londonderry, 25 June 1925 (PRONI, CAB/9D/1/5).
174 Colin Reid, 'Protestant Challenges to the "Protestant State": Ulster Unionism and Independent Unionism in Northern Ireland, 1921–1939', *Twentieth Century British History*, 19, no. 4 (2008): 419–45.
175 *The Times*, 18 April 1925.
176 Cabinet Conclusions, 4 June 1925 (PRONI, CAB/4/145/15).
177 *The Times*, 12 June 1915.
178 Craig to Londonderry, 13 June 1925 (PRONI, CAB/9D/1/5).
179 Andrews to Craig, 17 June 1925 (PRONI, CAB/9D/1/5).
180 Tallents' report to British Cabinet and diary, June 1922 (PRO, PRO/CO/906/24).
181 Craig to Wilfred Spender, 19 June 1925 (PRONI, CAB/9D/1/5).
182 Londonderry to Craig, 23 June 1925 (PRONI, CAB/9D/1/5).
183 Londonderry to Craig, 23 June 1925 (PRONI, CAB/9D/1/5).
184 Craig to Londonderry, 25 June 1925 (PRONI, CAB/9D/1/5).
185 Craig to Dixon, 26 June 1925 (PRONI, CAB/9D/1/5).
186 *The Times*, 10 July 1925; Craig to Londonderry, 2 July 1925 (PRONI, CAB/9D/1/5).

187 Londonderry to Lynn, 29 July 1925 (PRONI, D3480/59/57).
188 Éamon Phoenix, 'Michael Collins and the Northern Question 1916–1922', in *Michael Collins and the Making of the Irish State*, eds Gabriel Doherty and Dermot Keogh (rep. edn., Cork, 2006), p. 110.
189 Londonderry to Lionel Curtis, 5 October 1922 (DCRO, D/Lo/C/242 (2)); Cabinet Conclusions, 6 October 1922 (PRONI, CAB/4/54/13).
190 Londonderry to Wood, 1 December 1922 (PRONI, D3099/5/4).
191 Cabinet Conclusions, 29 October 1923 (PRONI, CAB/4/91/21).
192 J. A. Pauley, 'The Social and Political Roles of Edith, Marchioness of Londonderry, 1878–1959' (PhD thesis, University of Ulster, 1994), p. 255.
193 Farren, *Education*, p. 43.
194 Londonderry to Churchill, 5 August 1922 (DCRO, D/Lo/C/242).
195 Fionntán de Brún, '"Ulsteria": The Fortunes of the Irish Language under Stormont, 1921–72', in *Conflicts in the North of Ireland 1900–2000: Flashpoints and Fracture Zones*, eds Alan F. Parkinson and Éamon Phoenix (Dublin, 2010), pp. 202–22.
196 Cabinet Conclusions, 10 January 1922 (PRONI, CAB/4/29/15).
197 O'Donnell to Londonderry, 27 December 1924 (PRONI, ED/21/1/4).
198 Londonderry to O'Donnell, January 1925 (PRONI, ED/32/B/6/1/62).
199 Cabinet Conclusions, 27 January 1925 (CAB/4/134/28).
200 Farrell, *Arming*, pp. 129, 131.
201 *The Times*, 22 January 1925.
202 Carson to Londonderry, 6 June 1921 (PRONI, D3099/2/7/59).
203 *House of Lords Debates*, 16 June 1921, vol. 45, cols 625–6.
204 Graham Walker, *A History of the Ulster Unionist Party: Protest, Pragmatism and Pessimism* (Manchester, 2004), p. 47.
205 Londonderry to Lynn, 9 January 1928 (PRONI, D3480/59/68).
206 Cabinet Conclusions, 25 February 1925 (PRONI, CAB/4/135/18).
207 *The Times*, 5 August 1925; *The Times*, 20 November 1925.
208 Cabinet Conclusions, 20 October 1924 (PRONI, CAB/4/135/18).
209 *Irish Statesman*, 16 January 1926.
210 Don Handelman, cited in John Hutchinson and Anthony D. Smith (eds), *Ethnicity* (Oxford, 1996), p. 6.
211 Todd, 'Unionist', p. 197.
212 O'Leary himself qualifies his thesis, to some extent, on this formative period in education reform, but only to highlight, correctly, that Catholic autonomy was expensive and had the unintended consequence of reducing the legal options for redress (Brendan O'Leary, *A Treatise on Northern Ireland, vol. 2: Control: The Second Protestant Ascendancy and the Irish State* (Oxford, 2019), pp. 55–7).
213 Stephen Jackson, 'Religious Education and the Anglo-World: The Impact of Empire, Britishness, and Decolonisation in Australia, Canada, and New Zealand', *Brill Research Perspectives in Religion and Education*, 2, no. 1 (2020): 1–98.
214 *The Times*, 2 June 1926.

Chapter 5

1 John Campbell, *F.E. Smith, First Earl of Birkenhead* (London, 1983), p. 805.
2 Martin Pugh, *The Tories and the People 1880–1935* (London, 1985), p. 45.

3 Diane Urquhart, *The Ladies of Londonderry: Women and Political Patronage* (London, 2007), p. 87.
4 Campbell, *F.E. Smith*, p. 163.
5 Birkenhead to Londonderry, 26 April 1927 (PRONI, D3099/2/7/117).
6 Stuart Ball, 'The Legacy of Coalition: Fear and Loathing in Conservative Politics, 1922–31', *Contemporary British History*, 25, no. 1 (2011): 65–82.
7 Jeremy Smith, '"Ever Reliable Friends"? The Conservative Party and Ulster Unionism in the Twentieth Century', *English Historical Review*, 121, no. 490 (2006): 71–103; Alvin Jackson, '"Tame Tory Hacks"? The Ulster Party at Westminster, 1922–1972', *Historical Journal*, 54, no. 2 (2011): 453–75.
8 Londonderry to Stanley Baldwin, 13 April 1926 (Keith Middlemas (ed.), *Thomas Jones Whitehall Diary: vol. 2: 1926–1930* (London, 1969), p. 10).
9 *The Times*, 20 June 1928.
10 William Bridgeman, *The Modernisation of Conservative Politics: The Diaries and Letters of William Bridgeman 1904–1935* (London, 1988), pp. 229–30.
11 *The Times*, 9 January 1926.
12 Londonderry to Desborough, 1926 (H. Montgomery Hyde, *The Londonderrys: A Family Portrait* (London, 1979), pp. 168–9).
13 Beaverbrook to Londonderry, 23 January 1926 (HLRO, BBK/C/224).
14 Lady Londonderry to Beaverbrook, 4 February 1926 (HLRO, BBK/C/224); Beaverbrook to Lady Londonderry, 6 February 1926 (HLRO, BBK/C/224).
15 T. W. Moody and J. C. Beckett, *Queen's, Belfast 1845–1949: The History of a University, vol. 2* (London, 1959), p. 485. For Londonderry's appointment, see *The Times*, 9 May 1923; *The Times*, 30 June 1923. He was also made an honorary doctor of laws by Queen's University, see *The Times*, 11 July 1923.
16 Deirdre McMahon, *Republicans and Imperialists: Anglo-Irish Relations in the 1930s* (London, 1984), p. 153; Hugh Hanley, 'Monarchism, International Relations, and the Continuing Irish Revolution, 1926–29', *Journal of Imperial and Commonwealth History*, 49, no. 1 (2020): 93–117.
17 *The Times*, 18 March 1931.
18 Pauline Lynn, 'The Impact of Women. The Shaping of Political Allegiance in County Durham 1918–1945', *Local Historian*, 28, no. 3 (1998): 159–75.
19 Huw Benyon and Terry Austrin, *Masters and Servants: Class Patronage in the Making of a Labour Organisation: The Durham Miners and the English Political Tradition* (London, 1994), p. 323; Stuart Ball, 'The National and Regional Party Structure', in *Conservative Century: The Conservative Party since 1900*, eds Anthony Seldon and Stuart Ball (Oxford, 1994), p. 209; Stuart Ball, 'Introduction', in *Parliament and Politics in the Age of Baldwin and MacDonald: The Headlam Diaries, 1923–1935*, ed. Stuart Ball (London, 1992), p. 9.
20 Headlam, diary, 3 October 1926, 22 October 1926 (Ball, *Headlam*, p. 100).
21 Headlam, diary, 30 November 1926, 20 July 1929, 22 February 1930 (Ball, *Headlam*, pp. 105, 177–8, 185).
22 The remark was recalled by Lady Londonderry at the 1931 general election, when she spoke on behalf of the Conservative candidate for Newcastle Central, Arthur Denville, who went on to take the seat from Trevelyan (*The Times*, 27 October 1931). Shortly afterwards, Londonderry wrote to the former editor of the *Daily Express*, Ralph Blumenfeld, that 'you have been paying a certain amount of attention to Sir Charles Trevelyan. My interest is revived, because instead of leaving me alone, he had to make a reference to me in one of his election speeches. I think the man must be

literally mad because he talks of nothing but his riches, but takes no steps whatsoever to reduce them. I should have thought that there was nothing easier than for a rich man to become poor' (Londonderry to Blumenfeld, 4 November 1931 (HLRO, BLU/Lon/8)).

23 Lady Londonderry to J. C. C. Davidson, 11 December 1929 (Robert Rhodes James (ed.), *Memoirs of a Conservative: J.C.C. Davidson's Memoirs and Papers, 1910–37* (London, 1969), pp. 311–12).
24 *House of Commons Debates*, 8 May 1929, vol. 227, cols 2287–98.
25 Robert Pearce, *Britain: Industrial Relations and the Economy 1900–39* (London, 1993), pp. 74–5.
26 Lewis Mates, *The Great Labour Unrest: Rank-and-File Movements and Political Change in the Durham Coalfield* (Manchester, 2016).
27 Pauline Lynn, 'Seaham Revisited: The Fruits of the Electoral Franchise?', *North East History*, 33 (2000): 4–5.
28 Londonderry afterwards offered it to Durham County for 'hospital purposes' and in 1928 it was opened as a sanatorium for tuberculosis sufferers (*The Times*, 24 April 1923; *The Times*, 27 February 1928).
29 *The Times*, 13 May 1922; *The Times*, 4 January 1923.
30 Benyon and Austrin, *Masters*, pp. 203–5.
31 *The Times*, 21 August 1922; *The Times*, 28 August 1922. He later unveiled a memorial tablet to his chief mining agent, V. W. Corbett, in Seaham Church (*The Times*, 29 December 1929).
32 *The Times*, 27 December 1922.
33 *The Times*, 2 July 1923; Beynon and Austrin, *Masters*, pp. 296–8.
34 *The Times*, 27 August 1923.
35 Beynon and Austrin, *Masters*, p. 298.
36 *The Times*, 15 January 1923.
37 *The Times*, 30 August 1923.
38 *The Times*, 8 September 1923.
39 *The Times*, 26 May 1924.
40 *The Times*, 19 November 1924; *The Times*, 30 May 1927.
41 Londonderry to John Strachey, 17 May 1924 (HLRO, STR/9/15/11).
42 *The Times*, 2 December 1924.
43 *The Times*, 30 March 1925.
44 M. W. Kirby, *The British Coalmining Industry, 1870–1946* (London, 1977), pp. 66–91; Pearce, *Industrial*, p. 76.
45 *The Times*, 14 August 1925.
46 *The Times*, 17 August 1925.
47 *The Times*, 24 August 1925.
48 Richard B. Simons, 'The British Coal Industry-a Failure of Private Enterprise', *The Historian*, 16, no. 1 (1953): 9.
49 Londonderry to Baldwin, 18 December 1925 (CUL, Baldwin 13, ff. 105–7).
50 *The Times*, 9 January 1926.
51 *The Times*, 11 January 1926.
52 *The Times*, 12 January 1926.
53 *The Times*, 23 January 1926; Marquess of Londonderry, *Wings of Destiny* (London, 1943), p. 34.
54 Beaverbrook to Londonderry, 23 January 1926 (HLRO, BBK/C/224).
55 *The Times*, 27 January 1926.

56 *The Times*, 28 January 1926.
57 Castlereagh to Adrian Holman, 1926 (Hyde, *Londonderrys*, p. 169); *Sunderland Echo*, 23 January 1926.
58 Londonderry to Sir Ronald Waterhouse [Prime Minister's Office], 1 March 1926 (CUL, Baldwin 13, f. 144); Waterhouse to Londonderry, 2 March 1926 (CUL, Baldwin 13, f. 145).
59 Londonderry to Baldwin, 13 April 1926 (Middlemas, *Jones*, p. 10).
60 Thomas to Londonderry, 14 April 1926 (PRONI, D3099/2/4/36).
61 Margaret Morris, *The General Strike* (Harmondsworth, 1976), p. 224.
62 Cited in Stewart Mews, 'The Churches', in Morris, *General*, p. 326.
63 Julian Symons, *The General Strike: A Historical Portrait* (London, 1957), pp. 182–6.
64 Londonderry to Baldwin, 15 May 1926 (CUL, Baldwin 137, f. 87).
65 Londonderry to Jones, n.d. [June 1926] (CUL, Baldwin 20, f. 235).
66 *The Times* cites the *Colliery Guardian* (*The Times*, 18 June 1926).
67 Herbert Henson to Londonderry, 23 June 1926 (PRONI, D3099/2/4/39).
68 *The Times*, 30 June 1926.
69 Londonderry to Beaverbrook, 25 May 1926 (HLRO, BBK/C/224); Beaverbrook to Londonderry, 31 May 1926 (HLRO, BBK/C/224).
70 Hester Barron, *The 1926 Miners' Lockout: Meanings of Community in the Durham Coalfield* (Oxford, 2010), pp. 54, 117.
71 *The Times*, 25 June 1926.
72 *The Times*, 18 August 1926.
73 *The Times*, 20 August 1926.
74 Barron, *Miners*, pp. 118–19; *Durham County Advertiser*, 18 June 1926.
75 *House of Lords Debates*, 6 July 1926, vol. 64, cols 827–33.
76 Jones, diary, 26 August 1926, 5 September 1926 (Middlemas, *Jones*, pp. 68, 76–7).
77 Robert Rhodes James, *Churchill: A Study in Failure 1900–1939* (Harmondsworth, 1973), pp. 180–1.
78 Henry Pelling, 'Churchill and the Labour Movement', in *Churchill*, eds Robert Blake and Wm. Roger Louis (Oxford, 1996), p. 121.
79 Londonderry to Churchill, 6 September 1926 (PRONI, D3084/C/C/3/8). See also Londonderry and D.R. Llewellyn to Baldwin, 6 September 1926 (CUL, Baldwin 18, f. 64).
80 Londonderry to Baldwin, 12 September 1926 (CUL, Baldwin 18, ff. 149–54).
81 Baldwin's office to Londonderry, 20 September 1926 (CUL, Baldwin 18, f. 155).
82 *The Times*, 16 October 1926.
83 *The Times*, 26 October 1926. See also *The Times*, 2 November 1926.
84 *The Times*, 24 November 1926.
85 Londonderry to Churchill, 1926 (Hyde, *Londonderrys*, p. 172).
86 Churchill to Londonderry, 3 November 1926 (PRONI, D3099/2/5).
87 *The Times*, 4 December 1926.
88 *The Times*, 17 December 1926.
89 Londonderry also took the opportunity to deny that he owned 'all the old property at the centre of Seaham Harbour . . . he did not own a single house in that area . . . and he would never allow his rights as a ground landlord to stand in the way of the removal of unsatisfactory dwellings' (*The Times*, 20 December 1926).
90 *The Times*, 10 January 1927.
91 *The Times*, 14 January 1926; W. R. Garside, *The Durham Miners, 1919–1960* (London, 1971), p. 234.

92 Paul Davies, *A.J. Cook* (Manchester, 1987), p. 137.
93 Ross McKibbin, *The Ideologies of Class: Social Relations in Britain, 1880–1950* (rep. edn., Oxford, 1991), pp. 289–90.
94 Stuart Ball, *Portrait of a Party: The Conservative Party in Britain 1918–1945* (Oxford, 2013), p. 159.
95 *The Times*, 12 April 1927.
96 N. C. Fleming, *Britannia's Zealots, vol. I: Tradition, Empire and the Forging of the Conservative Right* (London, 2019), p. 147.
97 *The Times*, 13 April 1927.
98 *The Times*, 2 May 1927.
99 *House of Lords Debates*, 30 June 1927, vol. 68, cols 28–9; *House of Lords Debates*, 12 July 1927, vol. 68, cols 339, 375–8; *House of Lords Debates*, 13 July 1927, vol. 68, cols 503–4, 513.
100 *The Times*, 15 August 1927.
101 A. J. Heesom, 'Entrepreneurial Paternalism: The Third Lord Londonderry (1778–1854) and the Coal Trade', *Durham University Journal*, 66 (1973–4): 238–56; A. J. Heesom, 'The Northern Coal Miners and the Opposition to the Coal Mines Act of 1842', *International Review of Social History*, 25, no. 2 (1980): 236–71; A. J. Heesom and Brendan Duffy, 'Coal, Class and Education in the North-East', *Past and Present*, 90 (1981): 136–51; Beynon and Austrin, *Masters*, pp. 25–7, 33, 38.
102 *The Times*, 29 July 1927; Royal Commission on London Squares, Minutes and Papers (PRO, HLG/10/1).
103 David Cannadine, *The Decline and Fall of the British Aristocracy* (rev. edn., London, 1992), p. 581.
104 *Aberdeen Journal*, 27 September 1928; *House of Lords Debates*, 21 February 1929, vol. 72, cols 1022–3.
105 Richard Kelly, 'The Party Conferences', in *Conservative Century: The Conservative Party Since 1900*, eds Anthony Seldon and Stuart Ball (Oxford, 1994), p. 241; Ball, *Portrait*, pp. 224–5; Philip Williamson, *Stanley Baldwin: Conservative Leadership and National Values* (Cambridge, 1999), pp. 219–20.
106 Macmillan to Londonderry, 9 October 1927 (PRONI, D3099/2/13/A/4B).
107 *Aberdeen Journal*, 7 October 1927; R. T. McKenzie, *British Political Parties: The Distribution of Power within the Conservative and Labour Parties* (2nd edn., London, 1967), p. 225.
108 *Manchester Guardian*, 7 October 1927.
109 John W. Hills to Londonderry, 8 October 1927 (PRONI, D3099/2/13/A/3B).
110 Churchill to Londonderry, 22 October 1927 (PRONI, D3099/2/21/A/274).
111 Benyon and Austrin, *Masters*, p. 348.
112 James, *Davidson*, p. 405. See Quentin Outram, 'Class Warriors: The Coalowners', in *Industrial Politics and the 1926 Mining Lockout: The Struggle for Dignity*, eds John McIlroy, Alan Campbell and Keith Gildart (Cardiff, 2004), pp. 107–36; Keith Gildart, 'The Miner's Lockout in 1926 in the Cumberland Coalfield', *Northern History*, 44, no. 2 (2007): 169–92.
113 *The Times*, 30 May 1927.
114 *The Times*, 5 March 1928.
115 *The Times*, 19 June 1928.
116 *The Times*, 14 September 1928; *The Times*, 15 September 1928.
117 G. W. McDonald and Howard F. Gospel, 'The Mond-Turner Talks 1927–1933: A Study in Industrial Co-operation', *Historical Journal*, 16, no. 4 (1973): 818–19.

118 *The Times*, 15 August 1927.
119 *The Times*, 23 December 1927.
120 *The Times*, 30 December 1927.
121 McDonald and Gospel, 'Mond-Turner', p. 821.
122 McDonald and Gospel, 'Mond-Turner', pp. 819–20.
123 *The Times*, 2 March 1928.
124 *The Times*, 14 May 1928.
125 *The Times*, 18 June 1928.
126 *The Times*, 19 June 1928.
127 *The Times*, 5 July 1928.
128 *The Times*, 19 October 1928.
129 *Aberdeen Journal*, 20 October 1928.
130 *The Times*, 26 October 1928.
131 See *The Times*, 26 January 1929.
132 *The Times*, 27 November 1928.
133 *The Times*, 28 November 1928.
134 *The Times*, 8 March 1929.
135 Beynon and Austrin, *Masters*, p. 204.
136 Lewis Mates, '"We Want Real Live Wires, not Gas Pipes": Communism in the Inter-war Durham Coalfield', *Twentieth Century Communism*, 23 (2022): 77.
137 Londonderry to Baldwin, 5 March 1929 (CUL, Baldwin 85, ff. 144–6).
138 Londonderry to Baldwin, 1 February 1929 (H. Montgomery Hyde, *Baldwin: The Unexpected Prime Minister* (London, 1973), p. 297). Londonderry accused the vicar of Dawdon of having socialist sympathies (Rev. James Duncan to Londonderry, 29 May 1929 (D3099/2/4/75)). See Barron, *Miners*, p. 170.
139 *The Times*, 3 January 1929.
140 *House of Lords Debates*, 25 March 1929, vol. 73, col. 834.
141 *The Times*, 8 May 1929; Mates, 'Communism', pp. 72–7.
142 Londonderry to MacDonald, 22 July 1929 (JRUL, RMD/1/14/69).
143 *The Times*, 22 October 1929.
144 *The Times*, 5 November 1929. See also *The Times*, 11 December 1929.
145 Rodney Lowe, 'The Government and Industrial Relations, 1919–39', in *A History of British Industrial Relations, vol. 2: 1914–1939*, ed. Chris Wrigley (Brighton, 1987), pp. 185–210.
146 Simons, 'British', p. 12.
147 David Marquand, *Ramsay MacDonald* (London, 1977), pp. 525–31.
148 *The Times*, 2 December 1929.
149 *The Times*, 6 January 1930.
150 Barry Supple, *The History of the British Coal Industry: vol. 4: 1913–1946: The Political Economy of Decline* (Oxford, 1987), p. 417.
151 *The Times*, 28 March 1930.
152 Simons, 'British', p. 11.
153 *The Times*, 28 March 1930.
154 Salisbury to Londonderry, 19 March 1930 (PRONI, D3099/2/4/77).
155 *House of Lords Debates*, 29 April 1930, vol. 77, cols 180–92. See *The Times*, 28 April 1930.
156 *House of Lords Debates*, 13 May 1930, vol. 77, cols 487–588; *House of Lords Debates*, 14 May 1930, vol. 77, cols 593–662; *House of Lords Debates*, 24 June 1930, vol. 78, cols 93–112.

157 See Trevor Boyns, 'Strategic Responses to Foreign Competition: The British Coal Industry and the 1930 Coal Mines Act', *Business History*, 32, no. 3 (1990): 133–45.
158 *The Times*, 25 October 1930.
159 Mates, 'Communism', p. 77.
160 *The Times*, 20 February 1930.
161 *The Times*, 1 August 1930.
162 Londonderry to MacDonald, 19 March 1930 (JRUL, RMD/1/5/14). See Barron, *Miners*, p. 98.
163 *The Times*, 5 January 1931. See also Stuart Ball (ed.), *Conservative Politics in National and Imperial Crisis: Letters from Britain to the Viceroy of India 1926–31* (Aldershot, 2014), pp. 249–50.
164 *The Times*, 8 January 1931.
165 Lynn, 'Seaham', p. 20.
166 *The Times*, 20 October 1931.
167 MacDonald to Londonderry, 23 October 1931 (PRONI, D3099/2/12/2).
168 Cannadine, *Decline*, p. 352.
169 Headlam, diary 13 January 1927 (Ball, *Headlam*, p. 110).
170 Urquhart, *Ladies*, p. 150.
171 Channon, diary, 8 June 1935 (Robert Rhodes James (ed.), *'Chips': The Diaries of Sir Henry Channon* (London, 1967), p. 35).
172 *The Times*, 25 May 1937.
173 Robert Vansittart, *The Mist Procession: The Autobiography of Lord Vansittart* (London, 1958), p. 452.
174 Viscount Castlereagh, 'Memorandum', August 1936, in *Baldwin Papers: A Conservative Statesman, 1908–1947*, eds Philip Williamson and Edward Baldwin (Cambridge, 2005), p. 370.
175 Diane Urquhart, 'Peeresses, Patronage and Power: The Politics of Ladies Frances Anne, Theresa and Edith Londonderry, 1800–1959', in *Irish Women's History*, eds Alan Hayes and Diane Urquhart (Dublin, 2004), p. 55.
176 Hyde, *Londonderrys*, p. 258. Annabel Goldsmith recalls that Mount Stewart in her childhood, the 1930s–40s, had 'several dozen servants, the residential staff . . . outnumbered the family by five to one' (Annabel Goldsmith, *Annabel, An Unconventional Life: The Memoirs of Lady Annabel Goldsmith* (London, 2004), p. 11).
177 *The Times*, 18 March 1927.
178 Theresa, Lady Londonderry, general notes, 11 January 1919 (PRONI, D3084/C/C/B/1/15).
179 Ross McKibbin, *Class and Cultures: England, 1918–1951* (Oxford, 1998), p. 24; Marchioness of Londonderry, *Retrospect* (London, 1938), p. 251.
180 Londonderry, *Retrospect*, pp. 236–50.
181 Urquhart, *Ladies*, pp. 141–2.
182 Bernays, diary, 8 February 1934 (Nick Smart (ed.), *The Diaries and Letters of Robert Bernays, 1932–1939: An Insider's Account of the House of Commons* (Lampeter, 1996), p. 119); Hugh Hunt, *Sean O'Casey* (rep. edn, Dublin, 1998), pp. 5, 57, 63, 85, 121; R. F. Foster, *W.B. Yeats: A Life, vol. 2: The Arch-Poet 1915–1939* (Oxford, 2003), pp. 330–2, 314, 336.
183 MacDonald to Londonderry, 16 February 1926 (JRUL, RHD/1/14/68).
184 Malcolm Muggeridge, *The Thirties, 1930–1940 in Great Britain* (London, 1940), p. 49; Marquand, *MacDonald*, pp. 687–8; R. Bassett, *Nineteen Thirty-One: Political*

Crisis (London, 1958), p. 320; Hugh Dalton, diary, 9 July 1930 (Ben Pimlott (ed.), *The Political Diary of Hugh Dalton: 1918–40, 1945–60* (London, 1986) pp. 116–17); Beatrice Webb, diary, 14 February 1928, 5 September 1930 (Margaret Cole (ed.), *Beatrice Webb's Diaries 1924–1932* (London, 1956), pp. 161–2, 249). See also Patrick Balfour, *Society Racket: A Critical Survey of Modern Social Life* (London, 1933), p. 125.

185 Roy Boulting (dir.), *Fame is the Spur* (1947); David Giles (dir.), *Fame is the Spur* (1982).

186 Webb to Women's Section of Seaham Labour Party, 14 October 1931 (Norman MacKenzie (ed.), *The Letters of Sidney and Beatrice Webb: vol. 3: Pilgrimage, 1912–1947* (Cambridge, 1978), p. 369). See Austen Morgan, *J. Ramsay MacDonald* (Manchester, 1987), p. 225.

187 Headlam, diary, 24 August 1931 (Ball, *Headlam*, p. 214).

188 James, *Davidson*, p. 405; Bernays, diary, 22 November 1932 (Smart, *Diaries*, p. 18).

189 Urquhart, *Ladies*, p. 151.

190 Martin Green, *Children of the Sun: A Narrative of 'Decadence' in England after 1918* (rev. edn., London, 1977), pp. 241–305.

191 Headlam, diary, 17 December 1930 (Ball, *Headlam*, p. 183).

192 Headlam, diary, 20 November 1933 (Ball, *Headlam*, p. 284).

193 Londonderry to Baldwin, 19 May 1936 (PRONI, D3099/2/17).

194 Londonderry to Baldwin, 11 October 1930 (CUL, Baldwin 165, f. 209).

195 Patrick Gower to Baldwin (memorandum), 29 November 1930 (CUL, Baldwin 165, 170, ff. 136–137); J.C.C. Davidson to Londonderry, 17 June 1931 (HLRO, DAV/191); Londonderry to Davidson, 19 June 1931 (HLRO, DAV/191).

196 *Probation*, 2, no. 1 (1935): 5–7.

197 Londonderry, *Retrospect*, p. 253.

198 Evelyn Waugh, *Vile Bodies* (rep. edn., London, 2000), pp. 106–7.

199 Beaverbrook to Londonderry, 3 January 1932 (HLRO, BBK/C/224); Londonderry to Beaverbrook, 5 January 1932 (HLRO, BBK/C/224); Beaverbrook to Londonderry, 12 January 1932 (HLRO, BBK/C/224).

200 A. J. P. Taylor, *Beaverbrook* (London, 1972), p. 339.

201 Beaverbrook to Londonderry, 12 January 1932 (HLRO, BBK/C/224).

202 Lady Londonderry to Beaverbrook, 11 February 1932 (HLRO, BBK/C/224); Lady Londonderry to Beaverbrook, 22 February 1932 (HLRO, BBK/C/224). Lord Londonderry commented to Baldwin that having 'the Beaver' against them would do the government more favours than if he were with them (Londonderry to Baldwin, 22 February 1932 (CUL, Baldwin 118, ff. 164–9)); Urquhart, *Ladies*, pp. 175–6.

203 *The Times*, 20 November 1934.

204 Headlam, diary, 20 November 1933 (Ball, *Headlam*, pp. 284–5).

205 *The Times*, 5 May 1930.

206 *The Times*, 17 November 1930; James Barfoot, *Plâs Machynlleth: A Historical Guide* (Norwich, 1997), pp. 1–4.

207 Kenneth O. Morgan, *Rebirth of a Nation: Wales 1880–1980* (New York, 1981), pp. 254–6.

208 *The Times*, 26 February 1937.

209 Headlam, diary, 17 October 1928 (Ball, *Headlam*, p. 155).

210 Londonderry, *Wings*, p. 35; *The Times*, 19 October 1928.

211 Castlereagh, 'Memorandum' (Baldwin and Williamson, *Baldwin Papers*, p. 369).

212 Londonderry to Craig, 17 October 1928 (PRONI, T/3775/23/2).

213 *The Times*, 3 March 1926; Churchill to Londonderry, 6 March 1928 (PRONI, D3099/2/5/17).
214 Churchill to Londonderry, 14 August 1927 (PRONI, D3084/C/C/3/9A–B).
215 Churchill to Londonderry, 24 August 1927 (D3099/2/5/20).
216 Lord Stamfordham to Londonderry, 20 October 1928 (PRONI, D3099/2/4). According to Londonderry's youngest daughter, Lady Mairi, he carried the Cap of Maintenance instead of the Marquess of Winchester, whose family had 'always carried it', owing to Winchester's connection to a recent financial scandal. See Lady Mairi Bury to the author, 6 July 2005.
217 Londonderry's ministry oversaw repairs to Westminster Palace (Londonderry to Baldwin, 28 January 1929 (CUL, Baldwin 59, ff. 333–6)).
218 Londonderry to Baldwin, 13 February 1929 (CUL, 64, f. 103).
219 Londonderry, *Wings*, p. 36; A. Hardinge [Buckingham Palace] to Sir Edward Bridges [Cabinet Office], 11 June 1942 (PRO, CAB/21/2677).
220 For Cecil's bill, see *House of Lords Debates*, 12 December 1928, vol. 72, cols 562–571; Wilfred Ashley to Londonderry, 6 December 1928 (PRONI, D3099/2/4/45); Londonderry to Ashley, 7 December 1928 (PRONI, D3099/2/4/46); Londonderry to Ashley, 13 December 1928 (PRONI, D3099/2/4/49); Londonderry to Cecil, 7 January 1929 (PRONI, D3099/2/4/57); Cecil to Londonderry, 9 January 1929 (PRONI, D3099/2/4/60); *House of Lords Debates*, 29 January 1929, vol. 72, cols 801–803; Ashley to Londonderry, 20 April 1929 (PRONI, D3099/2/4/71); Cecil to Londonderry, 23 April 1929 (PRONI, D3099/2/4/72). Lady Londonderry was one of the first motorists to have seat belts fitted in her car (Hyde, *Londonderrys*, p. 183).
221 *The Times*, 10 September 1920; Sean O'Connell, 'Motoring and Modernity', in *Twentieth-Century Britain: Economic, Cultural and Social Change*, eds Francesca Carnevali and Julie-Marie Strange (2nd edn., London, 2007), pp. 111–26.
222 *The Times*, 4 January 1929.
223 *House of Lords Debates*, 18 February 1931, vol. 79, cols 1112–21.
224 Stuart Ball, *The Conservative Party and British Politics, 1902–1951* (London, 1995), p. 82.
225 Neil Riddell, *Labour in Crisis: The Second Labour Government, 1929–1931* (Manchester, 1999), pp. 2–3.
226 Amery, diary, 3 March 1930 (John Barnes and David Nicholson (eds), *The Empire at Bay: The Leo Amery Diaries 1929–1945* (London, 1988), p. 65).
227 Stuart Ball, *Baldwin and the Conservative Party: The Crisis of 1929–1931* (London, 1988); N. C. Fleming, 'Lancashire Conservatives, Tariff Reform, and Indian Responsible Government', *Contemporary British History*, 30, no. 2 (2016): 151–76.
228 *The Times*, 25 October 1923.
229 Londonderry to Baldwin, 18 November 1929 (CUL, Baldwin 164, f. 161); Londonderry to Beaverbrook, 16 December 1929 (HLRO, BBK/C/224); Beaverbrook to Londonderry, 19 December 1929 (HLRO, BBK/C/224).
230 *The Times*, 15 February 1930.
231 Amery, diary, 3 March 1930 (Barnes and Nicholson, *Empire at Bay*, p. 65).
232 *The Times*, 17 July 1930.
233 Londonderry to Beaverbrook, 19 July 1930 (HLRO, BBK/C/224).
234 *The Times*, 6 August 1930.
235 Londonderry to Baldwin, 11 October 1930 (CUL, Baldwin 165, f. 209).
236 *The Times*, 11 November 1930.
237 *House of Lords Debates*, 29 February 1932, vol. 83, cols 667–75; Buchan to Londonderry, 3 March 1932 (PRONI, D3099/2/16/4).

238 *The Times*, 6 December 1923.
239 *The Times*, 1 March 1929.
240 Londonderry to Amery, 6 June 1936 (DCRO, D/Lo/C/237 (3)).
241 Londonderry to Baldwin, 31 October 1930 (CUL, Baldwin 165, f. 214).
242 *The Times*, 24 November 1930.
243 Londonderry to Beaverbrook, 5 March 1931 (HLRO, BBK/C/224); Beaverbrook to Londonderry, 9 March 1931 (HLRO, BBK/C/224).
244 *The Times*, 14 May 1931.
245 Londonderry sat on the boards of both Sun Life Insurance Office and Sun Life Assurance Society (*The Times*, 10 July 1929; *The Times*, 26 July 1929). He received a DCL at Durham (*The Times*, 16 December 1929), was voted chancellor in 1930 and installed in 1931 (*The Times*, 21 November 1930; *The Times*, 21 May 1931).
246 Lord Stamfordham to Londonderry, 21 January 1931 (PRONI, D3099/2/4/80).
247 Londonderry to George V, January 1931 (Hyde, *Londonderrys*, pp. 186–7); George V to Londonderry, 25 January 1931 (PRONI, D3099/2/4/82).
248 Urquhart, *Ladies*, pp. 169–70.
249 *The Times*, 26 August 1931.
250 Londonderry to Baldwin, 25 August 1931 (CUL, Baldwin 44, f. 2).
251 *House of Lords Debates*, 8 September 1931, vol. 82, cols 3–4, 7 October 1931, cols 288–93; *The Times*, 19 September 1931; *The Times*, 9 October 1931; *The Times*, 20 October 1931; *The Times*, 21 October 1931.
252 *The Times*, 6 November 1931.
253 Londonderry, *Wings*, p. 44. See MacDonald to Londonderry, 28 February 1932 (PRONI, D3099/2/12/9); Donald Southgate, 'Baldwin 1923–1932', in *The Conservative Leadership 1832–1932*, ed. Donald Southgate (London, 1974), p. 224.
254 *House of Lords Debates*, 20 March 1924, vol. 56, cols 932–7.
255 Hoare to Londonderry, 4 April 1930 (PRONI, D3099/2/4/78).

Chapter 6

1 Winston S. Churchill, *The Second World War: vol. 1: The Gathering Storm* (rep. edn., London, 1949), p. 113.
2 *House of Lords Debates*, 14 March 1934, vol. 91, cols 191–2. For Londonderry's paternalistic treatment of staff at Air Ministry, see, for example, Christopher Bullock to Londonderry, 15 June 1935 (PRO, AIR/2/223); Sir John Salmond to Londonderry, 12 July 193[?] (PRONI, D3099/2/16/68); Air Ministry Employees to Londonderry, March 1932 (PRO, AIR/20/6259); Londonderry to Ramsay MacDonald, 3 May 1932 (PRO, PREM/1/114).
3 Peter Gray, *The Leadership, Direction and Legitimacy of the RAF Bomber Offensive from Inception to 1945* (New York, 2012), pp. 141–21.
4 *The Times*, 10 November 1931; Correspondence file of congratulations to Londonderry, 5–8 November 1931 (PRONI, D3099/2/9/16–82).
5 *House of Lords Debates*, 17 November 1931, vol. 83, cols 61–4; David E. Omissi, *Air Power and Colonial Control: The Royal Air Force, 1919–1939* (Manchester, 1990), p. 95.
6 *House of Lords Debates*, 14 June 1932, vol. 84, cols 842–8.
7 *House of Lords Debates*, 1 November 1932, vol. 85, cols 961–6; *House of Lords Debates*, 20 July 1933, vol. 88, cols 993–8.

8 *House of Lords Debates*, 14 December 1932, vol. 86, col. 413.

9 *House of Lords Debates*, 19 July 1934, vol. 93, cols 856–9; *House of Lords Debates*, 4 April 1935, vol. 96, cols 600–3. Later, in 1938, he objected to a proposal that would have allowed government ministers to address both houses of parliament, despite having exercised this right in the parliament of Northern Ireland (*House of Lords Debates*, 6 July 1938, vol. 110, cols 589–92, 605).

10 *The Times*, 8 November 1933. Londonderry defended the existence of a separate transport ministry (*House of Lords Debates*, 15 February 1933, vol. 86, cols 742–51). Londonderry resigned his seat on the board of the London and North Eastern Railway Company (Extract from minutes of London and North Eastern Railway Company, 28 January 1932 (PRO, RAIL/390/875); *The Times*, 30 January 1932).

11 *The Times*, 2 March 1933. During the Road and Rail Traffic bill debates, Viscount Cecil attempted an amendment to compel vehicles to display an external speedometer; Londonderry dismissed it as impractical (*The Times*, 16 November 1933). He gave the same reason when asked why parachutes were not fitted on all commercial aeroplanes, arguing that they were of little use when taking off or in most accidents (*House of Lords Debates*, 25 July 1933, vol. 88, cols 1095–8). Londonderry had a flying accident the following year (*The Times*, 8 June, 9 June 1934).

12 Headlam, diary, 19 June 1934 (Stuart Ball (ed.), *Parliament and Politics in the Age of Baldwin and MacDonald: The Headlam Diaries, 1923–1935* (London, 1992), p. 306).

13 *The Times*, 20 April 1934.

14 *House of Lords Debates*, 21 March 1935, vol. 96, col. 301.

15 *House of Lords Debates*, 30 May 1934, vol. 92, col. 536.

16 Marie Coleman, *The Irish Sweep: A History of the Irish Hospitals Sweepstake, 1930–87* (Dublin, 2009), pp. 95, 100.

17 Stuart Ball, *The Conservative Party and British Politics, 1902–1951* (London, 1995), p. 89.

18 *The Times*, 11 February 1933.

19 Viscount Snowden, *An Autobiography, vol. 2: 1919–1934* (London, 1934), p. 1016. The policy caused the cabinet resignations of Labour's Snowden and the Liberal, Herbert Samuel. Londonderry regretted the former but thought the latter to MacDonald's advantage (Londonderry to MacDonald, 28 September 1932 (JRUL, RHD/1/13)).

20 *The Times*, 3 January 1938.

21 *The Times*, 21 April 1934; Neville Chamberlain to Londonderry, 21 March 1934 (PRONI, D3099/2/4/90).

22 *The Times*, 9 November 1934.

23 Viscount Swinton, *I Remember* (London, 1948), p. 105. See *The Times*, 13 April 1933; *The Times*, 13 April 1934; *The Times*, 25 October 1934.

24 *The Times*, 28 September 1933. See also *The Times*, 29 September 1933; *The Times*, 9 December 1933.

25 *The Times*, 5 October 1933; *The Times*, 9 December 1933; *The Times*, 9 January 1935.

26 *House of Lords Debates*, 2 April 1935 vol. 96, cols 463–4.

27 Londonderry's statement on British commercial transport, 8 February 1934 (PRO, AIR/5/1427); Londonderry to Sir Robert Horne, 18 February 1935 (PRO, RAIL/257/55); Horne to Londonderry, 26 February 1935 (PRO, RAIL/257/55). See also *The Times*, 14 May 1935.

28 *The Times*, 13 December 1933.

29 *The Times*, 1 September 1934.
30 *The Times*, 4 November 1932.
31 *The Times*, 21 July 1934; Londonderry to David Margesson, 27 September 1934 (CUL, Baldwin 2, f. 362); *House of Lords Debates*, 21 November 1934, vol. 95, cols 59–63.
32 See Peter Ewer, 'A Gentlemen's Club in the Clouds: Reassessing the Empire Air Mail Scheme, 1933–1939', *Journal of Transport History*, 28, no. 1 (2007): 75–92.
33 Londonderry to C. W. Fisher, 8 December 1934 (Baldwin, 169, ff. 194–5); Londonderry to Baldwin, 10 December 1934 (Baldwin 169, f. 196); *The Times*, 19 December 1934. It appears from Leo Amery's diary that Bullock had harboured misgivings about Londonderry's competence as far back as 1932 (Amery, diary, 24 October 1932, in *The Empire at Bay: The Leo Amery Diaries 1929–1945*, eds John Barnes and David Nicholson (London, 1988), p. 284). Bullock was dismissed from the civil service in 1936 for misconduct, an outcome, he felt, of personal animosity against him (G. C. Peden, *British Rearmament and the Treasury, 1932–1939* (Edinburgh, 1979), p. 53).
34 See Londonderry to Baldwin, 19 May 1936 (Baldwin 171, ff. 166–7).
35 N. C. Fleming, 'Cabinet Government, British Imperial Security, and the World Disarmament Conference, 1932–1934', *War in History*, 18, no. 1 (2011): 62–84.
36 *The Times*, 13 November 1931.
37 *House of Commons Debates*, 12 November 1931, vol. 259, cols 281–2.
38 Uri Bialer, *The Shadow of the Bomber: The Fear of Air Attack and British Policies, 1932–1939* (London, 1980), pp. 42–3.
39 Paul Kennedy, *The Realities Behind Diplomacy: Background Influences on British External Policy, 1865–1980* (London, 1981), p. 21.
40 David Reynolds, *Britannia Overruled: British Policy and World Power in the 20th Century* (2nd edn., London, 2000), pp. 1, 16, 32; David French, *Deterrence, Coercion and Appeasement: British Grand Strategy, 1919–1940* (Oxford, 2022), p. 10.
41 French, *Deterrence*, p. 259.
42 Cabinet Conclusions, 9 December 1931 (PRO, CAB 23/72).
43 French, *Deterrence*, pp. 212–20, 381.
44 C. G. Burge (ed.), *The Air Annual of the British Empire 1933–34* (London, 1933), p. xxxv. For wider culture of racism in interwar RAF, see Barry Renfrew, *Wings of Empire: The Forgotten Wars of the Royal Air Force, 1919–1939* (Stroud, 2015), pp. 30, 67, 171–6.
45 Thomas Hippler, *Governing from the Skies: A Global History of Aerial Bombing* (London, 2017), pp. 56–100.
46 David Edgerton, *England and the Aeroplane: Militarism, Modernity and Machines* (London, 2013), pp. 66–79.
47 Charles Townshend, *Britain's Civil Wars: Counterinsurgency in the Twentieth Century* (London, 1986), pp. 93–9; Omissi, *Air*, pp. 51–2.
48 Scot Robertson, *The Development of RAF Strategic Bombing Doctrine, 1919–1939* (London, 1995), p. 31; Anthony Clayton, 'Imperial Defence and Security, 1900–1968', in *The Oxford History of the British Empire, vol. 4: The Twentieth Century*, eds Judith M. Brown and Wm. Roger Louis (Oxford, 1999), p. 287.
49 Brian Smith, *A History of Military Morals: Killing the Innocent* (Leiden, 2022), pp. 321–78; see Brett Holman, *The Next War in the Air: Britain's Fear of the Bomber, 1908–1941* (Aldershot, 2014).
50 Omissi, *Air*, p. 59.

51 J. A. Cross, *Lord Swinton* (Oxford, 1982), p. 48.
52 Londonderry to MacDonald, 19 July 1932 (PRONI, D3099/2/12/16).
53 See H. Montgomery Hyde, *British Air Policy between the Wars, 1918–1939* (London, 1976); Malcolm Smith, *British Air Strategy between the Wars* (Oxford, 1984).
54 Zara Steiner, *The Lights that Failed: European International History, 1919–1933* (Oxford, 2005), p. 565; Ian Clarke, *The Hierarchy of States: Reform and Resistance in the International Order* (Cambridge, 1989), p. 157; Andrew Webster, *Strange Allies: Britain, France and the Dilemmas of Disarmament and Security, 1929–1933* (London, 2019).
55 R. B. McCallum, *Public Opinion and the Last Peace* (London, 1944), pp. 140, 163.
56 Maurice Hankey, diary, 13 November 1932, in *Hankey: Man of Secrets, vol. 3: 1931–1963*, ed. Stephen Roskill (London, 1974), p. 63.
57 *The Times*, 3 December 1931; *The Times*, 11 January 1932.
58 Robertson, *Development*, p. 41; *House of Lords Debates*, 14 March 1934, vol. 91, col. 190. Londonderry complained to MacDonald about the schoolboy style of wording in official Foreign Office documents, the prime minister agreed (Londonderry to MacDonald, 11 August 1933 (PRO, PRO/30/69/706); MacDonald to Londonderry, 18 August 1933 (PRO, PRO/30/69/706)). For 'frat-house atmosphere' of Foreign Office, see Paul W. Doerr, *British Foreign Policy 1919–1939: 'Hope for the Best, Prepare for the Worst'* (Manchester, 1998), p. 134. Simon informed Londonderry that it 'grieved' him to differ with Londonderry on policy (Simon to Londonderry, n.d. (PRONI, D3099/2/16/61)).
59 *The Times*, 6 February 1932; *The Times*, 25 February 1932.
60 Sassoon to Londonderry, 20 January 1932 (PRONI, D3099/2/16/1).
61 David Marquand, *Ramsay MacDonald* (London, 1977), p. 693; *The Times*, 3 March 1932. The general committee had one member from each country (*The Times*, 9 March 1932).
62 Londonderry to Baldwin, 22 February 1932 (CUL, Baldwin 118, ff. 164–9).
63 MacDonald to Londonderry, 28 February 1932 (PRONI, D3099/2/12/9); Londonderry to Baldwin, 10 March 1932 (CUL, Baldwin 118, f. 170).
64 Londonderry to Baldwin, 22 February 1932 (CUL, Baldwin 118, ff. 164–9); *The Times*, 20 February 1932.
65 *Daily Express*, 17 February 1932.
66 R. Bassett, *Democracy and Foreign Policy, a Case History: The Sino-Japanese Dispute, 1931–33* (London, 1952), pp. 103–4.
67 Londonderry to Baldwin, 10 March 1932 (CUL, Baldwin 118, f. 170).
68 He added that he did not want to write too much in a letter 'as one is never sure under whose eyes they come' (MacDonald to Londonderry, 13 March 1932 (PRONI, D3099/2/12/10)).
69 Bassett, *Sino-Japanese*, p. 115.
70 Maurice Hankey to Londonderry, 20 April 1932 (PRONI, D3099/2/16/10).
71 *The Times*, 4 March 1932.
72 Sassoon to Londonderry, 20 January 1932 (PRONI, D3099/2/16/1); *The Times*, 9 March 1932.
73 Hyde, *Air*, p. 279; Robert Paul Shay, *British Rearmament in the Thirties: Politics and Profits* (Princeton, 1977), p. 35.
74 Hyde, *Air*, pp. 279–80.
75 Keith Middlemas and John Barnes, *Baldwin: A Biography* (London, 1969), pp. 731–2.

76 The lecture was announced weeks in advance (*The Times*, 19 April 1932); Londonderry, notes for a public lecture, 4 May 1932 (PRONI, D3099/2/16/22).
77 Hyde, *Air*, p. 280.
78 Simon to Londonderry, 1 June 1932 (PRONI, D3099/2/16/25).
79 Salmond to Londonderry, 8 June 1932 (PRONI, D3099/2/16/26).
80 Londonderry to MacDonald, 9 June 1932 (PRONI, D3099/2/12/13).
81 Roskill, *Hankey*, p. 42.
82 Londonderry to MacDonald, 10 June 1932 (PRONI, D3099/2/12/14); MacDonald to Londonderry, 29 June 1932 (PRONI, D3099/2/12/15). See *The Times*, 7 June 1932; *The Times*, 11 June 1932.
83 Hyde, *Air*, pp. 280–1; Londonderry to Sir Clive Wigram [Buckingham Palace], 21 July 1932 (PRONI, D3099/2/16/29A).
84 Londonderry, notes for a public lecture, 4 May 1932 (PRONI, D3099/2/16/22); Londonderry to Mrs Lees [Tonbridge Women's Adult School], 5 May 1932 (PRONI, D3099/2/16/24).
85 *The Times*, 7 July 1932.
86 Salmond to Londonderry, 12 July [1932] (PRONI, D3099/2/16/68).
87 Londonderry to MacDonald, 19 July 1932 (PRONI, D3099/2/12/16).
88 Londonderry to MacDonald, 28 July 1932 (JRUL, RMD1/14/73).
89 Londonderry to Lady Londonderry, 17 July 1932 (Marquess of Londonderry, *Ourselves and Germany* (London, 1938), pp. 47–8); MacDonald to Londonderry, 23 July 1932 (PRONI, D3099/2/12/17).
90 Marquand, *MacDonald*, p. 717; Londonderry to Hankey, 24 July 1932 (PRONI, D3099/2/16/31).
91 MacDonald to Londonderry, 28 July 1932 (PRONI, D3099/2/12/18).
92 Londonderry to MacDonald, 19 July 1932 (PRONI, D3099/2/12/16); Londonderry to Hankey, 24 July 1932 (PRONI, D3099/2/16/31); Alex Cadogan to Londonderry, 25 November 1933 (PRONI, D3099/2/16/41).
93 Londonderry to Clive Wigram, 21 July 1932 (PRONI, D3099/2/16/29A).
94 Londonderry, notes for a public lecture, 4 May 1932 (PRONI, D3099/2/16/22).
95 *The Times*, 19 October 1932. See also *The Times*, 28 October 1933; *Sunderland Echo*, 29 April 1941.
96 Hans J. Morgenthau, *Politics among Nations: The Struggle for Power and Peace* (New York, 1948), p. 398; Salvador de Madariaga, *Morning without Noon: Memoirs* (Farnborough, 1974), p. 48; Carolyn Kitching, *Britain and the Problem of International Disarmament, 1919–34* (London, 1999), pp. 8–11.
97 Simon to Londonderry, 7 November [1932] (PRONI, D3099/2/16/66).
98 Hyde, *Air*, p. 284.
99 Salmond to Londonderry, 6 November 1932 (PRONI, D3099/2/16/32); Bullock to Londonderry, 7 November 1932 (PRONI, D3099/2/16/33); MacDonald to Londonderry, 9 November 1932 (PRONI, D3099/2/12/20).
100 *House of Commons Debates*, 10 November 1932, vol. 270, cols 630–8.
101 Salmond to Londonderry, 10 November [1932] (PRONI, D3099/2/16/67).
102 Hyde, *Air*, pp. 286–7.
103 *The Times*, 3 February 1933.
104 J. F. Coakley, *The Church of the East and the Church of England: A History of the Archbishop of Canterbury's Assyrian Mission* (Oxford, 1992), pp. 354–7.
105 Londonderry to MacDonald, 16 August 1933 (PRO, PRO/30/69/706).
106 MacDonald to Londonderry, 18 August 1933 (PRO, PRO/30/69/706).

107 Charles Tripp, *A History of Iraq* (3rd edn., Cambridge 2007), pp. 30–78.
108 *The Times*, 31 January 1933; *The Times*, 3 February 1933.
109 Marquess of Londonderry, *Wings of Destiny* (London, 1943), p. 68; *The Times*, 3 February 1933.
110 Eden, diary, 9 February 1933 (Robert Rhodes James, *Anthony Eden* (London, 1996), p. 124).
111 *The Times*, 21 February 1933.
112 *The Times*, 28 February 1935.
113 *The Times*, 9 March 1933.
114 Chris Cooper, 'Conservatism, Imperialism and Appeasement: The Political Career of Douglas Hogg, First Viscount Hailsham 1922–38' (PhD thesis, University of Liverpool, 2012), pp. 248–9.
115 Londonderry to Hailsham, 8 March 1933 (PRONI, D3099/2/16/40).
116 Londonderry to Churchill, 14 March 1933 (PRONI, D3084/C/C/3/10A–B).
117 Londonderry, *Wings*, p. 90.
118 Alexander Cadogan, diary, 13 March 1933 (Churchill Archives Centre, Cambridge, Cadogan Papers ACAD 1/1).
119 *The Times*, 17 May 1933.
120 Robert Rhodes James, *Churchill: A Study in Failure, 1900–1939* (Harmondsworth, 1973), pp. 286–7.
121 Londonderry to Baldwin, 29 May 1933 (CUL, Baldwin 121, ff. 35–7).
122 *The Times*, 31 May 1933; *The Times*, 1 June 1933.
123 B. H. Liddell Hart, *Memoirs, vol. 1* (London, 1965), p. 206.
124 *The Times*, 8 June 1933. Londonderry did briefly return to London, probably to keep in touch with cabinet developments (*The Times*, 5 June 1933).
125 *The Times*, 9 June 1933; *The Times*, 10 June 1933; Londonderry, *Wings*, pp. 78–9.
126 David Carlton, *Anthony Eden: A Biography* (London, 1981), p. 42.
127 *The Times*, 23 June 1933.
128 Chamberlain to Hilda Chamberlain, 5 March 1932 (Robert C. Self (ed.), *The Austen Chamberlain Diary Letters: The Correspondence of Sir Austen Chamberlain with His Sisters Hilda and Ida, 1916–1937* (Cambridge, 1995), pp. 408–9).
129 Londonderry to Chamberlain, 24 June 1933 (PRONI, D3099/2/16/44).
130 Chamberlain to Londonderry, 26 June 1933 (PRONI, D3099/2/16/45).
131 *House of Commons Debates*, 5 July 1933, vol. 280, col. 371.
132 Philip Sassoon, 'Air Power in the Middle East', *Journal of the Royal Central Asian Society*, 20, no. 3 (1933): 394–405.
133 *The Times*, 25 July 1933.
134 Londonderry to MacDonald, 20 August 1933 (PRO, PRO/30/69/706). See James S. Corum, 'The RAF in Imperial Defence, 1919–1956', in *Imperial Defence: The Old World Order, 1865–1956*, ed. Greg Kennedy (London, 2008), pp. 152–75.
135 *The Times*, 10 June 1933; *The Times*, 11 July 1933.
136 *The Times*, 4 November 1932; *The Times*, 3 August 1933; *The Times*, 17 May 1933; *The Times*, 2 August 1933; *The Times*, 4 October 1933; *The Times*, 8 June 1934; *The Times*, 18 May 1934; *The Times*, 5 June 1934. He was also made an Honorary Colonel of the Artists Rifles (*The Times*, 24 April 1934).
137 *The Times*, 19 May 1934.
138 *The Times*, 22 June 1934.
139 *The Times*, 5 April 1932; *The Times*, 29 June 1932.
140 *The Times*, 23 June 1933.

141 *The Times*, 18 July 1933.
142 *The Times*, 3 July 1933. See Peter Adey, 'Airports and Air-Mindedness: Spacing, Timing and Using the Liverpool Airport, 1929–1939', *Social & Cultural Geography*, 7, no. 3 (2006): 343–63.
143 *The Times*, 3 July 1933; *The Times*, 4 July 1933; *The Times*, 17 July 1933.
144 Londonderry to editor of *The Times*, 8 July 1933 (PRONI, D3099/2/16/46).
145 *The Times*, 20 July 1933.
146 Londonderry to Baldwin, 20 November 1933 (CUL, Baldwin 55, f. 225).
147 *The Times*, 28 October 1933.
148 Martin Ceadel, *Pacifism in Britain 1914–1945: The Defining of a Faith* (Oxford, 1980), p. 134.
149 *The Times*, 28 October 1933.
150 *The Times*, 28 October 1933.
151 *The Times*, 6 November 1933.
152 *House of Lords Debates*, 29 November 1933, vol. 90, cols 178–86.
153 *House of Lords Debates*, 7 December 1933, vol. 90, cols 370–9.
154 *The Times*, 8 November 1933; Diane Urquhart, *The Ladies of Londonderry: Women and Political Patronage* (London, 2007), p. 185.
155 Hailsham to Londonderry, 28 December 1933 (PRONI, D3099/2/4/89).
156 *The Times*, 28 November 1933; *The Times*, 14 December 1933.
157 *The Times*, 29 December 1933.
158 *The Times*, 2 January 1934.
159 *The Times*, 3 January 1934.
160 *The Times*, 3 February 1934.
161 *The Times*, 5 January 1934; *The Times*, 26 January 1934.
162 *The Times*, 8 January 1934.
163 *The Times*, 10 January 1934.
164 *The Times*, 13 January 1934.
165 Omissi, *Air*, pp. 48–9.
166 *The Times*, 15 January 1934; *The Times*, 16 January 1934; *The Times*, 24 January 1934.
167 Londonderry, *Wings*, p. 91.
168 Marchioness of Londonderry, *Retrospect* (London, 1938), p. 60; *The Times*, 3 February 1933.
169 Londonderry, *Retrospect*, pp. 58–9.
170 *The Times*, 30 January 1934; Denis Mack Smith, *Mussolini* (London, 2001), p. 182.
171 *The Times*, 31 January 1934.
172 *The Times*, 1 February 1934; *The Times*, 2 February 1934; *The Times*, 3 February 1934.
173 French, *Deterrence*, p. 305.
174 *The Times*, 3 March 1934; *The Times*, 10 November 1934.
175 Londonderry to Francis Humphrys [British ambassador to Iraq], 13 March 1934 (PRONI, D3099/2/16/34).
176 Nick Smart, *The National Government, 1931–40* (London, 1999), p. 91.
177 French, *Deterrence*, p. 268.
178 *The Times*, 15 February 1934.
179 Philip Williamson, *Stanley Baldwin: Conservative Leadership and National Values* (Cambridge, 1999), p. 306.
180 *The Times*, 25 May 1934.
181 *The Times*, 18 June 1934.
182 *The Times*, 11 July 1934; *The Times*, 6 August 1934.

183 Kenneth Harris, *Attlee* (rep. edn., London, 1995), p. 118.
184 *House of Commons Debates*, 13 June 1933, vol 279, col. 34.
185 Omissi, *Air*, pp. 152, 162–3, 171, 174–5.
186 Londonderry to Baldwin, 17 July 1934 (CUL, Baldwin 1, f. 106); *House of Commons Debates*, 19 July 1934, vol. 292, cols 1273–8.
187 *House of Lords Debates*, 23 July 1934, vol. 93, cols 943–58.
188 Londonderry, *Wings*, pp. 115–16.
189 Ellington to Londonderry, 2 August 1934 (PRONI, D3099/2/16/50).
190 *The Times*, 23 October 1934. See also *House of Lords Debates*, 11 December 1934, vol. 95, col. 185.
191 *The Times*, 10 November 1934.
192 Londonderry to Hailsham, 23 November 1934 (PRONI, D3099/2/19/5A).
193 Notes of a meeting between Göring and Mr and Mrs Oliver Stanley, 5 October 1934 (PRONI, D3099/2/19/3).
194 Londonderry to Hailsham, 22 November 1934 (PRONI, D3099/2/19/4A).
195 William Carr, *Arms, Autarky and Aggression: A Study in German Foreign Policy, 1933–1939* (London, 1972), pp. 21–44.
196 Londonderry to Hailsham, 22 November 1934 (PRONI, D3099/2/19/4A).
197 Hailsham to Londonderry 29 August 1939 (PRONI, D3099/2/17/52A).
198 Middlemas and Barnes, *Baldwin*, pp. 790–5.
199 Londonderry to Simon, 11 December 1934 (PRONI, D3099/2/16/52).
200 Londonderry, memorandum, 26 November 1934 (PRO, PREM/1/155).
201 Londonderry to Baldwin, 30 November 1934 (CUL, Baldwin 1, f. 147).
202 Middlemas and Barnes, *Baldwin*, pp. 787–9.
203 Londonderry to Simon, 11 December 1934 (PRONI, D3099/2/16/52).
204 Middlemas and Barnes, *Baldwin*, p. 790.
205 Lothian to Londonderry, 7 February 1935 (PRONI, D3099/2/17/56).
206 *The Times*, 25 February 1935.
207 *The Times*, 18 December 1934; Londonderry to Craigavon, 3 January 1935 (PRONI, T/3775/23/4); *The Times*, 18 January 1935; *The Times*, 21 January 1935; *The Times*, 23 January 1935; *The Times*, 28 January 1935; Graham Stewart, *Burying Caesar: Churchill, Chamberlain and the Battle for the Tory Party* (London, 1999), p. 135.
208 N. C. Fleming, 'Diehard Conservatism, Mass Democracy, and Indian Constitutional Reform, *c.* 1918–35', *Parliamentary History*, 32, no. 2 (2013): 337–60.
209 *The Times*, 17 March 1933.
210 *The Times*, 23 October 1934.
211 *The Times*, 27 November 1934.
212 *The Times*, 28 January 1935.
213 *The Times*, 20 February 1935.
214 *The Times*, 6 March 1935.
215 *The Times*, 14 March 1935.
216 Londonderry to Baldwin, 14 March 1935 (CUL, Baldwin 1 ff. 152–4).
217 Brett Holman, 'The Air Panic of 1935: British Press Opinion between Disarmament and Rearmament', *Journal of Contemporary History*, 46, no. 2 (2011): 288–307; *The Times*, 28 March 1935.
218 Rothermere to Londonderry, 13 May 1935 (PRONI, D3099/2/21/A/274); see Viscount Rothermere, *My Fight to Rearm Britain* (London, 1939).
219 Robert Rhodes James (ed.), *Memoirs of a Conservative: J.C.C. Davidson's Memoirs and Papers, 1910–37* (London, 1969), p. 404.

220 French, *Deterrence*, pp. 33, 240. 284.
221 Wesley K. Wark, *The Ultimate Enemy: British Intelligence and Nazi Germany, 1933–1939* (London, 1985), p. 47. See John R. Ferris, '"Now that the Milk is Spilt": Appeasement and the Archive on Intelligence', *Diplomacy and Statecraft*, 19, no. 3 (2008): 527–65.
222 Simon's memoirs barely mention Londonderry's opposition (Viscount Simon, *Retrospect: The Memoirs of the Rt. Hon. Viscount Simon GCSI, GCVO* (London, 1952), p. 202).
223 Londonderry to MacDonald, 10 April 1935 (CUL, Baldwin 1, f. 165).
224 David Dilks, '"The Unnecessary War"? Military Advice and Foreign Policy in Great Britain, 1931–1939', in *General Staffs and Diplomacy before the Second World War*, ed. Adrian Preston (London, 1978), p. 110.
225 W. J. Reader, *Architect of Air Power: The Life of the First Viscount Weir of Eastwood 1877–1959* (London, 1968), pp. 201, 230; Churchill, *Gathering*, p. 114.
226 It is noteworthy in this context that the *Air Annual of the British Empire 1935–36*, in contrast to previous years, had nothing to say about the RAF's role in Iraq except the briefest allusion to it in the annual's reprint of Londonderry's memorandum accompanying the 1935 air estimates (C. G. Burge (ed.), *The Air Annual of the British Empire 1935–36* (London, 1935), p. 33).
227 French, *Deterrence*, p. 291.
228 Middlemas and Barnes, *Baldwin*, pp. 814–15.
229 James, *Davidson*, p. 405. See also Vansittart to Londonderry, 12 July 1933 (PRONI, D3099/4/20).
230 Chamberlain to Ida Chamberlain, 12 January 1935 (Self, *Chamberlain*, p. 472); Londonderry to Baldwin, 14 March 1935 (CUL, Baldwin 1, ff. 152–4). See also Ronald W. Clark, *Tizard* (London, 1965), pp. 105–27.
231 Cross, *Swinton*, pp. 135–44.
232 Londonderry, *Wings*, pp. 134–5.
233 Londonderry to Lady Londonderry, 27 April 1935 (Hyde, *Londonderrys*, p. 212).
234 Londonderry to MacDonald, n.d. [1935] (JRUL, RMD/1/14/75); Londonderry to MacDonald, 2 May 1935 (JRUL, RMD/1/13/4).
235 Londonderry to MacDonald, 6 May 1935 (JRUL, RMD/1/13/5).
236 Londonderry to Cunliffe-Lister, 11 May 1935 (CUL, Baldwin 1, f. 182); Ellington to Cunliffe-Lister, 11 May 1935 (Hyde, *Air*, p. 339).
237 Copy of cabinet minutes from Hankey to Londonderry, 21 May 1935 (PRONI, D3099/2/15/8).
238 *House of Commons Debates*, 22 May 1935, vol. 302, cols 359–82.
239 James, *Davidson*, p. 404.
240 John Charmley, *Lord Lloyd and the Decline of the British Empire* (London, 1987), p. 205; N. C. Fleming, *Britannia's Zealots, vol. 1: Tradition, Empire and the Forging of the Conservative Right* (London, 2019), p. 181.
241 *House of Lords Debates*, 22 May 1935, vol. 96, cols 1002–19.
242 Londonderry to Strabolgi, 23 November 1937 (PRONI, D3099/2/17/22).
243 Londonderry, *Wings*, p. 143.
244 *House of Lords Debates*, 23 May 1935, vol. 96, cols 1094–6.
245 *The Times*, 25 May 1935.
246 *The Times*, 25 May 1935. See also *The Times*, 28 May 1935; *The Times*, 4 June 1935.
247 Churchill, *Gathering*, pp. 113–14.
248 Marquand, *MacDonald*, p. 774; Robert Blake, *The Decline of Power 1915–1964* (London, 1986), p. 180.

249 Hailsham to Baldwin, 28 May 1935 (Maurice Cowling, *The Impact of Hitler: British Politics and British Policy, 1933–1940* (Cambridge, 1975), p. 60).
250 Channon, diary, 8 June 1935 (Robert Rhodes James, *'Chips': The Diaries of Sir Henry Channon* (London, 1967), p. 35); Marquand, *MacDonald*, p. 783.
251 A. J. P. Taylor (ed.), *W.P. Crozier: Off the Record: Political Interviews, 1933–1943* (London, 1973), pp. 46–8.
252 Londonderry to Baldwin, 6 June 1935 (CUL, Baldwin 171, ff. 152–9).
253 Londonderry to Baldwin, 6 June 1935 (CUL, Baldwin 171, ff. 152–9).
254 Baldwin to Londonderry, 6 June 1935 (PRONI, D3099/2/17/4A).
255 Londonderry to Alexander Cadogan, 18 June 1935 (PRONI, D3099/2/17/5).
256 *The Times*, 8 June 1935; Air ministry memorandum, 17 June 1935 (PRO, AIR/2/223) published in the press (*The Times*, 21 June 1935). He received his letters patent as His Majesty's Keeper of the Privy Seal the same day (L.C. Ridley to Londonderry, 17 June 1935 (PRO, LCO/6/1240)).
257 French, *Deterrence*, p. 321.
258 Cowling, *Impact*, p. 60.
259 Londonderry to Baldwin, 9 July 1935 (PRONI, D3099/2/17/6A).
260 Hailsham to Londonderry, 17 September 1935 (D3099/2/17/7B).
261 Craigavon to Londonderry 5 June 1929 (D3099/2/10/2/13); Craigavon to Londonderry, 6 August 1929 (PRONI, D3099/2/10/2/14).
262 *The Times*, 6 February 1926.
263 Londonderry to MacDonald, 28 July 1932 (JRUL, RMD, 1/14/73); *Irish News*, 9 August 1932; Paul Canning, *British Policy Towards Ireland, 1921–1941* (Oxford, 1985), pp. 142–3.
264 John Andrews to Londonderry, 26 July 1933 (PRONI, D3099/2/7/128); Deirdre McMahon, *Republicans and Imperialists: Anglo-Irish Relations in the 1930s* (London, 1984), pp. 31, 60, 110, 132.
265 *The Times*, 21 October 1933.
266 See Londonderry to Hailsham, 16 December 1935 (PRONI, D3099/2/15/6).
267 Cunliffe-Lister to Londonderry, 9 September 1935 (PRONI, D3099/6/11); *The Times*, 28 June 1935; Charles Hendriks to Londonderry, 20 September 1935 (PRONI, D3099/2/4/91A). The Duke of Northumberland was Londonderry's parliamentary private secretary (*The Times*, 12 July 1935). Londonderry had Hendriks transferred, with difficulty, from the Northern Ireland civil service (Londonderry to MacDonald, 11 August 1933 (PRO, PRO/30/69/706)); Hendriks to Londonderry, n.d. (PRONI, D3099/5/14/3). When Londonderry was appointed Lord Privy Seal, Hendricks was appointed as his private secretary, see *The Times*, 28 June 1935.
268 Londonderry to Craigavon, 16 October 1935 (PRONI, D3099/6/11).
269 Londonderry to Baldwin, 17 October 1935 (CUL, Baldwin 171, ff. 157–8).
270 *The Times*, 29 July 1935.
271 *House of Commons Debates*, 30 July 1935, vol. 304, cols 2484–7.
272 *House of Lords Debates*, 22 October 1935, vol. 98, cols 1090–100.
273 Pauline Lynn, 'Seaham Revisited: The Fruits of the Electoral Franchise?', *North East History*, 33 (2000): 27–8.
274 Reuters-Gaumont British Newsreel, 28 October 1935.
275 F. W. S. Craig, *British General Election Manifestos, 1900–1974* (London, 1975), p. 108. Hendriks advised Londonderry that this was a libel as he had acted at Geneva on behalf of the government, but nothing, at least in the courts, was pursued (Hendriks to Londonderry, 29 October 1935 (PRONI, D3099/2/16/58)).

276 Londonderry to Lord Derby, 14 November 1935 (PRONI, D3099/2/8/19).
277 *The Times*, 6 November 1935.
278 *The Times*, 8 November 1935.
279 *The Times*, 13 November 1935.
280 *The Times*, 14 November 1935.
281 Jon Lawrence, *Electing Our Masters: The Hustings in British Politics from Hogarth to Blair* (Oxford, 2009), p. 123; Marquand, *MacDonald*, pp. 779–80.
282 Baldwin to Londonderry, 21 November 1935 (PRONI, D3099/2/17/11).
283 Hyde, *Londonderrys*, p. 226.
284 Urquhart, *Ladies*, p. 189.
285 Londonderry to Baldwin, 19 May 1936 (PRONI, D3099/2/17).
286 Londonderry to Baldwin, 22 November 1935 (CUL, Baldwin 171, f. 162).
287 Chamberlain to Ida Chamberlain, 20 June 1936 (Self, *Chamberlain*, p. 509).
288 Headlam, diary, 5 December 1936 (Stuart Ball (ed.), *Parliament and Politics in the Age of Churchill and Attlee: The Headlam Diaries 1935–1951* (Cambridge, 1999), p. 101); Philip Zeigler, 'Churchill and the Monarchy', in *Churchill*, eds Robert Blake and Wm. Roger Louis (Oxford, 1996), pp. 193–5.
289 *The Times*, 30 December 1935.
290 *The Times*, 31 December 1935. Attlee's letter in turn provoked a reader, H. S. Tasker, of Sheffield, to write to *The Times* in Londonderry's defence (*The Times*, 2 January 1936).
291 Marquess of Londonderry, 'Bombing from the Air', *Nineteenth Century and After*, 125 (March 1939): 269–81. See also Londonderry to Lord Kemsley, 23 September 1940 (PRONI, D3099/2/17/62).
292 Londonderry to Baldwin, 18 May 1936 (CUL, Baldwin 171, f. 163).
293 Reader, *Architect*, pp. 289–92; Cross, *Swinton*, pp. 209–19.
294 Richard B. Simons, 'The British Coal Industry-a Failure of Private Enterprise', *The Historian*, 16, no. 1 (1953): 13.
295 Barry Supple, *The History of the British Coal Industry: vol. 4: 1913–1946: The Political Economy of Decline* (Oxford, 1987), p. 422.
296 *The Times*, 11 January 1932.
297 Huw Beynon and Terry Austrin, *Masters and Servants: Class Patronage in the Making of a Labour Organisation: The Durham Miners and the English Political Tradition* (London, 1994), p. 336; Headlam, diary, 27 September 1933 (Ball, *Parliament*, pp. 279–80).
298 *The Times*, 27 July 1933.
299 The gift was on condition that they had been in receipt of a coal allowance when employed (*The Times*, 18 December 1933).
300 Pauline Lynn, 'The Impact of Women. The Shaping of Political Allegiance in County Durham, 1918–1945', *Local Historian*, 28, no. 3 (1998): 168.
301 A. Susan Williams, *Ladies of Influence: Women of the Elite in Interwar Britain* (London, 2000), p. 21.
302 *The Times*, 2 November 1932; Ball, *Headlam*, p. 318.
303 Lynn, 'Impact', p. 166.
304 *The Times*, 19 December 1932; *The Times*, 22 October 1934. See also *The Times*, 21 June 1935.
305 Londonderry to Beaverbrook, 20 October 1934 (HLRO, BBK/C/224).
306 J. B. Priestley, *English Journey: Jubilee Edition with Eighty Illustrations* ([1934] London, 1984), pp. 244–61.
307 George Orwell, *The Road to Wigan Pier* (London, 1937).
308 Lynn, 'Impact', p. 171.

309 Simons, 'British', p. 13.
310 Supple, *British*, pp. 422–3.
311 *House of Lords Debates*, 11 December 1935, vol. 99, cols 181–7.
312 Londonderry to Beaverbrook, 26 December 1935 (HLRO, BBK/C/224); Beaverbrook to Londonderry, 30 December 1935 (HLRO, BBK/C/224).
313 Philip Noel-Baker, *The First World Disarmament Conference, 1932–33 and Why it Failed* (London, 1979), pp. 103–34.
314 Robert Vansittart, *The Mist Procession: The Autobiography of Lord Vansittart* (London, 1958), p. 445.
315 Londonderry to Beverly Baxter, 28 April 1947 (PRONI, D3099/2/21/A/264).
316 See, for example, Hailsham to Londonderry, n.d. [November 1935] (PRONI, D3099/2/4/94); Lord Templemore to Londonderry, 23 November 1935 (PRONI, D3099/2/4/100); Salisbury to Londonderry, 26 November 1935 (PRONI, D3099/2/4/113A); Lady Desborough to Londonderry, 23 November 1935 (PRONI, D3099/2/6/25); Charles D'Arcy to Londonderry, 25 November 1935 (PRONI, D3099/2/4/108).
317 *The Times*, 28 November 1935; Kipling to Londonderry, 30 November 1935 (PRONI, D3099/2/4/119).
318 John F. Kennedy, *Why England Slept* (New York, 1940), pp. 63, 98–9, 109. Kennedy mentions Londonderry and cites his article in *Nineteenth Century and After*.
319 Robert Sencourt, *Winston Churchill* (London, 1940).
320 McCallum, *Public*, p. 186.
321 Hilary St George Saunders, *Per Adua: The Rise of British Air Power 1911–1939* (London, 1944), p. 285.
322 Swinton, *Remember*, pp. 104–5.
323 Churchill, *Gathering*, pp. 114–15.
324 Vansittart, *Mist*, p. 499.
325 Cato, *Guilty Men* (rep. edn., London, 1998), p. 33; *The Times*, 15 March 1935.
326 Malcolm Muggeridge, *The Thirties, 1930–1940 in Great Britain* (London, 1940), p. 136.
327 B. H. Liddell Hart, *Europe in Arms* (New York, 1937), pp. 26, 153–4.
328 Hart, *Memoirs*, pp. 157–8.
329 A. J. P. Taylor, *English History 1914–1945* (rep. edn., Oxford, 1990), p. 365.
330 Andrew Webster, 'From Versailles to Geneva: The Many Forms of Interwar Disarmament', *Journal of Strategic Studies*, 24, no. 2 (2006): 225–46; Andrew Webster, 'Entente and Argument: Britain, France and Disarmament, 1899–1934', in *Britain, France and the Entente Cordiale since 1904*, ed. Antoine Capet (Basingstoke, 2006), pp. 64–77.
331 Carlton, *Eden*, p. 35.
332 Shay, *British*, p. 38.
333 Martin Gilbert and Richard Gott, *The Appeasers* (rep. edn., London, 2000), p. 333.
334 Robert Rhodes James, *The British Revolution: British Politics, 1880–1939* (London, 1978), p. 554.
335 French, *Deterrence*, p. 314.

Chapter 7

1 Oliver Harvey, diary, 16 March 1938 (John Harvey (ed.), *The Diplomatic Diaries of Oliver Harvey 1937–1940* (London, 1970), p. 118).

2 Kazuo Ishiguro, *The Remains of the Day* (London, 1989); Michael Schwarz, 'Appeasing the Past: Denying History, Destroying Memories, Creating Myths', in *Ethics, Values and Civil Society*, eds Michael Schwarz, Howard Harris and Stephen Cohen (Bingley, 2013), pp. 156–7.
3 Ferdinand Fairfax (dir.), *Winston Churchill: The Wilderness Years* (1981).
4 B. H. Liddell Hart, *Europe in Arms* (New York, 1937), p. 23.
5 *The Times*, 18 February 1938.
6 Londonderry to J. C. Gibbs, 8 February 1939 (PRONI, D3099/2/19/242).
7 David Dutton, *Neville Chamberlain* (London, 2001), pp. 84–5.
8 Londonderry to Lady Milner, 11 March 1937 (DRCO, D/Lo/C/237 (8)).
9 Dutton, *Chamberlain*, pp. 84–85.
10 Cato, *Guilty Men* (rep. edn., London, 1998); R. A. C. Parker, *Chamberlain and Appeasement: British Policy and the Coming of the Second World War* (London, 1993), p. 1.
11 David Lukowitz, 'George Lansbury's Peace Missions to Hitler and Mussolini in 1937', *Canadian Journal of History*, 15, no. 1 (1980): 67–82; Stella Rudman, *Lloyd George and the Appeasement of Germany, 1919–1945* (Newcastle, 2011), pp. 186–263.
12 Geoffrey Hicks, 'Conservatism Obscured, 1935–1939', in *The Tory World: Deep History and the Tory Theme in British Foreign Policy, 1679–2014*, ed. Jeremy Black (Aldershot, 2015), pp. 293–310.
13 R. B. McCallum, *Public Opinion and the Last Peace* (London, 1944), pp. 52–3, 58–9, 88–113; A. J. P. Taylor, *The Trouble Makers: Dissent over Foreign Policy 1792–1939* (London, 1969), pp. 152–82.
14 Londonderry to Lord Noel-Buxton, 11 May 1938 (PRONI, D3099/2/19/83); Noel-Buxton to Londonderry, 16 March 1938 (PRONI, D3099/2/19/63); Noel-Buxton to Londonderry, 16 July 1938 (PRONI, D3099/2/19/112); Marquess of Londonderry, *Ourselves and Germany* (London [Penguin edn.], 1938), pp. 178–9.
15 Eric Hobsbawm, *Age of Extremes: The Short Twentieth Century, 1914–1991* (London, 1995), p. 123; Peregrine Worsthorne, *In Defence of Aristocracy* (London, 2004), pp. 30–2.
16 Wolfgang Michalka, 'Joachim von Ribbentrop: From Wine Merchant to Foreign Minister', in *The Nazi Elite*, eds Ronald Smelser and Rainer Zitelmann (London, 1993), pp. 166–7.
17 David French, *Deterrence, Coercion and Appeasement: British Grand Strategy, 1919–1940* (Oxford, 2022), pp. 15–65.
18 David Cannadine, *The Decline and Fall of the British Aristocracy* (rev. edn., London, 1996), pp. 547, 554–6.
19 *The Times*, 18 June 1934.
20 Bernhard Dietz, *Neo Tories: The Revolt of British Conservatives against Democracy and Political Modernity (1929–1939)* (London, 2018).
21 For contrasting interpretations of support in parliament for British fascism, see Richard Thurlow, *Fascism in Britain: From Oswald Mosley's Blackshirts to the National Front* (London, 1998), pp. 69–70, and Martin Pugh, *'Hurrah for the Blackshirts!' Fascists and Fascism in Britain between the Wars* (London, 2005), pp. 75–91.
22 P. G. Wodehouse, *The Code of the Woosters* (London, 1938); P. G. Wodehouse, *Jeeves and the Feudal Spirit* (London, 1955).
23 Marquess of Londonderry, *Wings of Destiny* (London, 1943); Anon. to Londonderry, n.d. [1941/2] (PRONI, D3099/2/21/A/277).

24 *The Times*, 10 March 1926.
25 C. K. Webster, *The Foreign Policy of Castlereagh, 1815–1822: Britain and the European Alliance* (London, 1925); C.K. Webster, *The Foreign Policy of Castlereagh, 1812–1815: Britain and the Reconstruction of Europe* (London, 1931); H. Montgomery Hyde, *The Rise of Castlereagh* (London, 1933); J. A. R. Marriott, *Castlereagh: A Political Biography* (London, 1936).
26 *The Times*, 31 August 1937.
27 Londonderry, *Ourselves*, p. 147.
28 Londonderry to Halifax, 24 December 1936 (PRONI, D3099/2/18/18B).
29 Londonderry to William McKee [editor of *Belfast News-Letter*], 5 January 1938 (PRONI, D3099/2/21/A/4).
30 McCallum, *Public*, pp. 120–2.
31 Londonderry to Dr Seton-Watson, 21 April 1938 (PRONI, D3099/2/21/A/36).
32 Cited in H. Montgomery Hyde, *Baldwin: The Unexpected Prime Minister* (London, 1973), p. 543.
33 J. R. M. Butler, *Lord Lothian (Philip Kerr) 1882–1940* (London, 1960), pp. 190–237; Andrea Bosco, 'Lord Lothian and Appeasement', in *The Round Table, the Empire/ Commonwealth, and British Foreign Policy* , eds Andrea Bosco and Alex May (London, 1997), pp. 473–509.
34 Londonderry indicated that his voluminous correspondence might fend off unkind treatment by historians (Londonderry to Baldwin, 18 May 1936 (CUL, Baldwin, 171, f. 163); see *Evening Standard*, 7 October 1936; Londonderry to Baldwin, 7 November 1939 (PRONI, D3099/2/17/55).
35 *The Times*, 27 June 1936.
36 Londonderry to Baldwin, 29 December 1938 (CUL, Baldwin 171, ff. 178–91).
37 *The Times*, 1 August 1936; Londonderry to editor, *Rotherham Advertiser*, 20 July 1936 (DCRO, D/Lo/C/237(4)); Londonderry to Lord Strobolgi, 19 November 1937 (PRONI, D3099/2/17/21).
38 *Evening Standard*, 7 October 1936.
39 Londonderry to Attlee, 17 November 1937 (DCRO, D/Lo/C 237 (11)). See also Londonderry to Herbert Morrison 17 November 1937 (DRCO, D/Lo/C 237 (11)).
40 Richard Griffiths, *Fellow Travellers of the Right: British Enthusiasts for Nazi Germany, 1933–9* (London, 1980), p. 140.
41 *The Times*, 27 August 1923.
42 *The Times*, 25 October 1923.
43 Typed copy of Londonderry's broadcast on the BBC, 7.35 pm, 11 November 1924 (PRONI, D3099/5/13).
44 *The Times*, 1 March 1929.
45 *The Times*, 25 June 1931.
46 Londonderry, notes for a public lecture, 4 May 1932 (PRONI, D3099/2/16/22).
47 *The Times*, 20 July 1931.
48 See Londonderry, *Wings*, pp. 118–119.
49 Londonderry to Cadogan, 18 June 1935 (PRONI, D3099/2/17/5).
50 Londonderry to Sir Walford Selby, 24 January 1946 (PRONI, D3099/2/22/90).
51 French, *Deterrence*, p. 419.
52 G. T. Waddington, '"An Idyllic and Unruffled Atmosphere of Complete Anglo-German Misunderstanding": Aspects of the Operations of the Dienststelle Ribbentrop in Great Britain, 1934–1938', *History*, 82, no. 265 (1997): 46.
53 Londonderry to Lady Milner, 11 March 1937 (DCRO, D/Lo/C/237 (8)).

54 Ian Kershaw, *Hitler, 1889–1936: Hubris* (London, 1998), p. 241; Ian Kershaw, *Hitler, 1936–45: Nemesis* (London, 2000), p. 21.
55 William Carr, *Arms, Autarky and Aggression: A Study in German Foreign Policy, 1933–1939* (London, 1972), pp. 15–16.
56 Londonderry to Papen, 9 June 1939 (PRONI, D3099/2/19/306A).
57 W. A. Sinclair, *The Voice of the Nazi: Being Eight Broadcast Talks Given Between December 1939 and May 1940* (London, 1940), p. 10.
58 Gerwin Strobl, *The Germanic Isle: Nazi Perceptions of Britain* (Cambridge, 2000), p. 32.
59 Londonderry, *Wings*, p. 171.
60 Londonderry, *Ourselves*, pp. 81–2.
61 *The Times*, 6 February 1936.
62 Michael Burleigh, *The Third Reich: A New History* (London, 2000), p. 246. For alternative view on Nazi-aristocratic relations, see Manuel Sarkisyanz, *Hitler's English Inspirers* (Belfast, 2003), pp. 210–28.
63 Londonderry to Ribbentrop, 21 February 1936 (PRONI, D3099/2/19/17B); Londonderry to Göring, 25 February 1936 (PRONI, D3099/2/19/19B).
64 Lady Londonderry to Hitler, 21 February 1936 (PRONI, D3099/3/35/9D).
65 Reich Chancellery to Lady Londonderry, 29 February 1936 (PRONI, D3099/3/35/6); Hitler to Lady Londonderry, 2 April 1936 (PRONI, D3099/3/35/9D).
66 Lady Londonderry to Göring, 21 February 1936 (PRONI, D3099/3/35/4).
67 Londonderry, diary notes 30 January–7 February 1936 (PRONI, D3099/2/19/9B). For complete diary notes, see N. C. Fleming (ed.), *Aristocracy, Democracy, and Dictatorship: The Political Papers of the Seventh Marquess of Londonderry* (Cambridge, 2022), pp. 239–47.
68 *The Times*, 24 February 1936.
69 Londonderry to Dr F. W. Pick, 26 November 1946 (PRONI, D3099/2/21/A).
70 Amery to Londonderry, 26 February 1936 (PRONI, D3099/2/19/20).
71 Minutes of the 1922 Committee, 29 June 1936 (vol. 1, April 1923–July 1928, Bodleian Library, 1922/1).
72 Bosco, 'Lothian', p. 480.
73 Nicholson to Sackville-West, 20 February 1936, Nigel Nicholson (ed.) *Harold Nicholson: Diaries and Letters, 1930–1939* (London, 1966), p. 245.
74 Londonderry to Lady Londonderry, 30 March 1936 (PRONI, D3099/3).
75 Amery, diary, 25 April 1936 (John Barnes and David Nicholson (eds), *The Empire at Bay: The Leo Amery Diaries 1929–1945* (London, 1988), p. 414).
76 *Evening Standard*, 26 November 1935.
77 *The Times*, 5 May 1937.
78 *The Times*, 26 October 1937.
79 H. Montgomery Hyde, *Londonderry House and Its Pictures* (London, 1937); see also *The Times*, 25 May 1937.
80 Diane Urquhart, *The Ladies of Londonderry: Women and Political Patronage* (London, 2007), pp. 190, 202; *The Times*, 12 July 1938; *The Times*, 13 May 1939.
81 Göring to Londonderry, 24 March 1937 (PRONI, D3099/2/19/34A); Ian Kershaw, *Making Friends with Hitler: Lord Londonderry and Britain's Road to War* (London, 2004), pp. 194–6.
82 Lady Londonderry to Ribbentrop, 9 May 1936 (PRONI, D3099/3/35/15); Ribbentrop to Lady Londonderry, 5 June, 1936 (PRONI, D3099/3/35/20). Ribbentrop had

attended the jubilee ball at Londonderry House in May 1935, but it did not lead to any communication with Londonderry who was still in the cabinet.

83 Urquhart, *Ladies*, p. 196.

84 *The Times*, 16 November 1936; Kershaw, *Making*, p. 182. Recollections vary, however, about whether it was the anthem or a hymn that resembled the anthem, uncertainty that has been exacerbated by the failure of most accounts to make any reference to original or reliable sources.

85 Ribbentrop to Lady Londonderry, 5 June 1936 (PRONI, D3099/3/35/20); *The Times*, 16 November 1936; Henry Channon, diary, 29 May 1936 (Robert Rhodes James, (ed.) *'Chips': The Diaries of Sir Henry Channon* (London, 1999), p. 62).

86 John Weitz, *Hitler's Diplomat: Joachim von Ribbentrop* (London, 1997), p. 15; Norton Medlicott, 'Britain and Germany: The Search for Agreement, 1930–37', in *Retreat from Power: Studies in Britain's Foreign Policy of the Twentieth Century*, ed. David Dilks (London, 1981), pp. 78–101.

87 *The Times*, 12 March 1936.

88 Lady Londonderry's correspondence with leading German figures, 1936–39 (PRONI, D3099/3/35/1–42).

89 Beaverbrook to Londonderry, 19 March 1936 (HLRO, BBK/C/224).

90 Londonderry to Beaverbrook, 22 March 1936 (HLRO, BBK/C/224).

91 Beaverbrook to Londonderry, 29 March 1936 (HLRO, BBK/C/224).

92 N. J. Crowson, *Facing Fascism: The Conservative Party and the European Dictators, 1935–1940* (London, 1997), p. 66.

93 *House of Lords Debates*, 17 March 1936, vol. 100, cols 37–43.

94 *House of Lords Debates*, 8 April 1936, vol. 100, cols 540–6.

95 N. C. Fleming, 'Diehard Conservatives and the Appeasement of Nazi Germany, 1935–1940', *History*, 100, no. 3 (2015): 412–35.

96 Richard Whiting, 'The Empire and British Politics', in *Britain's Experience of Empire in the Twentieth Century*, ed. Andrew Thompson (Oxford, 2012), pp. 161–2.

97 Londonderry to Amery, 10 October 1937 (DCRO, D/Lo/C/237 (10) (i–iii)).

98 Londonderry to Göring, 3 June 1936 (PRONI, D3099/2/19/28B). See also Göring to Lady Londonderry, 16 May 1936 (PRONI, D3099/3/35/16); Göring to Lady Londonderry, 3 July 1936 (PRONI, D3099/3/35/24B).

99 Londonderry to Churchill, 9 May 1936 (PRONI, D3099/2/5/29).

100 Londonderry to Baldwin, 19 May 1936 (CUL Baldwin 171, ff. 166–71).

101 Göring to Lady Londonderry, 16 May 1936 (PRONI, D3099/3/35/16); Londonderry to Baldwin, 21 May 1936 (CUL Baldwin 171, ff. 171–3).

102 *The Times*, 27 June 1936; *House of Commons Debates*, 2 July 1936, vol. 314, cols 605–6.

103 Halifax to Londonderry, 1 July 1936 (PRONI, D3099/2/18/7).

104 Londonderry to Halifax, 4 July 1936 (PRONI, D3099/2/18/8).

105 Halifax to Londonderry, 16 July 1936 (PRONI, D3099/2/18/10); G. Bruce Strang, 'The Spirit of Ulysses? Ideology and British Appeasement in the 1930s', *Diplomacy and Statecraft*, 19, no. 3 (2008): 481–526.

106 Londonderry to Halifax, 17 July 1936 (PRONI, D3099/2/18/11).

107 Halifax to Londonderry, 25 August 1936 (PRONI, D3099/2/18/12).

108 *The Times*, 1 August 1936; Londonderry to Baldwin, 1 December 1936 (Baldwin 171, ff. 175–7); Lloyd George to Londonderry, September 1936 (Londonderry, *Wings*, p. 176).

109 Londonderry to Halifax, 16 September 1936 (PRONI, D3099/2/18/13).

110 Londonderry to Halifax, 19 December 1936 (PRONI, D3099/2/18/17); *The Times*, 16 December 1936.
111 Londonderry to Halifax, 24 December 1936 (PRONI, D3099/2/18/18B).
112 *The Times*, 5 October 1936; *The Times*, 24 October 1936; *The Times*, 31 October 1936; *The Times*, 2 November 1936.
113 Londonderry to Halifax, 19 December 1936 (PRONI, D3099/2/18/17); Londonderry to Halifax, 24 December 1936 (PRONI, D3099/2/18/18B).
114 *The Times*, 1 February 1937.
115 *The Times*, 26 October 1937.
116 Pugh, '*Hurrah*', pp. 269–72.
117 Norman Rose, *The Cliveden Set: Portrait of an Exclusive Fraternity* (London, 2000).
118 Charles Spicer, '"Ambulant Amateurs": The Rise and Fade of the Anglo-German Fellowship' (PhD thesis, University of London, 2018), pp. 260–2.
119 Londonderry to Countess de la Feld, 23 March 1938 (PRONI, D3099/2/19/70).
120 Spicer, 'Ambulant', p. 192.
121 Rose, *Cliveden*, pp. 116–17, 175, 179. For example of erroneous claim, see Lois G. Schwoerer, 'Lord Halifax's Visit to Germany: November 1937', *The Historian*, 32, no. 3 (1970): 353–75.
122 Urquhart, *Ladies*, p. 143.
123 W.W. Astor to Londonderry, 20 December 1938 (PRONI, D3099/2/19/207); Londonderry to Astor, 21 December 1938 (PRONI, D3099/2/19/208).
124 Londonderry, notes, 22 September 1937 (PRONI, D3099/2/19/36).
125 Londonderry to Ribbentrop, 26 October 1937 (PRONI, D3099/4/44). Lady Desborough assumed that Londonderry had met with Mussolini (Desborough to Londonderry, 1 October 1937 (D3099/2/6/26)).
126 Londonderry to Göring, 29 September 1937 (PRONI, D3099/2/19/37A).
127 Ben Pimlott, *The Political Diary of Hugh Dalton, 1918–40, 1945–60* (London, 1986), p. 237.
128 Ribbentrop, 'Strictly Confidential and Personal Conclusions Concerning the Report "German Embassy London A5522" on the Future of Anglo-German Relations', 2 January 1938 (Alan Bullock (ed.), *The Ribbentrop Memoirs* (London, 1954), pp. 206–7).
129 Londonderry to Halifax, 7 October 1937 (PRONI, D3099/2/18/27); Baldwin to Londonderry, 11 November 1937 (PRONI, D3099/2/19/39).
130 A. W. Baldwin, *My Father: The True Story* (London, 1955), p. 324.
131 Londonderry to Nevile Henderson, 7 October 1937 (DCRO, D/Lo/C/237 (9)).
132 *The Times*, 8 October 1937; Headlam, diary, 30 March 1939 (Stuart Ball (ed.), *Parliament and Politics in the Age of Churchill and Attlee: The Headlam Diaries 1935–1951* (Cambridge, 1999), p. 153).
133 Stuart Ball, *Portrait of a Party: The Conservative Party in Britain 1918–1945* (Oxford, 2013), p. 255.
134 Londonderry to Walford Selby, 24 January 1946 (PRONI, D3099/2/22/90).
135 Londonderry to Halifax, 2 November 1937 (PRONI, D3099/2/18/28); *The Times*, 6 November 1937; *Evening Standard*, 13 November 1937.
136 Andrew Roberts, '*The Holy Fox*': *The Life of Lord Halifax* (London, 1991), p. 67. In his role as chancellor of Durham University, Londonderry had recently conferred Eden with the degree of DCL, with evident reluctance (Headlam, diary, 25 March 1937 (Ball, *Parliament*, p. 109)). Londonderry had been appointed chancellor in November 1930 and installed in May 1931 (*The Times*, 21 November 1930; *The Times*, 21 May 1931).

137 *The Times*, 6 November 1937; Halifax to Londonderry, 8 November 1937 (PRONI, D3099/2/18/29); Halifax to Londonderry, 12 November 1937 (PRONI, D3099/2/18/30); Londonderry to Halifax, 13 November 1937 (PRONI, D3099/2/18/31).
138 Collin Brooks, diary, 15 February 1939 (N. J. Crowson, *Fleet Street, Press Barons and Politics: The Journals of Collin Brooks, 1932–1940* (Cambridge, 1998), p. 243).
139 Ribbentrop to Londonderry, 4 December 1937 (PRONI, D3099/2/19/40A); Londonderry to Ribbentrop, 8 December 1937 (PRONI, D3099/2/19/41); Londonderry to Ribbentrop, 20 January 1938 (PRONI, D3099/2/19/53).
140 Republished in *The Times*, 3 January 1938.
141 Londonderry to Garvin, 5 February 1938 (PRONI, D3099/2/21/A/19).
142 Londonderry, *Ourselves*, pp. 166–7, 178–9.
143 *The Times*, 5 April 1938.
144 Londonderry to Ribbentrop, 21 February 1936 (Londonderry, *Ourselves*, p. 97).
145 Gladys Hirsch to Londonderry, 6 April 1938 (PRONI, D3099/2/21/A/1); Londonderry to Hirsch, 14 April 1938 (PRONI, D3099/2/21/A/29); Hirsch to Londonderry, 18 April 1938 (PRONI, D3099/2/21/A/32).
146 Rothschild to Londonderry, 8 April 1938 (PRONI, D3099/2/21/A/22A); Londonderry to Rothschild, 11 April 1938 (PRONI, D3099/2/21/A/24A); Rothschild to Londonderry, 12 April 1938 (PRONI, D3099/2/21/A/25A); Londonderry to Rothschild, 13 April 1938 (PRONI, D3099/2/21/A/28A).
147 Londonderry to Rothschild, 7 June 1938 (PRONI, D3099/2/21/A/1/1/9).
148 See N. J. Crowson, 'The British Conservative Party and the Jews during the Late 1930s', *Patterns of Prejudice*, 29, no. 2 and 3 (1995): 15–32; Harry Defries, *Conservative Party Attitudes to Jews, 1900–1950* (London, 2001); Annabel Goldsmith, *Annabel: An Unconventional Life* (London, 2004), p. 13.
149 Londonderry to Hitler, 5 April 1938 (PRONI, D3099/2/19/73).
150 Londonderry to F.C. Spenser-Davison, 14 November 1938 (PRONI, D3099/2/19/171); Londonderry to S. S. G. Parker, 29 December 1938 (PRONI, D3099/2/19/210).
151 See Dan Stone, *Responses to Nazism in Britain, 1933–1939: Before War and Holocaust* (Basingstoke, 2003), p. 88.
152 Hobsbawm, *Extremes*, p. 27.
153 Geoffrey Saviour to Londonderry, 18 January 1938 (PRONI, D3099/2/19/50); Londonderry to Hitler, 5 April 1938 (PRONI, D3099/2/19/73).
154 Rennie to Londonderry, 7 April 1938 (PRONI, D3099/2/19/75).
155 Wachstein to Londonderry, 26 October 1938 (PRONI, D3099/2/19/38).
156 Paul Müller to Londonderry, 7 September 1938 (PRONI, D3099/2/19/120).
157 Edwart von Selzam to Londonderry, 24 May 1938 (PRONI, D3099/2/19/88).
158 *Daily Express*, 27 July 1938.
159 Londonderry to Ribbentrop, 17 February 1938 (PRONI, D3099/2/19/56); *House of Lords Debates*, 24 February 1938, vol. 107, cols 901–6.
160 Londonderry to Countess de la Feld, 23 March 1938 (PRONI, D3099/2/19/70).
161 *House of Lords Debates*, 16 March 1938, vol. 108, cols 139–44.
162 Londonderry to Ludwig Noe, 3 May 1938 (PRONI, D3099/2/21/A/42).
163 Lady Londonderry to Ribbentrop, 19 March 1938 (PRONI, D3099/3/35/33); Göring to Lady Londonderry, 22 March 1938 (PRONI, D3099/3/35/34B); Ribbentrop to Lady Londonderry, 27 April 1938 (PRONI, D3099/3/35/35); Selzam to Londonderry,

24 May 1938 (PRONI, D3099/2/19/88); Londonderry to Selzam, 30 May 1938 (PRONI, D3099/2/19/90).

164 Urquhart, *Ladies*, p. 201.

165 Londonderry to Hitler, 5 April 1938 (PRONI, D3099/2/19/73).

166 Hitler to Londonderry, 10 April 1938 (PRONI, D3099/2/19/77); Londonderry to Göring, 18 July 1938 (PRONI, D3099/2/19/115); Wolfgang Müller-Clemm to Londonderry, 6 September 1938 (PRONI, D3099/2/21/A/75B).

167 Londonderry to Beaverbrook, 24 May 1938 (HLRO, BBK/C/224); Beaverbrook to Londonderry, 26 May 1938 (HLRO, BBK/C/224).

168 Londonderry to Beaverbrook, 31 May 1938 (HLRO, BBK/C/224).

169 *Daily Express*, 27 July 1938; Londonderry to Beaverbrook, 30 July 1938 (HLRO, BBK/C/224).

170 Beaverbrook to Londonderry, 2 September 1938 (HLRO, BBK/C/224).

171 *The Times*, 25 June 1938; Oberführer Görnnert to Londonderry, 15 June 1938 (PRONI, D3099/2/19/95).

172 Harvey, diary, 14 June 1938 (Harvey, *Diplomatic*, p. 153).

173 Londonderry to Halifax, 28 June 1938 (PRONI, D3099/2/18/38B).

174 Londonderry to Halifax, 20 July 1938 (PRONI, D3099/2/18/39).

175 McCallum, *Public*, pp. 119, 123–4.

176 Londonderry to Horace Wilson, 17 September 1938 (PRONI, D3099/2/19/124); Londonderry to Chamberlain, 1 October 1939 (PRONI, D3099/4/52).

177 Churchill to Londonderry, 5 November 1938 (PRONI, D3099/2/5/33B).

178 Londonderry, *Wings*, pp. 208–9; Londonderry to Karl Silex 4 October 1938 (PRONI, D3099/2/21/A/83A).

179 *The Times*, 3 October 1938.

180 *House of Lords Debates*, 3 October 1938, vol. 110, cols 1336–42.

181 *The Times*, 11 October 1938.

182 *The Times*, 12 October 1938.

183 Londonderry to Viscount Powerscourt, 26 October 1938 (PRONI, D3099/2/21/A/107); Londonderry to Churchill, 14 November 1938 (PRONI, D3099/2/5/37A).

184 Londonderry to G.H. Perry, 16 November 1938 (PRONI, D3099/2/19/175).

185 Londonderry to Göring, 24 November 1938 (PRONI, D3099/2/19/184A).

186 Dr Gritzbach to Londonderry, 12 December 1938 (PRONI, D3099/2/19/199).

187 Strobl, *Germanic*, pp. 161–83.

188 *House of Lords Debates*, 30 November 1938, vol. 111, cols 232–40.

189 *The Times*, 14 December 1938. Arising from this speech, Londonderry was both thanked for taking a strong stand (Dr Irvin Leatherdale to Londonderry, 14 December 1938 (PRONI, D3099/2/19/201)) and urged to consider concessions (Marjorie D. Brooks to Londonderry, 13 December 1938 (PRONI, D3099/2/19/200)).

190 Londonderry to Douglas Veale, 17 November 1938 (PRONI, D3099/2/19/176).

191 *House of Lords Debates*, 30 November 1938, vol. 111, cols 232–40; *The Times*, 14 December 1938; Londonderry to Marjorie D. Brooks, 14 December 1938 (PRONI, D3099/2/19/202).

192 Londonderry to F.C. Spencer-Davison, 14 November 1938 (PRONI, D3099/2/19/171); Londonderry to Mrs S. S. G. Parker, 29 December 1938 (PRONI, D3099/2/19/210).

193 *The Times*, 21 January 1939.

194 C. E. Carroll to Londonderry, 31 January 1939 (PRONI, D3099/2/19/233); David Lamont to Londonderry, 4 February 1939 (PRONI, D3099/2/19/238).
195 Londonderry to Carroll, 4 February 1939 (PRONI, D30992/19/239).
196 *The Times*, 8 February 1939.
197 Marchioness of Londonderry, *Retrospect* (London, 1938), pp. 81–7, 229–36.
198 Lady Londonderry to Beaverbrook, 3 January 1931 (HLRO, BBK/C/224).
199 *The Times*, 29 July 1931.
200 Lord Phillimore to Londonderry, 17 January 1938 (PRONI, D3099/2/19/49); Pugh, *'Hurrah'*, p. 268.
201 *The Times*, 13 March 1939.
202 *The Times*, 14 March 1939.
203 Londonderry to German embassy, London, 10 March 1939 (PRONI, D3099/2/19/256); *The Times*, 13 March 1939.
204 Hedin to Londonderry, 16 March 1939 (PRONI, D3099/2/21/A/2/1/1); Londonderry to Hedin, 20 March 1939 (PRONI, D3099/2/21/A/2/1/2).
205 *The Times*, 20 April 1939.
206 Londonderry to Göring, 23 May 1939 (PRONI, D3099/2/19/297).
207 Londonderry to Papen, 9 June 1939 (PRONI, D3099/2/19/306A).
208 Londonderry to Price, 28 March 1939 (PRONI, D3099/2/19/271).
209 Robert Jamieson to Londonderry, 8 April 1939 (PRONI, D3099/2/19/280).
210 Londonderry to Herbert von Dirksen, 17 June 1939 (PRONI, D3099/2/19/310); Dirksen to Londonderry, 21 June 1939 (PRONI, D3099/2/19/315).
211 Londonderry to Halifax, 12 June 1939 (PRONI, D3099/2/18/41A).
212 *The Times*, 22 June 1939.
213 Conwell-Evans to Londonderry, 21 June 1939 (PRONI, D3099/2/19/316). See Peter Hoffman, 'The Question of Western Allied Co-operation with the German anti-Nazi Conspiracy, 1938–1944', *Historical Journal*, 34, no. 2 (1991): 437–64.
214 Londonderry to Halifax, 10 July 1939 (PRONI, D3099/2/18/43).
215 *The Times*, 22 June 1939; Londonderry to Halifax, 4 July 1939 (PRONI, D3099/2/18/42); Halifax to Londonderry, 11 July 1939 (PRONI, D3099/2/18/44).
216 Londonderry, *Wings*, p. 224; Londonderry to Silex, 29 July 1939 (PRONI, D3099/2/19/328); Londonderry to Count Deym, 13 July 1939 (PRONI, D3099/2/19/326). Winterton does not mention in his memoirs advising Londonderry to take such a course (Earl Winterton, *Orders of the Day* (London, 1953)).
217 French, *Deterrence*, pp. 475–8.
218 Londonderry to Halifax, 2 August 1939 (PRONI, D3099/2/18/46).
219 Harold Macmillan, *Winds of Change* (London, 1966), p. 399.
220 Halifax to Londonderry, 2 August 1939 (PRONI, D3099/2/18/47).
221 Londonderry to Halifax, 12 August 1939 (PRONI, D3099/2/18/50); Halifax to Londonderry, 23 August 1939 (PRONI, D3099/2/18/51).
222 *The Times*, 16 August 1939.
223 Hailsham to Londonderry, 29 August 1939 (PRONI, D3099/2/17/52A); Londonderry to Chamberlain, 19 September 1939 (PRONI, D3099/2/17/53).
224 Sir Thomas Barnes [Treasury Solicitor] to Sir Rupert Howarth, 11 February 1938 (PRO, TS/27/451).
225 Chamberlain to Londonderry, 27 September 1939 (PRONI, D3099/2/17/54A). See also Edward Bridges to Chamberlain, 2 October 1939 (PRO, CAB/21/2676).
226 Londonderry to Chamberlain, 1 October 1939 (PRONI, D3099/4/52).

227 See, for example, Sarkisyanz, *Hitler's*, p. 257.
228 *The Times*, 16 August 1939.
229 *Daily Mail*, 19 September 1939; *The Times*, 20 September 1939.
230 *The Times*, 4 October 1939.
231 *The Times*, 14 October 1939.
232 Londonderry to Halifax, 25 December 1939 (PRONI, D3099/2/18/54).
233 Roberts, *'Holy'*, pp. 177–82.
234 Londonderry to Halifax, 25 December 1939 (PRONI, D3099/2/18/54). The letter also expressed concern that lords lieutenant were not being utilized.
235 Cannadine, *Decline*, p. 623; Ian Packer, *Lloyd George* (Basingstoke, 1998), pp. 106–7; Minutes of the 1922 Committee, 4 October 1939 (vol. 4, November 1938–May 1943, Bodleian Library, 1922/4).
236 *The Times*, 23 May 1930; *The Times*, 6 April 1937; William Goode to Londonderry, 6 December 1938 (PRONI, D3099/2/20/6); Goode to Londonderry, 13 December 1939 (PRONI, D3099/2/20/9).
237 Circular to members of Anglo-Hungarian Society, 1 January 1939 (PRONI, D3099/2/20/9).
238 Londonderry to Goode, 27 August 1940 (PRONI, D3099/2/20/17); Goode to Londonderry, 6 September 1940 (PRONI, D3099/2/20/18).
239 Londonderry to Goode, 14 September 1940 (PRONI, D3099/2/20/19).
240 András Bán, *Hungarian-British Diplomacy 1938–1941: The Attempt to Maintain Relations* (London, 2004), pp. 100–1.
241 See Peter Hadfield, *Hess: The Führer's Disciple* (rep. edn., London, 2001), p. 150.
242 *The Times*, 14 October 1939; *The Times*, 24 April 1940.
243 Londonderry to Wood, 21 October 1939 (PRO, AIR/19/27); Wood to Londonderry, 26 October 1939 (PRO, AIR/19/27).
244 *House of Lords Debates*, 15 November 1939, vol. 114, col. 1819.
245 Londonderry to Churchill, 7 September 1939 (PRONI, D3099/4/52); Londonderry to Churchill, 17 November 1939 (PRONI, D3099/4/52).
246 Londonderry to Halifax, 27 November 1939 (PRONI, D3099/2/18/52); Londonderry to Halifax, 2 December 1939 (PRONI, D3099/2/18/52); Londonderry to Halifax, 25 December 1939 (D3099/2/18/54).
247 Londonderry to Amery, 6 June 1936 (DCRO, D/Lo/C/237 (3)). They shared a dislike of the 1938 Anglo-American Trade Agreement (Scott Newton, *Profits of Peace: The Political Economy of Anglo-German Appeasement* (Oxford, 1996), p. 120).
248 Londonderry to Swinton, 23 March 1940 (PRONI, D3099/4/56); see John Ramsden, *An Appetite for Power: A History of the Conservative Party since 1830* (London, 1999), p. 228.
249 Salisbury to Londonderry, 1 April 1940 (PRONI, D/3099/4/56).
250 Larry L. Witherell, 'Lord Salisbury's "Watching Committee" and the Fall of Neville Chamberlain, May 1940', *English Historical Review*, 116, no. 469 (2001): 1149.
251 Londonderry to Salisbury, 11 April 1940 (PRONI, D3099/4/56).
252 Londonderry to Salisbury, 22 April 1940 (PRONI, D3099/4/56).
253 Londonderry to Salisbury, 11 April 1940 (PRONI, D3099/4/56); see Lady Londonderry to Swinton, 9 April 1938 (PRO, AIR/19/28).
254 Londonderry to Salisbury, 13 April 1940 (PRONI, D3099/4/56); Salisbury to Londonderry, 16 April 1940 (PRONI, D3099/4/56).
255 *The Times*, 12 June 1940.
256 Londonderry to Prime Minister's office, 26 October 1937 (PRONI, D3099/4/44).

257 Paul Canning, *British Policy Towards Ireland, 1921–1941* (Oxford, 1985), pp. 205–6.
258 Londonderry to Chamberlain, 21 January 1939 (PRONI, D3099/4/50); Chamberlain to Londonderry, 31 January 1939 (PRONI, D3099/4/50).
259 John Bowman, *De Valera and the Ulster Question 1917–1973* (Oxford, 1982), p. 197.
260 *The Times*, 4 March 1939.
261 *The Times*, 8 July 1939.
262 J. A. Pauley, 'The Social and Political Roles of Edith, Marchioness of Londonderry, 1878–1959' (PhD thesis, University of Ulster, 1994), pp. 384–285.
263 Goldsmith, *Annabel*, pp. 38–9.
264 *Belfast News-Letter*, 10 July 1933; Gillian McIntosh, *The Force of Culture: Unionist Identities in Twentieth-Century Ireland* (Cork, 1999), p. 46.
265 Alvin Jackson, 'Unionist Myths 1912–1985', *Past and Present*, 136 (1992): 164–85.
266 Londonderry to Richard Dawson Bates, 8 September 1939 (PRONI, D3099/4/52); Hyde, *Londonderrys*, p. 258. See Maggie Andrews, *Women and Evacuation in the Second World War: Femininity, Domesticity and Motherhood* (London, 2019), pp. 133–40.
267 See, for example, Headlam, diary, 6 April 1940, 3 May 1941, 8 December 1942 (Ball, *Parliament*, pp. 186–7, 250, 346).
268 Headlam, diary, 23 March 1939 (Ball, *Parliament*, p. 152).
269 Clive Scoular, *John M. Andrews: Northern Ireland's Wartime Prime Minister* (Killyleagh, 2004), p. 59.
270 Londonderry to Bates, 8 September 1939 (PRONI, D3099/4/52); Bates to Londonderry, 13 September 1939 (PRONI, D3099/4/52); Brooke to Londonderry, 11 June 1940 (D3099/4/57). See Brian Barton, *Brookeborough: The Making of a Prime Minister* (Belfast, 1988), pp. 158–9.
271 Londonderry to Wood, 12 July 1939 (PRO, AIR/19/27).
272 John P. Duggan, *Neutral Ireland and the Third Reich* (Dublin, 1989), p. 100.
273 Londonderry to Eden, 16 May 1940 (PRONI, D3099/4/57); Eden to Londonderry, 21 May 1940 (PRONI, D3099/4/57).
274 Londonderry to Eden, 11 June 1940 (PRONI, D3099/4/57); Brian Barton, *Northern Ireland in the Second World War* (Belfast, 1995), pp. 43–52; Philip Ollerenshaw, *Northern Ireland in the Second World War* (Manchester, 2013), pp. 16, 39–40.
275 Londonderry to Eden, 23 May 1940 (PRONI, D3099/4/50); Eden to Londonderry, 30 May 1940 (PRONI, D3099/4/50).
276 Londonderry to Eden, 11 June 1940 (PRONI, D3099/4/57). Londonderry afterwards wrote Craigavon's obituary notice (Lady Desborough to Londonderry, 29 November 1940 (PRONI, D3099/2/6/35)).
277 Londonderry to Churchill, 21 June 1940 (PRONI, D3099/4/57).
278 Churchill to Londonderry, 22 June 1940 (PRONI, D3099/4/57).
279 Salisbury to Londonderry, 8 July 1940 (PRONI, D/3099/4/57).
280 Londonderry to Salisbury, 19 July 1940 (PRONI, D3099/4/57).
281 See Lady Desborough to Londonderry, 30 June 1940 (PRONI, D3099/2/6/31); Eden to Londonderry, 14 August 1940 (PRONI, D3099/4/57).
282 Channon, diary, 19 May 1943 (James, *'Chips'*, pp. 258–9).
283 *The Times*, 5 October 1936; *The Times*, 11 July 1939.
284 *The Times*, 23 September 1937; *The Times*, 10 July 1937.
285 *The Times*, 27 January 1937.
286 Wood to Londonderry, 7 December 1939 (PRO, AIR/19/27).

287 F.H. Sandford to Londonderry, 11 May 1938 (PRO, AIR/19/28); *House of Lords Debates*, 12 May 1938, vol. 108, cols 1082–92.
288 Londonderry to Kingsley Wood, 21 June 1938 (PRO, AIR/19/28).
289 Air Ministry, memorandum, 29 June 1938 (PRO, AIR/19/28).
290 Wood to Londonderry, 13 July 1938 (PRO, AIR/19/28).
291 *The Times*, 29 August 1938; *The Times*, 30 August 1938.
292 *The Times*, 23 July 1938; see also *The Times*, 1 August 1938.
293 A. W. Street [Air Ministry] to Londonderry, 2 August 1938 (PRO, AIR/19/28).
294 *House of Lords Debates*, 1 August 1939, vol. 114, cols 750–5.
295 *The Times*, 29 April 1942; *The Times*, 23 July 1942.
296 Guy Warner, 'Civil Aviation in Ulster – A Brief Survey', *Due North*, 1, no. 4 (2001): 18.
297 Londonderry to Wood, 20 August 1938 (PRO, AIR/19/28); Wood to Londonderry, 24 August 1939 (PRO, AIR/19/28); Londonderry to Wood, 21 September 1939 (PRO, AIR/19/27).
298 Londonderry to Wood, 10 July 1939 (PRO, AIR/19/28).
299 Londonderry to Sir Edward Campbell, 19 April 1939 (PRO, AIR/19/27). See also Lady Londonderry to Swinton, 9 April 1938 (PRO, AIR/19/28); Londonderry to Wood, 12 January 1939 (PRO, AIR/19/27); Londonderry to Wood, 18 April 1939 (PRO, AIR/19/27).
300 Wood to Londonderry, 24 April 1939 (PRO, AIR/19/27).
301 Wood to Londonderry, 4 August 1939 (PRO, AIR/19/27); Wood to Londonderry, 22 August 1939 (PRO, AIR/19/27).
302 Londonderry to Wood, 18 October 1939 (PRO, AIR/19/27).
303 Londonderry to Oliver Stanley, 18 March 1940 (PRONI, D3099/4/56).
304 *House of Lords Debates*, 16 October 1940, vol. 117, cols 511–26.
305 *Daily Express*, 9 January 1940.
306 Londonderry to Beaverbrook, 9 January 1940 (HLRO, BBK/C/224).
307 Londonderry to Beaverbrook, 13 February 1942 (PRONI, D3099/4/64); Londonderry to Beaverbrook, 25 September 1943 (HLRO, BBK/D/139); Londonderry to Beaverbrook, 11 October 1943 (HLRO, BBK/D/139); Londonderry to Beaverbrook, 11 May 1944 (HLRO, BBK/D/139); Londonderry to Beaverbrook, 12 May 1944 (HLRO, BBK/D/139); Londonderry to Beaverbrook, 2 November 1944 (HLRO, BBK/D/139); Londonderry to Beaverbrook, 1 June 1945 (HLRO, BBK/D/139).
308 Londonderry to Beaverbrook, 21 January 1944 (HLRO, BBK/D/139).
309 Londonderry to Beaverbrook, 3 December 1943 (HLRO, BBK/D/139); Beaverbrook to Londonderry, 24 January 1944 (HLRO, BBK/D/139); Beaverbrook to Londonderry, 31 March 1944 (HLRO, BBK/D/139). See file of documents among the Beaverbrook papers solely concerned with Londonderry and the Civil Aviation bill, May 1944 (HLRO, BBK/F/160).
310 When Beaverbrook left his post at the end of 1944, Londonderry commented that he would never take it on because Churchill 'destroyed' him, and adding that he was too old (Londonderry to Beaverbrook, 13 October 1944 (HLRO, BBK/D/139)).
311 See Londonderry to Beaverbrook, 3 April 1944 (HLRO, BBK/D/139); Beaverbrook to Londonderry, 16 May 1944 (HLRO, BBK/D/139); Beaverbrook to Londonderry, 17 May 1944 (HLRO, BBK/D/139); Londonderry to Beaverbrook, 18 August 1944 (HLRO, BBK/D/265); Beaverbrook to Londonderry, 13 November 1944 (BBK/D/139); Beaverbrook to Londonderry, 5 June 1945 (HLRO, BBK/D/139); Londonderry to Beaverbrook, 16 November 1945 (HLRO, BBK/D/224).

312 Londonderry to Selby, 7 July 1945 (PRONI, D3099/2/22/74); *House of Lords Debates*, 8 July 1953, vol. 183, cols 351–5. See Walford Selby, *Diplomatic Twilight 1930–1940* (London, 1953).

313 Londonderry to Lord Kemsley, 23 September 1940 (PRONI, D3099/2/17/62); Londonderry to Peter Masefield, 9 October 1940 (PRONI, D3099/2/17/65).

314 Lynn to Londonderry, 15 March 1941 (PRONI, D3099/8/1). In September 1940 the 81-year-old humanitarian and archaeologist, Arthur J. Vogan, wrote to Londonderry that people in Australia – where he lived – read *Ourselves and Germany*. The thrust of his missive, however, was to request Londonderry's patronage for a new archaeological project on the Yasawa Islands, Fiji (Vogan to Londonderry, 25 September 1940 (PRONI, D3099/2/21/A/249)).

315 F. Elwyn Jones, *The Battle for Peace* (London, 1938), pp. 228–9.

316 Simon Haxey, *Tory MP* (London, 1939), p. 221.

317 Wickham Steed, *The Fifth Arm* (London, 1940), pp. 109–11.

318 Londonderry to Steed, 9 July 1940 (PRONI, D3099/2/21/A/3/3/1).

319 Steed to Londonderry, 15 July 1940 (PRONI, D3099/2/21/A/3/3/3).

320 Londonderry to Steed, 1 August 1940 (PRONI, D3099/2/21/A/3/3/9).

321 H. Montgomery Hyde, *The Londonderrys: A Family Portrait* (London, 1979), p. 256.

322 Memorandum, n.d. [1941] (PRONI, D3099/2/21/A/277).

323 Londonderry to Hyde, 9 October 1938 (PRONI, D3099/2/21/A/85). Kershaw argues that Londonderry was not helped by Hyde and repeats the view of Sir Edward Bridges that it was written by a Fleet Street 'ghost' (Kershaw, *Making*, p. 448).

324 Londonderry to Beaverbrook, 26 June 1941 (HLRO, BBK/C/224); Londonderry to Sir Rupert Howarth, 5 July 1941 (PRO, CAB/21/2676).

325 Londonderry to Clementine Churchill, 1 January 1942 (PRO, PREM/4/6/12); Clementine Churchill to Londonderry, 5 January 1942 (PRO, PREM/4/6/12); Desmond Morton to Clementine Churchill, 30 January 1942 (PRO, PREM/4/6/12). See David Reynolds, *In Command of History: Churchill Fighting and Writing the Second World War* (London, 2004), pp. 30–1.

326 Alexander Cadogan to Edward Bridges, 28 May 1942 (PRO, CAB/21/2677).

327 Sir Alexander Hardinge [Buckingham Palace] to Bridges, 1 June 1942 (PRO, CAB/21/2677); Hardinge to Bridges, 11 June 1942 (PRO, CAB/21/2677).

328 Bracken to Londonderry, 5 June 1942 (PRO, CAB/21/2677).

329 Bridges to Churchill, 6 June 1942 (PRO, PREM/4/6/12).

330 Churchill to Bridges, 16 June 1942 (PRO, PREM/4/6/12).

331 Cripps to Bridges, 29 June 1942 (PRO, CAB/21/2677); Londonderry to Bridges, 4 July 1942 (PRO, CAB/21/2677).

332 Thomas Barnes to Bridges, 10 August 1942 (PRO, TS/27/529).

333 Bridges, memorandum, 11 November 1942 (PRO, CAB/21/2678).

334 Cripps, memorandum, 14 November 1942 (PRO, PREM/4/6/12); War Cabinet minutes, 18 November 1942 (PRO, CAB/21/2678).

335 Bridges to Londonderry, 19 November 1942 (PRO, CAB/21/2678); Londonderry to Bridges, 20 November 1942 (PRO, CAB/21/2678).

336 *The Times*, 20 August 1941; *House of Lords Debates*, 25 March 1942, vol. 122, cols 457–62; Peter Masefield and Bill Gunston, *Flight Path: The Autobiography of Sir Peter Masefield* (Crawley, 2002), pp. 106, 126.

337 *House of Lords Debates*, 26 February 1942, vol. 122, cols 77–86.

338 Halifax to Londonderry, 12 December 1942 (PRONI, D3099/2/18/56).

339 Channon, diary, 4 December 1943 (James, *'Chips'*, p. 381).

340 Clementine Churchill to Londonderry, 5 January 1942 (PRO, PREM/4/6/12).
341 Londonderry to Churchill, 30 October 1944 (PRONI, D3099/2/5/44); Churchill to Londonderry, 23 December 1944 (PRONI, D3099/2/5/45). Londonderry afterwards complained that his correspondence with Churchill on Pickard had been badly handled by officials at Downing Street (John Colville to Londonderry, 16 February 1945 (PRONI, D3099/2/5/46); Londonderry to Colville, 22 February 1945 (PRONI, D3099/2/5/47); Colville to Londonderry, 23 February 1945 (PRONI, D3099/2/5/48); Londonderry to Morton, 22 February 1945 (PRONI, D3099/2/5/49); Morton to Londonderry, 27 February 1945 (PRONI, D3099/2/5/50)).
342 Churchill to Lady Londonderry, 29 April 1953 (PRONI, D3084/C/C/3/12).
343 Londonderry to Lady Desborough, n.d. [1943] (PRONI, T/3201/54).
344 *The Times*, 21 April 1938.
345 *The Times*, 19 November 1938.
346 *The Times*, 23 November 1945.
347 Londonderry to Selby, 27 November 1945 (PRONI, D3099/2/22/84).
348 Londonderry to Selby, 5 January 1946 (PRONI, D3099/2/22/88).
349 Hyde, *Londonderrys*, p. 262.
350 Headlam, diary, 22 June 1942 (Ball, *Parliament*, p. 320).
351 Headlam, diary, 2 October 1943, 3 October 1943 (Ball, *Parliament*, pp. 386–7).
352 Headlam, diary, 18 April 1948 (Ball, *Parliament*, p. 554).
353 *The Times*, 23 November 1945.
354 *The Times*, 29 November 1945; *The Times*, 28 February 1946; Telford Taylor, *The Anatomy of the Nuremberg Trials: A Personal Memoir* (London, 1993), pp. 320, 351–3.
355 Kershaw, *Making*, pp. 330–1.
356 Weitz, *Hitler's*, pp. 298–306.
357 Viscount Templewood, *Ambassador on Special Mission* (London, 1946).
358 Londonderry to Bridges, 11 March 1946 (PRO, CAB/21/2678).
359 Bridges to P. J. Dixon, 14 March 1946 (PRO, CAB/21/2678). See also Bridges to Thomas Barnes, 17 April 1946 (PRO, TS/27/529).
360 Bridges to Londonderry, 29 April 1946 (PRO, CAB/21/2678).
361 Londonderry to Bridges, 6 May 1946 (PRO, CAB/21/2678).
362 Londonderry to Stansgate, 13 August 1946 (PRONI, D3099/2/21/A/254).
363 R. C. Chilver to E. A. Armstrong, 8 February 1947 (PRO, CAB/21/2678).
364 Bridges to Chilver, 13 February 1947 (PRO, CAB/21/2678).
365 Baker to Londonderry, 28 February 1947 (PRONI, D3099/2/21/A/260). This was confirmed by the Committee on the use of Official Information in Private Publications, April 1947 (PRO, CAB/21/2678).
366 Londonderry to Baker, 7 March 1947 (PRONI, D3099/2/21/A/261).
367 Londonderry to W. S. Mann [Northern Ireland Governor's office], 1 May 1947 (PRONI, D3099/2/21/A/268).

Conclusion

1 Harold Nicolson, diary, 8 May 1945 (Nigel Nicolson (ed.), *Harold Nicolson Diaries and Letters, 1939–45* (London, 1967), pp. 458–9).

2 Harold Nicolson, *Why Britain is at War* (London, 1939), p. 157.
3 Nicolson, diary, 8 May 1945 (Nicolson, *Diaries*, pp. 458–9).
4 Londonderry to Lady Desborough, n.d. [1943] (PRONI, T/3201/54).
5 Londonderry to Desborough, 21 September 1947 (PRONI, T/3201/55). For similar assessment of Churchill, see Sebastian Haffner, *Churchill: Life and Times* (London, 2003).
6 Annabel Goldsmith, *Annabel, An Unconventional Life: The Memoirs of Lady Annabel Goldsmith* (London, 2004), p. 17.
7 Londonderry to Lee, 7 March 1947 (PRONI, D3099/2/21/A/262).
8 *The Times*, 27 May 1936. A similar event had been announced the previous year (*The Times*, 2 October 1935).
9 Pauline Lynn, 'Seaham Revisited: The Fruits of the Electoral Franchise?', *North East History*, 33 (2000): 15; R. J. Cooter, 'Lady Londonderry and the Irish Catholics of Seaham Harbour: "No Popery" Out of Context', *Recusant History*, 13, no. 4 (1976): 288–98.
10 *The Times*, 13 December 1937.
11 *The Times*, 7 October 1938.
12 *The Times*, 6 May 1937.
13 Barry Supple, *The History of the British Coal Industry: vol. 4: 1913–1946: The Political Economy of Decline* (Oxford, 1987), p. 406.
14 *House of Lords Debates*, 5 May 1938, vol. 108, cols 912–20; *House of Lords Debates*, 26 May 1938, vol. 109, cols 628, 632–3, 674.
15 *The Times*, 19 June 1939.
16 Supple, *British*, pp. 400–1.
17 *The Times*, 20 August 1941.
18 Richard B. Simons, 'The British Coal Industry-A Failure of Private Enterprise', *The Historian*, 16, no. 1 (1953): 12–13.
19 Simons, 'British', p. 16.
20 *The Times*, 28 January 1946.
21 Diane Urquhart, *The Ladies of Londonderry: Women and Political Patronage* (London, 2007), p. 205.
22 *The Times*, 12 February 1949.
23 *The Times*, 17 February 1949; *The Times*, 18 February 1949. Viscount Swinton commented on Londonderry's youthful qualities when he paid a tribute to him in the House of Lords (*The Times*, 16 February 1949).
24 Headlam, diary, 1 May 1949 (Stuart Ball (ed.), *Parliament and Politics in the Age of Churchill and Attlee: The Headlam Diaries 1935–1951* (Cambridge, 1999), pp. 585–6).
25 H. Montgomery Hyde, *The Londonderrys: A Family Portrait* (London, 1979), pp. 258–61. The ninth Marquess of Londonderry resided in England, as does his son, the tenth marquess (Graham Turner, 'The Stronghold of Labour', in *Mining and Social Change: Durham in the Twentieth Century*, ed. Martin Bulmer (London, 1978), p. 125).
26 *The Times*, 12 February 1949.
27 *The Times*, 17 February 1949.
28 A. Susan Williams, *Ladies of Influence: Women of the Elite in Interwar Britain* (London, 2000), p. 21.
29 Goldsmith, *Annabel*, p. 53.
30 D. H. Akenson, *Small Differences: Irish Catholics and Irish Protestants, 1815–1922: An International Perspective* (Kingston and Montreal, 1988), p. 125.

31 Stuart Ball, 'Introduction', in *Parliament and Politics in the Age of Baldwin and MacDonald: The Headlam Diaries, 1923–1935*, ed. Stuart Ball (London, 1992), p. 9.
32 Excerpts republished in Pat Walsh, 'The Apprenticeship of Bomber Bull', *Irish Political Review*, 19, no. 6 (2004): 19–22. See Brian Murphy, 'J.J. O'Kelly, the *Catholic Bulletin* and Contemporary Irish Cultural Historians', *Archivium Hibernicum*, 44 (1989): 71–88.
33 Marquess of Londonderry, *Wings of Destiny* (London, 1943), p. 44.
34 N. C. Fleming, 'Lancashire Conservatives, Tariff Reform, and Indian Responsible Government', *Contemporary British History*, 30, no. 2 (2016): 151–76.
35 Kennedy, diary, 16 December 1938 (Gordon Martel, *The Times and Appeasement: The Journals of A.L. Kennedy, 1932–1939* (Cambridge, 2000), p. 282).
36 Londonderry to Churchill, n.d. (PRONI, D3099/2/17/77).
37 Londonderry to Baldwin, 7 November 1939 (PRONI, D3099/2/17/55).
38 *House of Lords Debates*, 22 May 1935, vol. 96, cols 1002–19.
39 David E. Omissi, *Air Power and Colonial Control: The Royal Air Force, 1919–1939* (Manchester, 1990), p. 211.
40 Earl Winterton, *Orders of the Day* (London, 1953), p. 198.
41 Headlam, diary, 1 July 1938 (Ball, *Parliament*, p. 132).
42 Headlam, diary, 1 December 1938 (Ball, *Parliament*, p. 145).
43 Kennedy, diary, 7 February 1939 (Martel, *Appeasement*, p. 285).
44 Martin Gilbert (ed.), *Winston S. Churchill, vol. 5, Companion. Part 2, Documents. The Wilderness Years, 1929–1935* (London, 1981), p. 933.
45 Amery, diary, 5 September 1941 (John Barnes and David Nicholson (eds), *The Empire at Bay: The Leo Amery Diaries 1929–1945* (London, 1988), p. 713).
46 Kennedy, diary, 16 December 1938 (Martel, *Appeasement*, p. 281).
47 Peter Mandler, *The Fall and Rise of the Stately Home* (London, 1997), pp. 225–63. For noteworthy if marginal exception, see Bernard Dietz, *Neo Tories: The Revolt of the British Conservatives against Democracy and Political Modernity (1929–1939)* (London, 2018).
48 David Cannadine, *The Decline and Fall of the British Aristocracy* (rev. edn., London, 1992), p. 217.
49 Headlam, diary, 1 December 1938 (Ball, *Parliament*, p. 145).
50 Headlam, diary, 1 July 1938 (Ball, *Parliament*, p. 132).
51 Headlam, diary, 6 April 1940 (Ball, *Parliament*, pp. 186–7).
52 Headlam, diary, 29 January 1938 (Ball, *Parliament*, p. 122).
53 Headlam, diary, 4 April 1940 (Ball, *Parliament*, p. 185).
54 Viscount Castlereagh, 'Memorandum', August 1936, in *Baldwin Papers: A Conservative Statesman, 1908–1947*, eds Philip Williamson and Edward Baldwin (Cambridge, 2005), p. 369.
55 Headlam, diary, 11 February 1939 (Ball, *Parliament*, pp. 572–3).
56 Channon, diary, 11 February 1949 (Robert Rhodes James (ed.), *'Chips': The Diaries of Sir Henry Channon* (rep. edn., London, 1999), p. 434).
57 Robert Boothby, *I Fight to Live* (London, 1947), p. 140.
58 Channon, diary, 17 February 1949 (James, *'Chips'*, p. 434).
59 Tom Paulin, *The Invasion Handbook* (London, 2002), pp. 62–3.

Bibliography

Primary sources

1. Personal papers

Cambridge University Library (CUL)

Stanley Baldwin (Baldwin)

Churchill College Archives Centre, Cambridge

Alexander Cadogan (ACAD)
Winston Churchill (Chartwell trust) (copies at PRONI, D/3084/C/C/3)

Durham County Record Office (DCRO)

Londonderry (D/Lo)

Hertfordshire County Record Office

Lady Desborough (copies at PRONI, T/3201)

John Rylands University Library, Manchester (JRUL)

Ramsay MacDonald (RMD/1)

Liverpool Record Office and Local History Department

Lord Derby (920/DER)

Parliamentary Archives, London (HLRO)

Lord Beaverbrook (BBK)
R.D. Blumenfeld (Blu/Lon)
Andrew Bonar Law (BL)
J.C.C. Davidson (DAV/191)
David Lloyd George (LG/F)
J. St L. Strachey (STR)

Public Record Office of Northern Ireland (PRONI)

Lord Carson (D/1507)
Lord Craigavon (T/3775)
H. Montgomery Hyde (D/3084)
Londonderry (D/3099)
R.J. Lynn (D/3480)

2. State and Institutional Records

Bodleian Library, Oxford

1922 Committee minutes

National Archive, Kew (PRO)

Cabinet Office (CAB)
Domestic papers of Public Record Office (PRO)
Foreign Office (FO)
Home Office (HO)
Lord Chancellor's Office (LCO)
Ministry of Air and Royal Air Force (AIR)
Ministry of Housing and Local Government (HLG)
Ministry of Munitions (MUN)
Pre-Nationalization Railway Company (RAIL)
Treasury Solicitor and HM Procurator General's Department (TS)

Public Record Office of Northern Ireland (PRONI)

Cabinet (Northern Ireland) (CAB)
Ministry of Education (Northern Ireland) (ED)
Ulster Unionist Council (D/1327)

Trinity College Library, University of Dublin

Irish Convention

3. Newspapers and journals

Aberdeen Journal
Aeroplane
Belfast News-Letter
Belfast Telegraph
Books and Bookmen
Colliery Guardian
Daily Express
Daily Mail
Durham County Advertiser
Evening Standard
Irish News
Irish Independent
Kent Times
Lamp
Llandudno and North Wales Weekly News
Manchester Guardian
Morning Post
Navy League Journal

New Statesman and Nation
Newcastle Journal
News Chronicle
Northampton Mercury
Probation
Punch, or the London Charivari
Rotherham Advertiser
Spectator
South Eastern Gazette
Standard
Sunday Chronicle
Sunday Express
Sunderland Echo
Surrey Herald
Teachers' World
The Times
T.P.'s & Cassell's Weekly
Tribune
Westminster Gazette
World

4. Published autobiographies, letters, diaries, and minutes

Ball, Stuart (ed.), *Parliament and Politics in the Age of Baldwin and MacDonald: The Headlam Diaries 1923–1935*. London, 1992.
Ball, Stuart (ed.), *Parliament and Politics in the Age of Churchill and Attlee: The Headlam Diaries 1935–1951*. Cambridge, 1999.
Ball, Stuart (ed.), *Conservative Politics in National and Imperial Crisis: Letters from Britain to the Viceroy of India 1926–31*. Aldershot, 2014.
Barnes, John and David Nicholson (eds), *The Empire at Bay: The Leo Amery Diaries 1929–1945*. London, 1988.
Boothby, Robert, *I Fight to Live*. London, 1947.
Bridgeman, William, *The Modernisation of Conservative Politics: The Diaries and Letters of William Bridgeman 1904–1935*. London, 1988.
Buckland, Patrick (ed.), *Irish Unionism 1885–1923: A Documentary History*. Belfast, 1973.
Buckmaster, Herbert, *Buck's Book: Ventures-Adventures and Misadventures*. London, 1933.
Bullock, Alan (ed.), *The Ribbentrop Memoirs*. London, 1954.
Callwell, C. E. (ed.), *Field Marshal Sir Henry Wilson: His Life and Diaries*. London, 1927.
Cole, Margaret (ed.), *Beatrice Webb's Diaries 1924–1932*. London, 1956.
Croft, Lord, *My Life of Strife*. London, 1948.
Crowson, N. J. (ed.), *Fleet Street, Press Barons and Politics: The Journals of Collin Brooks, 1932–1940*. Cambridge, 1998.
Fleming, N. C. (ed.), *Aristocracy, Democracy, and Dictatorship: The Political Papers of the Seventh Marquess of Londonderry*. Cambridge, 2022.
Gilbert, Martin (ed.), *Winston S. Churchill, vol. 5, Companion. Part 2, Documents. The Wilderness Years, 1929–1935*. London, 1981.
Goldsmith, Annabel, *Annabel, An Unconventional Life: The Memoirs of Lady Annabel Goldsmith*. London, 2004.
Goldsmith, Annabel, *No Invitation Required: The Pelham Cottage Years*. London, 2010.

Harvey, John (ed.), *The Diplomatic Diaries of Oliver Harvey 1937–1940*. London, 1970.
James, Robert Rhodes (ed.), *'Chips': The Diaries of Sir Henry Channon*. London, 1967.
James, Robert Rhodes (ed.), *Memoirs of a Conservative: J.C.C. Davidson's Memoirs and Papers, 1910–37*. London, 1969.
Liddell Hart, B. H., *Memoirs, vol. 1*. London, 1965.
Lloyd George, David, *War Memoirs of David Lloyd George, vol. 2*. London, 1938.
Londonderry, Marchioness of, *Retrospect*. London, 1938.
Londonderry, Marquess of, *Wings of Destiny*. London, 1943.
MacKenzie, Norman (ed.), *The Letters of Sidney and Beatrice Webb: vol. 3: Pilgrimage, 1912–1947*. Cambridge, 1978.
Macmillan, Harold, *Winds of Change*. London, 1966.
Madariaga, Salvador de, *Morning without Noon: Memoirs*. Farnborough, 1974.
Martel, Gordon (ed.), *The Times and Appeasement: The Journals of A.L. Kennedy, 1932–1939*. Cambridge, 2000.
Masefield, Peter and Bill Gunston, *Flight Path: The Autobiography of Sir Peter Masefield*. Crawley, 2002.
Middlemas, Keith (ed.), *Thomas Jones Whitehall Diary, vol. 2: 1926–1930*. London, 1969.
Middlemas, Keith (ed.), *Thomas Jones Whitehall Diary, vol. 3: Ireland, 1918–1925*. London, 1971.
Midleton, Earl of, *Records and Reactions 1856–1939*. New York, 1939.
Nicolson, Nigel (ed.), *Harold Nicolson: Diaries and Letters 1930–1939*. London, 1966.
Nicolson, Nigel (ed.), *Harold Nicolson: Diaries and Letters, 1939–45*. London, 1967.
Ó Bróin, Leon (ed.), *In Great Haste: The Letters of Michael Collins and Kitty Kiernan*. Dublin, 1996.
Petrie, Charles (ed.), *The Life and Letters of the Right Hon. Sir Austin Chamberlain KG, PC, MP*. London, 1939.
Pimlott, Ben (ed.), *The Political Diary of Hugh Dalton: 1918–40, 1945–60*. London, 1986.
Priestley, J. B., *English Journey: Jubilee Edition with Eighty Illustrations*. [1934] London, 1984.
Roskill, Stephen (ed.), *Hankey: Man of Secrets, vol. 3: 1931–1963*. London, 1974.
Rothermere, Viscount, *My Fight to Rearm Britain*. London, 1939.
Self, Robert C. (ed.), *The Austen Chamberlain Diary Letters: The Correspondence of Sir Austen Chamberlain with his Sisters Hilda and Ida, 1916–1937*. Cambridge, 1995.
Simon, Viscount, *Retrospect: The Memoirs of the Rt. Hon. Viscount Simon GCSI, GCVO*. London, 1952.
Smart, Nick (ed.), *The Diaries and Letters of Robert Bernays, 1932–1939: An Insider's Account of the House of Commons*. Lampeter, 1996.
Snowden, Viscount, *An Autobiography, vol. 2: 1919–1934*. London, 1934.
Swinton, Viscount, *I Remember*. London, 1948.
Taylor, A. J. P. (ed.), *W.P. Crozier: Off the Record: Political Interviews, 1933–1943*. London, 1973.
Templewood, Viscount, *Ambassador on Special Mission*. London, 1946.
Thorpe, Andrew and Richard Toye (eds), *Parliament and Politics in the Age of Asquith and Lloyd George: The Diaries of Cecil Harmsworth MP, 1909–22*. Cambridge, 2016.
Urquhart, Diane (ed.), *The Minutes of the Ulster Women's Unionist Council and Executive Committee 1911–40*. Dublin, 2001.
Vansittart, Robert, *The Mist Procession: The Autobiography of Lord Vansittart*. London, 1958.
Williamson, Philip and Edward Baldwin (eds), *Baldwin Papers: A Conservative Statesman, 1908–1947*. Cambridge, 2005.

Winterton, Earl, *Pre-War*. London, 1932.
Winterton, Earl, *Orders of the Day*. London, 1953.

5. Contemporary works and works by contemporaries

Armstrong, H. C., *Grey Wolf: Mustafa Kemal: An Intimate Study of a Dictator*. London, 1932.
Baldwin, A. W., *My Father: The True Story*. London, 1955.
Balfour, Patrick, *Society Racket: A Critical Survey of Modern Social Life*. London, 1933.
Burge, C. G. (ed.), *The Air Annual of the British Empire 1933–34*. London, 1933.
Burge, C. G. (ed.), *The Air Annual of the British Empire 1935–36*. London, 1935.
Cato [pseud.], *Guilty Men*, [1940] rep. edn. London, 1998.
Churchill, Randolph S., *Lord Derby 'King of Lancashire': The Official Life of Edward, Seventeenth Earl of Derby 1865–1948*. London, 1959.
Churchill, Winston S., *The Second World War, vol. 1, The Gathering Storm*, rep. edn. London, 1949.
Colvin, Ian, *The Life of Lord Carson, vol. 2*. London, 1934.
Craig, F. W. S., *British General Election Manifestos, 1900–1974*, rev. edn. London, 1975.
Davitt, Michael, *The Fall of Feudalism in Ireland, or, The Story of the Land League Revolution*. London, 1904.
Dugdale, Blanche E. C., *Arthur James Balfour, First Earl of Balfour, KG, OM, FRS, etc, vol. 1*. London, 1936.
Fingall, Countess of, *Seventy Years Young: Memories of Elizabeth, Countess of Fingall*, rep. edn. Dublin, 1991.
Haxey, Simon [pseud.], *Tory MP*. London, 1939.
Hughes, Philip, 'Castlereagh', *Studies: An Irish Quarterly Review*, 26, no. 102 (1937): 249–66.
Hyde, H. Montgomery, *The Rise of Castlereagh*. London, 1933.
Hyde, H. Montgomery, *Londonderry House and Its Pictures*. London, 1937.
Jones, F. Elwyn, *The Battle for Peace*. London, 1938.
Kennedy, John F., *Why England Slept*. New York, 1940.
Liddell Hart, B. H., *Europe in Arms*. New York, 1937.
Londonderry, Marchioness of [Theresa], *Robert Stewart, Viscount Castlereagh*. London, 1904.
Londonderry, Marchioness of [Edith], *Henry Chaplin: A Memoir*. London, 1926.
Londonderry, Marchioness of, *Character and Tradition*. London, 1934.
Londonderry, Marchioness of, *Mount Stewart*. Privately printed, 1956.
Londonderry, Marchioness of, *Frances Anne. The Life and Times of Frances Anne, Marchioness of Londonderry and her Husband Charles, Third Marquess of Londonderry*. London, 1958.
Londonderry, Marquess of, 'The Irish Problem, 1922', *Nineteenth Century and After*, 92 (December 1922): 895–8.
Londonderry, Marquess of, 'Public Education in Northern Ireland: The New System', *Nineteenth Century and After*, 95 (March 1924): 328–34.
Londonderry, Marquess of, *Airways of the Empire: Their History and Development*. Nottingham, 1936.
Londonderry, Marquess of, *Ourselves and Germany*. London, 1938.
Londonderry, Marquess of, 'Bombing from the Air', *Nineteenth Century and After*, 125 (March 1939): 269–81.
Marjoribanks, Edward, *The Life of Lord Carson, vol. 1*, 3rd edn. London, 1932.

Marriott, J. A. R., *Castlereagh: A Political Biography*. London, 1936.
McCallum, R. B., *Public Opinion and the Last Peace*. London, 1944.
McNeill, Ronald, *Ulster's Stand for the Union*. London, 1922.
Morgenthau, Hans J., *Politics among Nations: The Struggle for Power and Peace*. New York, 1948.
Muggeridge, Malcolm, *The Thirties, 1930–1940 in Great Britain*. London, 1940.
Nicolson, Harold, *Why Britain is at War*. London, 1939.
Nicolson, Harold, *George V: His Life and Reign*. London, 1952.
Noel-Baker, Philip, *The First World Disarmament Conference, 1932–33 and Why it Failed*. London, 1979.
O'Neill, Hugh, 'Ireland', in *The New Order: Studies in Unionist Policy*, edited by Earl of Malmesbury. London, 1908.
Orwell, George, *The Road to Wigan Pier*. London, 1937.
Oxford, Margot, *More Memories*. London, 1933.
Priestley, J. B., *English Journey*. London, 1934.
Sassoon, Philip, 'Air power in the Middle East', *Journal of the Royal Central Asian Society*, 20, no. 3 (1933): 394–405.
Saunders, Hilary St George, *Per Adua: The Rise of British Air Power 1911–1939*. London, 1944.
Selby, Walford, *Diplomatic Twilight 1930–1940*. London, 1953.
Sencourt, Robert, *Winston Churchill*. London, 1940.
Sinclair, W. A., *The Voice of the Nazi: Being Eight Broadcast Talks Given Between December 1939 and May 1940*. London, 1940.
Steed, Wickham, *The Fifth Arm*. London, 1940.
Taylor, Telford, *The Anatomy of the Nuremberg Trials: A Personal Memoir*. London, 1993.
Ulster Unionist Council, *The Ulster Unionist Demonstration of 1912: In Royal Agricultural Show Grounds, Balmoral, Belfast*. Belfast, 1912.
Ward Price, G., *I Know these Dictators*. London, 1937.
Webster, C. K., *The Foreign Policy of Castlereagh, 1815–1822: Britain and the European Alliance*. London, 1925.
Webster, C. K., *The Foreign Policy of Castlereagh, 1812–1815: Britain and the Reconstruction of Europe*. London, 1931.
Wyatt, Harold Frazer and L. Graham H. Horton-Smith, *The Passing of the Great Fleet*. London, 1909.

6. Literature, film, and television

Boulting, Roy (dir.), *Fame is the Spur*. 1947.
Fairfax, Ferdinand (dir.), *Winston Churchill: The Wilderness Years*. 1981.
Giles, David (dir.), *Fame is the Spur*. 1982.
Glyn, Elinor, *Did She?* London, 1934.
Ishiguro, Kazuo, *The Remains of the Day*. London, 1989.
Milton, John, *Areopagitica*. London, 1644.
Paulin, Tom, *The Invasion Handbook*. London, 2002.
Ritchie, Alice, *The Peacemakers*. London, 1928.
Sackville West, Vita, *The Edwardians*. London, 1930.
Spring, Howard, *Fame is the Spur*. London, 1940.
Waddell, Helen, *Peter Abelard*. London, 1933.

Waugh, Evelyn, *Vile Bodies*. London, 1930.
Wodehouse, P. G., *The Code of the Woosters*. London, 1938.
Wodehouse, P. G., *Jeeves and the Feudal Spirit*. London, 1955.

7. Reference works

Butler, David and Gareth Butler, *Twentieth-Century British Political Facts, 1900–2000*. London, 2000.
Cahill, Kevin, *Who Owns Britain: The Hidden Facts behind Landownership in the UK and Ireland*. London, 2001.
Fleming, N. C. and Alan O'Day, *The Longman Handbook of Modern Irish History since 1800*. London, 2005.
Moody, T. W., F. X. Martin, and F. J. Byrne (eds), *A New History of Ireland: A Chronology of Irish History to 1976: A Companion to Irish History Part 1*. Oxford, 1982.
Walker, Brian M., *Parliamentary Election Results in Ireland, 1918–92*. Dublin, 1992.

8. Official papers

Coal Industry Commission: Report and Minutes of Evidence, vol. 2. Cmd. 360, Parliamentary Papers (1919), XII.
Parliamentary Debates, House of Commons (Hansard), series 4 and 5.
Parliamentary Debates, House of Lords, (Hansard), series 5.
Parliamentary Debates, Northern Ireland House of Commons, (Hansard), series 1.
Parliamentary Debates, Northern Ireland Senate, (Hansard), series 1.
Plunkett, H. C., *The Irish Convention: Confidential Report to His Majesty the King by the Chairman*. Dublin, 1918.
Plunkett, H. C., *Report of the Proceedings of the Irish Convention*. Dublin, 1918.

Secondary sources

9. Articles, biographies, and monographs

Adams, R. J. Q., *Bonar Law*. London, 1999.
Adey, Peter, 'Airports and Air-mindedness: Spacing, Timing and using the Liverpool Airport, 1929–1939', *Social & Cultural Geography*, 7, no. 3 (2006): 343–63.
Adonis, Andrew, *Making Aristocracy Work: The Peerage and the Political System in Britain, 1884–1914*, rep. edn. Oxford, 2002.
Akenson, D. H., *Education and Enmity: The Control of Schooling in Northern Ireland, 1920–50*. London, 1973.
Akenson, D. H., *Small Differences: Irish Catholics and Irish Protestants, 1815–1922: An International Perspective*. Kingston and Montreal, 1988.
Allen, Nicholas, 'National Reconstruction: George Russell (Æ) and the Irish Convention', in *Ireland in Transition, 1867–1921*, edited by D. George Boyce and Alan O'Day. London, 2004.
Andrews, Maggie, *Women and Evacuation in the Second World War: Femininity, Domesticity and Motherhood*. London, 2019.

Aristotle, *The Politics*, trans. T. A. Sinclair, rep. edn. London, 1992.

Balfour-Paul, Glen, 'Britain's Informal Empire in the Middle East', in *The Oxford History of the British Empire, vol. 4 : The Twentieth Century*, edited by Judith M. Brown and Wm. Roger Louis. Oxford, 1999.

Ball, Stuart, *Baldwin and the Conservative Party: The Crisis of 1929–1931*. London, 1988.

Ball, Stuart, 'The National and Regional Party Structure', in *Conservative Century: The Conservative Party Since 1900*, edited by Anthony Seldon and Stuart Ball. Oxford, 1994.

Ball, Stuart, *The Conservative Party and British Politics, 1902–1951*. London, 1995.

Ball, Stuart, 'The Legacy of Coalition: Fear and Loathing in Conservative Politics, 1922–31', *Contemporary British History*, 25, no. 1 (2011): 65–82.

Ball, Stuart, *Portrait of a Party: The Conservative Party in Britain 1918–1945*. Oxford, 2013.

Bán, András, *Hungarian-British Diplomacy 1938–1941: The Attempt to Maintain Relations*. London, 2004.

Barfoot, James, *Plâs Machynlleth: A Historical Guide*. Norwich, 1997.

Barron, Hester, *The 1926 Miners' Lockout: Meanings of Community in the Durham Coalfield*. Oxford, 2010.

Barton, Brian, *Brookeborough: The Making of a Prime Minister*. Belfast, 1988.

Barton, Brian, *Northern Ireland in the Second World War*. Belfast, 1995.

Bassett, R., *Democracy and Foreign Policy, A Case History: The Sino-Japanese dispute, 1931–33*. London, 1952.

Bassett, R., *Nineteen Thirty-One: Political Crisis*. London, 1958.

Beckett, J. V., *The Aristocracy in England, 1660–1914*. Oxford, 1988.

Bennett, G. H., *British Foreign Policy during the Curzon Period, 1919–24*. New York, 1995.

Beynon, Huw and Terry Austrin, *Masters and Servants: Class Patronage in the Making of a Labour Organisation: The Durham Miners and the English Political Tradition*. London, 1994.

Bew, Paul, *Ideology and the Irish Question: Ulster Unionism and Irish Nationalism, 1912–1916*. Oxford, 1998.

Bew, Paul, Peter Gibbon and Henry Patterson, *Northern Ireland 1921/2001: Political Forces and Social Classes*. London, 2002.

Bew, Paul, *Churchill and Ireland*. Oxford, 2016.

Biaggi, Cecilia, 'Reforming Education in post-partition Northern Ireland: State Control and Churches' Interference', *History of Education*, 49, no. 3 (2020): 379–97.

Bialer, Uri, *The Shadow of the Bomber: The Fear of Air Attack and British Policies, 1932–1939*. London, 1980.

Blackett, Monica, *The Mark of the Maker: A Portrait of Helen Waddell*. London, 1973.

Blake, Robert, *The Decline of Power 1915–1964*. London, 1986.

Blewett, Neal, *The Peers, the Parties and the People: The General Elections of 1910*. London, 1972.

Bogdanor, Vernon, *The Monarchy and the Constitution*. Oxford, 1997.

Bond, Brian, *British Military Policy Between the Two World Wars*. Oxford, 1980.

Bosco, Andrea, 'Lord Lothian and Appeasement', in *The Round Table, the Empire/Commonwealth, and British Foreign Policy*, edited by Andrea Bosco and Alex May. London, 1997.

Bowman, John, *De Valera and the Ulster Question 1917–1973*. Oxford, 1982.

Bowman, Timothy, *Carson's Army: The Ulster Volunteer Force, 1910–22*. Manchester, 2007.

Boyce, D. George, 'British Conservative Opinion, the Ulster Question, and the Partition of Ireland, 1912–21', *Irish Historical Studies*, 17, no. 65 (1970): 89–112.

Boyce, D. George, *Englishmen and Irish Troubles: British Public Opinion and the Making of Irish Policy, 1918–1922*. Boston, 1972.

Boyce, D. George, *Nineteenth-century Ireland: The Search for Stability*. Dublin, 1990.

Boyce, D. George, 'Respectable Rebels: Ulster Unionist Resistance to the Third Home Rule Bill, 1912–14', in *Conflicts in the North of Ireland, 1900–2000: Flashpoints and Fracture Zones*, edited by Alan F. Parkinson and Éamon Phoenix. Dublin, 2010.

Boyns, Trevor, 'Strategic Responses to Foreign Competition: The British Coal Industry and the 1930 Coal Mines Act', *Business History*, 32, no. 3 (1990): 133–45.

Buckland, Patrick, *Irish Unionism: One: The Anglo-Irish and the New Ireland 1885–1922*. Dublin, 1972.

Buckland, Patrick, *Irish Unionism: Two: Ulster Unionism and the Origins of Northern Ireland 1886–1922*. Dublin, 1973.

Buckland, Patrick, *The Factory of Grievances: Devolved Government in Northern Ireland 1921–39*. Dublin, 1979.

Burk, Kathleen, 'The Treasury: From Impotence to Power', in *War and the State: The Transformation of Government, 1914–1919*, edited by Kathleen Burk. London, 1982.

Burleigh, Michael, *The Third Reich: A New History*. London, 2000.

Butler, J. R. M., *Lord Lothian (Philip Kerr) 1882–1940*. London, 1960.

Campbell, John, *F.E. Smith, First Earl of Birkenhead*. London, 1983.

Cannadine, David, *Aspects of Aristocracy: Grandeur and Decline in Modern Britain*. London, 1994.

Cannadine, David, *The Decline and Fall of the British Aristocracy*, rev. edn. London, 1996.

Cannadine, David, *Ornamentalism: How the British Saw their Empire*. London, 2002.

Canning, Paul, *British Policy towards Ireland 1921–1941*. Oxford, 1985.

Carlton, David, *Anthony Eden: A Biography*. London, 1981.

Carr, William, *Arms, Autarky and Aggression: A Study in German Foreign Policy, 1933–1939*. London, 1972.

Casement, Anne, 'The Management of the Londonderry Estates in Ulster during the Great Famine', *Familia: Ulster Genealogical Review*, 21 (2005): 56–68.

Ceadel, Martin, *Pacifism in Britain 1914–1945: The Defining of a Faith*. Oxford, 1980.

Charmley, John, *Lord Lloyd and the Decline of the British Empire*. London, 1987.

Chilston, Viscount, *Chief Whip: The Political Life and Times of Aretas Akers-Douglas, 1st Viscount Chilston*. London, 1961.

Clark, Ronald W., *Tizard*. London, 1965.

Clarke, Ian, *The Hierarchy of States: Reform and Resistance in the International Order*. Cambridge, 1989.

Clayton, Anthony, 'Imperial Defence and Security, 1900–1968', in *The Oxford History of the British Empire, vol. 4: The Twentieth Century*, edited by Judith M. Brown and Wm. Roger Louis. Oxford, 1999.

Coakley, J. F., *The Church of the East and the Church of England: A History of the Archbishop of Canterbury's Assyrian Mission*. Oxford, 1992.

Coleman, Marie, *The Irish Sweep: A History of the Irish Hospitals Sweepstake, 1930–87*. Dublin, 2009.

Colley, Linda, *Britons: Forging the Nation, 1707–1837*. London, 1992.

Cooper, Chris, 'Conservatism, Imperialism and Appeasement: The Political Career of Douglas Hogg, First Viscount Hailsham 1922–38', Ph.D. thesis, University of Liverpool, 2012.

Cooter, R. J., 'Lady Londonderry and the Irish Catholics of Seaham Harbour: "No Popery" Out of Context', *Recusant History*, 13, no. 4 (1976): 288–98.

Corum, James S., 'The RAF in Imperial Defence, 1919–1956', in *Imperial Defence: The Old World Order, 1865–1956*, edited by Greg Kennedy. London, 2008.
Cowling, Maurice, *The Impact of Labour 1920–40: The Beginning of Modern British Politics*. Cambridge, 1971.
Cowling, Maurice, *The Impact of Hitler: British Politics and British Policy, 1933–1940*. Cambridge, 1975.
Craig, Gordon A., *The Politics of the Prussian Army, 1640–1945*. New York, 1964.
Cross, J. A., *Lord Swinton*. Oxford, 1982.
Crowson, N. J., 'The British Conservative Party and the Jews during the Late 1930s', *Patterns of Prejudice*, 29, no. 2–3 (1995): 15–32.
Crowson, N. J., *Facing Fascism: The Conservative Party and the European Dictators, 1935–1940*. London, 1997.
Daly, T. P., 'James Craig and Orangeism, 1903–10', *Irish Historical Studies*, 34, no. 136 (2005): 431–48.
Dangerfield, George, *The Strange Death of Liberal England*, rep. edn. London, 1966.
Davies, John, *A History of Wales*, rev. edn. London, 2007.
Davies, Paul, *A.J. Cook*. Manchester, 1987.
De Brún, Fionntán, '"Ulsteria": The Fortunes of the Irish language under Stormont, 1921–72', in *Conflicts in the North of Ireland 1900–2000: Flashpoints and Fracture Zones*, edited by Alan F. Parkinson and Éamon Phoenix. Dublin, 2010.
De Courcy, Anne, *Circe: The Life of Edith, Marchioness of Londonderry*. London, 1993.
Defries, Harry, *Conservative Party Attitudes to Jews, 1900–1950*. London, 2001.
Dietz, Bernhard, *Neo Tories: The Revolt of British Conservatives against Democracy and Political Modernity (1929–1939)*. London, 2018.
Dilks, David, '"The Unnecessary War"? Military Advice and Foreign Policy in Great Britain, 1931–1939', in *General Staffs and Diplomacy before the Second World War*, edited by Adrian Preston. London, 1978.
Doerr, Paul W., *British Foreign Policy 1919–1939: 'Hope for the Best, Prepare for the Worst'*. Manchester, 1998.
Dooley, Terence, *The Decline of the Big House in Ireland*. Dublin, 2001.
Duggan, John P., *Neutral Ireland and the Third Reich*. Dublin, 1989.
Dutton, David, *Austen Chamberlain: Gentleman in Politics*. Bolton, 1985.
Dutton, David, *'His Majesty's Loyal Opposition': The Unionist Party in Opposition, 1905–1915*. Liverpool, 1992.
Dutton, David, *Neville Chamberlain*. London, 2001.
Edgerton, David, *England and the Aeroplane: Militarism, Modernity and Machines*. London, 2013.
Egremont, Max, *Balfour: A Life of Arthur James Balfour*. London, 1998.
Ervine, St John, *Craigavon: Ulsterman*. London, 1949.
Evans, Stephen, 'The Conservatives and the Redefinition of Unionism, 1912–21', *Twentieth Century British History*, 9, no. 1 (1998): 1–27.
Ewer, Peter, 'A Gentlemen's Club in the Clouds: Reassessing the Empire Air Mail Scheme, 1933–1939', *Journal of Transport History*, 28, no. 1 (2007): 75–92.
Fair, John D., *British Interparty Conferences: A Study of the Procedure of Conciliation in British Politics, 1867–1921*. Oxford, 1980.
Fair, John D., 'F.S. Oliver, *Alexander Hamilton*, and the "American Plan" for Resolving Britain's Constitutional Crises, 1903–1921', *Twentieth Century British History*, 10, no. 1 (1999): 1–26.

Farrell, Michael, *Arming the Protestants: The Formation of the Ulster Special Constabulary and the Royal Ulster Constabulary, 1920–7*. London, 1983.
Farrell, Michael, *Northern Ireland: The Orange State*, rep. edn. London, 1992.
Farren, Sean, 'Unionist-Protestant Reaction to Educational Reform in Northern Ireland 1923–1930', *History of Education*, 14, no. 3 (1985): 227–36.
Farren, Sean, 'Nationalist-Catholic Reaction to Educational Reform in Northern Ireland, 1920–30', *History of Education*, 15, no. 1 (1986): 19–30.
Farren, Sean, *The Politics of Irish Education, 1920–65*. Belfast, 1995.
Ferris, John R., *Men, Money, and Diplomacy: The Evolution of British Strategic Policy, 1919–26*. New York, 1989.
Ferris, John R., '"Now that the Milk is Spilt": Appeasement and the Archive on Intelligence', *Diplomacy and Statecraft*, 19, no. 3 (2008): 527–65.
Fitzpatrick, David, 'Militarism in Ireland, 1900–1922', in *A Military History of Ireland*, edited by Thomas Bartlett and Keith Jeffery. Cambridge, 1996.
Fleming, N. C., 'Lord Londonderry and Education Reform in 1920s Northern Ireland', *History Ireland*, 9, no. 1 (2001): 36–9.
Fleming, N. C., 'The Marquess of Londonderry: A Political Life', Ph.D. thesis, The Queen's University of Belfast, 2002.
Fleming, N. C., 'Lord Londonderry and Ulster Politics, 1921–6', in *Irish History: A Research Yearbook, 2*, edited by Joost Augusteijn, Mary Ann Lyons and Dierdre McMahon. Dublin, 2003.
Fleming, N. C., 'The Landed Elite, Power and Ulster Unionism', in *The Ulster Crisis 1885–1921*, edited by D. George Boyce and Alan O'Day. Basingstoke, 2006.
Fleming, N. C., 'The First Government of Northern Ireland, Education Reform and the Failure of Anti-populist Unionism, 1921–1925', *Twentieth Century British History*, 18, no. 2 (2007): 146–69.
Fleming, N. C., 'Cabinet Government, British Imperial Security, and the World Disarmament Conference, 1932–1934', *War in History*, 18, no. 1 (2011): 62–84.
Fleming, N. C., 'Diehard Conservatism, Mass Democracy, and Indian Constitutional Reform, *c.* 1918–35', *Parliamentary History*, 32, no. 2 (2013): 337–60.
Fleming, N. C., 'Education since the Late Eighteenth Century', in *Ulster since 1600: Politics, Economy and Society*, edited by Liam Kennedy and Philip Ollerenshaw. Oxford, 2013.
Fleming, N. C., 'Political Extremes and Extremist Politics', *Political Studies Review*, 12, no. 3 (2014): 395–401.
Fleming, N. C., 'Diehard Conservatives and the Appeasement of Nazi Germany, 1935–1940', *History*, 100, no. 3 (2015): 412–35.
Fleming, N. C., 'The Imperial Maritime League: British Navalism, Conflict and the Radical Right, *c.* 1907–1920', *War in History*, 23, no. 3 (2016): 296–322.
Fleming, N. C., 'Lancashire Conservatives, Tariff Reform, and Indian Responsible Government', *Contemporary British History*, 30, no. 2 (2016): 151–76.
Fleming, N. C., *Britannia's Zealots, vol. 1: Tradition, Empire and the Forging of the Conservative Right*. London, 2019.
Fleming, N. C., 'The Conservative Right, Ulster Unionism, and the Partition of Ireland', in *Ireland and Partition: Contexts and Consequences*, edited by N. C. Fleming and James H. Murphy. Clemson, 2021.
Follis, Brian, *A State Under Siege: The Establishment of Northern Ireland, 1920–1925*. Oxford, 1995.

Foster, R. F., *Paddy and Mr Punch: Connections in Irish and English History*, rep. edn. London, 1995.

Foster, R. F., *W.B. Yeats: A Life, vol. 2: The Arch-Poet 1915–1939*. Oxford, 2003.

French, David, *Deterrence, Coercion and Appeasement: British Grand Strategy, 1919–1940*. Oxford, 2022.

Fulford, Roger, 'The King', in *Edwardian England 1901–1914*, edited by Simon Nowell-Smith. London, 1964.

Fussell, Paul, *The Great War and Modern Memory*. London, 1977.

Gailey, Andrew, 'King Carson: An Essay on the Invention of Leadership', *Irish Historical Studies*, 30, no. 117 (1996): 66–87.

Gailey, Andrew, 'The Destructiveness of Constructive Unionism: Theories and Practice, 1890s–1960s', in *Defenders of the Union: A Survey of British and Irish Unionism since 1801*, edited by D. George Boyce and Alan O'Day. London, 2001.

Gardner, Sophy, 'Whitehall Warriors: The Political Fight for the Royal Air Force, 1917–1929', Ph.D. thesis, University of Exeter, 2019.

Garside, W. R., *The Durham Miners, 1919–1960*. London, 1971.

Gash, Norman, *Aristocracy and People: Britain 1815–1865*. Cambridge, MA, 1979.

Gilbert, Martin and Richard Gott, *The Appeasers*, rep. edn. London, 2000.

Gildart, Keith, 'The Miner's Lockout in 1926 in the Cumberland Coalfield', *Northern History*, 44, no. 2 (2007): 169–92.

Gilmour, David, *Curzon*. London, 1994.

Girvin, Brian, 'The Party in Comparative and International Context', in *Conservative Century: The Conservative Party since 1900*, edited by Anthony Seldon and Stuart Ball. Oxford, 1990.

Gottlieb, Julie V., *'Guilty Women', Foreign Policy, and Appeasement in Inter-War Britain*. Basingstoke, 2015.

Gray, Peter, *The Leadership, Direction and Legitimacy of the RAF Bomber Offensive from Inception to 1945*. New York, 2012.

Gray, Peter and Olwen Purdue, 'Introduction: The Irish Lord Lieutenancy, c. 1541–1922', in *The Irish Lord Lieutenancy c. 1541–1922*, edited by Peter Gray and Olwen Purdue. Dublin, 2012.

Green, E. H. H., *The Crisis of Conservatism: The Politics, Economics and Ideology of the British Conservative Party, 1880–1914*. London, 1995.

Green, Martin, *Children of the Sun: A Narrative of 'Decadence' in England after 1918*, rev. edn. London, 1977.

Gregory, Adrian, *The Last Great War: British Society and the First World War*. Cambridge, 2008.

Griffiths, Richard, *Fellow Travellers of the Right: British Enthusiasts for Nazi Germany, 1933–9*. London, 1980.

Grigg, John, 'Churchill and Lloyd George', in *Churchill*, edited by Robert Blake and Wm. Roger Louis. Oxford, 1996.

Hadfield, Peter, *Hess: The Führer's Disciple*, rep. edn, London, 2001.

Haffner, Sebastian, *Churchill: Life and Times*. London, 2003.

Hamilton, J. A., *revised by* Roland Thorne, 'Stewart, Robert, first Marquess of Londonderry (1739–1821)', *Oxford Dictionary of National Biography*. Oxford, 2004.

Hanley, Hugh, 'Monarchism, International Relations, and the Continuing Irish Revolution, 1926–29', *Journal of Imperial and Commonwealth History*, 49, no. 1 (2020): 93–117.

Harris, Jose, *Private Lives, Public Spirit: Britain 1870–1914*. London, 1994.
Harris, Kenneth, *Attlee*, rep. edn. London, 1995.
Harris, Mary, *The Catholic Church and the Foundation of the Northern Irish State*. Cork, 1993.
Harrison, Brian, *Separate Spheres: The Opposition to Women's Suffrage in Britain*. London, 1978.
Hartley, Stephen, *The Irish Question as a Problem in British Foreign Policy, 1914–18*. Basingstoke, 1987.
Havighurst, Alfred F., *Britain in Transition: The Twentieth Century*. Chicago, 1979.
Heesom, A. J., 'Entrepreneurial Paternalism: The Third Lord Londonderry (1778–1854) and the Coal Trade', *Durham University Journal*, 66 (1973–4): 238–56.
Heesom, A. J., 'The Northern Coal Miners and the Opposition to the Coal Mines Act of 1842', *International Review of Social History*, 25, no. 2 (1980): 236–71.
Heesom, A. J. and Brendan Duffy, 'Coal, Class and Education in the North-East', *Past and Present*, 90 (1981): 136–151.
Hennessey, Thomas, *Dividing Ireland: World War I and Partition*. London, 1998.
Hicks, Geoffrey, 'Conservatism Obscured, 1935–1939', in *The Tory World: Deep History and the Tory Theme in British Foreign Policy, 1679–2014*, edited by Jeremy Black. Aldershot, 2015.
Hippler, Thomas, *Governing from the Skies: A Global History of Aerial Bombing*. London, 2017.
Hobsbawm, Eric, *Age of Extremes: The Short Twentieth Century 1914–1991*. London, 1995.
Hoffman, Peter, 'The Question of Western Allied Co-operation with the German Anti-Nazi Conspiracy, 1938–1944', *Historical Journal*, 34, no. 2 (1991): 437–64.
Holman, Brett, 'The Air Panic of 1935: British Press Opinion between Disarmament and Rearmament', *Journal of Contemporary History*, 46, no. 2 (2011): 288–307.
Holman, Brett, *The Next War in the Air: Britain's Fear of the Bomber, 1908–1941*. Aldershot, 2014.
Hopkinson, Michael, *The Irish War of Independence*. Dublin, 2004.
Hoppen, K. Theodore, 'Gladstone, Salisbury and the End of Irish Assimilationism', in *Gladstone: Ireland and Beyond*, edited by Mary E. Daly and K. Theodore Hoppen. Dublin, 2011.
Hoppen, K. Theodore, 'A Question None could Answer: "What was the Irish viceroyalty for?"', in *The Irish Lord Lieutenancy c. 1541–1922*, edited by Peter Gray and Olwen Purdue. Dublin, 2012.
Howe, Anthony, *Free Trade and Liberal England 1846–1946*. Oxford, 1997.
Hunt, Hugh, *Sean O'Casey*, rep. edn. Dublin, 1998.
Hutchinson, John and Anthony D. Smith (eds), *Ethnicity*. Oxford, 1996.
Hyde, H. Montgomery, *Carson: The Life of Sir Edward Carson, Lord Carson of Duncairn*. London, 1953.
Hyde, H. Montgomery, *The Strange Death of Lord Castlereagh*. London, 1959.
Hyde, H. Montgomery, *Baldwin: The Unexpected Prime Minister*. London, 1973.
Hyde, H. Montgomery, *British Air Policy between the Wars, 1918–1939*. London, 1976.
Hyde, H. Montgomery, *The Londonderrys: A Family Portrait*. London, 1979.
Jackson, Alvin, 'Unionist Myths 1912–1985', *Past and Present*, 136 (1992): 164–85.
Jackson, Alvin, *Sir Edward Carson*. Dundalk, 1993.
Jackson, Alvin, *Colonel Edward Saunderson: Land and Loyalty in Victorian Ireland*. Oxford, 1995.

Jackson, Alvin, 'Irish Unionism, 1870–1922', in *Defenders of the Union: A Survey of British and Irish Unionism since 1801*, edited by D. George Boyce and Alan O'Day. London, 2001.
Jackson, Alvin, *Home Rule: An Irish History, 1800–2000*. London, 2003.
Jackson, Alvin, 'Ireland, the Union, and the Empire, 1800–1960', in *Ireland and the British Empire*, edited by Kevin Kenny. Oxford, 2004.
Jackson, Alvin, 'Stewart, Charles Stewart Vane-Tempest-, Sixth Marquess of Londonderry (1852–1915)', *Oxford Dictionary of National Biography*. Oxford, 2004.
Jackson, Alvin, 'Stewart, Charles Stewart Henry Vane-Tempest-, Seventh Marquess of Londonderry (1878–1949)', *Oxford Dictionary of National Biography*. Oxford, 2004.
Jackson, Alvin, '"Tame Tory Hacks"? The Ulster Party at Westminster, 1922–1972', *Historical Journal*, 54, no. 2 (2011): 453–75.
Jackson, Stephen, 'Religious Education and the Anglo-World: The Impact of Empire, Britishness, and Decolonisation in Australia, Canada, and New Zealand', *Brill Research Perspectives in Religion and Education*, 2, no. 1 (2020): 1–98.
James, Lawrence, *Aristocrats: Power, Grace and Decadence: Britain's Great Ruling Classes from 1066 to the Present*. London, 2009.
James, Robert Rhodes, *Churchill: A Study in Failure 1900–1939*. Harmondsworth, 1973.
James, Robert Rhodes, *The British Revolution: British Politics, 1880–1939*. London, 1978.
James, Robert Rhodes, *Anthony Eden*. London, 1996.
Jeffery, Keith, *Field Marshal Sir Henry Wilson: A Political Soldier*. Oxford, 2006.
Johnson, Gaynor, *Lord Robert Cecil: Politician and Internationalist*. Farnham, 2013.
Johnson, Matthew, *Militarism and the British Left, 1902–1914*. Basingstoke, 2013.
Kelly, Richard, 'The Party Conferences', in *Conservative Century: The Conservative Party since 1900*, edited by Anthony Seldon and Stuart Ball. Oxford, 1994.
Kendle, John, *Ireland and the Federal Solution: The Debate Over the United Kingdom Constitution, 1870–1921*. Kingston and Montreal, 1989.
Kennedy, Paul, *The Realities Behind Diplomacy: Background Influences on British External Policy, 1865–1980*. London, 1981.
Keohane, Nigel, *The Party of Patriotism: The Conservative Party and the First World War*. Aldershot, 2010.
Kershaw, Ian, *Hitler, 1889–1936: Hubris*. London, 1998.
Kershaw, Ian, *Hitler, 1936–45: Nemesis*. London, 2000.
Kershaw, Ian, *Making Friends with Hitler: Lord Londonderry and Britain's Road to War*. London, 2004.
Kershaw, Ian, 'Personality and Power: The Individual's Role in the History of Twentieth-Century Europe', *The Historian*, 83 (Autumn 2004): 8–19.
King, Carla, 'Defenders of the Union: Sir Horace Plunkett', in *Defenders of the Union: A Survey of British and Irish Unionism since 1801*, edited by D. George Boyce and Alan O'Day. London, 2001.
Kirby, M. W., *The British Coalmining Industry, 1870–1946*. London, 1977.
Kitching, Carolyn, *Britain and the Problem of International Disarmament, 1919–34*. London, 1999.
Koss, Stephen, *Nonconformity in Modern British Politics*. London, 1975.
Koss, Stephen, *The Rise and Fall of the Political Press in Britain*. London, 1990.
Lawrence, Jon, 'Class and Gender in the Making of Urban Toryism, 1880–1914', *English Historical Review*, 108, no. 428 (1993): 629–52.
Lawrence, Jon, *Electing Our Masters: The Hustings in British Politics from Hogarth to Blair*. Oxford, 2009.

Lees-Milne, James, *Harold Nicolson: A Biography 1886–1929*. London, 1980.

Lloyd, E. M., *revised by* A. J. Heesom, 'Vane [formerly Stewart], Charles William, Third Marquess of Londonderry (1778–1854)', *Oxford Dictionary of National Biography*. Oxford, 2004.

Lowe, Rodney, 'The Government and Industrial Relations, 1919–39', in *A History of British Industrial Relations, vol. 2: 1914–1939*, edited by Chris Wrigley. Brighton, 1987.

Lukowitz, David, 'George Lansbury's Peace Missions to Hitler and Mussolini in 1937', *Canadian Journal of History*, 15, no. 1 (1980): 67–82.

Lyman, Richard W., *The First Labour Government, 1924*. London, 1957.

Lynch, Robert, *The Partition of Ireland 1918–1925*. Cambridge, 2019.

Lynn, Pauline, 'The Impact of Women. The Shaping of Political Allegiance in County Durham, 1918–1945', *Local Historian*, 28, no. 3 (1998): 159–75.

Lynn, Pauline, 'Seaham Revisited: The Fruits of the Electoral Franchise?', *North East History*, 33 (2000): 1–34.

Lyons, F. S. L., *Culture and Anarchy in Ireland, 1890–1939*. Oxford, 1979.

Mack Smith, Denis, *Mussolini*. London, 2001.

Malcolmson, A. P. W., *The Pursuit of the Heiress: Aristocratic Marriage in Ireland, 1740–1840*. Belfast, 2006.

Mandler, Peter, *The Fall and Rise of the Stately Home*. London, 1997.

Mansergh, Nicholas, *The Unresolved Question: The Anglo-Irish Settlement and its Undoing 1912–72*. London, 1991.

Marquand, David, *Ramsay MacDonald*. London, 1977.

Martin, Peter, 'Unionism: The Irish Nobility and Revolution, 1919–23', in *The Irish Revolution, 1913–1923*, edited by Joost Augusteijn. Basingstoke, 2002.

Marwick, Arthur, *The Deluge: British Society and the First World War*, rep. edn. London, 1978.

Mates, Lewis, *The Great Labour Unrest: Rank-and-File Movements and Political Change in the Durham Coalfield*. Manchester, 2016.

Mates, Lewis, '"We Want Real Live Wires, Not Gas Pipes": Communism in the Inter-war Durham Coalfield', *Twentieth Century Communism*, 23 (2022): 51–95.

Matthews, Kevin, *Fatal Influence: The Impact of Ireland on British Politics, 1920–1925*. Dublin, 2004.

McBride, Lawrence W., *The Greening of Dublin Castle: The Transformation of Bureaucratic and Judicial Personnel in Ireland, 1892–1922*. Washington, DC, 1991.

McCarthy, Helen, 'Whose Democracy? Histories of British Political Culture between the Wars', *Historical Journal*, 55, no. 1 (2012): 221–38.

McCavery, Trevor, *Newtown: A History of Newtownards*. Belfast, 1994.

McCoole, Sinead, *Hazel: A Life of Lady Lavery 1880–1935*. Dublin, 1996.

McDonald, G. W. and Howard F. Gospel, 'The Mond-Turner Talks 1927–1933: A Study in Industrial Co-operation', *Historical Journal*, 16, no. 4 (1973): 807–29.

McDonnell, A. D., *The Life of Sir Denis Henry: Catholic Unionist*. Belfast, 2000.

McDowell, R. B., *The Irish Convention, 1917–18*. London, 1970.

McGrath, Michael, *The Catholic Church and Catholic Schools in Northern Ireland: The Price of Faith*. Dublin, 2000.

McIntosh, Gillian, *The Force of Culture: Unionist Identities in Twentieth-Century Ireland*. Cork, 1999.

McKenzie, R. T., *British Political Parties: The Distribution of Power within the Conservative and Labour Parties*, 2nd edn. London, 1967.

McKibbin, Ross, *The Ideologies of Class: Social Relations in Britain 1880–1950*, rep. edn. Oxford, 1991.
McKibbin, Ross, *Class and Cultures: England 1918–1951*. Oxford, 1998.
McKibbin, Ross, *Parties and People: England 1914–1951*. Oxford, 2010.
McMahon, Deirdre, *Republicans and Imperialists: Anglo-Irish Relations in the 1930s*. London, 1984.
McMahon, Timothy G., '"It Does Not Matter What the Authors Meant": Covenanters in Conflict, 1916–1920', in *Ireland and Partition: Context and Consequences*, edited by N. C. Fleming and James H. Murphy. Clemson, 2021.
Medlicott, Norton, 'Britain and Germany: The Search for Agreement, 1930–37', in *Retreat from Power: Studies in Britain's Foreign Policy of the Twentieth Century*, edited by David Dilks. London, 1981.
Mews, Stewart, 'The Churches', in Margaret Morris, *The General Strike*. Harmondsworth, 1976.
Michalka, Wolfgang, 'Joachim von Ribbentrop: From Wine Merchant to Foreign Minister', in *The Nazi Elite*, edited by Ronald Smelser and Rainer Zitelmann. London, 1993.
Middlemas, Keith and John Barnes, *Baldwin: A Biography*. London, 1969.
Moody, T. W. and J. C. Beckett, *Queen's, Belfast 1845–1949: The History of a University, vol. 2*. London, 1959.
Morgan, Austen, *J. Ramsay MacDonald*. Manchester, 1987.
Morgan, Austen, *Labour and Partition: The Belfast Working Class, 1905–23*. London, 1991.
Morgan, David R., *Suffragists and Liberals: The Politics of Woman Suffrage in England*. Oxford, 1975.
Morgan, Kenneth O., *Consensus and Disunity: The Lloyd George Coalition Government, 1918–1922*. Oxford, 1979.
Morgan, Kenneth O., *Rebirth of a Nation: Wales 1880–1980*. New York, 1981.
Morris, Margaret, *The General Strike*. Harmondsworth, 1976.
Mowat, Charles Loch, *Britain between the Wars, 1918–1940*, rep. edn. London, 1966.
Murphy, Brian, 'J.J. O'Kelly, the *Catholic Bulletin* and Contemporary Irish Cultural Historians', *Archivium Hibernicum*, 44 (1989): 71–88.
Murphy, James H., *Abject Loyalty: Nationalism and Monarchy in Ireland during the Reign of Queen Victoria*. Washington, DC, 2001.
Murray, Bruce K., *The People's Budget 1909/10: Lloyd George and Liberal Politics*. Oxford, 1980.
Newton, Scott, *Profits of Peace: The Political Economy of Anglo-German Appeasement*. Oxford, 1996.
Nicholson, Colin, 'Edwardian England and the Coming of the First World War', in *The Edwardian Age: Conflict and Stability 1900–1914*, edited by Alan O'Day. London, 1979.
Nietzsche, Friedrich, *Untimely Meditations*. Cambridge, 1983.
O'Brien, Patrick, 'Is Political Biography a Good Thing', *Contemporary British History*, 10, no. 4 (1996): 60–6.
O'Connell, Sean, 'Motoring and Modernity', in *Twentieth-Century Britain: Economic, Cultural and Social Change*, edited by Francesca Carnevali and Julie-Marie Strange, 2nd edn. London, 2007.
O'Day, Alan, 'Introduction', in *The Edwardian Age: Conflict and Stability 1900–1914*, edited by Alan O'Day. London, 1979.
O'Day, Alan, *Irish Home Rule 1867–1921*. Manchester, 1998.

O'Day, Alan, 'Ireland and the United Kingdom', in *Problems and Perspectives in Irish History since 1800: Essays in Honour of Patrick Buckland*, edited by D. George Boyce and Roger Swift. Dublin, 2004.

O'Halpin, Eunan, *The Decline of the Union: British Government in Ireland 1892–1920*. Dublin, 1997.

O'Leary, Brendan, *A Treatise on Northern Ireland, vol. 2: Control: The Second Protestant Ascendancy and the Irish State*. Oxford, 2019.

Offer, Avner, *Property and Politics 1870–1914: Landownership, Law, Ideology and Urban Development in England*. Cambridge, 1981.

Ollerenshaw, Philip, *Northern Ireland in the Second World War*. Manchester, 2013.

Omissi, David E., *Air Power and Colonial Control: The Royal Air Force, 1919–1939*. Manchester, 1990.

Outram, Quentin, 'Class Warriors: The Coalowners', in *Industrial Politics and the 1926 Mining Lockout: The Struggle for Dignity*, edited by John McIlroy, Alan Campbell and Keith Gildart. Cardiff, 2004.

Packer, Ian, *Lloyd George*. Basingstoke, 1998.

Parker, R. A. C., *Chamberlain and Appeasement: British Policy and the Coming of the Second World War*. London, 1993.

Parkhill, Trevor, '"Chivalrous rather than Administrative": The Career of the Third Marquess of Londonderry, Soldier, Diplomat, Landlord', in *Politics and Political Culture in Britain and Ireland 1750–1850: Essays in Tribute to Peter Jupp*, edited by Allan Blackstock and Eoin Magennis. Belfast, 2007.

Patterson, Henry, *Class Conflict and Sectarianism: The Protestant Working Class and the Belfast Labour Movement 1868–1920*. Belfast, 1980.

Pauley, J. A., 'The Social and Political Roles of Edith, Marchioness of Londonderry, 1878–1959', Ph.D. thesis, University of Ulster, 1994.

Paxman, Jeremy, *Black Gold: The History of How Coal Made Britain*. London, 2021.

Pearce, Edward, *Lines of Most Resistance: The Lords, the Tories and Ireland, 1886–1914*. London, 1999.

Pearce, Robert, *Britain: Industrial Relations and the Economy 1900–39*. London, 1993.

Peden, G. C., *British Rearmament and the Treasury, 1932–1939*. Edinburgh, 1979.

Pelling, Henry, 'Churchill and the Labour Movement', in *Churchill*, edited by Robert Blake and Wm. Roger Louis. Oxford, 1996.

Phillips, Gervase, '"Who Shall Say that the Days of Cavalry Are Over?" The Revival of the Mounted Arm in Europe, 1853–1914', *War in History*, 18, no. 1 (2011): 5–32.

Phillips, Gregory D., *The Diehards: Aristocratic Society and Politics in Edwardian England*. London, 1979.

Phoenix, Éamon, 'Michael Collins and the Northern Question 1916–1922', in *Michael Collins and the Making of the Irish State*, edited by Gabriel Doherty and Dermot Keogh, rep. edn. Cork, 2006.

Porter, Bernard, *The Absent-Minded Imperialists: Empire, Society and Culture in Britain*. Oxford, 2004.

Powis, Jonathan, *Aristocracy*. Oxford, 1984.

Pugh, Martin, *The Tories and the People 1880–1935*. London, 1985.

Pugh, Martin, *'Hurrah for the Blackshirts!' Fascists and Fascism in Britain between the Wars*. London, 2005.

Purdue, Olwen, *The Big House in the North of Ireland: Land, Power and Social Elites, 1878–1960*. Dublin, 2009.

Quinn, James, 'Dublin Castle and the Act of Union', in *The Irish Act of Union: Bicentennial Essays*, edited by Michael Brown, Patrick M. Geoghegan and James Kelly. Dublin, 2003.

Ramsden, John, *An Appetite for Power: A History of the Conservative Party since 1830*. London, 1999.

Reader, W. J., *Architect of Air Power: The Life of the First Viscount Weir of Eastwood 1877–1959*. London, 1968.

Reid, Colin, 'Protestant Challenges to the "Protestant State": Ulster Unionism and Independent Unionism in Northern Ireland, 1921–1939', *Twentieth Century British History*, 19, no. 4 (2008): 419–45.

Rempel, Richard A., *Unionists Divided: Arthur Balfour, Joseph Chamberlain and the Unionist Free Traders*. Newton Abbot, 1972.

Renfrew, Barry, *Wings of Empire: The Forgotten Wars of the Royal Air Force, 1919–1939*. Stroud, 2015.

Reynolds, David, *Britannia Overruled: British Policy and World Power in the 20th Century*, 2nd edn. London, 2000.

Reynolds, David, *In Command of History: Churchill Fighting and Writing the Second World War*. London, 2004.

Riddell, Neil, *Labour in Crisis: The Second Labour Government, 1929–1931*. Manchester, 1999.

Robbins, Keith, *Munich 1938*. London, 1968.

Roberts, Andrew, *'The Holy Fox': The Life of Lord Halifax*. London, 1997.

Roberts, J. M., *Europe, 1880–1945*, 3rd edn. London, 2001.

Robertson, Scot, *The Development of RAF Strategic Bombing Doctrine, 1919–1939*. London, 1995.

Robins, Joseph, *Champagne and Silver Buckles: The Viceregal Court at Dublin Castle 1700–1922*. Dublin, 2001.

Rose, Norman, *The Cliveden Set: Portrait of an Exclusive Fraternity*. London, 2000.

Rubenstein, William D., 'Henry Page Croft and the National Party 1917–22', *Journal of Contemporary History*, 9, no. 1 (1974): 129–48.

Rubinstein, William D., *Men of Property: The Very Wealthy in Britain since the Industrial Revolution*. London, 1981.

Rudman, Stella, *Lloyd George and the Appeasement of Germany, 1919–1945*. Newcastle, 2011.

Russell, A. K., *Liberal Landslide: The General Election of 1906*. Newton Abbot, 1973.

Sarkisyanz, Manuel, *Hitler's English Inspirers*. Belfast, 2003.

Scholes, Andrew, *The Church of Ireland and the Third Home Rule Bill*. Dublin, 2010.

Schwarz, Michael, 'Appeasing the Past: Denying History, Destroying Memories, Creating Myths', in *Ethics, Values and Civil Society*, edited by Michael Schwarz, Howard Harris and Stephen Cohen. Bingley, 2013.

Schwoerer, Lois G., 'Lord Halifax's visit to Germany: November 1937', *The Historian*, 32, no. 3 (1970): 353–75.

Scoular, Clive, *John M. Andrews: Northern Ireland's Wartime Prime Minister*. Killyleagh, 2004.

Shay, Robert Paul, *British Rearmament in the Thirties: Politics and Profits*. Princeton, 1977.

Simons, Richard B., 'The British Coal Industry-a Failure of Private Enterprise', *The Historian*, 16, no. 1 (1953): 3–17.

Smart, Nick, *The National Government, 1931–40*. London, 1999.

Smith, Brian, *A History of Military Morals: Killing the Innocent*. Leiden, 2022.
Smith, Jeremy, '"Ever Reliable Friends"? The Conservative Party and Ulster Unionism in the Twentieth Century', *English Historical Review*, 121, no. 490 (2006): 71–103.
Smith, Jeremy, 'Sir Edward Carson and the Myth of Partition', in *Politics and Power in Victorian Ireland*, edited by Roger Swift and Christine Kinealy. Dublin, 2006.
Smith, Malcolm, *British Air Strategy between the Wars*. Oxford, 1984.
Southgate, Donald, 'Baldwin 1923–1932', in *The Conservative Leadership 1832–1932*, edited by Donald Southgate. London, 1974.
Spicer, Charles, '"Ambulant Amateurs": The Rise and Fade of the Anglo-German Fellowship', Ph.D. thesis, University of London, 2018.
Steiner, Zara, *The Lights that Failed: European International History, 1919–1933*. Oxford, 2005.
Stevenson, John, *British Society: 1914–45*, rep. edn. London, 1990.
Stewart, A. T. Q., *The Ulster Crisis: Resistance to Home Rule 1912–1914*, rep. edn. Belfast, 1999.
Stewart, Graham, *Burying Caesar: Churchill, Chamberlain and the Battle for the Tory Party*. London, 1999.
Stone, Dan, *Responses to Nazism in Britain, 1933–1939: Before War and Holocaust*. Basingstoke, 2003.
Strang, G. Bruce, 'The Spirit of Ulysses? Ideology and British Appeasement in the 1930s', *Diplomacy and Statecraft*, 19, no. 3 (2008): 481–526.
Strobl, Gerwin, *The Germanic Isle: Nazi Perceptions of Britain*. Cambridge, 2000.
Stubbs, John, 'Lord Milner and Patriotic Labour, 1914–1918', *English Historical Review*, 87, no. 345 (1972): 717–54.
Supple, Barry, *The History of the British Coal Industry: vol. 4: 1913–1946: The Political Economy of Decline*. Oxford, 1987.
Sykes, Alan, *Tariff Reform in British Politics 1903–1913*. Oxford, 1979.
Sykes, Alan, 'The Radical Right and the Crisis of Conservatism before the First World War', *Historical Journal*, 26, no. 3 (1983): 661–76.
Symons, Julian, *The General Strike: A Historical Portrait*. London, 1957.
Taylor, A. J. P., *The Trouble Makers: Dissent over Foreign Policy 1792–1939*. London, 1969.
Taylor, A. J. P., *Beaverbrook*. London, 1972.
Taylor, A. J. P., *English History 1914–1945*, rep. edn. Oxford, 1990.
Taylor, Tony, *The Politics of Reaction: The Ideology of the Cecils and the Challenge of Secular Education, 1889–1902*. Leeds, 1997.
Thackeray, David, 'Rethinking the Edwardian Crisis of Conservatism', *Historical Journal*, 54, no. 1 (2011): 191–213.
Thompson, F. M. L., *English Landed Society in the Nineteenth Century*. London, 1963.
Thompson, F. M. L., 'Britain', in *European Landed Elites in the Nineteenth Century*, edited by David Spring. London, 1977.
Thompson, F. M. L., *Gentrification and the Enterprise Culture: Britain 1780–1980*. Oxford, 2001.
Thompson, J. Lee, *Northcliffe: Press Baron in Politics, 1865–1922*. London, 2000.
Thorne, Roland, 'Stewart, Robert, Viscount Castlereagh and Second Marquess of Londonderry (1769–1822)', *Oxford Dictionary of National Biography*. Oxford, 2004.
Thurlow, Richard, *Fascism in Britain: From Oswald Mosley's Blackshirts to the National Front*. London, 1998.
Tindley, Annie, *The Sutherland Estate, 1850–1920: Aristocratic Decline, Estate Management and Land Reform*. Edinburgh, 2010.

Tindley, Annie, *Lord Dufferin, Ireland and the British Empire, c. 1820–1900: Rule by the Best?* London, 2021.

Todd, Jennifer, 'Unionist Political thought, 1920–72', in *Political Thought in Ireland since the Seventeenth Century*, edited by D. George Boyce, Robert Eccleshall and Vincent Geoghegan. London, 1993.

Townshend, Charles, *Britain's Civil Wars: Counterinsurgency in the Twentieth Century*. London, 1986.

Tripp, Charles, *A History of Iraq*, 3rd edn. Cambridge 2007.

Turner, Graham, 'The Stronghold of Labour', in *Mining and Social Change: Durham in the Twentieth Century*, edited by Martin Bulmer. London, 1978.

Turner, John, *Lloyd George's Secretariat*. Cambridge, 1980.

Turner, John, *British Politics and the Great War: Coalition and Conflict 1915–1918*. New Haven, 1992.

Urbach, Karina, 'Flirting with Hitler: Biographies of the German and British Nobility in the Interwar Years', *German Historical Institute Bulletin*, 29, no. 1 (2007): 64–74.

Urquhart, Diane, 'Peeresses, Patronage and Power: The Politics of Ladies Frances Anne, Theresa and Edith Londonderry, 1800–1959', in *Irish Women's History*, edited by Alan Hayes and Diane Urquhart. Dublin, 2004.

Urquhart, Diane, *The Ladies of Londonderry: Women and Political Patronage*. London, 2007.

Waddington, G. T., '"An Idyllic and Unruffled Atmosphere of Complete Anglo-German Misunderstanding": Aspects of the Operations of the Dienststelle Ribbentrop in Great Britain, 1934–1938', *History*, 82, no. 265 (1997): 44–72.

Walker, Graham, *A History of the Ulster Unionist Party: Protest, Pragmatism and Pessimism*. Manchester, 2004.

Walsh, Pat, 'The Apprenticeship of Bomber Bull', *Irish Political Review*, 19, no. 6 (2004): 19–22.

Ward, Alan J., *Ireland and Anglo-American Relations 1899–1921*. London, 1969.

Wark, Wesley K., *The Ultimate Enemy: British Intelligence and Nazi Germany, 1933–1939*. London, 1985.

Warner, Guy, 'Civil Aviation in Ulster – A Brief Survey', *Due North*, 1, no. 4 (2001): 17–19.

Wasson, Ellis, *Born to Rule: British Political Elites*. London, 2000.

Weber, Max, *The Theory of Social and Economic Organization*, edited by Talcott Parsons, rep. edn. New York, 1964.

Webster, Andrew, 'Entente and Argument: Britain, France and Disarmament, 1899–1934', in *Britain, France and the Entente Cordiale since 1904*, edited by Antoine Capet. Basingstoke, 2006.

Webster, Andrew, 'From Versailles to Geneva: The Many Forms of Interwar Disarmament', *Journal of Strategic Studies*, 24, no. 2 (2006): 225–46.

Webster, Andrew, *Strange Allies: Britain, France and the Dilemmas of Disarmament and Security, 1929–1933*. London, 2019.

Weitz, John, *Hitler's Diplomat: Joachim von Ribbentrop*. London, 1997.

West, Trevor, *Horace Plunkett, Co-Operation and Politics: An Irish Biography*. Gerrards Cross, 1986.

Weston, Corrine C., *The House of Lords and Ideological Politics: Lord Salisbury's Referendal Theory and the Conservative Party, 1846–1922*. Philadelphia, 1995.

Whiting, Richard, 'The Empire and British Politics', in *Britain's Experience of Empire in the Twentieth Century*, edited by Andrew Thompson. Oxford, 2012.

Williams, A. Susan, *Ladies of Influence: Women of the Elite in Interwar Britain*. London, 2000.

Williams, Gwylmor Prys and George Thompson Brake, *Drink in Great Britain 1900–1979*. London, 1980.

Williamson, Philip, *National Crisis and National Government: British Politics, the Economy and Empire, 1926–1932*. Cambridge, 1992.

Williamson, Philip, *Stanley Baldwin: Conservative Leadership and National Values*. Cambridge, 1999.

Wilson, Keith M., *A Study in the History and Politics of the Morning Post 1905–1926*. Lampeter, 1990.

Witherell, Larry L., *Rebel on the Right: Henry Page Croft and the Crisis of Conservatism, 1903–1914*. London, 1997.

Witherell, Larry L., 'Lord Salisbury's "Watching Committee" and the Fall of Neville Chamberlain, May 1940', *English Historical Review*, 116, no. 469 (2001): 44–72.

Worsthorne, Peregrine, *In Defence of Aristocracy*. London, 2004.

Young, John W., 'Introduction', in *The Paris Embassy: British Ambassadors and Anglo-French Relations*, edited by Rogelia Pastor-Castro and John W. Young. Basingstoke, 2013.

Zeigler, Philip, 'Churchill and the Monarchy', in *Churchill*, edited by Robert Blake and Wm. Roger Louis. Oxford, 1996.

Zeman, Z. A. B., *Nazi Propaganda*, 2nd edn. Oxford, 1973.

Index